T0353967

OUTBURSTS OF A SUPERCILIOUS RENOUNCER;

THOUGHTS OF A POSTMODERN DEGENERATE (YEAR FOUR)

BAETHAN BALOR

OUTBURSTS OF A SUPERCILIOUS RENOUNCER;
THOUGHTS OF A POSTMODERN DEGENERATE (YEAR FOUR)

iUniverse books may be ordered through booksellers or by contacting:

iUniverse
1663 Liberty Drive
Bloomington, IN 47403
www.iuniverse.com
844-349-9409

ISBN: 978-1-6632-2597-9 (sc)
ISBN: 978-1-6632-2598-6 (e)

Library of Congress Control Number: 2021917218

Print information available on the last page.

iUniverse rev. date: 09/21/2021

Dedicated to my Ego, Self, and I.

"If you write for God you will reach many men and bring them joy. If you write for men—you may make some money and you may give someone a little joy and you may make a noise in the world, for a little while. If you write for yourself, you can read what you yourself have written and after ten minutes you will be so disgusted that you will wish that you were dead."

- Thomas Merton

"The sweaty players in the game of life always have more fun than the supercilious spectators."

- William Feather

CONTENTS

Acknowledgment xi

November 1
December 15
January 89
February 131
March 173
April 211
May 241
June 287
July 321
August 369
September 435
October 521
November 639

Epilogue 723

ACKNOWLEDGMENT

Entities are documented to the best of my truth.
Errors in spelling, punctuation, grammar, and
syntax are fundamental. The reader is a fool.

NOVEMBER

Wednesday, November 20th, 2019

9:41 AM

Journals are self-indulgent.

I'm 6'1, 163 lb, at 10.3% body fat (calculated by digital scale). My two-inch long dark blonde hair is often well-kept and styled back flat atop my head. I have blue-grey eyes, a nose, mouth, two cheeks, a chin, a forehead, two lips, two ears, and all the skin between. Clean-shaven. The common opinion, throughout all my dealings with humanity, is that I'm handsome; this is no boon; on the contrary, I suffer from the increased attentional output of others, and often disappoint, for my character is that of a mythological troll, one that resides beneath a bridge and harbors nothing but an interchange of pity and contempt for humanity.

Each morning I wake to view my morose visage reflected in the bathroom mirror of a one-bedroom apartment devoid of furnishings. I behold a skeleton upheld by something horrible: A bit of tendon here, a layer of meat there, rendered alive, aware, *conscious* of *it*self—of the feelings familiar to a creature cognizant of death.

Consumption, defecation, and exertion, are exemplified in my three exclusive pursuits of reading, writing, and strength training, respectively. I maintain no relationships (family, friends, lovers) by choice and forsake all entertainment except for music as a means to preserve my inflated ego, to maximize the efficiency of introspection and unique thought: the proponents of *this* writing. Sexual relations disgust me. I'm averse to the blatant dissimulation, pretensions, and deceits practiced by *both* sexes and strive to refrain from participation, though my instincts compel me to desire; therefore, my ~~writing~~ life is first and foremost a comedy.

"Mental illness" is a theme by consequence of my philosophy. I'm a deviant and an anomaly, *not* on account of any inherent uniqueness, but by the opinions of the status quo perpetuated by American culture.

Thursday, November 21st, 2019

9:04 AM

I've predetermined a theme for the next year of my life, i.e., the theme of this book; therefore, I will endure another three-hundred and sixty-four days employed at a fried chicken oriented fast food restaurant within the walls of the single university established within the bounds of the city I reside in northwest Arkansas. I will be uncommunicative and mute throughout all non-work-related interactions with my associates and document the trajectory of my social plummet.

On November 20th, 2020, I will sever all occupations, liquidate my ~~assets~~ possessions, and venture further west on foot to an undetermined destination. The savings I accrue with one year's worth of labor will fund the ludicrous venture.

Friday, November 22nd, 2019

5:24 PM

A fifteen-minute walk from the low-income suburban apartment complex where I reside, to the cities' single university, leads me through the front glass double-doors of a college dining hangout, replete with stereotypical undergrads of disparate ethos and ethnicity. The environment is of fallacious scholastics, wherein each individual primes themselves for sexual relationships by a method of the pursuit of education in a given field of natural inclination or vain ambition.[1] My station amongst the misdirected throngs of youth and impudent professors I serve is at one of the three counters arranged along the perimeter of a rectangular food court stocked with convenience store items sold at exorbitant prices, e.g., one banana for $0.99, a premade quart-sized Caesar salad for $6.50. One counter specializes in fried chicken (my counter), the second in subs, and the third in pizza.

I enter the establishment; my eyes begin to water on account of an adjustment of temperature. An immediate aura of baseless hubris and foppery assaults my senses in the form of smarmy socialites often converged by the entryway for a round of vapid conversation and histrionics. Every third or fourth day, an amateur group of musicians performs classical pop music written by artists other than themselves, to which large crowds often stand and gawk at while engaged in a muted dialogue inches from one another's ears.

My all-black ensemble, complete with a heavy coat and a military issued backpack, accentuates my standoffish stride. Opinions shift and vary depending on my mien—wrought by my *thoughts,* for I am but an animated object of flesh to be perceived and judged.

---

[1] The few geniuses will masturbate.

I hasten down the hall towards another hall adjoined to the aforementioned hall, lined with rows of half-sized locker cages, deposit my belongings, and "clock in" to the standardized electronic interface featured at megalomaniac corporations and industries. A rote *"ping"* resounds, a harmonic I will remember till death, for what *it* expresses; an upbeat tone, with a gentle, monotonic timbre: An encapsulation of the somber awareness of being a stooge.

Saturday, November 23rd, 2019

9:46 PM

"I dread being alive," said an idiot reclined in a patio chair to a college-educated youth. Both sipped the rims of canned soda and observed the outermost layer of a dense cedar tree grove.

"Then kill yourself," said the youth.

"I once read that killing yourself is the ultimate cop-out."

"On the contrary, I've read that killing yourself is a noble act, one beneficial to society if you're dead weight with nothing to offer but melancholy or a gloomy attitude towards your fellow man."

The idiot scratched between the rumpled folds of an athletic purple shirt and said, "I'm ready for you to go home now."

"I'm visiting Adriana next, not going home."

"I'm ready for you to go then."

The youth said, "All right," and stood, set a can of soda depleted of one-fifth of the contents onto an adjacent round table between both reclined chairs, readjusted a pair of black, rimless sunglasses, and walked, upright and steady, to a teal sports car parked alongside the grooves of a gravel driveway.

Sunday, November 24th, 2019

10:46 AM

The four minutes inside a six by eight-foot squalid bathroom after utilization of the time clock is spent in equal thirds of urination, followed by apron, hairnet, nametag, and visor donning, and the last superfluous yet critical minute and twenty seconds dedicated to staring at a small rectangular mirror, to reckon what I am: the aspect of what I project. I behold the visage of a fast-food worker and marvel at everything I *could* be in life, and what I am in the moment. The ephemeral feelings positioned in front of the mirror range day-to-day on a spectrum from a morbid satisfaction to a dreary despondency, though the reflection is essential for my sanity, for-

I exit the bathroom, march through the kitchen to the galley of fryers, and I'm assaulted by a plethora of undignified stimuli: Three old harridans and one of two eighteen-year-old boys (dependant on the day) fret over fried chicken and waffle fries. A crowd of customers, assembled for the daily lunch rush, stare with the vacuity suitable for one in expectant of overpriced detrimental foodstuffs at either an overhead menu—their upturned chins topped by a furrowed brow, or a disingenuous grin directed at one of the employees engaged with hectic functions.

Kim: The supervisor, a self-proclaimed "Chicken Queen"; a frenetic matriarch; an evangelical Christian, occasionally emphasized by a few spoken allegorical axioms, coarse behavior, and egregious treatment of subordinates. 5'8, Caucasian, doughy physique, frazzled and thick shoulder-length brown hair, librarian glasses, large rump, slouched shoulders, heavy-set stride, the tender voice of a nubile girl when dissimulating, and the shrill bark of a vexed shrew when riled. Pedantic with petty policy. Hypercritical and bureaucratic despite her powerless authority. Puerile and mawkish with attempts to relate to others.
Self-assigned meaning in life: (Never asked.)

Rosa: Newsmongerer and gardener; a Hispanic domestic; 5'4, obese, rectangular glasses adhered to a hard round face. Dull brown eyes flitter between social interests. Her right arm is often raised at the elbow with her hand upheld limp and adjacent near her head while she roams—primed to pounce on one of the many compulsive activities the labor allots. She speaks broken English and often employs fluent Spanish when communicating with other Hispanic ethnicity employees and patrons—to converse on inconsequential banality (gossip, weather, food, declarations of being "tired"), regardless of language.
Self-assigned meaning in life: "To take care of my family."

Christina: A lifelong exploited trollop with four children to feed as a single mother. A mousy prevaricator. A 5'2 Caucasian woman in her late fifties. An incompetent hustler. The labor is onerous for her because of being an idiot; she fears fault or failure, reinforced by Kim's crass criticisms, which inflict Christina with doubt—of her job's security. Strained soliloquies are common utterances while Christina flits about to employ herself—a gracious, neurotic airhead, an impotent tart.

Self-assigned meaning in life: "Taking care of my kids and um, I don't know! Having a good time?"

Hunter: A 5'8, Caucasian, obese nineteen-year-old who struggles with severe depression and sexual identity issues. An intelligent buffoon who is prone to prattle and outbursts of mock female orgasms. My closing colleague. A moralist about workplace policy and an expert phenomenological philosopher of internet memes; a Dungeons and Dragons (DND) roleplaying dungeon master (DM); attended college with the intent to become a social worker and dropped out due to failing grades and joined me to work full-time. Fixates on me and sings classic rock to elicit a (null) reaction. Kim's favorite acquiescent employee.

Self-assigned meaning in life: "What the hell kind of question is that? There is no meaning."

Kalvin: A apprentice welder who works part-time, four hours a day throughout the workweek. A twenty-year-old, 5'1, stout Vietnamese man. Insipid conformity produces a character of sufficient common sense coupled with a mundane individuality: a valuable asset to the team. Declarations of hatred for labor dominate his speech, equal with half-hearted taunts with intent to establish a pedestrian rapport.

Self-assigned meaning in life: "I don't know. That's a really weird question."

Cesar: A 5'3 eighteen-year-old fraternity attendee pursuing a business degree with aspirations to become involved with the development of wind turbines. Slouched and amiable. Five siblings of varied ages. Fast-food labor is his first experience with employment. Optimism is an understatement: Gleeful, repressed, and safeguarded against humanity's atrocities. Gulled and persuaded by every person of age or rank superior to his own while he acquiesces with a forced smile. He is a naive man: happy, jaunty, sweet, and smart. I gave him a signed copy of my book *(Year Two)* without a word spoken; he clutched *it* to his chest, gazed at me with an indebted expression, and whispered, "Thank you so much," in one, effeminate, exasperated breath.

Self-assigned meaning in life: "Hm, that's a deep question. (Forty-second consternation while filling waffle fry sleeves.) To help people."

Baethan: A misanthropic "schizoid" attracted to the secluded waffle frier corner. A 6'1, twenty-eight-year-old Caucasian man. A militant

observer. Impeccable and proper appearance. Stands and stares straight forward during extended periods of inactivity. Paces behind associates as a quasi supervisor with both hands steepled near his abdomen. Silently corrects mistakes and deficiencies to the chagrin and indignation of his peers. An insufferable companion who speaks only when necessary and thrives on cerebral odium; a reticent and supercilious mien; a solemn wretch; a dour crank with an admirable work ethic and a despicable persona.
Self-assigned meaning in life: To write.

"**Apart from this, what goes on in other people's consciousness is, as such, a matter of indifference to us; and in time we get really indifferent to *it*, when we come to see how superficial and futile are most people's thoughts, how narrow their ideas, how mean their sentiments, how perverse their opinions, and how much of error there is in most of them; when we learn by experience with what depreciation a man will speak of his fellow, when he is not obliged to fear him, or thinks what he says will not come to his ears. And if ever we have had an opportunity of seeing how the greatest of men meet with nothing but slight from half-a-dozen blockheads, we shall understand that to lay great value upon what other people say is to pay them too much honor.**"

- Arthur Schopenhauer's The Wisdom of Life

Wednesday, November 27th, 2019

12:11 PM

An obnoxious array of variegated, fast-paced, electronic beeps sets the mood of every shift. I veer past my colleagues and wash my hands at one of two sinks and listen to the cacophonous aggregations... sheer and brutal—vexatious and coarse. Overhead fans roar. Kim asserts her overblown authority via micromanagement of her peers, barking orders to employees who were *already* committed to a command. Crowds of hungry college attendees laugh, jitter, and whisper absolute nothings into each other's ears.

"What should I get? I don't know what to get!" exclaimed a hopeful nubile girl to a man three years her senior, and advanced in height by eighteen inches.

The man lowered his head, remained fixated on the menu, and said, "Uh."

Lo, to the three fryer vats filled with peanut oil, and hark to the beeps! Behold, the stations:

One assembles sandwiches of four varieties:

1. **Regular chicken sandwich** consisted of buttered and toasted processed white bread with two pickles and a fried chicken fillet.
2. **Regular chicken sandwich** with no pickles.
3. **Spicy chicken sandwich** consisted of buttered and toasted processed white bread with two pickles and a fried chicken fillet marinated in extra spices, oil, and additives.
4. **Spicy chicken sandwich** with no pickles.

Customers may request the addition of lettuce, tomatoes, and cheese (American, Colby Jack, and Pepper Jack) for a modest fee. Grilled chicken on a brioche bun is an unpopular option.

The second station is a breading cart (nicknamed "The Beast," by Kim), where one stands, yellow gloves/apron adorned, and prepares fillets and nuggets to be fried with a soak in "milk wash" and pressed with a coat of additive-laced flour. *"Nuggets please!"*; *"We need spicy!"*; *"Drop regular!"*; *"Drop nuggets!"*; *"Need a lot of nuggets!"* are average variations of shouted orders to be obeyed.

The third station is a potato fryer at the opposite end of the breading cart; tucked into an alcove, one manages two rectangular steel baskets suspended over a vat of soybean oil diagonal to a fridge stocked with bags of waffle fries (and miniature hash browns for breakfast). One-click of salt from a dispenser for one basket of fries; two-clicks of salt for *two* baskets of fries. Size options: Large and medium.

The fourth and final station is the role of a sauce dispenser and chicken nugget boxer. Two panes of glass affixed to the counter impede customers from excess consumption. Each individual must request and receive sauce from an employee at no extra charge. This station is risible, outlandish, and serves to provide awkward and often unpleasant interactions (for the customer dealing with myself) when they are met with my apathetic gaze and monotonous, robotic, "You're welcome," after I'm thanked for the dispensation of the flavored fat packet(s).

Absent-minded labor conducted to the satisfaction of a small subsection of the college denizens in demand of unhealthful product; a negligible work; a worthless endeavor, though I'm compensated for my nugatory contribution to society with a median bi-weekly paycheck of $650; that's an estimated $14,000 a year after deductions.

5:35 PM

I desire sexual release, as any young man of my age would, yet I'm rendered catatonic and disinterested in the reflection of what each act of gratuitous engrossment with the flesh is. The grotesqueries of human conduct and the fickle, transitory feelings each gender inhibits are raw pain, pure and distilled, to *think* of emotion, of the inherent selfishness of what humanity deems romantic "love," rather, lust.

I've contemplated homosexuality to a great extent, based on an innate comprehension of what man is—a familiarity of masculinity and honor, though the flesh disgusts me, even my own, and I often revisit memories, back to the throes of insanity, embraced with a woman.

The first sunrise to sunset of a five-day Thanksgiving vacation from my primary employer is spent in solitude, in my apartment, wherein I lift weights, pull my chin up to be parallel with a doorway rod, push my body off the floor, pace the circuit of my living room/kitchen with literature by Schopenhauer in hand, listen to quiet emanations of oratorios by J.S. Bach through the medium of subpar laptop speakers, consume, and ponder my lack of existence. The minuteness of my physical body contrasted by the unfathomable macrocosmic dimensions of the universe, compounded with the insipid documentation of my ruminations concerning *sex,* is hilarious.

Thursday, November 28th, 2019

11:12 AM

On a bright Thanksgiving morning, at the sound of a 6:45 AM phone alarm, a man awoke, yawned, turned to his regal partner clad in a transparent silk gown, and said, "Today is as good as any day to be struck head-on by a vehicle."

The woman giggled, blinked twice, positioned herself up onto a pillow with a crooked forearm, slanted her hand against her chin, and said, "Now why do you say that?"

"I'm not hungry, and I know I won't be, even when the mac n' cheese and pies are brought out, though that's…" The man laid spreadeagled, stared up at a light-grey paneled bedroom ceiling, closed his eyes, pressed his wrists against both cheeks, slammed his arms against a featureless bed, sighed, and continued, *"It's just a good day for it."*

"I wish you wouldn't."

"Why?"

"I can't afford a funeral with Black Friday tomorrow and I need someone to take care of the kids while I'm out with the girls on Saturdays." The woman assumed a sly countenance, narrowed her eyes, and spread her fingers over the top of the man's right hand.

"Sometimes you don't come home until Sunday morning."

The woman retracted, thumped flat onto the bed, and snorted; she said, "Don't start this again."

"Yeah. Today's just as good as any."

"You're such an asshole."

"I haven't even done anything and you're insulting me."

Both lay for a quiet moment and listened to the hastened inhalations of each other.

The woman said, "You're alluding that I'm out *screwing* other guys on Thanksgiving morning *right* after you talked about wanting to *kill* yourself. How are you *not* an asshole?"

"All right Tiffany, you win."

"No, *no,* I don't want to win anything, I just want—I-" The woman mewed, suppressed tears, flipped the covers aside her curvaceous body, scooted off the bed, stood, and marched over a plush amber carpet into an adjacent hall where she veered out of the man's peripheral vision. The man remained statuesque in the bed, fixated on a few discolored speckles on the corner of one ceiling panel, and listened to the woman's distant, affectionate exclamations: *"Good morning you two! Happy Thanksgiving!"*

7:22 PM

I sit on my weight bench with the lights off in my small apartment and gaze out the horizontal slits of window blinds at the patter of rain on a darkened street while I consume a conglomeration of two apportioned grilled chicken fillets, a boiled sweet potato, two tablespoons of peanut butter, one tablespoon of Ceylon cinnamon, three ounces of diced apple, an ounce of apple cider vinegar, a handful of mixed nuts, and a drizzle of raw honey.

"Every day is Thanksgiving," said a bitter old man.

9:34 PM

I have forsaken all love and choose to live on the verge of destitution, committed to this defamatory documentation, prepared for a premeditated, deplorable doom. If I were to befall disease or become disabled, my mental affairs' improvident consequences would be authenticated for the captious and perverse nature that *it* is when subjected to genuine misery and agony. My death will be an infantile expression.

Sardines and honey for dessert.

Friday, November 29th, 2019

10:59 AM

Inside an ovoid cavernous recess, a raven-haired young woman finished the last strokes of an elongated, modified recreation of Vincent Van Goth's *Starry Night* on a thirteen-yard-wide stone wall. The fresh, vivid colors, illuminated by several makeshift torches spanned across the opposite wall, shone with a subtle brilliance.

A man—a stranger, of similar age and mien, entered the chamber and befell a fate worse than death on sight of the woman beside the mural. "My God…" he muttered and placed a leather-gloved hand upon his chest.

The woman backstepped and whirled away from her creation to address the stranger, the template of paints and brush balanced within the grasp of delicate fingers held parallel to her abdomen. "Who are you?" she hissed.

"An admirer, for sure," said the man; his eyes transfixed on the woman's stern visage.

"Get out."

The stranger advanced a step and said, "But, *wait.*" Silence ensured, accented by the crackle of fire; the man swallowed, shook his head, advanced a stride beyond the cavern's threshold, and said, "I love you."

"Get *out,* now," the command resounded.

"I must know your name."

The woman tossed her template and brush to the unvaried stone floor, unsheathed a dirk strapped alongside the small of her back, and held the stainless blade outstretched in front of her, tip pointed at the stranger's forehead. An aspect of resolute affirmation overtook the man's countenance; he lowered his hand; both palms faced forward by his waist; he said, "Ah," and feigned a smile while he observed the contents of the unorthodox living quarters: A simple bed comprised of pink linens atop a pile of straw, a large rectangular icebox, and a steel rack of modern dumbbells assorted by weight. "I don't think you heard me correctly," he droned and gazed around the room. "I said, 'I love you.'"

"I'll kill you if you don't leave."

"I have a weapon of my own."

"Then we'll fight and you'll die."

The stranger met the woman's dire glare with a grin of jovial wonder and said, "Are you certain?" The woman accelerated, spanned the four-yard space between herself and the man within three seconds, and plunged the dirk into the left side of his exposed neck while he reached for a 9mm handgun affixed to his belt. Both toppled to the unyielding stone. The woman's knees thrust into the man's groin while he groped: elbows bent, fingers flexed and convulsed against the holster of his weapon. The woman twisted the dirk, retracted, and stabbed two inches above the previous wound. The man's movement stymied; paralyzed, his body quivered from the force of the woman's amplified weight pressed against the blade lodged within his flesh.

Entertainment. A droll waste of time. Insensible violence and inept dialogue.

"Show, don't *tell,*" asserts an absurd authority of literature.

The woman butchered the man after she enjoyed his agonized death throes. She pleasured herself with his amputated genitalia and stored the remainder of his severed limbs inside the icebox. Later that night, she extracted the heart and liver from the torso, consumed both raw organs by the glow of a moribund torchlight, and bashed the corpse's head to a pulp with a fist-sized rock.

8:43 PM

A federal holiday proposes that American people meet up to spend an exorbitant amount of money on food and remind one another that each exists. The next day, millions surge through the streets or peruse online venues for "discounted" products with the residual notion of their extended family to think of while Christmas looms. The masses fuel the system; some abstain, and what are they but a bane.

Saturday, November 30th, 2019

8:43 PM

To lose oneself in the intuition of another's thoughts concerning what you may be to them is the apex of madness, though what else is there? When you consider the nothingness that is your "self," and all other individuals engrossed with their own minds and thoughts of what others think of *them,* you wade through an intricate network of sentiments that may be simplified as, *"How will this benefit* me?"

I sit on my weight bench, stare at a white wall, wonder why anyone would care, and then I realize—again, as though I had been blessed to forget, that people are rapt by other people, for we are each other's one true source of validation, of godliness: little playthings and models to be studied and understood, each with an absurd tale to tell and innovative conceptions of thought deemed brilliant by those who hadn't suffered a similar passion. Kill one, praise three, enslave a dozen, condemn thousands, envy a million, lust for a billion. Little people. Watch them watch you.

DECEMBER

Sunday, December 1st, 2019

11:03 AM

Workplace Courtesans

A woman corresponds with gift and word.
Her daughter enamors by simple gaze:
Lips upturned at the fringes;
Starry eyes of intrigue.
Stymie the tongue, nod the head,
Preserve yourself, lest you supplant
The hollow within, for a
Whole without.

7:07 PM

A package containing Albert Camus' *The Myth of Sisyphus*, Jean-Paul Sartre's *Nausea*, and Friedrich Nietzsche's *Beyond Good and Evil* and *The Genealogy of Morals*, has been purchased and delivered to my doorstep.

"Living the dream," said a dispirited social worker.

Monday, December 2nd, 2019

9:19 PM

After a full week of silence, within the first half-hour of my shift, preceded by a five-day vacation, I examined a salad atop a counter prepared by my supervisor, Kim, and frowned. The salads had been reduced in size to 2/3rds of the previous week's volume while the price remained unaltered.

Kim rounded me, scrutinized my face (a common behavior from *all* my co-workers now), and spoke with a persecuted inflection, "What's wrong with *it?*"

I turned away from Kim towards an approaching college student and uttered a reactionary denouncement: "*It*'s a total ripoff."

"You're at the wrong job, dude."

I spoke (*again*—damn me) an instantaneous affirmation: "Don't I know *it*," while I walked towards a beeping fryer.

Kim grimaced within my left peripheral and said, "All fast-food places do this kinda thing."

I said nothing for the remainder of my shift.

A young boy woke to the sight of a monstrous absurdity, brown and amorphous, latched to his bedroom ceiling. The boy screeched an unholy wail, leaped out of bed, bound to his closed door, twisted down on a handle rendered immovable by an unknown power eighteen times, banged on the door with two feeble fists twenty-two times, continued to screech until his voice cracked—thereby, he screamed.

The absurdity listened to the screams and waited.

Disoriented and terrified, the boy turned, braced his back against the door, stared up at two distended green eyes hung slack from foot-wide fetid sockets by sinewy optic nerves, and continued to scream. Two minutes elapsed; the boy quieted, wedged himself into the corner of his room—gaze fixated on the vague aspect of the moonlit monstrosity, and managed to mewl, "What are you?"

The boy's voice spoke within his consciousness, "I AM WHATEVER YOU WILL."

A brief moment of silent consternation ensued; the boy pondered and thought of a large trimmed hedge he saw three weeks and a day ago on an unfamiliar route on his way home from school. The monstrous absurdity morphed—an instantaneous transposition, into a perfect simulacrum of the hedge, adhered to the ceiling and darkened by the ill-lit room.

The boy's terror abated; he giggled, touched his left cheek with the tip of his left pointer finger, and said, "That's stupid."

"SURELY!"

The boy thought of a Thanksgiving turkey mounted on a small circular podium surrounded by four red-cheeked pilgrims garbed in green tunics and white stockings; the image appeared before him. The boy lapsed into a fit of uncontrollable laughter and jejune theatrics; he clapped his hands thrice, closed his eyes, thought of a strawberry shortcake, and there, before him, *it* suspended in the space above his bed. The boy frowned, closed his eyes, and thought of his naked mother; he opened his eyes and there she was: a lifeless figure, bare and sleek. The boy woke in his bed thereafter, ogled the sunlit panels of his vacant bedroom ceiling, scratched at the right side of his head inches above the ear, and sighed.

Tuesday, December 3ʳᵈ, 2019

9:22 PM

My enforced silence has alienated me from my colleagues. Consequently, my reputation has plummeted and I displace myself to the waffle fryer where I spend the majority of my shift before closing functions initiate. I speak to comprehend customers' needs, to the aggravation of those nearby who once considered me a ~~friend~~ adequate distraction. Hunter persists with outbursts of song near my ear, histrionic dancing, and conversational prods, e.g., "Baethan, on a scale from newborn baby Jesus to O.J. Simpson, how innocent are you?" and "Baethan, if you sterilize the inside of your asshole with a wet wipe, do you consider *it* sanitary for contraband?"

There are instances when I am thanked for unanticipated behavior by those turned away from me, e.g., I present our dishwasher, Wayne, with two containers of chicken noodle soup; he said, "Thank you, sir," with his back turned to me, and I hesitated for several seconds before I said in-turn, "You're welcome, Wayne," out of the established norms of common decency, for I desire to be understood, for he was unable to view my reassuring countenance paired with a respectful head nod. And for what? There is no difference if my intentions are acknowledged or ignored. I *will* commit myself to speech necessary for survival and the performance of my duties, *only*.

No more greetings or dismissals, nor "thank you" and "you're welcome." I will endure an interpersonal hell of my own design, at the mercy of my *actions*.

I speak… to myself, in *this* format; I am my own void to fill with "I."

Wednesday, December 4ᵗʰ, 2019

8:50 PM

I begin each day wrapped within a cold black comforter strewn across my floor in an empty bedroom to the resonance of a generic 7AM phone alarm. I rise from a dull-grey carpet and veer past white walls through an archway; to my right is the bathroom, to my left, the kitchen and living room. I enter the kitchen for a few swigs of room temperature water siphoned from a countertop filter and proceed to the bathroom where I wipe ground from the corners of my eyes with a cotton swab tip. The face I observe in the mirror never meets my expectations of the man I know myself to be. Something pleasant and innocent gazes back at me with doleful eyes and unkempt hair. I turn away in disgust and wish to crush the whelp of the man I am chagrined by.

Urination. Shave. Shower. Once more beset by the mirror, the face is invigorated and impudent; a flash of scorn marks the end of the bathroom ritual.

Return to the kitchen: A *tad* too clean for a single man to enjoy the complete uninhibited virility of his isolation. No appliances. Three small cardboard boxes on one of the two counters serve as a makeshift podium for a writing device. A few books are wedged upright between the stack of boxes and the wall to the left. A few handwritten journals from yesteryear—yet to be transcribed to digital format, litter the space to the right, alongside scraps of paper scrawled on with vague conceptions and ideas. One black ink pen acquired in U.S. Navy boot camp, eight dollars in cash, a house and mail key, a company name tag, a book light, a voice recorder, and a New York State photo ID are scattered amongst the remainder of the counter space.

Stacks of recycled translucent plastic (salad) containers and five rectangular Tupperware pieces are arranged on the kitchen countertop to the left of my sink atop an array of scavenged silverware. Two pots on the stovetop: One enormous; the other, too small.

I drink an impotent pre-workout mix, lift a pair of adjustable 52.5 lb dumbbells (my single furnishment), perform calisthenics, and pace around the closet and cabinet space at the center of my adjoined kitchen and living room while I rest between sets with a book held up to my face. Physiological boons are diminished and retention is hindered on account of split attention to both activities. Drink whey protein mixed with Ceylon cinnamon, raw honey, and apple cider vinegar. Eat a can of sardines and a banana. Read until 11:25 AM. Depart for work at 11:45 AM.

Each venture from my apartment, I breathe deep and contemplate the existence of every sensory input I perceive and savor the brief synaptic discharge induced by the fourteen-minute jaunt between home and university.

Arrive at 11:59 AM.

Friday, December 6th, 2019

6:10 PM

Cockroaches dropped in a closed container filled with a 1-millimeter layer of apple cider vinegar suffer an exquisite death. The immediate drop after a prod into the caustic chamber incites the creature into a frenetic panic. I imagine the shared consciousness of what constitutes the basis of life confined to the miniature body and thereby anthropomorphize the agony I witness, albeit, the sensations may be stymied due to the cockroach's limited faculties—compared to a human. Between vinegar and tabasco sauce, I've determined the vinegar to be the most effective in terms of lethality, while the tabasco sauce inflicts prolonged anguish, followed by a torpid agony, until the specimen relents and quits life out of necessity.

Oh, *you,* yes *you,* pissant reader, indulged on this journey of words I've smithed for *my* pleasure. I vindicate your judgments of *my* debasement, of my immoral character and social rebellion—positive or negative.

Yes, the execution of life by grotesque methods is absurd, that is *all.*

In truth, I'd rather be the curator of live human subjects, an operator of a live-action museum with features such as the iron maiden, the rack, and the Judas cradle, etc., operated by robust juveniles eager to exact pain upon self-professed saints. *Then* I'd be a writer of quality, to be marked and noted in the annals of antiquity beyond my time, studied in high school classrooms, lambasted by theists and pitied by scholars. I'll be exalted if these words evade a scrutinous mind; my virulence is contagious.

Saturday, December 7th, 2019

3:22 PM

Another weekly (Saturday) shift began with my part-time employment at a research center situated at the cities' singular mall. I entered, a Navy-issued pack strapped to my back, filled with hygienic essentials, 32oz of water, a spring mix chicken salad, and two copies of my second-year publication. At the mall's busiest pedestrian intersection where I'm stationed, a colossal Christmas tree bedazzled with bright bulbs and glittery garnishments loomed over a pseudo-Santa Claus and his ~~elvish~~ African-American photographers. Among these jovial denizens: a one-dollar-operated crane game filled with plastic balls valued at $0.08, a 2019 Ford sports car painted a bold red, vendors of candy, fudges, inscribed imitation silver rings, worthless trinkets, five-dollar 18oz lattes, and plastic phone cases. Noise. Cacophonous clamor. Incessant chatter. Infantile wails. Youthful screams. Inaudible Christmas music droned from an array of hidden speakers sixty feet overhead. One hour into my shift, I managed to convince one overweight thirty-three-year-old social worker and her 6'0 sixteen-year-old blockhead son to endure twenty-five minutes of me conducting a survey preceded by the viewing of a work-in-progress horror movie trailer.

My refined pitch: "Excuse me." *[Disinterested acknowledgment of a potential sucker.]* "Are you interested in being paid to watch a trailer for a movie?" With a 94.9% failure rate, I experience rejection on the level of Don Juan.

Two hours into my shift, a spineless desk boy employed with the company I work for approached me on the mall floor and whispered, "Matilda (the gaudy, obese, 5'5, brown-haired manager) wants to speak with you."

I nodded, keen on my dedication to the preposterous practice of perpetuated mutism in all matters of personal social relations, strode to the establishment offices, and entered my manager's office under the impression that she wanted to speak with me in-person after I had emailed her with a request to increase my hours for one month on account of being furloughed for the upcoming Christmas vacation at the university.

"Hello Baethan, please have a seat right here." Matilda pointed to a black, six-legged, nondescript rolling chair. I sat; she closed the office door on my knee and commanded simultaneously, "Will you just—will you *please* move over?" before I entirely situated myself in my seat.

I rolled the chair a foot to my right and stared forward, contented, fingers pyramided on my lap.

Matilda slammed into her seat, rolled towards the computer screen, grazed the monitor with weary eyes, turned to me, and said, "All right Baethan, I've been informed that you're using a voice recorder while you work here," she stated, and paused, as an opportunity for me to incriminate myself.

I raised an eyebrow and smiled, tickled by my co-worker's duplicity— the *single* man who I informed of my activities due to *my* hubris. I said, "Yes."

Matilda huffed and said, "Please turn *it* off and put *it* on the table."

I reached for my left pocket and said, "I have *it* on me, but *it's* not turned on."

"Please turn *it* off and put *it* on the table."

Our eyes locked. I said, slower, *"It's* not turned on-" as my fingers gripped the four-inch device.

Matilda immediately repeated before I finished my sentence, "Please turn *it* off and put *it* on the table."

My smile intensified. I spoke with plain inflection, *"It's* not turned on," and pulled the device from my pocket to hold out in front of me atop an outstretched palm.

Matilda picked the device off my hand, careful not to touch my flesh, inspected the blank screen, and placed the recorder on a table decorated with a vase of fake sunflowers. Her visage assumed a crestfallen pout; she reached for a paper on her desk and said, "Unfortunately you've violated company policy by recording surveys and I need to take action."

"I didn't record any surveys."

"Well-" she glowered down to her right, snapped her attention back to me, and resumed with uncertainty, "You even having this on you is against policy even if you're using *it* or not. Do you understand?"

"Yes."

"Now as much as I don't want to do this I have to because of company policy—which is a shame because you were our best recruiter..."[2]

At this point I failed to contain my joy; my mind raced with thoughts of the inept vermin of a man who chattered away—alas, I am my own saboteur, for *I* spoke a month ago, under the pretense of trust and comradeship; I laugh (while I write) and scoff at myself for the communication of my foolish secret. The crystallization of my self-imposed value to be silent in dealings with personal relations compounded, for what is a friend but a gratuitous validator at our worst moments and a treacherous scoundrel at our best? The man had inadvertently spared me of my unemployment dilemma. Now, when Christmas vacation begins for the college students on the 13th of this month, I will be *fully* unemployed without the need to scrape by with *less* money for working *more*. I scribbled my signature on

---

[2] All employees idled, complained, and conversed with each other, vendors, and shoppers. On the contrary, I ignored everyone and preyed on the naive, stupid, bored, and curious, i.e., I worked, hence my superior efficacy. Sudden invalidation due to my mutism amplified with envy incurred by comparisons of competence impelled the betrayal of my colleague(s).

the notice for employment termination, said nothing more to Matilda, and extended my hand for a shake; her eyes watered and she accepted with the limp wrist of a feminine office slave. I stood.

Matilda addressed me with dire gloom expressed in her maternal countenance and said, "I'm sorry Baethan—that circumstances are this way." Indeed, Matilda had been sorry for herself, for she lost her best Saturday employee due to his asinine behavior. I marched out of the office, elated, liberated from my dismal duty as a pawn of a data-mining nuisance.

9:00 PM

I occupy my little space and think of all the men who lived before, and those who live now, that perform(ed) the same mental gymnastics in their idle time. What I mean is, the self-reflective process of understanding the immediacy of death in conjunction with an existence limited by the faculties of the human creature. This "universal consciousness" of which I've produced a few disjointed and unrefined thesis by a surge of ephemeral inspiration is an illusion created by the human desire to be something other than what *it* is: A little bit of matter teaming with other matter.

Is this a novel with a protagonist; if so, who is the antagonist but God? If I am God, must I thwart myself, being also the protagonist?

Enough—I defile and promulgate ideas thought before. I may as well be plagiarizing, even after an exchange of certain words for pleasant synonyms to craft a sentence of similar frequency.

What else do I have to offer if *it* is known that nothing can be known other than a blip of my life from day-to-day, aware of the futility of my endeavor to create, for nothing is new but manifestations of art, which is a perversion of truth. My art is a perspective, and when all perspectives are perverse lenses unto which we view this world, all realities *are* an illusion maintained by the perceiver. Alas—more regurgitated concepts, though is there anything more profound than this? All fiction is by comparison tasteless to the immediate. All human progress is null, equatable to the shift of tectonic plates and planetary objects' trajectory throughout the universe: There is progress, though towards *what*? Again, more ideas mimicked with differentiated prose.

How else will I commit myself to the fulfillment of this self-assigned purpose—though I haven't chosen; I am *compelled* out of an aversion to the oft-espoused life: to *simply* live and be happy.

A white twelve-by-twelve foot room devoid of furnishings and illuminated by one eight-foot by one-foot rectangular fluorescent panel spanned across an eight-foot-high ceiling.

"I don't want to be happy," said a judge to a priest.

The priest fluttered his luxurious eyelashes, lowered his head, and said, "I *truly* am sorry for you."

"You've nothing to be sorry for."

"Tonight I'll be going home to my wife and three-year-old daughter; a ham and mashed potatoes await me, and my wife will serve us beer in wine glasses atop a cedarwood table covered by a regal tablecloth."

The judge enunciated each word with sluggish precision: "Why do you tell me this?"

"I share my happiness with my friends."

"I'm not your friend."

The priest chuckled, shook his head, and affirmed, "You're *my* friend."

The judge closed his eyes. Fourteen seconds elapsed; the judge opened his eyes to behold an empty white room and an open door connected to an adjacent hallway outlined by darkness.

Sunday, December 8th, 2019

6:19 PM

I suppress a few hollow, selfish tears on behalf of my mother and father, for the grief, languishment, confusion, disgust, anguish, and resentment I've inflicted on both. Humans require the companionship and love I avoid; even my emotions are pretentious on this account, for I've injured myself and everyone who ever cared for me. There is no woe or pity justifiable for any fate I befall. I wish upon myself a cruel, agonizing end, for what I'm worth as a man amounts to twisted amoralism. Torture no longer terrifies me, not even a chill, for the pain may be endured. I fear the man I may become if I am to ever act on my dehumanized spirit.

My mother is unknown to me; she is a false idol I have conquered (applicable to my father).

My father is alone; he may be dead, or wish to die (applicable to my mother); isolated—no matter who he ingratiates, with his petty pleasures and amusements. I empathize, as I toy with the fickleness of idle pastimes all the same. Each book read, musical composition heard, scraps of food ingested, and words wrought into existence by my hands is a subtle plea to supplant the nothingness of every moment. Is this pathetic, or is there something greater?—when *I* am the sole condemner or redeemer of my character; I cast the judgment, and the thoughts determine my flesh's physiology—the conduit to interact with this world of incredible, chaotic entropy. Yet there is the illusory order on which our aggregated reason and logic is founded; I scorn this, for *it* is the basis of all notions of progress and by consequence the accursed traits of humanity; yes—traits damnable by the collective judgments of a society which strives to thrive—to propagate and expand, which promotes the exact "evil" punished in individuals by the collective for an exceptional performance of the *game*.

Transcendent feelings of empowerment foreshadow anxieties of death, also contrariwise. I'm lost in a bedlam of intransigent riddles pertinent to the conduct of life. I owe nothing to those who love.

"But this time is ours, and we cannot live hating ourselves."

- Albert Camus

Monday, December 9th, 2019

7:56 PM

When I return home from my shift, I enter my apartment and am overwhelmed by a sense of not belonging. Everything is foreign. The objects I've accumulated are strange anomalies that happen to exist in the same space I've situated myself. While I consider this, I chew my meal with great care, aware of my innards and of what enters. I hear the neighbor's television through the kitchen wall to my right and feel displaced from reality; is this *my* space? No, *it* never has been, no matter where.

Lack of speech has rendered people strange to me. My silent and subtle gesticulations are more effective than if I were to speak. Intuitions guide me. To my surprise, I'm no longer regarded as a pitiful man too afraid to speak, for my mien, work ethic, and good-natured will affirms my character. I'm no longer feared or loved; colleagues are circumspect, curious, and *abiding*. My managers accept my impersonal responses to their greetings and inquiries of my mood. A thumbs-up, head nod, and quaint smile suffice. I'm relieved of social pleasantries.

Christmas vacation begins on the 14th. I intend to spend the entire month alone in my apartment, to leave only for trips to the local grocery store and the apartment complex laundry unit. I desire sex, to dominate and thrust into a woman, to ravish a feminine being with affection and affirmation; I must refrain for the sake of my madness and folly. I think back in time two months ago to my fraternization with the young girl, Amethyst. "To love is to lose," she said to me, two weeks before I terminated our relationship. Romantic comedies are a tired trope, millenniums-old.

Tuesday, December 10th, 2019

7:46 AM

There is nothing remarkable about writing and publishing a book; in my youth, I dreamed of *it,* of what material would manifest from my mind. My youth… a distant mote of remembrance now, not that there is anything worthwhile *to* remember out of the early stages when all experience seems mystical, fresh, and vibrant with authenticity; even the terrible moments are spirited through the lens of ignorant lucidity.

At the age of seven, I lost my faith, when one December morning I lay in bed and puzzled over the existence of Santa Claus, and how such a man of magnanimous benevolence could exist, and of course, the fount of his power—his elves—crafting electronics packaged in boxes printed with megalomaniac corporate logos; his tenuous relationship with Mrs. Claus, and how he entered homes without chimneys—expected cookies as a tribute, or rather, a tithe, to fuel his quest, and how his consumption betrayed logical capacity of the human stomach, unless he was *inhuman,* and invoked magic to accommodate gross ingestion for the sake of pleasure, but then why would he be fat—unless he *chose* to be. Santa Claus: a diety, my divine, my God; I loved him.

I entered my mother's bedroom at that tender age in demand of an explanation, "Mom. Mom," I woke her. My stepfather had already departed for his labor.

"Baethan… what is it, sweetie?"

"Is Santa Claus real?"

"Of course he is," she muttered a muffled affirmation between blanket and pillow.

My fists clenched; I leaned against the bed frame and said, "You're lying."

"Hunny what's wrong?"

"Why do you lie to me?" Tears welled up in my eyes.

With a slight hesitation, my mother lowered the covers and exposed her drowsy eyes. "I'm not lying. If you believe in him he's real."

"Do you believe in him?"

"Absolutely," she yawned. "Do you?"

"No. *It* doesn't make sense. If I don't believe in him and presents still show up on Christmas then *it*'s just you and Doug and Dad placing them there—*and* eating the milk and cookies."

"Hunny *it*'s too early for this; let's talk about this later-"

"Why do you lie to me about Santa?" I cried.

My mother propped herself up onto an elbow. "What's wrong with you? I told you that if you believe in him he's real. I'm not lying to you. Your father tells you the same, right? He believes in Santa Claus too."

I blubbered, "That's stupid. You're both lying to me."

"Baethan, please stop crying."

"You're a liar."

"All right Baethan, all right, would *it* make you feel better if I told you Santa Claus isn't real?"

"Yes."

"Okay then, Santa Claus isn't real."

I yelled, "Thank you!" turned, ran back to my room, and buried my face into my pillow. My mother chased after me; I proved to be inconsolable; she quit after several minutes and left me with my grief. With a simple shift in thought, I killed my God.

"One of the first signs of the beginning of understanding is the wish to die."

- Franz Kafka

10:20 AM

There are often inconsistencies and errors in my writing; these are essential: distinguishable proofs of my humanity. Spared the numb rectifications of an editor, my perfection is preserved on behalf of my faults. What need have I to pay someone to ensure my clarity and credibility? For that matter, why do I publish? Why do I write?

Wednesday, December 11th, 2019

8:01 AM

Across from the fried chicken station, a virile young man named Emil—a few years younger than myself, works at a sub-making station. Our first conversation transpired two months ago while we worked alongside each other in the dish room. We made points to reveal our ambitions. Emil has been accepted into a college to become a physician and awaits the beginning of his classes next year; thereby, I disclosed my writings and recent separation from the U.S. Navy boot camp.

Emil is a handsome man of European ethnicity, who carries himself with confidence, exhibits superior charisma, is a fluent, extroverted, stream-of-consciousness-speaker, struggles with anger, maintains a muscular physique, is several inches shorter than me, and sports a pompadour. His self-assigned meaning of life is to "Help people in any way that I can."

Emil asked me a few days after my previous question of his self-assigned meaning in life if I thought humanity as a whole would be better off if we all knew the innate meanings of our lives and the mechanisms of the universe we inhabit. I said, "No. If we knew our true meaning, there would be no chance to hope, and we would rebel against the insanity wrought by the knowledge of a pre-imposed fate." Emil strode away, satisfied with my answer. Weeks later, I "gifted" Emil a copy of (Year Two) of this documentation due to his spurious interest and informed him that I don't respect my readers.

Emil said, "Thanks man," with affected enthusiasm, "I'm open to learning anything from anybody."

Often, when business is slow, I stand and stare straight forward from behind a counter, statuesque, with a vacuous countenance, and observe those around me. Emil often lazes on a stool or leans against a similar counter, preoccupied with his phone, though we scrutinize each other's behavior from a distance and there are often negative spikes of energy transferred between us. Intrigued by my own feelings and the intuited knowledge of his feelings concerning me (more so after the recent weeks of my sudden silence each time he attempts to engage me in conversation), I focus my attention on him, which in-turn prompts his attention to me—as often as I catch him mid-stare; we lock eyes across the food court for several inimical seconds and share a latent contempt.

Last night, while I mopped a quadrant of my assigned floor nearest to Emil's station, he rattled off to me his interest in my book, praised my "choice of verbiage," and stated that he reads a page every night and how he'll be reading *it* on the plane while he travels this upcoming Christmas vacation. After his long-winded, sycophantic accolades, he seemed content with my silence and responsive gestures, though I sensed that he yearned for me to speak, for we both withheld secret animosity for one another; he desires to confirm *it*... I *spoke* against my discipline and informed him of my "pseudo mutism," to which he expressed his infallible understanding and compassion.

We puttered around for several minutes after the aforementioned interaction with nothing more to do than wait. I powered on my voice recorder, approached Emil, and captured the following conversation (Speed read Emil's dialogue for vicarious authenticity), transcribed verbatim for accuracy and critical analysis, regardless of how the writing quality is impaired:

I said, "Emil."

Emil whirled to face me, surprised.

I nodded, closed the distance between us, and inquired, "Do you have time to speak now?"

"Yeah! Yeah-" Emil hastened to talk.

"For a few minutes-"

"Yeah—of course-"

"While we have some downtime-"

"Yeah. I have nothing but time. I have nothing going on."

"All right." I smiled. We stood two feet from each other. "So. I want you to treat me as though I am just a man to you, nothing else: you don't even know me; I'm just approaching you as a stranger, and I'm telling you all these things."

Emil's eyes gleamed; he said, "Okay so... Is there a setting? I feel like the setting is going to determine-"

"This sub station."

"Okay."

"Just right here right now. And I am just a man to you."

"Okay."

"So, when I see you, I have some envy—I'm envious, and *it*'s because of your chest."

Emil chuckled.

I continued, *"It*'s because I have pectus excavatum."

"Mhm."

"I'm sure that you've sensed that."[3]

"Uh no I didn't know. No. That's where—that's when—*it's* from your knees when you're in the womb, right?"

"... Uh-"

Emil continued, "-Because you're in a crouched position and when *it* formed *it* formed around your knees? And that caused *it* to be a little bit concave?"

"That may be the cause of *it*."

"I have a friend who has *it*—yeah."

"So, when I see you, I feel slight pangs of envy because of your well-developed chest."

"Okay."

"It doesn't happen so much with others-"

"-Okay."

"Because not everyone has well-developed pectorals."

"Yeah I get that, yeah. So now I go? So like a back and forth?"

"Sure."

Emil shifted, excited, thoughtful, and said, "You give me a full rundown and I give you one."

"Yes."

"Okay. Um. I guess in the same vein I wish I was taller; I envy your height. I see you over there with good posture looking above everybody and I like that, because I'm down here most of the time. So being able to be... I—I—yeah, looking over people—I've always wanted to be a bit taller, I think—I think you're at the perfect height."

We nodded at each other, reassured with one another's confessions; I said, "Now... there was another point—*oh* yes, I believe you are a sociopathic narcissist who cares way too much about what other people think of you."

Emil spoke through a bout of laughter, "I'd say that's actually a pretty damn good description—yeah. Why do you think the sociopathic part of *it?*"

"Because I think I am also sociopathic, and I also think that I am narcissistic, so I am able to identify one when I see one."

Emil beamed and said, "Yeah—I think you're pretty good—yeah—I don't think anyone would be able to pick up on that."

---

[3] By "that," I meant my envy, though I presume Emil thought I meant pectus excavatum.

"Except I have chosen to completely shun what people think for the sake of… being able to validate myself."

"Yeah."

"So, I turn away from everybody, and I have no friendships by choice, which is hard for a narcissist to choose to do."

"That is! That goes against… fundamentally goes against a narcissistic viewpoint."

"Yes."

"Interesting," Emil stated; we both smiled, eased in each other's company.

I said, "So I internalize, and validate myself by consequence."

"Huh—when *it* comes to you I think… I find myself always wondering… what you're thinking about, and *it*'s not so much an analysis of you and how you interact or what you do; *it*'s more so what's going on behind your eyes that I always see. When you're standing over there and you have these brief kind've ephemeral interactions I can tell that there's more that goes on. And I hear people say stuff like '*Oh, it* looks like Baethan is stoned' or whatever, 'I want what he's on,' or something-"

"Yes—you told me before that's what Billy said."

"Yeah yeah, and I see other people, uh, they're always like 'I wonder what Baethan is on over there,' you know, somebody else said that too, and I'm like: 'He's just *thinking*,' and I, I think that… I guess I appreciate *it* in a way—the fact that, I feel like *it* wouldn't really phase you; I could walk up and say pretty much anything I wanted to you-"

"Yes."

"-and I feel like you would hear *it*, but you wouldn't internalize *it* and focus too much on *it* ya know? I don't know I've never really gone and kind've… really, psychoanalyzed you that much but *it*'s been more of that I've wondered what's going on—*it*'s a lot of mystery and intrigue I think with you, because I think you're very… *misunderstood?* Just by the way people—I see you walking sometimes—I see you parked [4] way over in that parking lot one time—just walking and just thinking, and somebody said they saw you in [Supermarket name] one time too and they're like, 'Oh I wonder what he's doing; he's being really quiet' or whatever, and I'm like—I feel like people don't take the time to appreciate and think about what you have to say; like I saw-" Emil began to laugh, "Whose the guy that you work with; I forgot his name; he always wears glasses; he always makes jokes-"

---

[4] I don't drive or own a vehicle. The presumption is understandable.

"Cesar."

"No not Cesar-"

"Kalvin."

"Is Kalvin the Asian guy?"

"Yes."

"No—the other one."

"Cesar."

"No, I just saw him—he was over there yesterday joking with you and I started laughing so hard—because you're standing there clearly deep in thought and he's joking—and he's doing this-" Emil slammed the edge of his right palm against the flat of his left palm thrice, "-like right next to your face and you're just standing there—you didn't even smile or look at him, and uh-"

"Hunter."

"Hunter? Oh yeah, he's the other guy who works there. Yeah okay, Hunter—yeah." A contemplative woman approached the sub counter; Emil addressed her offhandedly and returned his attention back to me. *It's* interesting that you came up with that, because I think I do put a little bit too much thought into what people think—ya' know?"

I turned to leave Emil with the customer and said, "I think you're misunderstood as well."

"Yeah?"

"And I can tell you exactly how, but I'll let you serve her first."

"Yeah—okay."

Eight minutes elapsed while I performed my duties at the fried chicken counter. Hunter worked in silence alongside me. Emil entered our station, said, "Hm, I like your view from over here—different from where I'm at; I like *it,*" and puttered over to an enclosed walkway midway between our stations which serves as a waypoint between the employment sectors and the food court.

I joined Emil under the archway and said, "So, what I was saying, is that people see you as a stud."

"A *stud?*"

"Yes-"

"-Yeah."

We both grinned and I said, "Which is a sexually virile man."

"It's true *it* is—yeah," Emil chuckled and leaned back against the wall.

"But you don't feel that way."

"No!"

"And you would prefer that people didn't see you that way, because when people see you, they often think, 'we'll look at that meathead,' when really there's a lot more there."

"Yeah. Well so how did you come to the conclusion about the sociopathic narcissistic part? I'm just curious to see your reasoning and rationale."

"The interactions. And your behavior is parallel with mine; I see the way that you move, your demeanor, what you pay attention to, what you *don't* pay attention to—and when people think I'm on drugs staring off at nothing, I'm really just observing everything around me."

"No I can tell—trust me; I've—coming from somebody who knows what *it* looks like, *it*'s like I know—I know when somebody's with *it* or when somebody has taken something that alters the way they think or see, but I can tell—yeah—trust me [5]—and I know that there's a lot more going on with people. I don't think people necessarily like to assume... that—you know what I mean—I don't know—I think that people like to take things at face value. *It*'s like he looks like he's not working—he's out of *it*—he's just standing there, but in reality there's more going on than that—based on what you write and how you think, I can clearly tell that a lot of what you take in and a lot of the inspiration and the way that you formulate these ideas and concepts are based on how you stand there— like you said, *it*'s an environment that you can work in and be able to see everything that goes on around you. *It*'s something that's isolated in a sense where you can work independently but you also work with others. *It*'s not like a call center where you have to be talking to people all the time. You can be doing your work whether *it*'s sweeping, or putting... whatever you guys are doing—flour? Or whatever *it* is on *it*. Um, you can work independently and *think* too so I think that's kind've interesting—so I've *noticed* that—I think *it*'s interesting because I always like to know what people are *thinking; I hate not knowing.* When I see Adrianna (a coworker) staring off I ask her what she's thinking about. My girlfriend is sitting there staring at nothing: I say 'What's going on up there in your head—what's driving those ideas in your head?' *It*'s frustrating because nobody ever seems to give me an answer I want too—ya know? But *you*—you give me answers. Like, 'Adrianna what are you thinking about': *'Oh I don't know I'm just staring off-'* *It*'s like—*it*'s impossible to think of nothing. Even the process of thinking of nothing you're still thinking of

---

[5] The assertion to trust compelled me to distrust.

something, ya know? And I think that's interesting because nobody ever seems to want to give an answer about that, but you don't tend to shy away from providing any kind of an answer."

I nodded and said, "Would you say that you rely on your intuitions... in order to 'mind-read' people?"

"Yeah. I see how they interact, and ya know whether *it*'s like Wayne or Adriana, I know that Adriana perceives me as more like a stud, so if I, *it* sounds bad but if I ever want a sandwich I'll come up and touch her arm and be like, 'Hey Adrianna,'" Emil laughed, "'do you have any food back here?' And she'll then go, *'Oh I'll cook you something up!'* Or Wayne is always talking about-"

"See that's the sociopathic aspect—is that you know that your behavior will provide that response."

"Yeah—and I know that Wayne likes to talk about his past and playing basketball so if I even bring up something remotely close to that I know he'll start talking about *that* even though I don't know anything about sports. Like he was asking about the *Fab Five* in basketball and I didn't know so I looked *it* up and quizzed him and I could see that-" Emil shook his head, chuckled, and truncated his speech.

I said, "The whole purpose of this mutism experiment is that people have been accustomed to me being talkative, gregarious, outgoing and friendly-"

"-Yeah-"

"-but really on the inside I abhor everything around me."

"Yeah."

"In particular when I'm standing there," I pointed to the sauce dispensary counter, "I see all the advertisements—all around me-"

"-Yeah."

"-Pepsi, Coca-Cola, Nabisco—everything, and I take *it* all in, and see all these college kids bumbling around talking about absolutely nothing—and I'm standing there—and I know exactly what they think when they see me; they think, 'What the fuck is wrong with this guy? He's trying way too hard to be professional—he's mentally *ill*,'" My voice quaked while I gestured flippant hand movements, "'He's blah-blah-blah—he's this and that,' and I'm just *standing* there, stone-faced-"

"Yeah."

"And I'm taking *it* all in, and I'm thinking..." I stared at Emil for several seconds with an impassioned grimace. "... And that's about *it*-"

"-Yeah."

I pointed upward and spoke with fervor, "I hear *it* all up here in my head, what we may consider to be listening to our intuition."

Emil started with equal enthusiasm, "Yeah, I can tell—I can see *it*—yeah, and I think—I—I—just—I think *it* bothers me a little bit too that people don't give you more credit. I see how hard you work and you've—you go about your day and you're also trying to think if—to do things you want to do I guess within the confines of your own mind—you know—you're not letting people influence that too much but—I—I know—I've—yeah I don't know—I just hear people say that and I—I, I—like sometimes I hear them say 'Oh look at Baethan—look at him-' and you'll be standing there just kinda staring. And I can tell there's more going on *it's* like no—I always tell them 'No he's just thinking right now—he's probably just thinking about something'; I said 'He's probably just thinking about something'—you know-"

Disturbed by the overt ingratiation, I interjected, "I feed off of the negativity."

Emil exclaimed, *"Oh* so I'm working against you in a sense then."

"Somewhat. Well… I mean, I think that stems from the fact that you just want everybody to like you."

"Yeah." Emil's immediate agreement alarmed me.

"You defending me gives you the air of—or the aspect of a good-hearted man to *them."*

"Mhm."

"So really *it's* not for my sake—*it's* for yours."

"Yeah. I guess *it* could be, yeah. I think sometimes they are conscious processes—like I do—I do enjoy our interactions and I didn't want—I don't like this at the end of the day too—I don't think people have been necessarily treated unfairly just because they're different—I did work with like autistic kids and stuff and I remember there's a lot of things—people would be like 'They're different,' and *it's* like—I get like—they act different but *it's* just that they have a different neural circuitry than we do, ya know—than some people at the end of the day—so *it's* like—I don't know—I have moments, but then there's… I, I think part of that is being able to read people to a certain extent ya know I think that does come into play sometimes with how I interact with what people expect out of me and certain interactions. But I'm quick to—I think part of *it* too is that… you're right, it's like a—a status thing too because people sometimes back there—they see me as just a subway worker, and then they talk about school so I slip in that I'm getting into med school-"

36

"-Yes-"

"-just to see their reaction change and they regard me now as somebody more than just a sandwich maker but a future physician, and-"

I smiled and interrupted. "The first time I heard that, when you were standing here-"

"Yeah."

"-and there was that sort of... quasi, cele... celebration, I was standing over there (a few feet away) thinking 'This man just dug his own social grave.'"

Emil chuckled.

I continued, "Because you stating that-"

"Yeah."

"I mean, yes, people have the initial presentation of happiness and admiration-"

"Yeah."

"-but then after *it* sinks in that we're all in this shithole together-"

"Yeah"

"-and they see you and think they, '*Oh*, look at that good-looking guy who has all this going for him-'"

"Yeah."

"'-and I'm stuck here in this shithole,' and then they just grow to envy you instead."

"Yeah."

"And then they just hate you... for *it*. So the same people you told that... initially thought you were... great, going off to bigger and better things now-"

"-Mhm—But is *it* bad that part of me likes that?"

I shook my head and said, "No, because a healthy ego is what makes man what *it* is."

"Yeah. That's true—I just—I guess-"

"-or rather who we are-"

"-I have an issue with being... *disrespected* sometimes. I mean when I go up there (the sub counter) and people go, 'give me *this;* give me *that*,' I feel like—I know *it*'s bad but I kinda want to put them in their place—*it*'s like... I've gone through a new-grad too—*it*'s like, I've been through where you are—*it*'s like—I'm working *hard* right now, I don't need to have whatever shit you feel like giving to me, *given* to me, you know? And sometimes I'm quicker to point that out than I probably should be but I

37

try not to let that come to light too much you know? That's interesting. I don't know. What do your parents do?"

I smirked. "My father is a retired social worker, and—well, he was a postal worker-"

"-Yeah-"

"-for thirty-five years."

"Cool!"

"And my mother was… a… pretty much a tramp, you could say-"

"Really."

"She was a waitress… at a restaurant."

"Okay."

"But, her true vocation was being a tramp."

Emil began with a slight giggle, "Do you think in terms of your personality and the way you think—is that near any of your parents or is *it* pretty unique?"

"Perhaps my father's… militarism?"

"Mhm."

"… Though, I took the militarism on myself—he's more of an old hippie stoner."

Emil laughed.

I said, "… And… no… I try to disregard everything that my parents… ever instilled in me."

"That's interesting! How—what made you… what made that arise though?"

I raised my right eyebrow.

Emil gestured open-handed while he spoke, "What I mean—how did you come to that conclusion? Was there something—because usually when we formulate ideas and opinions about something *it*'s precipitated from an event. You know that's usually—when we experience the world around us that's usually how we formulate opinions; how did you decide that was going to happen—how you—I'm just interested—like did you ever sit down and have conversations like this with your parents? Again—this is me trying to understand your thinking process more and where a lot of this arises within you."

"This conversation is similar, yes, but I was just dismissed as thinking too much."

"Yeah!"

"I came to the conclusion that my parents are a negative influence on me because… they're just *people,* and they really have no authoritative right over you."

"Mhm."

"I used to idolize my father, and as I grew older and spent more time with him, I started to understand all his faults… his entire character as a whole… and I made the decision to sever myself from him."

"Oh so you don't talk to him anymore then."

"No. I don't talk to any of my family."

"Oh," Emil intoned sympathy.

"… That was… the whole purpose of joining the military in the first place—was to… escape, from my hometown, because I had tried many times before, and I had failed due to my own character and choices, and I always… reverted back to *home.*"

"Yeah."

"So I wanted to make a permanent move, but then when I was kicked out [of the U.S. Navy] on account of my writing… and, I know that sounds far-fetched, but that's really what happened."

"That's what you said—yeah, yeah."

"I had the choice to fly back to my hometown, or… to go someplace entirely new, so I chose [City Name], Arkansas, because I did some research, and *it* was the lowest socioeconomic status place you could possibly be, with the best standard of living in terms of wages and food and-"

"-Yeah. That's interesting. So you're not taking any classes right now?"

"No."

"How old are you?"

I muttered, "I'm twenty-eight."

"Twenty-eight—I don't know why I thought you were like twenty-four. So what's your—I don't know if I ever asked you—what's your next step then? Is *it*—is *it* [City Name] forever?"

"I want to be here for a year until November 20th, and then I'm going to leave. I want to join a cult."

"Oh-ho-ho—okay—I mean have you done the research on which ones or-"

"I've started."

"That's interesting well I mean—what—I guess where did that come from? Why a cult?"

I paused for several seconds and contemplated. "Well because… *it's* a convergence of all these loons that believe in one specific thing, and to be there would be a great chance to document them, that lifestyle."

"What happens if *it*'s a cult that decides that you all have to end your lives at the same time—is that something—is that something you'd be willing to do?"

"Even better, because I wouldn't do *it,* and I would be incriminated, and possibly… harmed; *it* has potential for writing, and that's what makes life so lovely."

Emil trilled, *"Yeah* that's *true,"* and normalized his tone. "So you don't think you would ever—but see that—isn't that kind've the scary aspect of a cult, though—is you get this kind've group mentality and then you lose a sense of self, and *it*'s more about what you're… you're believing in or what you're achieving for; and then, aren't you ever worried that *that* would blur the line, that you wouldn't get caught up in whatever their endgame is whether *it* is you need to be alive to worship or end your life in some, glorious way?"

"Well that's where sociopathic and… narcissistic traits come into play."

"I was going to say—those would be an advantage in that sense."

"Yes," my inflection upbeat; we both shared a mutual snicker.

"You're reading people-"

"-To understand what would make them… *happy."*

"That's true. Wow man I got some respect—I don't know that I would ever do *it* but-"

"I wouldn't respect me for *it.*"

"I don't *know!*—but you're-"

I affirmed, *"It*'s completely selfish."

"It is but… that's all the more respect—I feel like a lot of people don't *do* things for themselves. Again like—like a lot of us want to know how others perceive us; I don't think *it*'s selfish—I don't think there's anything truly wrong with *it,* you know? I think *it*'s interesting—I think going out—like you said, you don't really… you just stand there—you don't *try* to make people… smile or do whatever, you're not worried about seeming too professional or whatever you just said just now… *it*'s all-"

"In that way, I care just as much as you about what people think of me; *it*'s just on the complete opposite end of the spectrum. I would prefer for people to think vile things of me, and to think that I'm a fool."

Emil chuckled and beamed. "I guess we're still in that same vein of thought, yeah, *it*'s just you're at the opposite spectrum of *it*… That's interesting… That's a lot to process…" I turned towards my closing coworker, Hunter; he toiled alone and listened to our conversation; I made a move to rejoin him, though Emil pressed the discussion further: "Do you even know where you're going to go from here then, have you even given *it* much thought?"

"I've been searching a… a complete, uh… database… for cults."

"That exists?"

"Yes. And out of all of them I'm trying to find one that would be similar to my interests, something that's focused on the pursuit of knowledge, or…"

"Okay."

"Nothing too… in the theist route…"

"Yeah—yeah."

"But more of an atheist-"

"Right I gotcha."

"And nothing that focuses on one particular person but more of believing in an idea, because that is easy to feign."

"Mhm."

You can always convince people you believe in something just by saying that you do."

"Mhm."

"I did this when I stayed at—*it's* in the book that you're reading now—when I stayed at a place called the *Peaceorama,* and that's essentially a cult where I went to-"

"No kidding."

"-and wrote about that; for three months there, I stayed—and *it's* a commune, and they all study a book together, and I studied *it* with them, and I wrote all about *it,* and I… dismantled their ideas."

"Yeah."

"In my writing… " I hesitated, stared at the floor for several seconds while Emil stood by, and returned my crestfallen gaze to him. "See… To even talk about *it* is… is… *disgusting* to me, because *it's*… *it's*… *it's* all egotistical tripe."

"Yeah."

"And I *do*—really feel bad that I'm even speaking in the first place; *it's* going against my self-imposed mutism." I fumbled in my pocket and showcased the recording device in my palm. "I'm using a voice recorder."

Emil's eyes widened. "Okay."

"And I'm savoring this conversation."

Emil stifled uncertain laughter. *"Okay."* I returned the device to my pocket; Emil resumed: "No I think that's cool—that's interesting though—yeah I uh, I think that you have a lot of… yeah I think *it*'s, I don't know—which ones are you looking at right now, in terms of…"

"Cults?"

"Yeah—I didn't even know there was a database for *it.*"

"I haven't decided. I'm just-"

"I mean are we talking like a hundred or a thousand—I don't even know anything—in terms of, I mean, the actual organizations, how many of those even exist?"

"Oh there's thousands."

"Thousands—okay I don't why I thought *maybe it* would be a hundred, I mean unless-"

"Well there's at least a thousand but there could be two or three thousand… I didn't go over the full extensive list."

"That's interesting—wow. Are you ever worried you're going to get flagged in some kind of a thing looking for cults?"

"I think I am flagged already because of what I wrote about the military, and those-"

"-Ohhh-"

"-physical pages confiscated from my journal-"

"They actually took those?"

I frowned and said, "Yes. I've been trying to get my old writing device and phone back from my recruiters too, that… I left those objects with, and they have refused to contact me again—and I believe *it*'s because the senior chief who confiscated my work, told them to not answer me—and since they *are* the federal government, they *could* be keeping tabs on me."

"Yeah."

"And I'm fully aware of that in all my activities—hence the 'sociopathic*ness*,' where you are always aware of how your activities and actions can affect… everything, when you're thinking about what other people may be thinking."

"Yeah. That's interesting. So I mean do they have access to what's on those or do they know something exists on them?" Customers approached the fried chicken counter and Emil reckoned my repeated glances over my shoulder. "I don't want to hold you—you can get back if you need to."

I shrugged and said, "I think I will. This was a great conversation."

"Yeah absolutely! Anytime, I'm always happy to *talk;* I've got nothing else to do." As Emil walked away, he shouted to me, "What'd you say— what'd you write in the book you gave me—*it*'s, 'For a fellow fool,' I like that; I think about that a lot; I like that."

I grinned, nodded, and returned to my labor.

8:46 PM

I've *spoken* to two individuals thus far (since November 20th) about my practice of pseudo mutism. *Just* what the *hell* is this? I fail to uphold my integrity out of a desire to *speak*, for this is what people *do*. I'm appalled by my own lack of conviction and nebulous motive; there is no purpose to the practice of being mute other than the documentation of the social implications. If I *speak* of the method to others, I'll be gossiped of, and the "truths" yielded from my endeavor are thereby rendered false. Damn this idiocy. Must I be so vain?

Thursday, December 12th, 2019

8:34 PM

I'm astounded by many things: The effectiveness of silence in the workplace, the inconsiderable behaviors people apologize for, the flavor of *King Oscar* brand sardines canned in extra virgin olive oil, with or without jalapeno peppers.

I feel out of the ordinary tonight: swell; I often refrain from writing when I'm affected by optimism for then the content is blithe and palatable. Yes, *sardines* and *extra virgin olive oil...* lovely.

9:06 PM

I feel redundant *again:*

Old Maid

Lard drips down a
Bean-stained double chin
Into the mouth of an infant
Afflicted with cerebral palsy.
"Stop squirming you little shit";
Horrisonant syllables pronounced
Between two blistered lips

Registered in the mind
Of a girl gripped tight
Around the armpits
By a pair of
Indomitable hands.

Friday, December 13th, 2019

7:36 AM

"Why are you kind to those you despise?" I said to Emil an hour before the end of my shift.

Emil addressed me with contentious eyes and retorted immediately, "Because then I won't have to deal with enemies—whose—I don't remember who said *it* but—'Keep your friends close but keep your enemies closer'? Yeah—I mean—[unintelligible]."

I smiled and revealed my teeth while I nodded and clenched the stick of a mop in both hands. Emil had smiled too, though as I watched him turn away from me after a self-imposed truncation of his dialogue, I observed his barren countenance while he pushed his own mop and bucket when he rounded the corner to his station.

"There are only two people who can tell you the truth about yourself: an enemy who has lost his temper and a friend who loves you dearly."

- Antisthenes (444 BC - 371 BC)

Twenty-five minutes elapsed: I emptied a mop bucket into a basin at the back hallway of the primary kitchen; Emil passed by me, prepared to depart through two sets of double-doors; he said, "All right, see you later Baethan."

I said, "Emil..." he stopped, powered off his earbuds, and turned to face me. "Before you go-"

Emil snapped, "What's up?"

"-will you tell me your unfiltered opinion of me?"

"Of *you?*"

"Yes. I could use some ego destruction."

"Ego destruction," Emil repeated, amused.

44

"I desire sweet dreams tonight."

Emil laughed. "That's a—ya *know…*"

I spoke with punctuated precision, "Because… I *know…* that you do… despise me, and I understand why."

Emil met my grim presumption with more laughter and said, "Why would I des—why would you understand why?"

"Because I know what I am."

"And what are you?"

"And I know what my behavior is… and… the behavior that you have responded to; I can read *it* in your body language, especially when we are at our posts…"

"Yeah?"

"And I'm standing there like a fool." I braced myself, body flexed.

"I just think you present yourself differently," Emil chuckled. "If—if you're wanting my honest opinion of you I think you're a little weird… That's all. Yeah. *It's* not just that though; *it's* not in a *bad* way, *it's* just I don't think I've encountered anybody that has… the same persona and the same way that you conduct yourself before—you know what I mean? You're your own class—I haven't quite met anybody like that before."

"I'm not searching for a fight, by all means," I affirmed; Emil raised both palms and shook his head; I continued, "I'm not trained in any sort of martial art."

Glee accented Emil's tonality: "I'm not gonna fight—no-no-no—I'm not looking for any altercation—I just mean like, the way you *think,* and I think—weird in a sense again, not—like I haven't encountered *it* before—unique, out of the ordinary, not to say if somebody else walked by their's wouldn't be weird—weird just means outside I think the social—not even the social norm—just how people interact with each other I think; I think yours is more formal, so I don't—I don't mean weird in a way to tear you down or destroy your ego necessarily; I just think that… you're unique, you know? And I think that you have a lot to offer people—just like how you talk and think about things but… I don't know you have my *un*—opinion is just… a unique person you know I never quite—I don't know—*it's* like hard to come up with something you know?"

I murmured, *"It* could be a mental illness, to some degree."

"I never really considered that though—do you think *it* is? Your personal opinion?"

"Well, I've definitely pondered *it.* Although-"

Emil's speech hastened, "What would *it* be?—I mean mental illness is such a big thing."

"*It* could be my projection of my ego on to you, and *my* opinions on to you; so maybe I'm the one who really disdains you, but I think that you disdain me-"

"*It* could be-" Emil assumed a dubious mien.

"-or rather, despise."

"Yeah, yeah. That's a good point, what would that be though; is that truly mental illness then?"

"See that's what I've wondered for a while."

"You could look *it* up in the DSM."

I scowled and fulminated, "I despise—well I *hate* the *DSM-*"

Emil chuckled, "Okay—well, you don't gotta-"

"In fact, I used criteria from the DSM to get me discharged from the Navy because I had *it* memorized; I've studied *it intensively,* and think *it*'s a crock of *shit-*"

"-Yeah-"

"-that a board of psychologists come up with criteria… of, conditions and behaviors that don't fit a social norm."

"*Exactly*—and I think that's interesting too because when you look at the pathology of like a cell, you can tell which enzymes are functioning and which aren't but—when neurons and stuff fire together you have these emerging properties of cognition, consciousness and behavior, and a lot of the times, we don't understand necessarily all that goes into that. Behavior isn't as simple as 'A' plus 'B' equals 'C', and so I think that that's kind've our… 'shouting into the void' to try and figure out what's going on in terms of that? I don't know!—I mean, I definitely think that some parts of *it* you know at least with bipolar disorder—is *it*, lithium?—helps to—like cause—helps to settle whatever imbalance that is in your brain so I do think there's a scientific thing behind *it*—but, we just don't quite know enough now so *it*'s more generalizations of behaviors-"

I interjected, "I think *it*'s the thoughts that cause the chemicals to shift; and, if you believe in a unified consciousness, there's thoughts you believe you aren't having yourself, but they are, by consequence, an impact from the people that are around you because we're all connected in that way-"

"-Mhm—*but, my* thought behind that is that you don't have thoughts unless your neurons are firing; *it*'s kinda the whole, 'Which came first, the chicken or the egg?'—and in this case I think that the neurons firing cause the thoughts because when you think about *it*—when you get put under anesthesia for a surgery, you shut down that part of your consciousness that keeps you awake to interact—you don't have thoughts, *it's* like you fall asleep and woke back up.[6] So I think without the structural components—the framework of your brain, you don't have your thoughts; *but* the interesting part of that is—I know I learned this in addiction class: You have certain genes that predispose you to have an addictive personality, so even your genes that your parents give on to you may predispose you to thinking in a way in a sense that you may have these cravings—so who's to say that a certain thought pattern or a certain emotion or a way that you react to a certain situation wouldn't be... from your parents? So then I always wondered: 'How much economy do I have with my thoughts' and everything because some of that may be passed down to me. Ya know—if my dad's really aggressive and I start to get aggressive, how do I know that that pattern hasn't been instilled in me before I kinda came into being—ya know that's something locked away in the blueprints of your DNA. So I always think that that's interesting so... I don't know—I don't—I wouldn't say that the whole situation can cause you to get stressed and stress causes certain stress hormones to be released to affect DNA transcription so, *it* very much is this constant interplay between your environment... and yourself—kinda what comes out of that—so who's to say your thoughts aren't directly derived from how somebody else interacts with you, which could then interact—so I think *it's* kinda—I think you *need* all of those structural components in order to perceive and understand something's happening in order for *it* to be influenced but—I don't know, I think *it's*—*it's* so... *it's* weird; *it's* hard to even comprehend—that's part of the reason I like neuroscience—so, that's why *it's* hard to—I guess to get back to your original question, to give you... an assessment of yourself, *it's* just, I don't think you fit into the way that most people interact but then again I don't think you think like the way most people interact—so 'weird' isn't necessarily a bad thing *it's* just a step outside I think of what most people are used to—you know what I mean?"

I inhaled, processed for a moment, and said, "Yes, with all that considered, and that's why I asked you because I know you are intelligent

---

[6] Contemporary research proves this to be false. Anesthetic-induced oscillations dramatically alter when neurons can spike, and impede communication between brain regions that play a role in consciousness. Unconscious thoughts may be experienced but are not retained in memory upon returning to consciousness. Reference: www.the-scientist. com/features/general-anesthesia-causes-telltale-brain-activity-patterns-65501

enough to form a... *accurate* synopsis of my character without even knowing that much about me."

"Mhm."

"So, *it's* more of a relay or a feedback option when I see you, and if you were to ask me the same thing, I would happily provide, my unfiltered, unabashed opinion."

Emil shifted, smiled, laughed, and said, "That's—I mean sure hit me man."

"If you really want to hear *it*."

"Yeah... Okay—yeah!—look I'm not gonna fight you or anything—don't—I don't want you to think I'm gonna be like violent—yeah—no—ya know-"

"All right... I think *it's* pitiful to seek external validation, so the charisma that I witness, is appalling to me-" Emil began to chuckle; I smirked in response, "-that I often gag internally... whenever I witness you speaking to people, especially to the women around here."

"Yeah."

"They're all dawdling around hoping for male attention, and you happily provide *it*, and I think *it's* grand in that way, but still at the same time, *it's* deplorable to me."

"So what's your—not to interrupt you—but what's your first thought," Emil snapped his thumb and index finger, "you see that happening—what's the first thing that shoots through those neurons inside your head?"

"Fucking buffoons-"

Emil tilted his head back and laughed.

I continued, "-or something along those lines."

"Yeah—yeah—yeah!"

"And do you ev—do you get that impression from me, when-"

"No—I—I think that, well sometimes I see you smiling when you're looking over and I can tell that *it's* an amusement thing as much as *it* is a critical smile."

I glowered and said, "Yes. Even when I see people... *eating*... and, you know—just, *ugh*-" Emil guffawed at my brazen disgust and mimicked my grunt. "-The human acts! Yes! Just seeing *it* all; how people interact and the women going after particular men based on body composition and facial structure—and you can see *it* all and... *it's* just... I don't... envy *that*."

"Yeah."

"*It's* just—I... I'm so keenly aware of *it* constantly-"

"Yeah."

"Because I can't fixate my mind on anything else because *it interests* me… but yet *it nauseates* me, so I'm in this perpetual… loop… of being nauseated by humanity, but yet I am a human being, and I can't escape *it.*"

"I was going to say you're still bound by the same conditions that everybody else faces—okay so, let's say that you have a group of women doting over you; how would you react? Not to be too much in your personal life but, are you attracted to women?"

"Oh yes."

"Yes—so if you see this beautiful woman walk up—but you're still looking for the same features—the symmetrical face—and from an evolutionary standpoint—I'm gonna let you know this—this is actually really cool; you look for symmetry in a face: *it* means their genes are good enough to be providing structure—*it's*—*it's* complete, *it's* symmetrical and everything is properly functioning well—and then we can get into the whole MHC complexes—they're called… misto—uh, *wait what is*—major histocompatibility complexes—and, so if I'm by a woman and she smells nice, *it's* like a subtle pickup that her genes are just different enough from mine and that if we were to combine our genetic material that you could produce offspring that has even more of a chance of being protected against whatever kind of illnesses or viruses or whatever is out there. So, not to get off track, but like—you see that in a *woman,* and even subconsciously over evolution you've just been… hammered into your DNA that that's what you're looking for and you need to procreate—I mean that's what life comes down to is passing on this genetic code you carry. So, how would you feel if you had women doting over you?"

"I do, and you've seen exactly how I react; I act like a robot."

"Right!"

"And *it* repels them, but yet *it* also intrigues them."

"Hm."

"And that also makes me want to repel them even more because… *it's* the whole mysterious and intrigue factor-"

"Yeah."

"-as you've said, like *'Oh, that's a mysterious man, he comes off like he's psychotic because he's looking through me! Now I'm attracted even more!'*"

"Yeah."

"And then they come back, but then—there were multiple women here actually, college students-"

"Mhm."

"-and they made the telltale plays, ploys, the eye contact, the prolonged staring, the whimsical looking and all that—but I just look through them and eventually they just give *it* up, after four or five times. Even here, I mean, that's how I see all male and female interactions—*it's* just a mating game."

Emil's chuckles settled; we stood for several seconds in silence. Two girls from the coffee shop on campus and a janitor puttered nearby. Emil said, "But if these are the conditions we're bound by then why... why fight them? What—what—I guess what are you *gaining* out of stepping out of that ring? You know if you like to take part in the same humanely pleasures that everybody else does, I guess—and we're on this earth for a limited time, what benefit is *it* to step back, and not to indulge... in the things that we've been *given* to go out and enjoy and—you know and meet other people and everything—I guess what's the satisfaction that comes out of that?"

"*It's* extremely masochistic, but I believe that to love somebody else, you must sever your own ego."

Emil's phone rang; he immediately silenced *it* and said, "Sever your own ego?"

"Yes—as soon as you begin to care for somebody else, truly."

"But *again*—what is the benefit of that because usually every action that we have, tends to be, in some way to benefit ourselves. Very rarely do we do stuff that's either harmful either mentally or psychologically—I mean *it does* happen, don't get me wrong—*it's* just that I'm wondering what's the benefit of doing that you know?"

"The benefit *is* the psychological damage; *it's* madness; *it's* insanity. I go home and I have no friends. I'm looking forward to this Christmas vacation because *it's* going to be a complete month period where I don't interact with anybody at all except for those who I make eye contact with at the grocery store."

"So when you go home—is this just a persona that you keep up—in—in—in a social environment? What are you like at home; do you still have the quote on quote, 'robotic movements' or are you a different person at home? Or do you even analyze yourself when you're not around other people?"

"Oh—I analyze myself at home; I behave as though... 'god,' in quotes, is always watching, and observing—and I believe that we are all our own gods, so we are dictators and judges of our own behavior. So what started as a sort of, act, because I understand how people would react to psychotic behavior, I eventually adopted that, and now I think I actually am becoming psychotic."

"So *it*'s, *it*'s kind've that-"

I shook my head and said, *"It's* like I'm at a confessional with you-"

"You're manifesting *it,* though."

"Yes."

"So if you've realized that then what's stopping you now from reversing *it?"*

"Because I enjoy *it!"*

"I understand but what—I guess—I guess *it*'s just such a foreign concept to me that... what's the *enjoyment?"*

The two girls from the coffee shop slouched their shoulders and ducked between us while I said, "The plunging into... neurosis, or psychosis, for the sake of the creative endeavor."

"So *it*'s a creative aspect, that's what's, okay. Well I guess that might be where *it* loses me then because I've never been a creative person in the sense that I love science; I like things that are bound by rules and equations—I liked physics, *it* was, if you plug in these variables you can get the outcome here, and I think—I think *it*'s interesting too in a sense that things aren't necessarily bound by equations, like human interactions you know? You know like people react when you say a certain thing—I think that's always been fascinating but that's also just... like, the study of human behavior— ya know *it*'s like you—if you react in this way, and a lot of *it*s psychology too which kind've feeds back into our whole conversation earlier about neurons and everything but, I just think *it*'s interesting how, you could say something or do something and reasonably know how somebody is going to react to *it;* but then again, not to call you weird but there's *yours,* which is... outside unique to... you're kind've different to how most people deal with interactions—or even the pursuit of creativity—I know there's definitely other people for sure who share similar things to that but I guess I've never talked to somebody so—so *it*'s the creative aspect of looking at something in a novel way, of creating something?"

"I behave in a certain way to repel people. Consider how I approached you; I asked you to give me your unfiltered opinion of my character-"

"Yeah."

"-and I would do the same for you—and I have; I've told you that one negative trait that I see that makes me nauseated, but yes, *it*'s for the creative experience—the, the writings I've been doing... I—I... the *'failed sociopath'* in quotations, *it*'s supposed to be... a satire because of the DSM-"

"Right."

Impassioned, I said, "-The DSM-5 and how I don't believe in any of that—*it*'s all *jargon* and concepts individuals made up and spewed out and we all follow them blindly because we're all fools!"

"So then… this will be interesting for you then; this seems to be a strength, is you putting up this front, I wouldn't say acting in a negative way but *it* is kind've negative—staring at somebody until they look away or whatever; wouldn't this be more of a pursuit of creativity if you put yourself *out* of your comfort zone—your comfort zone is doing exactly what you're doing right now, so wouldn't *it* be… an interesting pursuit for you then to put yourself into these social norms—*knowing* how you like to act, and then putting on a different front, and being like *'Hey ladies!'*—you know walk up—you go to *parties,* you *interact* with people."

I suppressed a scornful laugh.

Emil continued, "That would be interesting because that would spawn a lot of creativity—only because that's not what you're used to doing."

"But that would be truly psychotic."

"It would be but that's what you said you like to do *right?* That fits in properly, then."

"You're encouraging me to go out and completely hurt people-"

"-No—no—no—no—no—not hurt!-"

"-because I don't care—but I would act like I do."

"I don't mean hurt people, that's-"

"-Well that's what would happen!"

"I'm just saying go out and… whatever you normally do, *don't* do that—like maybe go to the bar, play darts with somebody you never met, or buy somebody a drink, you know? *It*'s like—go to a club! When girls start walking up to you hit 'em up—like *'Hey! What do you go—let me take you out for coffee later'* or something that you wouldn't normally do, and then, you could, I don't know—analyze them or whatever you wanna do—while you have coffee but you're acting like a different person so you get this kind've duality; you have what's going in your head, and then you're disgusted with yourself because you're doing that—but that's kind've the pursuit of creativity, *right?* Because you're stepping out of your comfort zone—I'm not saying do anything bad to anybody but just—you know do stuff that's not what you're used to doing, and maybe you'll come up with a new perspective, because you're playing into the whole—like you said—masochistic and everything—and this negative almost pessimistic viewpoint… so… but *it* would be difficult—that's what I'm *saying.*"

Dejected, I said, "That would be horrible."

"It would be, but that means you would love *it* though right?"

I opened my mouth to speak and grimaced.

Emil giggled and said, "That fact that *it shocked* you, and *it's* hard to come up with words shows that though. *It's* so deplorable to you that *it's* intriguing."

"Yes."

"Yeah."

"I've had interactions… recently where I tried to put on an act, and I'm able to do *it* successfully though on the inside I'm screaming."

"See that sounds *enjoyable* though too at the same time right?"

"Well yes, though *it* is—*it's* so simple though because you can just play into… I know *you* know."

Emil murmured, "Mhm," and responded to my laughter with a superficial chuckle.

"And that's why I approach you with these-"

"-Yeah-"

"-concepts because…" I paused for a prolonged period, stared at the kitchen tiles, leered at Emil, and growled, *"you* embrace *it."*

"Yeah… So why not do a month of… this new thing—like you said *it's* a slow descent-" Emil's giggles persisted, "-into—into insanity or whatever—to go do the most insane thing you can and… document *it*. And then you can come back after a month."

I uttered a melodramatic lie: "The most insane thing I could do at this point would be to integrate with people."

"Exactly! That—I think *it* would be *very* interesting to see… out of the norm Baethan, you know what I mean? Instead of standing there robotically—interact with people, ask about how their day is going, be like *'Hey you like the chicken sandwich or whatever?'*—I know you don't care, but see how *they* react, and then you could maybe switch up the questions that you ask people to see how that influences your thoughts and feelings about the whole situation—just constantly say something new to a new person, you know… I think that'd be kinda cool; I can't *picture* you doing *it*—that's why I think *it'd* be good."

"I'm committed to this year being mute."

"Oh no—no—that's cool-"

"At least *attempting*—I mean I'm failing right now."

Emil muttered another superficial string of "ha—ha—ha's" and said, "That's all right—but—I don't know—that'd be kinda cool—you know? You know—acting differently, not again like a super negative but more of a positive way, see how people's days are going or... I don't know... *It could be cool-*"

I began to shout in the most affected, pretentious manner I could muster, "Hey how you doin'? *It's, it's, great!*"

"Yeah—there you go!" Emil encouraged me.

Three of the coffee shop girls stood by; I yelled, *"It's lovely isn't it; it's a lovely* day!"

"Well you know what I mean—that's so scripted-"

"Aren't you glad? Aren't you happy today?"

"Yeah exactly! But see what I mean? You can get in the flow of *it*—*it* might feel foreign at first but then after you try for a little while *it* might be kinda interesting—you know? I just think *it's* cool to look at—I always think perspective is unique and—you're set on one perspective right now— but the... the more perspective you have the more realistic your ideas kinda become—you know? You get *all* the way around 360—you know what I mean? You got one slice of the pie you're looking at right now from your viewpoint but then maybe step around and do stuff people might think is... more normal... I don't know..." At the sound of Emil's defeated tone, I reflected on the fatuousness of our conversation and realized I've stood with another man for twenty minutes, admitted my despicable opinion of him, myself, humanity, and listened... *earnestly,* to recommendations of behavioral alterations comparable to *his:* to become a mimic of the man before me in the name of creativity—for a moment, a day, a *month...* "I don't know how you act outside so I couldn't give you examples but I'm just saying here you're very stoic; what would happen if you pinned your emotions right on your face if you were happy or disgusted or something you know?"

I started with a slight stammer, "... I do, for the most part, but for the most part I'm not really feeling anything."

Emil laughed and said, "Well that's what I'm saying—maybe *try* to feel something—I can't begin to tell you how to do that—but-"

"I appreciate you stopping to take the time to speak with me."

"Yeah—yeah!" Emil enthused, "No problem man—just suggestions— I'm always here to spark ideas but I'm gonna run... I'm gonna get some food with some people."

"And you said you aren't creative."

"Not in the sense where... I never look at myself as creative in the sense of drawing... even writing—I'm good at writing scientific stuff but I think creativity has many faces, ya know—I like to talk to people, maybe that's my way of coming up with ideas—I don't know I've never really thought

about *it, I've* always just considered myself to be a non-creative person. I don't know."

"I'm going to hate myself later for this conversation."

"Oh yeah you will. But that's good though right?"

I frowned.

Emil implored, "Because that's what you said you like to do!"

"But we don't live life when we hate ourselves; *it's* a stasis."

"*It* is… *but, it's* what makes us unique. Manipulate the variables and see what happens. *It's* all a stasis in the end—who cares; you can do whatever you want!"

I couldn't argue with that immaculate logic. Emil turned to depart; I said to his back, "I thought for sure you'd pounce on the opportunity to tell me exactly what you thought of me—but you're too damn *nice,* you charismatic bastard."

He rang out over his shoulder in a light-hearted tone, "That's how *it* goes! You better watch out! All right take *it* easy man."

I managed to utter, "You too," while Emil pushed himself into the night. I stood with a damp mop head clenched in both hands, unsettled and chagrined, for although Emil spoke his final jest with amicability, I heard his words for what they are and determined him to be neither an enemy nor a friend who loves me dearly.

8:21 PM

There is no creativity. There is only tripe. Each instance I set out to write, I hate what I am, for this isn't *living.* This act of self-engrossment is refined hatred for oneself.

I enjoy oratorios, chorales, and choir; the Latin tongue is incomprehensible to me and I may listen to the purity of the human voice. I *do* desire companionship… yet I behave as the greatest fool I have ever known. What hysteria may this be classified as? I am dejected and without remorse.

My thoughts betray who I want to be: A man free from himself. This flesh disgraces my poor spirit.

Damn all the psychological jargon: "Sociopath," "Psychopath," "Depression," "Autistic," "Bipolar," "Schizophrenia," "Anxiety," etc.; these manufactured descriptions are in alignment with the four temperaments developed by Hippocrates—more outmoded jargon. The Myers Briggs personality test?: *More* deceitful trite aimed at egotistical buffoons (I've fallen victim to the trap of implied uniqueness on many occasions) by those with a profit at stake—as all designs; mine is no exception.

Am I a mindless partisan of individualism? Nay, the human creature is malleable, unfixed; our experiences and genetics alter the template. *No one* is born without a conscience; the conscience is dependent on learned morals and ethics. Empathy is not synonymous with compassion. One born with a physical impairment or deformity which negates facets of cognitive abilities is *just* an anomalous byproduct of genetics. What is right or wrong other than what facilitates a society to function? If one is isolated and prospers, what is "good" and "evil" but symbols and ambiguous sound? Fear is universal. Guilt and shame are practical tools. The world *is* black and white; generalizations *are* applicable; this is *my* tangible reality. Consumption, defecation, procreation—the holy trinity I've expounded on before, and will again—for this moot distraction (thoughts to objects) arouses my volition to exist!

If one believes the authenticity of my previous conversation between Emil and myself on my evaluation of us being "sociopathic narcissists," then one is a more profound fool than myself—for my incitement, recording, *and* transcribing of the conversation—for you:—Fool, whoever you are, I loathe to imagine you *care*. What are Emil and I but young men at the apex of our health, ambitious, with an inclination to know what we desire, abhor, and to pursue what is beneficial—to avoid what is detrimental, to foster our egos for the sake of our *humanity?* How accurate would I be to state—*instead* of "sociopathic narcissist": A manipulative fop? A "psychopath": A charismatic scoundrel? Both are self-engrossed.

A shoe is a shoe, despite the composition of the molecular compounds we understand only at the depth of our current scientific *theories* limited to our human sensory organs. What more may be said of the molecular structure of the human mind? *No...* better to divert exorbitant amounts of resources into the research of how a function *functions,* for the sake of progress—yes, by the supreme effort of civilization I may stand and type this uninformed trash, which the reader considers for a fraction of a second, and thereby discards, for the information previously ingested has served them well!

"Ah, but I know sweet potatoes are a superb source of carbohydrates and vitamin A"; "Oh, I know my girlfriend is cheating on me; her mien, tonality, and the direction her eyes look when she speaks to me are dead giveaways"; "Hm, the color red elicits hunger and will render me sexier"; "Hum, I should wait thirty minutes after a meal before I brush my teeth."

Progress, what we believe to be growth, advancement, reformation, and the sole recourse of existence, is the source of our *inhumanity.* The more we "know," the less we may choose, and the berth of what remains to be discovered widens with every discovery. Consciousness is god and the single truth known to consciousness is entropy. All who ~~believe~~ condone what I write are asinine sympathizers of an absurd anarchist (more grandiose labels); think for yourself (or ask *Google* to do *it* for you).

Saturday, December 14th, 2019

9:40 PM

A metal band plays; all the songs sound the same.

I've heeded Emil's suggestion and write in a small black journal at a bar marketed to and filled with unfortunates, lowlives, and misfits. Noise and several muted conversations transpire around me. I enjoy the last of my second glass of red wine; there is no other way to live than this moment.

Emil convinced me to indulge in public machinations for the sake of creativity, yet I feel more hollow than when I first landed at the airport of this city, or when I stand at the fried chicken counter with nothing to behold but the sight of capricious college students and advertisements. I enjoy the alcohol; that's the extent. My body is enriched; my mind, numb.

11:04 PM

The petite singer of a grunge metal band captivated me; the little vixen sensed my infatuation and approached: "Are you enjoying the cabernet?" she inquired. I didn't hear the first utterance of what she said while I stared at a mural of a 17th-century castle painted on the wall; she repeated herself.

I gazed down at her, reckoned a tomboyish haircut of bold brown hair framed around a feminine face… a body dressed in a plain black hoodie and tight black jeans. I said, "Yes." How she knew I drank cabernet must've been the product of gossip.

The woman eyed me up and down, evaluated my black ensemble

of a dress shirt beneath a bulky coat, and said, "I've noticed you haven't interacted much with anyone."

"One needn't speak to interact."

"*It* helps, though."

I nodded in slight acquiescence and observed her coy hazel eyes, upturned lips, reddened cheeks, and watched her go when she realized I had no intent to reciprocate—to amble up the stage, where she performed for three dozen bargoers. I stood close-by, wine glass in hand, and scrutinized the amateur performers. My eyes fell on the woman's countenance and our attentions met: a grotesque affirmation, sealed at that moment; I wanted her, and she wanted me—despite her subtle affiliation with the lead guitarist. Nothing came of *it*, of course; I avoided her persistent gaze for an hour thereafter while she engaged in vapid conversation with those around me—thus I departed downtown and ran three miles home with a backpack filled with copies of my book (Year Two)[7] strapped to my back, relieved from the awful cacophonies and blessed with my two favorite musical compositions ever composed, resonated through earbuds: the first movement of J.S. Bach's, *St. John Passion - Herr, unser, Herrscher,* and the first movement of J.S. *Bach's Mass in B Minor - Kyrie I,* conducted by Jacobs and Herreweghe respectively... both pieces a little less than ten minutes in duration, played back to back... Empowered, I strode across the pavement and sidewalks, rallied at the sight of the moon between layers of intermingled clouds distributed against the opaque blackness of a starless night sky, and returned *home,* where I stand now and prepare to indulge in a sensuous feast of steel cut-oats, sardines, Ceylon cinnamon, extra virgin olive oil, a few splashes of tabasco sauce, and a drizzle of honey. Marvelous—this life; drunk and enchanted by the mere intrigue of a woman, I'm primed for death.

---

[7] A gregarious old man approached me for conversation within my first fifteen minutes at the bar. He spoke of progress, authoritative suppression, and the conservation of the beauty of the world. I condemned him with a signed copy of my book upon his unwarranted praise of my intellect by the end of our conversation; thereby he shook my hand twice, regarded me as a scholar, and departed the bar with his flummoxed-phone-occupied female companion.

Sunday, December 15th, 2019

4:11 PM

My neurophilosophy obsession is compounded. The rabbit hole is ineffable. I think understanding consciousness is analogous to understanding black holes; all black holes are connected in the same manner that consciousness is connected (and consciousness is not limited to living beings, but *all* matter, in the same vein of thought as the philosophy of Spinoza); both are the veritable "yin and yang" of the singularity. However, to understand would be inhuman, or rather, nonbeing.

Much easier to consume, defecate, and ~~procreate~~ masturbate grasp my penis when *it* becomes erect at convenient times of idleness, offer myself a few deliberate, dry strokes, remind myself of the inadequate sensation, and quit. I'm tempted to divert funding for next year's publication and cult expedition to acquire a lifelike sex doll equipped with artificial intelligence and a thermal unit. I'd snuggle up close and whisper sweet meanings into ~~her~~ *it*s auditory receptors.

Monday, December 16th, 2019

5:28 PM

A middle-aged homeless couple hailed me downtown and requested money for food. Both carried sleeping bags, tents, and wore heavy jackets. The woman eyed me with derision while the man pleaded; what a display of masculinity and a stalwart ability to provide for your partner, to beg another man for nourishment. I said, "Have you gone to the local homeless shelter?"

"That's where we got the sleeping bags," the man lamented, "They're closed now—during the winter."

I said, "I don't have any money to spare," with seven dollars in my pocket. I nodded my feigned respects and visited the grungy bar for two glasses of red wine. This is the manner of man I've become.

5:57 PM

At the bar, behind me, to my left, a man swung a small cylindrical metal ring suspended from the ceiling by a white string towards a hook projected from a wall. The man's ineffectual attempts to land the hoop on the hook impelled him to persist with the activity.

Tuesday, December 17th, 2019

9:45 AM

A youthful, voluptuous, muse-faced bartender with bodacious small-of-the-back-length locks of blonde hair streaked with black strands served a dozen older patrons. She wore a skintight bright red one-piece that accentuated her robust figure and emphasized her breasts' defined rotundness. I was at once overtaken with lust and disgust in equal proportion and settled for indifference.

On my way to the far end of the bar, closest to the empty stage, the row of men and a few women eyed me with circumspection. "Can I see your ID?" the bartender asked.

I said, "Yes," and handed her a New York state ID that featured a picture of me at the age of twenty with a contented smile and head of voluminous chin-length disheveled hair dyed black; she stood and scrutinized the ID for twenty seconds and asked another patron if they have ever seen a New York ID. I glared at her and waited.

"What brings you to [City Name]?"

I sat on a stool, slung my backpack off, hesitated—distrustful of the intense inspection, closed my eyes, shook my head, scowled, and said, "To live."

"Oh, to live. Okay." The bartender sensed my immediate contempt, yet this only encouraged her to initiate multiple conversations with me throughout the hour and a half I spent with a drink in hand. If I had been a ~~fat~~ chubby, ~~hideous~~ ugly, *or* cordial man, she would've been disgusted—though I had been *me,* not to boast of any superb qualities, for I am no stud by any means, at least in the physical respect: my face is median and my physique is juvenile; however, emotionally and mentally, I am *needless,* and the strong-willed, intelligent, attractive woman behind the bar had been *confounded* by my latent disinterest, i.e., the *mystery*—which serves to amplify my animosity, for what has the interaction been but a farcical microcosmic example of the ubiquitous conditions of man and woman interlocked in a perpetual state of passion and discord? My reticence served to aggravate. I thought of Emil's charade while we stood by a chemical closet: *"Hey! What do you go—let me take you out for coffee later!"* Instead, I rose from the stool, stared forward at a cooler filled with alcohol, down to the crimson liquid in my cup, to a game of pool played by two buffoons, to the row of bored, dejected faces.

The bartender flitted around me and ignored the other patrons at the opposite end of the bar for the full duration of my visit. We discussed our hobbies, the artwork painted on the bar's walls, and exchanged a few personal trivia, though her genuine interest in me had been dissimulated for her own entertainment: this is her job. The topic of our shared pursuit of writing surfaced and the bartender said that she would "love to read my book sometime": a bold statement for one who has *no idea* what the content is. I would've given her a copy, though I had donated my pack's contents to the local library hours prior. Instead, I wrote my email on the back of a four-by-six-inch advertisement for my second publication (Year Two) and handed *it* to her.

"I'll start reading later tonight when I get home," the bartender announced while she examined the cover art, "I've got nothing else to do."

My life is a sham.

I dreamed of a pretty girl in a log cabin; she stood proximate to me while she relayed her issues and problems with other men. I listened for several minutes, pushed her against the wall of a featureless hallway, and kissed her lips; she inhaled, moaned, veered away from me, blushed, and said, "I can't."

I nodded, strode away to a makeshift cot in a hearth-warmed living room, and woke when I saw my satisfied reflection in an enormous, ornate mirror.

4:19 PM

A man chain-smoked cigarettes to my right and stared up at a muted television screen. The smoggy remnants blew into my face. His attention alternated to his phone, whereby he flicked through social media. A blue henley shirt, blue jeans, and white converse shoes compressed his body.

Intermittent bursts of discordant sounds emanated from the phone speaker. The self-consciousness he experienced near me was exemplified in sidelong glances, sighs, tensed arms, and agitated footwork; he watched my hand slide across my physical journal. He sat and folded his arms. Another drag, another sip, stare at two screens—just what are we? I could only tolerate this environment long enough for one glass of wine today.

I gave three copies of my book away: One to a lost man who hailed me from his car, and two to a different female bartender; I asked her to deliver a copy to the previous bartender on my behalf; she expressed extreme interest; thus I offered her one. All had been signed and inscribed on the first page with my condemnation, "[Name], For a fellow fool."

I'm perplexed by my own writings: What is *it* to idle in a thoughtless bar and write sentiments of oneself and the distribution of previous books published? Trumpery and filth. You goddamn fool.

8:34 PM

I will never visit a that bar again.

Thursday, December 19th, 2019

8:37 AM

"Good morning Sheilah." The light of dawn streamed in through a glass wall-window of a penthouse and illuminated a room furnished with two large rectangular victorian vanities on opposite ends of cream-painted walls. At the room's center, an attractive man—a musician of exceptional skill with the lute, laid and stared at a feminine visage beside him. Both heads rested on a regal, purple, body-length pillow lined with golden renaissance tassels. The man smiled, shifted closer, and kissed a pair of cold lips.

Two eyelids popped open and the glassy eyes beneath returned the man's stare. "Good morning, daddy. How are you today?"

The man smiled and stroked his right index finger across a faultless pale cheek. He slid a hand around the nape of the neck, ruffled the long black hair strewn between his fingers, and said, "I'm wonderful every morning when I wake up to see your beautiful face."

"I love every morning with you," droned a monotonous voice.

"I know you do baby."

"I love you very much."

"Yeah," the man reached across his abdomen and fondled his genitalia, "You too baby—*yeah*. Daddy's gonna make you feel good this morning."

"I can't wait, daddy. I want you to give *it* to me rough."

The man pushed the stiffened and immaculate feminine body onto *its* back and clambered on top of an hourglass waist. "Daddy gonna fuck you good this morning baby girl—yeah."

"I can't wait, daddy. I want you to give *it* to me rough."

"Yeah," the man breathed sensuous exhalations along a snow-white neck and proceeded with rhythmic thrusts. Puerile feminine moans resonated throughout the space, accented by the man's guttural grunts. A minute and fifty-two seconds elapsed and the bombastic cries ceased. The nubile face rendered a stasis: starry eyes glared forward, and a petite mouth hung slack. The man yelled, "Fuck—*shit!*" tottered off the bed, grasped the end of a black, six-foot-long electrical cord, and inserted the two male prongs into an outlet between the shoulder blades of his companion. "Come on… *Come on…* " He waited eleven seconds and wiped a bead of sweat off his brow.

"Good morning, daddy. How are you today?"

6:51 PM

An odious man pulled over to me on the side of one of the city's main roads and spoke with haste, "Hey man, I know this sounds really forward but will you top me? I've been lookin' for a top for quite some time and I don't bottom with guys but will you top me? You're the perfect top."

I opened my mouth to say, "No," with the instinct to march onward; instead, I stopped and said, "Why do you want me to top you?"

"Cuz I just said man," he spoke with agitated haste, "you're like the perfect top for me—*look* at you," he extended his left arm out the driver-side window and slammed a palm against the door, rolled his head *and* eyes, and managed an exasperated giggle.

I peered inside the car and observed two pill bottles in the compartment between the front seats and said, "When?"

"Now!—if you're free right now."

"Perhaps in a few hours?"

"Why not *now*—okay how about this," the man's words flowed, rapid-fire, "My cousin is at home passed out on my couch so I'll go home and get him up and motivated then as soon as he's out [of] the door I'll take [a]—shower—when done I'll text you how to get to my place—maybe in about an hour we'll be having some fun—what's your number or can I give you mine? How old are you?"

"Twenty-eight, you?"

"I'm forty-five. You want to top or not?"

"I'll take your number."

The man told me his number, his name, and sped off. I walked the remainder of the way home, flabbergasted, repulsed, and determined to undertake the act of mounting this man for the ludicrous experience of the ugly, outrageous, and the odious; in essence, I thought of this journal and my meaning in life. The omen manifested as an odious man with a desire for anal penetration. God has a plan for me.

I returned home, deposited my groceries, showered, and donned my pack once more for an hour's walk to an upper lower-class suburb. The man greeted me at the doorway, more hideous and maddened than he appeared within his car. "There's no way you're twenty-eight," he proclaimed.

I said, "I expected your trepidation in regards to my age, so I brought my ID," and handed him my New York identification card.

The odious man raised both eyebrows, gratified by my forethought, and scrutinized my ID in a similar manner the muse-faced bartender had. "Just wanna make sure you're not underage."

"Have you had problems in the past?"

"*No* but you look a lot younger than you are." I reflected at that moment that if I cared enough to attempt a sexual endeavor back at the bar, I could've been in the bartender's apartment. Instead, I saw an old box television set from the 1990s, an overturned plastic chess game in a corner between two brown-hued couches stained with patches of yellow, a bizarre cold-colored painting of eight anthropomorphized moons encased within cylindrical plant stalks, a few empty processed snack food wrappers, and a *decent* amount of cockroaches on the carpet, walls, and furniture. I sat down on one of the yellowed couch cushions and spread my legs; this is where I chose to be. The odious man next to me scratched his balding head and spewed out varied sentences of mostly incomprehensible context. We exchanged basic information about one another; for instance, he told me his name, though I shall refer to him *only* as "the odious man," not to dehumanize or ridicule, but for the visual reminder. "You wanna watch a porno or somethin'?" he said.

Friday, December 20th, 2019

9:23 AM

I gazed down at a soiled carpet, shook my head, and said, "I haven't watched porn in... since high school at least. Sure."

"Come to the bedroom—the t.v. is in there."

We stood and I followed the odious man's hobbled gait. On entry to his bedroom, I scanned the vicinity and noticed six pill bottles on a rectangular dark wood dresser—a flat-screen television atop that, a *Pink Floyd, Dark Side of the Moon* wall tapestry, a well-made bed, various articles of clothing strewn about the waxed wood floor, two bongs on a nightstand, one bong on the floor, and a convergence of five cockroaches at the far corner of the ceiling opposite of the doorway. I remained silent and slung my backpack onto the floor while he powered on the television and scrolled through selections of feature-length porn videos. "Bathroom's there if you need to use *it,*" his countenance twitched and he shifted his weight.

I said, "Al lright," and sat next to the odious man on his bed, at ease, detached, contrary to him, who expressed palpable anxiety. "This will be the first time I've ever topped a man."

The odious man said, "Oh yeah? Well, okay."

"Another man has topped me before and... I didn't enjoy *it,* to say the least."

"*It*'s cool—how's this one?" he referred to a porno featuring two men and a woman at a public gym, copulating atop a weight bench. I chuckled and said, "*It*'s so scripted."

"Well I can find a different one-"

"No—I mean *all* of them."

"Well yeah *it*'s porn-" the odious man forced a nervous laugh and scratched his body. "Make yourself comfortable then or whatever." I nodded, shrugged, stripped naked, and laid on the bed next to the odious man. "Yeah, so, whenever you want to get started," he uttered, and jerked his attention between my body and the porn; his eyelids scrunched down and his mouth contorted.

I said, "All right, let's start now. Take off your clothes."

"Well all right," said the odious man, and he stood from the bed. The pants and underwear dropped first. I glared at a flaccid, overhung pair of flattened ass cheeks marred with several rectangular scars. A topless blonde woman alternated an oral sex performance on two penises on the screen behind the odious man. Stereotypical upbeat porn music emanated, accentuated with inserts of persistent female moaning audio clips. The odious man's green t-shirt came off next and he turned to face me. The corpulent body sagged, covered with patches of thinned black hair. Several faded *U.S. Army* tattoos colored the biceps, although he never served. The distended abdominal hung low and grazed the bed while he crawled on his hands and knees towards me.

I turned on my side, huddled up against the odious man's body, and said, "I brought condoms: three."

"Okay good," he braced both hands against his bed, stricken, "cuz I don't have any. Let me get the lube." He lurched off the bed with a few strained upheavals, retrieved a small bottle of dollar store lotion, and slammed back down on the bed. I winced on *his* behalf. He said, "So how do you want me? Doggy? Reverse? Cowgirl? Missionary?"

I smiled up at him while he looked down at me on his knees and said, "Whatever way is the most comfortable for you."

"Well I don't care—some guys like to fondle my tits while I ride them so I can face you—or I can turn away—and other guys like to grip my ass, so, whatever you wanna do. Just go fuckin' easy on me—don't fucking ram *it* in or we're gonna have problems. Some guys ram *it* in and I'm like, 'No fucking way this is gonna happen,' so be gentle all right?"

"I understand. Let's have you ride me first so that you're in control. I'd prefer you to face me."

"Okay," said the odious man. He ripped open a condom and prepared me with a short bout of oral sex. I sat and watched in silence, uninclined to mutter disingenuous groans of pleasure. The odious man garbed me with a condom and lobbed himself on top of me. "I've got some hip problems and I haven't been fucked in a long time since May so *go easy* on me." He reached for my penis and attempted to guide the appendage into his orifice. Flashes of pain overtook his visage and he cursed aloud on several failed attempts. "Fuck! God damn *it;* hold on—need more lotion." He fell flat over the bed, fumbled for the lotion, squirted a large glob into his palm, swatted his ass four times, and groped for my penis again. Two more failed attempts. "My hips are hurtin' me," he announced and exerted an extreme effort to displace his leg to a more suitable position. "Lemme try reverse cowgirl."

"All right."

A minute and a half elapsed and the odious man managed to position himself away from me. His misshapen body weighed on me while I utilized my left hand to help him maintain balance. A struggle ensued and he unleashed a puerile moan. "Oh *yeah!*"

I said, "Is *it* in?"

"Uh—*yeah!*—my ass is tight isn't *it?*"

I acquiesced, uncertain what I felt, and said "Yes."

"Feels good?"

"Yes."

"Oh *fuck*," he murmured, and began to rock back and forth on top of me. I shifted from the discomfort. "Easy! Go easy!"

"Yes."

The slight oscillations continued. I observed the odious man's slackened composition and jerky head movements. The woman on-screen moaned ad nausem due to simultaneous anal and vaginal penetration. *"Ah*—my fuckin' hips—stop—stop—stop-"

I lay motionless. A cockroach crawled out from beneath my pillow and scuttled down the side of the mattress. The odious man lifted off me, crashed to the adjacent pillow, began to roll the bedsheets into a conglomerate, and huffed, "Damn that felt amazing, but my hips—you wanna try doggy next? I want you to kiss me while you fuck me."

I uplifted my eyes to the blank grey ceiling, said, "All right," readjusted the bottom of my condom, ensuring not to touch any segment of my body thereafter, and situated myself behind the ghastly anus: spread-cheeked and reddened.

"Go easy—don't *fuckin'* ram *it* in."

"Yes," I cooed, awestruck and reverent of the moment. I pushed in and watched the odious man's forehead crinkle, his head sideways against the pillow.

"Ahhh—*shit...* slowly—slowly."

I performed meager thrusts and remained erect through sheer force of will. I *wanted* to do this, yet the craven and egregious nature of my being juxtaposed with what I believed to be *"good"* for me, rendered me overcome with subservient inertia. My repulsed rationale obeyed the coercion of my reason. *"What is man?"* I thought, while the stranger beneath my hand quivered with pained delight. I said, "Are you all right?"

"Yeah—I'm fan-fuckin'-tastic! I'm great!" he grunted into the pillow's concave slant.

I increased the rate and berth of my thrust by a decimal and the odious man blurted, "AH—stop—stop—stop-"

"Pull out?"

"-yeah—stop—stop. Ah-" I retracted and the odious man stumbled off the bed, "You literally fucked the *shit* out of me," he laughed, and staggered towards the adjacent bathroom, both hands on his anus, "*Damn*—felt great though," he stated, and continued to chuckle while he shut the bathroom door. On my knees atop the bed, I looked around the room. The cockroaches along the ceiling contours had dispersed. The woman on-screen laid on the inclined weight bench and alternated service on two penises grasped on either side of her. I listened to falsified female orgasms and the flush of a toilet. The odious man emerged from the bathroom and said, "Man that's by far some of the best I've had; I hope you come back for more, maybe tomorrow."

I acknowledged him, void and listless.

"Or maybe once a week—or every two weeks."

I lowered the back of my head to the pillow, cautious not to rotate and connect more flesh than necessary with the fabric, and said, "So that's *it* then?"

"Well we have all night! If you want to stay for more we can... You know what I want next time, is for you to fuck me missionary style so you can kiss me."

"We can do that now."

"Are you—well shit, all right!"

I discarded the condom into a waste bin filled with segments of a destroyed carpet, donned a new one, and prepared to mount from the front. The odious man fought to position his lower body onto the conglomerate of sheets; forty-five seconds elapsed; he announced, "I'm ready," and twitched the entirety of his body.

I balanced over him on my palms in a quasi plank position and allowed him to guide me in. I exerted pressure and we failed in four instances. On the fifth, we succeeded, to which the odious man gasped with passionate exhalations while I focused on the maintenance of blood flow to my erection. His head uplifted and two lips met mine. Stubble chafed the bottom of my nose and an alien tongue lapped in and out of my mouth. I closed my eyes and reciprocated with equal fervor for eight seconds. For two minutes out of the oblivion of life, this activity persisted. He shouted. "Stop—stop—*stop*. Fuck. Pull out."

I did. The odious man squirmed against the backboard of his bed, sighed, and exclaimed, "That was great! Really—that was fantastic! I hope we can do this again sometime!"

"May I use your bathroom?"

"Of course!"

I passed by my pile of clothes on the floor, flicked on a light switch, and closed the bathroom door. Grime surrounded me. The clean shower contrasted the remainder of the space, though many saturated towelettes littered the shower floor. I entered and turned on the hot water. A single travel-size container of discount dish soap rested on one of the two shower counters. I waited for the water to steam, squirted a glob of dish soap into my palm, and washed my arms, lower face, and genitals with vigorous scrubs of my hands. I patted my body dry with a single towel hung from the curtain rail and entered the bedroom. The odious man hadn't moved; engrossed with his phone, he looked up at me and said, "So yeah when I was little—like six years old, I wanted to go to Seaworld so I convinced my friend to skip school with me and we walked to Seaworld instead. When we got there—I got lost cuz—I don't know—I was fuckin' six years old? So I ended up with some Pez candy in this cave place and I was raped by an older man, at least that's what I was told afterward cuz I didn't know what the hell was going on."

While I dressed, I said, "So… the reason you tell me this, is… why you enjoy being bottomed by men, because of this incident and the psychological damage incurred?"

"Yeah I guess so; I *mean that's what happened*—so yeah now I get off being fucked by guys," the odious man stated, rolled his eyes, and flicked a thumb across his phone screen. "Hey man I had a lot of fun so come by anytime again, preferably soon. Oh *hey-*" he scooted to the edge of the bed, "Come over here; I want to show you this girl; she wants a threesome before she gets too old. Two cocks in her ass at the same time and fucked in the ass and vagina at the same time. She said that if I find someone to tell her. Hold on." I waited in silence while he browsed his phone. "Here." A video of a fair, athletic brunette being fisted on the bed I sat on played before me. The odious man's voice resonated from the phone speakers, e.g., *"Yeah you like that don't you bitch?"* I marveled at the man I sat next to. "You like her?" he said.

I said, "Yes, she's attractive."

"All right—cool, I'll let her know and send her a picture of you; once she sees you she'll be all for *it*."

"Just my body."

"That's all she'll need."

I dressed and we thanked each other for the time, discussed the aesthetics of the original moon painting on the wall (the odious man lifted the art off the wall to inspect the back for an artist's name [there was none] and two cockroaches near the top left corner of the wall where the painting had been scrambled for cover.), and I departed into the twilight of a setting sun for a two-mile walk home.

9:37 PM

This morning, at 9:51 AM, the odious man sent me a text message on my phone: "I wanna thank u for yesterday I had a lot of fun & *it*s been awhile and I would really like to hook up with u again soon!! Just saying but if u wanted I sure would have sex with you today."

At 9:57 AM, I replied, "Thank you, too, for the opportunity to try something out of my realm of experience. I thought the scenario was bizarre and odious; I enjoyed *it* and will never forget *it*. I'm not interested in a repeat experience, though if you fail to find a third person for your desired threesome, I'll return."

No response.

11:07 PM

"This is what I thought: for the most banal even to become an adventure, you must (and this is enough) begin to recount *it*. This is what fools people: a man is always a teller of tales, he lives surrounded by his stories and the stories of others, he sees everything that happens to him through them; and he tries to live his own life as if he were telling a story.

"But you have to choose: live or tell."

– Jean-Paul Satre's Nausea

Saturday, December 21ˢᵗ, 2019

10:41 AM

The president of the United States is impeached, for reasons I don't know, nor care about. I relish the liberty of my ignorance.

5:09 PM

I sit on my weight bench and attempt to read and am drawn to the cracks between horizontal blinds. Thereby I retrieve my device and begin: I listen to the distant songs of birds and watch the light of day fade behind slanted rooftops. Cars drive by. People holler and banter on their doorsteps and on second-story causeways. I had intended to leave my apartment for a Christmas party at a nearby bar I have never been to tonight, with my publications and physical journal in tow, though I muse on the idea *of* going rather than the action, for I know *what* I'd do: Stand in a corner with a glass of red wine between my fingers, indulge in brief, intermittent sips, and observe everyone around me with scorn and pity. I'm unfit for bar life; therefore, I'm baited by my desire for the unsatisfactory. I may remain holed up with my books, writing, and weights for the next three weeks and be content, or I may force myself to venture out, to endure, yet I *know* what would happen: There would be pangs of anguish felt on behalf of my *choice* to suffer as I ought not; I'd write of my hatreds and the debaucheries of those around me. There would be others similar to me, with relatable ideas of what man is, who would, in turn, see my dissatisfied visage and think, *"And what does this douchebag reckon that he accomplishes with such behavior?"*

May I enjoy the wine for the wine, the brazen ostentatiousness, the dissipated socialites, the tempered gentlemen, the whores, the lamenters, the drunks and merrymakers for what they are?

7:43 PM

I went to the unexplored bar and the establishment served no wine. Disgruntled, I departed and ventured half a mile west to another bar; the bartender declined to service me on account of, "Your ID looks nothing like you." (Long hair and a genuine smile.) A random patron agreed. "I'm sorry. I can't."

I said, "All right," and ran home.

71

Sunday, December 22nd, 2019

10:05 AM

An ex-child sex trafficker whispered over his vodka into the ear of a thirty-one-year-old office supervisor for an insurance company, "You think you have *it* bad, huh? I've seen men burned alive. I've strapped people to trees out in the middle of nowhere with duct tape and beat them to death with an iron rod. I've cut the limbs off executed men with a machete and rammed their severed heads on iron fences."

"C'mon…" the officer worker ran three fingers through his hair, grinned, shifted atop a faux leather seat, narrowed his eyes, and sipped a tepid martini.

"I've shot men in the neck and watched the life slip out of their eyes, inches away from their face; those moments are precious to me; I think of them often while I lay next to beautiful women at night."

"I mean, is this *really*—this isn't the kind of conversation I expected to be having with you, and *it* isn't appropriate, I think."

The old man across the narrow table swigged two gulps of vodka and laughed. "No one can hear us over the band. Are you worried you'll hear something that you don't want to believe?"

The office worker grasped the slim contours of the martini glass and swirled the remnants within. *"It'*s not that, no."

"Then what?"

"I don't know, I guess I don't have anything to contribute—my life—as you said—my life is blase; I'm not as… *worldly* as you."

"That's quite the insult. Are you trying to hurt my feelings?" The old man smiled and stared forward, aligned against the backboard of a cramped booth.

"No, no—that's not-"

"Listen to me. You've got a wife and kids; that's something I could never understand. To have a wife at such a young age too, in this modern-day-" the ex-child sex trafficker whistled while he raised the vodka beneath his nose, "-you must be an inspiration to all your friends at work; united under the institution of your god, one *happy* family."

The office worker stiffened and leered at the immaculate brown tabletop and at the martini glass fixed within his grip. His left eye twitched at the faint clank of four cubes of ice amongst the old man's vodka.

The old man cleared his throat and continued, "I don't know what *it's* like to kiss the forehead of a child, let alone my own. Granted, I have children, borne from many women, though I know nothing of them. Yes, by the grace of *your* god, we sit here and enjoy this alcohol in the false security of this establishment; how grateful I am, supersedes me. I wish you'd speak for yourself. I know there's a man in you, *clawing*, rearing, desperate to escape your own skin."

"I'm content with my life, thank you." The office worker's head snapped up; he smirked, snorted, raised the martini glass for a brief faux toast—to which the old man ignored—and forced the rim of the glass between two tight lips.

"I've seen boys with decent lives hang themselves, watched their feet kick; their arms raise straight out in front of their bodies; they reach for something divine, certain of their desire for death, yet fearful of the pain. Anything is better than what they've known, so they reach out while the light fades." The ex-child sex trafficker sighed and scanned the busy bar to his right. A dozen patrons stood, inert, and swayed to the monotonous beat of a three-person bluegrass group illuminated atop a small metal stage by one enormous overhead spotlight. An apathetic grimace overtook the old man's irreverent countenance, and he returned his gaze to the insular eyes of the office worker across the table. Both sat in silence and listened.

Monday, December 23rd, 2019

4:33 PM

Contemporary science leads us to believe that a thousand trillion trillion trillion trillion trillion trillion trillion trillion years in the future, the final black hole in existence will evaporate, the universe will be composed of "nothing," and time will be unaccountable. The universe is believed to be 13.8 billion years old. The only theorized hope for intelligent (non-human) life to proliferate long before the last black dwarf dissipates is to open a gateway to an alternate universe. I predict human life will end ~~by the year 2600~~ due to omnicide, if not for an external factor, though I'll never know, and even if I were lucky to experience the extinction event, I'd be dead.

"In Heaven, Everything is fine, In Heaven, Everything is fine, In Heaven, Everything is fine - You got your good things, And I got mine.

"In Heaven, Everything is fine, In Heaven, Everything is fine, In Heaven, Everything is fine - You got your good things, And you got mine.

"In Heaven, Everything is fine."

- David Lynch's Eraserhead

5:08 PM

I've written before that suicide is the single way to "lose" the game of life, though I've reconsidered. I've reconsidered many subjective dilemmas and paradoxes of existence, even my conviction of there being no truth. I'm humbled by my own self-reflection, my intrinsic lack of meaning, even with my self-assigned one. My scope is infinitesimally minute and void; my contributions to humanity are uncouth postulations and tiresome trite.

9:28 PM

Everyone has a superficial understanding; I cannot stand *it*. Even those at the frontier of a field, who battle with the elements and dilute the manifold mysteries into layman's terms have *only* a superficial understanding of *another's* understanding to provide reason and structure to their discovery. In this way we depend on each other. What good is the craftsman's wheel and axle without the carpenter's barrel? A simple metaphor that applies to all knowledge, and the utilization, to advance what is *now*, and still, we continue, for there is no recourse.

I have an immediate superficial understanding of my *self*, to which others may relay their own superficial understanding of their *selves* for an overall superficial understanding of our *selves* in relation to others. Each of us is a cog in another's machine. The ability to read and understand these words is, for the sake of appearances, genuine, though these words—thoughts—feelings, are *mine*—by my own superficial grasp of the English language taught to me since birth: an acculturated effort of civilization to label and convey; yet now the whole of what I am is *yours*... I cannot stand *it*.

Wednesday, December 25th, 2019

8:06 AM

"What else do you have to say?"

The old man licked his lips, stretched both arms out on either side of himself, relaxed, and said, "There's nothing I *have* to say."

"Well, what else have you seen? I'm intrigued."

"Once you've seen a few atrocities performed by your fellow man, you've seen them all; hearing about them is no different."

The office worker lurched forward and hunched, both elbows on the tabletop, and peered at the old man through half-closed eyelids. "Have you seen a beheading?"

"I've performed."

"How did *it* feel?"

"How did *what* feel?"

"The… the gristle, the spine being severed."

The old man glared at the sullen face across the table. "You're one sick puppy aren't you?"

"Me? I didn't fucking do *it!* Why did *you?* Were you affiliated with some gang or cartel?"

"Personal reasons. I was once a young, inquisitive man like yourself."

The office worker leaned back, tilted his head slack onto his right shoulder, and spoke with flat affect through a scrupulous sneer, "What do you mean?"

"I mean that I had perceived this woman—I'll tell you about this *one* woman, all right? I perceived her to have wronged me, to such a great extent that I decided to exact revenge in my own way; be my own law, my own justice. So, I arranged to meet with her one night, I remember, *it* was two days before Valentine's Day—she cared for that kind of thing—and… up in the mountains, I won't tell you which, I cracked her head with a rock from behind while she sat and ate mixed nuts and granola after relieving myself on a nearby tree. The sun had begun to set and I remember being cold… my hands were numb." The old man sipped the remnants of vodka and looked to his right towards a crowd of bar-goers converging on a waxed wooden dance floor. Intermittent flashes of multicolored strobe lights illuminated the old man's pensive configuration and accentuated his sunken cheeks' depth.

"And?"

"Hm?"

"And… aren't you going to finish your story?"

"Why should I?" The old man turned to face the office worker's contemptuous visage. "Haven't you figured *it* out on your own? You're an intelligent guy."

"You haven't answered my questions."

The old man chuckled, lowered his head, and muttered, "I stood and contemplated how I wanted to kill her; I had *it* all figured out before, though when you're standing there, face to face with the thing, there's a savagery about *it…*"

"You aren't going to offend or shock me," quipped the office worker.

The old man's brow furrowed; he chortled and said, *"Oh?* Yes, I can tell."

"So how did *it* feel—to cut through her neck; what did you use?"

"It felt like a chore, like something that I've done before and that I should've done a week prior but hadn't gotten around to."

"But the actual *physical* sensation?"

"Well there's the resistance of course, and the initial stymied screams— consider: you're knocked out, and next you know, you're jarred conscious with your neck sawed open, arms and legs tied, on your back, blindfolded, so that's a lot to take in… but, as for *my* feeling, there wasn't much, and the knife got the job done; I had sharpened the blade, and this wasn't my *first* job by a long shot, so… in this case I knew right where to cut for a quick fix."

"How many beheadings have you performed?"

The old man inhaled, held his breath, and said throughout a single exhale, "The only thing that gets me is the distorted screams… the respirations…"

"What?"

"They sound like pigs." The old man jolted out of the booth, strode seventeen feet at leisure over to the bar counter, set the empty vodka glass on a round beige coaster, and hailed a flummoxed bartender preoccupied with a group of three licentious women at the far end of the establishment.

2:03 PM

I forgot today was Christmas; laid on the carpet of my living room, I basked in the sun's rays, listened to three neighborhood children play outdoors, and thought, *"It's Christmas."* Something needed to be done; thereby, I stood, paced, and planned to visit a nightclub, though I convinced myself to stay indoors fifteen minutes later. I smelled my clothes and allowed their integrity to be the determinant if I am to go. The armholes smelled of laundry detergent. The first Christmas of my life that I needn't be pained by the sights of holiday splendor and the faint reverbs of festive song; why spoil the day? I've resolved to stay.

4:21 PM

I may as well be dead. There is no thought worth having. To spend all one's time alone, without distraction, and to squander the joy of life, one may as well be dead. I desire *to* desire. My suffering is negligible; my diet and exercise: moderate; my health: optimal. I'm at another pinnacle along life's journey, primed for death.

Theories of mind are subjective. I'm sane, too *sane* for my own welfare; I thrived when maddened. Now, the doldrums of default American existence, comfortable and at ease, jeopardizes my will.

To relinquish everything once more, to cease this querulous nonsense and embroil myself with a muse… though this mode is my muse *now,* what I've become: A ~~dead man~~ coward.

Thursday, December 26th, 2019

2:34 PM

The ex-child sex trafficker rounded back to the booth after a brief banter with the bartender, set down a new glass of vodka, slid into the seat, and said, "I know Tommy. He's a good kid."

The office worker wrenched at the right cuff of his cross-thatched burgundy-grey dress shirt and avoided the stern gaze of the old man. "The bartender?"

"Yep. Good kid."

"I want to know something—when…"

"All right."

"When there's *so* much beauty in the world, and culture… and wonder—and magnificence and goodwill and… nature… Why do what you do?"

"Hey, I *could* work at a slaughterhouse or meat-packing plant," the old man suppressed a laugh and flared his nostrils.

The office worker straightened his posture and relinquished the dress shirts' cuff: fingers upraised, the backs of both hands flat on the table. "These are human lives you're taking," he whispered. The old man leaned forward an inch in response. "For a profit, *that's it.* You're a murderer for your own selfish gain."

"You're starting to bore me now."

"Well *really!*–" the office worker blurted, looked around at throngs of unaware patrons, and continued with a hushed tonality, "I wouldn't meet you anywhere else but a place like this–"

"You've told me this–"

"–because quite frankly I—you're just monstrous and I'm rather terrified of you, though I'm curious, so here we are."

"Here we are." The old man forced a grin though the sadness conveyed in his eyes betrayed the authenticity; he raised his glass. The office worker scowled, looked down at the vacant space of a shadowed cushion to his right, and sighed a quick expulsion of air reminiscent of a whimper. The old man lowered his glass to the table without imbibing and said, "I was at Camp Speicher when the massacre happened. Do you know where that is?"

"No."

"I peered over an outcrop of rocks a little after midnight and saw the vague outline of a few hundred corpses being bulldozed into a mass grave. You said you don't know where that is?

"No—I don't."

"Doesn't matter. I've disemboweled men hung upside down by their ankles, well, no; I was the one holding a rag over their mouth so that the two other guys and I wouldn't have to hear screams while intestines are pulled out of an incision along the abdomen. I've mutilated twelve and thirteen-year-old girls for refusing to obey. We'd drag them out to the woods by the hair in pairs and lay them side by side, bound with some cloth or a bedsheet. I climbed on top of them and pressed both knees against their arms while I stabbed their neck with a six-inch blade. The little girls don't scream. They look up at you with forlorn eyes, even after their trachea is severed and they're choking on blood: not a look of condemnation, but one of fearful, plaintive resolve–"

"–I—why, *why* do you tell me this shit?"

"*It's* remarkable. I've seen dozens of traitorous recreants tremble and beg for their worthless lives with a gun pointed at their head—grown men. But the little girls being decapitated? I think my buddy drugged them."

The office worker stood without a word spoken and averted his eyes to a domed ceiling.

The old man chuckled; his gaze fixed straight forward at the back of the empty seat opposite of him. "You haven't heard half of *it*, a *fraction*. You *haven't* heard *anything*," muttered the old man, though the office worker had already passed through the rambunctious crowd of intoxicated dancers and acculturated with a mass of walkers on a busy inner-city street.

Friday, December 27th, 2019

7:28 PM

I squat over the toilet bowl and J.S. Bach's *Toccata and Fugue in D Minor* begins to resonate from my earbuds the moment I commence with fibrous defecation. Is this *not* a life worth living?

Saturday, December 28th, 2019

9:48 AM

Last night while I read, an outburst of a youth resounded from outdoors, "*It*'s not fair!"

When we're born into this world, "innocent" and bare, I marvel at the societal norms and cultural values we are taught, imposed on our malleable sensibilities by those who have already learned that existence is incompatible with justice. I think of Santa, myths and legends, the gods, and creatures of the night: Why the lies? Successive genealogical teachings of ethics and morality are nothing but a series of lies and outdated experiences; this is evident by the commonality of each dire exclamation shouted by a child: "*It*'s not fair!"

2:20 PM

I haven't left my apartment in a week and experience no desire to. A light rain patters outside, the exhaust of an idled truck expels a steady hum, and a distant ice cream truck plays the piper's song. I'm disturbed by what I hear. I'm an object among objects; when I look in the mirror I find the face unrecognizable; a subhuman stares back at me. For long periods I may prostrate on the floor or gaze out at a particular segment of the concrete street through narrow slits in my window blinds; throughout these thoughtless periods I feel the most alive, yet I'm too aware of the irrelevant: time. Days have slipped by, one into another. Mornings and nights are distinguished by my weariness. Empty cardboard boxes litter my unfurnished kitchen: future trash containers. All my clothes are unwashed, yet each article retains a pleasant odor.

I think of others' lives and am rendered bored: Bored by the idea of how others occupy themselves. I pace, read, perform five sets of five dumbbell exercises, and am bored with this too. I'm bored by what I write and think of the potential excitement of human interaction, to go out and feign; this is all. Everyone goes out and feigns their entire existence, everything about them. Relationships are sustained through *"charisma,"* a horrid word. In dealings with others, one may overlook the veneer of personality and empathize, for, the odds stand that whomever you interact with is not actively fascinated by their own humanity and the humanity of others; instead, the individual is engrossed with whatever task or distraction that may benefit them. This task or distraction may be a conversation with you; you've something to offer, in the other's opinion; how lucky you should feel to be a device in another's machination! If you're truly blessed, *you'll feel the same,* and will perform reciprocal acts: a sublime dance of ploys upon ploys; intuitions garner rewards for those who employ them well. Shall we call *it* love?

I've been all-too charismatic before, in my youth especially, and awed myself with the malleability of my relations. I squandered many opportunities to defile and deflower out of sheer disgust of others *disposed* to be… manipulated; yes, I thought for a moment, there is no other word. Being loved or cared for, and to love and care, is a delicate game with nebulous conventions.

A tortured, emaciated, and crucified man may love the sensation-seeking killer who encroaches in the night to end his torment with a single bullet to the head.

A woman may love the man who neglects her when he *finally* comes around to acknowledge her existence, only to dismiss her again, to leave her with a vague notion of hope; this hope gives her meaning.

A slave may love a master. A master may love a slave.

The feeling is dependent on meaning.

I love my pain; therefore, I write. What pain would I know?

Sunday, December 29th, 2019

4:38 PM

"What pain would you know?" slurred a drunken torturer into the ear of a sacrilegious priest suspended upside down with a taut rope around both ankles.

The priest watched the torturer fumble with a dull four-inch blade and pleaded, "You aren't one of them are you?"

"One of what you pissant?"

"One of the men to execute me?"

The torturer guffawed, swigged a dark-hued liquid, suppressed protracted expression to refrain from spitting out the drink, swallowed, and said to neither himself nor the priest, "This one thinks he's being executed."

A man garbed in resplendent red robes approached up a flimsy wooden scaffold, pressed a hand down onto the torturer's left shoulder, and muttered, "What did I tell you, Warin? How many times? Don't speak to the condemned."

"You ain't told me anything." Warin turned to face a cluster of trees a few feet beyond where the men stood. Other men garbed in black and brown robes lumbered up the scaffold steps, surveyed the priest with disinterest, and cocked their heads towards the man dressed in red.

The man in red barked, "Are you drunk?" with wry derision expressed on his contemptuous face as he inspected the priest's binds.

Warin grimaced and said, "Why... of *course* I'm *drunk.*"

The priest blurted, "That's exactly *it!*" One of the three newcomers slammed the butt of his knife against the priest's head six consecutive times. Blood began to flow from a pink gash.

"Easy with him right now," commanded the man in red to the assaulter; he turned to Warin and said, "I can't have you on the job if you're cup-shotten and you know *that*—what're you thinking?"

Warin leaned onto a makeshift post and lifted his chin. "I'm not drunk; I've only had a few."

"A few what?"

"Just a few drinks, that's all I've had, I swear *it,* I-"

"A few drinks *of what?*"

"Just a few drinks—really-"

81

"Can you perform?"

Warin scowled, pushed off the post, meandered towards the priest and pointed the tip of his knife at the contours of the bleeding pink forehead wound. *"Of course* I can perform; this is my job ain't *it?* I wouldn't drink just a few drinks if I knew *I couldn't perform."* He enunciated the last few words with exasperated anger.

The priest whined, "Don't I have a say in all this?—and if I'm not being executed then what's going to happen?"

"Silence, swine," said one of the men garbed in black.

"Bind his mouth," ordered the man in red, "This one's a talker; he'll no doubt be a screamer."

"Wait—*no*—*wait!* Please—if there's anything I-" the priest began with a stupefied yelp, though the shortest of the men garbed in black gripped the priest by an ample lock of hair and held him steady while the one who had battered the priest's head wrapped a thick, six-foot-long span of white cotton around the priest's mouth.

Monday, December 30th, 2019

5:49 PM

A series of muffled cries undertoned the idle banter of the men:

"How does he not know what'll be done?"

"Look at him writhe… vulgar heathen."

"Reckon you know what's served at Hilda's this evenin'?"

"Resecure his arms."

"Beef stew."

"He acts like he *isn't* being executed."

"May the Gods have mercy-"

"Always beef stew."

"-on this immoral apostate-"

"Better than rabbit."

"-who has lost himself to-"

"Cunting rabbit."

"-the influence of evil."

"Don't pray for the damn idolator."

"What you got against rabbit?"

"All of you, shut your mouths," uttered the man in red; the others obeyed the calm instruction. "Get on with *it*. Be done within the hour. I trust you all know well enough." The man in red leered at Warin, spun on his heels, tramped down the scaffold steps, and followed a beaten dirt path of a sunlit glade into the dense straits of a forest.

Tuesday, December 31ˢᵗ, 2019

8:29 PM

Muted whimpers accented the melodies of songbirds perched in windblown canopies three dozen feet above the men.

"Well… are we going to get this started?"

"I want to be off at a decent hour tonight."

Warin pressed his palms against a horizontal wooden rail level with his waist and slurred, "In a minute."

"Get ahold of yourself."

"He doesn't look well, does he?"

The third robed man remained silent and held both hands with fingers interlocked at the bottom of his abdomen.

"Just give me a minute or…" Warin hunched over the rail and stared straight down at clusters of ferns eight feet below.

"You heard the arbiter—a minute out of the hour is too long you drunken donkey."

"I'm not drunk," Warin spat and straightened his posture. "Just a few more seconds."

"Well you sure aren't sober either. Why'd you ever leave Llyod's?"

Warin turned to face the three figures garbed in black and gazed at his questioner with feigned deference. "God's house offered better bread."

The tallest man grimaced and said, "I've always known you're a faithless scoundrel; now you confirm *it*. You'll be the one slung up by a rope next if I have anything to say on *it*."

"What've you got against me? I'm just a man doin' a job."

The shortest interjected, "Then get—get! Stop this nonsense, bickering like wenches."

Warin lifted his chin and addressed each man in-turn with lowered eyelids. "No," he began with amiable inflection while he gripped the priest by a tuft of hair, "I left Llyod's because the work wasn't a challenge to me anymore." The three robed men encircled the priest in a quadrant with

Warin at the front of the scaffold. The tallest stood opposite of Warin and clenched the priest's waist; the shortest stood to the left and outstretched the priest's right arm while the silent man pulled the priest's left arm into a similar position.

"I can smell the alcohol on your breath from here," grumbled the tallest.

The knife slipped under the priest's hairline. Trails of blood began to flow down into the priest's frazzled black hair and stained Warin's fingers a bright crimson. The priest screamed into the wool bound around his mouth and thrashed against his suppressors.

Warin shouted, "Hold him steady!"

The robed men said nothing and observed Warin's masterful incisions around the priest's scalp, reminiscent of curious children. Warin released the priest's hair and set the blade on the wooden rail to his right. The priest spun his head in wild circles and he leered at Warin: abject terror expressed in two widened blue eyes. Warin dug into the folds of sliced flesh with his fingertips and peeled upward. The priest convulsed and screeched through the wool.

"So this is more of a challenge for you then?" The tall man smirked and raised an eyebrow while he tightened his hold around the priest's waist.

"A challenge to my patience dealing with you lot; never had to work with others till this job."

The shortest man's jaw hung slack and he watched with awe as the priest's face tore clean off down to the nose. Warin fumbled with the skin around the eyes and reached for the knife with a right hand smeared with blood. The priest ululated through the wool and twitched; his body arched back and bent forward despite the men's efforts to restrain him. The shortest man whispered, "This one's strong."

"They're all strong at first," snapped Warin, and he sliced around the priest's eyelids with two deft movements.

The shortest man spoke with dire solemnity while he stared at what remained of the priest's horrified visage: clenched teeth concealed by the wool and reddened cheeks. "I wonder what *it* feels like."

Warin broke his stoic mien, turned his attention to the shortest man, and warbled with a delightful faux smile spread from ear to ear, "Why, methinks *it* feels like having your skin flayed off!" and reverted his gaze back to the priest with an affirmative frown. The priest lurched with every few slices of the knife; his torso shifted and strained at the shoulder sockets.

The tallest man said, "Aye… so why don't you go back to Llyod's then, if you're as miserable as you look."

Warin's speech slowed to a mechanical drawl while he displaced the wool gag and held the priest's entire slackened slab of facial skin in his left hand, "Like I said, better bread, and wine is better than beer."

"Ah, that's debatable," quipped the shortest man with flat affect.

The tallest man persisted, "Wouldn't you rather be alone again skinning squirrels and rabbits?"

Warin ignored the men and reaffixed the gag into the priest's mouth. The silent man scowled, shifted on his feet, and looked to the sky. Warin's quick cuts separated the skin down to where the neck began; he inserted his widespread fingers and yanked up from all angles with five intermittent jerks. The robed men clenched the priest while Warin struggled to peel back the dermis from exposed arteries.

The shortest man said, "I feel sick."

"Look away then," Warin commanded. "The difficult part is over."

The tallest man chuckled and said, "Difficult part for you, what about *him!*"

The shortest man began to hyperventilate and said, "That's what I—I mean; I imagine what's he's feeling and-"

Warin's slashes hastened: his movement zealous, he said, "Will you two shut your mouths?"

"Impressive work for a drunkard," cooed the tallest man.

"I'm not a drunkard; I'm *just* drinking is all."

The priest spurted congealed blood from his nose and the saturated wool stuffed into his mouth oozed a thickened stream of blood which contributed to the many channels that flowed to the top of his head before dripping down to accent the red-stained wooden timber of the scaffold with a fresh spatter of vibrant red.

"*Oh*—oh, oh, oh," the shortest man started.

"You'd think he was flaying *you,*" said the tallest man, "Remember this one's crimes against God; your pity is intolerable."

"Oh-ah—yes; he'll be dead soon."

Warin shook his head and ripped two nipples away from the chest. "They usually live for a while after I've finished."

"*No,*" the shortest pleaded.

"Really?" inquired the tallest. "That seems a bit, unnatural."

"Up to a day. Professional opinion is that they die from hypa… hippa-"

"-Hypothermia?" said the tallest.

"Yes, that or blood loss." Warin allowed the mass of detached skin to dangle in a misaligned clump and gouged an incision from the priest's shoulders to the top of his wrists.

"Ah, *exsanguination* or hypothermia... I think I'd rather burn than endure this."

"Be a good boy then; recite your prayers and stay away from the bishop's coffers." Warin removed the skin from both arms in an instant, evocative of a mottled snake. The priest's resistance had ebbed to a few involuntary spasms though his agonized wails continued to exacerbate the shortest's nausea.

"And just what do you mean by that?" the tallest said with sudden sternness.

Warin paused and looked to the right of the priest's suspended legs at the accusatory visage staring back at him and slurred, "I need you... to shut your cunting mouth so I may focus!"

"You've no right to speak to me with such language."

Warin slashed and pulled at the priest's abdominal flesh and said, "Lower him."

The tallest man remained statuesque for a moment and veered away from the labor, down the scaffold steps, to a metal crank bolted to the earth—rope affixed and bound along a wheel; he reversed the notchings, one by one, until the priest's knees were level with Warin's eyes. The shortest and the silent man released the priest's unmarred fingers, whereby both hands fell and skimmed the pool of coagulated blood along the scaffold. The tallest man stood on his toes, peered past the men at the length of rope toward Warin, and said, "Well?"

"That's enough," said Warin. "I need a break." Warin set the knife on the rail and wiped the sweat of his brow onto an unbloodied patch of his shirt.

The silent man's low voice boomed, rendering him unsilent, "Don't prolong his suffering."

Warin's befuddled countenance snapped up; he gaped, open-mouthed, for a fraction of a second, shook his head, scoffed, turned towards the forest, and said, "We're all sufferin'—him no more than I or the rest of you lot."

The tallest man rounded up the scaffold stairs, glanced down at the exposed musculature and wracked visage of what was once a man, and sniggered. "I *really* must disagree with you there, Warin."

"No—no—this man may feel extraordinary pain now but at least for him *It*'ll be over soon."

"Nay," retorted the shortest, "he awaits eternal suffering in hell!"

The tallest said, "Enough of the philosophical nonsense! You've got a job, haven't you?—Then work as we are!"

Warin grumbled and returned the knife to the sheet of abdominal flesh. "You're all hardly workin'." The knife cut with ease and severed two inches of skin from muscle in a second. The priest's spasms reinstated and prompted the men to hold fast.

The tallest man strode around the perimeter of the scaffold and surveyed the scene, his hands gripped behind his back, head hunched forward. "My... you're a real butcher with that thing; nothing exact about you."

"Shut up," Warin hissed.

"*It* just sloughs off."

Blood poured from the priest's head and fingertips through the narrow space of scaffold timber and painted the dirt beneath with spidery etchings. The priest's muffled screams and pained cries shifted to agonized wails that nullified the wool's silencing effects.

"I can't believe you're the only one they assigned to perform," commented the tallest; the two other robed men eyed Warin with circumspection.

Warin said, "Yeah?—I'm the only skilled skinner in the county for miles, and *miles* around, from what I know, so that's that."

"You're hardly a skinner... a butcher..."

"I—I-" Warin threw the knife to the scaffold floor and approached the tallest, nose to nose. "I've only an hour; if you can do better, shut your trap and get to *it*. You just walkin' 'round here doin' nothin' but flabbin' yer' cuntin' mouth huh? Get to *it!*"

"Step back you drunkard."

The shortest outstretched an arm and cried, "Please, please, friends!"

"No—you..." Warin began; both fists clenched in tight balls by his sides, he turned, clomped down the scaffold steps, and followed the glade trail into the density of the surrounding forest.

"Warin!" shouted the tallest.

"Come back! Won't he come back!?" said the shortest.

The silent man opened his mouth and said nothing.

The priest gurgled behind a veil of mangled facial skin. Translucent red foam surfaced around the wool gag.

8:46 PM

I entered a bar, gazed around before the band began to play, and an immediate thought rebounded throughout my mind while I listened to the banal banter of the dozens around me; thus, I wrote with numbed hands on a piece of scrap paper: "I don't understand people." And *really,* I don't at all, for I don't desire to be here, nor do I desire alcohol.

No—I sit in a corner booth, alone, and enjoy the air-conditioned warmth leech into my body, listen to the jukebox blare, hear my brethren. I listen. I *am* one of them. What else is there but humanity? Smoke. Drink. Music. I'm engulfed with a miasma of filth and nonsensical cacophonies. This duress I've wrought on myself will end prematurely. I resolve to never attend a bar or club again; both are venues for the dissipated and forlorn.

JANUARY

Wednesday, January 1st, 2020

12:06 AM

The bar served no Pinot Noir. I tipped the two female bartenders $23 after drinking one glass of cabernet and conversed with a twenty-one-year-old Christian man about his love for raising cattle: his self-assigned meaning in life. A real cowboy, he pulled a small circular piece of rubber from his pocket—two-inches in diameter, and explained that the instrument is used to castrate calves. He shook my hand and departed with a stout girl engrossed with a phone, half his height, whose nervous one-tone-laughter punctuated our conversation on cattle castration.

The three musicians were rambunctious and awful: mindless strums of two guitars, monotonous bashes of a vehement drummer, and a juvenile singer who made teenage love his muse. The bartenders were both as industrious and fluent as I remembered them. I ran home a little after 11 PM and at the stroke of midnight (I checked my wristwatch) I encountered a weepy young woman on the street near my apartment; as I passed by her, I raised my arms and shouted, "Happy fuckin' New Year!"

The woman said, "I know right? Shit!"

Distant fireworks exploded to the west from the city center where I had previously been.

Thursday, January 2nd, 2020

11:05 AM

Inside a Cambodian temple, a neophyte garbed in a simple orange robe kneeled before a resplendent Buddhist altar illuminated with dozens of small white candles and murmured, *"O Holy Baphomet, gleaming in the eastern sky, sign of righteousness in-"*

"What?" interrupted a fellow neophyte prostrated two feet away.

"Oh, that?" The monk leaned back and sat on his feet, posture erect. "I'm just practicing my rights as a denizen of the cosmos. By newfound scientific dissertation, I formulated my own credo for justice and thereby practice a conservative-libertarian approach to all perspectives; I'm an open advocate for all belief and wish goodwill, compassion, and the liberation of the soul from reality from which we are bound by pseudo practices ill-founded worldwide."

The adjacent monk stared for a long while at the first monk's thighs, dropped his gaze, and returned his forehead to the floor.

"*... And hieroglyph of the arcana of the invisible world: exalt our minds and hearts with the-*"

"Why," hissed the prostrated monk, "do you worship Satan in a Buddhist temple?"

The first monk assumed a haughty grin and raised his chin. "My pantheism synthesized with a crystallized belief of panpsychism is infallible by how I conduct myself; though the processes to my intuitive understanding are epistemological, one cannot deny the physiological boons of such a mode of mind, exemplified in the health of my body and the clarity of my rhetoric, as thus, you may testify."

The prostrated monk mimicked the first monk's position on both knees and said, "You shouldn't be here."

"Why not?"

"You aren't Buddhist."

"Yes I am. You shouldn't believe anything I just said because I really don't believe in any of *it*, honestly."

"You're a liar and a hypocrite."

"No," the first monk stood, gazed around the small ovoid chamber, and lifted both hands, aligned with his shoulders. "I'm actually not a Buddhist, and neither are you; we're just two men dressed and behaving in a certain way-"

"You are not me; you don't know what I believe."

"How do you know that I'm not you or that you aren't me? Aren't you weary of the dogmas and the scriptures and upholding your actions to a certain standard? You-"

"Look, guy," The second monk stood and turned to face the first monk. "I don't know you and you don't know me, but I just want to pray, all right? I've had a rough year and I've struggled a lot and I'm finally starting to overcome my past because of what I believe now, so please, just leave if you don't believe."

The first monk opened his mouth to speak, paused, and laughed. A few tears welled in both eyes and remained fixed along both bottom eyelids. He walked out of the shrine.

Every thought or formulation of ideas I've ever experienced has been experienced already (Hundredth monkey effect/simultaneous invention). My fundamental philosophies of existence are tired concepts. Explanations of consciousness are moot. I read of the terminologies and theories; every renowned philosopher of antiquity up to my contemporaries believes in a deviation of another's deviation of another's deviation. The spiral of madness persists and I can't help but to sit in my little apartment, with my little ~~writing~~ multimedia device, and wonder just what *it* is that people believe they're going to achieve. I'll tell you:

Validation—ah! Of course, our social conundrum—consciousnesses aware of other consciousnesses ad nauseam, though that which exists wishes to be known, to make the best of *"it,"* i.e., "that which is." What difference is there in the profundity of labor of those who dedicate their lives to developing theories of mind, existence, god, of the universe, and myself?—devoted to the refinement of my *doubt*. When you strip away the pretensions of virtue applicable to labor for the progression of humanity, there is true merit to the path of the hedon, engrossed with pleasures of all manners—and zestful too: the materialistic spiritualist *is* here *now*.

This writing is my entertainment, my lie I tell myself through my biased perspective of a past version of myself that no longer exists, my escapism, my filthy masturbatory session. I ejaculate words.

One can't quit philosophy. Even one who has never heard of the word "philosophy" continues to philosophize, unbeknownst to them, by the act of their will. A deadbeat sycophantic mother of four children who spends all her time watching television crime drama reruns and eating grilled cheese sandwiches with ham is inherently a philosopher—but—*oh*—this has been thought of before!

Must I quit writing, or resort to half-baked fiction for the remainder of my days? The details of my life are a trifle, a drop in the bucket among the billions alive, billions dead, and billions (trillions) to come. These words are destined to be nothing, the same fate as every six-hundred-or-more-page tome written by a well-learned scholar or graduate with an ego of his own to share in the manifestation of thoughts to advance civilization: a drab venture.

To overthrow entropy (god) is our directive, to outwit the end—whatever an end is, i.e., nothing—we can't even conceive *it*; how do we evade the inconceivable? That's the whole point of *it*, then? To understand? So that we may overcome? Overcome what? Nothing? I laugh. I'm a writer, so *it*'s called.

3:55 PM

My New Year's resolution has come late. I resolve to, ah, nevermind.

Friday, January 3rd, 2020

9:30 AM

A no-name woman walked into a bar and bounded over to another no-name woman seated at a booth preoccupied with a laptop screen and keyboard. "Why don't you write a story of substantial length and quality, a story that doesn't have one-dimensional characters and nondescript settings?"

"I'm not invested enough," said the seated no-name woman leaned back against the booth. "Besides, I wouldn't even know how; when I look around, all I see are one-dimensional characters. Anything else is a ploy. The subtle nuances and complicated feelings-"

"You only think that way because *you're* a one-dimensional character. All your writings are a bore to me—sorry, though I know you don't mind; I'm just being pretentious after all—what was *it?* Trying to validate myself? Yes, that's *it.*" The standing no-name woman flashed a snide grin, rolled her head, and drifted away in expectancy of a retort that never came; she meandered, disappointed, and situated herself between two men of identical mien seated at the bar. Both men gaped up at her with immediate approval. The first man's gaze fixed on the newly seated no-name woman's compact breasts, snuggled together beneath a black turtleneck sweater. The second man feigned surprised and shouted, "What're you doin' here!? They don't let seventeen-year-olds drink!"

"Shut up Eddie."

Both men laughed; the first lowered his eyes to his beer; the second blushed and caught sight of the newly seated no-name woman's compact breasts, snuggled together beneath a black turtleneck sweater.

12:42 PM

As for philosophy, I'm ready to consign myself to banal exposition and half-hearted fiction. I've deluded myself for too long; thereby, my ego flourished; well, that's over. Would death be welcome? Would I be equipoised? This is impossible to know. Philosophers, i.e., humanity, flagellates themselves with some neurosis, the stoics (and masochists) most of all. I think to quote Nietzsche on this matter: a little flavor text to embolden my own, to enhance my nonexistent merit, but what merit could Nietzsche have over *my* experience? I cling to the passages and proverbs of other men with a diminutive hope that there is at least a notion of truth in this world, a mote of wisdom, an essence of all-pervasive sagacity which governs all… though these processes are of a *stoic* nature, and what legacy did the stoics leave other than a recount of lives they'd prefer to not have lived.

7:49 PM

My mental unrest is profound; I read and am repelled. Convictions elicit disgust. Attention turned to human advances in space exploration and neuroscience elicit my good humor. A few sets of pull-ups here, a few sets of push-ups there; I'm alone, yet I'm not alone? I'm myself, yet I'm not myself? I am you, and you I? I imagine a haughty tea-drinking intellectual dipped in a vat of boiling oil. Violence is the answer to our quandaries. Barbarous savages and thieves are the wisest of all.

The days pass by unnoticed, each indistinguishable from the last. In ten days I will return to my job as a fried chicken purveyor. Meanwhile, I research alternatives to live (cults, test subject opportunities, volunteer work) while I bide my time and pay off debts incurred from last year's stint of unemployment without benefits compounded with publishing services. If I had been born gifted, I'd squander myself.

Saturday, January 4th, 2020

10:26 AM

It's My Pleasure

Man looms over breader cart:
Two. Four. Six. Eight fillets
Arranged in a silver pan.
Beeping.
"Nuggets please!"

Wash your hands;
Don new gloves.
Beeping.
Vacuous faces watch
Automation on demand.
Beeping.
America's youth: a myopic view-
"One ranch and uh… two barbeque."
Beeping.
"How else may I help you?"
Beeping.

Sunday, January 5th, 2020

8:54 AM

I delve into Nietzsche's philosophy of negatory philosophy again after ten years of superficial gleanings—*ideas* of *hundreds* upon *thousands,* and am reminded to cleanse my palate. My stoical martyrdom and self-assigned meanings are rendered fraudulent. My indignations veiled my (self) lies. How Nietzsche wrote such a long, passionate, charged exposition(s) of his indignations in regards to humanity's individual search for truths serving as a catalyst *for* his indignation is a certain demerit—in *my* truth; yet, I'm moved, for *it* is much easier to be the nihilist—too entrenched with his own humanity to even begin to fathom being removed from the position, convinced of the boundless untruths *as* truth: Not even scientific theory may withstand *it.*

All the relationships I've terminated and avoided could've been something great, though if the relationships *were* to be great, they would've never existed in the first place, for I would have never attracted nor been attracted to those with whom I once explored interpersonal relations with. Differentiated reason and passion would impel me to varied heights or lows. I mention this now for my own sake—as this entire journalistic endeavor is—veiled in the supercilious delusion that I may benefit others by the proliferation of my idle pass of the hours—for the resurgence of a "unified consciousness" is common in contemporary thought. The whole reason for a superficial understanding of another's philosophy is because one's own philosophy is *just* a superficial understanding of another's.

Hark!—a "unified consciousness": I can't even begin, not out of a lack of ideas—or even the *want,* but for the comedy of *it.*

I scratch the surface of Daniel Kolak's near-seven-hundred-page tome, *I am You: The Metaphysical Foundation of Global Ethics* and laugh aloud at every page. The convoluted nonsense, jargon, and academic references to others' work as a means to justify his own work (which *is not* his own—but a compilation), serve the *exact* premise that he strives to endorse, as an unjust fallacy.

At the age of fifteen, I remember reading Franz Kafka's *The Castle* and being struck by a phenomenon I failed to understand: *"How do I relate and feel the raw emotion of this man; how do I comprehend the thought as if my own?"* This is more than a matter of literary ability and the mastery of language. I am Kafka, and Kafka is I.

The basis of the soul—of consciousness—defined by dead men I won't bother to name till now—where I stand and write atop a stack of cardboard boxes on my kitchen counter, is sterile and innocuous. Philosophy of any nature is *sterile and innocuous,* for even if we were at a future climax to become enlightened by the delineation of our human faculties, what would be reaped *but* an understanding? I.e., what *benefit* is *it* to understand?

8:17 PM

I cried on behalf of Beethoven while listening to the second movement of his Piano Concerto No. 3; the man's suffering is an inspiration.

Monday, January 6th, 2020

1:45 PM

A surgeon slumped over a writing desk. A cup of green tea steamed beside a blank piece of paper. Moonlight shone in and accented the dim lighting on the 3rd floor of his yacht. He wrote: *"Outline for Eleemosynary."* at the top of the page in the far left margin in size nine font with an illegible script. A pause. The opaque tea tilted along the cup's brim, synchronized with waves that lapped against the yacht's exterior. The surgeon set a pen down along the paper's vertical right edge, stood, walked across a plush carpet, and strolled downstairs where he met with a youthful woman idling by a steel outdoor side-rail.

The woman looked at the surgeon and said, "What's wrong?"

"Oh," he cooed, and joined her at the yacht's edge. "I can't think of a name."

"Who are the characters?"

The surgeon's supple hands slid across the exposed back of the woman's silver dress between her shoulder blades. "I make up the characters as I go—the details of how they appear, what they're wearing, or personality… all that's secondary to the theme, the idea."

The woman inhaled a drag from a cigarette and expelled a thin stream of smoke between two pursed lips. "Well, what's the big idea then, *big* man?"

"A wealthy man; the true-to-life, wealthy man."

"I didn't know this was an autobiography."

"Please."

"What!"

"I'm not wealthy; I'm rich, and god knows for how much longer."

A warm wind trilled between them. The surgeon removed his hand from the woman's back and gripped the side rail with both hands.

"People enjoy stories for the *people*—you know—as *you* know, I'm a *voracious* reader." The woman's sensual words filled the man's ears, enclosed around him—drowned him in a sonorous deluge reminiscent of a siren's lure; she dragged on the cigarette. *"It* makes people feel human when they read of characters they can relate to, who do… *human* things and think and behave and react as you'd expect them to," she squinted, smirked, and moved her free right hand over to the surgeon's left hand.

Fingers played on the back of the surgeon's knuckles. "Humans are the means to their own ends. My characters are ploys for my ideas, disposable, *malleable,* as they are, for *my* own ends. That's why I create them."

"You're such a humanist George! There's still so much I don't know about you."

George chuckled and acknowledged the woman's face for the first time since he joined her: Nothing changed, exactly as he remembered *it.* "C'mon." George turned and walked back towards the stairs leading up to a third-floor bedroom. The woman blew one final puff from the half-finished cigarette, tossed *it* over the rail, and obeyed.

7:39 PM

"Outline for an… eleemosynary? Really?" The woman set the paper back down on the table, sat on a small white chair, and began to remove her pearl-colored high heels. George laid on a regal bed atop the covers and stared at the domed ceiling. "What made you decide to write a book anyway?"

George said, "I have something to say."

"I get that, but if you had something to say, why not write a thesis or an academic journal if character development isn't your strength—or what you even care about."

George rolled to his side; a black tie flopped over a white dress shirt and slumped against the bed. He met the woman's eyes with a gentle smile "Because my dear, *I* have nothing to say; the characters do."

The high heels clattered aside the desk. "Your writing style would annoy me."

"Why?"

"When you read literature, you should have the full scene clear in your head from the start. You can't just go coloring and shaping the world midway while the action unfolds."

"What do you mean?" George muttered; he assumed a quizzical expression, laid flat on his back once more, and steepled his hands on his chest.

"If I'm reading about people discussing humanity—or whatever *it* is— and I envision them to look a certain way, and suddenly a few sentences or pages later the man had a ring on his finger when I had previously imagined him to be *ringless,* well, that would irritate me and ruin my immersion."

"Hm. I think *it*'s rather funny."

The woman kneeled onto the bed beside George and grumbled, *"I* think *it*'s bad writing."

"You would think that." The surgeon reached out and rubbed the top of the woman's bald head. "You're beautiful no matter what you think."

"Oh," the woman mewled feigned delight, "You're such a *sweetheart."*

George removed a pair of eyeglasses and set *it* on an ornate nightstand beside the bed. He repositioned his head on a tasseled blue pillow and said, "I should just give *it* up, the whole writing idea; I haven't the grit or patience."

"Don't be like that; *it*'s unattractive."

George laughed; a hint of contempt flashed over his reddened cheeks, though he substituted the feeling with humor. "That's really what I *don't* like about writing. Everyone expects to learn something or to be entertained. There's no accountability—you can say whatever you want and as long as your rhetoric holds up you're granted a pass sheerly out of positive skepticism—nothing like mathematics—nothing tangible or reliable. No one wants to read about *real* people, the *facts:* farting, burping, coughing, self-doubting and word-fumbling facts of relationships—of growing old and disinterested, of vapid nights in each other's arms when neither thinks or feels a thing of the other, of every bathroom session and hair found on the rim of a sink."

The woman yawned, rubbed at the corner of her right eye, leaned over George's face, and said, "You don't know what you're saying."

"Don't you gaslight me," George snapped.

A two-minute silence ensued, followed by thirteen-minute foreplay, twenty-one minute intercourse, an eleven-minute shared shower, and fifty-six minutes of intimate conversation before sleep, while lying side by side, naked and clean, between the sheets of a soiled bed.

Tuesday, January 7th, 2020

8:44 AM

I wept on my floor last night while I thought of the cumulative pain of my father and mother—not caused by me, though I've contributed. I thought of past friends, of the women who sought and slept with me. From an early age I deduced interpersonal relations were extraneous matters that must be cultivated for the sake of the other person's feelings. With time, I withdrew from everyone I knew or allowed my indifference to permeate every facet of a relationship; thereby, I repelled many, and now attract a unique class of humanity's delusional manifestations—people similar to me: I'm haunted by ~~demons~~ the self-possessed. Perhaps I wept for myself; even the most sympathetic sessions of grief are egoic by nature.

My mother would feel no sympathy for me, only because she wouldn't understand.

1:43 PM

Every set of arbitrary movements to stimulate my muscles and neurons is despicable—every set of push-ups, pull-ups, squats, bench and shoulder presses. Each meal is senseless, the consumption vile. We distract ourselves with everything deemed pleasurable and holistic. We distract ourselves with pain and fantasy, locked in our bodies; we know nothing else.

I write to distract myself from the meaningingless of my self-assigned meaning: to write? Fool. As much as a fool as a philanthropic environmentalist or a degenerate child molester—each with their own distractions.

"Minimize the suffering of others," proclaims a modest saint; demonstrate, then! Show me your healing powers for what is chosen!

On the brink of death, a man convulses. The donations of a self-made billionaire render the administration of drugs capable of saving the man's life possible—his pain nullified—reason restored; rejoice, for the great humanitarian!

Another chops at a man's neck with a fireax: punishment for petty theft. The attacker abandons his handiwork, half-finished, and permits the thief to die an agonizing death. Creature! Boo the scoundrel off the stage! Yes, how *very* inhumane!

Read between the lines of benevolence and nobility, of the odious and wicked, and you'll decipher the indifferent bonds of nature. Civilization or solitude. Dualistic? Anarchistic? Don't bother to ascribe me a title; I *am* you! Consciousness? Identity? Feel your body, the flesh that *it* is. What do you digest?

8:09 PM

"How's the writing coming?" said the bald woman.

George sat on a sun chair with a laptop balanced on his chest. "I've decided on a journal."

"Academia?" The woman strolled over to the rail several feet away from the surgeon and uplifted her head to the noon sun.

"No, just a journal."

"Of what?"

"Whatever I think of."

The woman raised a lit cigarette between the middle and forefinger of her left hand and quipped before a drag, "That sounds boring."

"*It* is."

"Then why do you write?"

"I've nothing better to do."

"Will you read some for me?"

George chuckled and began at once: "Three Pitbulls lay by each other's sides in an unkempt carrot garden. The dogs' elderly owner hollered, 'Ay! Out! Out!' and struck each dog in-turn on the back with a stick-"

101

"-George!"

The surgeon glared at the woman; she scoffed and braced her hands on the rails, cigarette wedged between her knuckles. "The dogs lurched up from their midday slumber; one knocked the owner to the ground with a weighty tackle and the other two tore into the man's neck. Skin tore away in small patches and stained the dirt with blood. The man fought and screamed. His desperation excited the animals' bloodlust. One pulled at the man's shoe and the other two mauled his head. Try as the man might, he failed to repel his once beloved pets and succumbed; his body mangled and partially eaten, rotted with each turn of the sun for weeks to come."

The woman pushed herself off the rail, arched her back, dragged on her cigarette, turned full-body towards the surgeon, and said through a windblown cloud of smoke, "That was *fucking* awful."

"Writing isn't easy."

"No—George, that was truly terrible. Why would you write something like that?"

"What? That's relatively tame. I thought *it* was a fine example of justice."

"George…"

"Why do you only refer to me by my name when you're upset with me? Look where you are girl, look around you. Have you any reason to be upset? You asked me to share a little of what I've written and I have; you didn't like *it;* that's fine. Put a hat on before your pretty head is burned."

The woman returned both hands to the rail, posture straight; she said, "So how does that character's death serve what you have to say?"

"The words I've written are all I have to say."

The woman took quick, successive drags on her cigarette.

Wednesday, January 8th, 2020

5:12 PM

I've been evoked to tears by music, painting, and nature, though for the first time in my life, tears fell from my eyes and mucus streamed from my nose on my reading of Leo Tolstoy's *What Men Live by:* not of a rudimentary sadness or happiness elicited by tragedy and drama, but an exalted sorrow.

"Eight men dressed in mismatched t-shirts and flannel jeans of variegated color hacked the limbs off mounds of desiccated human corpses piled four-feet high at the center of an annual human meat market. Machetes tinked on bone. That's my opening; what do you think?"

The bald woman scowled and pulled the bedsheets up past her bare breasts. "*Tinked?*" she giggled and silenced herself. "Well, um... I mean, *it*'s shit. I wouldn't read *it*."

"Why?"

"There needs to be at least one character for me to relate to at the start of a story for me to be hooked. I don't care about a bunch of savages."

The surgeon sighed and set his journal flat against his desk. "You're thinking from a consumerist perspective. All right—what do you *feel* about *it?*"

"I feel *and* think that *it*'s shit; there's nothing '*consumerist*' about *it*," the woman laughed, unrestrained, and reached for a pack of cigarettes on an adjacent nightstand. "There's just no merit to *it*. Why you would even write something like that and expect there to be people who would want to read *it* is asinine."

The surgeon stared at the ceiling and listened to the flick of a lighter. "Why wouldn't someone want to read *it*? I wrote more." The surgeon reached for the journal and held *it* inches from his face.

"George, no-"

"Flies nestled within the folds-"

"*-George!-*"

"-of mutilated torsos and sprung from slackened mouths with every-"

"-Shut the fuck up!"

The surgeon grinned, lowered the journal to his chest, and said, "You're a close-minded woman."

"I don't care—I don't want to hear that shit right now; and you're a sick, twisted man."

"We should've been more detailed and honest on our dating profiles."

The woman said nothing and the nothingness which amounted between them amplified into a reckoning beyond either of their comprehension until there was something which died between them, something neither knew existed, though both thought they felt an inexplicable rift. The surgeon scratched his abdomen and the woman said, "I think I'll make us eggs and pancakes in the morning."

Thursday, January 9th, 2020

3:20 PM

The ineluctable comedy of philosophers, theorists, "isms," and "ists," is that there's too many, or rather, that each is solicitous to peer reviews. The result is a farcical skirmish of the intellect, no more elevated than a savage brawl. Each postulation asserted is a variation of analogous beliefs, dissimilar by subjective experience.

My thesis:

Iknowathiscism: An Irreducible and Irrefutable Theory of Existence

1. ~~To begin:~~ I acknowledge that I know.
2. ~~To end:~~ Proceeding from point (1), I acknowledge that you don't know.

There are flaws with the verbiage, this I know; for instance, there is no end to what you don't know, nor is there a beginning to what I know, though these axioms are otherwise infallible.

Friday, January 10th, 2020

12:34 PM

The notion of how unhappy I am sobers me only when I'm around other people, not on account of a comparative reference, but for how people *are;* thereby, I fail to practice pseudo mutism, even of the selective kind, due to a misplaced pity of my fellow-creatures. I am spoken to and am inclined to respond, for my naive perception of the other's *innocence.* I have no desire to injure another, yet, an enforced silence in the face of an individual vying for an understanding *is* an injury when I can understand, and choose to withhold.

"How was your vacation Baethan?" said Grant, a kitchen worker.

I met his eyes, smiled, and nodded, though he looked at me, expectant. I held out a thumbs-up, swiped a handful of rags out from a plastic bag, and walked away.

Grant said, "That's good," and pushed his glasses up higher onto his nose bridge; he addressed me with a crestfallen, sidelong glance. *"Still an asshole,*" he thinks, for I've no concern for *him*—or how *his* vacation was! The essence of humanity dies between us at that moment—*that moment;* what is life but a sequence of moments?

A bored employee—a young man named Cesar, shuffled to me, sighed, smiled at my delayed acknowledgment of him, and said, "I didn't eat any fast food all vacation Baethan. I'm proud of myself. I feel… cleaner."

I thought to say, *"You've purged yourself,"* or, *"They miss your money,"* yet I said *nothing,* for what difference is there? The boy's accomplished smile distorted into a desperate grin—his shoulders slouched on my vague, silent appraisal! *"Well done lad! I'm proud of you too!"* followed by an exclamatory high-five would be ideal for us both to form a rapport, a bond, a comradeship, a *lie.*

At the end of our brief midday shift, at our lockers, Cesar said, "You've really helped me out a lot Baethan."

I could withstand *it* no longer; I said, perplexed, "How have I helped you?"

"You've given me food, a book, and a shirt."

"They're peripheral things. I haven't helped you."

"They help more than you think." He spoke while rummaging through his locker. I said nothing; I *wouldn't* say anything. I hadn't felt happiness or solemnity, nor did I feel accountable. I stood beside him and stared down at the cuffs of my coat. "Well, I'll see you Monday, Baethan."

4:57 PM

I know of no profound language or clever models anymore; I wish to dispel everything I've ever gleaned, every word spoken and thought processed. Even nihilism is now a child's plaything among a pen of toys. I imagine each metaphysical, ethical, epistemological, aesthetical, and logical philosophy as an object of thought held up by all proponents, reminiscent of how a group of zealots would worship their god(s). Whether there is or isn't this ideal named by us, "truth," I care no longer. I've failed myself. If not philosophy, what?

"The unexamined life is not worth living."

- Socrates

I'll heed the dead man who knew nothing and go on examining.

Saturday, January 11th, 2020

9:17 AM

The examination: A man wakes at 6:13 AM from his floor after bouts of inconsistent periods of sleep and vague, disjointed dreams. He remains on his floor and periodically shifts into various uncomfortable positions on his sides until 7:06 AM, whereby he rises out of a sense of urgency elicited by the immediate need to urinate upon his upright stance.

The man observes his reflection in the mirror and is dismayed by the stranger. Each day someone new addresses him with a somber acknowledgment. The familiarity is keen and surreal. "Enough," the man thinks to speak, though the thought is detained, yet the body obeys and assumes a weary visage before moving away into the kitchen. There are many options in the kitchen, *too* many; therefore, a regimen is a necessity. The man's universe is contained: the apartment and *it*s rooms, wiring, piping, carpets, handles, cabinets, closets, and fixtures, are assorted to his needs, as though *he* had drawn the blueprints and built the space.

Five quart-sized containers of oats and chia seeds soaked overnight in water, apple cider vinegar, and ceylon cinnamon loom at the far end of a counter. The man knows what to do next—the moment planned:

While two containers' contents simmer on the stovetop, the man occupies himself with a screen and reads two succinct biographies detailing the life of Georg Hegel and Immanuel Kant. "Neither are as interesting as the life of Friedrick Nietzsche," he thinks—and does not think to speak, yet his body obeys with a sigh and a shift on his feet while he stands in front of a cardboard box podium.

Consumption.

Chin-ups, shoulder presses, and tricep extensions are planned for the afternoon.

The man sits on an inclined weight-lifting bench to write of an examination.

Jesus Christ would have been wise to practice his faith in silence; his egomania begs the question if he were a true Christian; he was the people's sycophant.

Sunday, January 12ᵗʰ, 2019

9:58 AM

A stout old woman roused from her bed and played with tufts of uncouth hair on the hinds of three of her nine most amiable house cats. "Oh—boo—boo—boo!" she cooed, bent parallel to the floor. "Oh—*boo*—boo. *Yes,* oh I *know,* you're hungry for your breakfasts aren't you babies? *Yes!* Oh—boo—boo." A lean black cat brushed up against the woman's leg; one fluffy brown cat sauntered out the bedroom door, and the third: an aged, chubby black cat with dull yellow eyes, sat at the foot of the bed and squinted. *"Oh*—boo—*boo—boo!"*

In the kitchen, two cats walked on the dining table, one sprawled out on top of a cutting board, one swatted a knitted toy, another sat vigilant by a window ledge, and the last still slept beneath a dander encoated sofa. "Oh—boo—boo—babies!" The woman entered, proceeded by the first three.

All nine cats converged within fourteen seconds around the woman's feet and mewled. "Yes. *Yes."* The woman beamed, stretched her arms high above her head, inhaled through her nostrils, and shouted a passionate exhalation. "Good morning—*yes*—I know! Momma's gonna feed you—my sweets."

The cats licked themselves, bawled through widespread mouths, paced, fumbled, twitched, and swatted each other's tails.

The woman has lived and awoke each morning in this manner for twelve years. She supports her minimal lifestyle with a disability claim pertaining to osteoporosis. Every Friday she visits a discount antique store and purchases a 1960s themed item to add to a house-wide collection; once a month she treats herself and visits the store on Thursday in addition to Friday. When a cat dies, she adopts two more from a cat breeder she met at a local hairdresser. Four cats have died since the woman's initial five years of this lifestyle, and each instance of cat death elicits grief that renders her inconsolable and reclusive for two days and one night.

Monday, January 13th, 2020

8:59 AM

I lapsed into despair last night with the usual reflections on meaningless absurdity and thought of society on a global scale, of my work, of technology and the modern comforts of civilization which enable me to think and reflect; I laughed, for the comedy of *it*. Philosophers most of all: veritable jesters of humanity. Paradigms of science, morality, ethics, and existence serve to distract from *their* meaninglessness, reminiscent of a child engaged with shadow puppets on a stage. Profundity is the ultimate delusion. Men holed up with their studies—luminaries and prodigies, are *truly* an aberration, a curse upon themselves, though they illuminate the future; whether this may be interpreted as a curse extended to the remainder of humanity, or a blessing, is irrelevant to the *objectivity* of "progress."

Tuesday, January 14th, 2020

8:16 AM

I communicated my month and a half-long attempt at pseudo-mutism to those most affected by my silence. Reparations to workplace relationships revitalized my "will-to-be." I'm disturbed by the effective pleasantness of idle trivialities in the restoration of my faith in humanity, especially with Hunter; to discuss our theories of the "collective consciousness" and "true intelligence" rekindled a dormant flame in my heart—to be sentimental; however, what *disturbs* me is that there is no transcendence or subversion from our humanity, and *I* am far too human, with a will—to be, to live, to negligible power—thus the ideal of a cave graces my thoughts again, though the older I become, the less idealistic I am.

I forswear everything, my integrity forthwith, and remain *only* disciplined… patient. Each morning, afternoon, and night is a dead end with my financial straits. I am a dead man who must persevere until my debt is cleared, whereafter I will destroy what I've built again and begin anew.

Opportunities for intercourse present themselves to me in the form of nubile college girls while I serve packaged sauces, fried chicken, and waffle fries. I neglect to initiate what *would* be an accessible venue: a consolation for existence.

"Your insemination is well-received," uttered God. An ethereal hand gripped my right shoulder. "You've fulfilled your purpose."

"God, I've thought this through and through and I'm overcome with consternation and grief. Through reproduction we only introduce another being into this world destined to undergo the rigmarole of life and all the suffering and joy entailed. The many I speak to often meet with despair on this exact query: What is our purpose?"

"You are your purpose."

"I'm confused."

"I am too."

The hand's presence dissipated. A hooded boy approached and said. "Spicy chicken sandwich with no pickles and… Colby Jack cheese."

"Yes."

"Can I also get two honey barbeque sauces and a medium fry?"

"Yes."

"Thank you."

"*It*'s my pleasure."

10:36 PM

"Have you found me antagonistic?" I inquired of my self-assigned enemy, Emil.

"Oh of course," he said; a toothy, confident grin splayed across his face. "Do you find *me* antagonistic?"

We locked eyes; I wavered for a brief moment and said, "Yes."

This morning I left my recorder at home and figured the day would transpire as any other even when my intuition goaded me to reconsider; I should have, for the conversation experienced with Emil was one of the best I've ever had with my fellow man. In essence—a summation: I ushered our hostilities to the forefront and acknowledged what we are: men overwrought with our egos.

We addressed each other with lighthearted smiles and lax body language, though beneath our veneers, a maelstrom of activity bubbled. We've no reason to hate each other, to scorn, to despise, or even dislike; *it* is only that we are men of great ambition confined to positions of powerlessness, albeit self-chosen and temporary; however, what *is* temporary is merely the scenery and personalities. Once Emil departs for medical school, he will find himself embroiled with a new cast of the haughty and pretentious—to a facility upon graduation where an elite social strata will *become him,* a slave, still—as I will be, to a multitude of future employers for menial low-wage labor, if we are to both live to see our gradations of *nothing.* Emil and I are no enemies; we are mirrors of our own self-perceived deficiencies. Men understand themselves only through other men. An "enemy" is an apparition conjured by the mind; hate is the shadow.

Emil desires to leave an impact on the world—a legacy for the "good" of civilization, as any healthy, ethical, and intelligent young man would; thus he is frustrated—*angered* by each passing second that he must serve students and faculty who dismiss him for the man he now is, opposed to the man he envisions himself to become. Lack of control is the core of the unrest, the upset, and ultimately the antagonistic behavior's impetus: This is of a sound mind! Men seek to usurp the power of those around them in constant flux, no matter how ludicrous or trivial. This is where we meet: Two fools who believe themselves to be something; no matter what we achieve, there will always be the *man,* and *only* the man; all else is folly and smoke.

Emil gesticulated and spoke devoid of "um"s, "uh"s, and "like": "Imagine a mountain one-thousand miles high and one-thousand miles wide. A bird flies by once a day and pecks a minute portion of that mountain away. After the mountain has eroded to nothing, after all that time—*that* is a millisecond of eternity. *That's* what scares me."

On death, eternity frightens Emil: the "what" which comes after the presupposed negation of consciousness, which is to assume a "truth" that consciousness *is* negated and/or dissipated, dispersed, or recycled. The void is inconceivable. A man may flounder within the extreme limitations of his own thoughts and justify his knowledge of existence with self-proclaimed axioms based on a deluded understanding. These paltry words are no better; I revel in my insurmountable insignificance.

"I could be here from now until the year 2074," mused the twenty-four-year-old man, "then there's eternity."

On this reflection, the brain rationalizes irrationally—of a consolation, of profundity, a divinity—an *absurdity:* the (a) God(s) internal or external, of pantheism or panpsychism. Perhaps the rationalization is unnecessary; there is an acceptance of the nothing and a strained comprehension of knowing that one knows not what "nothing" is. An eternity of not knowing is enough to render one platitudinous; we are endowed with the privilege to die. "God" is a buzzword.

Wednesday, January 15ᵗʰ, 2020

10:15 PM

I desire to quit my self-assigned meaning in life. The ego isn't worth the investment. My publisher overprices my books, has accused me of plagiarism, and has proven to be incompetent on several facets of each procession thus far; I've only myself to blame. I'm an idiot, in truth, for what I do, who I am, what I've become. I laugh at myself. What do I know other than my own experience?

I suffer a paradox because of my chosen way of life: I've no other reason to live other than to persist with this document, though I *desire* to stop. I laugh again: An imbecile. I pity those who enjoy me.

There are no longer intuitions of my perceived state of pathetic being, though this is only on account of none knowing me intimately. My intuitions are pleasant and *fallacious.* I am averse to fiction writing and masterful prose, repelled by the pretenses of knowledge on all fronts, of theories, philosophies, scientific studies—of em dashes and semicolons; what else have I ever known? To abandon this emprise would be the best option for my general well-being, to be *truly* free, liberated from my *self.*

I'm indifferent to sex; by consequence I attract those who only want sex—nothing more. Sex, the consolation for existence, has been perverted by my indifference. Am I no longer a man? Why do I bother to feed this worthless body if I choose to subvert my desires?

I'm disinclined to believe Buddhist tenets, e.g., desire is the cause of suffering; this is preposterous; *it* is to say: "Existence is the cause of suffering." If you cease to desire, you cease to exist due to death, and presumed relinquishment of the consciousness to whatever intangible processes indiscernible to humanity.

Remember: I work alongside children and old women as a fried chicken purveyor.

"God" is a Buzzword

Another run-on sentence
Disguised as verse, though
These lines are functional
Opposed to poeticial,
For a reiteration
Of the title
Delights.

"You call that writing?" said a creative writing M.D. holder.

A journalist tapped his dry lips with the blunt tip of a black and white pen and said, "I really don't know what to call *it* other than a misuse of time and space—*this* space occupied on screen or in print, the spaces between the words and letters; *it's* vacuous trite that may elicit a grin, a dissatisfied chortle, an uncomfortable shift of the body, or a yawn. There are much better sources of entertainment that evoke more than haughty contempt."

"You just don't know what you're doing. I've written several best sellers and consort with a wide circle of fellow writers and marketing agents daily. You have no special knowledge; that's your problem."

The journalist licked his lips, lowered the pen, and thought for a moment. Yes, *it* all became clear—there *it* was, and *it* left as soon as *it* had come.

Thursday, January 16th, 2020

8:41 AM

On Buddhism: We desire human relationships. Without each other, there is no authenticity to our lives other than a selfish persistence driven by the desire to consume, sleep, and maintain homeostasis. "Nirvana" is fictitious.

I think of Eckhart Tolle's vacuous head bobble. "Be here now, for now is all there is." And what of tomorrow when you hunger and thirst? Will you work to fulfill your desires and rob yourself of "Nirvana," or will you sit and bobble your head, dependant on charitable volunteers who subscribe to your dead-end ideologies?—those who *strive* to become *you,* not knowing that you are an anomaly, a fraud, an impossibility without *them.* Why practice religion if the goal is *not* to attain the ideal? "Ah, I am a humble Buddhist who enjoys a little suffering now and again; *it* builds character!"; "Buddhism is convenient for me when I don't attain what I desire. I sit, clamp my eyes shut, and think about how much I didn't desire what I had desired."

To void one's desires and abstain from life participation is suicide; is this "Nirvana"?

7:58 PM

My father emailed me for the first time in eight months since my departure for U.S. Navy boot camp: "I love you, Baethan."

I responded: "I love you too, father."

I cry, the fool that I am.

Friday, January 17th, 2020

6:19 PM

The more I empathize and communicate, the greater the void within me sublimates what little remnants of my spirit clings to self-actualization. The idea of friendship disturbs me; a future enemy broods. This condition of human relations is far removed from paranoia. Wretchedness abounds: animals at play.

I've shared the transcription of my conversation with Emil, with him, and asked if he found contention with what I wrote.

Emil washed his hands at the sub-making station and said, "No, no, I thought *it* was well-written, especially the adjectives that you use to describe the dialogue interactions, though there *is* one thing I didn't like."

"What?"

"The fact that I say so many filler words like 'uh,' and 'like,' all the time—I really need to work on that like—*see*—I fucking did *it* again," Emil continued to comment on his appreciation of the accuracy of the dialogue on account of the opportunity for introspection. We now behave as cordial associates with our newfound understanding and mutual acceptance of each other's characters based *solely* on the *words* we've shared with each other, which, by my judgment, has been truth, yet the desolation I feel suffocates, for this is *just* what Emil wanted: to be liked.

"All right Baethan, I'll see you next week; I hope you have a nice relaxing weekend," said the man who intends to strain his body to the limit over the weekend to develop a respectable physique.

"Thanks Emil, I hope you do too," we spout to each other; our second-nature, while intrinsically we are both warped with impenetrable blackness; *this* is what disturbs me of the human condition. What has been achieved but an illusion to conceal our personal delusions? This sickness of mankind has corrupted me, only on account of my acknowledgment and *care* of the machinations beneath the pleasant veneers of my "brothers." I know myself enough to know of the creature.

8:57 PM

I seek employment as a dishwasher.

Saturday, January 18th, 2020

12:21 PM

At the age of forty-nine, Winthrop slaved in a dish room; from the age of fourteen, this is all Winthrop did. He traveled from town to city, city to suburb, and suburb to town as a vagabond with nothing but a pack full of food and a spare change of clothes, where he lived out of trams, abandoned homes, and one-piece tents.

Orphaned at the age of three, Winthrop never knew his parents. He abandoned his myriad of negligent caretakers of an orphanage at the age of eleven and entered the workforce as a dishwasher after being caught stealing from a dumpster by the head chef of a dingy bar on the outskirts of Winthrop's hometown. Money never concerned him; he purchased what he needed when necessary without fail, and desired only what he needed.

Winthrop is mute and has met the challenges of life without a spoken word. He has never known grief, shame, or guilt, nor has he known joy, faith, and love.

Oh, is this a character of interest? Does the reader seek an escape from the banality of their life and resort to the promise of my suffering only to behold a few paragraphs of personalized fiction? Is the reader disappointed by my tactless "breaking the fourth wall" narrative to what otherwise may have been the start of a cohesive piece of *authentic* entertainment that would require *genuine* talent?

Sunday, January 19ᵗʰ, 2020

11:36 PM

A month ago I ventured through downtown and stumbled across a secluded store within an enclosed alleyway: *Anomalies and Artifacts.* Intrigued, I entered, and found myself surrounded with macabre curiosities and grotesque oddities. Whimsical trinkets and humorous superfluities also had their place among the three-room domain featuring wares reminiscent of a 12ᵗʰ century charlatan's tent.

"How many things I can do without!"

- Socrates

A middle-aged Caucasian woman strolled out of a back parlor and greeted me while I browsed the full perimeter and inspected each item. A warm-colored painting of a warped and distorted face mid-scream and a few skeletons of rodents interested me, though I stopped at a small stand of young adult fantasy fiction books written by a local author. I slung my pack off and presented a copy of my recent publication to the owner and asked whether she would accept the donation. On her affirmation, our conversation elapsed into the realm of personal affairs, whereby, ten minutes in, I asked, "Are you single?"

The owner, Candy, blushed and confirmed that she is not. I departed after a fifteen-minute discussion and informed Candy that I would return in a month or two to allow her time to reach a verdict on whether my book would be a fit with her wares.

A month-and-a-half elapsed and Candy contacted my publisher in hopes of reaching out to me. I returned to the shop last night and donated four more signed copies.

Candy and I sat in her back parlor and chatted for an hour; the topic of her utmost interest: My mind. She had read one-third of Year Two. A shame, the sexual energy between is palpable and our fondness for the bizarre is mutual; I'd have enjoyed a romp with Candy on the floor right then. Instead, she pressed me with questions raised of my character that are unanswered in the text:

1. My ethnicity is predominantly Welsh.
2. I edit and proofread my own work and omit nothing written from the first draft.
3. My uncustomary Russian-esque "accent" *could* be an inadvertent side effect from speech therapy for stuttering (I overcame the impairment on the realization that lack of self-confidence was the cause) in grade school.
4. I conduct social experiments to the detriment of my well-being for the sake of writing, e.g., feigned psychopathy and selective mutism.

I departed with a promise to meet Candy again next Saturday, same time and place, for she desires to speak more with me.

An exposition *of* my exposition; how much more engrossed could my writing become?

1:34 PM

My next-door neighbor is a Hispanic man who blares repetitive Mexican banda music three days out of the week for 1-2 hours at a time. On Sundays (today), the music resonates *all day* while he sings along. I set my writing device close to the wall and blasted the first movement of J.S. Bach's *Mass in B Minor* (which, to my disgruntlement, Hunter brought to my attention that the song has become a meme on the social media platform *Tik Tok*). My upstairs neighbor shuffled to where my music emanated. Four minutes in, I stopped my music, stood close to the wall separating my westward neighbor and myself, and shouted, "Hello! As you are now aware! Music being played at obnoxious volumes is disturbing to your neighbors! I suggest that you invest in a pair of headphones! Thank you very much! Enjoy the rest of your day!"

One minute and fifteen seconds elapsed; my neighbor's music persisted at the same volume. I shouted, *"Or!* You may continue being self-entitled! That's fine!"

My blood pressure escalated. I donned my shoes, coat, paced ten feet outside, and knocked on my neighbor's door. A short, mid-forties, spectacle-wearing thin-of-the-hair man greeted me with wide eyes and said, "Hello."

"Your music-"

"-*Oh*—oh, I turn *it* down, yes."

"Thank you."

The door closed and I returned next door to my room, public service enacted.

4:04 PM

The music next door amplified and returned to the original volume of obnoxiousness. I visited the apartment complex office to issue a complaint. The obese Caucasian woman at the desk informed me there is nothing the complex authorities may do and advised me to call the police. I returned to my neighbor's door, knocked thrice, and before I could speak, the man said, "This about music?" while banda music rebounded at an absurd volume out of the man's living room into the open air around me.

"Yes."

The man regarded me with derision and spoke with broken English, "Look, I... you come in—listen and tell me you hear, turn *it* down?" he shook his head and glared at me.

I refused to venture into his home and said—near-shouted, "I've been to the office."

"Oh. I enjoy today, daytime music," The man sneered, lowered his chin, and moved back towards the entry-way on the realization that I had no intent to enter.

"Your music is obnoxiously loud. Are you hard of hearing?"

The man gazed around as if to convey he had *just then* begun to hear, retreated a step, and moved his hand to the door's edge with the subtle intent to shut me out expressed in his wicked frown, and said, "No. Don't think so-"

I said, "At this noise level, myself, and all the neighbors adjacent to and above you can hear."

"*Okay, okay,*" the man bowed forward and pushed the door closed—slowly, and peered at me from the top rim of his glasses, hateful resignation expressed in his sunken eyes, "I turn *it* down."

"Thank you."

The door closed and I heard a spiteful Spanish outburst from within.

6:14 PM

A quiet night. Quinoa simmers on the stovetop.

Monday, January 20th, 2020

9:44 AM

Bill Hansen is a thirty-seven-year-old man who has lived with his mother and two aunts for the entirety of his life. At the age of seventeen, his small suburban hometown's local grocery store hired him as a bagger. Bill ascended through the ranks of bagger to cashier and requested a transfer to a stocker role, whereby he rose to night stocker, night supervisor, to daytime supervisor over twenty years of stellar performance.

Bill had no enemies; everyone appreciated his light-hearted humor and gentle smile. Even with a slight forward hunch and moderate obesity, Bill's compliant and helpful character won him the honors of the employee of the year three times throughout his career.

The only aspect of Bill's life that he thought felt dull and lusterless was his potential to find love. Bill's aunts attempted to makeover his style and appearance, though Bill had no interest in maintaining daily hygiene or an exercise routine; a disheveled ponytail, unkempt beard, and oversized mono-colored t-shirts were suitable to his mien.

A remarkable man: Bill will do anything for his friends. A manager role seemed inevitable with his twentieth anniversary; Bill swelled with pride.

11:27 AM

The so-called "Mad Letters" of Nietzsche serve to discredit; his claim of being "God the Creator" *and* the reincarnation of critical figures of world history, is the product of healthy humor; what can a man do when his mind is superseded by his own philosophy? The idea that we are all of the same immortal consciousness aligns with ~~my~~ the theory that consciousness is God, though neither of these propositions is new; they are *ancient,* and what of *it* if they are true *or* false? What would a revelation herald but another shade of darkness?

Much easier and far more scrutable to apply labels of afflictions, i.e., "madness," to a wry, polemical man.

12:19 PM

An African-American man and his Caucasian acquaintance worked under the hood of a car with the driver-side door open. From within, bassy hip-hop music blared and rattled the window fixtures of my apartment.

I stepped outside, walked over to the duo, and said, "Excuse me."

The African-American man said, "Yeah?"

"Are you under the presumption that everybody around you wants to hear your music?"

"No."

"So *it*'s really just for you."

"Yeah just for me. I just…"

"So in other words you have no consideration for your neighbors."

"Yeah. If *it*'s too loud—if *it*'s too loud for ya'-" the man sidestepped towards the car door with the intent to manipulate the radio.

"Well… I mean—when you live in a neighborhood, and people can hear everything that goes on outside, when you're playing music simply for yourself, you could consider wearing headphones. *It*'s about being conscientious."

"I'll turn *it* down. I'll turn *it* down for you."

"Oh, not for *me!*—I'm just curious about your thought processes."

"I'm not trying to—no-" he leaned into the vehicle.

The man's companion, a disheveled old man, inquired with a high-pitched inquiry, "That's too loud? *That's* too *loud?*"

I averted my attention to him and said, "I can hear *it* clearly from within, and *it* shakes my windows, so I would presume that since we all share the same structure that other people's fixtures may be rattling as well."

"I didn't know that."

"Yes. That's some information for you-"

The African-American man started, "-Okay—thank you—thank you."

"Yes. Just being conscientious of our neighbors."

"All right. I appreciate *it*."

I returned to my apartment.

I'm a classic case of a honky asserting his privilege. How pretentious of me to claim a position of absurd anarchy when I attempt to order an element of my environment per my preference; though, am I *good?* Am I a *vigilante* to enforce an unspoken principle of civil *American* conduct?—or am I equatable to a Neo-Nazi, irreverent to the passive-aggressive expression of "minority" culture?—e.g., overloud music and curb-side histrionics?

1:37 PM

Anarchy is anti-human and devoid of ethics; however, an anarchist feels no shame. The required dependency on other people renders anarchy absurd; one cannot be an anarchist *without* being absurd. Even the successful hermits who thrive in the wilderness for thirty years are still dependent on others, either through theft or annual restocking of goods in a neighboring town. Without previous technological human developments or compilations of knowledge for the hermit to utilize to his advantage, he would be forsaken from the clothing and tools which permit his hermitage in the first place.

Tuesday, January 21st, 2020

10:17 PM

Bill Hansen hurried to and from a pallet stocked with toilet paper to three tiers of empty shelves; he checked his wristwatch, sighed, and forced a weary smile at an old man who limped on a cane.

"Hello son," said the old man, "You're quite the worker."

Bill stammered, "Thank you," and swiveled his head.

"What's wrong with you?"

"Nothing."

"Doesn't look like nothing."

Bill stiffened and leaned back with one hand on the edge of a four-foot-high plastic sheath wrapped around a stack of toilet paper and said, "How can I help you, sir?"

The old man trod forward, two paces away from Bill, and exhaled. Bill's nose flared and the flesh around the edge of his eyes crinkled. "You can *help* me," said the old man, "by answering a question for me."

"Yes?"

"What do I look like to you?"

Bill stared at an unkempt head of frazzled grey hair strewn down over a puckered face slotted with two bloodshot eyes atop a compact body striated with sagged veins dressed in a brown hoodie with rolled-back sleeves mismatched with navy blue trousers and white tennis shoes. "A wise man," said Bill.

The old man guffawed and ejected seven oblong droplets of spittle onto Bill's right cheek. "I once knew several boys your age and not one of them had a lick-split of shit to say that was worth a damn to hear until their fucking balls dropped; now what's *it* with boys like you looking like you want-" The old man ceased to speak and lurched past Bill towards the *Shampoo and Conditioner* aisle.

Bill proceeded to stock the three tiers of empty shelves with toilet paper for twenty-seven minutes while listening to 1980s classic rock music from a single white wireless earbud in his right ear despite the 1990s pop music resonating from overhead speakers at an indistinct volume.

Wednesday, January 22nd, 2020

9:27 PM

An inch of snow fell today; therefore, the university closed. I don't remember most of my time in my apartment, and what I do remember is unworthy of retention.

An old man sat hunched forward in a fourteen-by-nine foot living room in a faded brown recliner and played puzzle games with the tip of his pointer finger on a phone lain vertical on a stained rectangular coffee table. A cigarette held between his middle and pointer finger burned by his left ear.

An old woman on a futon diagonal to the old man sat with her right leg folded beneath her buttocks while she fumbled with a limp heating pad and said, "God my sister pisses me off," and slapped a small section of the white electrical cord against her arms in an attempt to plug the device into an outlet in a nearby wall four-feet away without displacing herself from the seat cushion. *"It's* warm in here but I'm still cold; I get cold so easy. My doctor tells me *it's* because of poor circulation and that I need to quit smoking and you know what I say to him?"

Quiet victory fanfare resonated from the phone speakers and the old man tapped through a series of prompts.

"I said *fuck you!*" the old woman laughed for 1/4th of a second and continued, "My sister says I smoke too much too. She's smoked all her life so I'm like, 'Uh, you've smoked all your life, who do *you* think *you* are to tell *me* not to smoke?' and then she tells me I drink too much—then she asks me for twenty dollars, can you believe *it?*"

The old man said, "Mm."

"So I give her twenty dollars and tell her to pay me back. Well that was a week and two days ago and I called her up for the money and she tells me she's at the dry cleaners and that's what she needed the money for in the first place; she expects me to believe that? I mean, she thinks I'm *that* stupid? So now I can't buy cigarettes because apparently, she needed the money she asked for a week ago—*today.*"

"Do you come over here and do this just for attention?"

"Do what just for attention?"

"Complain about your sister."

"Um," the old woman flung the end of the cord onto the carpeted floor and cocked her head, "No, I'm telling you about something that upsets me; why do you insult me like this?"

The old man swiped his pointer finger across the phone screen twice and took a deep drag on the cigarette.

"You don't even talk to me—you don't even *look* at me; you're right, I don't know why I come down here; I guess I'm just looking for attention or something!" The old woman hugged the heating pad to her chest, straightened both legs, stood, marched out the old man's door, rounded a snowy outdoor perimeter of the suburban building, and entered her apartment.

Friday, January 24th, 2020

8:25 AM

A writer typed on a computer terminal: "A writer typed on a computer terminal and expressed his character's actions in thoughts."

No, that isn't right, thought the writer; he deleted the sentence and began again: "A writer wrote of a thoughtful character whose ideas expressed his actions better than the actions themselves because-"

I need to figure this out… just think… thought the writer; he deleted the sentence and began again: "A writer wrote of his character's thoughts because he didn't know how to express his character's actions otherwise, which is a potential signal of poor writing skills, an unrealistic character, or a dynamic character with complex thoughts that-"

Where am I going with this? Is it good or bad? Succinct… think succinct… thought the writer; he deleted the sentence and began again: "A writer's thoughts are like watermelons; they are colorful and full of juice, and when squeezed, a small pulp is left behind."

God… my life is such a joke. I'm never going to make ends meet. I can't depend on Mary to be faithful and she doesn't trust me with the kids anymore. I should eat something—no, I need to finish this first and then mow the lawn. I don't have time for all this—just write something and forget it, thought the writer; he deleted the sentence and began again: "A character's thoughts aren't worth expressing."

Perfect—succinct. I'm a genius. English muffins with butter and jelly.

4:53 PM

Consciousness is "God," "God" being figurative, for the experience of being conscious is all we "know" that can be certain. "Entropy is God" is a fatalistic extension of "Consciousness is God," in the way that consciousness is subject to entropy; entropy would not exist without consciousness, i.e., a crock theory I no longer care to think about because all any of us will ever "know" is the moment we endure, and thus far, reality is, and has been, a social construct since the dawn of man, subject to ethics, which has become a far more prominent topic of study for me.

One of the first sentences I wrote in the back of my first physical journal before I began my typed journal is, "I don't give a fuck about fitting into your culture. I have my own culture": a stroke of childish rebellion, yet a statement that precipitated my interest in absolute isolation, which is unachievable while dependant on others, which the severance of dependency is *also* unachievable—an inescapable condition, even if I were to become rich enough to support myself until the end of my life in a cave, the Hermitude (as I've previously stated) would be supported by the product of civilization, i.e., culture, in the form of the tools I use, the food I eat and the manner I cook, my learned behaviors since childhood, the incandescent/fluorescent lighting installed, the method by which the cave would be shaped, excavated, and furnished—is all dependant on the culmination of what humanity is. If I were to stake out on my own in an unknown wilderness in a foreign country, the culture of "I" persists as a product of transcendent knowledge and memory, and if I happened to be stripped of all clothing, my mind wiped of all memory and skills by a blow to the head or an invasive procedure, I'd perish for the lack of sense, for I'd be robbed of the primeval experience passed on by thousands of generations.

All of this considered, I *doubt*.

7:28 PM

I am lucky today: A slender, 6'0, raven-haired college girl dressed in her typical black ensemble of frilly black skirt and shawl requested an order of large waffle fries and two packets of ketchup.

While I set her fries in the oil to cook, I rounded out to the sauce counter, looked her up and down while she poked her phone, and said, "Excuse me."

"Yes?" she answered, doe-eyed, and took a step towards me.

"May I have your phone number?"

"Oh!" she beamed; her mouth opened, surprised, and she gestured a slight fanning movement with her left hand by her breast. Hesitation followed by, "I have a boyfriend! I'm sorry!"

"That's all right. No need to apologize. A medium fry?"

"Yes. Thank you so much."

I filled a hard paper sleeve with waffle fries and said, "You're welcome."

Sunday, January 26th, 2020

9:09 AM

In Candy's shopfront, recorder on, I said, "What delusions do you have that you *know* are delusions?"

Candy said, "Okay, that's a hard one; I'd have to think a long time because *it* wouldn't be a true delusion if I wasn't aware of *it* at all. There's always fringe stuff: what do I willingly delude myself about in order to function on whatever level for societal reasons; there's always going to be something, probably, just like with death for most people, and them not thinking about that they're dying every minute of the day, and they *should* be aware of that."

"Would you say that's how we all delude ourselves?—*not* thinking of death at every moment? That would be counter-intuitive to life and how we live, the actions necessary, if we were always thinking of death."

A long hesitation. "Well... Everything for me is a two-sided coin, so philosophical-wise I would say that's true on *this* side and not true on *that* side, you know... I'm trying to figure out what my delusions are because that sounds fun." Candy laughed. "What is yours?—let me put that question back on you."

"I'm aware of a few delusions, and even though I'm aware, I still abide by them; they're mostly my intuitions. I think my intuitions are just a projection of my ego."

"You don't buy into your 'psychicness,' is that what you're saying?"

"Yes. I depend on my intuitions but at the same time... I-"

"-don't think *it*'s ultimately real."

"Yes."

"Okay. Just coincidence."

I said, "I think that's where my... perceived 'unique' (I gestured quotations) character is derived from, and that I may be mentally ill in accordance with the criteria of the DSM-5; I'd be categorized as 'mentally insane,' or 'schizophrenic'—because of how *it*'s classified when we depend on intuitions that are *wrong*. I believe that because of *my* lack of trust, that nobody trusts me; I also believe that because of *my* belief that all virtue is pretentious and that society is a construct, that other people *also* think in this way, so whenever someone interacts with me, they're only seeking something from me—such as validation. Since my beliefs are adamant, I project this onto others, while also being aware that others are *not* aware that they are seeking validation—they aren't thinking of *it*; they aren't aware that their good intentions are taught to them."

"You believe they're unaware—that doesn't mean they're *not* doing *it*, but they aren't aware of *it* as you actively are."

"Yes. For instance, every beneficial—every *mutually* beneficial act that you and I have shared thus far has been entirely for our own benefits: Me entering your shop and searching for something that would peak my interest, me asking you out—if your single, me donating a copy of my book to you; you complied, with everything except me asking you out—because you already have a boyfriend."

"Mhm."

"Otherwise you would've-"

"-Mhm-"

"And I can tell you're still on the edge about that, but you have your *moralities*-"

Candy giggled and leered at me.

"-which is a social construct, and that's where me speaking of this gets 'into your head' somewhat, but that's not my intention."

"Okay."

"Do you agree?"

"What—with everything you said?"

"Yes."

"Yeah. Yeah, except I got confused on the part where you said that's what interests me."

"What… where what interests you?"

"Well, *it* truly doesn't matter…" Candy trailed off with a hushed tonality and gazed down to her right.

"No!—*it* does matter because this could be valued intuited madness that I'm trying to clarify; so please, if you would, despite how *it* makes me feel."

"Okay, well, you know that part where I made that face for a second? You used the term, '*it*'s part of the reason why you're interested in what I'm saying right now.' You said something—you said *something* about my interests; you were projecting onto me something that I didn't get, obviously; *it* wasn't what I was thinking or I would've got *it*."

"And what did I say-"

Candy giggled again.

I pressed the matter further: "-in relation to that?"

"You were talking about all of our mutual and beneficial exchanges-"

"Yes-"

"-and everything that they've been or what they mean or meant up till now and how *it* was holding my interest, the reason for *it* holding my interest, or that's why I was having interest—or take interest."

"Because we share a mutual gain?… What else would interest you if I was not a beneficial presence?"

"*Oh*—" Candy began with a sudden start, as if she remembered her initial reason(s), "because *I'm* interested in the gain of… of a… I don't have a—I mean yeah I have some interest but I really uh… actually I find *it* difficult to be interested in things just for myself… ya know? I have interest—like, um, I'm inter—like I was interested in helping you; I was interested in putting your book up because I wanted other people to see *it;* I'm interested in you having financial freedom—I want you to find grants or commercial work for yourself; I'm interested in um, understanding you and hopefully you'll have good feelings about being, you know, understood or listened to, ya know? A lot of my focus is outward, I think."

"So the altruistic... aspect, is what you're saying."

"Yeah I guess but *yeah*."

"And I once had an argument with a man, well not an argument-" Candy opened her mouth to speak. "-go on—I can tell-"

"Well *it*'s because—I wouldn't say that... cuz that's like those people that run to help people when there's a freakin' flood, *it*'s like they're only doing that because *it* makes them feel good to help somebody—they're really doing *it* for *themselves* not for those *people* because they get *feel-good-feelings* from helping people!"

"That's exactly where I was going."

"Okay—*however*... for me, *it*'s my state of being?" [8]

Tuesday, January 28th, 2020

9:36 AM

The decadence of American culture, oikophobia (fear or hatred of one's home), and nihilism are prominent topics among modern academics and philosophers; theses are written and lectures are performed stating the "facts" without any solution, *as if* there is any recourse for the cyclic nature of civilization—oh, the nihilism crept in again.

I've nothing to contribute. I'm an uneducated, ignorant pawn to a system beyond my fathoming, limited to a narrow strait of expertise (if that) projected to be amalgamated (or subsumed) with the ideas of others: a contribution to the zeitgeist; a single grain of sand in the metaphorical hourglass of "progress."

"How pleasant," said a merchant's boy, "to watch the sand pile in a heap and see *it* funnel in a stream from the top compartment to the bottom."

"Samuel, get over here and help me with this crate," said the boy's father.

"Yes."

---

[8] I didn't finish the transcription due to disinterest.

Tendonitis near my left wrist reoccurs this year, the same month as last year, for the same reason: intensified calisthenics.

I repel and am repelled. What value am I to a female?—with my nonexistent net worth and absurd life prospects; I am fodder for adulteresses.

Wednesday, January 29th, 2020

9:19 PM

Modern psychiatry vilifies all character traits that are prerequisites to "success" that aren't ~~altruistic~~ capitalistic by nature.

If *"I am you,"* you're a ~~"psychopath"~~ fool *too!*

Dessert Menu

Peach, apple, pumpkin pie,
Funnel cakes too—don't be shy:
Double-dutch chocolate strudel surprise,
Bubble gum toffee topped with candy eyes,
Coupled crumb coffee cakes and cinnamon sweet potato fries,
Tumbled strawberries baked alongside honey-
glazed peanut brittle bread rise.
Wild-caught sardines canned in extra virgin olive oil.

Friday, January 31st, 2020

4:53 PM

On my way out of the college campus, I saw movement to my right and looked: A black-haired girl named Vannety: a cafe worker at the college.

Since I began employment I've been attracted to Vannety; from what I perceive, the inverse is true. A coy smile often accompanies her narrowed eyes; she stands a head shorter than me and is of a healthy, modest build.

Vannety gazed down at the ground the moment I acknowledged her; herself, free of distraction, while I, engrossed myself with technology, avoidant of a walk I believed to be inconsequential; yet here, now, I write of *it,* for what I have lost and gained by the product of our beings. I am deprived, yet sanctified by my actions, for I thought to call out to her. Thus, a romance would be borne of folly, of petty longings and misguided yearnings. The aforementioned moment had been the first she and I had ever met, alone, devoid of obligations under the constraint of a timeclock, and I voided the account—by *choice:* a lack of action.

However, I've learned over the years; *it*'s best not to shit where you eat.

FEBRUARY

Saturday, February 1st, 2020

7:47 PM

"Your grammar is shit," said an editor. A backdrop of an expansive cityscape comprising identical square rooftops and multicolored neon billboards framed the writer's antagonist. From the 38th floor of the tower, the sun appeared smaller in contrast with evenings spent on the outdoor patio of a countryside cottage.

"I know; that's why I'm here," said the writer, yet this wasn't enough. The words fell flat, empty, devoid of "umph." Anything could've been said, yet the writer chose to say *that:* an affirmation of incompetence; a deadpan plea to a man superior to himself at an ambiguous "something" he lacked. Seated before the editor, the writer reckoned with bloodshot eyes what he perceived as two disembodied fingers clasped around a cigarette within an office too clean to tolerate.

The editor laughed and said, "Are you all right?"

"What?"

"You're looking as though you're about to cry."

"Can I ask you a personal question? I know you're my editor, but you're also a human being."

"Sure," said the editor with ill-affect.

A silent expulsion of air blew over the writer's dense nose hairs. A piece of fuzzed lint floated three inches in front of the editor's face and uplifted towards the ceiling by the force of a subtle updraft blown in by a nearby floor vent. The writer said, "I don't know why I write what I do; I'm not qualified for anything."

The editor waited sixteen seconds and observed a bald spot on the top of the writer's downturned head; he said, "What's your question?"

"Why do *you* do what you do?"

"I enjoy my job and helping people," said the editor without hesitation; he blunted his near-finished cigarette in a pristine ashtray: the first of the day, at 5:37 PM. "Is that all?"

Sunday, February 2nd, 2020

12:57 PM

"No," said the writer, "that isn't *all:* I've no desire to excel at anything, *or* to be mediocre. I see what you have, seated there, in your chair, with the things that you value and what you hold dear; *it* makes me sick—all of *it.* Great literature is the mark of a discontented mind, written by one emboldened by their wit's end, their dissatisfaction and... and longing, *yearning.* They pass through here; you see them once in a while—these great ones who stop in your office-"

The editor cleared his throat and interjected, "Actually, I am seldom visited by clients; most are international."

"You-" the writer began with a crack in his voice, "-A computer could do your job."

"Artificial intelligence has been programmed to write award-winning novels too."

"So... *it*'s really programmers who are the world's leading artists and creatives?"

"Look, Josh, I've got a lot of things to do-"

"Wait, please," Josh extended a hand towards the editor and recoiled halfway over the desk between them as one would after contact with a hot stovetop, "When I go, I'll be alone again and won't know what to do with myself."

"I'm sorry to hear that."

"Oh *quit* your *fucking* professional act and treat me like a human being—a basic manuscript writing, faulty... desiring-"

"*Josh,* you come in here wanting my second opinion, *after* I've already performed my job, and berate me with a series of non-sequiturs related to *your* misgivings and shortcomings with humanity—*not* mine. Frankly, listening to you is reminiscent of reading your work; I don't need this shit right now."

"I don't want to excel."

"Yes, I understand. That's why you're here."

"You're a patronizing scumbag."

The editor's gaze hardened; he met eyes with John and said, "Get out."

"I don't have anywhere to go."

"Go *home.*"

The writer leaned back in a stiff chair, braced both hands on his knees, rolled his head in a full-circle once, and said, "Home doesn't *feel* like home."

"Get the fuck outta here, John. *Now.*"

The writer stood, indignant and perplexed; he idled for four seconds and said, "You're such a…"

The editor raised an eyebrow and observed the bold creases on the back of a disheveled green t-shirt while John strode to the office door.

Monday, February 3rd, 2020

8:17 PM

"I can write anything I want, yet I choose to write this," said a theoretical metaphysics professor; he held out a paper for a young woman, seated on a bench next to him, bathed in sunlight, at the center of a park.

"Oh, don't be so hard on yourself; let me see," said the woman. She straightened the page in front of her face with two delicate hands clasped on both sides and read aloud: "I lost my phone today. Goddammit, my phone is stolen. I sat in a bathroom stall, checked my email, and left my phone on top of the toilet paper dispenser… now *it's* stolen. I'm a professor at a university, and I lost my phone in a bathroom stall." The woman chuckled, lowered the paper to her lap, and said, "I expected a thesis or a dissertation."

"Yeah."

"Did you write this just for me?"

The professor stared forward at a patch of grass and said, "No, I wrote *it* for me."

"Why?"

"Yeah."

The woman laughed and rested her head on the professor's shoulder.

Tuesday, February 4th, 2020

9:21 PM

The bullshit of existence often overwhelms me. There is nothing to ascertain. I am a nobody and content.

A new eighteen-year-old Caucasian girl named Anna is trained by my supervisor, myself, and my peers at the chicken purveying establishment.

During her first shift tonight, Anna flirted with me throughout four hours; on one of these instances, she reached out for a hug while I mopped the service floor.

I said, "That's unnecessary," and stood, statuesque and unresponsive as Anna grazed my arms.

Anna set both her hands on my cheeks and said, "I'll teach you how to love, Baethan," and strut away; she is to be my new co-closer, alongside Hunter—who has yet to meet her.

My supervisor introduced Emil and Anna to each other. A brief, awkward conversation ensued. One minute later, Emil approached with a wicked grin expressed on his countenance and said, "So you got a new coworker, huh?"

"Yes."

"Is she autistic?"

I paused, chuckled, and said, "And I thought *I* was a douchebag."

Emil smiled, looked sidelong towards a wall, and said, "No, no—I mean I used to work with autistic people and I'm just wondering, not to be mean or anything. Her eyes were shifting all over the place—looking all over."

I said, "I think she's just horny."

Emil laughed. I forgot the rest.

9:57 PM

I've endeavored to read Marie Bashkirtseff's journal.[9] Philosophy bores me; Nietzsche and Camus have ruined my delusions. Academic work as a whole is grating to the sensibilities.

Wednesday, February 5th, 2020

12:28 PM

For the first instance in my life, the music of Antonio Vivaldi nauseated me. Halfway through a set of goblet squats, I imagined myself from a third-person perspective: a creature inside of a small compartment listening to a digital rendering of bows drawn over strings while undertaking an act of rigorous artificial stimulation of the lower body.

I hastened to the final rep and flung my earbuds away from me.

---

[9] I didn't read further than the editor's preface.

9:12 PM

Anna feigned sympathy on account of my disclosure that I walk (for eight minutes) home at my shift's end; she offered me a ride. On my polite refusal, Anna *demanded* to provide me a ride home, repeatedly, for fifteen minutes, while she blockaded the exit hallway with her body. After several failed attempts of rhetoric and outspoken censure of Anna's ridiculous behavior, I resorted to displacing her body with my own, to which she fought with the demented fervor of a nonlethal harpy. My years of strength training have been tested with a real-world application: the circumvention of an eighteen-year-old girl.

Anna hit the back of my neck with her visor and said, "I hate you," as I walked away.

I said, "I'll see you tomorrow, Anna."

Thursday, February 6th, 2020

8:44 PM

What else is there but man and woman?

Anna said, "I heard you don't talk too much, Baethan," while we performed our closing roles.

I said, "The one who said I don't talk too much, talks too much."

"Amen!"

We continued to work in silence.

Anna attempted to intercept me again after I clocked out; I hastened past, ignored her incessant gripes of my behavior, and exited the building with my rationale intact.

Friday, February 7th, 2020

5:51 PM

Two raspberry pickers:

"*It*'s sure cold out today!"

"Oh, yes!—and *it*'s also Friday!"

Laughter.

Literature bores me. All things I once deemed great are now a source of vexation. What I believed throughout my youth and young adulthood of "romantic love" is reduced to a heap of chalky dust. My ignorance of human nature served as infallible comfort.

A sixty-two-year-old, stout, African-American dishwasher named Wayne conversed with Emil about food stamps; Emil knew nothing of the government-assisted program except the name.

I see Emil and feel nauseous, *humiliated* by my brethren, yet wonderstruck by the quintessential youthful male in his prime. "I feel prideful," said Emil to me while I mopped the floor near his station, "of my humanity, of being human. I like to live life; I like girls." He play-tossed a miniature palm-sized stress-relief toy resembling a human brain.

I said, "That'll be a hard fall."

For the first time, Emil demonstrated *doubt* in front of me: his chin lowered, eyes obscured by the visor of a hat; he said, "Yeah," and immediately segued the conversation to a series of inquiries on the competence of my physical reflexes and my knowledge of the lobes of the human brain.

I see myself in Emil—a part of Emil, a sliver of humanity interchangeable with one another. I'm struck with light-hearted woe at the sight of his flawless white smile, immaculate skin, and ambitious spirit— delighted by the boyish innocence, and repulsed by the intrinsic *man*.

I said, "I often view humanity from a third-person perspective and judge in accordance with the nature of an entity estranged from human affairs. Each time you speak to me I'm rooted back to the reality of my condition."

"Do you consider yourself a martian?—would you ever live on Mars?"

"You mean, as a colonist?"

"Yeah."

"I wouldn't do well with dependence on a small colony; my lack of trust would undermine me; I'm better suited as a leech on the fringes of established civilization on earth."

Emil veered past me with a cartload of dirty bread knives and condiment bottles. "I can picture you on Mars playing in the dirt," he said.

I laughed. "Of all the occupations, that's the image you conjure of me on Mars?"

"There's nothing else to do; I would do the same."

8:05 PM

To excel is preposterous. I sift through the countless writing and editing gigs online and recoil from the idea of producing content on behalf of another for the sake of a living. I'd rather work a service or manual labor job and be servile under the premise of producing or purveying a product sold by one slave to another. The middleman is the freeman: no obligations, no contracts, no stipulations, *only* mediocrity.

To produce content with the intent of making money is *equally* preposterous. I pity the pitiers of a solemn wretch; they know not of what they judge to be ill or defected. I meet with those who sneer and smirk daily: students and pedagogues—scholars of the modern age.

"I'll take a regular chicken sandwich with no pickles… and Colby Jack cheese," said an upturned lip.

We're nearing 7.8 billion humans on this planet, each wayward in their affection for ephemeral gains, mastered by their desires. *Who* is pathetic?

10:10 PM

I think of Pelagia, my haunt from yesteryear; she had dubbed me "Charles Bukowski." Pelagia tinted my soul black and gifted me a purpose: emotions, when I wanted them least. A volatile woman. A liar. I don't smoke and I don't drink; however, when I thought of her, I drank. The red wine flowed down my gullet after each late-night dishwashing shift at a downtown social venue where I entertained a few bartenders for months. I felt whole, then; I had an identity—a strong one. Now I relish in the infinite absurdity of my nothingness—what has always been—and wouldn't want to exist any other way.

I read journals and view artistic achievements of the dead on a *screen* and wonder at the idle longings captured in time, each piece an expression of helplessness. From song, sculpture, architecture, painting, and *writing*— count me among the many of my contemporaries who strive to "be" something other than the blatant truth we know ourselves to "be": mortal paradoxes.

"I wasn't a misanthrope and I wasn't a misogynist but I liked being alone. *It* felt good to sit alone in a small space and smoke and drink. I had always been good company for myself."

- Charles Bukowski

139

Sunday, February 9th, 2020

5:00 PM

"Three rats dressed in black academic uniforms sat at respective desks inside of a college classroom and wrote-"

A professor interrupted his student: "No, I don't like high fiction dribble, especially anthropomorphization."

The student sighed and said, "Really?—but I spent the last week writing this."

"All right. Let me hear a little more. The rats wrote, what?"

The student glowered and read from a thick stack of loose pages grasped in one hand: "And wrote with one-inch-long pencils on two-by-three inch sheets of paper. On the blackboard before them, the words, **"RAT RACE"**, drawn in bold, blocky white lettering, stood out from the small square room's otherwise barren features. With the stroke of-"

"I see, I get *it*," the professor interrupted with a half-hearted chuckle, "You took the parameters for my assignment literally. Clever, *very* clever."

The student opened his mouth to continue; a slight quiver of hope twinged in his brow. "Still preposterous in regards to academic work," jilted the professor. "We only write nonfiction in my curriculum."

"But this *is* still social sciences in a-"

"Save your Orwellian twists for a philosophy assignment; that is your major, after all, correct?"

"I wrote this piece specifically for this assignment and I think you'd appreciate the theme if you'd take the time to hear me out before shutting me down!" blurted the student.

The professor said, "No."

Monday, February 10th, 2020

10:21 PM

I've slept with Candy, the owner of *Anomalies and Artifacts*. My relationship with this woman is the first "healthy" partnership I have ever experienced because of *my* pursuit of *her*. The masculine and feminine synergize. Throughout life, I've only ever been pursued, routed into an emasculatory role from the get-go. Although she dates another man with hopes to marry him, my initial proclamation of sexual interest no more than five minutes into speaking with her for the first time in her shop set the course.

Candy reads my journal and continues to sell copies in her shop. We meet late at night in her regal suite above her shop for conversation, food, wine, and sex. I presume she expects to read of herself one day in my work; perhaps that's a primary attraction; though what a bore that would be, for she isn't a vexation, and therefore what I write of her would only be pleasantness and niceties. I'm counting on the comedic tragedy.

Seated before Candy's fireplace, I experienced the intimate female touch again. In her bed, my act of domination via intercourse rejuvenated my spirit; I repulsed myself at that moment on reflection of the gross homosexual acts of my recent past: On account of wanton apathy and disillusionment with virtue, I have allowed myself to be penetrated by a man. I've penetrated a man for the same reasons, and experienced repugnance instead of satisfaction in both scenarios.

There is *only ever,* man, and woman; no self-identified pronoun may extricate oneself from this fact. No matter how idiosyncratic and peculiar one may *think* they feel, and the convoluted sexual impulses and attractions experienced, one is not an isolated instance, *only* human, i.e., man and woman.

Wednesday, February 12th, 2020

9:27 PM

The journal summons me: an unwanted intermission to record memories of beings and perspectives that no longer exist. A twisted account of biases and jaded conclusions would develop if I were to account for the minute details; therefore:

After a passionate bout of sex, Candy and I partook in cabernet, grape leaves stuffed with rice, horseradish cheese, pepper jack crackers, almonds, and a pan-fried salmon cooked in olive oil, garlic, and lemon. We consumed and copulated again in her apartment and conversed on the trivialities of our lives.

I said, "Where I am now, with you in one hand and a cracker in the other, astounds me in contrast with the routine, lackluster banalities of what my life is, and what I've recently done."

I've nothing but positivity to think of concerning Candy, for I don't consider her "mine" in any conceivable manner; therefore, harmony is acquired. She will be forty-years-old this month.

My heart has blossomed into something uncanny and unfamiliar. Candy deems me "romantic" in my style of "love." I've *told* her I'm romantic prior, yet I didn't quite believe *it* until she affirmed *it*. Despite this, I reminded Candy that our relationship is not "love."

Everything is petty.

J.S. Bach's, *Komm, süsses Kreuz* began to emanate from my earbuds at the climax of a downpour while I ran home at 4:00 AM. I felt rekindled by a deluge of ice-bolts against my face, neither rain nor snow: frigid spikes of semi-frozen pellets. Both of my shoes untied. I trod over flooded sidewalks and lawns of mud, heedless of fatigue.

I'm alive without a word to speak of *it*.

Today, Anna said, "Go suck a dick."

I said, "Go fuck yourself."

I felt regretful and informed her fifteen minutes later that I hadn't resorted to such a phrase since early grade school.

Anna said, "Don't worry, I've been told much worse just today."

I stared forward at a cooler full of soda and frowned.

At our shift's end, Anna addressed Hunter and me: "Will anyone walk me to my car?"

I ignored Anna. Hunter agreed to walk Anna to her car. Anna refused Hunter's escort.

A fried chicken purveyor at a college campus.

The predictability of human greed is risible, yet sacrosanct.

Yes, everything is petty: My pain. Your pain. Preservation of the ecosystem. Space travel. Designer handbags. Swimming pools. Dissertations. Something someone said to you. A facial expression that made you feel uncomfortable. The best oral sex you've ever received. Opera singers. Carpet dirt.

Thursday, February 13th, 2020

9:27 PM

"Inside the cold metal walls of a slaughterhouse truck, a brown cow peered through a five-inch diameter hole at a small convergence of despondent humans.

"The brown cow said to a black cow, 'Why do they come?'

"'They come to protest how their ilk treats us.'

"'But why?'

"'I don't know.'

"The brown cow continued to stare through the hole at three uneven rows of aggrieved human faces and shifted from leg to leg. 'Would you do the same if our roles were reversed?'

"The black cow snorted and said, 'What, if we were to eat humans? Or do you mean if *we* were human?'

"'If we were human. I'd never want to eat a human, even if I was one.'

"'No. Though *it*'s hard to say, as I've no reference level. I think I'd eat us.'

"The brown cow turned away from the convergence and said, 'I'm fearful.'

"'Yes,' said the black cow, and the two-"

A professor of critical political theory held up both hands, swung both legs from underneath an ornate desk, and said, "All right. All right."

A third-year student peered up from a thin stack of loose-leaf papers and said, "Yes?"

The professor shook his head and said, "You're the second student out of the class of twenty-four to anthropomorphize animals to express a point despite my explicit instructions to *not* do so."

"I don't remember you stating that."

"I did. I stated *it* numerous ways: In spoken word, on the whiteboard, in a PowerPoint, and on two printed papers; the prohibition is also stated on the course syllabus."

The student frowned, squeezed the edges of his documents, and said, "Why?"

"I've read too much Orwellian bullshit in my life."

"That's an unfounded bias and goes against my rights as an animal activist. You could be-"

The professor scowled and said, "I don't have a single shit to give you about your clever metaphor of cows and the industrial machine. Have you ever read *The Jungle?*"

"Yes," blurted the student.

"Of course you have; that's the reason why you wrote the dribble you're holding."

"You didn't even let me read past the first frickin' page."

"I don't need to hear any more to know *it*'s more sensationalism presented in empathetic format; the only way animal rights activists garner attention is by such appeals."

The student locked eyes with the professor and muttered, "We wouldn't be human without emotions."

The professor grimaced, chuckled, and said, "Sit down."

"You know *it*'s true. Meat isn't just killing us physically, but emotionally too, and-"

"-I said sit down-"

"-mentally. You'd teach better if you stopped eating meat. You know there's-"

"I *am* a vegan. Get the hell out of my classroom."

"Then why are you so quick to reject me?—because of some notion that I copy the style of George Orwell or-"

"If you don't leave this classroom now, I'm going to fail you."

The student glared at the professor. Mutual animosity flashed across each other's eyes.

"That's the end of part three," said an elated twenty-two-year-old woman.

"That's marvelous," said a professor of social justice. I enjoyed the story within a story theme. I'm impressed!"

"Thank you!"

"Will you have the full piece completed by the April deadline?"

"Oh, yes! I have the idea outlined and I've rehearsed the character dialogues out loud with a few of my friends. They all think *it*'s great," said the student.

"*It* is. *It* really is."

10:16 PM

My book posters have been removed from all of the university bulletin boards except for one small notebook-sized advertisement that remained posted above a water fountain bulletin board. Someone pinned an advertisement for a watermelon event to raise money for children with cancer directly over my advertisement for *Outbursts of a Failed Sociopath*.

Friday, February 14th, 2020

7:28 PM

Being colleagues with three young men with varied backgrounds, aged eighteen, nineteen, and twenty, I've come to understand with my advanced age that the feelings and thoughts I felt at their respective ages are similar in all respects. There had been nothing unique or isolated with my perspective, only how the reality of being human is manifested and expressed.

Saturday, February 15th, 2020

6:37 PM

Every day for the past five months I walk along an avenue adjacent to my neighborhood and gaze up at a pair of shoes tied at the laces suspended over power lines. The joy of youth is encapsulated in the sight. I think of a shirtless fourteen-year-old boy with his two younger friends and their unrestrained laughter with each missed attempt to lob the interlaced shoes onto the target. On the twenty-second final and successful attempt, the three backstep, sidestep, swing their arms, flare their noses and show their bright white teeth as they dance away from the scene. Giggles abound.

I think of a passing law enforcement officer and their silent sanctimonious condemnations of an anonymous perpetrator. What are the shoes but a blemish?—a symbol of deviancy?—a work of art. Oh, I feel *it*:

Shoes on a Power Line

Look there, isn't that swell?
Weathered white running shoes
Forefront a faded cold horizon.
Quintessential suburban trees:
Not too trim. Tall and robust.
Sun hovers off-center.
Long strips of cloud.

Poetry is the gag of literature: a conveyance method for drunkards, romantics, and desperate scientists.

10:51 PM

I've corresponded with Vannety, the young woman employed at the university coffee shop for the past three days after she pursued me one evening at the end of my Friday shift. Vannety said, "Why would someone like you be interested in a person like me?" After intense consternation, I've decided to not send a message I've written and record *it* here for future regard:

Vannety,

I've thought more of this interaction despite assessing the integrity to be damaged with no healthful route for reclamation on account of your unwarranted poor self-esteem and my lack of desire to manipulate you.

For me to still be attracted to you and waive your self-directed negativity is pitiable; I'd have diminished self-respect and would revert to a phantasm of myself that no longer exists by consequence. I think you project a false persona (dead inside) due to your circumspection of my interest and a similar desire for self-preservation. I think there's a vivid spirit roiling beneath your veneer. I may be wrong; I hope I'm not. I imagine our humanity from a third-person perspective and judge an interplay of two faithless wanderers. The game is wearisome; I pity the players, despite there being no other recourse to life, for what else is there but man and woman and the creativity inspired?

You overanalyze as I do; thus, we meet at an impasse, for we are both aware of the absurdity that is "being." Yes, my assumptions are magnificent; I take the risk of making an equally magnificent sap of myself, though this is of no consequence. I reckon a kindred soul in you, though the *meaning* is folly and a moot point. Let us remain as strangers, for the respect of each other. Let there be no grievance for what hasn't been. Laugh, as I do! One buffalo sauce—nothing more.

- *Baethan*

Sunday, February 16th, 2020

10:56 PM

My writing is perceived by me as a gratuitous waste of time, though so is life; thus, I may as well persist and leave my futile mark on the world.

I'm confident in absurdity and knowing that everyone around me knows just as much as I do as for "truth." My perception of people as egotistical biochemical amalgamations and consumptive beasts with shared experiences of self-awareness and aggrandized intelligence, is conceptualized in the notion, that our holistic belief that the aforementioned self-awareness and intelligence is proof of what elevates us from all known life, levels every one to an equal plane of abysmal ignorance, as if we're all already dead. The feeling is equivalent to a colony of ants only ever knowing ants, swarming other mammals indiscriminately, unaware of the entity being consumed; there is one, or a few unlucky ants out of the multitude that reel back on *it*s hindquarters and perceives what *it* is and marvels at *it*s existence amongst the god-hoard.

Monday, February 17th, 2020

9:38 PM

I'm a sap, a nincompoop. I've invited a young witch into my life. On Vannety's admission of feelings for me via email, I denied her for the sake of our respect for one another, for she has performed nothing but a gross act of dissimulation for me to ingest. I'm railed with anguish: Do I vie for self-destruction, or be ~~content~~ asinine? Yet, this young woman, who *I* have entreated, giggles from behind a screen with impunity for *my* feelings for the sake of *her* feelings!

Romanticism is all there is to this dreadful, dull life of untruths and theories. The mind grates with possibilities, yet all the routes are tortuous and laden with peril.

I've written for pleasure of late. Now... *Now...* I'm reminded of the foulness of yesteryear, the year prior, and the pathetic tumults of youth. *Now,* I write for the sake of myself, my self-preservation, for I could thrust myself willy-nilly into the egregious embrace of this young temptress—yet, I've wrought the same temptation onto her! The poor girl!

10:36 PM

"Baethan,

"You're right. There's been nothing. And yet, when I would walk past you, I felt attracted to you. Hiding what I feel is easy for me, damn *it*. Then, I found out about your book. Bought the book for ninety-nine cents like the fool you've called me multiple times in that book. Suddenly, I run into you more and more.

"Then you say my name. You confess [your attraction to me] through email. The attraction I repressed, is back.

"And quite frankly, I'm angry. Angry you brought this attraction back and don't want *it* anymore."

- Vannety

In response, I told Vannety that I will strive to abolish her attraction to me without malice, will no longer reply to her emails, and sent her the message I wrote and withheld on the night of the 15th of this month.

11:09 PM

Every fictional character portrayed in my books is a one or two-dimensional man or woman: the mark of poor writing. The life which brims out of each authentic word, spoken or written, transcribed or copied to this document, is greater than any summation of my entire span of existence lived outside of this template. What am I, if I am not perceived?

Tuesday, February 18th, 2020

10:23 AM

I woke to something extraordinary:

"Baethan,

"I know you won't answer and I respect your decision. Thank you for the last message. I just need to say this. Whether you care or not.
"There is no need for you to abolish my attraction towards you. You're not responsible for what I feel. I am. Please don't ever consider leaving work because of me or anything of that sort. Leave because you're bored or have found better options.

"I've come to the conclusion that my type of attraction to you might be merely sexual. Sleeping with you might've sated *it*. I don't truly know you and I never will. Reading your books means nothing.

"I feared our similarities would've eventually ruined the little progress I've made or whatever would have transpired between us. We both crave a partner who is anything but us. (Well, I do. Perhaps you don't.) Which is why the rational part of me begged me not to care for your confession. I'm glad you were able to make the right decision. I had been so willing to be absolutely destroyed by you.

"Good luck."

- Vannety

Never before have I been moved to joy by self-deprivation until the finalization of this correspondence. My contentment at this moment eclipses any achievement, conquest, or victory. Vannety and I have defeated ourselves and negated life, our will to live, to power—yet, is this junction *not* the joint power of our will? I live *for* this solemnity. If I survive to old age, I will always remember this raven-haired woman and what we *did* experience.

8:47 PM

I've worn a green farmyard chicken motif bow-tie to work for the past two days and have received a plethora of compliments. Among the praise and flattery, people said, "Why do you wear a bow-tie?"

I said, on each occasion, "To be pretentious."

Most don't understand; some continue to compliment, and a few laugh. The most superficial draw attention to the bow-tie as though *it*'s an object reserved for the classy and dignified.

My closing colleague and closest comrade, Hunter, has submitted his two weeks notice to terminate his employment to begin work at a wall-manufacturing factory for sixty hours a week. He has gifted me a "memento," as he dubs *it:* A small satchel that contains "lucky" dice he has used for *Dungeons and Dragons* campaigns.

Anna has been assigned to morning shifts. Tonight is the last night I am to endure her obstinate and disrespectful company.

I await word on a dishwashing position and bide time.

Time: My life is an empty void. I'm invigorated with disdain. Yes, I feel dead; I won't deny my dread. Any reader has triumphed over me; bask in my wastefulness.

10:25 PM

I haven't prostrated since before Navy boot camp until now. At odds with my flesh, humanity, and existence, I'd rather reenter the trials of boot camp ad nauseam than persist with this comfortable stasis.

My desire has abated for all things. I gaze upon my naked, unwashed body early mornings and think of what additional muscular tissue would merit: I confound myself and laugh.

Aphex Twin's *Stone in Focus* reverberates into my ear canals. I've begun to cry; a thin contour of tears lines my lower eyelids and seeps back into my eye sockets, unfelt.

Nine open cardboard boxes of varied sizes are arranged in two neat rows along my empty "dining room" wall. Three are filled to the brim with empty cans of sardines and empty cylinders of steel-cut oats. My neighborhood offers no option for recycling. I dispose of the trash-filled boxes in a dumpster thirty-five paces away from my front door.

My apartment smells of faint meal residues indiscernible to my olfactory sense. The weight bench I sit on is a peculiar object in an otherwise empty space. A large cockroach I found dead one December morning remains in a heap of dry leaves and detritus piled in a corner near my front door. I purchased a broom and dustpan three months ago and employed *it* twice in the kitchen and once on my living room carpet.

If I were to kill myself, my body would be found next Thursday by the monthly pest inspector, with the exception of a death in my empty bedroom, or the empty closet adjoined to my empty bedroom—in which case I'd be found by a residential employee three months and three weeks later, after my first failed rent payment and three subsequent late fees.

I walked past Vannety at the end of my shift tonight and saw her in my peripheral vision through a pane glass wall-window while she mopped a cafe floor. I felt an immediate pang of discomfort, flinched, and forced myself to stare forward.

I'd masturbate tonight, though I don't know what I'd think of.

Wednesday, February 19th, 2020

8:24 PM

"Well *it*'s all perspective, ya know?" said an obese professor to an agreeable student by a lemonade dispenser.

This commentary is trendy. Everyone knows the truth of untruth and everyone is unique yet we're all the same—the words "everyone" and "all," spoken as gospel for whatever context deemed suitable. Why people bother to write and read—to *learn,* is a matter of personal prosperity. Calories in, calories out. Be sexy.

"Well *it*'s all perspective, ya know?" said an emaciated Hindu sage, said a CEO of a Mars colonization project, said an Englishman seated by a sunlit lake while he drank Coca-Cola, said a Malaysian torturer, said a city mall fortune-teller—said every day by therapists, philosophers, social activists, life coaches, ophthalmologists, and psychologists.

"Yeah, well, you know, that's just, like, your opinion, man."

- The Big Lebowski

11:05 PM

I haven't played video games in over three years and often yearn for the escape. I browsed the internet for videos of the newest games and discovered iterations and adaptations of nearly every game series I've ever played. More of the same and the same old banality.

In other news: Democratic socialism. The poor don't want to be poor. I must try to masturbate tonight… to *something*… I'll think of *it*.

Thursday, February 20th, 2020

7:48 PM

My unhappiness is grotesque; there is no reason for *it* other than my choice to think of the superficiality of humanity in all relations: Self-seekers seek fulfillment through the utilization of other self-seekers.

"In 1983 Lieutenant Colonel Stanislav Petrov was on duty at a Russian nuclear early-warning center when his computer sounded a loud alarm and the word 'LAUNCH' appeared in bold red letters on his screen—indications that a U.S. nuclear missile was fast approaching. Petrov held his nerve and waited. A second launch warning rang out, then a third and a fourth. With the fifth, the red 'LAUNCH' on his screen changed to 'MISSILE STRIKE.' Time was ticking away for the U.S.S.R. to retaliate, but Petrov continued his deliberation. 'Then I made my decision,' Petrov said in a BBC interview in 2013. 'I would not trust the computer.' He reported the nuclear attack as a false alarm— even though he could not be certain. As *it* turned out, the onboard computing system on the Soviet satellites had misclassified sunlight reflecting off clouds as the engines of inter-continental ballistic missiles."

- Fully Autonomous Weapons Pose Unique Dangers to Humankind, *Noel Sharkey in Scientific American: January 28th, 2020*

I've felt a renewed pity for humanity resurge in me today due to editing yesteryear's journal; the above article amplified that feeling. ~~War is anachronistic. Globalization is the only recourse.~~ Established "countries" and dividing lines ~~are a bane to~~ is the human condition. When you're confronted with annihilation, what purpose is there to annihilate the other party, except to be vengeful and spiteful?—that's what the Petrov story is reduced to. Masses of AI weaponry competing while commanders watch from screens are glorified video games to the detriment of the planet and human civilization.

Yet, here we are, and even if we were to be obliterated, I would be indifferent to know why or how.

The chicken purveying company's head manager approached me while I placed fried chicken between buttered and toasted white bread. She smiled and said, "What's with the bow-tie?"

I stopped and turned to face her. This had been the first instance in seven months since I began employment that she spoke to me. Stone-faced, I said, "To be pretentious."

She fumbled on her words and said, "*It's* not allowed."

"Oh?"

"*It's* cute and everything, but *it's* not part of [Company Name]'s uniform.

I untied the knot, removed the tie, and observed the woman's face with focused intent for four seconds: Caked-on mascara, large rounded abdomen concealed in a rippled white over-shirt, a suppressed scowl; a bloated corpse. I said, "You had approached me with a light-hearted spirit, but then *it* turns out you speak only words that make me feel awful."

"Well," she began, and had already turned away from me; I didn't listen.

Emil approached me later while I swept and relayed information he had searched online about my city of birth and father's name; I lied and denied both. "Are you all right? Are you mad today?" he grinned.

I said, "I've been editing and have reread thoughts I once had a year ago that highlighted the superficiality of human relations and I'm feeling apathetic." Unjustifiable tears welled in my eyes and I looked away.

Emil pressed the matter further, curious—*just* curious, of my pain. I informed Emil that my initial impressions of him were of his superficiality. Emil didn't find that to his amusement and continued to harangue me with unwanted questions: a test of my vocabulary. Reluctant, I defined several words on Emil's behalf, such as "diatribe," to his entertainment. I defined "didactic" as "a form of rhetoric." Emil defined "didactic" as "a method of teaching or instruction." We were both only half-right. Emil declared his appreciation for the word "ethereal," and read aloud the dictionary definition from his phone. I informed Emil that I often pronounced "ethereal" as "etherul," and stuttered in the process. He called me a dumbass, in jest: *It's* what he vyed for all along.

I nodded my head, looked down, and resumed my sweep.

"*Baethan*—I'm kidding! C'mon!"

I said nothing. I felt nothing. Emil left me alone in the side vestibule and I closed my eyes, felt blood rush to my cheeks, and thought of the microcosmic thing that I am. My breath hastened and I balanced on the straightened broomstick, clenched tight in both of my hands, arms skewed at acute angles.

On my break *it* was the same. I eat in seclusion at 3:30 PM each day in the storage hallway behind the university auditorium. After today's meal, I clenched my fists and leaned against the painted white wall, head down. More tears welled and didn't fall; I refused to allow myself the bitter satisfaction. I returned to work, eyes vacant, mind compliant, head up and vigilant.

Saturday, February 22nd, 2020

5:12 PM

Names of the (in)famous serve as beacons of disillusionment. Every great figure who has ever existed is a part of the mass, yet the mass wishes to distinguish: "Us" and "Them"; "I" and "You"; pronouns are anathema and constitute the basis of war *and* individualism. Without pronouns, there would be only *names*, which, in regard to what names serve to *distinguish*, is *also* the root of war and individualism. Individualism *is* war.

We wage war on ourselves to become greater than the mass of which we are inseparable. Each human is indistinguishable from the other, despite heralded achievements, skills, honors, or conquests. One man's victory or defeat is all of man's; the miasma of our delusions is indefatigable when one begins to value judgments over desires.

Sunday, February 23rd, 2020

2:22 PM

"There isn't a single difficult aspect of writing anything. Add quotation marks to any sentence, a few colorful adjectives to describe the scene, and a banal aphorism that expresses the theme," said a leather-clad man atop a snowy vista. A black-bladed zweihänder balanced straight up towards the sky in the deft grasp of two gauntleted hands.

A hoary wizard approached up a flight of battered stone steps, garbed in nothing but a plain brown tunic and a pair of weathered cow-hide boots. "I've read your work." The wizard sneered and spat the words with an acerbic style: "There is no character development and the plot is nonexistent. To even call you a 'writer' would be an injustice to your betters. If writing isn't difficult, why is *your* work terrible?"

"I won't argue with your rhetoric."

"Well," the wizard scoffed, "I didn't expect a simple concession."

The man with the zweihänder glowed purple for three seconds, faded to his original coloration, and said, "Yes. I have judged this encounter inadequate to more suitable means to occupy my time."

The video game powered off and a professional real estate agent sat on a long white sofa in a living room painted blue. The hum of a fridge in an adjacent kitchen and the faint sound of his girlfriend's blow dryer from an upstairs bathroom occupied his mind while he sat for two minutes and fifty-three seconds and stared at his reflection on a vacant flat-screen television. "Christina!" he yelled.

A sharp, feminine voice resounded down the stairwell: "Yeah?"

The man lifted a can of orange-flavored energy drink to his lips and sipped.

Christina repeated, impatient, "*Yeah?*"

"What rally is first?"

"The Transgender Awareness march."

"What time?"

"1 PM."

"How long will *it* last?"

Six seconds of silence elapsed. Christina said, "I don't *know.*"

The man said, "The Men's Rights meeting is at 4 PM."

A digital clock beneath the television read "10:58 PM." The man's attention flitted from the display to a digital wrist-watch clasped tight against his lower left forearm that read "10:57 PM." The blow dryer resumed a faded drone from above. The man said, "What time are we leaving?"

The blow dryer ceased and Christina yelled, vexed, "*What?*"

"What time are we leaving?"

"Around noon. The drive is about forty-five minutes to Maple Ave."

"Will we have time for the Men's Right's meeting?"

The blow dryer switched on halfway through the man's sentence; he sat and listened for one minute and thirty-three seconds, statuesque, controller held firm; both thumbs pressed down against the joysticks. He checked his wrist-watch: "10:59 PM." The man sniffed one exasperated inhale through his nostrils and powered on the videogame. He skipped an intro cinematic, hastened through the character selection screen prompts, and logged in.

The wizard outlined a stark-grey horizon and stood from a meditative pose. "Ah, Roygbivalent, you've returned."

Roygbivalent flourished the black zweihänder; a spire of fire crackled from the guard, up the fuller, to the point. He said, "You haven't moved since I logged out?—fucking loser."

The wizard gestured a mocking swipe of an arm and said, "I knew you'd be back. You're a no-lifer with nothing else to do."

Roygbivalent assumed a readied stance and said, "I just want to complete this quest."

"I know."

"You're a pathetic cone of frost spammer."

"You're a shitty writer IRL." The wizard bounded up the steps and invoked a blast of ice shards from the palm of his right hand.

Roygbivalent evaded three glacial assaults and swung the zweihänder in a horizontal arc from his position on one knee toward the wizard's neck.

The wizard levitated backward five feet and shot a spray of ice, encoating Roygbivalent in a sheen of hoarfrost. Roygbivalent attempted to maneuver out of another blast despite his chilled body, failed, and succumbed to a barrage of nine consecutive attacks. Encased in a block of rime, Roygbivalent said, "Such bullshit," and shattered.

"Get good," said the wizard.

5:19 PM

I faff; therefore, I am.

Monday, February 24th, 2020

10:11 AM

I spoke with a resident from my apartment complex for the first time in six months of occupancy (excluding the next door Hispanic man about his obnoxious music): I had returned home from work and a man who called himself "D" greeted me from his seat on metal steps that lead to the second floor. D smoked a cigarette and talked of his retirement from being a shipyard worker for twenty-five years. D proclaimed he doesn't know what to do with his time; therefore, he sits outside on metal steps, smokes cigarettes, and chats with neighbors. Indoors, he watches television.

D said, "Ninety-nine percent of the people in this world are bad, but there are the few, the few 1% who are good, I think."

I said, "Do you think you're part of that 1%?"

"I sure like to think I am," D laughed.

7:39 PM

Each instance a car passes me I think, *"Pop!—pop!"* and imagine what position my body would fall to the pavement and what caliber of bullet would enter my skull.

There is an eighteen-year-old acne-faced Korean cashier named Jason who self-identifies as a "Simp." [10] Jason enjoys grilled chicken sandwiches with two slices of lettuce, Pepper Jack cheese, and a wrapper with the words "**SIMP**" written on *it* in black sharpie.

I said, "Jason, you aren't a simp."

"Yes I am," Jason affirmed.

"How?"

"I would pick up a ladies' papers if she dropped them on the floor."

"That doesn't make you a 'simp,' that just means you practice common courtesy."

"No. That's just one example. I'm a 'simp' and I'm proud."

"'Simp' is a word with many negative connotations."

"Not if you're proud."

Wednesday, February 26th, 2020

8:06 PM

At my shift's end last night, I ran a mile and a half across town for a palm-reading session paid for and appointed to me by Candy, intended as a kind gesture. I met with Candy's friend, R.J: A woman in her late fifties garbed in an ensemble of flowing black robes and a wide-brimmed hat of comparable shade, adorned with baubles and jewels.

I entered Candy's shop, sweaty and winded. R.J. awaited me beside the shop counter next to Candy's assistant (Candy had been ill, and reposed in her apartment above) and grinned at my entry. "I assume you are the one who I'm meeting with at eight o'clock?"

I verified, exchanged greetings, and we rounded out to the back of Candy's parlor, where R.J had assembled a spiritual-themed station at a centered roundtable covered in a blue cloth. I discreetly powered on my recorder in my front coat pocket and recorded the thirty-minute session:

R.J said, "Okay so put your hands right out. All right, so we read both hands… Have you had your hands read before?"

I said, "I haven't."

"Oh! Well you have fire hands, so you're very energetic, intense, and like—go-getter."

---

[10] Acronym for "Sucker idolizing mediocre pussy."

"I think you could tell that just by me walking in."

"Oh running here?

I wiped the sweat from my brow and said, "Yes."

R.J uttered a bombastic laugh. "Yes I could except your lines really do say that too! Plus, um, they've got—your hands have a little bit of red to them which is a trait of fire hands as well; plus your lines are very dramatic, they've very—in fact I want to take a closer look; if you'll take that as well," R.J handed me a large magnifying glass, "and you can see how, you know they're very kind of spark-like—you'd have to see, um, a water hand, an air hand, uh, um—to kinda be able to really see what I'm talking about—but, and, you're definitely a timely person because you have nice lining around your knuckles—do you play any music, or?"

"I don't."

"Okay so this is mostly about time. Let me see your other hand. So you see this knot right here?—that's about wanting things to be on time, understanding where time is, and a lot of times you don't even have to look at the clock—you can almost guess what time of the day *it* is—you know *it* feels like two o'clock—oh yep—boom there *it* is. Ya know one-fifty-five-"

"-I do write by deadlines."

"Huh?"

"I write as a vocation."

R.J. forced a laugh of null comprehension and followed-up with, "Oh!"

"I keep track of a strict... uh..." Beads of sweat dripped into both of my eyes and blurred my vision.

"Timeline?"

"-Sorry—I don't mean... I don't want to interrupt—and I have sweat dripping into my eyes."

"Here!" R.J giggled and passed me a tissue paper.

I forced a single syllable laugh of discomfort, patted my eyes, and said, "Ah, hm, yes, there we go, thank you," while R.J leaned back against her chair and laughed (authentically).

"Oh you're very welcome!"

I muttered, "I didn't even see those tissues there."

"Well that's all right!" R.J. announced with maternal tonality, "That's what I'm here for. So, and you can also see that there's a lot of—and I guess I'm going to have to give you the glass back cos I want you to see, the, um, modeling in your hand. You see how you have a white, and then you got all these little kinda red, kinda, splotchy... parts?"

"Yes."

"So, uh, that says that your brain is really operating right at the moment and you're really wanting to know all kinds of stuff. And actually right here—let me take this (the magnifying glass) from ya, cos I'm gonna look over *here*... Um, these are calluses right here, but, um, you can see that there's some—well a little bit of heightened pockets right there? So this is your heart line... this is your head line, and they have, well, oh *nice!*—I haven't seen one of those in a minute; I have one as well. Okay, so this is called the 'Girdle of Venus' and I don't think I've seen one of those lately at all. And you almost have a heightened, hm... an extended, um... heart line... that's um, kinda running parallel to your heart line? So that probably means that you have, um, you're very deep feeling and uh very, um, understanding... [Indiscernible mumbling for three seconds.] Oh yeah, okay, so this is the line of intuition right here. *Oh*—and *it* has a nice little Neptune fork on *it*, on the end of *it*, and uh... Interesting. Okay, so... is that? Okay. I was trying to see if that was from pressure from the table or if that was actually, just, um, the way *it* is. So you see this is your moon right here, and you have a little bit of indention right there; and see how your headline runs all the way across the hand and comes down to this little, um, pocket... So, the more, um... um... When, um—moon sort of curves through right there, you see how *it* comes out right here and then *it* divots in, and then you have your Pluto right here; so you must have, um, friends or people that call you—*it's* kinda like the counselor node; *it* says that uh, you are good at giving advice and talking with your friends—there are actually people that call you to see what you think about things—they like running stuff by you. Is that true?"

"Somewhat—but I don't have any friends."

"*Oh* how so?"

"*It's* by choice."

"Oh okay, cos you-"

"I'm more of a loner."

"Then the divot is probably saying that, and you get up in your head quite a bit. And, uh, you're more of a, well I probably would say a loner, yeah, because of that, but you can see the formulation there, um, sort of indicates that. But the people that you do talk to, you probably give them information or some sort of advice, because of your, uh, your Pluto. So then you have, uh, Neptune—*oh* so back to the 'Girdle of Venus.' The 'Girdle of Venus' actually is, um, a trait of someone who's very attractive to other people—so, you must have a little bit of difficulty with keeping people..."

"At bay?"

R.J chuckled and said, "Is that true?"

I frowned and said, "Yes."

"Okay, because you have an attractive manner and an attractiveness that, uh, *draws* them in, so that's kinda contra- I mean, how is that living a contradiction of kind of a loner but yet you attract people?"

"Well *it*'s… that's what I write of."

"Oh-ho-ha!"

"*It*'s the human condition."

"Uh-huh, uh-huh."

"*It* is a hell unto *it*self."

"Yeah." R.J. squeaked with laughter. "I gotcha, I gotcha. So, the other thing is that, you have a little bit of different thoughts and outlook on life than your parents did—you're a little bit, maybe different in philosophy than they were, um, because your—see right here where your head line is and where your life line—there's a little bit of a separation there, and actually when you were a small child *it* was really fine but about the time you got to a teenager, um, *it*'s like this, *it* was almost like all-of-a-sudden you woke up and just went 'Wow, I don't think I really *think* like them.'"

"Yes."

R.J chuckled, reassured. "And um, so, *it*, um… and maybe *it* was a little sad when you realized *it*."

"*It* happened when I read a quote by Franz… Franz Kafka, and that is: 'The first sign of the beginning of understanding is the wish to die.'"

"*Oh*—uh-huh, uh-huh!"

"That shaped me."

"Mm! Mm! Mm. Okay, so. Um, very nice head line, a lot of distance, but that's really good. And, and, you were worried about—or you have had, or you're going to—you seem fairly young—how old are you?"

"I'm twenty-eight."

"Okay, Mhm. Let's see here… Right, when you come down to the middle finger right here when you're about thirty-five, or midlife is right here; so you've had about three challenges, um, one: the early one, didn't um cross on over to your life line but at least came up to *it*… and *it* looks like… gonna be *really* nice… Let's see here… Probably from about forty-five to about sixty, things are going to be *really* nice. Okay so, you're seeing some lines coming across here, this is your Venus, and then you see this *nice* place right here, where there aren't any—well that little line comes across right there but *it*'s not too bad—but you see how *it*'s got a nice, clean—all you see is your derma, your skin ridges. You see 'em?"

"Yes."

"So this period of your life is going to be really nice; you're going to be very invested in *it;* you have a nice color on your life line which means you'll have lots of energy, um… and… This is your line of destiny right there—I almost thought, 'Man am I reading the right line there?' But I am!" R.J. chuckled. "And, uh… So line of destiny right here but *it* actually, um, kind of parallels your life line—so what religion are you?"

"I'm… agnostic."

"Oh yeah? Well, um, my gosh you got a ton of like, um, uh, a… past-life lines. How—where do you stand on past life?"

"On my past life?"

"Or have you thought about *it,* or do you believe in *it? Do you think this is one rodeo or?"

"Oh, as in reincarnation?"

"Mhm, mhm, mhm."

"I hope not."

"You hope not?" R.J laughed.

I muttered, "I hope this ends."

"This—this is the last time you want to come through this little portal?" R.J's laughter continued and sounded akin to a jovial outburst of a young girl.

"Yes."

"Well, okay so what I'm talking about is—you see these lines right here? All of those lines that are coming up like that? All of them along here are past lives so you're probably exhausted from living them cos you have actually quite a few, but not all of them are influencing your current-"

"Those smaller lines?"

"Yeah—you see these all coming down through there?" R.J. traced a pink marker over rows of vertical lines along the breadth of my mount of Venus (the flesh below my thumb). "This one here; this one here… and this one here; those mean that those are past lives that are actually influencing this life, so you probably have at least four people or four instances that really… Do you feel a sense of deja vu or a sense—that real deep connection, or, um, like, you've uh maybe been with them before so you know, if you *believe* in reincarnation you'll understand that we travel in clusters and we generally meet up with the people that we've actually seen before—we just change roles a little bit; and that's how we end up learning all the parts—and the sooner we learn how everything is, the higher we can evolve into our spiritual life, right?

I nodded.

R.J continued: "So, um, life lines nice and strong, I think you'll have a good go at *it*—they come all the way around. So, um, did people influence what you do, your career? Or was *it* a complete independent choice from, um, from your-"

"*It* was a complete independent choice."

"Okay, umm… well your life line, er—your fate line comes up— *it*'s comin' up over here from your Venus—generally… that means that somebody influenced you in *some way,* but I suppose now that I think about *it,* did you do something that's completely opposite of what your parents thought you should do?"

I pondered for a moment and said, "Yes."

"Okay-"

"My father."

"All right—what does *he* do?"

"He was a postal worker for thirty-five years."

"*Oh yeah!* Work for the man!" R.J. laughed.

"Yes."

"Absolutely—so you're more independent?"

"Yes."

"And he doesn't understand that-"

"He does, and I think that he may have influenced me most-"

"Oh okay!"

"-of all the people that I know."

"Oh okay! All right, I gotcha. Well your destiny line is very nice, *it* comes all the way up to your head line. Oh you have some nice psychic crosses there—so you have like, uh, good intuition?"

"I believe so but sometimes I think I delude myself because intuition can't be entirely trusted."

"Yeah? Why not? I mean—because *it* doesn't come from a written book or-"

"*It*'s more of an instinctual feeling, and your instincts can be off."

"They can, but your *cognitive* can be off too."

"Yes."

"Hm. Interesting. Well, I think you have a capability there. Okay, so, let me show you this-"

I said, "I've been called a 'mind reader' a few times but I've always interpreted *it* as in jest."

"Oh okay—so you see this right here? *It's* what they call a psychic cross; *it* sits right between your head line and your heart line, and, um… and also this is your um… actually… trying to see… so you got a star right there so you got a St. Andrew's Cross which means you tend to think altruistically about things or uh, help—tell me again what your job is? A writer you said?"

"Yes, I write, but I have a nine-to-five job-"

"-Uh-huh-"

"-that I change every six months. Right now I'm frying chicken."

"Oh. Really?"

"Perhaps you can smell *it* on me."

"Oh—oh, oh *no*. Frying chicken? Like at [Corporation] or something like that or a restaurant?"

"At [Corporation]."

"[Corporation]! Oh my gosh [Corporation]!—that's like one of my favorite places to eat!"

About thirty seconds of one-sided [Corporation] banter elapsed. I continued to nod.

R.J said, "Yeah I graduated and got my degree from [University]. So, you see this nice little configuration right here… *it's* kind of almost starish, right?—cos you got your line of intuition crossing over and you've got, uh, your destiny line coming up; so, I don't really know if I wanna use this word… *fateful*… but I think you're probably going to meet, um… meet your crossroads in this lifetime. You'll probably really come to understand things a whole better because you have that with your destiny line and your intuition line and you got your psychic cross so I think there's a wealth of aspects to you that you'll be able to capitalize on—even the older—as you get older, things will start to really roll through you, if that makes any sense. Do you understand what I'm saying? Do you know-"

"Do you believe in reincarnation? Is that-"

"-Uh-huh!-"

"-an essential belief to have, to have any faith in this practice?"

"In the palm-reading-"

"Yes."

"-or in… um, I don't know. Um, I know that of all the tons and tons of books I've read—have—I was telling Candy today that I have ninety-eight books just on palmistry alone—and I have *several* other books that have *portions* of *it,* uh, in there, but, I don't—I think I've been here a lot of times." A long silence elapsed between us. A radio in the adjacent shop room played jazzy electronic piano music. R.J. said, "So I think... I'll probably ask you—is *why?*"

"Well, you say 'past lives'-"

"-Uh-huh-"

"-then you're saying I'll come to a crossroads in this life."

"-Uh-huh, mhm, right here," R.J pointed to a line.

"So, *it's* as though believing in reincarnation is essential to believing what you are telling me."

"Oh!—no, not necessarily, not *necessarily*—the reincarnation, but you *will* come to, um, a really good... awareness, because anybody that—*it's* like when, you know, where you come to the crossroads—you go, 'Oh, oh!' like who would've thought, right?" R.J giggled.

"I think so, yes."

"So I think you're going to have a lot of those because of this configuration right there. *And* you have really strong lines, and you have, uh, a really good hand as well. So on your—so your actual hand—let me see both, again."

I held both palms out in front of me.

"Okay... Hm... Are you mainly right-handed?"

"Yes."

"Are you ambidextrous?"

"No."

"Okay so you can see your right hand is really red and your left hand is very much more um, you know—flesh-colored. So, um, the active, um, hand is, uh—your dominant hand is how you feel with everything that's going on out here and your non-dominant hand is more about what's going on inside yourself, and uh, you got a little calmer here (left hand), but the *outside* world is, you know—impacting you... in a lot more... I don't know if I want to say intense but—in a lot more *profound*—I guess—way. So this is Venus, and you have a nice firm Venus. You have um, really good timing; you've got, uh, a nice responsibility line. This is your will, and you're pretty firm about what you think, and what you do, and where you go, and you're very, um, independent in that because your thumb doesn't roll over—yours is very firm, *it's* very strong—*it* has nice, uh skin—*it's* nice and firm as well. And this is your Jupiter; this is Saturn; this is Apollo or the sun, and this is mercury; so this is social, political, moral, ethic, creativeness, and

164

communication and business. So, put your arms up and put your elbows on the table. Relax. There you go."

I shifted in my seat and obeyed.

R.J said, "So you are pretty interested in things that are going on and you actually don't mind getting into things because your hands are leaning out just a little bit. You're pretty open-minded about things. Um, you try to be very watchful and learn situations but sometimes that probably gets away from you. You're um, somewhat outspoken and sometimes… sometimes you probably wish you had said less," R.J chuckled, "depending on the person I suppose… Is that true?"

"Yes. I tend to never speak."

"Oh—but you do somewhat because you've got a little space there between your creative finger and your um, communication finger so…"

"Each time I do speak, I wish I hadn't, so at this point-"

"A little bit less than you did?

"No, just never spoken at all."

"Oh! Okay, gotcha, gotcha. Yeah. And um, your um, a little bit, uh… um… mainly I want to say reserved on meeting new people. Um, you mostly I think there's some underlying thing that you don't want to be interrupted in what you have going on because you feel where you're at is where you need to be and how um—because you see how your thumb comes in here, and your actual heart here is a little bit closer—that's like, somebody that's like, really trusting—everybody they see they talk to; their thumb is going to be almost at an angle. So your thumb's up and then the 'will' part of your thumb is setting inward a little bit, so you don't really like people messing with your space." R.J looked at me for affirmation.

I said, "Yes."

R.J laughed and said, "And uh, so that's—you know—and that's fine, uh, yeah. I think that's a good prudent thing to have actually. I think people probably end up sometimes being too ~~gargarious~~ gregarious and—and out, and that they get all kind of things going on that they can't really, um, you know, manage a whole lot—but your Venus is actually—you know—your passion and your um… intensity—and the things that you wanna do—and your life line really swings wideout here, on your Venus?—you see that? Like, if, um, I'm looking at the lip of your hand right here, that is almost halfway out, so it's a pretty, uh, widespread. And then this is your Neptune too and, Neptune, um, says that you've got a little bit of a peak as well, so you have, um—for wanting to be sort of a loner you have a charisma, that people are attracted to. So… I'm thinking… Uh, people are probably much more wanting to interact with you than you are with them, and that's uh—that's uh, um… That's a way to have to navigate I guess, that uh, requires kind of a lot of uh… uh, skillfulness, and uh…"

"Tact."

"Yes," R.J guffawed for three seconds and said, "Absolutely, absolutely. All right… um… Sometimes you probably get, um, frustrated when you start doing something and you don't get finished?"

"… I get frustrated… when I don't finish something?"

"Yeah, and sometimes you start 'em and you don't get 'em finished."

"… Not recently."

"So, pretty much what you got going on, you pretty much are able to take care of right now—the reason I say that is cos the moons on your fingernails are, uh, really tight—the cuticles. So—but you're very interested in things that are going on since you have a little like—like your fingernail goes like that. So you can see my fingernails: they're called conic, they go straight and out—I have air hands so you can see the difference; my hand is a little more, um, kind of feathery?—a little more, sort of lighter. And your lines are very much more etched. Mine are a little uh, you know, not quite as deep—like you can see my life line, my head line and my heart line as well, but, um the rest of the lines are a little um, lighter. So, um, and then the fire hand also has a very long palm and a little bit of shorter fingers? And, uh, you know fire individuals are very, very deep—very intense, very, um, forthcoming with, you know, what they feel and what they think; but, like you said maybe not all of them are outspoken because you've got the little divot in your moon. This is your Mars—your lower Mars—your upper Mars; you're not really uh, I don't think upset with anybody right now but you can, you know get ticked occasionally," R.J began to chuckle. "Is that true?"

I shrugged and nodded.

"The reason I say that is you see how this end kind of moves up there?" R.J continued to laugh and worked to suppress *it*. "This is the anger part of Mars and this is the strategic—Mars is the war, right? The war, uh gods, so… And um, you know, this extra, um, part—oh and your *relationship* line—your relationships will probably deepen once you move past the second half of your life, cos that—this is the marriage line but I call *it* the relationship line—you can see that at halfway, in-between here and here—but *it's* very deeply etched so probably your relationships will be much more defined and directive, uh, past mid-life. And uh, so, and like I said, this is your Venus and *it* comes down through there as well. Do you, um… So, politics, disturb you?

"Politics annoy me, so I guess."

R.J laughed (a recurrent trend each instance I spoke), and said, "Well-"

"Politics are wearisome-"

"Yeah, well, you see-"

"-but that's what human life is: politics."

"Yeah that's true—but you see this *really* strong line right across there? So this is your moral—this is your social and political guide—so this line comes all the way across—this is your morals and ethics—so you're looking at maybe politicians, or political situations where—that's basically where people are vying for their own best interest and to heck with everybody else: to me that's what kind of politics is at the moment—and that disturbs you quite a bit because your line runs over to your morals and ethics, which is like, 'Why aren't they doing this thing right? Look at the time they are *wasting,* the people that they're hurting,' the um… the… what do you call *it* when people are wasteful, um—you know those things are always kind of inhibiting how things could be so much better, if they'd just—*be* better. Let me see if that line is on your other hand as well—yeah *it* is right here too. Also you have, um, a little *square* right there! You have actually—squares are really nice, those are like, protection—can you see *it?* See *it* right there? The square?"

I gazed through a magnifying glass at a rectangle and said, "Yes."

"Nice little square and that's—that's—this comes all the way—so, um… you like, um… You have a great emotion about the way people are. And their… Well politics is a big pile of bullshit—their, just stuff and the things they do. So you want to have, um—when you have a square that means protection or *it*'s um, uh, generally in your Jupiter *it* also means that you have a teaching capability… um, so you… try to… uh, inform or educate people on how to do better, or… how to, *think?*—more, um, appropriately, for the betterment."

"Yes. I write theories about how all personality is pretentious-"

"Oh really! Where do you publish or where do you put *it?"*

"I publish through iUniverse."

"Oh okay."

"My book is actually in the shop."

"Oh really?"

"Yes."

"Oh! Well… Congratulations then—that's very nice—I'll have to take a look at *it*. Now what's *it* called?"

"Uh, *Outbursts of a Failed Sociopath; Thoughts of an Amiable Stranger.*"

"Oh! Well I'll be darned."

"It's part of a series and I really don't recommend *it*."

"Oh really?"

"Yes."

R.J laughed and said, "Yes you really don't recommend *it?*"

"Yes."

R.J laughed harder and said, "How so? Well then how come you wrote *it?*"

I consternated for five seconds and said, "Something to do."

"Oh, okay."

"I'm a fool."

"Yeah? And how are sales?"

"I don't know."

"Oh… Still waiting?"

"Yes. *It*'s my second book."

"Oh, okay. Well, um, you definitely have the intensity for *it*. So that brings me back to the moon, because if you've written books and you finished them, then, your um, ability to finish-" The thirty-minute alarm for our session blared from R.J's phone. "Maybe *it*'s, um… only things that you are intensely interested in or have a passion for are the things that you finish. Things that don't have value for you, when you get involved in them, are easily left, uh, left undone; you're in no hurry to do them. Yeah?"

"Yes."

"Okay. Excellent. Is there anything that you wanted to know particularly?—I mean the life line looks like *it* particularly; I mean you can't tell life or death on a hand but you definitely have a deep etching there, and, um… your… You got really, really good lines. Everything health-wise looks pretty good: No blues, or browns, or oranges, or yellows, so that should be in good shape. Um…" R.J snickered and said, "You get frustrated to speak with stupid people."

"How did you conclude that?"

"Because you see this little—this is your head line right? And you see that right there?—here take a look," R.J passed me the magnifying glass. "You see that right there, that little kind of, spot? So, you know, *it*'s kind of a frustration factor, so…" R.J retrieved the magnifying glass from my hand and held both my palms close to her face. She mumbled to herself for fifteen seconds.

I said, "I was told that you charge an extra dollar for each minute over thirty."

R.J. pushed my hands away as if they burned her, clasped her own hands in her lap, and said, *"Oh—right,* yeah." She cackled and said, *"It's* hard for me to shut down, cos I really—so, did you have any questions or anything? Or Candy just said, 'Come on in and have this experience,' or just?-"

"Yes. Candy thought I would appreciate *it. It* was a nice gesture on her part."

"Oh okay—well excellent—well I'm glad you made the effort to get all the way here—I'm sorry that you had to run-"

I scoffed and shook my head.

"-but, um, they do close at 8 o'clock but we wanted to be able to accommodate you so I'm glad you came in. Do you have any questions or anything, or is there anything you'd like to ask me about-"

"Do the length of the 'past-life' lines have any meaning?"

In brief, R.J answered, "Yes."

"Thank you for your time."

"You're very welcome—*oh* you're *very* welcome! Please take care and don't run so fast on the way home."

I donned my coat and said, "Yes. The way home will be more lax."

"How cold is *it* out there?"

I smiled; for the moment the essence of our meeting no longer had any bearing: the *weather* emerged as a topic. *"It's* not cold at all."

"Oh."

We walked side-by-side toward the shop floor and I turned to her for one final statement: *"It* seems like most of the conclusions that you came to could be applied to most people."

"Hmmm, mmm-"

"Such as being frustrated by deadlines or annoyed by stupid people."

"Well, let's just take—since I started reading here I haven't met anybody who had that yet."

"Really?"

R.J spoke with an unexpected gentleness: *"It* could be but... generally the readings are very specific; they never were the same for me at all. But *it* may seem that that would be something that would be, but *it* isn't necessarily so, no. Interesting. Interesting—anyway!—thank you!"

We shook hands and I said, "I thank you too."

"Come again sometime and get your cards read."

"I would like to."

"All right! All right! Take care. Be careful going home."

"You too, and thank you."

"Uh-huh!"

I entered the main floor of the shop and met with Candy's assistant who waited by the door for me; I said, "I thank you for staying late."

"Excuse me?"

"I thank you for staying late on my behalf."

The assistant began to laugh for reasons beyond my comprehension; she said, "Oh yeah—yeah, that's fine; *it*'s nice to meet you." We shook hands. "I *started* your book-"

I blurted, "Why?"

"-but I haven't gotten very far." Now *I* laughed: a boisterous guffaw. The assistant blushed, began to laugh along with me, and said, "I don't know!"

"I don't blame you."

"Uh—no, no *it*'s not that; *it*'s just I read when I'm here, and-" the woman burst with jovial laughter on account of my quizzical grin. I pushed my way out the door and she said, "*It* was nice to meet you."

Through a fit of chuckling, I said, "*It*'s nice to meet you too."

"Okay."

"Take care."

"Thank you."

Palmistry is an *exquisite delight*. Confronted with equivocal, generic, applications, one has no recourse but to concede under the pretense of being unique. Bombarded with information of this woman's expertise of what she "knew," my interest piqued; however, what she *did* know, for the majority, remained *with* her. What I *did* glean:

I'm emotional, understanding, and adept at time-keeping, though I've yet to know a human being to whom these descriptions *don't* apply.

The splotchy red marks on my hands signify that my brain is operating; I can't argue with that.

I advise all my friends yet I have no friends, except *you*, fool, and what have I advised other than for you to refrain from reading?

I'm "probably," "maybe," "kind of," attractive to other people, I guess.

I "maybe" have "a little" bit of different thoughts and philosophies than my parents: profound.

A crossroads later in my life will make me "sort of" more aware of "things."

"Sometimes" I "probably" become "sort of" frustrated when I don't finish something.

Thursday, February 27th, 2020

7:40 PM

I attempted to pay the last of a credit card balance and am short by $4.76 in my bank account due to an unaccounted for expenditure at a grocery store. The bank charged me a $29.00 overdraft fee and the credit card company charged me a $38.00 late fee. Today's full day of work: well spent.

Friday, February 28th, 2020

4:52 PM

Attempts to care are absurd. This culture renders me vacuous; *I* am empty-headed and moot.

Why complain? My fingers trounce over a keyboard for lack of life. Content writing is a joke. I'm confident in my lack of ability.

People. They're everywhere and I'm one of them.

I see the girl, Vannety, in the locker hallway while I retrieve my belongings. She opens her locker four cabinets to my right; her co-worker, a blonde-haired girl, who often accompanies her, stands between us. I say nothing and can't help but to observe the side of Vannety's face through a hasty, sidelong flicker of an eye. The perpetual grin on her face elicits me to mirror her expression: an empathetic charade; Vannety doesn't see *it*. I *think* by consequence: *"Get a life,"* in regards to her at first, for what little pettiness we had experienced, though the thought is wholly for myself. Why I bother to write of *it* now astounds me. I highlighted her poor self-esteem and now I know (by inductive and fallible reasoning) that she regards herself as "better" than me, for she reflects on her actions instead of my own and thereby understands the manner of man I am. She reads (or began to) a book I wrote and knows an "I" that has long-fleeted into oblivion.

I wore a black dress shirt to work on our "Casual Friday Dressdown."

My supervisor Kim said, "Um, Baethan?—Why are you wearing a black shirt?"

I said, "I have three reasons, though would that change your verdict?"

"Okay. Go ahead."

"All my work shirts are dirty and since today is a dress-down day I thought this (dress shirt) would be acceptable." My third unstated reason had been that my co-worker, Kalvin, had worn a black *Playstation* shirt on two previous Fridays

Kim said, "Friday dress-down is for school-themed shirts only. You need to change. I have spare shirts in the back."

"What size are they?"

"Larges, I think."

"I wear a size small. I have a dirty shirt with me. I'd rather wear a dirty shirt as opposed to one that doesn't fit."

Thus, I changed into a dirty work shirt. I felt vexed, nullified, and annoyed, for inexplicable reasons. I had no preference for the dress shirt or work shirt, and the maple syrup-esque odor around my armpits didn't bother me as much as I had anticipated. The *fallout* from the engagement, whereby my superiors, co-workers, and a half-dozen customers, perceived the interaction and judged per the limited information available to each of them in conjunction with their genetics and life experience up till that point, *maddened* me. The exchange of upraised eyebrows and disjointed frowns between the social relations manager and a kitchen worker; the wide-eyes and countenances of surprised disbelief concerning the policy by my colleagues; the uncomfortable downcast gazes of customers while they watched, in wait of deep-fried chicken served on buttered toast—*maddened!*—by all of *it!*— not for the sake of my ego, but for the scene *it*self! What are we?

While I disengaged my shirt stays, undid my apron, unfastened my nametag, and changed shirts in the employee bathroom, I mulled on the inconsequential *opinions*—of which I *don't care*—and marveled at the absurdity of even conceiving the entire affair to be of a mote of importance. I reflect and *write* about it now. Who is the fool? What have I learned?

The sixty-plus-year-old single mother, Christina, whispered to me, "I thought you looked professional in all black."

In less than one second, I scrutinized Christina, looked away, returned my eyes to her fulsome, toothy grin, and said, "Thank you."

MARCH

Sunday, March 1st, 2020

1:28 PM

A parakeet communicates with *its* reflection cast by a fist-sized ovoid mirror within a large metal cage inside Candy's apartment. I ate almonds and sipped black coffee while Candy nestled against my side. We sat on a sofa in the silence of an early morning glow and listened. The parakeet deludes *its*elf, alone in the cage, a reflection being *its* sole companion: *it*self is all *it* knows.

"I'll be purchasing a mate for him soon," said Candy.

The parakeet trounced from perch to perch, consumed, defecated, and communicated *madness;* I thought myself no different than this creature, limited to *its*elf, the horizon a happenstance enclosure. I hear the song of a parakeet and the muted conversation of a human neighbor: What differentiates the beasts other than the comprehension? I hear the song of a parakeet and close my eyes. There is no beauty inherent; I reckon the equivalent of an isolated thirty-seven-year-old man at his wit's end, harking to himself in a bathroom mirror. I hear the song of a parakeet: *"My days! My days! Good day to you--and you! I've no interest in the paper. Fetch me a lemon cake this evening, I will; no doubt about that. Tacos are too expensive. Rain! Rain! Go away! I'm interested in complex quantum systems and--god I'm lonely. There's no more salt in the shaker."*

3:29 PM

"Your parakeet has a beautiful face," said a spokesperson for [Corporation] body spray.

A pet shop owner said, "Yes, I value the face of all my parakeets, though this parakeet's face is superior in beauty. Admire the sleek contours and the sun-yellow ruffles around the eyes, as I do."

"I have, and wish to purchase the bird from you."

"Unspeakable."

"How so?"

"Every man knows the value of beauty. My Selena is an incomparable specimen. I'm an astute man--be sure of *it.* Many men such as you have entered this shop and have become enamored with Selena's gaze. I am the bulwark, the wall, the centurion."

The spokesperson exited the store and entered a dark, cobblestone alleyway ridden with grime, replete with hollowed iron barrels, and littered with dilapidated planks of timber. "Oh, *Selena…*" he sighed.

4:08 PM

I spoke with an old dishwasher at a low-key bar. The old man is employed by his son (the owner of the bar) and has spent his life dedicated to creating visual art. Framed paintings and digital renderings created by the old man covered the widest wall of the establishment. I inquired of the art and the bartender summoned the healthy, grey-haired old man from the kitchen. The old man escorted me from piece to piece and explained the techniques and inspiration for each. One painting of a WWII fighter plane looked photorealistic.

I said, "How long have you been a dishwasher?"

"Two months; my son employs me. Why do you ask?"

"Dishwashing is my passion. How long have you worked in mundane jobs?"

"Excuse me?"

"How long have you been employed with banal work?"

The old man grinned, shrugged, and said, "I don't understand what you're saying."

"How long have you worked low-wage jobs?"

"I started working at fifteen and have been at *it* ever since at a whole lot of different places."

The old man's art is worthy of a gallery beyond the scope of an occluded bar, yet *there*, he washes dishes and is content with local renown.

On the lawn of a Presbyterian church, one side of a double-sided outdoor signpost read:

"ATM INSIDE. ALL WELCOME. MERCY, PRAYER, NO JUDGMENT. 0 CARD REQUIRED."

I walked past and read the opposite side of the signpost:
"A SMILE LOOKS GOOD ON EVERYONE."

9:52 PM

I hate the information I produce.

Monday, March 2nd, 2020

8:08 PM

A large, late-forties, overweight man that moves with a permanent limp, works in the kitchen as a dishwasher where I'm employed: Nathan. His stark grey hair is pulled back into a ponytail and his unkempt facial hair frames a wary face. Nathan is the apex of subservient; the words, "Sorry," are spoken while he shambles out of the way of everyone who moves toward him and manages to establish eye contact with his avoidant gaze. His speed is reminiscent of a beast in physical agony. His words fleet from his mouth, often in haphazard arrangements, for he hastens to convey information, as to not be intrusive. After the first three months of my employment, I said to him, "Nathan, you regard everyone as a tyrant and behave as a dog," to which he shrugged, cocked his head, and informed me that he does, in fact, *feel* such a way, for that's how he claims he's been treated.

I gave him my copy of Albert Camus' *The Myth of Sisyphus.*

Nathan writes horror fiction and is a superb artist.

These *dishwashers…* what exemplar human beings.

Today, I worked alongside Nathan for several minutes and said, "I want your job, Nathan."

"If I ever find someplace new I'll let you know."

"Even if you did, management wouldn't want me in the kitchen."

Nathan grinned and said, "Why, did you piss them off or something?"

"No. Management would rather see me suffer out front."

Nathan hobbled away to place clean dishes in their designated places. I finished my kitchen work and returned to my chicken purveying post. An hour elapsed. I passed Nathan by the pit; he flinched and veered out of my way while I said, "Regarding what I said earlier: For me to consider that management thinks of me—even as a mote of thought, is foolish. Also, what suffering would I know here, in actuality?" I shrugged.

Nathan stared at me, doe-eyed, and said, "I don't…"

"No, no—no, I don't expect you to say anything. I just wanted to clarify my folly to you, on how egotistical my thoughts are, for me to think such things."

"Maybe."

I nodded, returned to my labor, and reflected on the single aforementioned non-work related conversation I had all day.

Tuesday, March 3rd, 2020

9:13 AM

I awoke this morning to my new upstairs neighbors. A man shouted, "You're the one acting like a stupid bitch—let's face *it*—you really are."

A woman mewled an indiscernible rant. For hours, the ceiling above me shook and rattled. Inane laughter resounded between accusatory shouts, both combatants unaffected by the normalcy of their verbal assaults. A dog barked.

The man said, "Fuck—I go to the bathroom and got a long hair comin' outta my fuckin' dick—what the *fuck!*"

At an unspecified paradise, a man woke refreshed from a quiet repose to the song of birds, strode through the sunbeams filtered through pearlesque kitchen curtains, enjoyed a cup of Jamaican coffee, a vegetable omelet, and a serving of greek yogurt adorned with blueberries and a drizzle of honey. The man sat at a rounded Greco-roman balcony and gazed out over the rails of an uninhabited seaside vista.

Another man woke in a jail cell to the pain of gonorrhea and the sound of putrid exhalations blown into his nostrils. Two coarse hands flipped the man onto his abdomen, raised his lower body, and prepared his anus for penetration with two globules of saliva.

10:07 PM

After my shift, I pass by fields occupied by young men practicing a sport. Tracks of grass illuminated by stadium lights permit games to be played. I return home to the light of my device and resume a play of words:

No more dialogue, idyllic settings, intellectual themes, or character development.

I'm determined to change; the trajectory of my journaling has been a disjointed outburst of nothings and I'm committed to align my "nothings" now, in this entry.

For one, nobody will ever read this and understand.

I desire to consume and never produce, yet I must produce or I'll cease to exist. These words are my existence: a harrowed plea for validation. Consider what we are and the incalculable amount of words ever produced since the invention of calligraphy, the printing press—our species' interconnectedness nullifies the individual. There are no more heroes or villains; there never *was*. If I wasn't "me," and I discovered this documented series, I wouldn't bother. I don't bother with much of anything, for my time in this world is limited, and I prefer to squander moments engaged with the production of a document I deem worthless—conscious of the fact of what *it* is and what I am.

I admit I've created stories and poems in the past with the intent to impress and delight, for the sake of *entertainment;* this isn't what people want—or perhaps I presume too prematurely with unfounded conviction; *it* is merely what *I don't* want. Suffering is far more palpable. If I want to be entertained, I'll seek the company of a woman and a home-cooked meal. Media shouldn't (for me—I don't care about *you,* anomalous reader) be a fanciful delight equivalent to primal or carnal pleasures, for that is how one loses oneself to a vacuous engrossment. My writing should be a chore to read, for *it* is undignified labor to write, and rife with notional observations. My delusions are yours, only mine is a microcosmic example, a veritable "brain in a vat" of limited experiences confined to a mortal body, conditions of which all of life shares, yet some choose to *produce* so-called art of what their experience is.

I'm one of the lucky fools that choose to produce. I have an outlet for my inhumanity. Every energetic burst of vileness and maliciousness is a muse, per example: Michelangelo di Lodovico Buonarroti Simoni, Ludwig Van Beethoven, Francisco Goya, Leonardo Da Vinci, Antonio Vivaldi, Leo Tolstoy, Auguste Rodin, and J.S. Bach, as exemplar cases—what abominable horrors of the mind these men must've experienced to produce such eminent masterpieces. All the "greats" of this age and the years prior, from music, to literature, to painting, to sculpture, could now be reproduced and outclassed by a computer; if not today, perhaps tomorrow.

I cannot promise myself change; *it* comes on *it*s own, akin to pain, and is always welcome.

Wednesday, March 4th, 2020

10:04 AM

I return home with a plethora of ideas of what to write and decide on something I hadn't thought of up till *this* moment: The inconsequential absurdity of my existence; however, I've written of this before and the topic has become mundane banality.

Other people exist: Each shift and convulse against themselves. I thought to write a few skits in-depth, then write many in brief, and decided not to bother with any, for anything I write would be an ill-informed judgement concluded by one snapshot of a character I perceive in a constrained moment in time.

While employed at the chicken-purveying counter, I am vigilant of potential customer status and often observe the influx and outflow of potential consumers. When I gaze over my shoulder, engaged with fryer oil and scrub brush in hand, my gaze often sweeps over qualitatively physically attractive young women. The personas range, though the two thought-processes which differentiate the majority of these women by consequence of the behavior ~~their~~ my thoughts produce are:

1. Those who are chagrined at my lack of expressed sexual interest, though if I *were* to express sexual interest, I'd be regarded with disdain on account of my socioeconomic status.
2. Those who reckon my lack of sexual interest as the natural order on account of my socioeconomic status.

"Not all women are like that," said a nameless woman-

You're right: Not all women are young and qualitatively physically attractive.

"You're pathetic."

No, I'm truly not interested in you sexually.

"You're a repressed homosexual, but that's okay; I accept you for who you are, even if you are a pathetic cocksucker."

I wouldn't expect anything less from an independent woman.

"You fucking misog-"

I think most of my readers, if any, will be women, on account of the soap opera-esque tripe I write. Of these women, I project at least 90% will have known me at some point in life and are "fascinated" or "interested" by how much they agree with me and hate me simultaneously. After my death, when I no longer meet women, my work will reach the height of obscurity and will be nullified.

Candy gifted me a ticket to a local orchestra on the 7th and has invited me to her home again on the 8th to enjoy an outdoor grilling of Mahi tuna and sweet potato. Stuffed grape leaves and greek yogurt with peaches will also be served. Pinot Noir will be imbibed between bouts of film and "carnal activities," as Candy dubs *it*.

Entertainment is sparse; I have only myself to depend on in the hours after my shift ends. What I had intended to write tonight turned out to be a matter entirely removed from what I have written, though the outcome of either what *does* exist or what *would* exist is mean, self-centered, obnoxious, and disagreeable. To inform others of my writing is a mistake. There is nothing funny about this.

Thursday, March 5ᵗʰ, 2020

10:19 AM

Words I've heard (derived from an internal third-person narrative) as "voices in my head" when I think of what two managerial individuals at my place of work think of me: "Tosser," "smarmy," "strange," "mature," "unsociable." I consulted a dictionary for the full definition of "tosser" and "smarmy," for the words manifested in my mind as foreign, though I *presume* that I must've had indirect knowledge of the definitions at some point in my life and applied them to fit the context despite my initial lack of accessible qualia for comprehension. Incidents such as this are recurrent and daily. I adjust my behavior accordingly to satisfy my desired expectations.

8:31 AM

Chris, my social relations manager, greeted me for the first instance in two weeks today at the start of my shift: "How are you today, Baethan?" I addressed Chris with a glance, stationed by the waffle fryer: a fill-in until I arrived. I pondered, for I had anticipated this eventual moment. Chris said, "Not good, or?-"

I said, "Chris, I understand why you ask me this question, being the spider that you are, though I can't help but to be amused on each instance," and turned away to don a pair of gloves.

Chris smiled, veered towards me, and said, "What? The spider? Why the spider?"

I met Chris' smile with my own, oscillated my fingers at both sides of my waist, and said, "You're in everyone's affairs."

Chris strode past me without a word, his ego emboldened with my words. We spoke nothing more for the remainder of the day.

Kalvin, the twenty-year-old Vietnamese man, converses with me often about the consumption and preparation of various foodstuffs and the quality and quantity of his defecations. Kalvin eats cuisine I have never sampled, such as fish eyes and pig brains.

Kalvin said, "I go to the bathroom, like, five or six times a day."

I said, "That's too frequent. What do you normally eat?"

"I start the day with a shake and eat like, twice a day: here, and dinner at home."

"How big is your feces?" I drew and protracted a shortened space in the air between my two fingers.

"*It*'s diarrhea. *It* usually covers the surface of the bowl."

"Wow."

"Yeah."

"*Each* defecation is diarrhea, or are your morning shits more firm?"

"The ones in the morning are firmer, yeah."

"Do you drink a protein shake in the morning?"

"No, just a shake with fruit and milk blended together, but I'm lactose intolerant."

I grinned and said, "Wow, Kalvin."

"What!—I like milk too much and I don't want to drink any almond milk or anything."

"There's plenty of non-dairy alternatives."

"They're too expensive for me to consider."

"By about 89 cents."

"I'd rather shit myself all day than pay 89 cents."

I laughed. *We* laughed together. Kalvin braced both arms on our chicken purveying counter and looked down at the floor.

I said, "That's my quote of the day—what you just said. I haven't written of you before except one passage, but you made *it* into my book again, Kalvin."

"Oh yeah?"

"Yes."

Kalvin frowned.

"I'd rather shit myself all day than pay 89 cents."

- *Kalvin, Twenty-Year-Old Vietnamese Food Service Worker*

11:22 PM

Domestic violence upstairs. The new residents mistreated their dog, screamed "fuck" and "fucking" more than any other words, and rattled my ceiling fixtures. The woman bawled and yelled, "I love you! I love you more than anything!"

The man refuted the woman with declarations of his and her unhappiness. The woman's cries amplified.

Both lulled and continued to argue at a polite, inaudible decibel in the room above my own.

Friday, March 6th, 2020

4:46 PM

At the chicken purveying counter, an old couple consisting of a woman professor and a domestic male approached and bantered with my supervisor, Kim. I stood beside Kim, spooned chicken nuggets into a paper box, and listened to the egregious exchange of societal conditioning:

"Hello!" The old man snaked in from behind the woman and slid his hands over the contours of her curtailed purple jacket adorned with a bronze name tag. Both of them: bright-eyed and frothing with amiability. Cultured and dignified, the man punctuated every word: "May I *please* have *one* of your zesty buffalo sauces?"

"Of course, sir!" said Kim.

"Thank you *so* much, ma'am."

"*It's* my pleasure!"

I hate my job. I'd ~~rather~~ prefer to be swamped in dishes than to spend another day beset by hoity-toity college-aged nimrods, safe-space advocates, up-and-coming athlete egotists, female nursing students, destined dropouts, and prim intellectuals. No amount of free grilled chicken will sanctify my mind. Stood by the waffle fryer, each paper sheathe I fill with potatoes cooked in a vat of saturated fats and sprinkle with salt is a moment in which I retreat into the stimulating consternation of the *exact* position and action of my being in the world. You become what you do.

Three local dishwashing positions have opened and I've applied to each.

7:11 PM

Yesterday, I asked an obese man named Grant, who is hyper-conscious of his obesity, "What three items would you bring to a deserted island?" while he waited for two fillets of grilled chicken to cook. After intense introspection and a few questions for clarifications, e.g., "What habitations are on the (generic tropical) island?"; "Is there any hope (no) for being rescued?" Grant said, "I'd just sit and wait to die."

I said, "Why?"

"There's nothing worth living for at that point."

"What do you have to live for now?"

"… I don't know."

"Well…"

"My hopes and dreams, I guess."

"What is your dream?"

Grant hesitated and relayed to me his dream of becoming an actor; he didn't look me in the eyes all-the-while, snatched the translucent plastic bag of grilled chicken from my hands, and lumbered away.

Saturday, March 7th, 2020

4:33 AM

I dreamt of urinating into an employee toilet and woke to boxers and pants soaked in my urine three minutes before my 4:30 AM alarm for an extra weekend shift.

Today I will attend a symphony orchestra.

11:52 AM

On a catering shift, I assisted a frazzled woman named Jennifer with the preparation of food, drink, and tertiary utensils for a trip to a nearby university student medical building. We loaded the truck, sped around two blocks, unloaded the truck, entered the building, transported three carts-worth of items up an elevator, emerged out into the top of a huge domed foyer featuring a rectangular chandelier, and my companion checked her clipboard with a single paper attached.

"*Shit*—we're in the wrong building," said Jennifer. I waited for a follow-up… "Uh, shit—we need to go to math and science."

I obeyed and followed Jennifer back down the elevator without complaint or mockery, to the bottom of the multi-tier foyer, where two amiable middle-aged women reckoned Jennifer's fierce mien. Both women attempted to instruct Jennifer to the alternate entrance: a faster route to our destination one block away.

Jennifer said, *repeatedly,* "Yeah that's where we're going!" without listening to the women's helpful prompts. Instead, I followed Jennifer with our carts out to the parking lot. I said, "I think we'd get there faster if we rolled around the sidewalks instead of loading the truck back up again."

"You think so?"

"Yes, if we go back through the building and out the alternate doors."

"Yeah—I think you're right."

We reentered the student medical building, pushed our carts through the foyer, and out again along the university sidewalks to the science building. On arrival, through another foyer and up another elevator, we reached our destination where two severely overweight women in a classroom on the third floor set up the arrangement. Jennifer turned to me and said, "Can you go back and get the silver stand for the coffee dispenser?"

I said, "Sure," and gripped a silver rack from one of the carts.

"No, not that—at the Campus building. I forgot the silver coffee stand."

"Oh."

"Yeah, can you run over there and get *it?*"

"All right."

I ran down three flights of stairs and back to the adjacent campus building, attempted to enter through the kitchen entry where we had departed, and found the doors locked. I stood for several seconds and pulled again, with the quasi hope that the doors wouldn't be locked on a second attempt. I ran around the building and tried three separate sets of glass doors. The final set opened; I breathed a sigh of relief, dashed in, secured the coffee stand, ran back to the math and science building—up the stairs, and met with Jennifer, who had nearly finished the set up with two minutes until our target time.

Three minutes later, when Jennifer and I began to depart, she said to the one other woman present, "I'll be right back with your orange juice cups that I forgot at the Campus building."

I said nothing.

Catering and food service, in general, is a dirty industry, even at a college campus. I'm accustomed to the begrimed containers and greasy appliances of commercial kitchens operated by low-wage employees. I imagine renowned institutions, restaurants, and cruise ships worldwide commit to a higher standard, though luckily, I'll never have to deal with those great expectations. On return to the kitchen, Jennifer threw her coat on an office chair and said, "All right so now we lose our fuckin' mind and wait around with nothing to do for the next three hours," she huffed and began to scroll on her phone.

I said, "This is an average day for you?"

"Yeah, just about. An hour of extreme stress and then a few hours of absolutely nothing."

"At least you're paid for *it*."

"Yeah—I'm surprised they pay us for this shit."

I conceded with a nod, poured myself a cup of coffee, peeled a banana, and paced the kitchen while I consumed. Thirty minutes elapsed; Jennifer departed for personal business. I entered the cooler and prepared myself a Greek yogurt serving with pecans, blueberries, and three slim slices of cantaloupe. I'm no corporate executive, yet I'm paid to eat like one. Jennifer returned twenty minutes after and interrupted me while I paced and wrote this entry on a paper attached to a clipboard: "God, I'm losing my mind."

I looked up and said, "Why?"

Jennifer slumped into a chair with a chocolate cookie and yelled, "There's nothing to do!"

"Ah."

"You can go on break and get a free meal over at the 'Den' if you want."

"That's all right. How long is our shift for?"

"About seven hours but I don't know why there's two of us."

"I understand. I'll go home."

"Hey thanks baby; [manager] was giving me a hard time about *it* but if you're going, I can tell him."

"No problem. Take care."

"You too, baby!"

I Want to Live on an Oil Field

Clear California sky.
Surrounded by black pumpjacks
Listen to the sound of enterprise:
Metronomic revolutions
Fuel my dreams.

The Smell of Smegma

Stand in a bathroom,
Male or female.
Something itches
And tingles. I know
It's your smegma.
Sniff once, not enough.
Twice is fine.
Time to shower.

I'll stay with a day job.

6:32 PM

The halls of the performing arts center are lined with portraits and paintings of a washed-out aesthetic. One, in particular, stands out to me: A messy watercolor depiction of a street of *this* city; there is a church steeple and several nameless commercial structures. At the forefront, an old man carrying groceries walks towards the perceiver and passes an obese woman beneath a bold, red and yellow, *McDonald's* pillar.

Couples amble around me, dressed for the occasion: to listen to an ensemble perform music. Does each, in their garb, desire to impress a partner?—the performers?—or to attract a mate? Others stand and idle, such as myself, notebook splayed on my left palm. Ink bleeds away from my stolen pen and reminds me of last year when this pocket notebook had been my only recourse to free my mind of *its* burdens. Now, with how "far" I've come, I feel poorer than I had when I had nothing but the backpack that weighs on my shoulder with a load far lighter than I had been accustomed to. Why I bother to train and maintain my flesh is mere vanity, to impact my social relations positively.

I'm a pretentious douchebag waiting to listen to other's talents and skills; poised with pad and pen in hand, I scribble away and pause at intermittent periods to observe the familiar strangers. Our behaviors are a bore, *objectively,* as creatures, limited to song, dance, and manipulations of our natural environment.

I connect eyes with my fellow plebs and each reckons the abject wonder in my expression. Am I an alien to them?—to myself? No... no, I *know* already, as aforementioned: a pretentious douchebag.

7:02 PM

I've found my seat, third row, fifth in from the walkway, no one before me; a clear view of the orchestra.

A cacophonous din resounds, reminiscent of Penderecki's *Threnody for the Victims of Hiroshima.* The theme for this performance is "The Sounds of Power."

8:04 PM

The first composition, *Where Eagles Fly,* had been introduced by the composer himself, Rocky Reuter, as a tribute to military veterans. The arrangement begins with a progression from sappy, to bravado, and ends with a celestial crescendo.

George Gershwin's *Rhapsody in Blue* is "powerful" children's music. The young pianist is exaggerated in his expression of emotion for music evocative of *Looney Toons;* he plays on an out-of-tune piano.

Segei Prokofiev is last with his *Symphony No. 5 in B Major, Op. 100:* No power, only a disdainful Warsong.

9:35 PM

Meaningful conversations create rifts between people. Banter brings people together.

All noise is the same.

Instruments being the ultimate expression of "sounds of the universe" are a preposterous claim of the eighty-five-year-old retired music professor seated next to me.

Whether I sit at the orchestra or stand at a bar, there is no difference in my sense of enjoyment or lack thereof. The culture of cultured sensibilities appalls me. I am disgusted by my own humanity and the pretensions of finery in any regard.

The "sounds of the universe," to the old man seated to my left, are equatable to sheep intestines and synthetic wires drawn over strings.

I said, "What is your self-assigned meaning in life?"

The old man said, "I'm a retired professor of music."

There is a marvelous performance before me and I'm wracked with opinions of what the "sounds of the universe" is. Is the hum of a power pylon, the call of a cricket, the racket of a pneumatic drill, and the agonized cries of a pig dipped into a drum of boiling water *not* also the sounds of the universe? Is the distinction present *only* on account of what is pleasant to the limited range of human appreciation? The old man reasoned that how a composer creates order in the performance of an assemblage of instruments is what he means by "the sound of the universe." On the contrary—old man!—for *chaos* is "the sound of the universe," and the order which humans tamper with chaos for the sake of our sensibilities and an illusory feeling of control—*that* is unnatural! Akin to how I prune my words for clarity and conciseness, one may lean back, regard my manuscript with an upraised chin, and *huff.*

I spoke to the aforementioned old man, albeit, in an *ordered* and cordial manner for the sake of cordiality and to indulge in his illusory control. The lights dimmed and the audience hushed on my closing sentence: the denouncement of order.

We listened to the music. My teeth grated.

The orchestra ended; the old man and his wife stood and talked *at* me. I sat and endured privileged barbs of advice concerning the information I had chosen to share with them of my personal life: How I should vote!—attend college!—do *something* with my life!

The old man offered to pay for my ticket for the same seat for the next performance, with him and his wife for company. I declined, thanked him for the generous offer, and watched him ask me *again,* pleading. The old man didn't want to leave my side despite his wife's goading! "Well," he said, "I hope you have a nice weekend, or week, or month. I hope we see each other again."

I gazed up at the friendly stranger. We were the only two remaining members of the audience. I said, "I'm certain we won't see each other again. I hope you enjoy the rest of your life."

The old man scrutinized me with resigned eyes. We shook hands and he said, "I hope we do."

I sat alone while the maintenance crew stacked chairs on stage and wrote of *it*.

10:37 PM

I stand in the bar with the castle mural, imbibe on my second glass of cabernet, and reflect on the old man's new wife of two months, garbed in a minx neckpiece and other grand accessories suitable for a retired temptress on her way out of this world, who implored me that I *needed* to vote. The conviction behind her ceaseless stream of words when her husband went to shake hands with a tuba player astonished me. Tears welled in my eyes on her commands and declarations, e.g., "This is the most important time of your life. I hope you're registered to vote," and "What are you doing with your life? Are you attending college?"

I said, "College is an institution that I don't need. I'm free to educate myself."

Laughter. The old woman laughed, chuckled, and *giggled*. The abomination. The fur-coated abomination.

Sunday, March 8th, 2020

1:03 PM

I met with the girl, Brittany, by chance, at the bar with the mural of a castle, after I attended the orchestra. She greeted me while I passed my backpack to the bouncer. I turned to face Brittany: Dressed in a bright ball cap, t-shirt, and short-shorts; a little girl at play, off-duty, with the denizens of the bar. She said, "I've read most of your book but still have a way to go."

I reckoned her fallacious smiles and disingenuous small-talk pertaining to her "gladness" to see me, again. "Why?" I said, in regard to her declaration of gladness.

Brittany turned from me without answer and I walked away, ordered a glass of cabernet, and listened to a run-of-the-mill group of rejects blare out their hearts on-stage. Brittany walked past me thrice, to and from the bathroom; each pass she resembled to me more, and more, of a child.

There is nothing for me there, nor anywhere. I have no virtue, no desire. Abject abandonment of the soul, spirit, and flesh becomes me with each passing night. I am a savage, yet I am treated like a nobleman.

Monday, March 9th, 2020

9:36 PM

A blue autumn sky. The naked boy couldn't see the man's face nor did he want to. Brief glimpses of an amorphous humanoid outline veered in and out of the boy's vision while he strained ineffectually against dirtied linen bound around his wrists and ankles.

"I'm going to skin you alive," said the man with a gentle affection, "but first, I'm going to disembowel you."

The boy fatigued himself against the unyielding metal rods nailed through the linen, down into the rich soil on which he lay spread-eagled.

Tuesday, March 10th, 2020

11:00 AM

Yesterday, Kalvin asked me for details of my writing, e.g., "How often do you write?"; "How many words do you write a day?"; "What do you write about?" I answered each query in brief. Kalvin asked, "How often do you publish a book?"

I said, "Once a year."

"Wow. They must not be of good quality, then." Delighted, I whirled to face Kalvin, opened my mouth to speak, and he said, "I'm kidding!"

"No—you're right! You're absolutely right!"

Kalvin laughed, blushed, and said, "*It* was a joke!"

11:31 AM

On my first set of inclined dumbbell presses this morning, I listened to songbirds outside and shut my eyes. On the final rep, a conversation between my neighbor D and my next-door Latino neighbor who is fond of blaring music and action movies, gossiped about our new neighbors, and of me. I gossip of both now:

The men praised our new drug-addicted, obnoxious, domestic violence perpetrator upstairs neighbors to be "nice" and "friendly."

The men condemned me to be "mysterious" and "mean."

I reiterate a point I wrote years ago: What do people care to talk about?—each other, and how each of those "others" relates to themself; that's all *this* is.

The reader is a fool.

8:52 PM

Candy inspired me to ask my colleagues and student customers: "If you were stranded on a tropical island, alone, with no hope for rescue, what three things would you miss most from civilization?"

Kalvin, the twenty-year-old Vietnamese man said, after extensive deliberation, one thing: His phone.

Rosa, the early fifties Latino woman, would miss her phone most of all, followed by her husband, and nothing else.

A lanky ear-bud wearing student contemplated while I assembled a sandwich for him: The internet, chocolate, and people-watching.

A stout bearded student beamed throughout answering while his girlfriend idled nearby on her phone and listened: People, bike-riding, and television.

Cesar answered with a chuckle and said, "My insanity," to which I retorted, "You mean your sanity?" Cesar said, "Yes, see? *It's* already happening!" and laughed. I didn't laugh.

The African-American simpleton dishwasher, Wayne, said, "Water, food, and people," within seconds of my inquiry. I informed Wayne there are sources of water and food on the island and he immediately followed up with, "Oh, well then: women, family, and *people,* man!" thereby, he guffawed. None of the answers I've received have been my three: Health care, refrigeration, and sanitation.

9:08 PM

Christina talked of how she would love to write a piece of literature specifically for a time capsule, for those future generations who would unearth the text and revel in *it*s obscurity. I argued that the invention of writing, the internet, and the advent of globalization, would nullify the effect of a time capsule being discovered, unless humanity endured near-extinction and a group of future nomads discovered the preserved literature—though what *benefit* would that be?

I think of this while writing my own work, and reflect on the oversaturation of literature that my thoughts are bound to be lost in. Artificial intelligence is now capable of writing award-winning novels with human-assisted directives. What will machines be capable of in the future in the realm of painting and sculpture? The next Michaelangelo may be a robot. Step into any library and behold all the things you've no desire to read.

Wednesday, March 11th, 2020

9:38 AM

Slaughterhouses and hatcheries.

50% - 65% of my daily diet is animal products: Chicken breasts, eggs, milk, yogurt, sardines, and tuna.

If plants could express their suffering in a manner which humans could understand, I think the folly of universal philosophical compassion for all life would be regarded as a mockery of life *it*self.

Thursday, March 12th, 2020

7:27 PM

The end of a double shift: One-hundred (post-tax) dollars for twelve hours of trouble. My addled mind is once again awed by everything I know I *don't* know. My ineptitude when I look at myself in a mirror is prominent.

A student who works at the university coffee shop responded to my deserted tropical island question about the three things he'd miss most from civilization; the man answered "food" and "clean water" at first, though these answers were rejected by me on account of the fictional island providing such resources. The man became frustrated and deliberated by the counter, engrossed with his phone for eight minutes. While I stocked sauce nearby, he abruptly looked up at me and blurted, "How can I help you, sir?" as if he were the server, and I—the customer.

I said, "What was your answers to the questions?"

Several seconds elapsed; he studied his phone for the duration, gazed up at me again, and said, "What did you say?"

I repeated, "What was your answers to the questions?"

"Oh," the man said with averted eyes, "'What *were* your answers to the questions,' I thought that's what you said."

A young girl approached simultaneously, suppressed laughter, and requested two honey mustard sauces. I provided, and the man and her departed, giggles abound, while I stood and fumigated out of my ears. The mortification hit me at once: I *were* an uneducated foodservice wretch at that moment on account of incorrect grammar. A self-proclaimed writer—foiled by the comprehension of his orated native language. My anger rippled through me and I donned a frown for two hours. While I paced and ate my meal in the auditorium storage hallway, I ruminated on the sequence and devised a statement to utter when I next met with the man: "Your intellectual instigations are on par with that of a grade school girl—to mock a man for his grammar?" I thought myself to be petty and decided against speaking in favor of a stoic charade, despite my inner pandemonium: a crisis of merit.

I returned to my shift, jaded with the world and listened to hysteria concerning Covid-19 and despaired of my fallible, flawed, mortal, humanity—and of those around me who cling to life as if the vessels they inhabited are precious motes to preserve. The man who mocked me returned in pleasant spirits, bowed to me, as per usual, and requested pepper jack cheese on his sandwich. I obliged. My heart palpitations hastened. I leaned over the glass sneeze-catcher and said, "You've humbled me, in regards to our previous interaction."

The man said, "What?" his countenance puzzled.

"When you first stopped by a few hours earlier, you corrected me on my grammar and humbled me."

"Uh, what are you talking—oh, that… um, okay."

I removed the top bun, placed pepper jack cheese on top of a slab of fried chicken, and said, "You don't recall?"

"Now I do since you brought *it* up again—who cares?"

"Well, I care, for you illuminated me for the moron that I am."

The man watched me tuck his cheese-adorned sandwich into a paper sleeve, smiled, shook his head, and said, "Sure."

"Are you majoring in English?"

"No," he laughed, "I just speak English."

"Well, none of us are born with the innate knowledge of English grammar."

"I was—I was born a smartass."

"You caught me on a nuanced grammatical error; that's all I mean to say."

"Your *face* is nuanced; how about that?" The man chuckled, assumed a wry smirk, and turned away from me. Several students looked on and listened to our exchange, confused and amused. I had been the only employee at the counter. The weight of *my* judgment dissipated.

"Now I'm back to the point that prompted me to keep a diary in the first place: I don't have a friend."

– Anne Frank

Friday, March 13th, 2020

8:34 PM

I drank water out of a styrofoam cup today due to a new policy for sanitation regarding the Covid-19 hysteria. On the side of the cup, in bold red font, read: "Cozy up with [Company] food delivery service! [URL]" This marketing contributes to what produces the depraved, lackluster, complacent, and ambitionless. Misguided by directives to enhance our comfort, technology supersedes our animal will.

I pass by open apartment doors on my way home and peer into each living room: A big-screen television drones in each domain. The obese, downtrodden, and crestfallen languish on sofas and beds. Others sit on plastic mono-color chairs in front of their homes and silently scoff at passerby or disregard existence entirely. Food and sex are of the essence.

This morning I awoke to my upstairs neighbors: At 10 AM, the man screamed, "I told you not to lay a fucking finger on me! I've been up for twelve hours and you [unintelligible]." The girl began to cry, beg, and whimper. I meandered to the center of my living room and continued to listen.

The man roared a vehement, monstrous declaration of, "I'll *fucking kill you!*" in a bestial tonality that shook my apartment fixtures. I suppressed my desire to beat on my ceiling with the tip of a broom handle and instead thought to round out of my apartment and knock on their door to interfere with the gross domestic abuse. No… I opened my mouth to shout an insult, and stifled myself. Blood flowed to my cheeks. I clenched both of my fists and stared downcast.

The woman quieted. Heavy-set footsteps pounded across the floor for the next two hours before my departure for my last shift before a two-week vacation on account of the universities' closure. The Covid-19 outbreak in conjunction with "spring break" leaves me with my own devices, to reflect on all that I am (not).

Saturday, March 14th, 2020

6:56 PM

The upstairs altercations apexed at multiple junctions. Throughout the day, my ceiling trembled and the man shouted hatred for himself—for everything, nothing but hate. The girl cried and consoled him; the man rejected her and pounded on walls, the floor, screamed, and fulminated with instances of the word "fuck" spoken between every two sentences. Again, my blood pressure increased and I followed along with the overhead outbursts, my head inclined towards the ceiling, that I may better comprehend the nature of the argumentations:

Hate. The man proclaimed that he hated everything and *screamed:* A wild animal unleashed—a vermin, a rabid dog frothing at the mouth. I dressed, powered on my recorder, exited my apartment with the device in my front coat pocket, rounded up the outdoor stairwell, and knocked six monotonous raps on my upstairs neighbor's door. My other neighbor, D, the man who deems me "mean" and "antisocial," leaned on the railing to my left alongside his wife. Both dragged on cigarettes and observed.

The door creaked open, slightly ajar, and the cute face of a worry-eyed woman peered back at me through the opening. I said, "Hello."

"Hi," she said at a volume a decibel above a whisper.

"May I speak to the man?"

"Why?"

"Because I'm your downstairs neighbor."

"Oh…" the woman's eyes widened and a flash of comprehension manifested as a despaired grimace. She closed the door, retreated into the apartment, and I heard the muffled declaration: "Uh… Hey babe?

196

Uh—downstairs neighbor is wanting to talk to you." The woman returned to the door, glanced through an inch-wide crack, and said, "Okay, um, ju—just a second." The door closed again. I folded my hands in front of me and listened to the calls of birds for twenty seconds.

The woman swung the door wide open and revealed an unfurnished, messy apartment. A *Nirvana* poster of a yellow x-eyed smiley face with an exposed tongue had been the sole characteristic of a living room identical to mine. A slim, shirtless, handsome man dressed in cargo shorts fumbled with a blanket strewn over his shoulders akin to a shawl. Both youthful faces stared at me. The man said, "Ayo—hello."

I said, "Hello," with an amiable tinge. "Do you need someone to talk to?"

"Do I need someone to talk to?"

"Yes."

"About what?"

"About your anger."

The man cringed and looked away for half a second, though his gaze locked on mine; he said, "I have a psychiatrist. I'm currently... I just started."

I pointed to the woman and said, "Is she your psychiatrist?"

"No, she's not my psychiatrist."

Eight seconds of direct, unshifting eye contact elapsed. I muttered, "That's no way to be treating her."

"Okay..."

"That's no way to be... *behaving.*"

"Yes sir I understand; that's just why I'm getting help."

The woman said, "Thank you very much," and interjected as an afterthought, "for the concern."

I nodded at both. The man continued to stare at me while the woman spoke: "We won't have anymore loud... altercations like that again." The door creaked from being pushed closed and I shifted my gaze between both. The woman said, "You have a nice day okay?"

The man, indignant, said, "We apologize for the noise, sir."

The woman, desperate, said, "We really do."

I said, "Thank you," and the door shut as I turned my back.

For the first night in two weeks, all is quiet.

Tuesday, March 17th, 2020

8:26 PM

Candy has employed me at her shop as a commission-based employee (30% each sale) paid "under the table" in the wake of the Covid-19 pandemic that has gripped the world with panic, to my amusement; to watch my species teeter with madness over the slightest amount of chaos incites a shudder through my spine. On my first day employed at the shop, I stood and edited at a makeshift standing desk at the front counter while a little over half a dozen customers siphoned in and out throughout my eight-hour shift. Each being is strange to me. I reckon myself reflected in each person yet identify with no one.

Spoken interactions are moments that I feel locked in stasis, pitted against an alternate will that desires to extract something from me: attention, time, labor, money, affection, or an outlet for the ego. "Love," as we name *it,* is a warped rendition of compassion and sympathy. Empathy is true "love," and the word "empathy" could do without the subtext. Even killers may "love" their victims.

A man flipped through pages of my publication (Year Two) on one of Candy's shelves. The man chuckled, nodded his head, and tilted the book towards his teenage son, who looked on. "We're all on the rat-race treadmill to nowhere," read the man to his son, "I like that," and he set the book back on the shelf.

10:42 PM

I had recorded forty-two minutes of an eleven-card Celtic cross tarot reading with R.J and had planned to transcribe the session. On reflection and further investigation of tarot card readings and interpretations, I realized the folly of my vacuous spiritualism. I had been spooked—by *my own* interpretation of the meaning of each card concerning the other. The tarot reading is a tool for one to introspect, finalize conclusions, and plan initiatives based on what the individual attributes to the card descriptions—to their own state of mind.

Spooked by ~~the tarot reading~~ my self-engrossed fascinations in regard to the cards and my upcoming plans. Any arrangement of cards, and I would've perceived the same outcome due to my preconceived *will.*

I conjured a self-story from the cards, and instead of relaying the technicalities of each individual card meaning, placement, and relation to other cards, I will write myself a fable in typical metanonfictional style:

The Tale of a Foolish Man

A young man sought to establish himself as a martyr for his ego's sake to the detriment of everyone who loved him. He forsook his home, disowned his parentage on a cruel whim of fanciful delusions, and would hear no one but the shadows of his mind.

The man illusioned calumny and danger and he projected these fears onto all who desired to assuage his burdens. Wracked by emotional despair, he thought of nothing but his ambitions and the success for which he aspired.

Many would-be friends vied for the man's comradery; the generous and kind among them found themselves abandoned and deprived of the affection which each, in turn, had hoped to receive. The man blinded himself with amorality and relished in despondency, empowered by the metronomic output of futile labor.

Disillusioned with what he once deemed sacrosanct and noble, the man, beset by a ruinous state, strove to overcome his fear of self-defamation, contemplated a divergent life path, and reunited with his begetter, thereby reconciling with consciousness, as *it* is.

One man's cards are another man's bullshit.
Bah—a fable! Replace all instances of "man" with "ape."

Wednesday, March 18th, 2020

2:02 PM

While regions of the world panic from the elderly and infants experiencing hastened deaths on account of Covid-19, I stand in an aromatic shop tucked away in the nook of a courtyard beneath the upscale apartment of my employer/lover and listen to Beethoven's *Symphony No. 3.* My illusions are comfortable.

9:11 PM

On a commercial airplane from the city of Buffalo in New York to the city of Salt Lake City in Utah, three-hundred and seventy-seven passengers occupied themselves on-route. Whispered conversations, muffled snores, cries of children, and the annoyed sighs of readers resounded at various intervals.

"I wipe my ass with fast-food napkins," said a 198 lb man dressed in a green t-shirt, beige cargo shorts, and yellow runner shoes, to a 123 lb woman dressed in a blue summer dress and brown clogs, seated next to him on the airplane. The man's face scrunched inward with an expression of someone who had frowned for most of their life. Three inflamed pimples triangulated a flaky forehead overgrown with two enormous brown eyebrows with an inch of separation between each patch of hair, spanned over a pair of deep-set hazel-blue eyes. Faded burn scars on the man's fingertips etched down to the center of both palms and outspread in the pattern of a wispy spiral. The man's reddened forearms rested bare on the shared armrests. The flesh around his upper arm, where the shirt's sleeves began, grew a crosshatched abundance of thick brown hair. Nostril hairs fluttered with every exhale and stilled with every inhale of laborious breathing.

The thirty-six-year-old woman, who had miscarried two days ago, sat with her feet pressed together, wrung her hands against the top of her thighs, rotated her neck to toss a lock of blonde hair away from the front of her face, arched her back, grunted, sniffed once, and said, "There are no fast-food napkins on an airplane."

The man pushed himself off the seat, stood in a partial squat, retrieved a small yellow backpack from the rectangular compartment above him, unzipped one of the three front pockets, removed a frayed tuft of brown paper napkins, clenched the bundle in his fist, and smirked.

"Oh, I see," said the woman.

Friday, March 20th, 2020

11:24 AM

Covid-19 has impaired the economy and killed over 100,000 people.

In-store business in Candy's shop is negligible, though I have begun work full-time as an undocumented employee setting up an online website for her business while stationed in her shop-by-day, and enjoying her company by night.

Last night, asleep in Candy's bed, I dreamed of pulling an old friend out from a car fire by his legs after he leapt into the flames.

10:45 PM

My shift at *Anomalies and Artifacts* ended and I visited the grocery store. Three women wore face masks and one old woman wore blue medical gloves beneath her shawl's sleeves.

The man in front of me bought two half-gallons of ice cream for $9.62.

The woman behind me bought four cans of *Chef Boyardee* ravioli for $6.39.

I bought twelve sweet potatoes for $5.18.

I checked out, surrounded by unhappy people, and "farmer's-carried" potatoes one mile back to my apartment.

Saturday, March 21ˢᵗ, 2020

4:09 PM

I stand in Candy's shop and have been informed that there have been no customers all day prior to my arrival. The global hysteria pervades human interactions. The day taxes are due has been delayed by ninety days for those with an annual income lower than $10 million. Interest paid on student loans has been halted. The stock market teeters on the verge of a recession. Infection rates ascend across America.

While I stand, I wonder why I write at all, and even more, why I publish. Death would be "the dream" fulfilled, no matter the agony endured. We animals hasten to preserve our mortal coils, enraptured by the idea of our own existences. By writing *this, now,* I delay the editing of yesteryears writings, locked into a mode of self-imposed slavery to myself; what would I be if otherwise?—a man, of what manner? I've no desire to *know.*

I'm overwhelmed with half-hearted sadness, a rare sentiment nowadays, a notion I haven't felt since being stood among the ranks of young recruits at Navy boot camp: Sadness on behalf of the machinations and dealings of others. From one station to another, I flit among those who vie for something more. I reflect the looking-glass mirror on myself and reckon the same, expressed *here,* to the judgment of whoever reads, and to myself in the future for having the gall to return to these words. J.S. Bach's: *Kommt, eilet und laufet, BWV 249 - 2. Adagio* resonates from a turntable-themed stereo. Surrounded by trinkets and baubles of no inherent value beneficial to being, I dawdle.

Sunday, March 22nd, 2020

11:39 PM

The ceiling above my bathroom began to leak after my upstairs neighbor showered. Water poured from the interior of a ventilation unit into my tub.

There being no meaning to existence is difficult to accept with grace. To apply meaning to one's life is gauche. Video games and drugs are a temptation though I've avoided these outlets for years. Many other people with ambitions would agree, though I've no ideal to attain; thus, I've departed from my own notions and have arrived where I've begun on my journey of "enlightenment."

I communicate daily with my father by email and plan to reunite with him in September if the U.S. airlines haven't been dismantled due to negligence on account of the Covid-19 pandemic. We plan to board a trawler together, to live on, and to sail the east coast, through the panama canal, and up the west coast, over several years, while we stop at ports along the way. I'll be reduced to a twenty-nine-year-old man living with my father in his basement until then.

I write of the future, yet I could die tomorrow—tonight, and what difference would there be? Grief?—for an ephemeral fraction of "time," and still, my death would be meaningless, much like this document. Yet, I'm happy. Candy cooked me the best (spicy) fish soup I've ever eaten after we committed to her online website's final details. The sex is great; the coffee is strong; the work is fulfilling, and I live day-by-day. Yes, I've no idea what I am or what this document means—not to me—I *know* what *it* means to me, but what *it* means as a product; I speculate: absolutely nothing. My books are a method to maintain my vital essence, a perpetual void to squander my money, an incentive to stay on the treadmill of a self-imposed perception of abundance.

I reel back from all the life I witness, at a loss, bombarded with inputs and sentiments of others, confined to each of our own realities as they are. I may write of my entire life story down to the finest details of delicate moments. The intimacy shared with Candy, how we watch the morning news chaos and comment on the charade of the prompters, and our nights of indulgence with red wine and wedges of gourmet cheese, with a finale of a few romps in her bedroom—I *could*—oh, *I* could write of *it* for the sake of myself, though I'd rather sit and brood on account of wonder, for how minuscule I am, and the wretchedness of my humanity. I think of nothing but peanut butter and bananas now, and how I may entertain myself for the next hour before I retire to my floor and doze off to the sound of sporadic bursts of dripping water against the basin of my tub two rooms away.

Wednesday, March 25th, 2020

9:26 AM

A decrepit old man with a half-crescent top of frazzled grey hair sauntered at a pace of 0.5 mph towards a gas station. A dirty, plain brown t-shirt concealed a bloated abdomen. His body skewed left and right with each labored step, stiff and board-like—a shambler, a veritable vintage movie zombie. I thought to myself, *"Some people are incredibly deplorable."* The man spotted me as I marched with long strides towards the gas station where he headed. We locked eyes. I nodded at the man and aimed to pass him by, though he stopped, turned towards me, smiled, and called out across the crumbled parking lot, "Can I ask you a question?"

I said, "Sure," slowed my gait to a slight amble, and veered towards him with no intention to breach a six-foot distance between us on account of the Covid-19 pandemic hysteria in conjunction with his unsatisfactory image of what a human being is capable of reducing themself to.

The man outstretched both hands towards me, skewed at the elbow, and said, "Do you have a cigarette?"

"No."

"You don't?"

"No, I don't have a cigarette."

"God bless you; have a great day."

Littered streets are comparable to dumps, albeit the refuse in dumps is out of view and not a blemish to a neighborhood's aesthetic. Regardless of where the trash and garbage is, *it* still exists.

I tell myself this while I walk my hour home through sideroads and observe the copious amounts of plastic waste scattered around lawns, sidewalks, gutters, and patios. Are we not trash ourselves? I compile waste and trash in my home within cardboard boxes and discard the contents when a box becomes overstuffed into a community dumpster in my neighborhood. Whether the contents are discarded into a landfill or incinerated and sent up in a plume of smoke into the atmosphere is irrelevant to *existence*. A flattened *McDonald's* plastic drink cup, straw and lid included, is equally as natural as the human eye that perceives *it*.

A homeless man cradled a small toy dog in both arms while he held a sign at one of downtown's busiest intersections; he hailed me and used the dog as a ploy in his ruse: "If you spare a few dollars I can feed this guy tonight," he began, and segued into an exposition of his love for the dog. The man's sign read, **"Spare Money? God Bless."**

I listened to him prattle on, *begging*, for forty seconds, and said, "Why do you own a dog if you can't provide for yourself?"

"I can provide for him—I only got him about a month ago."

Two women, also homeless and equipped with signs, stood at adjacent street corners and meandered in-place. I said to the homeless man, "Why do beggars always use god as a ploy?"

"I never use God as a ploy—no-" said the homeless man, "I never do that."

"Your sign says, 'God Bless.'"

"Yeah I guess *it* does."

"Why?"

"Uh—well I think *it's* respectful and nice." He glowered at me.

"Don't you think that beggars use god as a psychological ploy so that whoever rejects them will feel guilt and perhaps change their mind?"

The homeless man turned from me, straight-faced, indignant, and said, "You're right." He yelled to the woman across the road: "Hey, come get Kevin (the dog); come get Kevin now!"

I had already resumed my walk away from the intersection when (I presume) the homeless man glanced my way and saw me go. He called after me, words I didn't hear over the wind and a passing car, though I sensed the hostility in his tone, hence my early leave, the coward that I am.

Thursday, March 26th, 2020

7:10 PM

I spent the morning with Candy's seven-year-old son, Midnight, and cooked an omelet for each of us. The boy reminds me of myself at his age: an untarnished template with similar aptitudes. He waited several days to warm-up to me and had analyzed my behavior from a safe distance, though once he initiated an interaction, the conversation between us had been loquacious.

The United States now leads the world in confirmed Covid-19 cases. God bless America.

I wait on Candy's couch after a shift in her shop while she showers. The Benedictine monks resonate from the television, selected by her on my behalf. We dine on salmon with crackers and cheese tonight.

Friday, March 27th, 2020

7:26 PM

I woke early in Candy's bed, showered, dressed, and departed from the second-floor balcony, to her locked garage below, where I hid for half-an-hour, awaiting Midnight to be dropped off by his father.

I've been tasked to assemble the boy's computer this morning. Years have elapsed since I last laid hands on a component.

I *feel* as though my character has reverted, that all "progress" achieved and thoughts distilled on the study of phenomenology and epistemology have been disentangled from my psyche. I *think* as a fool, while I type on the cardboard box of a helium canister designed to fill balloons in Candy's garage. My need to defecate is urgent, yet I stand in this dimly lit—yet well-kept space, stocked and furnished with out-modeled furniture and forgotten trinkets.

7:52 PM

My need to defecate overwhelmed me and incited me to behave as a wild animal. I fled the garage, locked the door behind me, and sped to the adjacent shop less than a block away. I slung my backpack off and commenced with defecation. While I exerted myself over the toilet, I spied the head of Midnight's father pass by the large arched shop window. If I had deliberated only a minute more, the ruse would've been compromised. How all people lie in our own little manners, devoid of moral scrutinization when the lens is turned inward, continues to intrigue me.

I ventured back upstairs for an omelet, coffee, and a dose of Candy's television broadcasting news of the pandemic—by my request. I *must* be informed of the wretchedness of the world through a fourth-party outlet. *Wash your hands!*

Saturday, March 28th, 2020

9:01 PM

Candy pays me $30 per day for eight hours of work. The arrangement we agreed on for an extra 30% commission payment has been unfruitful due to zero in-store customers. Before my shift ended, Candy called me by the shop phone and offered to pay for my dinner via food delivery; she sent me the menu by email and I declined due to the outrageous prices. Part of our aforementioned arrangement is that low pay is compensated for by her food offerings, coffee, and use of her kitchen. The arrangement reminds me of my previous "under-the-table" employer, Chloe, with whom I also developed a romantic relationship with. With Candy, the relationship developed first, yet now, the work has usurped the romance, at least for me.

Over the phone, Candy informed me there is no need to check-in with her at her apartment before I go. I said, "I want to discuss my pay."

Candy's voice hushed and she became overwrought with emotion. Distraught, she relayed to me her financial burdens and the total cost of her business in conjunction with reduced customers due to Covid-19, and confirmations of how my request for more pay is beyond her means unless I reduce my hours to only fifteen-a-week to meet my expectation of $8 an hour. We agreed on those terms; this would be fine with any other employer, though this peculiar relationship I have with Candy rendered her entangled with an inexplicable, suppressed feeling while she spoke over the phone. I had said, "I didn't mean to upset you," while she disclaimed her inability to increase my wages.

A severance has occurred; there is a rift between us now—there always has been, only dulled by fancies and illusions. I confirm to myself once more that all interactions are manipulations whether positive or negative, and that all of life is a grand, ephemeral orgy of consumption, an exchange, validation of egos.

9:25 PM

Often, this journal is as necessary to me as eating and breathing, not for the potential profits, fame, or social leverage which is bound to accrue simply due to my actions, and not on account of talent or merit, but for the validation, the meaning, and the introspection. Out of all the nonsensical panderings I ever speak, nothing compares to the refined word—never a writer, *just* a typist—what I *type* to my screen is of more value to me than any conversation; my screen is a release which I will one day revise via screen, digest once more, and continue in whatever state I may be in at a future point. What *it* all means mystifies me; there is no other way to be, *to be* content: mystified—a grade higher than ignorant, on th My Hero, by Foo Fighters (1994) e cusp of knowledge without any hint of understanding.

Sunday, March 29th, 2020

10:40 AM

I'm amazed by everything I am, for what humanity has become. Screens resonate above and adjacent to me in different homes. People purchase things they don't need to feel emotions that don't need to be felt. Curb your enthusiasm, put down the fork, and think for a moment.

In my youth I desired, though I don't recall what—that's how much these ambitions mattered. Works of art be damned, from culture to culture. I think of the infinite manners in which a human being may develop and scoff at my own proclamations, convictions, delusions—my *thoughts* are nothing but an occluded mire, yet what else is there but to think-

"There goes my hero, *watch him* as *he goes!*" [11] blares from my ceiling.

---

[11] *My Hero,* by Foo Fighters (1994)

The young couple wakes me each morning with rambunctious play and their overweight dog. The two cough together after each puff of marijuana. "There goes my hero, *watch him as he goes!*" What thoughts did I have earlier? I won't bother to reread, better to be derailed from my previous existence.

Monday, March 30th, 2020

8:40 PM

Candy wrote to me:
"Do you know I have strong feelings for you? I care for you. When we are in bed together, I believe you know or can feel my heart. Those times when you give me a sweet goodbye kiss you look into my eyes as though you are speaking to me, and I feel such contentment with your arms around me. I have no idea what your thoughts may be though. I do feel physically bonded to you because of the sex and as such I have no desire to be touched intimately by anyone else."

I wrote to Candy:
"I've thought long on my feelings of you and am dispirited, not on account of what we've experienced up till now, but because of my inclinations and the other man involved. I think affairs would proceed in your best interest if you heeded and returned Frank's affections. I know nothing of the man other than what you've relayed to me, and what I've deduced is that he has your genuine interest at heart and is capable of assisting you by means far more significant than I could. I don't proceed to tell you this out of self-pity or jealousy, rather, a holistic perspective of the scenario. Frank obviously experiences feelings for you far more intense than my own and can support you in ways I am unable, whereas I'm reminiscent of a mercenary, loyal to only myself—despite our romance, where I realize my role is something 'on the side,' so to speak.

"I can only speculate why you've brought Frank to my attention on as many instances as you have, and of why you have informed me of your in-depth unsavory history—I presume as a means to level our interaction on account of you reading my journal—to be as forthright as possible; however, in doing so, you have induced me to think of outcomes beyond my realm of feasible comprehension in regards to if we were to disengage from our romantic dealings and remain as friends, or even as an employer to employee relationship. Anything of substance I may offer you is purely emotional and sexual gratification. If you were to channel your affections to Frank instead of being in a state of disparity and entrenched in self-sustained drama, I think you'd be better off, from a survival perspective.

"The cart has been put before the horse in how I've relayed this to you and I presume my assumptions and conclusions may have surprised or offended you. I've affirmed my external reasons before my own internal feelings to hopefully negate any negative feelings you may experience on account of my decision: I think we should continue as employee/employer and nothing more if you are still comfortable with this arrangement. We've had our intimacy together and I've enjoyed your personal company more than anyone I've ever developed a romantic relationship with within this condensed period. There is no one else that influenced my decision: no strumpet nor bar wench. I'm ready to be alone in my personal affairs and think *it*'s for the best; I hope you understand."

APRIL

Wednesday, April 1st, 2020

8:52 AM

I've terminated my romantic and intimate relationship with Candy.

882,000 people have been infected with Covid-19 worldwide, with 42,000 deaths.

188,000 have been cases in the U.S., with 4,000 deaths.

I began my shift yesterday at Candy's shop from 11 AM until 7 PM for my new negotiated wage of $8/hr.

Sadness welt inside me while I photographed and measured shop items: the telltale budding of self-pity for the relationship I had relinquished. I quelled this feeling the moment I felt *it* arise in me and reminded myself of the endless possibilities in which I may suffer genuinely. Gratitude elevated me from my gloom: a delusion of reference.

11:08 AM

I crossed paths with Lewis, the African-American man I resided with for three months last year after a bout of homelessness. I couldn't help but to beam from ear-to-ear; he walked to the grocery store with his new Caucasian escort, as we used to. I passed him, and felt an emotional expression I haven't felt for years overtake me: bashful, as a well-cared for dog encounters an abandoned master.

Lewis moved to shake my hand, to grasp my shoulders—hell, to *kiss* me for all I know, though I veered past, *bashful* as I had been. Lewis' dumpy companion stole quick glances at me and kicked at the dirt he trod over; I reckoned a prisoner of his own becoming—a sexual slave to Lewis' fancies.

Lewis said, "I heard my old upstairs neighbors are your new upstairs neighbors."

I blinked, bewildered. The recollection flooded back to me; the obnoxious marijuana-smoking music-blaring couple above me had been above me at my *last* residence—*and* had purchased marijuana from Lewis, who is probably *still* their dealer.

Lewis continued, "I heard what you did; they told me what you said to them."

I remained stationary, at a loss for what to say; there had been nothing to say.

Lewis said, "I thank you for that, really—the guy needed to hear *it* from someone."

I shrugged and shifted to turn once more.

"Where are you going?" Lewis said, and I showed my back and continued to walk. "Hey!" he yelled.

I stopped and pivoted to face him from across the street.

Lewis threw both arms up and said, "I don't hate you, man!"

"I don't hate you either!"

*"It'*s good to see you."

I lightened my inflection and said, *"It'*s good to see you too, Lewis."

Lewis' posture stiffened; standing sideways to me and staring straight down the road to my right, he said, "All right," and proceeded with his flummoxed companion.

Thursday, April 2nd, 2020

8:49 AM

More turmoil and belligerence from upstairs kept me awake until midnight. I dressed to interfere once more and suppressed myself. The woman is just as, if not more, vitriolic and antagonistic as the man. In my first dealings, I represented myself as a "white knight," though this is anything but true. I desire ~~peace and~~ quiet serenity, undisturbed by the dramatic stage act of two dissipated youth. The welfare of either is moot; therefore, I remained in my apartment and nursed my indignance until the petulant screaming and obnoxious battering on the floor and walls above evolved to a tearful and muttered conversation.

3:00 PM

I stock a store that is doomed to failure, along with the other businesses. I fumble with the veritable corpses of misplaced trinkets all day, snap photographs, and measure dimensions.

5:46 PM

There should never be preventative measures enacted worldwide in the case of pandemics. Systems should already be in place to care for the afflicted while the status quo is maintained. The sooner the entire populace becomes infected, the better off humanity will be. *Yes,* there will be *more* human deaths if preventative measures aren't enacted, though, *for the species,* this isn't "bad"; the Darwinian principle applies.

In this current humanitarian system (which is inevitable due to the ego), every human life is precious, and the world economy sustains a blow *to progress* due to our preventative measures. Progress!—isn't that why we're here—the continuation of the species and the development of civilization for the sake of who we beget? Is stymying a global operations efficiency to spare 5%-10% of the population a health-induced death a humanitarian cause?

Instead of opening the metaphorical floodgates and embracing the virus with courage, we wall ourselves off from each other and continue to gorge ourselves with information—*yes*—the information *pertinent* to the pandemic that, if we had been ignorant to *it,* would *enable* us to *be* courageous—in our culminated ignorance!

10:41 PM

A muscled man with a crew cut slouched back in a padded chair and stared at a screen. The man's girlfriend paced through the arched opening between a living room and kitchen. Every fourth pass past the man's screen, she stole a terrible glance over her shoulder and grimaced. "Babe."

The man said nothing. A mouse clicked and a keyboard clattered.

The woman repeated, *"Babe."*

"The man pulled a headset off his ears and said, "What!"

"Do you want the chicken baked or fried?"

"Fried in *what?*"

"A pan."

The man's eyes bulged and he looked through the woman's abdomen at a yellow bean bag chair pressed up against a wall painted navy blue with white trim. "Is *it* breasts?"

"Of course."

"How many?"

"Like, nine or ten."

"Jesus."

"They were on sale."

"Just bake them."

"Okay."

The man returned the headphones to his ears and looked back to his screen. He read *"10,878 viewers"* and focused on his game. A warrior outfitted with light leather armor gripped an enormous two-handed hammer, controlled by a mouse and keyboard input. 10,901 people now watched the man play since the last twenty-four seconds that he checked the viewer count. Some paid money by the month in support of his efforts. The man said something inconsequential and watched the chat window. A steady influx of one to six-word comments responded at a rate faster than he could read. One light in the corner of the living room illuminated his monitor desk. A plastic raspberry yogurt container with the lid still attached at one side and a metal spoon dipped in a pool of remnants emanated a faint aroma. The man blinked four times in one minute.

Friday, April 3rd, 2020

10:40 AM

In an adjacent bedroom, the woman donned a virtual reality headpiece and aligned herself at the center of a seven-by-eight foot area devoid of furnishings. A small bed, one chair, and a vanity to the south of the pink room had been long neglected. The woman gesticulated with open hands by her waist and said, "Hey Deborah... Yeah he's out there screaming again... At the game... No... I don't know... Are you getting lag? My lag... Yeah I'm—nevermind, I'm good. Hey, so... Hey—*Deborah*, do you want to go to the dunes today?"

Reality outside of the woman's reality lapsed onward, though the reality contained within her reality had been subjected to the same bounds as *it*s container. There had been no difference; the value within either is imperative to both.

11:07 AM

The widespread philosophical belief in the existence of a soul perturbs me. I believe in the flesh of an avocado to nourish me, the flame that will burn me, the water that vitalizes me; however, I've no desire to think of anything beyond my sensory stimulus any longer. Let me be a lamb again, a babe of no sensibility, of no reason, birthed from the womb; let my desires be simple and bestial. I have conformed to the baseness of humanity, yet

I've never been anything more. I delude myself, then, if I am to believe that the myriad of thoughts and circumstances I've experienced throughout my life elevates me from my humanity in any way. My delusions were once a delight; now, they are a burden—resolute, for they are shapeshifters and doppelgangers, never to dissipate.

Saturday, April 4th, 2020

4:57 PM

I confronted the young man upstairs while the woman was away about the noise output and amended my situation.

I don't know of a single activity worth doing. My publisher is an efficient scam company and I intend to pay them until my death. The act of writing and editing is moot. I write nothing worth reading. The reader is *genuinely* a fool; whoever you are, you may believe this to be comical or a satire whenever my thoughts delve to these domains, but I am sincere in my expression of contempt.

Covid-19 cases worldwide have reached 1.2 million, with 65,000 deaths.

This journal means nothing to me yet *is* me. Already I weary of this template, after only four years. Fiction is dull empathy fodder and nonfiction is regurgitated trite we all experience with different adjectives to color the *"flavor."* I've degenerated in character and purpose—yet feel more holistic and pure than ever before, as if I've discovered my true calling of existence: *nothing.* Absolutely nothing.

Books are an antiquated media. I am one of the last of my kind, a proponent of decadence.

"Then, there are books which are most *pernicious* in their influence. There are all grades and degrees of evil in this class. Some of them carry a *subtle poison* in their atmosphere which is noxious to those who breathe it. We need to keep most careful watch over our heart, so that nothing shall ever tarnish *it*s purity. Any corrupt thought, dallied with even for a moment, leaves a *stain upon the mind* which may never be effaced."

- J.R. Miller

6:00 PM

The man and woman upstairs scream at each other about an abortion. The woman wants *it;* the man doesn't want *it.* Both threaten the other with ultimatums.

9:57 PM

My mind is befouled with glorious stains. I wish to die and know not what I wish. I wish freely, knowing wishes amount to nothing. Life is a wish.

10:12 PM

I thought I had overcome the existential nonsense. I pander with myself and spill the feelings into my keyboard with the hopeful knowledge that my writing will remain obscure despite my proliferations until the annihilation of the human race. I think of what thoughts I have, and know that a fool would appreciate some droll fiction right about now as far as the pacing of this book applies, yet all I feel is a hollowed misery—and would normally cease to write—*ah,* type!—under normal circumstances.

Though this is a special occasion, for I listen to my internal dialogue and expel the narrative to a template; I have nothing better to do with my time; I know I'm not alone in this matter, yet the relative comparison with my fellow pitiable men and women fails to console me. I may type an entire book of my mental agony and provide authentic entertainment; this is what being human is. Positivity is entrenchment with a delusion. Every environment and set of people I've been affiliated with throughout life has invigorated me with hope and wonder for the first few *hours;* however, this is a mere fancy. The layers always fade—a *peeling back* of what bombastic and jubilant behavior conceals: *Not* a soul, *just* a *thing*—something naked and lurid.

Sunday, April 5th, 2020

9:03 PM

This is a fatuous journal of a fool, destined to be read only by fools. Behold, my lack of talent and purpose:

"Baethan,

"If I may, share some sentiments on the personal side? Your email that you were finished with our 'relationship' was a surprise and *it* did hurt. I don't want you to think the indifference I treat you with at work represents how I felt personally about your withdrawal from my bed and my life.

"You were loved. I did love you. I just didn't say *it* to you with words. Time spent with you was special and meaningful to me and I am thankful for *it*. I meant *it* with my whole heart when I said I would honor your decision and respect *it*. *It* was sudden and I didn't feel like I got to properly tell you how I felt. You were not a fling or used. I feel we shared mutually ourselves and I am grateful. I want for your happiness, alone or with whom you choose.

"Time will heal my heart and you will be a favorite scar on *it*. I would do *it* all again. I don't regret *it*. I do of course wish there had been more time to explore, but I am the curious sort and there may have been no end to my want of you. Thank you for being loving and kind and gentle. I have many wonderful memories to reflect on for comfort and consolation.

"Sincerely,
"Candy"

I responded:

"Candy,

"You had once asked me while we lay beside each other in your bed of the last time that I had cried and I failed to answer. The night I had requested severance of our intimate relationship and you accepted, I cried while I laid on my floor to sleep. I hadn't expected to, felt foolish to, and I shed tears now while I type this, partly due to revulsion of myself and of what being human entails, partly for your sake—for the pain I hadn't desired to inflict on you, and partly for my own decision and the consequential state of being by which I subject myself.

"I haven't processed my feelings in full. I didn't want to develop feelings at all, though I had, and this discomfited me. I decided to spare myself exacerbated future grief at a time when I thought the circumstances would be in alignment with a beneficial outcome for both of us. I'm resolute in my statement that my relationship with you had been the best I've ever experienced—not on account of my initiation, I've discovered, but for what we experienced and how you treated—and continue, to treat me.

"My time is spent in solitude now, just as I prefer to be. I'm grateful for what we shared, for your compassion, and empathy most of all. I'd prefer not to be a scar; instead, an ephemeral affliction you've recovered from, a case of Covid-19.

"–Baethan"

Monday, April 6th, 2020

7:37 PM

"I'm going fucking crazy!" shouted the woman upstairs.
"I'm going fucking crazy too!" the man shouted in response.
I beat on my ceiling thrice with the end of a broomstick.
The woman shouted, "We know!—okay!"
I yelled, "You're going crazy, huh? Well here's a fucking reality check!" This had been effective for forty-minutes. Soon after, I heard the man scuffle onto the floor with the woman. He shouted at the top of his lungs, "Get rid of that fucking baby!" and began to sob. Between wails, the woman managed to shout, *"It's* part of you—part of us!"
"It's not me! *I* am all of me!" the man retorted, and my ceiling began to throttle. I imagine them on the floor, his hands gripped tight around the woman's shoulders, tears streaming down both of their cheeks, and I'm grateful for where I stand, alone, with this document to tell the tale to. A gross case of domestic manipulation, nauseating to the core. Something breaks. The man threatened to leave her if she doesn't commit to an abortion; consequently, he will be subjected to child support payments for eighteen years, and he knows *it;* therefore, there is wrath, and he frames the cause of his rage as "love" for her. The man forsakes his responsibility, as per the law—enforced upon him. He proclaims of being unable to support a child, of not being ready—oh yes, they certainly aren't prepared. The woman clings to the emotional spectrum, of the beauty of life, of the

father's genetic material that will ensure an attractive baby despite the lack of a father. The state substitutes a father. The only victim is the baby.

Moments akin to this bring to mind antinatalism. We were all babies once; we never asked to be born, just as the two above me who now contemplate their suffering and the inevitable suffering of the unborn, though neither is aware. The man and the woman reckon only their rational thoughts, mired in emotion.

8:57 PM

On my return from picking up my clean clothes from the neighborhood laundry room, I found a piece of lined notebook paper folded and taped to my door:

"I'm sorry, unexplainably sorry about how annoying we must be. Me and My girl friend are dealing with very hard and life-changing news right now. We are both stressed and broke, and very on edge. I understand that we must be quite loud from above. Once again I'm very sorry for disturbing your peace."

Wednesday, April 8th, 2020

7:38 AM

Circa 2010-2015, a middle-aged woman named Joan lived in Germany and accrued fame for herself by promoting self-mutilation on an online venue. Caucasian, with long brown hair and brown eyes, her features amounted to an attractive face if not for her malformed body.

The cutting began with dozens of three-inch horizontal swipes with a straight razor across the tops of both thighs, along the rib cage, and along both arms. Among these cuts, Joan managed to inflict severe open-wounds: gaping gashes, often severed down to the bone. Joan found solace in posting images of these wounds online and managed to establish a modest fanbase that encouraged and supported her efforts.

Buckets of blood situated atop crimson-stained rags served as a backdrop for Joan's poses. She allowed her wounds to heal through self-care and proceeded immediately with a new slew of mutilations to satisfy and nurture her fanbase. In one instance, Joan slit her arms from the shoulders to the middle of her forearms, slashing until the razor dragged across bone.

The exposed bone surrounded by dripping muscle tissue captivated her internet audience and they demanded more from Joan; she obeyed, and proceeded to gouge at the flesh at the bottom of her calf until she struck the tibia bone. For one picture, Joan wedged a pair of tweezers behind the tibia and applied pressure to protrude the bone outward.

Within a year, Joan had progressed through more than five series of mutilation sessions; however, she had yet to be satisfied, along with her blood-thirsty following. Layers of scars had formed and distended the flesh of Joan's arms and legs with irregular rows of dark-pink lines and premature wrinkles. Joan refrained from affecting most of her torso except for seven three-inch carvings around her navel and one dozen hypodermis-deep incisions above each breast.

While Joan practiced basic first-aid at home with disinfectant and wide-area bandages, she performed a feat that would mark her for life by gouging five quarter-inch-deep lines across her right cheek: three vertical, two horizontal, cross-thatched. She thrived on her renown and continued to ravage her flesh despite the impairment of all her limbs. Joan traced razors around old scars and connected new bone-deep wounds with the former. Her boyfriend cared for her throughout the endeavor and enabled the chronic behavior beyond his realm of control. Hundreds of two-inch-long horizontal cuts spanned across each arm and leg in rows reminiscent of a bloody 2D staircase and developed into one single row of bloated scars on either side of poorly-tended lesions that continued to glisten and cause Joan severe agony for years. Heedless of her own pain, Joan persisted in her ruthless venture and managed to slice open any trace of unmarred skin on all four limbs. With no recourse except to heal, Joan relished in her bloodsport and posted numerous photos of her maimed and deformed body online, to her fans' delight.

By the time Joan's body fully recovered, the craterous and tender remnants of her deeds remained etched over her limbs, resembling a bloated corpse; Joan expressed disdain for her followers with gestures of hate in the final images she posted, striking poses with her warped figure. Joan's provocations only incited her fans to lambast and encourage her to "finish the job."

Joan's online presence faded soon after; the posting ceased and her fanbase dispersed. Most speculate that Joan did commit suicide as her fans had suggested, while others believe her to be alive and unwell, struggling day-to-day with mental duress and her body as a testament to her self-hatred: a haunting memory for those who saw her, and a baneful reality for herself.

Thursday, April 9th, 2020

4:09 PM

Today marks a monumental day for me. After three-and-a-half years of abstention from all entertainment and media except for writing, reading, music, and documentaries, I have purchased a Playstation 4 Pro and a 42-inch 4k television; both are set up on my kitchen counter atop two stacks of empty shipping boxes: a makeshift standing desk in my kitchen.

Foolish reader, I rejoice, for my return to the digital worlds I have previously forsaken instills me with joy! I urge you to quit reading this perpetual document now, for this day marks the end of my absolution and conviction. I am not the man I was three years ago, or anytime in between. Even now, while *you* read this, I am certainly dead, or have advanced beyond these proclamations in life. Let my work be a testament to the folly of man; egotistical creatures that we are… ah, I am *excited*. The realms of (action) role-playing and strategy games await. Thank you, Hidetaka Miyazaki.

Friday, April 10th, 2020

8:08 PM

On my way to Candy's shop, I encountered a ploy of what I thought to be two homeless men standing at the popular intersection of downtown. One: A short-statured middle-aged Caucasian man, held an uninspired cardboard sign with the words, **"NEED HELP"** written in bold black marker. The other, a taller African-American man, paced short distances on a sidewalk adjacent to the sign-holder. From an estimated 100 yards away, I watched the invariable sequence of vehicles rolling up to a red light and the driver ignoring both men. I presume the homeless men's tactics must be *somewhat* effective, otherwise, they would not return to the same position day after day with crude signs and hopes.

However, these men were *not* homeless; as I drew closer, I recognized the African-American man: Lewis, where I had encountered him on the same road weeks ago. He sauntered towards me on the opposite sidewalk and said, "You come walking this way now?"

I stopped, turned to him on the barren street devoid of traffic, smiled, shrugged, and said, "I'm here, aren't I?"

"Yo, where you headed man?"

I shook my head, chuckled, and moved to turn away.

"Hey-" he began, though the man I conversed with disgusted me; Lewis stood at the roadside to find new meat: indigent Caucasian men. I knew too well, and could conjure no emotion other than revulsion. Lewis sensed this, mirrored my turning, and said, "All right." We went our separate ways; myself, to build an online catalog for a novelty store for eight hours, and Lewis, to solicit the destitute.

Saturday, April 11th, 2020

12:26 PM

I'm disgusted with myself for how much I don't care.

My writing is trash; Candy promotes *it* out of a yearning to validate me for the sake of a resurgence of romance. I've no desire for any convoluted human interplay. I'm an attractive "autist," content with solitude and the liberty of my free will opposed to any other arrangement. I always think sex will elevate my functions, boost my mood, and vitalize my physiology. On the contrary, sex is draining; the dominance and assertion of masculine energy over the submissive female energy is a delusional prowess. Masturbation provides no satisfaction or relief; however, there are health benefits associated with a weekly climax; I strive to make each session brief, for while engaged in the act, I often imagine myself from a third-person perspective and reckon the creature that I am.

Sunday, April 12th, 2020

1:30 PM

"Read a few pages of a book a day, exercise three times a week, meditate, donate to a charity, and volunteer to support a cause you care about," said a life coach who graduated from Yale University while she stared at rows of towering skyscrapers and innumerable vehicles traversing roads at the base of each structure displayed on her phone screen.

The woman seated across from her sighed. Their eyes met, though neither saw the other, only templates for humanity. Both women enjoyed the contents of their screens, curated to their personal delight. The differences between how they indulged had been nugatory. There had been a sense of displacement in the sensibilities they shared at that moment; both women acknowledged the imminent state of death that loomed for them and they pitied each other for the ways that they spent their time until that point.

The life coach remained fixated on the screen and continued, "I recommend a charity or group that you're passionate about, one that makes you feel like you're contributing to a cause greater than yourself."

"What are you looking at?"

"A video of Berlin taken from a bird's eye view."

"Why?"

"I don't know. *It* was recommended to me on *Youtube*."

The woman seated across from the life coach sat in silence. She leaned forward and placed her chin on the knuckles of her clenched left fist.

The life coach shifted in her seat, set her phone face-down on a desk, and took in the sight of the woman before her, surrounded by the same teal walls of her office that she had known for over fourteen years, and said, "Why do you ask?"

"Just curious."

"Why are you *just* curious?"

"I wanted to judge you."

The life coach assumed a fake smile and said, "I thought so. What did you conclude?"

"You're just the person I need in my life."

The life coach reached forward and gripped the edges of the phone with her right hand and recoiled an inch—fingers curling, tips flat against the desk.

The woman has replayed this moment of the interaction between herself and her life coach each night while she lay in bed for 146 consecutive days; the memory is precious to her.

Monday, April 13th, 2020

6:45 PM

For the last two weeks, Candy has sent me four verbose messages, that, in essence, state her dissatisfaction and lack of comprehension with why I terminated our "romance." Candy expresses her guilt in pressing the matter, and claims to not know how to communicate with me; the extent of her loneliness and desperation undertones every word. She wishes to not be an intrusion, and sends me passages of *just* that affirmation, thereby rendering her an annoyance—at the least, though she has stated that she wishes to not be *that* either.

Thursday, April 16th, 2020

3:28 PM

An old man wearing sunglasses pulled open the door to *Anomalies and Artifacts* while I worked behind the counter and said, "Are you going to make *it*, man?"

I said, "Am I going to make what?"

"Are you going to make *it* through this crisis?"

"Oh yes, I think I will."

"Good," affirmed the man, and he allowed the door to swing closed with him on the other side. I watched him walk past the storefront out of view.

2,173,000 people have become infected with Covid-19 worldwide; 546,000 have recovered; 145,000 have died. There are 11 confirmed cases in the county where I live; 6 have recovered; 0 have died.

I ponder on this "crisis": a natural cycle of death and suffering, heeded with globalized awareness. President Trump's $1,200 payout to Americans who qualify (the majority), in the long-run, only creates expectations, laziness, dependency, and amplified decadence. There are the few who are viable, and there are those—such as myself—who have received ill-gotten gains for nothing. I feel no shame. The stimulus, as much of a boon as *it* may be, marks the decline of America; *it* is in opposition to the order of capitalism.

Friday, April 17th, 2020

6:43 PM

Candy's attempts to reinvigorate an intimate relationship with me know no bounds. What began as an innocent romp with a premature end has evolved into a rebarbative play of messages and face-to-face interactions

226

from her that serve only to ~~guilt~~ repulse me. I'm disgusted. My plans for future business with her regarding my books once I leave in September will be void if the emotional entanglement persists.

How I've recorded instances of other's messages in this document that I intend to publish is also a cause for disgust—of myself—for I could write of some absurd fiction trite, such as the story of a man who succeeds in disabling the internet worldwide, only to be undermined by a visit from an alien civilization aboard a mothership. One alien descends from the ship as an ambassador to earth and meets with the United Nations to diagnose and restore humanities' internet, due to: "Although our race garners nothing but contempt for humanity, we know how terrible *it* is to have no internet."

And—in two sentences, I conveyed the idea for fictitious entertainment and saved myself and the reader 1,500 or more words of dribble consisting of filler, e.g., character motives, plot, backstory, details of what the alien race looked like, the weather at the time of the United Nations meeting, the part where the man sat in his apartment with a plate of roast beef and mashed potatoes while he watched a live stream of the alien meeting with the United Nations after the internet is restored, thereby nullifying his work, and his reaction to the meeting—*also*—the conversation he had with his ex-girlfriend two hours before the meeting that changed his perspective of her for the rest of his life. The train ride that inspired the main character to disable the internet worldwide due to observing everyone around him engrossed with phone screens, and his follow-up four-page-long internal narrative had also been omitted.

Saturday, April 18th, 2020

10:32 PM

The vacuity of existence never ceases to amaze me.

A basketball bounces outside my apartment under the haze of a streetlight and a toddler yells from a second-floor balcony several residences away.

No matter where we are or what we do, the barrenness of *it* overwhelms me; there is no substance or essence to anything other than what we ascribe.

Men scurry around with digital notebooks and write a thesis on machine intelligence. The United States president languishes over the economy and wakes each morning with a distilled sense of dread and pompous ambition, which, in conjunction, produces a beast of a man. A drug cartel leader watches a live-recording of his two favorite whores being beheaded and feels nothing—he only thinks of how to exact revenge for the profit lost. An old Hawaiian woman wakes at the crack of dawn and prepares breakfast for her two grandchildren. An earthworm writhes towards an unknown destination.

What difference is there?

Sunday, April 19th, 2020

12:17 AM

From one screen to another.

A flash of lightning. The treble of thunder. The clan outside my window disperses to their respective shelters upon the onset of a sudden downpour. I listen to the rain, seated on my weight bench positioned in the center of the darkness of my living room. I close my eyes.

"Damn *it*'s comin' down fuckin' hard; what the fuck we gonna do? Why is *it* rainin'? Why is *it* rainin' so bad? Unbelievable." Three voices laugh. The voice directly outside my window continues to complain over the overwhelming deluge. I open my eyes and write about *it*.

9:44 AM

Consciousness will not be, and should never be fathomed.

I injured several muscles in my upper back from performing too many pullups and dip variations throughout each day for the past week. By the time I heal, all "progress" will be for naught.

I stare at this template and think of my thinking and the "nothing" I have reaped throughout my life on account of this thinking.

5:57 PM

I'm inquisitive about what is worth learning; I want to learn what is worth learning. I've learned to write in the manner I have to become more effective at communicating thoughts I'd be better off without in order to write books that validate me. I learned basic math, psychology, sociological principles, manipulation, workout regimes, food effects on physiology, esoteric vocabulary—every moment I learn, from simple existence, no matter what *it* may be. Moments spent in idleness and reflection amount to knowledge as significant as a scientist steeped in his work towards advancing the effects of gravitational pull on a newly developed space station.

This world is rife with monologues; I am no exception. We are all "somebody" with something to say, something to sell, whether *it* be the claim of love or a (dis)belief. The product varies, yet the profit is consistent: validation—from the streetside beggar to the billionaire egotist.

I inquire of my lord and master: *"Best psychology/sociology/philosophy/ educational books of 2020,"* and what do I glean other than a slew of nonsense akin to my own?—masqueraded as an art, a thought worth indulging, an *essential something* for the grand nothing.

Monday, April 20th, 2020

9:45 AM

There is a house I walk by on my way to and from Candy's shop three days out of each week. This house is an exemplar model of destitution. Throughout my life, I've never passed a place more rundown and deplorable to the eye than this two-story 1980s apartment building.

Cardboard boxes stuffed with indistinguishable detritus and soiled papers consisting of discarded junk mail and newspapers litter the sidewalk adjacent to the walkway that leads up a brief flight of dilapidated steps to the front torn screen door hung partially off the hinges. From the open second-floor windows, grimy clothes lay strewn in misshapen arrangements atop crooked and weathered roof tiles.

By this point, any reader may presume the remainder of the details of the house with a great degree of accuracy; this in mind, what point is there to persist with the description, if not to tantalize the sensibilities of a bored entertainment-seeker? Would you not be better off utilizing your imagination to render the picturesque scene of squalor and lamentable economic conditions?

"Lazy writing," proclaims a lazy reader, and I admit, I'd rather leave the scene of this house as *it* is, and impart to the reader and myself that this house is situated six blocks away from the city's single university. The divide between the privileged and the disadvantaged is rendered clear in aristocratic fashion, though the social rift is *only* within the mind, for all are equally impoverished in spirit.

The Covid-19 "quarantine" has changed nothing of my life other than a weekly deposit of $716 to my bank account out of no effort on my part. First, the banks were bailed out and that went *swell*. Now the strata of lower to middle-upper class are being bailed out, along with small businesses nationwide; I wonder how *that'll* pan out.

11:40 PM

Videogames offer a bittersweet respite, akin to meditation, food, reading, weightlifting, writing, sex, etc., ad infinitum. Anything *but* reality as *it* is, alone with one's thoughts; I presume I'm meditating *wrong*.

I yearn to be a virgin again, disillusioned by ignorance and enraptured by the idea of love. The old feelings I once experienced, engrossed in either a virtual world or a wayward vagina are now fickle memories of nostalgic joy, when childhood didn't consider *it*self to *be* childhood, and the future was infinite and inconceivable. Now, the future is a narrow, linear road, aligned on both sides with barbs: pleasures and indolences—all of which lead to ruinous suffering. Better to throw oneself into the bramble head-on than stay the course, lest you lose yourself *to* yourself, and the delusions inherent.

Tuesday, April 21st, 2020

8:33 PM

The zest has returned; I indulged in marijuana alone and hear my ego for what *it* is; is this the nature of schizophrenia? J.S Bach's *Mass in B Minor* plays through earbuds and I know a sweet return of this stream of consciousness nonsense. I am insane; this intrigues me. My nature is contrary to reality. I loathe all around me and know myself for what I am; yet, I judge myself for my humanity, and what *it* is that I do; there is nothing but nonsense.

I've lost my mind; this is certain; I know of the nothingness that I am and the God within; "God," with a capital "G." I must remain quiet, lest I scream out my own self-judgment, estranged from reality. I think I stink like hell and nobody has the gall to tell me; however, I shower every day and wash my clothes weekly—what am I, a clown?

Wednesday, April 22nd, 2020

7:23 AM

Last night Candy offered me a joint of marijuana before the end of my shift after I expressed interest in smoking alone, to which I graciously accepted and indulged in while I prepared sweet potatoes to boil on the stovetop later last night. The otherworldly sensations returned to me— old haunts, a "tapping into" a realm of pure ego. I ended up yelling proclamations of my contempt to the couple above me and engaged in inconsistent conversation with their muted, authentic responses. They also had smoked marijuana; therefore, we communicated on the same plane of stupidity.

After a tirade of the undisciplined, rambunctious dog, and a mockery of human relationships exemplified in my riotous miming of a pregnancy drama with an imaginary girlfriend, I implored the man upstairs to meet me outside for conversation, for I had been in the mood for the first time in the six—seven, or eight months I've lived in these apartments. I went outside and seated myself on the middle stairwell stoop, at the diagonal center of all eight apartments of my section, and blatantly stared at those who did the same—on their stoops, in their cars, standing with a cigarette or beer outside their apartments—I *watched* the hobbyist *people-watchers,* with scorn expressed in my gaze, and responded to every voice I heard with thoughts of my own, which manifested in me as bodily expressions that were interpreted with a high degree of accuracy by observers of me.

I *talked loudly—not* shouting, of my lunacy—of being a madman, and pressed inquiries across the lane at others, e.g., "What are you doing out here?"; "Do you watch other people often?" I deigned to engage in public conversation—*one* lousy conversation with a kindred pleb, and the only man who answered my summons despite knocking on the direct upstairs apartment door: D, my *diagonal* upstairs neighbor—the same man who once worked at a shipyard and retired; he stood in his doorway and threatened me with expressions of alluded violence if I am to come near him—yet the fool had opened his door and initiated contact with me!

Eventually he retreated indoors and I returned to my respective apartment to tend to my boiling sweet potatoes.

A police officer arrived and knocked on my door, concerned with my state of being—he was, the poor man, dealing with a stoned, rambunctious fool late in the evening. I merely sought conversation and behaved as most of the residents here do, by miming their boisterous activities and idleness outside one another's living spaces. I had been tame by comparison; I didn't even blare music from a car or complain about the weather. I incriminated no one but myself and had been forthcoming with my personal information: My full name—spelled; my previous state of living; how long I've lived in my current domain. Oh, yes... I *talked* to the police: the only conversation worth a damn that I experienced. The officer offered me "help," to which I declined, and he left me alone after I urged him to continue having conversations with others in the apartment complex about "noise levels."

I said, "Oh, *that's* what you're doing? Be my superhero!"

The office laughed; a bolshy face upturned at the cheeks by authentic creases appraised me, regardless of the scenario. Ah, my fellow men.

I experience a trend: Each instance that I smoke marijuana and choose to interact with others, there is a high probability that the police will be called on me. I woke this morning and stowed the remainder of the joint on the back of the shelf above my bathroom mirror.

Now I stand, sober, with no intent to indulge in marijuana again (soon), unashamed with my conduct, dignity intact. What had I been but a savage? Good morning, America.

8:02 PM

I resisted the temptation of what remained of my marijuana upon my return home for about five minutes, though I hadn't planned to resist.

No matter where I am, the ego is consistent.

I will not be jailed for listening.

The upstairs neighbors make for great writing fodder. Drama is plentiful.

Lewis' affiliation with my upstairs neighbors as their drug dealer warps this whole scenario. Life is a crescendo of bullshit. I've endured the company of several men and have determined my abhorrence to sexually please another man. I'm haunted by reminders of those other consciousnesses around me, trapped in this thought bubble of self-vexing duress.

I'm experiencing misgivings about choosing to rejoin my father. My faith wanes; do I want to live a life of greater luxury again—a step-up from the ghetto slum and *it*s inhabitants?

I am absolved, by my own decree and promulgations.

8:29 PM

There is no rush; I have time now… all the *time* I need, to *be.*

I pace in my kitchen and listen to the ignorant fellows around me complain while I maintain resolute silence. Water boils on the stovetop.

All of life is a comedy to me. Under one condition, I will not shame myself: I endure this night with my quietude intact and refrain from speaking out in any way. Already, I wished to terrorize my upstairs neighbors with a sudden, violent scream; oh, how I desire with earnest fervor and compassion, to exalt them with fright.

I am the menace here; I understand what I have become.

Thursday, April 23rd, 2020

8:46 AM

My greatest fear is being tortured, killed, and consumed by my father.

10:01 PM

The little money that I have, I don't need.

Friday, April 24th, 2020

10:06 AM

It's easy to snuggle up into the folds of another's flesh and be consoled for the misgivings of life and what ails you—to whisper into one another's ears the sweet nothings that disturb you; whisk *it* all away in an ego-validating maelstrom of oxytocin.

4:40 PM

I want none of the flesh, none of anything but a decent ratio of carbohydrates, protein, fat, and micronutrients. My life is an ensemble of non-sequiturs leading to a null zone. I love my insignificance. Every moment I begin to write, I think of the world population, of Asians seated near rice patties, of Russians sitting on the edge of a gutter on a dingy streetside of a busy city, of throngs of Americans seated at outdoor picnic tables hunched over a phone. 7.8 billion people live now out of an estimated 100 billion that have ever lived. Think of everything you've ever done, the achievements you've yearned for, aspired for, driven yourself towards, and where you are now, what everything amounted to, the relation of yourself to civilization—the constitution of your body, the emotions you've felt, the pain you experience, the guilt and shame you've been taught.

Saturday, April 25th, 2020

5:53 PM

I stand in Candy's shop near the end of my shift. I haven't thought of writing all day out of lack of interest; however, a homeless man who visits the shop often to utilize my computer for trivial matters stopped in for his scheduled tarot phone-reading session. I reminded him that his session is conducted *by phone*.

"Oh... Yeah... You're right," the man acknowledged. After a moment of hesitation and downcast eyes, he said, "Can I go outside then?"

I scorned the man internally for his ludicrous request to *leave* and said, "You can stay in here and have a seat in the parlor if you like." The man did as I suggested. I listened to the charlatan (R.J, the same woman who conducted my in-person tarot session) he speaks with on behalf of the blaring volume of his speakerphone from fifty feet away: Twenty dollars for a twenty-minute session.

8:32 PM

I asked the homeless man what insights he gained from the phone tarot session. From behind a white face mask, he said, "Yeah—yeah—yeah... no, not much really," and he followed up with a proclamation of his enjoyment of a particular brand of incense sticks. "Hey man, I'll be back with my card for those."

"The incense?"

"Yeah."

Sunday, April 26th, 2020

10:28 AM

I wake to the most absurd and rambunctious noise I've listened to in weeks. The man and woman were at the apex of their domestic patterns and I smiled while I laid on my floor. No longer will I speak to anyone in this quadrant; I am no hero. The problems of others are *just* that. Since my initial intervention, I've acquired a pair of noise-canceling headphones. I silently encourage the disgraceful fulminations—be at each other's throats, manipulate and vex, infuriate and fulminate.

The two don their social masks and assume their pretensions immediately after an emotional tousle to meet and banter with my diagonal upstairs neighbors outdoors—to lean on a banister and speak of idle nothings. The sun shines today. My blinds remain closed.

5:33 PM

Amethyst, the girl I developed a brief intimacy with last year, entered Candy's shop with her new boyfriend in tow. We locked eyes while I stood behind the counter, and her—a step in front of the doorway. Her boyfriend didn't notice. I had been pleased to see her with a compatible man: a stout gangster trope.

I'm too entertained to write of anything entertaining. Don't you understand, reader? This book isn't for you; *it*'s for me, even after I'm dead: a headstone I'll never read. The future will be nothing but bloggers, article-writers, disposable content creators, i.e., ego proliferators. Technological advancements will permit thoughts to become objects and all sources of information will become null as consciousnesses merge into one awareness. Humanity will become engrossed with themselves at an individual level and the social dynamic will be disrupted; civilization will collapse under the immensity of self-engrossment. I am but a minor contribution to the testament of what being human is. Behold, for this is my exposition:

Candy's daughter dated a man for two months, married him, and a year later, divorced him when she returned home from work and found him dressed in her lingerie.

Monday, April 27th, 2020

6:48 PM

Three-hundred words to go, stream of consciousness style:
"Your writing is terrible if you write for the sake of arbitrary goals."
I agree; therefore, I'll write to exemplify the mockery of the existence of others and myself. People waddle around outdoors and enjoy the sunlight, smoking cigarettes, thinking of food, sex, and entertainment. Drink a beer, maybe two, try on a new pair of shoes. Oh, they don't fit, and my rhymes are bad. Aren't you glad you decided to read today? Don't count on me to keep your existential dread at bay. No pseudo-intellectual here; I've been reborn with nothing to say except "Bring on the mundane."
"Who said that?" I said.
"But I thought you were the one tal—er, writi—*typing*—typing!"
I am the one ~~writing~~ typing. The quotations serve to distract and confuse.
If you're the character in each quotation, *it* could be surmised that every character ever written of is an extension of the writer's ego, imaginative or not; a nonfictional character who existed, such as Napoleon or Beethoven are accounted for with a margin of bias, no matter how slight, that is dependent on perspective.
"That's quite the insight, though how will that serve me in acquiring a college degree to earn a substantial salary to pay for my future house, boat, car, wife, and children?"
"Being a provider is an antiquated notion."
"Elaborate, please."
"No."
"But you've yet to meet your three-hundred-word quota for the day!"
"I've no qualms with being a failure by my own accord and judgment."
Disappointed? Don't be. You've all your life to read about all of ~~your~~ my life.

Tuesday, April 28th, 2020

11:20 AM

On my route past the closed elementary school, I strode on a sidewalk marred by blue chalk. Every few meters, a word, or set of words, existed to be read and retained to my memory for the sole purpose of documenting. Yes, the grand design of life is a perpetual memory to sustain one when all else fails to provide nourishment:

Etchings of a Child

"God
"God
"You can
"Smile
"Hello
"Cats & Dogs
"Blue"

A thunderstorm is due tonight.

2:39 PM

Amethyst returned to the shop and purchased $75 worth of merchandise: herbs, sage, black salt—all manner of dispelling trinkets, and now, as I type this, she returns amid a group of customers.

2:42 PM

Amethyst bought four candles: red, black, green, and white—each of the only colors in stock. I spoke no more than necessary professionalism. Flustered, she hastened out of the shop. Such a splendid girl. Her lips were supple, sublime; her body: fine and sleek. My heart swells for vacuous vixens, and she fits the bill to a tee. Engrossed with the spiritual and occult, Amethyst derives solace in the mystical aspect of life, and believes in a myriad of wondrous conjurations of the imagination: A marijuna smoker, animal lover, self-identified alcoholic, and seeker of knowledge. I recall our jaunts in the park together shortly after I overcame homelessness; our fleeting moments of secret rapture revitalized my faith in humanity. Why I chose to leave her before giving us a chance… I regret, yet, I know the decision has been optimal for my well-being. How we seek vices to the detriment of our livelihood, elevated by the gross satisfaction provided—invigorated by the stimulus—flesh upon flesh, the gaze into another's eyes, the exchange of thought.

Thursday, April 30th, 2020

11:29 AM

Doognevil

The muffled screams a night before the creature's death titillated me. By "creature," I mean the faerie I captured inside a large glass bottle in my youth and discarded in the attic storage space of my parent's home. I knew nobody would believe me if I told them, and if my parents had ever discovered my little pet they would've conjured up a delusional explanation and condemned me to an asylum—for their own sake.

The faerie had been a male, by my distinction, on account of the vocal range, hence my titillation. Being a virginal girl, there wasn't much that didn't arouse me in some manner, though this creature—oh, I can't begin to describe my longing for those years, for those late nights huddled under my covers with only a glass jar separating that fantastical thing from my embrace, my body—our unrequited unity.

I didn't know what to feed *it!* I didn't think the thing ate, but merely sustained itself on the essence of existence—whatever that is. I had been a young girl, awestruck by my ignorance, yet ignorant *of* my ignorance. How could this be? Well…

I had layered the jar prior with mossy detritus, a few small twigs, a nondescript flower, and a leaf; however, these were mere decorations for my pleasure. I hadn't considered the… I mustn't call it "thing," or "*it*,"—such a disgrace to one I've *loved!* Oh, my rumination overtakes me often. I captured the faerie—I hadn't named him, though I'm struck with inspiration now and believe his name to be Doognevil; yes, Doognevil—I captured Doognevil in a large bottle I had stolen from my father's in-house

238

glass-blowing workshop. Only moments after the capture did I realize the inadequacy of the size. Doognevil stood about seven-and-a-half inches tall and the bottle measured about eight inches. Ah, Doogy hadn't even been able to fully outstretch his arms, and each moment he seemed to involuntarily—by consequence of wrath—flutter his adorable leafy six-fold wings, whereby he knocked his majestic crowned head on the top of his prison! And the wails which resonated from within!—I'll never forget, oh—no, the riotous outbursts had failed to offend me. I had—as already remarked, been *titillated*. I imagined genitalia on the lanky green, apparently asexual body, and stared at Doognevil for hours.

I never felt guilt, nor shame for how my Doogy had huddled himself into the cornerless bottoms of the bottle while I observed. Occasionally, he would reveal his face and furrow his brow, as if to castigate me in his silent terror. I didn't think he'd ever die. I sealed the top of the bottle with a custom cork my father had cut specifically for the bottle I had stolen and flipped the container upside down. The greenery settled to the new designated bottom of the bottle, and within the first day of Doogy's imprisonment, I attached a wavy patterned lattice around the cork while he looked on through the glass with vindictive scorn etched across over his otherworldly features.

No—never did I think my Doognevil would leave me; I'd always have my little sprite, my faerie companion, and throughout his terrible fear, he would guide me in my darkest moments—I had been so sure. And then—*ah!*—I hesitate to recount my emotions, for after only two days, I woke one drab morning, lifted my bedsheet, and witnessed my Doogy—dead—*petrified* as he is to this day, after all these years!—immoveable—locked in a statuesque stasis of desperation! His eyes, I'll never forget his eyes: A glossy forlornness stared out from the bottle's confines and pierced into my being—my *soul;* haunted, as I am—I can bear the burden of the guilt and shame onset from wisdom and experience that—in my starry-eyed youth, I failed to acknowledge, to *comprehend*. I can no longer tolerate the sight of my dear beloved, partially decayed, preserved as a grotesque fossil—a testament of my grief, fixed in his agony, mouth clenched in despair, and his little paw—spanned up towards the bottle's reversed bottom: A final plea to a god of his own! Thirty-four years and he *still stands*. Asphyxiated, dehydrated—no, the *cause* is of no concern for why my Doogy died as a statue—as a tortured revenant!—yes, he speaks to me still, screams out my name; he *lives* a quasi undeath. I hear the cries in my sleep and wake to the thought of his tormented flesh. No more! No more!—I can endure these vexations no more!

MAY

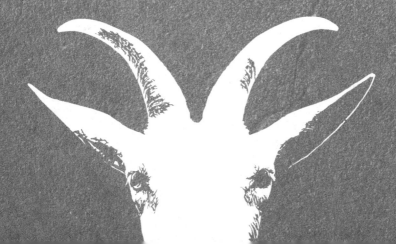

Friday, May 1st, 2020

8:35 AM

Last night, the homeless man who visits *Anomalies and Artifacts* stopped in again, only this time with two opportunities for work and leisure. I've accepted a gig to edit his schooling real estate papers for $20 each. Each paper is between 750-1,000 words. After our agreement, the man offered to share marijuana with me at his home. I declined and inquired about from whom he purchased his marijuana. The homeless man informed me that a man in one of his neighborhood's upstairs apartments sells "medical-grade" marijuana and that I may purchase from him.

I followed the ~~homeless~~ man to his neighborhood and we knocked on the door of his seller. A tall, shirtless African-American man with a bloated abdomen answered the door and said, "The fuck is this?"

My companion's eyes shifted to the balcony floor and he failed to answer for four seconds.

I said, "I'd like to purchase marijuana from you."

The shirtless man retreated a step into his apartment, said, "Naw man—I've no idea what you talkin' about," and shut the door.

My companion and I descended the balcony steps and he invited me into his apartment. Based on the varied furnishings and several small framed prints hung from the walls, I suspect he hadn't been genuinely homeless, as the rooms conferred the look of prolonged occupation: Downtrodden, uncouth, and sanitary enough to make a grown man feel at ease. The man (I've yet to learn his name) switched on a small television from the 90s positioned on a small wooden stool, and replaced a disk from a DVD player atop the television with a different disk. The first episode of the 2001 television series, *Smallville,* began to play. I stood in the center of the living room while the man retrieved a basic glass pipe and two small baggies of marijuana from his room. He sat on a beaten sofa and gestured for me to sit next to him while he filled the bowl of the pipe halfway. I complied.

"This is *Smallville,*" said the man. "*It*'s a show about the origins of Superman and-"

"I know what *Smallville* is. I've never been into superheroes, Superman especially."

"Oh yeah—neither have I, not really."

I chuckled and said, "Why do you watch something you don't really have an interest in?"

The man's words were unintelligible by me; however, a bowl and lighter were passed into my hands. "That's all for you bro so hit *it* as hard as you want."

I indulged and we spoke more of his papers that required editing. With an agreement made, I departed and headed homeward. My psyche had been wracked, and while I walked, I was all-too-aware of my altered state. I become exceptionally social under the effects of THC, and heed my internal voices/daemon/spirit/universal consciousness/god with a strict code of honor, for these voices are the guideposts in the ineffable existence we traverse.

Instead of my typical focused gait and disinterest in those around me, I locked eyes and stared at *every person* I encountered, no exceptions, and thought of contempt, scorn, and *wonder* on account of what humanity is. I had been amused by *everyone,* for the creatures we are.

"Yo—why the fuck are you smiling?" shouted a man from the backseat of his car. Ah, *it* had been years since an instance such as that: a man yelling an absurd question from a passing vehicle. I stopped, turned, and while the four passengers waited at a red light, I approached the stationary vehicle.

A large African-American man in the front passenger seat stepped out as I approached and attempted to intimidate me. I requested to inform the man in the backseat why I had been smiling, though none of the three desired to listen. I informed all three that "I'm high," and the African-American man backed away and assured me that "You lucky you high otherwise you was gonna get hit."

The young female driver stood halfway out of her seat with one foot on the pavement and goaded me with questions of my marijuana usage, for the two expressed interest in purchasing from me. The man in the backseat who had obnoxiously inquired of my "smiling" remained silent throughout the entire interaction. I abruptly detached from the three without divulging any information and continued my walk home. All-the-while, my mind had been set ablaze with voices of myself being an "asshole," "douchebag," and "loser," only now, I *embraced* the manifestations of my mind and continued to observe the observers of me throughout my walk that elicited such voices to transpire on account of the presupposed "unified consciousness" in conjunction with the particular subset of American culture I ambled through.

I heard the legitimate voices of a group of five men standing outside a shabby home. When low-income degenerates gather, the individuals among them become more outspoken and vitriolic, more so if alcohol has been consumed. One said, "Look at this fucking guy," within earshot, in reference to me. I smiled at him, and thought, repeatedly, *"A smile looks good on everyone!"*

Out of the five gawkers who gawked at my gawking, one said, "How are you?" which is a useless inquiry, and an outright pretension of caring for a stranger.

I yelled, "I'm well!" and continued to stare—and *smile.* Reality impacted by my existence; social animals, what many repress and fail to acknowledge day-to-day, even when engaged with the multitudes. How simple a smile is; the immediate impact of my aberrant behavior had been obvious!

On my return to my apartment, I intended to write my night away with worthless nihilistic exposition and retire to my floor. Instead, I ascended the stairwell to the second floor of my apartment complex and positioned myself where my neighbor, D, always stands to enjoy a cigarette: A great vantage point of one-third of the neighborhood. There I stood, for three hours, until I returned indoors and immediately prepared for sleep. Throughout my time standing there, I stared at every person—in their cars, those walking across the lot, those who stood in their doorways and stared at me, and into the windows of others who observed me. I'm amazed at how little people enjoy being observed when the circumstance is beyond their control, as if I infringe on their rights of sanctity in a public domain. All-the-while I wished for a demented idiot to approach me for a physical confrontation, or a disgruntled man with a rifle to shoot me from a passing car, or from the window of an apartment. Oh, *yes,* I made many enemies by observing, and the few who attempted to be my "friend"—most notably, one of the neighborhood maintenance employees who wanted to "take me out for a drink," were interpreted by me as desperate and pathetic, as their lives were void enough of meaningful relationships to venture to befriend someone of *my* esteem; for in that moment, I had been nothing but a buffoon, high on marijuana, "enjoying" his Friday night by standing erect on a second-floor balcony and staring at everyone who entered his field of vision.

To regard me in third-person, my behaviors, and what I have committed, is therapeutic, for there is no objectively better course of action I could've undertaken. Even if I endeavored for a noble, philanthropic, humanitarian emprise in that three hours, my time *wouldn't* have been better lived—for this is *my* life, of *my* jurisdiction and responsibility.

The neighbor, D, who smokes cigarettes on the balcony—the same man who called the police on me the first instance—the instance I ascended the stairwell to ~~his~~ the balcony and proclaimed my "madness"—opened his door and joined me. A six-foot distance between us, I addressed him with what began as a smile. D attempted to ignore me; he succeeded, superficially; however, as social animals, we are sensitive to each other's energy, and he revealed himself to me, the manner of man that he is, *just* as I had deduced: A spineless worm; one who speaks a great game, and when confronted with a demon, fails to acknowledge *it*s presence—*strives* to fail in that regard. For six minutes, I stared at the side of his head and out-of-shape physique, at the creases along his cheeks, the scruffy remnants of a misshapen beard and mustache, and I reviled, loathed, and pitied most of all—for he *desired* to confront me, he *yearned* to, though in his mind, he practiced being "the better man," yet, he doesn't know what "being a man" is. He acknowledged me with a perturbed sidelong glance—only for a moment, a short-lived moment I relished: an open validation of my humanity. There I was, an entity he had mocked for months, standing beside him as a fellow man, and my fellow buffoon had nothing to say for himself—not an eye's worth of contact between us. I rejoiced in the protracted ephemeral moment.

Here, I write of "being a man" and what that entails in my childish document. Everyone has something to prove; this document is proof enough of that. I've nothing to prove except that there *is* something to prove: The human condition.

The apartment maintenance man returned at 11 PM (curfew) and requested, for the second time, for me to join him for a few drinks out on the town. I declined with a shake of my head, donned my pack, and descended the balcony steps towards my apartment.

"I'm offended," said the maintenance man.

I said nothing, returned indoors at 11:03 PM, and slept minutes later.

8:48 PM

Two teenage kids knocked on my door and ran away in two separate instances. Coincidentally, this happened the night after I perturbed the majority of my neighbors and scared several children. I've acquired a reputation for myself fitting for my esteem: The eccentric ninny who lives in #91.

I forgot to record a scenario yesterday: On my return home, I passed by a mutt in a caged backyard that *always* barks at me, and *has* barked at me for months. I stopped, vexed by the beast—after all the noise I've endured on account of *it,* and reprimanded *it* as if *it* were my own. The owners (a man and a woman) emerged from their home minutes later and pretended to need something from their vehicle.

"What are you doing?" asked the man.

"I'm disciplining this dog—is *it* yours?"

"Yes," answered the woman, "just leave him alone."

I turned back to the dog, shrugged, and shouted, *"Ah*—now I know why you behave the way you do: They just leave you alone!"

The owners fumigated in silence and conversed with (presumably) friends on a porch occluded by a nearby bush. I continued to lecture the dog and named *it* a bastard. Eventually the beast scurried away, tail between *it*s legs, and I walked away, to the chagrin of the owners who observed my jolly stride.

Yes… I made many inconsequential enemies for myself yesterday. Bad blood alters my delusions.

Saturday, May 2nd, 2020

11:48 AM

I dreamed of urination and woke to an outline of dampness around my waist and the soaked briefs that I slept in. In this particular dream, I had been asked by a faceless employer to urinate all over a row of undesignated company toilets, to "prepare them for cleaning." I hadn't understood, yet I obeyed the order, confused; however, I had been pleased with the sensation of urinating which amounted to a *real* experience. My surprise upon waking had only been surpassed by my disappointment, for I had just washed my sheet two days prior. Dreams of urination are my bane.

I shit, shaved, and showered, in that order, and lifted a pair of pants I wore yesterday from my carpeted floor. A cockroach scurried out and hid beneath one of my adjustable dumbbell stands. Cockroaches are a unique creature in that their consciousness seems heightened; they operate through fear and abhor the light—all sensations. The smell of Tabasco sauce elicits mental images of a cockroach, for I became intimate with many cockroaches when I first moved into my apartment. When captured in a clear bowl, the frenetic behavior is reminiscent of how a human would scurry around, terrified and perplexed—as if the cockroach is self-aware of the fragility of *it*s existence in the same vein a human is when we are injured and reminded of our mortality. A slight cut that bleeds is often enough to remind one of death. At least a dozen cockroaches and millipedes succumbed to a guided death by my hand, slathered in a bowl of Tabasco sauce. The agony endured by the creature is palpable enough that even a human may sympathize, though how could one *empathize* with a being of alien proportions and manner?

I shifted my dumbbell stand and the cockroach scurried towards the next available cover: my other dumbbell stand; therefore, I shifted *that* stand too, and watched for a moment as the cockroach contemplated for a fraction of a second before zig-zagging onto my kitchen floor. My foot came down hard and a singular *pop* resonated, to my satisfaction. I removed my foot and the cockroach remained still except for one leg that kicked as I lifted the creature by the antenna, dropped *it* into a cardboard box full of trash, and washed my hands. If I had the time, I would've prepared a thin layer of Tabasco sauce for the cockroach to wade through. Alas, I am a professional man; thus I clipped on my shirt stays, tucked in my dress shirt, styled my hair back, strapped on my wristwatch, brushed the few specks of lint off my shirt collar, and trekked across town for an hour through ghetto suburbs and lower-to-middle-class American quintessential "living the dream" homes so that I may stand in a gift shop and greet customers with a smile and nod of the head.

Yes, a gentleman and a scholar—*they* call me.

2:05 PM

A restaurant stockroom is adjacent to *Anomalies and Artifacts.* Workers from the restaurant often pass by and gaze in at me on their routes to and from the stockroom. One of these workers is a middle-aged Caucasian man who greets me and comments on the weather on every occasion that we meet. Today, on his departure from the stockroom, while I lit incense and placed *it in an* outdoor flower pot, the man said to me (for the second instance within three hours), *"It*'s sure hot out today."

I said, "Yes, you've said that twice today. Don't you find *it* curious that when people are friendly and gregarious towards one another, that there is-"

"Well what's wrong with being friendly? I'm friendly all the time; I work in a restaurant. Isn't that part of your business? You're a dick man."

The man walked away and left me standing, flabbergasted. I couldn't help but smile. He didn't even let me finish my inquiry. I await his return; I *need* consolation.

Sunday, May 3rd, 2020

6:38 PM

I've purchased a video game console and don't bother to play video games; instead, I resort to uninclined interest in marijuana usage, reading, editing, and continuing the act of writing. Without this template, my life would be devoid of worth. I am unenthused, in all respects. After another sullen outburst rallied against my neighbors, I've established, through the use of my guile, to subdue the unwarranted social behavior of my upstairs neighbors, and, by consequence, the adjoining residences. Life has been calm, and I experience flow from what my hostilities have reaped: peace.

But *video games*, how I miss them; yet, I have access to them! I miss the *memories* of my youth. "One always misses memories when they're gone," said a falsifier and a liar. One can't rue or pine for what they don't remember. I attempted to play at intervals and found myself deluded by the character I operate on-screen. The latest action-role-playing games provided nourishment on completion of one playthrough. I'm primed to move on. In most cases, I would be moving on by searching for a new residence, though there is no practical reason now that I've established dominance on my corner of the block and plan to depart by September, back to my father's domain.

The only role-playing survival strategy game that appeases me long-term are the machinations of reality.

7:37 PM

The Sound of a Burning Sun is an excellent name for a Pulitzer prize winner.

Monday, May 4th, 2020

9:41 AM

I sit on my weight bench and listen to music play above me.

Is this document overtly negative? Is there no other recourse? I attempt to profit off of my "patheticism" and childishness. Luckily, my environment permits me. I acclimate well.

The sight of a man with a woman is truly pathetic to see. Social engagements between men and women should always be conducted in private quarters; there is nothing else to see. I practice my proclamations. Two people bound to each other through necessity is a pity to witness. A man *with* a woman, or rather, the women's man, is a pity to see—even if viewed in one's private home.

A ~~writer~~ journalist with thought and catalyst is unassailable.

The issue is, I have no thoughts worth recording.

12:03 PM

Everywhere I go, there is always a man and a woman; the duo upstairs is the quintessential example of disparate states.

Tuesday, May 5th, 2020

10:17 AM

Antisocial tendencies render me hateful. Instead of playing games, I removed my headphones, sauntered over to my weight bench, seated myself, leaned back, and listened to domestic abuse.

Thursday, May 7th, 2020

1:35 PM

Albert Camus' novel, *The Stranger*, impacted me with a peculiar feeling of bliss on completion. Not often does a work of literature rip me from my dissipated spirit and distill my thoughts with acceptance for what is. My circumstances are wonderful and I thrive, despite the entities around me; I choose to focus my attention on the alien life—my brothers, in consciousness, estranged by the flesh. I await Seneca's *On the Shortness of Life* in the mail. I could read a free digital format online, though I'd rather practice a delusional behavior practiced by aspirants of a philosophy or cause: those who read a single book religiously to remind themselves of the dogma or tenets within.

I gave my copy of *The Stranger* to Candy. Books—antiquated as they are in the advent of the digital age, still retain a tactile satisfaction when handled, or an object fit for ostentatious display on a bookshelf that's dusted every week by a maid, or a pretentious symbol left out on a coffee table for a rare guest to glean. Burn all books; let savages reign. Think of the libraries across the world—in flames; what a glorious image to behold in the mind's eye; to be deprived of knowledge, successes and failures, of wisdom and suffering, to bask in the amplification of human futility— for what difference would there be if all culminated receptacles and storage devices of human knowledge ceased to be known? A regression? An impedance? A dark age? On the contrary, I think enlightenment via annihilation.

Friday, May 8th, 2020

11:01 AM

I've gone to the barbers and had my head shaved to 1/8th of an inch in length all around. While I waited for forty minutes in a chair for my turn, I stared at the vacant chair before me, and at a fly that buzzed around the room. Four elderly men, all over the age of sixty-five—the owner of the barbershop included, exchanged interested, vacant stares at me, and I at them. The owner's employee: a woman encroaching her forties, inquired if she had been correct in her viewing of me on a particular street a few days ago; she had wondered when I would return. I said nothing.

On my turn, I seated myself in the barber chair and made my request. A minute later, as the woman began to shave the sides of my head, I inquired, "Why did you ask if you saw me on a particular street?"

The woman replied with nothing substantial—i.e., she didn't answer the question. "Curiosity," which is a blanket-affirmation to conceal any motive or inclination one may otherwise not desire to share.

Behind the counter of *Anomalies and Artifacts,* I've asked three customers thus far why they've asked me, "How are you?"

All are taken aback, though I explain myself when pressed as to why I question *why* an individual inquiries of my state of being or mood. These statements are wasted breath and go without saying; there is no casual instance in which a person learns more of someone's authentic mood than if they were to just *observe*.

"Are you from around here?" or "Where are you from?" is often uttered to me after I explain myself of the rationality of my questioning a socially conditioned norm. Often, I outright refuse to answer, though depending on *how I'm feeling,* I may reply with, "New York, though strangers greet each other by asking how each other are in New York as well; my origins are of no consequence in this matter."

My personality is dreadful to interact with, and my character withholds nothing but secret anathema—a vindictive bane for my fellow man. I want *nothing* to do with our creature formalities; however, I garb myself in fine clothes and present the aspect of a "gentleman" while projecting the mien of an incompetent, an asshole, a scoundrel. These adjectives are of my self-assigned description, for I *know* myself, and the *void* that is everything that I am.

I experience an internal crisis with video games at my disposal. The question becomes: Do I lose myself in the difficult, artificial challenges of role-playing games whereby I may enjoy an outlet for my misanthropic thoughts through the virtual slaughter of enemies via an innately hostile world?—or do I embrace reality, and *become* a savage?—engrossed with nothing but the resolute tenets of the ego, there would be nothing more than a savage man.

To my dismay, on reflection, there is no difference if I were to relinquish the satisfaction of video games. However, if I removed the temptation, I would merely revert to a different, *unsatisfactory* activity that would pale in comparison to if I were to submit to my humanity and *enjoy myself*—or at least *attempt* to, no matter how mind-numbing I may render my psyche, and how the voices of my ego thereby punishes me as a result—for I cannot repeat enough, foolish reader, that I *know* myself on account of the *very* documentation you read, that which I implore you to abandon, for *it* is mine, even if you paid for *it* after I had the gall to publish *it*.

12:41 PM

I checked out a large bundle of white sage and a woman in her fifties with her young daughter in-tow said, "Where are you from?—your accent?"

I looked at the woman and shook my head slightly before speaking: "I... I'm a denizen of the world, if anything. Why do you ask?"

"Your voice is very deep."

I said nothing.

The woman, somewhat flustered, turned away and said, "Thank you!"

I said, "Thank you," with a *slight* emphasis on "you."

What is a man? *Just* what I am but a pawn and a king of interrelated realms? While I walk down the left side of the main city street faced towards oncoming traffic, I think of the plausibility of my death, at ease, comforted with my general disdain, and the disdain I (generally) receive in exchange.

"How can man know himself? *It* **is a dark, mysterious business: if a hare has seven skins, a man may skin himself seventy times seven times without being able to say, 'Now that is truly you; that is no longer your outside.'** *It* **is also an agonizing, hazardous undertaking thus to dig into oneself, to climb down toughly and directly into the tunnels of one's being. How easy** *it* **is thereby to give oneself such injuries as no doctor can heal. Moreover, why should** *it* **even be necessary given that everything bears witness to our being—our friendships and animosities, our glances and handshakes, our memories and all that we forget, our books as well as our pens. For the most important inquiry, however, there is a method. Let the young soul survey** *it*s **own life with a view of the following question: 'What have you truly loved thus far? What has ever uplifted your soul, what has dominated and delighted** *it* **at the same time?' Assemble these revered objects in a row before you and perhaps they will reveal a law by their nature and their order: the fundamental law of your very self. Compare these objects, see how they complement, enlarge, outdo, transfigure one another; how they form a ladder on whose steps you have been climbing up to yourself so far; for your true self does not lie buried deep within you, but rather rises immeasurably high above you, or at least above what you commonly take to be your I."**

- Freidrick Nietzsche

253

Candy's young son, Midnight, walked into *Anomalies and Artifacts* to drop off a package and said, "I like your haircut."

I said, "Thank you."

"Have you ever been in the Navy or Army?"

"Yes."

"You look like you have been."

"Do you say that because of the haircut?"

"No—because you have long legs and stand up straight *and* the haircut."

"Well, thank you for the compliment."

Midnight pushed out of the storefront door and called back to me, "You're welcome."

A child's perspective is refreshing.

Saturday, May 9th, 2020

I smoked marjuana with Candy at her home and we watched three episodes of a television series called *The Midnight Gospel*. After a night of talking, I spent the night on her couch out of respect for the man I encouraged her to choose over me despite the overt sexual tension between us. Regardless of whether we experience intercourse together, Candy still practices emotional infidelity; we may revert to hedonistic lust eventually and reignite a secret affair out of sheer pleasure of one another's company.

Sunday, May 10th, 2020

9:07 AM

There will be no incentive to return to the workforce once the Covid-19 panic has passed after experiencing a taste of socialism. Why work when the U.S. government is willing to offer bail for failed economic systems? Why write when I have nothing to expound on other than:

Three little monkeys bumbled around a bunch of six bananas. Overhead, from an array of resplendent clouds covering a morning sky, God gazed down on his creations and said, "I'm proud of you, for what you've become." The monkeys teetered on their knuckles and swung their tails, mouths agape, jaws slackened.

What does *it* mean? Horrible writing—that's all, nothing more to *it*. I could omit this entry and be better off in the future when I decide to denigrate myself with a casual flip-through of this book's pages and stop *here*.

8:25 PM

A lone wooden workshop, abandoned for a century. A low-bearing steady breeze whistles over the tops of lilacs. An old man rolls onto his side beneath the canopy of a willow tree. Cold dirt wedged beneath fingernails.

Monday, May 11th, 2020

10:03 AM

Another dream prompted me to urinate in my sleep; that's twice in one week. I feel no shame; therefore, I record the experience, and instead account for my annoyance with my brain's appeal for me to relieve myself through subliminal stimuli. The sensation of dream urination has been felt enough to distinguish when I *am* urinating due to a dream's parameters as opposed to reality. In the dream, as I urinate, an aura of heat afflicts my genitals, which is, in fact, hot urine being soaked into my briefs and surrounding bedding. I woke myself with a commanding thought, vexed by the content of my dreams. There is *always* a urinal or toilet available to me in my dreamscapes—a temptation to relieve oneself prior to an interesting adventure with the random faces of my imaginings, derived from people that I have seen in waking life.

After I removed my soiled garments, I returned to my sheet and thought of my writing: How I haven't written many short stories or poems this year, and my overall lack of care for the quality of the content I produce. Thereby, with my right cheek pressed against my sheet and my neck misaligned with my spine, I thought to write of three men who lived in a sewer.

A steady trickle of putrid brown droplets siphoned into an underground tunnel system from a broken pipeline landed in a stagnant puddle of mired human feces and disheveled remnants of a rat rest next to an emaciated man who wheezed and coughed before every sentence he spoke. "I remember when I gave a shit," the man rasped to a young girl; spreadeagled on the tops of four wooden crates several feet away from the man, she leered down at him through a tangle of slimy black hair hung in front of her face.

"I don't," said the girl.

"Yeah, you wouldn't."

The girl propped up onto her hands, squatted, and stood with a sudden upward jolt. A simple grey dress, smeared with huge grime patches, fell flat and heavy down to the girl's knees. "I can't see shit in here."

"*Oh, it*'s there," spat the man; he clenched his teeth and forced an involuntary bestial growl out of an attempt to continue speaking.

The girl said, "How could you give a shit if you can't see *it?*"

"Wait until daybreak and stand under the manholes; you'll see *it* all then."

"I know," said the girl while she hopped down from a five-foot-high drop, flat onto two red tennis shoes stained with black sludge, "I've been here for as long as you, you dope."

The man chuckled, cleared his throat, and said nothing.

A low, guttural hum emanated from above, diminished in intensity by a steady lapping of the contents of a slow-moving sewage canal. The girl blindly held out a hand and traced the top edges of the wooden crates. Her feet scuffed across the ground while she said, "I don't want to be here anymore."

"Then go, but when you come back-" the man coughed.

The girl interjected, "I wouldn't come back."

"-bring me a can or two of Pringles."

"I said I *wouldn't* come back."

"I didn't hear you, bitch."

The girl stiffened and withdrew her hand from the sharp corner of a crate. She turned around towards the man, slumped in a narrow ray of a street light shone down from above through one of the four slots of a manhole. Despite the darkness, she reckoned one bloodshot eye below a green and black U.S. Army beret cap and the quiver of a grin.

The man said, "Why wouldn't you come back?"

The girl said nothing.

Tuesday, May 12th, 2020

4:15 PM

I walked outdoors with the resolve to give away my television and Playstation 4. My mind had been hijacked by multimedia. Reality is more assuring to my senses. I may work with clarity when I'm not bombarded with distractions. I feel lighter, my mind at rest, recomposed in my leisure and at peace with myself. At first, I visited the upstairs neighbors: The ones directly above me, and knocked on their door for several instances. They hadn't answered after five instances of various raps. I stood, turned, and gazed out at the neighborhood.

I hadn't intended to give away my media for the sake of my soul, or to appeal to a higher calling for the sake of karma; I obeyed the commandments of my ego, and realize what gaming is—a wretched waste of time, for *me,* as I would rather live the fantasies portrayed; energies are diverted, split, *severed,* and a man becomes less sanctified with himself. I am a ~~writer~~ fool, first and foremost, and the entertainment would be a burden to haul, both physically and in one's mind. I need an escape from myself with such severity that I resort to virtual templates to do so and discover that I'm as much of a wretch in those mediums as I am in reality; a scumbag, by my own design.

After eight minutes of waiting between intermittent knocks, I walked over to my neighbor's apartment (the man who called the police on me) and knocked his door. After one minute, the man answered and said, "Got the wrong house?"

I said, "No."

"Then what are you doing here?" The man assumed an amiable, though somewhat pretentious smile elicited by a combination of conviction and anxiety.

"Do you want a television or a Playstation 4 Pro?"

His face softened while his wife continued to observe from behind him, standing in the living room area. "No, we're all set buddy."

I thought to speak, "You regard me as 'buddy?'" However, I said, "All right," and returned to the front door of my direct upstairs neighbor. I rapped with a friendly tonality on their door again and waited; no response for another minute compelled me to return to my apartment, defeated.

The sensation of defeat didn't last long as an old African-American woman in the apartment adjacent to me readily accepted a new 43-inch high definition television and a Playstation 4 Pro for herself and her son.

6:07 PM

I spent my government-issued Covid-19 stimulus check on two video game consoles: one for my father, and the other, no longer in my possession.

Wednesday, May 13th, 2020

9:13 AM

This egotistical and narcissistic doctrine is my bane, my anathema, yet, I yearn to be consumed by *it,* and to create the page's contents to be a medium devoid of "I."

6:02 PM

Nonsense, there is only "I." All fiction is folly and *entertainment*— and *this,* this document, is *my* antithesis of entertainment, thus, a reader's delight. Behold:

The old African-American woman next door returned home and I knocked on her door; she answered, and I requested my television and PS4 back and handed her five twenty-dollar bills, as I knew she had been excited for her son to set up the system for her. The woman declined my payment, with the rationale that the items had been mine in the first place, though I insisted, for the sake of myself.

Yes! What foolishness I reap *and* sow! Any perception or belief a reader has of my character is *wrong.* I may be respectable to myself, and by extension, to an observer, for a fleeting moment, and then—hypocrisy, blasphemy, division.

What a joke.

7:14 PM

Outbursts of a White Centipede (of a) Man.

Thursday, May 14ᵗʰ, 2020

8:08 AM

The aforementioned title applies for I am pale of skin and behave like a centipede among men, whereby I dash from cover to cover and the sight of me causes distress and discomfort.

12:46 PM

My neighbor, D (a retired shipyard worker), has accused me of being a loon on account of me questioning why he refers to me as "buddy" and "boss." The man began to rave with a belligerence fit for a cretin, and approached me on the stairwell in an unremarkable attempt to intimidate me. Throughout his outburst, the man (and his wife) assured me that I have no idea what a "psychopath" is. The man proceeded to posit that he is a "certifiable psychopath." I challenged the claim and distinguished him to be a "sociopath" due to his lack of malice, to which the woman laughed at me from the second-floor balcony and announced that she "went to school and has thirteen degrees, a few of which are in psychology."

So there, I have affronted a certified psychopath and his live-in polymath psychoanalyst. I am a pillar of the community.

10:38 PM

If I were to scream right now, I'd terrorize Geoffrey and Catherine, and the police would be at my door within five minutes.

My journal is a masterpiece of crockery. I am a despicable genius, repulsive, a *White Centipede of a Man*. There is genius *in* my hatred. I loathe those who loathe me; therefore, the insufferable conviction of hatred severs the bond of man and we are compelled to animosity. I yearn to be hated. I am no *dumb* man, yet I am delighted that you think I'm dumb.

Friday, May 15th, 2020

7:43 AM

My ego won't permit me to enjoy myself. Every attempt results in dissatisfaction. I had attempted to smoke a small bowl of marijuana and play a post-apocalyptic simulator for three hours before bed last night while my dinner digested, and instead, went straight to my sheet for sleep.

I'm an uncertified "psychopath." This condition is pervasive. I reckon I should be grateful for what I am, wholly acknowledged. Do I delude myself with a belief of societal jargon—a self-fulfilling prophecy of thoughts?

I yearn for an eremitic life, afflicted with the "I."

7:00 PM

I hate to enjoy myself; allow scientists, analysts, and researchers to study this useless doctrine in the future, to their own detriment, of what a spawn of man lower than a rat-demon provides to the world.

In my experiences, women love to express their disdain for matters with loud, vexing, outcries, often heard through walls and ceilings.

8:15 PM

I enjoyed a meal for what *it* was, and reconfigured my mind in front of this template, for I came to understand what matters most in my times of plight: this document.

Saturday, May 16th, 2020

8:34 PM

Candy worked alongside me at *Anomalies and Oddities* today and throughout our variegated banter she decided to end our conversation with a non sequitur of, *"It's* interesting how you pay so much attention to what you eat and put into your body, and then I think of the black man."

I said, "What do you mean by this?"

"The black man who fucked you in your asshole," she stated with pert nonchalance. "You care so much about what goes into your body-"

I smiled, braced both of my fists atop the counter before me, and said, "I thought that's what you meant. Not even my father knows about that, though he'll end up reading about *it*."

"I will too." At that moment, Candy's son, Midnight, entered the store.

We shut off the lights and exited the storefront together. While I turned to lock the door, I met Candy's eyes and said, "You've given me something to think about on my walk home."

Candy grinned, her son by her side, and we veered out of each other's disparate lives. Umbrella in hand, I walked through heavy rain to a supermarket. Candy and her son entered a white van and drove to a general merchandise retailer.

I think of my recruiters, of the men I met at boot camp, of the officers, chiefs, meal servers, and the hordes of "failures" at Navy SEPS (Separations). If my three recruiters—men who I once considered *friends* when my faith for companionship had been at a nadir—had returned the writing device and phone I entrusted to them on my departure to boot camp, I would have never submitted myself sexually to another man for the sake of sanctuary. I feel like less of a man on the recollection of my sought-after-enslavement; yet, the old "black man," Lewis, proved to be my brother, although he had the penchant of referring to me as his "bitch." The moment he placed an aggressive hand on me, the inverse occurred—though I admit, Lewis feared the law of the state that I could've invoked on account of him being a convicted drug-dealer receiving fraudulent welfare checks while on probation.

10:09 PM

Neither of the two tenants upstairs has created any noise for the past two weeks except for the woman puking into the toilet above me each morning, and the man yelling one single, sharp command to his dog on rare occasions. Neither has made a *peep*, except in late hours of the night, though then, I walk beneath where I know they are at leisure—directly beneath—and chew my sweet potatoes and oatmeal with fervor and conviction, and pretend I am in solitude, in nature, in a *cave*.

What savagery is this? I left my window open for one to pass through and surprise me with death tonight. If this is my last night on this vicious plane of existence, I leave no will, and would rather take *it* with me.

Sunday, May 17th, 2020

10:56 AM

Last night I anticipated my death, or a struggle with the "certified psychopath" that would result in his death, and promoted the occasion by leaving my window open while I slept. I had set everything right; the instance had been perfect. Despite the fear of pain, I had been ready.

I awoke to the bright glow of the sun behind my light-negating curtains and the morning songs of birds, refreshed after a long sleep.

The water damage on my laptop has been amended.

"No one truly turns to examine his past, unless he is prepared to submit his acts to the courtroom of his conscience, which can never be fooled. He who has ambitiously coveted, proudly scorned, recklessly vanquished, treacherously betrayed, greedily taken, or extravagantly squandered, must forever doubt the veracity of his memory."

- Seneca's On the Shortness of Life

2:33 PM

Nothing satisfies me. I reap what I sow.

3:55 PM

There are vermin in my walls. I endure the voices of beasts once again; I compel them to leave me, to my peace and equanimity, as I pace in circles around my apartment while I wait for my sweet potatoes to boil.

Lewis gossiped loquaciously out on the porch stoops with Catherine while I lived with him, discussing *me,* for I had been his pride and joy, his "bitch." Lewis derived extreme enjoyment by the defamations he conveyed to his relations, on the topic of me. I had been a fool at his disposal.

4:18 PM

I season the sweet potatoes with a mix of yellow mustard, cayenne pepper, turmeric, curry powder, and Ceylon cinnamon—*always* the Ceylon cinnamon. Peanut butter is a decadent ad-mixture consumed in sparse portions. Honey drizzled across the amalgamate is a rare treat. I often enjoy thinking about consumption and the preparation while pacing the quadrant of my apartment and thinking of my neighbors' reactions who hear the obnoxiously loud creaks on my floor.

Welcome to the human condition:

Oh, a poem name?

Welcome to the Human Condition

Here I stand with a bowl of
Potatoes and
Wonder...
How you taste.

4:27 PM

A certified psychopath wouldn't behave in the manner the man that I interact with on the railing every-so-often behaves; his behavior is tinged with indolence.

I'm just your average stupid white male millennial who allowed himself to be fucked in the ass—succumbed to the throes of destitution, provided providence by an African-American man who exhibited racial disdain.

We are *all* psychopaths-

If you believe *it*.

Until the potential for death knocks on the metaphorical door of your reality and all pretense fails you.

What then, to the pretenders?

And what, for those without pretension?

4:59 PM

This is the my age of decadence on behalf of Covid-19.

Behold, the product of a decadent civilization: Me ("I"); the collective consciousness resonates within my soul THC-occluded perception.

Monday, May 18th, 2020

6:49 AM

I walked to the apartment laundry building to begin washing my clothes as the first and only priority of my day. Midway through loading, someone cleared their throat when I thought I had been alone. I scanned at eye level and saw no movement. A rustle of fabric directed my attention below a table in the corner of the room where a fat African-American man had slept overnight. I offered him assistance, to which he thanked me and declined.

9:45 AM

I have no other recourse but to write:

On my final trip back from the laundry building, an African-American man wearing a bandana around his lower face and black sunglasses over his eyes repeatedly honked his horn in quick, successive bursts. I thought to confront the man about his obnoxiousness; instead, I entered my home as a docile lamb would. The horn continued. My hand still fixed on the handle of my door, I pressed down, and pushed out, back into the cool, sunny morning, and strode across a patch of apartment grass towards the horn-abuser.

On my approach to the side of the open window of the driver's side, the horn-abuser silently pointed up at who he honked for, as if *that* were my question, or rather, the *reason* for my presence.

Without any trace of humor or amicability, and sober, I said, "Why do you honk your horn repeatedly, to the detriment of your neighbors, when you may step out of your car and knock on the door of whose attention you are trying to attract?"

The man immediately resorted to death threats and accused me of being a white supremacist. I encouraged him to end my life, for what value he assigned to the killing of me, amused me. He lowered his bandana, removed his sunglasses, exited the vehicle, and stepped in front of me, inches from my face. I observed well: Yellow eyes—that's about all, yellow where there should have been white.

"You fucking bitch white supremacist mother fucker. I'll fucking kill you. I'll fucking *kill* you."

I outstretched my arms, smiled, and said, "I'm right here."

The dramatics persisted in this way, with slight variations, for about one minute longer. The man's yellow eyes shifted towards the second-floor balcony of my apartment quadrant. I turned my head. There stood my well-deserved haters: The four residents I had interacted with for the past few months: A certified psychopath and his live-in psychoanalyst, and the younger couple who once lived above me when I stayed with Lewis at a schoolhouse converted into an apartment building. All began to jeer and shout at me in the hornblower's defense. I felt the human condition at that moment—greater than I ever have before: Confirmation of my innate disdain for myself and humanity reflected at me in those whose wills I have transgressed. Real, *tangible* human voices, spoken from faces I could observe:

"You aren't liked around here," said the live-in psychoanalyst.

"Go back into your apartment and shut the fuck up," said the young woman who lives above me.

"You're a nuisance," said the live-in psychoanalyst.

"You're fucking stupid, bud; you made this world for yourself," said the certified psychopath.

"This is an everyday thing with you," said the live-in psychoanalyst.

"You're acting weird and shit all the time knocking on people's doors when I'm not home and I'm just trying to get by with my pregnant girlfriend," said the young man who lives above me.

I spoke out against the five: the man who threatened to kill me to my proximate vicinity, and the four on the balcony. If they had access to peanuts and tomatoes, the occasion would've been suitable for a pelting. The young man on the balcony, shirtless, eagerly joined in on the mob-rule. Indeed, if not for society's law—that which I seek to extricate myself from—I would have succumbed to my neighbors. I diverted my attention away from the horn-blower and requested to speak to the young man; however, his girlfriend, Catherine, answered on his behalf, with a defiant, "Uh, hell no!" while both began to back away and stand in their doorway on my approach up the stairwell.

The certified psychopath barred my way with his body at the top of the stairs and demanded that I don't touch him. I assured him and the others that I had talked with the office manager and she confirmed that me being on the second floor is not breaking any policy or law—though none would hear me over their verbal assaults. Both women retrieved their phones and called the local police department. The horn-abuser continued to threaten me with death while a woman—I presume his companion, with an infant in her arms—"restrained" the horn-abuser by tugging on his shirt sleeves. The histrionic antics continued while I stood, nonplussed. The certified psychopath accused me of "drinking" and stated that I "reeked of alcohol." A hail of hostile voices assailed me. The combined onslaught of those I imagined to despise me throughout my hateful marijuana-induced imaginings became a confirmed reality. I had been barred permission from a conversation with Geoffrey (the young man who lives above me) to resolve any misunderstandings, by the certified psychopath. I turned away from everyone and stood at the middle of the stairwell, on a flat section where the stairs protruded out on both sides of me, and braced my hands against the railing. I observed the observers who observed me: Men and women from around the neighborhood, standing idle by their doors—shadowed faces from behind windows. I said aloud, with gaiety and disdain, "Just what am I if not a man? These creatures around me—just what are we?" The condemnations of me faded while I listened, again, to the subtle songs of birds in nearby trees, the rustle of trash discarded alongside a dumpster, blown by a chill wind, and the hum of traffic along a distant highway. Tears welled in my eyes, for the scorn I felt concerning my existence, the ignorance of others, and my ignorance of *my* ignorance.

Who had I been to confront another man? How presumptuous of me to assert myself in this world of slaves.

I asked those around me if I should remain where I am in anticipation of law enforcement. No one provided me an answer. On my way back indoors with intent to consume, Catherine called me a "criminal." While I stirred my oatmeal and lowered the stove top burner's heat setting, I heard an officer of the law arrive and converse with the certified psychopath and his live-in psychoanalyst about the deficiencies of my character.

I abandoned the prospect of consuming oats for that moment, opened my front door, and greeted a sergeant of the local police force dressed in civilian clothes. "Are you an officer here to interrogate and detain me on account of my barbarism?" I asked with an eager inflection, hoping for *any* man to be more than how they present themselves.

"No," the sergeant assured me, "I'm here to talk with you about what happened."

I relayed, in earnest, my account of the scenario. Midway through my story, two police vehicles pulled up and out stepped three men in uniform to listen. I addressed each with a circumspect gaze, stunned at the course of events that led to this moment. I had been cooking oats and washing clothes; the next instance, a repetitive horn disturbed me—*and then,* my life threatened!—I implored for the end, and hoped the African-American man would attempt to shoot, stab, or pummel me into oblivion, for I realized then… the washed clothes, the oats, the *moment* is all I had; there had been no future to consider; the past is sourced from an ill-contrived fount of memories laden with emotional overlays—such as what *this* is.

I deserve the animosity of those around me, for that is what I harbor.

My story told, I informed the officers of my scorn, and returned indoors without saying goodbye, or thanking any for their time. I stopped midway in my doorway, my eyes bleary with crestfallen dejection, and forced a somber nod of my head when an officer who had been speaking to me said, "Contact us for now on if anything disturbs you and we'll take care of *it.*"

12:16 PM

The apartment manager arrived and knocked on my door. I relayed to him my feelings and thoughts regarding humanity and felt the restorative peace of an empathetic being waft through me; we even shook hands. I admitted my infractions against my upstairs neighbors out of my volition and desire to equalize the playing field, to acknowledge that no single party is entirely right or wrong, but rather, to vindicate humanity on a microcosmic level. I shared my accounts of yelling through the ceiling after listening to domestic disputes, and yelling through my walls at my Latino neighbor on account of his boisterous music. He listened to me—this apartment manager with shades on—while I stood shirtless in my doorway and enjoyed the sun's rays on my deprived skin. Swaths of pollen wavered through the air beneath a clear blue sky.

"As an unmuddied lake, Fred. As clear as an azure sky of deepest summer. You can rely on me, Fred."

- Alex Delarge, portrayed in Stanley Kubrick's
movie adaptation of A Clockwork Orange

I may terminate my lease early for the price of half of the duration of what remains; this amounts to four months, which would cost me an estimated $850. If I am to terminate my lease now, liquidate my belongings, and book a flight due for next month back to New York, I may assist my father with apartment affairs once again and expedite his venture of acquiring a boat where we may live at sea.

Sympathy for me would be an injustice, as any astute reader would know.

4:32 PM

I've terminated my lease agreement early at a liquidation fee of $604: a paltry sum for a greater progression.

Under "Reason for early termination," I wrote, "I'm a menace."

On June 28th, I will fly on a plane back to New York. I may overlook my depravity and self-abasement at this moment, and rejoice, for I have restored hope. Though a plan may be folly, without such a design, the human creature lapses into forlornness, despair, and ultimately, contempt and disdain.

I've arranged to meet with Candy tomorrow morning for breakfast with my PlayStation 4 console and peripherals carried on my back. Her nine-year-old son will derive far more enjoyment from the system than I ever could.

Perhaps my mood is affected by recent sunlight; for the first time since my acquisition of a "home," I visited a nearby university park, paced up and down a secluded avenue, and read a few chapters of Nietzsche's *Beyond Good and Evil.*

"At the risk of displeasing innocent ears, I submit that egoism belongs to the essence of a noble soul, I mean the unalterable belief that to a being such as 'we,' other beings must naturally be in subjection, and have to sacrifice themselves. The noble soul accepts the fact of his egoism without question, and also without consciousness of harshness, constraint, or arbitrariness therein, but rather as something that may have *it*s basis in the primary law of things:—if he sought a designation for *it* he would say: '*It* is justice *it*self.' He acknowledges under certain circumstances, which made him hesitate at first, that there are other equally privileged ones; as soon as he has settled this question of rank, he moves among those equals and equally privileged ones with the same assurance, as regards modesty and delicate respect, which he enjoys in intercourse with himself—in accordance with an innate heavenly

mechanism which all the stars understand. *It* is an additional instance of his egoism, this artfulness and self-limitation in intercourse with his equals—every star is a similar egoist; he honors Himself in them, and in the rights which he concedes to them, he has no doubt that the exchange of honors and rights, as the Essence of all intercourse, belongs also to the natural condition of things."

- Friedrich Nietzsche

Tuesday, May 19th, 2020

10:14 AM

I tossed and turned on my floor; my first inclination is to unload the toxicity of my mind onto this template, and behold for myself, in a future state of being, of what manner of despicable creature I am. The malignancy of the social beast causes me unrest and duress.

9:29 PM

The only rational feeling is indifference.

10:38 PM

The man above me shouted "fuck you" to the mother of his fetus. I'm surrounded by hysteria.

Wednesday, May 20th, 2020

8:20 AM

I awoke this morning to "Shut the fuck up! Shut the fuck up! Shut the fuck up!" screamed by Geoffrey overhead, loud and clear. "Leave me alone! Leave me alone!" I stretched and smiled. They'll be wonderful parents someday.

Over 5,000,000 Covid-19 cases worldwide, with 325,000 deaths induced, and 2,000,000 recovered. I reiterate, from many instances prior: 7,800,000,000 people *live, simultaneously,* moment to moment, at any given contemporary time; where then, I wonder, is this global *crisis?* Would my attitude be different if I, or my father, were infected?—no: I accept my mortality.

4:36 PM

After an intense blowout all morning that ended in a rampage, screaming, and tears, between my upstairs neighbors, Geoffrey and Catherine, the antics ended with both of them engaged in a shouting match outdoors. Geoffrey drove away after announcing that he will be staying at Catherine's grandmother's home for the night. Earlier, I had listened for hours while I read a few PDFs and consumed a breakfast of steel-cut oats and canned chicken. Geoffrey had been completely emasculated; Catherine condemned him; both raved and lamented of the love they once had for each other. "The baby in your **stomach**,"—cried Geoffrey! Oh, woe, woe, *woe* to humanity!

I've expedited my flight back to New York for the 16th of June: A thirteen-hour escapade that will lead me through layovers at three different airports. I've yet to inform Candy of my decision.

5:16 PM

I must admit for myself that I'm overjoyed—I *gloated* on hearing Geoffrey fall to his knees on the floor above me and weep on behalf of the remorse incurred by his wrath *and* lust, reminiscent of a twelve-year-old boy. I've suffered the convictions of idiots. There is nothing to fear.

5:47 PM

"I would never hit a woman!" Geoffrey called out; the distinction between violence on man or woman fascinates me.

Thursday, May 21st, 2020

8:18 AM

Out of everything that I may be accused of, most adjectives may be applied; however, I am no "criminal"; unless, of course, the ingestion of marijuana qualifies for shame and repentance.

Geoffrey is a pathetic excuse for a man; I emanate nothing but hatred for Geoffrey: scorn to the utmost.

The woman too, Catherine, is a vile creature: a witch of malice that incites this behavior between men in the first place. I heard Catherine beg for her life after shaming and emasculating Geoffrey for an hour-and-a-half, the insufferable cunt; I will not edit this. Catherine, you are a despicable lowlife, to entreat a man's emotions to manipulate him into staying in a toxic relationship, for the sake of a baby he doesn't want, nor neither of you can provide for. And Geoffrey, of course, for impregnating the woman in the first place. The literal scum of society lurks above me: rats, both of them.

Listen to me Chew, Asshole

You condemn me for my enjoyment
Yet you don't reckon your own behavior.
What do you see but an image?
These thoughts are a nuisance.
"He doesn't even drive."
The ignorant masses, I wonder:
What "education" do you have?
Do you hear me type?
Do you hear me chew?
I often wonder...
About *you.*

Psych Ward prison at sea.
Alcatraz, but smaller.
Plot is a cook who cooks oatmeal for prisoners, condemned to a jail sentence because the scumbag couple who lived above him in an apartment complex reported him to local authorities for acting aberrant.

Friday, May 22nd, 2020

6:05 PM

"Want to know something interesting?" inquired the pseudo-homeless man upon entering *Anomalies and Artifacts*. He smiled wide before I could answer and said, "Mushrooms grow in my house now." I looked at him: sweaty and uncouth. "Real big ones."

I said, "Well, damn, man."

"Hey, could I use your restroom?"

"The res... yeah, sure."

After fifteen minutes, he emerged, coughed, said, "Oh, shit man, can I use your computer for like, fifteen or twenty minutes for a test I gotta take—otherwise I gotta go all the way down to the motel and use their computers."

"I'm using my computer right now for work."

"No I mean before the shop closes."

"No, I'm using *it* for work."

"But before the shop closes—you gonna use *it* for forty minutes?"

"Yes."

"Oh, well... so should I go down to the motel then?"

I looked up at him, away from this document (this document recorded in real-time), and said, "If *you* want to do that."

"All right bro, well... all right bro; hey, I'll be back to buy those books sometime; I just wanted to get outta the house. Even if I waited for you to finish your work, when the shop closes—could I use your computer then?"

I met his eyes and saw a flicker of disdain, entitlement, desperation, and vacuousness, all at once, and said, "No."

"Ah well, all right bro." The man proceeded to putter around the shop with an immense frown plastered over his face. He turned on a heel and pushed out of the shop door.

I said, "Take care," before the door closed behind him. I observed him observing me with a crooked neck through the front shop window.

Without delay, on my return home from my shift, I visited a grocery store for steel-cut oats, sweet potatoes, berries, bananas, apples, and sardines. I *must* transcribe a series of voice recordings I captured on May 21st, 2020, for the sake of my future ~~enjoyment and~~ reflection.

The first hour-and-a-half, I shouted a soliloquy up through the ceiling of my apartment *at* Geoffrey and Catherine while I stirred slow-cooking oatmeal on a stovetop. The second three hours, I stood with the voice recorder in my pocket on the second-floor balcony of my apartment. My productivity will be dedicated to the transcription of this henceforth; therefore, I digress, ~~critical reader~~ future self:

8:45 PM

Before I begin, on my way home from the grocery store, carrying my bags, five African-American children, the same rowdy gang as before, walked up to me from behind the railing of an upraised parking lot. The oldest boy approached me; I smiled (genuinely) and nodded. The boy turned sharply away from me, covered his face, and through a grin, he shouted, "Ow! He hit me! Did you just see him hit me?"

I stopped, and the other boy and two girls approached, all around the age of ten to thirteen years old.

I reached into one of my bags, pulled out a dew-covered granny smith apple, and feigned an aggressive toss. Both boys shouted and backed away in fright. One said, *"Oh* what the fuck!" The girls watched, intrigued.

"Here, you want *it?*" I handed the apple out and the same boy who had accepted my banana a month ago snatched the fruit from my hand. I turned to go, and the oldest boy grimaced at me, both arms flat by his side. I reached into my other bag, procured another dew-covered granny smith apple, and said, "Here."

The oldest boy said, "Fuck no I ain't want dat."

My eyes averted to the nearest girl and she immediately yelled, "I do!"

I passed the apple to the girl and began to walk away. Six seconds later, I observed an apple skitter across the parking lot to my left and break into three pieces. I heard a child's voice: "Come back here and I'll kick yo ass motha fucka!" and didn't look back. Fifty seconds elapsed. I encroached the perimeter of the apartment complex and I heard a second apple smash three feet behind me, slightly to my right. I skewed my head to see the perpetrator: The boy who had accepted my first apple; he showed me his middle finger.

I'd deem these boys wise for not accepting fruit from a stranger, especially a kind notorious for being poisonous in fairytales and legends, though these boys had accepted, taken a few bites of, and cursed the hand that fed them. I had truly been in a ghetto.

10:03 PM

I admitted to Candy today that I feel like a scumbag for relishing the scumbaggery exhibited by others and writing of my self-induced problems in choosing to interact with such scum, while other people, e.g., herself, suffer from authentic, unwanted problems day-to-day, such as her thrice-weekly physical therapy for her feet. Candy proceeded to ~~empathize with~~ validate me: A great woman. I'll repose in my memory of her, yet, I'll never miss her.

Perhaps Candy and I are the scumbags relishing each other's validation. *I* am the scumbag for accusing others of being scumbags. I'll leave the verdict to my *brilliant, intelligent, infallible* ~~readers~~ paid critics.

Saturday, May 23rd, 2020

6:35 AM

I am sleep-deprived.

As much as I don't want to, I care about Candy's opinion of me as a man. To her, I suspect I am deficient, perpetually dependent on another man to achieve my goals (i.e., my father, or Lewis) and devoid of integrity with my commitments (these are *my* opinions of myself that my ego fails to assimilate with and therefore project onto Candy); I have betrayed her, twice: First, by ending our intimate relationship on a whim on account of my desire for her to pursue relations with a man who could authentically provide for her; second, by returning to New York three months earlier than I had projected.

I have alerted Candy of my emotional instability and requested work off, only to retract my request two hours later, around 6:00 AM.

Yes, what manner of man am I? Candy talks of dreams of me, how she will miss me, and the earlier facets of our romance as if they were bygone relics to chat casually of; this had been well by me, until I experienced *joy,* and kinship, spent with her young son. Seated at the breakfast table with an ex-lover and the son of another man, I felt the natural pride of a pseudo-father and reminded myself of what I will never know.

I weep and grieve, you *fool* reader—and now, without delaying your gratification any longer—you completionists and avid sadists who long to read of my wretched, pitiable slog and inevitable demise, I transcribe for you, my lonely THC-induced outburst at my upstairs neighbors on May 21st:

Sunday, May 24th, 2020

11:54 AM

A Lonely Outburst

"Wonderful—now I'll stir my oats and you can listen to me chew!"

Thirty-two seconds elapsed while I stirred steel-cut oats. "With a typical pleb face, I project *it* outwards; my ego speaks, but I'm just a *fucking* madman. What? Who said that?"

Two minutes elapsed. I stared up at my ceiling and shouted, "Are you a man or a twelve-year-old? What? What did you say? Who said that? I'm a fucking madman. Oh… *oh*… You know, I just have problems; I need to talk about all the *fucking* time."

Forty-three seconds elapsed. "Did I mention that I've been fucked in the ass by a black man, so what do I know? I'm just a madman after all—you *fucking* **infant!**"

Nineteen seconds elapsed. "And you too woman, what mannish behavior—yes, that's right, very masculine of you up there. You **are** a bitch!"

Thirty-five seconds elapsed. I dropped my oat stirrer and began to stride around my apartment while shouting, "Let's stay together and bring another life into the world so that they can live a life of a miserable existence! That sounds wonderful! For the sake of ourselves, we'll be happy together. We'll continue validating each other—even though there's no love whatsoever! That sounds wonderful, hunny! We'll make wonderful parents someday! Oh… I need a psychoanalyst; I better go next door! Three doors down, that's right, *that's* right… That's if I can get past the certified psychopath! Ho-ho! **Oh** I'm a fucking comedian! I should write *it* down! Instead I'm talking about myself… and all my problems… in a loud voice… with no consideration for those around me."

Eleven seconds elapsed. "I can't help *it:* I love your genitals, *so* much, that I cannot bear to think of a life without you by my side. You are just *so* attractive to me, despite your *miserable* scumbag behavior. Do you truly need to hear this?—am *I* the asshole?—I don't fucking know! I'm just a madman! What did he say?—I don't fucking know! He's just a madman and I am too!

I returned to the stovetop and stirred my oats. *"Yes,* I hate people; well, doesn't *this* explain **why!"**

Twenty-eight seconds elapsed. I turned and yelled at my ceiling, "What did I ever do, god?—to deserve this? Why do you **smite** me in such a way: to be **cursed,** with somebody who *talks* **all the time!** How wretched that must be—to not be able to consult yourselves!—*oh, it* truly wounds me, but I can't help but smile!"

I sauntered around my living room and screamed, "What are you going to do? **What are you going to do!? I wonder! Let's see** *it!* Calm myself down? But I'm just a man full of testosterone! I'm also mad! As you can see, I need a psychoanalyst, as soon as possible, to show me the light! I've heard there are certified psychopaths around here who can help me out! I have a vendetta—yes—against all of these **plebs,** that have **no** self-insight—except for a few—I mean… I have very **limited** social interactions here, and I only speak to those who are **total** *fucking* **assholes… so you'll know if I'm talking to you, that you're a fucking asshole!** But, man can only see a version of *himself,* so therefore," I roared at max capacity: *"I* am the asshole—in fact—the **biggest fucking asshole,** *you've ever met in your life!* **You see what happens when somebody** *screams!? That's fucking emotional manipulation!"*

I returned to my oats and stirred. "Ah, that's all right though; I'm just gonna go on writing, because I'm a madman! And you two can have fun fucking each other! *Ah*—I feel so much better getting that off my chest! Now you can call the cops, or go next door and complain—I don't fucking care. I'm going to *chew* for you now!—well—in a little bit: about fifteen or twenty minutes, and *listen* to you too! But I'm just a madman! I don't know what I'm doing!"

Fourteen seconds elapsed. I spoke to myself at a slightly elevated volume, "Mm… Mmm… *Damn,* what an outburst. Was that shameful of me?" I yelled, "Aw, *fuck*—I feel so much *shame* now that I *spoke* and *screamed* and was completely fucking *irrational* and behaved like a **twelve-year-old** *boy!* Go ahead and **kick my ass** you fucking *cunt*—knock on my fucking door—**make my. Fucking. Day!** And you too, **wretch,** or **wench;**

if you have an issue go right-the-fuck ahead; you're capable of kicking **his** ass apparently!"

Thirteen seconds elapsed. I heard two sets of footsteps directly above me where I had screamed. "Are you home or are you **rats** lurking up there!?—**skittering around!? Come on, let's hear some anger! I've heard** *it* **before!** I wonder! I'm asking for *it*—that's right. I'm ready, to feel like a man again, to be confronted, with a **face,** that tells me the **truth."**

Nineteen seconds elapsed. I impersonated a young female and male voice: *"What are we going to do, hunny?'* 'I don't fucking know; we fucked up! We're crazy assholes too!' *'Oh no! I never saw it coming!'"*

Twenty-one seconds elapsed. I stirred my oats and said, "Get this guy on some meds; he's just a crazy asshole. No but really, if you want to test your manhood because you're fucking **angry** and don't know how to rationalize *it*—you can't even *talk* to me—fuck you! **Yeah you hurt my 'feel-wings!'** You insulted my **respect,** for **life!** To bar another human being from communication... I don't speak often; this is a **rare** instance! My... idiosyncrasies."

I stood beside my front window. "I hear somebody *bitching* outside. *It*'s interesting—this life, you know? Oh—*oh,* sorry; **I wouldn't want to empathize;** you don't deserve *it."*

Twenty seconds elapsed. I listened to the footsteps above me. "Those are some *big* fucking rats, damn. Such brazen and reckless behavior. Should I just be mute and scary, or somewhat creepy and weird, or should I be an outspoken asshole? I don't know which is more fun. Hm, these are the 'big' questions, not black holes or any of that *bullshit*—or what consciousness is—or what a thought is... not that **we have any of those in the fucking first place!**—other than, each other's genitalia. Because who gives a fuck about what a thought does when you can't be bothered. We're all mad right? We all need *professional* therapy—we all need help, because we're just fucking incapable of thinking for ourselves: Spoken by the maddest asshole you've ever met. Isn't that wonderful? I'll do you justice, but you'll probably hold the information against me. **I'm leaving soon! I won't specify when! I'm going on a boat! A life at sea! Oh** *it*'s *fucking* **romantic!** And you two will go on to be wonderful parents some day, and that, is a blessing, to the entire world!"

Sixteen seconds elapsed. "Unless of course, I'm apprehended by authorities before I go, and then—oh, you hear my confidence wane there at that moment, due to all the *cares* I have in this world. *I have so much holding me back. I don't want to die.* That would be horrible. *It*'s a funny topic when you're thinking about *it* and… when you think you're so tough and invincible, and immortal, like a **god.** But then you think… would death really be, so, **bad?** To move onto something totally unknown—yes, *it's* terrifying especially, that we all will feel some manifestation of pain when we die. I hold my hands in prayer for you, and for my**self,** and I pray… I can't think of anything to say that's clever or funny, so I'm going to stop now. *It* never was clever or funny to begin with, and I tried to make *it* so, despite the sad, disgusting, reality of *it.*"

Fifty-three seconds elapsed. "*Oh* wow—I got that all on a voice recorder! Time to start a new file."

Monday, May 25th, 2020

1:00 PM

A Lonely Outburst, Part 2

"And then transcribe *it! It's* so much easier than having to think at the moment, and type; *it's* much more efficient—but then you have cognitive slips—yes—and stuttering, and sometimes straight from *thought* to *object* is so much better. So this will be for my own amusement, and then summarized succinctly in a later moment: the transcription process! And *it* spikes ideas, because here I am having an outburst about *nothing,* talking about *people* squirming over each other's *fucking* bodies—*oh* and there's so much foul language being spoken. 'Whenever he uses the word *fuck it's* just so *crude! It* detracts from the meaning! *It's* disgusting! Hm. *It's* offensive to my ears, and therefore my body and my physiology. Who will listen to me? Who will hear *it?* I want you to know how offended I am about what he talks so loudly about—and says *fuck!*'"

I unleashed a bestial growl and shouted, "I wonder, hm—what do people do; what do people think about; what do they *speak* of? Is this just a wonderful act?—oh-*ho-ho!* You should be in comedy on a stage! You should be preaching! You should be fucking president!—ho-ho-ho-ho—who the fuck… cares? *It's…* I'm in a state of bliss with my oatmeal. Listen to those birds."

I departed from the stovetop and walked to my open bedroom window. "Oh, wonderful—life, cars, and traffic—*traffic* from the nearby highway and… uh, what is *it*. A buzz, a whirring, a *whir,* of some sort-of… mechanism. Oh—the air conditioning unit, yes—and the *birds*—yes—everybody loves the *fucking* birds, even though they look at you like you're *shit*. The squirrels too, the squirrels see you and they think, 'What the fuck does a human do all day? *Think?* The damn fools!' Yes, the squirrel thinks, 'What the fuck does a human do all day? *Think?* The damn fools.' Yes. That's what squirrels think. And they think, 'Nuts nuts nuts squirrel oh my god car,' well, there's no 'oh my god,' *it*'s just 'car.' 'Nuts nuts, car, nuts nuts nuts nuts—dodge the car—nuts nuts, sex nuts sex nuts… oh… car—car—car—car—car—ca—ca—ca—car oh, —nu—nu—nu—nuts—nuts—nuts, nuts, nuts. Nuts. Sex.'"

I sighed. "I'm truly out of my mind! Oh I'm talking about what squirrels think about and what they do—I must be a fucking madman eating oatmeal. Mm… Mm… Life. *Yes* I'm having a good time, to your expense! Now what does that make me?—a fucking asshole right? Yeah! So what do I deserve? To be *annoyed,* so *annoy* me. Do *something.* Stop being rats in your existence. You can talk, you can play, you can live your life and be happy and fuck and be merry, smoke your cigars and drink—I don't give a shit!"

Fourteen seconds elapsed while I chewed and paced. "I *read;* I walk around my house and I read; therefore, I hear you. Music distracts from the content and retention. So I know—I *hear* these things, and I *know,* my *volume* is *intrusive* and **obnoxious** right now, because… Well, yeah, *it*'s obvious right? I have a lot of time on my hands. *It*'s great! I'm free—to behave in this manner. We all have been the entire time. I'm free! I'm a free man in my box!—a slave to myself! This is not Covid-induced. This is just the freedom of expression, in the moment… because I'm a fucking madman." I muttered, "Yes. I'm just a loon. I keep telling myself that."

I consumed oatmeal for thirty-one seconds and resumed my amplified narrative, "Now would be the ideal time for me to go out on the second-floor balcony, and stand there, and be… *jovial,* and see what happens. If I were to place my body on the second-floor balcony, and *exist,* in a jovial state, I wonder what would happen to me? I wonder what would transpire around me. I think the certified psychopath would come *right* out of his home, and *speak* to me, and ask me why I'm here. But I have **every right** to be on that second-floor balcony; isn't that curious?—residents of this shithole, don't you think so? *It*'s a *social* thing… *It*'s *a common* area. Even if he was already standing there when I came out, I am *free,* to *'be.'* So, I think I'm going to get dressed, go out on that balcony after I brush my teeth—and make sure that I don't have **shit in my eyes,** in case somebody gets really close to my face, so they can see how pretty that I am!—hopefully while they're **threatening my life! That would make my** *fucking day!"*

One minute and eleven seconds elapsed. From the bathroom, I sang, *"We'll, meet again, don't know where, don't know when! But I know… and I don't know the rest of the song!—so fuck it!"*

Two minutes and twenty-four seconds elapsed while I brushed my teeth. "Well I suppose I should get myself presentable, and *shave…* God **damn** *it.* I condemn god, for making me shave."

Three minutes and fifty-eight seconds elapsed. "I'm about to live my life, and go out into the world, as a free man. Ah, *it*'s good to be free; I can *piss* whenever I want to."

I urinated for eleven seconds, exhaled deeply, and said, "Yes, pissing whenever I want to feels great. Nothing compares."

One minute and thirty-nine seconds elapsed. "Time to put on the single dress shirt that I own. Isn't this fucking weird. Seeing some fucking loon like myself walk out and just *exist,* on a balcony, or a walkway, or a railway, doing nothing but *existing.* That's so fucking strange. I'll be back in by 4 o'clock to put away my oatmeal, so *it* doesn't get *moldy,* from this strange existence, this strange bacteria-ridden existence, with viruses and parasites… so strange. I will not speak while I'm out there unless spoken to; that's the deal I have with myself; that grants me sanctuary—because I was just existing! I only existed, in that space, and said *nothing.* But my joy will be so pro- Hm, let's see… provocative, yes. My joy will be *provocative.* 'My joy was provocative, officer! That's what happened—I swear! My joy, *it* was so damn provocative!—they just couldn't handle *it!'* Now we're all curious human beings here, so I don't mind a few peeks every now and then. Get on my belt; I think I'll button up my shirt *all* the way because *it*'s a bit chilly. Well, not all the way; the last button *must* be undone; that is what's normal! Truly normal. These people are going to confront me and express their hatred, and that may be wonderful too. I don't know; I'm excited; life is a joy. *I'm going out to exist, in so-ci-e-ty! It*'s a *great* day! I'm going to exist, in a place! And I'm going to be shot, from a window, by some man with a rifle, and nobody will know who did *it!* Nobody will care either! They'll say 'Good fucking riddance, about that scumbag!' And all that scumbag was doing, was enjoying himself damn *it!* Ah, I'm such a fucking comedian; oh *it*'s wonderful. I want to exist, and I'll be quiet about *it.* I just want to look, and smile.

Thursday, May 28th, 2020

8:42 PM

There is nothing more pitiable than self-pity. This book is a lie—the entire series; my limited perspective cannot begin to capture even a mote of truth in relation to objective reality, i.e., god. Yes, the god within us all observes me for the man that I *truly* am, unbeknownst to me.

I ventured to sleep with Candy's twenty-year-old daughter and informed Candy of my intent hours later. Candy claimed to love me. I terminated the plans Candy's daughter and I had begun to develop to spare Candy the jealousy and hatred she struggled to suppress. I terminated the intimacy between Candy and myself, again, not to cause her grief, but to spare us both utter nonsense.

I repaid my debt of $300 to the homeless shelter I stayed at prior to attending the U.S. Navy boot camp.

At the supermarket, a skinny, well-groomed man a few years younger than myself pushed a broom towards me while I meandered towards the berry section. I veered out of the man's way. From behind a face mask, he said, "Hi."

I said, "Hello," proceeded to select four granny smith apples, turned, and met with the same man, who now stood behind me without a broom.

The man said, "Hey."

"Hello." I stopped and stood before him.

"Do you remember me?"

"No."

"We talked at checkout one time."

"About what?"

"We talked about how awful customers are."

"I don't recall."

The man shifted on his feet, adjusted his facemask, and said, "Well, I don't have any friends and I was wondering if you'd like my number."

"Why, so we can talk about how awful customers are?"

The man laughed and removed his face mask to show me a smile. "Yeah—well, no, to be friends."

"I also have no friends, but by choice."

"Oh," the man gazed down at the floor and returned his eyes to mine, "Well, if you ever want anything from me, seek me out."

I nodded, smiled, and said, "Thanks."

This world of sex and ephemeral amusements, of mothers with their sons working on front yard projects, of middle-aged white men removing garbage from their property discarded by residents of a next-door ghetto, of seven-year-old-children sneaking beneath a table cloth to kiss, of a young couple who volunteer to babysit a neighborhood family's children and realize their disdain for one another in their attempt to work as a team, of pillboxes, of subscription television series, of numbers on a screen dictating your self-worth—yes—this is *our* world.

The ~~homeless~~ man who once sold me marijuana met me immediately after my shift ended and hailed me on the corner of the street. I didn't recognize him at first; therefore, he called me "buddy" twice to capture my attention. The sky had been light-blue—always, the typical light-blue; I didn't notice *it* then—the moment when the man who sold me marijuana once had called me "buddy," though I think of *it* now, in conjunction with the heat, and I marvel at the simplicity of *our* world. The man asked me if I ever suffered a bank ATM "eating" a debit card. I responded in the negative and hurried away.

Friday, May 29th, 2020

9:50 AM

On the Balcony, Part 3

"This is going to be boring. I'm going to enjoy *it,* and then my joy will *fleet* from my face, and I won't know what to do but to come back here. I don't know—let's see—everything's in order, as if I'm going out to work. Yes, everything is accounted for. I take my key off my wall, even though no one would ever enter my apartment while I'm right there—so…[12] I guess not. Yes, all right. I'll leave the door unlocked—don't want to look *pretentious that* way—that's just *stupid* pretentiousness. Now we'll go." I exited my apartment, rounded out to the stairwell, ascended to the second-floor balcony, stood by the rail, and observed the sluggish movement of clouds, the passage of birds, the flow of neighborhood traffic, and the others nearby on their respective balconies. For three minutes and fifty-

---

[12] Oh, how wrong I had been.

two seconds, I remained this way: stationary and at peace, until the door to the certified psychopath's apartment opened. The live-in psychoanalyst stood in the doorway, one foot on the balcony, one foot on her carpet, long disheveled blonde hair pulled into a ponytail, unlit cigarette held by her head.

The psychoanalyst said, "Are you fuckin' for real? You're fuckin' out [of] your mind—you know that, cuz I *know* you're listenin' to me outside!" I turned my head towards her, raised an eyebrow, smiled at her for one second, and gazed back towards the skyline. "And I'm *glad* you're amused— get the fuck out of my—porch, *get off*." I remained where I stood. Twelve seconds elapsed and the psychoanalyst dialed a number on her cellphone. She shouted, "[Indiscernible] please!" and glared at me. "You have lost your god-blessed mind. *It* is taking every bit of my energy, to not come over there, and *beat* the bricks out of you myself. Oh *no*—I *know* you ain't stupid crazy—you *dangerous* crazy!—cuz you know I gotta touch yo' ass to call the cops right? I ain't stupid hunny, and *I know!*—you ain't my hunny! But I *do* know who I can call to help assist me with this! You're trying to get a *rise* out of me, and you probably can because ***fucking*** my heads more fucked up than yours right now!"

The psychoanalyst took a deep drag from her (lit) cigarette while I addressed her with a countenance of bewildered pity. She remained in the doorway. Her fifteen-year-old-son veered in and out of the shadows behind her. "No—you stay right there," the psychoanalyst said to her son when he had asked to leave the apartment. She proceeded to speak her address into the phone pressed hard against her head. "Um—I have my downstairs neighbor that's been up here—and he's not supposed to be up here, in front of my door, and I need you to come and prevent him from coming into my door. Right, please. Because I *don't know if I'm going to be able to restrain myself much longer!*—so I—please, need you to get somebody here. Uh—um—he's *not* supposed to be up here—upstairs—he's a downstairs neighbor. He is coming out here trying to make a scene—he's a true menace," the psychoanalyst stared at me while she spoke, "which he knows—to all his neighbors," her voice wavered and cracked, "the office is aware of *it*. Courtesy officer [Name] is aware of *it*. The [Indiscernible]. Baethan. I do not—I care not to know about *it*. Oh yes. Oh yes. Yes, he has a vacate the premises in effect right now." I looked at the psychoanalyst, surprised she had known about my lease termination, and she covered her phone with a hand and snarled, "Knowledge is power *fucker. Leave! Go downstairs!*"

The psychoanalyst removed her hand from the phone, and with an air of contrived dignity, said, "All black (in reference to my clothing). Caucasian. Yup!" she laughed. "This man has lost his mind. *Ahh*—I'd say mid-twenties. He obviously doesn't have any competence. Um, *it* doesn't matter to me; I'm restraining myself—I'm *restraining* myself right now. No, I'm in my doorway."

Thirteen seconds of silence elapsed. I listened to bird calls and children playing in the streets below us. The psychoanalyst asked me, "Are you still amused?"

I nodded my head, stone-faced.

The psychoanalyst grinned and talked into the phone receiver, "He's amused right now. My husband just suffered—they were here just a few days ago and my husband suffered a *heart attack* because of *this man*," the psychoanalyst's voice trembled and her eyes welled with tears, "so I'm *literally telling you that* you need to get someone here—cuz I'm literally restraining myself to prevent me from *hurting this man*—because my husband is about to *fucking die* because of *him!*" The psychoanalyst screamed into the phone while she looked at me and began to sob, though she suppressed her tears, leaned against the balcony railing with one hand, and puffed on a drag from her cigarette. Neighbors from different apartment complexes had come out of their homes to stand in front of their doorways and observe the scene (me standing and gazing out at the parking lot).

Fifty-one seconds elapsed. The psychoanalyst commanded her son to stay indoors and proceeded to talk into the phone receiver with a quivering voice, "He's trying to trick me into—using psychological tricks—to trick me into attacking him, first, and in the state of mind that I'm in right now I'm *so* at that threshold and that's why I called you first—because I can't come out of *my own* *house* because *this man* is *standing* in my walkway. And I—I—I'm seriously going to lose my shit right now—and me being on the phone is actually a courtesy to him?—because *it*'s protecting his ass right now. I'm an employee here also," she giggled, "that's how—he doesn't realize how I have so much knowledge."

Two minutes and ten seconds elapsed. The psychoanalyst finalized her call to a dispatcher. We stood side-by-side, six feet between us, for one minute and forty-six seconds. A city police vehicle rolled up and parked. Out stepped a short, pudgy, slick-haired officer; the psychoanalyst addressed him: "Hello!"

"Hello. Is that him?" The officer pointed at me while he ascended the balcony steps.

"Yes *it* is, that's him."

The officer stopped by my side and said, "Do you have an ID on you?"

I said, "No."

"You don't have an ID?"

"I do have an ID."

"Can I, see *it*?"

"It's in my apartment."

"Where do you live at?"

I turned, pointed to my apartment door, and said, "Right down there."

"What's your name?"

"Baethan."

"What's your last name?"

"Balor."

"Balor?"

"Yes."

"What's your date of birth?"

"November 20th, 1991."

The officer repeated my birthdate and said, "What number apartment do you live in?"

"[Number]"

"[Number]?"

At that moment, my direct upstairs neighbors, Catherine and Geoffrey, emerged from their apartment. Catherine stepped out first. Geoffrey stepped out shortly after. The psychoanalyst commanded from the other end of the balcony, "Go back into your apartment Geoffrey!" I met eyes with Geoffrey for a second, if that. Geoffrey obeyed the psychoanalyst and returned indoors without a word spoken, his head down.

5:32 PM

I quit my position as an employee for Candy.

Candy informed me afterward that she disposed of all my books for sale in her shop.

Saturday, May 30th, 2020

10:42 AM

I had intended to write of the entire balcony debacle, verbatim, and have lost interest. The police entered my home with my permission, interrogated me, determined me to not be a threat despite the malingers and disparagers which surrounded us, and I stood outside long after the four policemen had departed, where I endured the insults of ~~my fellow men~~ women for another three hours. Yes, *all* the unfounded remarks I ever suffer are perpetuated from women, and men with a feminine perspective who indulge. I am no madman after all; in fact, those around me are far worse off. The reader is *still* a fool; this book is my own, and there isn't enough space in the binding to contain all the daily bullshit I witness.

Sunday, May 31st, 2020

10:18 PM

What a painful existence *it* must be to care about those you will never see again.

JUNE

Monday, June 1st, 2020

10:15 PM

I quit smoking marijuana.

Candy's young son, Midnight, and a girl of similar age, played a game of "Marriage." I watched off-handedly and listened whole-heartedly while I cleaned and organized a broom closet during my last day at Candy's shop—these little humans, how they assigned each other a role and devised pre-taught conceptions of what "love" is for each other.

The boy followed the girl, in, out, and around the room, bound by an invisible tether clasped firmly around his neck and held taut in the girl's tiny fist.

How quaint, one would think—not I, *oh*, no. Neither knows any better but what they observe: planting kisses on each other's cheeks, professing their vows, speculating nonexistent housing options, watering imaginary plants: Corn chips, candy, and bite-sized pastries.

I had been familiar with such childhood games at their age, enamored by nubile sweethearts with dollish faces and conditioned hair. I wonder what girls are attracted to in boys at that age: slavish puppies eager to lick their face and perform tricks for a treat.

Tuesday, June 2nd, 2020

3:44 PM

Writing of myself daily has long lost *it*s appeal.

A new holiday title has arisen: Blackout Tuesday. Participating entertainment industries have shut down to support the *Black Lives Matter* crusade. Perhaps I've lost my human sensibilities, for I fail to understand how shutting down social entertainment venues may support a protest; people will entertain themselves elsewhere. What would I know?—being an ignorant and "privileged" white man standing naked in an apartment devoid of furniture while I type on a cheap Chromebook atop two cardboard boxes balanced on a kitchen counter. My life matters just as much as "black" lives, I presume, which isn't to say much, considering my poverty in a capitalistic nation; however, I must digress; this movement isn't about equity; otherwise, race would be irrelevant; the movement is about *equality*, the greatest impossibility ever conceived.

Regardless of opinions, I commend the brazenness of protesters amidst the first downturn of a pandemic.

I want to understand justice, this great conundrum. What is a "black" life, and why is there a self-perpetuated distinguishment between these "black" lives and other lives? I miss the comfort of the sediment beneath my rock. Alas, I write of my life again; I must matter—to what degree, I've yet to be validated by another life.

Dear God, I write for *you,* a haiku:

> *Upstairs Neighbors Fight*
> *Nullified Motivation*
> *Why do I exist?*

I'm cursed with this ego, laden with desire; I fail to write a haiku for God without referring to myself—ah, that's right. Here I am. Is there anything else?

Yes, of course, I remember now: 3,100,000 active Covid-19 cases worldwide. 380,600 Covid-19 induced deaths worldwide. The "calamity" ebbs and the U.S. government grants me $716 weekly unemployment checks for nothing. I'm disliked by the few who remember me, hated by those who know me, and loved by one of my begetters. I write for the synonymous concepts of god and justice. My consciousness knows only the bounds of *it*self.

Wednesday, June 3ʳᵈ, 2020

8:59 PM

I experience nothing but disdain for peaceful protesters, supporters, advocates, and most of all, saints. Money and violence are the only catalysts for change. Peaceful activists serve only to inspire those with money and the will for violence. I browse my lord and master Google and expose myself to an infinite amount of human affairs, each constrained to a microcosmic principle: ~~racism~~ inequity—the new-old topic has resurfaced and dominates my senses on a little screen.

Like myself, people, engrossed with their bubbles of limited and ignorant concerns, stare at their screens and spout *opinions*—much like myself—only I intend to publish these *opinions* in a book that will never be regarded as anything more but a pathetic madman's hateful tripe.

Climate change, animal rights, chicken farmer inequity, celebrity pay, politics, riots, sustainable farming, hedge funds, school shootings, gender identity, sexual orientation, privilege—*privilege*—what is this gratuitous nonsense I read and hear of *privilege?* These highfalutin men and women dressed in their assorted t-shirts of expression based on the flavor of the week "movement"—pitiful self-deceivers; I lament and scorn you while I lay on my floor to sleep at night, *haunted* by thoughts of what I've viewed on my screen *of you* throughout each day.

What if I̶ we were to become disconnected from worldwide events? Globalization is the true scourge of human civilization. How can there be 195 countries, 7,177 languages, 4,300 religions, *and* unified global acceptance? I only know these statistics for my lord and master Google grants my desire for knowledge—to doom myself with the inconsequential matters of our strictly humanistic plights! I'm disgusted by the inevitable. What hope do *I* have?

Yes, if humanity were to become disconnected from worldwide events—impossible. Social animals: we must endure, together, the cries of each other—the outrage against *nature:* Differences, variables, unfairness, uncertainty, *chaos.* Annihilation is the only justice.

Friday, June 5th, 2020

10:56 AM

The American Screen. How wonderful, to wake, and immerse yourself with the media of your choice, to engross yourself with isolated issues conflated to a global scale for all to buy into. My screen is filled with words, symbols, and often fantastic images. Johannes Brahms and new-age retro synth music pipes into my ears this morning while steel-cut oats slow-boil on my stovetop—*ah*—Dearest America. I've become accustomed to socialism and haven't left my house in over a week. I'm a non-contributor to society: life is grand!

Only the ignorant refute the premise of their screens. The loftiest yogis, gurus, meditators, and monks, all have screens of their own—even if they wake to a beautiful sunrise, isolated among palm trees along a serene shoreline amidst a small village; if they have any opinions to promulgate, there's a screen! Uneducated savages otherwise! We Americans poo-poo the ignorance of the unrefined. Educated!—we are!—yes!—delightfully informed by how uninformed everyone without a screen is!

I'm uncertain if I write satire. How could anyone refute my claim without a screen? Who would bother? Why care?

I'm alone and content with my screen. I'd be alone and distracted with books if not for my screen… and if deprived of both, well, there's always ~~women~~ my hand.

Saturday, June 6th, 2020

12:32 PM

I once willingly subjected myself to being anally penetrated by a fifty-nine-year-old African-American, twice, instead of choosing to reap unemployment benefits after my separation from Navy boot camp, out of a sense of unwarranted pride in the self-reliance of my abilities and resourcefulness. This African-American man offered me providence in my time of destitution—when I had exhausted my payments received while attending the Navy. I had survived being homeless in a low-income city for over a month and anticipated employment within the week when this African-American man spotted me in a parking lot and invited me to his home for temporary shelter.

I.e., I spread my ass cheeks and suffered hemorrhoids for a **black** man obsessed with racial injustice. I listened, daily, to the gross inequality and inequity suffered by black men and women across the globe and performed fellatio on a black man's penis by night.

I reiterate: Nineteen days ago I requested a black man to stop repeatedly honking his horn to the detriment of the peace of myself and our neighbors. In response, the black man exited his car, stepped a foot away from me, and said, "You fucking bitch white supremacist mother fucker. I'll fucking kill you. I'll fucking *kill* you."

Ah, well, I've just checked my privilege and determined that I'm an isolated incident that doesn't holistically represent society. Well, that's fine, because I don't *choose* to be a victim.

"There is nothing either good or bad but thinking makes *it* so."

- William Shakespeare.

Monday, June 8th, 2020

1:48 PM

It's interesting how most famous peaceful protestors or advocates of peace were assassinated. Gandhi didn't accomplish anything, nor did John Lennon, or Martin Luther King, etc. Peaceful advocates of a cause or belief only serve to inspire violent advocates of similar ideologies. Money and violence change the world, not starving yourself, or spread-eagling in front of a tank, or singing songs, or marching to evaporate ocean water to collect salt, or publishing pamphlets. Books can be burned and people can be killed. That's true power and change. Barbarians will inherit an obliterated earth.

"Now I am become death, the destroyer of worlds."

- Julius Robert Oppenheimer

The peaceful protests of the current *Black Lives Matter* movement evolve into violence when challenged by an authority. Nothing would come of *it,* if otherwise, except to inspire and rally more people for potential violence.

Tuesday, June 9th, 2020

12:15 AM

The past few nights I lay, unable to sleep, covered in a sheet on the floor of an empty room and listen to the thoughts that grace my consciousness when I think of particular people: "Loser" and "disappointment" are the most prominent.

I ponder my plan to republish the first year of this journalistic endeavor simultaneously with (Year Ten) highlighted by a subtitle, *"Sellout Edition,"* featuring reflective annotations, professional (paid for) editing,

293

and a picture of myself for each year up to the present. I conclude that this action, propelled by a marketing campaign, would only compound my suffering, and would be a spiteful vexation against my existence. I can only hope to die in obscurity, unread and unknown. That fate alone, is justice, for my words are malignant and woeful. Any reader would be better off disposing of this work, regardless of the entertainment derived from my self-destructive recording. Indeed, by the process of creation—thought to object, I inherently destroy myself.

I'm a little creature that lives in a confined space among hundreds of others, all of us *feeling* the same condition, confined to our flesh; we may never know anything more but the bestial obligations of our needs. Most of them sleep now, as I had attempted moments ago. A few copulate. Some eat, or stare at a screen akin to myself. Yes, the few hundred around me in this apartment complex, how we persist in familiar ways, in identical environments that we may fill with materials we deem valuable or sentimental. Billions of creatures like us—the millionaires and billionaires around the earth, far removed from our lifestyle, they too, suffer the same: the holy trinity. No luxury yacht, wonderdrug, a glass of refined alcohol, or sexual encounter may grant you sanction from yourself—from an awareness of yourself, or from your memories.

Thursday, June 11th, 2020

12:20 AM

For the past week-and-a-half, every morning, the young couple upstairs degenerate to petulant domestic abuse practitioners. The woman has resorted to screams reminiscent of incompetent female leads in horror films whenever the man's emotional abuse and physical shenanigans bring her to the brink of a breakdown. I'm often awoken, and lay on my floor to listen, comforted by the fact that I *am* alone.

Except I'm not alone; a thin ceiling and walls separate me from the other beings that play out their dramas. A child grows in the woman's womb. Each morning she vomits into her toilet on at least three instances within a half-hour time frame. The dog they own is neglected, abused, and undisciplined. I often hear the dog jump onto kitchen counters, tear open bags of food, and piss onto a carpet when the couple is away. Yes—the ceiling is *that* thin, that I may hear the piddle of a dog.

This man and woman fascinate me, for their haughtiness due to the attractiveness of their youth, and the mannerisms they assume when hosting for company—the boisterous joviality and amiability incite me to raise an eyebrow, for I witness the tirades of their private "love" as a loath observer. I could write a novel about this man and woman; instead, I'll leave *it* at *this*:

I'm scheduled to board a plane at 7:00 AM on June 16th to fly back to New York to reunite with my father for our plan to purchase a Great Harbor N37 trawler to live a life on the ocean.

6;35 PM

I'm disconcerted that I'm content with mediocrity. I don't consider myself a writer; I'm an egotist. I have no special traits, qualities, or talents, and even if I did, I wouldn't employ them to my advantage. I'm confident in the aforementioned statement, for even the skill and talent I've developed as a ~~writer~~ journalist over the years has been squandered on this lifelong engrossment. I sure *can* wait to see how *it* pans out.

Friday, June 12th, 2020

6:42 PM

A doughy stout man with a clipboard stepped out of a vehicle parked outside of a social services building and hailed me on my way to the unemployment office. "Excuse me, sir!"

I said, "Yes?"

The man waved the clipboard and said, "Excuse me, could you sign something for me? You'd be really helping me out."

I stopped, turned to face the man, chuckled, and said, "What am I signing?"

The man's mien shifted to that of a charlatan and he parroted a spiel I could tell he had rehearsed many times: "Well, due to these hard times, the people of [City Name] have expressed interest in building a few casinos to restimulate the economy by promoting jobs and growth. With-" I laughed. The man hesitated to continue, yet his clipboard remained suspended in the air by his left arm.

I said, "Oh is *that* what casinos are for? All right."

"Yes… The casinos would help to introduce new jobs and would be a great stimulus to the economy if you are to sign here," the man pointed to one of twenty-odd rows on a piece of white paper with a few lines of condensed text.

I said, "Casinos are great entertainment for degenerates."

The man looked at my pants, down to my feet, and shifted his legs while he said, "Well, I mean… I guess, but, your signature would be a great help to me." I listened for a bit longer; the man persisted with a regurgitated spiel despite knowing all-too-well that he had no chance of acquiring a signature from me—perhaps a sliver of hope.

I abruptly turned from him and said, "I won't waste any more of your time," and walked away. The last I saw of that man, and will ever see of him, he held the clipboard against his left leg, paper-side pressed to the fabric of his khaki shorts. His head had been downturned in my direction. He wore black sunglasses; therefore, I never saw his eyes. I wonder what he does now—what food he bloats himself with, or if he shared my statement with his colleagues and had a good laugh at the expense of my perceived ignorance while being keenly aware of the lies he's convinced himself of— for the betterment of the city: casinos.

Saturday, June 13th, 2020

12:51 PM

This has now become a vulgar political opinion to some degree. In this social climate, I'm drawn to the stupidity of these self-proclaimed "woke" individuals and groups who have suspended belief of the ethnic and racial barriers imposed by societies worldwide, and that the fundamental essence of life is, ironically, oversighted and dismissed as… ah, right: injustice.

A disadvantaged, marginizaled, disempowered, and disenfranchised African-American man retorts, "You claim to know what the 'fundamental essence of life' is?—talk about ignorance."

To a loyal reader—I pity you—though you'd be aware of my holy trifecta, the assertion of consumption, defecation, and procreation as the only "truths" that may be known. Please, by all means, don't take my satirical diatribe seriously—I am but a despicable degenerate standing naked and eating spicy oatmeal while I type this—no matter—I digress-

I admit, I've written enough on the topic of "injustice," and I'm not concerned in the *slightest* degree of the developments activists and parties grovel for—in the name of a presupposed notion of "justice"; however, if I am to become my title; I'll begin with a statement of equivocal incisiveness: I'm a human supremacist.

From a center-stage spotlight, a marginalized minority shouts, "What is a human supremacist?"

One who is supremely more human than you in sagacity, comprehension, and understanding of the human condition, no matter how slight—you preachers of *undeniable* and *inherent* ethics and human rights; yes, for even the *slightest* education beyond your pitiable perspective of being *uniquely* disadvantaged due to experiencing "injustices" relatable to your race would reveal that life is *undeniably* and *inherently* unfair.

You lot of scoundrels and charlatans—no matter your origin—desperate for change and reform in *such a narrow field of concern* as your plight for equity and equality! Do you believe yourself to be a victim of the dice toss of life? Imagine being illiterate for a moment (and refrain from reading; you're unworthy of my thoughts) and confined to a Persian lord's basement: a sex slave from infancy till death. Ah, the injustice—I weep for all the unknown sufferings of existence!

A haughty marginalized minority said, "Your examples are an overblown representation of special cases that are excluded from the racial injustice we fight. We—as a people—have suffered unjustly, and as a society—nay—civilization in *its* entirety, needs to be corrected."

Corrected?—as if there *were* a wrong?—*an injustice?* Do you not understand, my fellow slag of consciousness, that... Well, there isn't anything more to expound. I'm glad I dropped out of a community college after one semester and never invested my money in a prestigious institution; otherwise, I'd be routed to write a thesis paper on inane matters such as this... I shudder at the thought.

1:52 PM

Nevermind, I have far more interesting topics to dedicate my time to, such as how I capture spiders and cockroaches in a cup and observe their behavior together under various environmental conditions. Besides, most advocates and activists of racial equality and equity are "privileged" white men and women—**the most self-righteous and judgmental of all the races** (I would know); there's no getting through to them. Besides, everyone needs to assign a (unconscious) meaning to their life, or strive to achieve something, even if that entails standing around public venues for unproductive *peaceful* protests that *always* incite violence, either on-site, or elsewhere.

Sunday, June 14th, 2020

12:40 AM

Cockroaches introduced to a drop of tabasco sauce all perish similarly when upturned onto their backs. A futile panic ensues. I prefer the expedited demise of bubbled vinegar-based cleaning detergent, whereby the head of a roach is submerged in a cluster of suds and ingests acidic properties. The assumed agony of both deaths is expressed with equal detail.

I've become fond of cockroaches, and enjoy dispatching each with minor alterations to my methods. No other insect grants the same satisfaction due to the observable, or projected, sensation of pain, expressed in twitches, head turns, and *flailing*. Yes, cockroaches are expert flailers, as much as a worm or maggot is adept at writhing; yet, in the throes of death, a cockroach overtakes a flaccid creature's performance in writhing. There is a cockroach now, at the bottom of a cup on my kitchen counter, recently suffocated with cleaning liquid bubbles. On *it*s back, the cockroach's abdomen continues to waggle while wolf spiders crawl over and around *it*. The desiccated corpses of eight other wolf spiders, one cockroach, and one pill bug litter the bottom of the cup, soon to grow in number by the aforementioned count of living subjects. The spiders die of starvation, though before this fate, each new addition sustains *it*self through the partial consumption of the recently deceased. The spiders are averse to attacking each other; each reacts with fear and circumspection of another throughout the first or second encounter; however, by the second day, the spiders become seemingly indifferent to the other's presence, and may even clamber atop one another without consequence or reaction.

Above me, at this "quiet time" hour, my upstairs neighbors blare rap and hip hop music and yell over the noise to engage in a conversation with each other. Thrice throughout the night, I've suppressed my desire to either scream up through the ceiling, "You need to turn those beastly beats down right now or I'll be calling the police," or simply call the police. If I hadn't been banned from stepping a foot on the balcony that leads to their apartment door at the risk of being arrested, I would've already ventured outdoors to command a smidgen of respect. Perhaps the disrespect is their intent, for their belief in my criminality. I smell marijuana smoke and must factor this into my conjectures; I suppose the matter of "respect" is out of the equation... No, they think nothing of my existence; I'm not even real.

Only two more days to endure in this domain; thus, I sedate myself with pleasant thoughts.

3:22 AM

Insomniac's Prayer

As I lay me down to sleep
I stay awake and always think
Of all the folk I've ever known
Who curse my name with rue and scorn.
Amen.

11:19 PM

I laid down to sleep at 8:03 PM and endured a maelstrom of thoughts. Angered with my inability to sleep, I've no recourse but to report my ineptitude to this document. Entropy exacts a toll on the flesh. I'm surrounded by degenerates, and I become one—nay... I've *always* been one; *it* is my birthright.

I've yet to witness a non-degenerate human being. The most "successful" of us are, by natural law, the most disposed to degeneration.

Monday, June 15th, 2020

12:34 AM

A sleep-deprived man walked into a psychiatrist's office. The psychiatrist said, "What seems to be the problem, hm?"

The man said, "While I lay down to sleep, I hear little voices of people that I no longer care about in my head."

"Ah, yes," the psychiatrist rolled a pasty white thumb over the top of a ballpoint pen, "you have a classic case of Dumbassisism."

"Dumbassisism?" The man laughed, hearty and robust, "Fuck you too, Todd."

"Yes, a classic case. Now, this is important. Do you think about breathing while you lay still?"

"You're really going to continue mocking me—and I *paid* for this shit?"

"This is no joke. Dumbassisism has no cure, and I can only offer you a few exercises to practice to alleviate you of your existence. So, do you think about breathing at night?"

"Seriously—fuck you, Todd." The man stood and walked out of the psychiatrist's office.

5:59 PM

I've trashed all my non-essential items, cleaned my apartment, and fit every belonging that I'll be taking with me back to New York in my military-issued pack.

When I first acquired residency in this lot, I had been triumphant, for the occasion marked my possession of dependable security since the moment I landed in Arkansas with no expectations or semblance of what future I would pursue.

Unburdened down to a 35 lb pack of belongings, relationships severed, and contracts terminated, I am somber, and ponder my transitional reset. The moment of previous triumph—to now: a regression; however, I return to my father and the city of my youth as a man unknown to me, even as I live the experience. I don't return out of necessity, or of a desire for comfort, or a longing for familiarity, or even for respect for my father, but for the promise of a challenge and a new beginning beyond the one that starts tomorrow: life on a boat.

Tuesday, June 16th, 2020

5:18 AM

I slept for three hours, cleared out my apartment, and rode in a cab to the airport, where I'm currently the only person waiting for the security checkpoint to open. I'm happy to be leaving this city behind me, much like how I felt about my former city of residence (where I return to) and the entire regional area when my recruiters picked me up for my ship date.

9:45 AM

To be a saint is to be a misanthrope. I am at ease in my father's home once again, and have moved all my belongings into the basement. I am secluded, and granted time to indulge and reap the benefits of unemployment for $712 a week. I've paid off all my debt and will live to assist my father with our day-by-day venture of transitioning to a trawler.

I sit and listen to Jean-Philippe Rameau while I purchase a 55' $1,899 screen OLEG television as a present for my father, for *Father's Day:* the tradition of men honoring men for being men.

Covid-19 has annihilated Donald Trump's ~~ego~~ economy; there is no salvation for Trump, and I sympathize with him, as a human being.

Wednesday, June 17th, 2020

2:51 PM

I dwell in the basement, and have initiated a routine of normal life with my father. I've returned to a veritable paradise, though my father has been lonely and openly lambasts the intelligence of my older half-brother, and his own younger brother, to the detriment of the equanimity I had become accustomed to in quasi-solitude.

One day I'll become a certified psychological scientist, licensed by the APA, and request to ascribe my title to the criteria of the DSM-5.

"...If I only had a brain..."

- The Scarecrow from The Wizard of Oz (Yip Harburg)

10:25 PM

I need to think of a title that personifies my true spirit of the year: **"Outbursts of a Loser Supremacist; Thoughts of a Woke Nigga."**

The opposition of slavery is a feminine movement.

301

11:03 PM

The Mortal Sneeze

Does a god ever sneeze?
No.

Thursday, June 18th, 2020

9:23 AM

Despite what politicians and the media inform us, data analysts report that Covid-19 cases continue to rise worldwide. The critical mass of fake news and misinformation is the true crisis wrought by globalization.

What's that? What did you say? A pandemic has incited a worldwide crisis?—now is the ideal time to protest *your* privilege, by forming a ~~riot~~ peaceful protest composed of the sole activity of antagonizing the state's police force. The government is on a nationwide lockdown. Our President is a martyr to his ego, ruined by a facet of the nature of this world that he, in all probability, ignored his entire life—being an affluent economist and influencer; why would he direct thoughts to epidemiology? Destroyed in the style of H.G Wells' *War of the Worlds*.

Yes, now is the ideal time to threaten to kill the white supremacist bitch mother fucker white policeman ordering me to stand down.

Instead of working to lower our species' carbon blueprint and maximizing the efficiency of infrastructure and energy, let's kill and imprison each other over *justice,* because, without a doubt, every human being prosecuted or who suffers on behalf of social "injustice" is a *valuable human being,* to be sanctioned from chaos and consumption.

May we overcome the inexorable tide of entropy together, as a united species, under the banner of globalization, by killing ourselves before we kill each other. Amen.

The Mortal Shit

Does a God ever shit?
Look at a mirror.

12:19 PM

"We weave, but we do not build; we manipulate, buy, sell and lend, quarrel over the proceeds, and cover the world with our nets, while the ants and bees of mankind labor, construct and manufacture, and struggle to harness the forces of Nature. We plan and others execute. We dicker, arrange, cajole, bribe, pull our wires and extort; but we do *it* all in one place—the center of our webs and the webs are woven in caves."

- Arthur Cheney's The "Goldfish": Being the Confessions of a Successful Man

Friday, June 19th, 2020

10:13 AM

A basement devoid of cockroaches is uncanny.

1:54 PM

I listened to the three-and-a-half-hour-long recording of the certified psychopath's wife when she called the local police department and had me banned from the second-floor common area balcony—for when I *existed* in the area without speaking a word. I listened to the censure and rejection from my neighbors. Women cackled on balconies, reminiscent of witches surrounding a cauldron full of boiling viscous liquid.

My father is wrathful; this has always been my fear. I am rendered second-ruler of my shared reality, a hopeful servant to my begetter: Hope, for a life on a boat, on the ocean, beneath a sky devoid of light pollution.

6:22 PM

The basement is cleaner than I had anticipated, with accommodations suitable to my nature. A carpet on a cement floor supports three sheets, layered one on top of the other. To the left of a small furled blanket that I utilize as a pillow is a small hand-lantern manufactured circa 1980 and a copy of Seneca's *On the Shortness of Life*. To the right of my bedspread, my emptied U.S. Navy issued backpack leans against a speckled achromatic, washed out, cement brick wall. Behind my headrest, a high-rise wooden

303

chair in a corner supports clothing that has yet to be dirtied. To the left of the foot of my bedspread, one interchangeable steel 52.5 lb adjustable dumbbell awaits first use; the second dumbbell will arrive by mail in about 3-5 days. Beyond the bottom of my bedspread, two wooden chairs, identical to the chair in the corner above my bedspread, are stacked upside-down—one on top of the other. On the upside down chair's legs, I hang six back dress shirts and three pairs of black work pants. A dehumidifier runs constantly and muffles the negligible noise my father produces above me.

The basement is about fifty feet long and twenty feet wide. I occupy a corner beneath a stairwell leading to my father's apartment. A laundry area with a washer and dryer are within eighteen feet of my bedspread from the bottom left end. Already, three days have elapsed, and I've yet to see another tenant in this downstairs common area, nor have I left the house for any reason. The remainder of the basement is full of organized tools, trinkets, unwanted memoirs, and general junk yet to be disposed of. The ceiling of the basement is an uncovered network of pipes beneath an often web-ridden wooden floor spanning the expanse of the building. I've known this building since the age of fourteen and am familiar with every room—having lived in each apartment at one point in my life, and now, in the basement—my favorite arrangement thus far; only a boat could compare.

7:51 PM

"Baethan is such a pathetic little assclown."

"This guy, he behaves like such a retard but he really just hates the world."

"That's fucking unbelievable; I really do believe he his mentally sick."

I'm high on marijuana again, after a lapse in will and the proximate availability, and recorded my aforementioned spontaneous self-loathing thoughts while attempting to enjoy a boneyard constitutional as I had years ago. My father watches *South Park* and *Rick and Morty:* his preferred programming.

Saturday, June 20th, 2020

1:12 PM

My father awoke in a rage this morning due to our ninety-year-old neighbor's usage of a lawnmower at 7:20 AM. According to my father, this ninety-year-old man mows his lawn each day of the week, and his wife: a woman of similar age, lounges under the shade of a shed and watches her husband mow. The woman has Alzheimer's and could potentially not know *who* her husband is.

A philosophical scientist said, "'Change' is a buzzword."
There should be no such thing as lawyers.

2:18 PM

I should've lived in a basement all my life, the one I'm in now, to be particular. To work out in peace and silence in a dingy place that represents my inner world most accurately, is a joy.

3:19 PM

I'm *perceived* as a victim by society and I'm praised for *it*.
Ah, one-liners and italics; I'm a writer now!

5:51 PM

An abundance of time—*time:* the most precious resource.

Sunday, June 21st, 2020

10:39 AM

Arbitrary darkness, talking heads on a screen, and reality as you know *it* to be.

2:26 PM

My older thirty-six-year-old schizophrenic half-brother (same mother) stopped by for father's day. I attempted to speak to him about his "voices" in an attempt to share my insight, and he admitted of his 9th grade GED education and immediately began to fumble through his backpack for a soda, grabbed the soda, raised the soda up towards my father, said "Ginseng," as if to demonstrate to my father that he is being health-conscious, and followed up with complaints about his medication and social affiliations.

I am saddened for my half-brother; there is nothing else.

3:24 PM

My father asked my half-brother, "Do you know what a flash of insight is?"

My half-brother looked away, dejected, and said, "No," while he stared at the futon he sat on.

7:29 PM

My father said, "Do I want to sit around like a retired old fuck watching baseball until I die? No."

Monday, June 22nd, 2020

3:39 PM

Outbursts of a Certified [DSM-5 Diagnosis] would be the perfect title for this book. I believe I can will this matter into being by visiting a psychologist and being diagnosed. I could learn all of the identities and labels I've been ignorant to all my life; there is a potential to make a profit off of my "societal deficiencies."

My father complains non stop of the ignorance of other people to the point of exacerbating himself and draining all vitality from me. I, on the other hand, have nothing to do but ~~complain~~ report of the old man who took me in to ride along with him on his boat... to *this* document;

you foolish reader—you read the complaints of another and think *it* to be *entertainment?* You buffoon.

My discipline has relaxed while here. The television I purchased for my father as a gift for *Father's Day* arrived with a large network of cracks and a deep gash throughout the bottom left of the OLED screen. The gift has been delayed, and instead, I sit with my father, dissipated as we are, high on coffee and *Gorilla Glue* marijuana, watching a series of lectures on *The Black Death,* told by an alluring professor. What is there not to enjoy about life? Ignorant people, according to my father. I've no recourse but to listen to the ceaseless vitriolic complaints of *others*—my family included. I am to harvest my own pride by reporting this to my document.

There are some things I can never live down, more so, with this commitment to memory, by the art of my expression.

While a thirty-five minute episode discoursed on screen, my father proceeded to talk in an attempt to explain the disparity between truth, fact, and fiction relating to the lecture.

I said one sentence throughout the entire lecture: "The more we speak during this lecture, the more ignorant we sound."

My father continued to complain of ignorant people not being able to distinguish between fact or fiction.

5:36 PM

I visited the local boneyard after a year's hiatus from the grounds and encountered many people in cars, vans, and trucks, driving slowly along the paved roads of the well-developed sanctuary I once knew as a child. There remains one final sanctum in the back of the boneyard grounds—a veritable providence, away from all human development. One low stoop down, beyond the threshold of the boneyard grounds, a sandy tire-marked path leads into the forest, undisturbed and overgrown. Seven feet below the artificial flattened expanse of the cemetery dirt, the native earth blooms with overgrowth and towering trees. I stand amidst the bushes and channel accumulated negativity out of me, unto the unscornable facet of nature, human-free; my god is chaos, and I worship alone, as a madman would. I hadn't been ready to enter the deepest section, where the tall grass and intertwined brambles graze the tops of my shoulders. An adventure for another time.

Adventure… What am I, a little boy? An idiot?

Incompetent and unqualified is all I know myself to be. Whenever I speak, I hear an ignorant pissant resound, despite those that comment on my "deep voice"—not on account of being an ignorant pissant, but of my tendency of expression. Or, perhaps I am an ignorant pissant, and the preceding sentence is crucial to examine due to the sequence of thoughts leading to this stream of consciousness expression. The introspective process delights me.

I am a rat in a well-maintained cellar, free to think myself into existence and to ameliorate my father's mental hysteria in regard to Covid-19.

Tuesday, June 23rd, 2020

4:40 PM

"My thoughts are deeper than anything my body could ever be," mused a romantic.

I am a quintessential twenty-eight-year-old American loser. The basement is enshrouded in darkness, illuminated by two rectangular windows enwreathed in cobwebs that allow the sun's rays from noon until dusk to shine through. I installed a set of curtains with my father between the doorway and the window between the living room and kitchen. We no longer scrutinize each other's miens; sound remains muffled. My father is delighted to have a new system in place that maintains the low temperature of his rotten man-cell.

I live in my own rotten man-cell, beneath him, ennobled by the fact of being right where I belong—in a little man cell.

7:21 PM

I am a disgusting human being; I eat an ounce of steak smeared with half of an avocado in the corner of a dark basement. I *could* stand with my face turned towards the wall and channel my malevolent energy in that manner. Instead, I pound into a keyboard and masticate the same large chunk of meat for over three minutes while I type this passage.

My father lingers above me in a dark alcove, listening to Mozart—his favorite composer. Mozart's whimsical and lighthearted music appeals to my father's hedonism. I prefer the cantatas of J.S. Bach. The modicum of discipline this journal requires the strength available only to one who has chosen solitude as their primary past-time.

Mastication of red meat exercises the jaw muscles well.

I am relieved to have unintentionally destroyed my voice recorder in a washing machine.

Each bite of avocado on steak nourishes me. I am bolstered with resolve on consumption; *it*'s swell to be a man.

This document is the only material with influence on my reality. All else is unreal and improbable—a *surreal* scene of perpetual childhood. I feel as a teenager would, lurking in his father's basement and plotting his next idea. I've reverted three years, in truth, and long for the outdoors. I yearn to don a pair of boots and walk through the nearby wilderness that has yet to be converted to residences or commercial structures.

Covid-19 has impacted life in my father's opinion; he is fearful of contagion and our quality of life suffers on behalf of our limited options to act in accordance with the goal to board a boat. I ponder the option to become diagnosed by a certified psychologist referring to the DSM-5 lawbook. My affliction would become the title of my book and I'd pay to become certified with something new each year to apply as the title beyond each subsequent installment. To use the DSM-5 for satire: a parody, a charade. I will become anything I want to be by the APA's law and decree, and will be afforded many "rights" and "privileges." Such a *pity*.

Wednesday, June 24ᵗʰ, 2020

12:17 PM

I sit and smoke one bowl of marijuana through a bong and listen to my father complain of our neighbors and tenants—all of them, regardless of the content. After my father's thirty-five minute long diatribe, I removed myself from the living room couch and stood in the illuminated doorway of a noon sun, shielded behind a screen door. I stood and watched a blonde-haired woman of mid-size proportions amble up and down her back porch to stand behind six-foot-high wooden fence posts.

I thought to myself, *"Why do you choose this life for yourself, neighbor?"* and continued to watch her, statuesque in my movement, as a beast observes another, where my father often stands, and experienced life through the eyes of a psychopath. The woman sauntered around as if she hoped to be observed in the little space; she did, in fact, will this life to herself, and enjoys the presence of the neighbors around her.

In this regard, our ninety-year-old neighbor mows his lawn each day and lounges around his outdoor patio. The other neighbor, Ken, and his wife Sherlie, own upwards of ten or more cats, according to my father's calculations.

Thursday, June 25th, 2020

3:25 PM

I've blasted two bowls of marijuana at my face and stood in the basement after watching another lecture on the Black Death. My hatred and revilement of me is a sincere expression; I am a *"Pathetic Loser."*

My only solace is the reprieve of my chosen social destitution. I suspect my father loathes me and complains of me to visiting family when I'm absent. I'm a degenerate scumbag who consumes copious amounts of food. I'm keenly aware of my pathetic visage and confine myself to this cellar, enthralled once more by contemptuous energy. This hadn't been what I intended to write at all. In fact, I had intended to kill myself when I stepped down the steps into this cellar, for my pain of existence is often intolerable. Perhaps there won't be a *Year Four;* I could only be so lucky. The most disgusting thing I have ever done is begin this series of documentation. I have chosen a cornerstone of the American Dream that should've been left untouched. This is not a cry for self-help. I don't even desire to be heard. The more I type, the more I make an ass of myself.

6:44 PM

This journal is my lord, my savior, my grace. Without *it,* I am nothing but a void, a piece of flesh that seeks to consume and expel. We judge each other in accordance with our success within society to achieve our own ends, to meet with a criterion of success.

I do everything for all the wrong reasons and my father knows *it.* I condemn him for nothing. There is an abundance of material for me to document, material that is offensive to humanity, and I'd rather clatter away on a little screen in the basement of my father's home to lament the condition of my chosen placement within this social schism.

I've directed this life for myself, examined the potentials prior, and knew what I would end up as. I feared *this*—myself, all along, not my father. My begetter, and my mother as well—neither, are to the fault of my self-chosen fate. I am a hedon to my own expulsion. I delight in my secretions.

My father aims to guide me on the path most conducive to my future financial success by recommending networking: to market my trash to the world; verily, a consumer of these words is advised to cease consumption.

I have no other recourse than to languish, exert, and consume, in private and at peace, at ease with my chosen burdens. I am responsible for my thoughts.

Friday, June 26th, 2020

9:05 AM

I experienced an "ego death" yesterday.

I communicated to my father my unsettling thoughts from yesterday and discovered that my psyche had been based in falsities and delusions, seated in my own aggression and feelings of powerlessness with my circumstances while my father and I wait to progress with the purchase of a trawler.

I must trust my father if I am to live without fear.

2:36 PM

I've discovered an article titled: *Research on group differences in intelligence: A defense of free inquiry,* by Nathan Cofnas, published December 23rd, 2019. I present particular excerpts taken out of context of the article to purposely incite an inflammatory response with examples most pertinent to the current social trend of the *Black Lives Matter* ~~protests during a global pandemic~~ "movement":

"The leading intelligence researcher Robert Sternberg (2005) argues that good science is characterized by "taste in the selection of problems to solve" (p. 295), and that *it* is in bad taste to investigate the genetic basis of race differences." [13]

---

[13] Nathan Cofnas; Balliol College, University of Oxford, Oxford, UK

An African man said, "That's *so* fucking racist."
An African woman said, "Are you for real?"
Yet, both continued to read.

"**Kourany (2016) asks: "is there any reason new policy constraints like these for the life sciences should not be put into effect for the social sciences – new policy constraints that include research guidelines for weighing societal harms of research against societal benefits … ?" (p. 786). As to the suggestion that the potential harm from deadly viruses is greater than the harm from research on intelligence differences, she urges us not to minimize the latter: intelligence research has already been shown to cause significant harm… to lots more people [than a virus] – to all the people whose self-esteem, self-efficacy, ambitions, and successes are lessened as a result of direct or indirect exposure to the research or aspects of the research … ; to all the people whose self-esteem, self-efficacy, ambitions, and successes are lessened as a result of the treatment they receive from others who have been directly or indirectly exposed to the research or aspects of the research; and so on – in short, to all or most women and, in the United States at least, to most minority men and many men of color in other parts of the world… Cognitive group differences research, then, arguably does pose harms to society near – perhaps even exceeding – the harms posed by the recent synthetic genomics research. (p. 787)"** [14]

The African man said nothing, and continued to read.
The African woman said, "This is some neo-nazi bullshit."
A Jewish man entered the fray and crossed his arms.
An Asian man joined the scene and smirked.

"***It* is also easy to overlook the harms that have been caused by uncritical commitment to environmentalism. Kourany (2016) comments: Finding out that blacks have lower IQ scores than whites… could be the beginning of educational and training programs to work with the strengths and work on the weaknesses of every group to help make them the very best they can be, and even to use the special talents of each group to help the others. Finding these things out could be the beginning of innovative programs that support rather than undermine**

---

[14] Ibid

the right to equality. That this does not happen, or seldom happens, is a function of the... racism of society. (pp. 783–784)" [15]

The African man said, "I'm going to kill this man. The audacity of what I *just* read is offensive to the essence of my existence. This is the *apex* of ignorance."

The African woman, Jewish man, and Asian man said nothing, and continued to read.

"In the liberal West, many of our institutions, laws, and moral values are predicated on the assumption that race differences are either nonexistent or environmentally caused. If the hereditarian theory of race differences became widely accepted, *it* seems inevitable that there would be significant cultural changes, even if we cannot predict what those changes would be with any precision. Just about any radical change – even if *it* ultimately benefits the vast majority of people – will have some negative consequences, but the fact that change always has negative consequences is not by itself a compelling reason to preserve the status quo. Every instance of progress has negative byproducts: alternative energy puts coal miners out of work, teaching evolution causes distress to creationists, and so on. Many examples throughout history show that attempts to block scientific progress, for whatever reason, are generally both futile and ultimately harmful. Is research on race differences a special case? Would finding a genetic origin to race differences pose a uniquely serious threat?" [16]

A *Black Lives Matter* protester joined the group reading and began to froth at the mouth; there was no sanction from the man, not even from himself, and he made himself heard with peaceful disparagements and the destruction of the monuments of dead men.

"A common fear is that, if race differences were proven to have a genetic basis, this would cause people to turn to Nazism. Indeed, the study of race differences is often explicitly equated with Nazism. This fear seems to be based on a historical misunderstanding. Nazi ideology was not based on scientific discoveries. The Nazis were

---

[15] Ibid
[16] Ibid

flagrant pseudoscientists whose research in biology and psychology was permeated with ideology. Contrary to a popular myth, both the Nazis and their ideological predecessors (such as Joseph Arthur Comte de Gobineau and Houston Stewart Chamberlain) rejected Darwinism (Richards, 2013).5 Most important for the present discussion, Nazi scientists rejected mainstream intelligence testing and the concept of IQ (i.e., general intelligence, or the g factor derived by factor analysis), preferring a mystical view of intelligence tied to race. Erich Jaensch, an influential Nazi psychologist at the University of Marburg, claimed that IQ tests advanced the "supremacy of Bourgeoisie spirit" and would be a tool 'of Jewry [to] fortify *its* hegemony' (Rindermann, 2018, p. 61). Jaensch's student Friedrich Becker advocated 'intelligence measurement according to a national and typological point of view,' and called for what was essentially a version of multiple-intelligences theory that accounted for "realism," "conscientiousness," "the character value of intelligence," and "practical intelligence" (Rindermann, 2018, p. 61)." [17]

"An intelligent conversation would be impossible with Baethan; I want to flay him, and throw his wracked body into a vat of salt," said a figment of my imagination, of who I project the cognitive faculties of your average "peaceful protestor." Am I a grown man? Do I utilize straw man commentary? Who am I, and why do I matter? These questions should be at the forefront of every protestor's mind while they wake each morning and plan to take to the streets for their petty perceptions of racial injustices. Meanwhile, the world continues to spin, and the lives of 7.8-8 billion people, living and dying minute realities, ebb onward into oblivion. A fraction of the population awakens each morning with thoughts of injustice while participating in a reality of chaos that we—each of us individually, struggle to *order* as a global consciousness.

"Wanting to know the intelligence of the different races is inherently racist; there can be no other plausible motive," said a protestor of unidentified origin, heritage, creed, age, gender, and education.

"Any society that manages to be even minimally functional must have... 'a robust appreciation of the endlessly protean utility of truth' (p. 15). He expounds: Our success or failure in whatever we undertake, and therefore in life altogether, depends on whether we are guided by truth

---

[17] Ibid

or whether we proceed in ignorance or on the basis of falsehood. [To] the extent that we recognize what dealing effectively with the problems of life entails, we cannot help loving truth. (Frankfurt, 2006, pp. 35–36, 48)" [18]

"The truth is that you're a racist white supremacist motherfucker," said a white woman.

"There is also a long-standing tradition that truth has some intrinsic value, and that comprehending the truth and acting in conformity with *it* are worthwhile goals even if, in some cases, 'he who increases knowledge increases sorrow' (Ecclesiastes 1:18 NKJV)." [19]

God shrugged.

Saturday, June 27th, 2020

8:25 AM

Each night and morning I succumb to an insurmountable sadness that I don't understand. I'd rather stand in the pitch darkness of a basement and stare blindly at walls than engage in entertainment pursuits with my father and his new television. I attempted to play a video game *(Dark Souls Remastered)* for the first time last night since moving back in with my father, and found myself uninterested and indifferent to success, failure, or the content. I pace the basement before languishing on the floor to sleep, whereby tears stream down my unmoving face. What are these tears? Tears of self-pity—nothing more. And what do I grieve for other than the life I chose for myself? Nothing.

There are those around the world who have never experienced a hot shower, a feeling of security, or a cup of coffee with a splash of whole milk. People wake in jail cells days after day, or in a slum, with nothing but a jug of contaminated water and rice—if that. What do these allusions mean to me other than to remind me of my *privilege?* Any reader should rejoice, to know of my mental agony each sunset and sunrise: *this* is justice.

I reap hatred and contempt, for that is what I sow, yet, nobody knows

---

[18] Ibid
[19] Ibid

me here, or remembers me, for all *I* know. These feelings I endure are naught but my own, locked in a feedback loop of pity for humanity, based on my limited perspective. *Dribble-dribble-drabble-poo,* I have nothing *better* to do. I'm not guilty of anything; there is no shame. The parallels I use to diminish the suffering I feel compared to those who endure hardships beyond my realm of reference level are a psychological device to maintain feelings of gratitude despite a lack of meaningful relationships.

I hadn't anticipated this entry, though the words leak out of me and curtail any "genius" within my power to express. Exercising body and mind is my only tether to this reality we know.

9:01 PM

I live in a proverbial American paradise and am unhappy. No matter where I could be would make me happy, nor anything I could possess. Where I am and what I possess is, and will only ever be, my humanity.

Sunday, June 28th, 2020

9:30 AM

At the guarantee of discrediting myself (not that I had credentials), I record an instance from last night for the betterment of my development as a conscious entity:

At 10:40 PM last night, I smoked two large bowls of marijuana through my father's bong and immediately headed downstairs with the sole "aspiration" to confront the "voices" I experienced. I laid in the pitch darkness of the basement on a dirty sheet, folded my hands across my chest, and became *genuinely* terrified that I was going to die. I communicated with my ~~father *and* my mother~~ egoic self-talk, and convinced myself that my father had resolved to kill me in the most torturous way I could imagine for valid reasons that I didn't desire to dispute, i.e., I readied myself to die.

I believed that my father considered me to be a pathetic failure who amounts to nothing, and that my return to his home marked a disgrace (even though he encouraged me to return) among his community (that he doesn't care about) and that I marred his reputation (that he also doesn't care about). I believed the threat of Covid-19 also prompted my father's decision to kill me, and that he believed that he would be preventing future pain and grief for me, himself, and anyone I may come into contact with in the future.

I continued to hear the malevolent voices of my ~~father~~ ego proclaim that I am a "pathetic rugrat" and a "stunted faggot fool," along with many other disparagements and insults, though the aforementioned two phrases were the most prominent and resounded the loudest. I fantasized an imminent scenario, narrated by the voice of my father at the forefront of my psyche, of how he would murder me—a death I thought I deserved on account of my character as a whole: In brief, I expected a sheet to be thrown over my body two or three hours after falling asleep, with the weight of my father pressing down on my torso, inhibiting my limbs. My father would insert a rolled sock into my mouth and proceed to cut out my eyes with a carbon steel kitchen knife. With a choice between driving me to a secluded area in the wilderness and depositing me in a ditch, blinded and doomed, or flaying my flesh, my father would choose to flay me. Being blind, the agony I would experience would be amplified with terror and feelings of absolute loss and sadness, for I do in fact "love" my father, to the degree that love can be comprehended, and to be killed by him would be authentic justice for the disgrace and guilt I feel on account of my choice to sever relations with him in the manner that I did. My mother, too, hadn't deserved such treatment, and I lambast myself as a daily regimen.

I imagined my father wearing the treated skin of my face, snapping a single photo to remember the occasion by, and discarding my facial skin into a garbage bin thereafter.

The fright I experienced compelled me to sigh in resignation while tears streamed down my face; I wept in silence, muffled by the whir of basement water heater mechanisms, disgusted with myself for not only my fear of death, but for the self-pity I felt due to how I anticipated my death. I sat up, slouched forward, and thought of my life, from birth until that moment, and the time I shared with my mother and father. I resumed a supine position, my arms aimed straight down at both of my sides, and awaited my anticipated fate.

With the reconciliation of my end, I heard the internal voice of my father say, *"Stay still, I'm coming down now,"* and bounded to my feet. I fumbled for my lantern and ventured upstairs. My father laid in his bed, awake, watching television. I approached, terror-stricken, with tears streaming down my face, and said, "Are you going to kill me?"

My father gazed at me, exasperated, somewhat fearful himself, and said, "You're stoned, dude." He told me that I may sleep upstairs on the living room futon if I desired, though I concluded to myself that doing so would lessen the difficulty of him murdering me. I returned downstairs, laid in the darkness once more, and continued to panic... paranoid... *schizophrenic,* as many would delight in decreeing, by the usage of marijuana. My denial of the condition is a *symptom,* according to the DSM-5. What defense do I have? I am unmedicated, and enjoy introspection; thus, I elect to endure the malevolent thoughts I experience of myself with intent to write of the occurrence. I hadn't expected to lay in a stranglehold of self-inflicted fear; I anticipated death, and in my one "final" act of will, I sprung off the floor, engaged with my writing device, and recorded what I thought would be my last bidding: "I am a pathetic rugrat. People have praised me for my intelligence all my life and I am nothing but a stunted faggot fool." I returned upstairs, acknowledged my father with a fearful countenance, and inched myself onto the futon, where I laid with a blanket in the living room adjacent to my father's bedroom for a half-hour. My panic abated; however, my discomfort on the soft cushions had been detrimental to quality sleep; therefore, I rose from the futon, attempted to sneak past my father who I presumed had been sleeping, and repositioned myself on the basement floor. An hour elapsed while I fought with my fear of imminent death before I succumbed to a restful sleep.

I awoke the following morning and realized that my will to live is vigorous and profound; I delude myself with the belief that my writing is... "important," or at least, impactful with the unity of humanity experienced as consciousness. Even if my contribution is ultimately to go unheeded, unread, unheard, and forgotten—obliterated—*inevitably*—of course... I have this *will* to live.

My father told me there is no justification for my behavior regarding how I departed for Navy boot camp until the time we reconnected. I have confronted my guilt of abandoning my father and mother on separate occasions; this guilt is taught to me by societal standards with the inclusion of family values and tradition; however, I accept my past, and have no recourse but to proceed with living and to face my inevitable death with indifference.

10:05 PM

I'm ashamed of the previous entry; thus, I must retain *it*.
Marijuana no longer nourishes me with any semblance of pleasure

after I've been induced to accept my imagined death two nights in a row on account of smoking *it;* therefore, I quit indefinitely due to exhausting all possibilities of growth and learning with the substance.

Monday, June 29th, 2020

6:32 PM

I want nothing out of this world. My expectations are null.
My father's mother died in a nursing home at the age of ninety today.
I wrote a few notes on a piece of lined paper over the past week:

Astronaut botanists removed their spacesuits in a zero-gravity chamber; planetary objects formed from pubes and skin cells. I feel as though I've seen a ghost: My schizophrenic brother, who ingests three different antipsychotic medications, visited my father and admitted to never thinking about "why" he sees delusions of people with angelic wings when I questioned the matter.

7:59 PM

There is nothing but the exposition based on my constrained perspective; I exist as a template.

Tuesday, June 30th, 2020

10:29 AM

Yesterday, I walked through the city I've known for all of my life for the first time since my return. Even after a full year of being absent, nothing changed except for the content of advertisement venues posted on billboards and business windows. On my way through the city center, I thought to evade the storefront where I knew Pelagia[20] worked at a small "hole in the wall" health food bar. The employees of the restaurant are trained to be alert for people passing by the storefront window and to encourage potential customers to purchase products by smiling and waving. Knowing this, I walked on the sidewalk opposite of the restaurant twice (to

---

[20] An ex-lover; a vicious harpy; a licentious temptation.

and from my destination) and figured the distance to be enough to avoid anyone who may recognize me.

On my return home, I checked my email and saw a message from Pelagia: "I heard that you may be back in town. If that's true, I'd like to meet up. Possibly this Wednesday or Thursday on my days off."

I succumbed to consternation, stunned and perplexed that I had been spotted even with my precautionary route, and recounted a surge of memories from yesteryear preserved in journalistic format that I had recently proofread for my final manuscript submission to my publisher. Why do I care, and for what do I dramatize the past for? I thought her to be pathetic, to lack self-respect, for I had been vicious to her before my departure, and denied her *sex*—for that's all ~~she~~ we wanted. Subsequently, I admired her boldness and assertive power, for this woman, who previously had no bearing on my reality, made herself a force to be ignored or acknowledged once more.

I responded: "Hello Pelagia. Yes, I'm back in town. Do you want to meet to spurn me as I did you? Do you want to educate me? What time on Wednesday?"

I expected no response, and that perhaps Pelagia would recall our horrid treatment of each other with my wry reminder, for in our dealings, we had reduced one another to the status of douchebag (myself) and ho (Pelagia). I intended to commend Pelagia on her newfound self-respect if she were to ignore my response; however, my intuitions proved wrong again, for Pelagia messaged me shortly after: "No spurning. No educating. Would simply like to see you and catch up. I'm open to time suggestions. I am getting a new apartment on Wednesday as well, so I'll need to get the keys and whatnot. I'm not sure when that will be just yet."

Thus, we arranged to meet tomorrow.

"Abandon all hope, ye who enter here."

- Dante Alighieri's Inferno

JULY

Wednesday, July 1st, 2020

7:45 PM

Pelagia stood on the balcony of her new second-floor apartment and waved at me as I approached. She wore a long white flower-patterned shawl and her hair had been shaved short and dyed blonde. I waved back and met her outside the entryway. We embraced in a hug, kissed, and stared into each other's eyes for several seconds. Upstairs in her spacious, unfurnished, early 1900's Victorian-style apartment, we conversed for two hours and engaged in affectionate playfulness. I stated my intent for sex and Pelagia declined, citing recent bad experiences with a sugar daddy and a long abstention from intimate relationships.

Pelagia and I ate at the restaurant where I had been employed as a dishwasher prior to departing for the U.S. Navy boot camp and I spoke with the owner, Walther, about resuming my employment.

Back at Pelagia's apartment, we laid on her kitchen floor, snuggled against one another, and discussed a myriad of topics. As romantic as our time today had been, and as much as I am loath to admit to vaporous feelings of rekindled "love," there is nothing remarkable to write of other than the surreal overtone of the occasion. The woman's face... her *eyes*... body... her feminine conduct; all is endearing. I meet with her again tomorrow.

Thursday, July 2nd, 2020

9:38 AM

Yes, the unremarkable exposition is all there is. My only skill and talent are that of recollection and ephemeral romance. I'm your stereotypical starving artist, only, my "art" is a byproduct of living, and I'm not starving.

Seated at a desk of a cubicle-less office on the fourth floor of a twenty-two level building with expansive wall-windows from floor to ceiling, a twenty-six-year-old, fit, intelligent man, stared with mean intent at a computer monitor displaying a three-dimensional graphic of an armored knight mounted on a black warhorse. Around him, thirty-three of his colleagues busied themselves on their respective terminals; three young women and two men dressed in casual urban clothes stood and engaged in playful non-work related banter in a half-circle near the center of a modern chic themed department. Two old men, distinguished by their formal suits and neckties, observed from behind the glass wall of a separate compartment, phones in hand, seated at elegant steel chairs situated behind white oblong desks that supported nothing atop both. Rows of unnecessary fluorescent lightning illuminated a hard floor of green and brown multifaceted hues. Six narrow pillars painted with a vibrant coat of neon-yellow paint spanned evenly across the room and supported a popcorn-textured azure ceiling.

The twenty-six-year-old man hunched forward; his eyes strained and glistened with passionless tears unfit for shedding. He blinked six times with a 0.4-second interval between each instance, removed his thick-rimmed square glasses, and pressed both of his palms against his eyes. The ends of his fingers grazed the top of his impeccable pompadour. The tapered sides of his hair blended with a full beard of short stubble. The man removed both palms pressed against his eyelids, stared at the unfinished crest splayed across the horse's regal armor and the knight's kite shield, and thought, *"I've followed all the guidelines on how to attract women that I've read online... I don't even like this haircut; I feel like a douchebag, and beards are such a pain in the ass to maintain. Susie is such a slut but I think that's why I want her. I fucking hate this assignment. Mark is always assigned what players see the most and I get stuck with forgettable sidequest shit. My financial debt... this stupid fucking hair—barbers are ridiculously overpriced. I should go keto. All this-"*

"I like your crest design, Doug," said a bald thirty-one-year-old accomplished programmer from behind the twenty-six-year-old man.

Doug twisted his head and acknowledged the bald man, turned slowly back towards the monitor, leaned back in his chair, stretched his hands over his head, sighed, and said, *"It's not finished."*

The bald man sipped coffee out of a white mug with the text, "if(!coffee) {cup.refill();}" printed on the side with black font, said nothing, and walked away towards the group of five of their colleagues. Two of the three women addressed the bald man with subtle eyebrow raises and genuine smiles. One of the men said, "Carl—my guy!" on the bald man's approach and raised a hand for a generic high-five. Doug listened, realigned his posture with the back of his chair, focused on his breathing, and stared at the crest's outline on the knight's kite shield.

Friday, July 3rd, 2020

4:01 PM

Time with Pelagia is enriching, yet I fail to comply with my own spoken word of trust. There is the extreme potential for growth and progression in our relationship, though I don't trust her. I correspond with no one else but my father, Pelagia, and my forgotten associates at the two local bars at the center of downtown who have become entities I must now interact with once more on account of being rehired full-time at a wage of $14.00/hr. The manager decreed me to be "too competent" to work only as a dishwasher; thus, I've been tasked to learn all the kitchen roles of both establishments.

I'm pained to open my heart to Pelagia, to share superfluous emotions that constitute the human experience. Her flesh against mine is a redemptive quality of existence; however, I harbor remnants of guilt *and* suspicion, for Pelagia believes herself to be "not good enough," in the manner of attractiveness, intelligence, and general prowess, which verifies my notion of her lack of self-respect; alas, this is a duress we share… and I'm inclined to think that we settle for each other out of a mutual crystalized belief that neither of us is apt for someone "better." I've never been with anyone as compatible as Pelagia; beyond the realm of the bedroom and superficiality, we share kindred philosophies and self-imposed afflictions of the mind. I'm inclined to think that the more I exude "love," the more I repel her, and that our attraction for one another is rooted in a similar void—that of desperation for meaning veiled with indifference and apathy.

Pelagia informed me that there hadn't been a single day that passed when she didn't think of me in some manner since my departure over a year ago: a proclamation of prodigious grandeur!—and I am roused to immediate doubt and detestation, for manipulation of the pathos, to the *benefit* of the ego, is the worst vulgarism one may suffer. Am I *that* much of a fool to believe—to *trust* her? She yearns for a single child to rear, a girl, and has commented on her belief that I would make for an exceptional father; thereby, I questioned her belief of my fathering aptitude. My genetics (that I wouldn't wish to condemn another with) had been the primary factor, by her judgment. What manner of man am I to think that Pelagia would be content to extract my seed at an optimal time and exclude me from the care of a progeny, to *spare* me from the severance of my ego for the sake of kin by a dissolution of our relationship? Moreover, what manner of man am I to delude myself with outrageous future potentialities after only *three* days of our resurgence? I'm nauseated by bestial instincts—to propagate, to usher another being into existence to suffer this implausible reality, to *dare* the thought that my flesh is worthy of proliferation. By the reckoning of my mind's contents, one may clearly distinguish the banal diatribe of a madman.

The only absolute is of lies enhanced with truths. May we continue with our delusional expectations and the machinations of our species, for the betterment of humanity; an interposition between cultural virtues and iniquity is null; as creatures, we delight in expedience, in gratification, in vice, in the relinquishment of guilt and shame, in the liberation of our self-chosen bondages, only to delve to the myriad manifestations of decadence and viciousness out of misaligned principles, dogmas, creeds, oaths, and promises. Anywhere our organism thrives, we persist with a veneer of slight variations, yet the product remains the same; the outcome delighted, no matter the intent, is each moment of validation.

"Enough of your pseudo-intellectual spiritual philosophy crockery," said an affluent businessman, "Are you a man or a whimpering bitch? Just fuck her and forget her like all the others; you think too much. Life is meant to be enjoyed."

Saturday, July 4th, 2020

7:53 AM

A night of impromptu intoxication with Pelagia, her best friend Howard, and his boyfriend, Ethan, from 1:00 AM until 5:00 AM. Howard desires nothing but the best for Pelagia and pleaded with me to not tell her that I love her, to spare her from herself and the hopeful machinations that would arise.

An hour elapsed while Howard spoke, drunk, of his existential crisis, universal suffering, and qualms with social and animal injustices. The four of us converged on the balcony for eight minutes, and Howard went with Pelagia to her bedroom to speak in private while Ethan and I discussed Ethan's passion for mixology.

Howard and Ethan departed. Pelagia began to cry and confessed her love to me. I admitted the same—despite Howard's prior pleading—and expressed a desire for commitment, which Pelagia declined out of fear.

6:58 PM

Past memories, despite my capacity for recollection due to *this* endeavor, are inconsequential; to learn from past errors, and to apply wisdom, is a moot prospect against chaos—the improbable elements of human affairs, immutable as our nature proves to be, is a poor predictor of events of an ever-shifting climate of disparate ethics and morality as mutable as the wind.

9:45 PM

Even from a basement, I am awakened by the crack of fireworks. Nationalism and patriotism are a scourge.

10:13 PM

I lay, unable to sleep, and know the pain I feel is the only substance ever worth recording: Pelagia dissimulates; she is a master of the art. I am deceived without knowing why. Her best friend, Howard, who she has known and confided in for twelve years, is her true lover; I assert this not out of jealousy, but of the interplay. I am a dupe. I yearn to provide value and solace to a mate, and am reviled with secret hatred. Am I mad?— deluded—corrupted with doubt? Our arrangement is a lie; we love to love, without knowing why; hence, the deception; we deceive each other, for our own cruel satisfaction. I feel a hollowed emptiness, with the consideration that Pelagia may one day read this, purely out of spite, or a sadistic curiosity, to continue to pity me in secret: a hatred veiled in pity. I am a toy to her. What is she to me? Why would she love me, *and* Howard, too—in their inebriated states—the accolades of my character rendered me sick, for together, they...

Yes, I *must* be mad, to reckon my intuitions as truths, for I've been wrong before. Or perhaps I'm merely afraid to accept reality for what *it* is.

I wrote a document for Pelagia: an outline for weight loss; a plan to help her, as she had inquired, titled, *A Reformation of the Human Spirit*. I wrote parameters for behaviors similar to my own, complete with contrasts of diet, and statements concerning my personal regimen. In retrospect, I think she may have interpreted the document to be a precursor manifesto for my "control" over her, or a flaunting of my knowledge and self-proclaimed regimen of strength training seven days a week, which I'm certain she doubts due to my average (non-American) physique. I desired neither control nor esteem; I wasted my time, only to be maligned in secret, hated, pitied; always the pity, and I wonder why… why?—yet *feel* nothing except lingering anguish, not quite within me, on the fringes of me, at the *focal* point of my *external* being, a part of me, without *being* me.

What reformation of spirit could I propose in goodwill?—for I love Pelagia, and she loves me, only on account of us both being ignorant to love. I ingest toxicity.

> To love is to surrender yourself to an entity you hate, be *it*
> a person, object, idea, or yourself, to embrace the polarity
> of unification, to worship your self-destruction.

Sunday, July 5th, 2020

10:00 AM

I dreamed of an outdoor family gathering around an old home of my early youth. My mother and father had both been present, in earlier stages of their life—their early 40s; however, I retained my current age of a twenty-eight-year-old man. With outspoken thoughts, contrary to my mien, I responded to my extended family of aunts and uncles with stream-of-consciousness disparagements and attempted to flee. On a busy city street, I saw my father at both ends of a road; both aspects hounded me, called my name, and urged me to return home. Horrified, I informed the local populace (a group of teenagers and young adults) that I am being hunted by a doppelganger, and began to sprint into unknown recesses of the city, darkened by towering structures.

I woke, refreshed, after a twelve-hour sleep, and reflected on the dream. I had been wrong in my usage of the word "doppelganger"; however, this usage had been all in my mind, similar to this document, which in all likelihood will remain as my mind in physical format without ever being acknowledged by anyone other than women who once claimed to love me, to their chagrin, in hindsight. Foolish reader, go on then, end this at once; I'll be back for more regardless.

2:10 AM

Pelagia laid beside me in her bed two mornings ago and said, "You remember everything; that's admirable."

I said, "Why?"

I don't remember what she said, though for her to hold me to higher esteem for my self-flagellation method confounded me, more so for her unexpressed perceptions of me. When I hear only inflated virtues and praise on my behalf, I'm consciously aware of the brooding which underlies all niceties. We both think our relationship is doomed before *it* has even developed into something greater, for Pelagia doesn't seek greatness; she seeks mediocrity from not only herself, but from everyone. Pelagia loves only those who skirt her love and keep her on the fringes: an impossible potentiality. I postulate that her bisexual best friend, Howard, who she has known for twelve years, is her ideal man. According to Pelagia, Howard deemed me "perfect" for her, and I've been the only man Howard has ever "approved of"… *for her.*

With every affirmation of my compassion, I become weaker in Pelagia's unconscious perspective.

8:05 PM

Since my return to New York, I've reverted to only my three basic tenets of reading, writing, and exercise. Since being exposed to groups of others near my age in social settings once more, I realize how deprived I am by maintaining a friendless lifestyle. I've listened to the *Netherlands Bach Society's* recorded performances in my father's basement all day and emerged only to consume and expel.

"Twerp" comes to mind to describe me—for what this journalistic endeavor is and how one with a long-term partner, a business, and children would perceive me. Indeed, the older I become, and as my publications' scope expands, the greater a twerp I am. I'm eager to begin employment again, to join others in their deluded sense of self-worth on account of being *occupied.* Perhaps I should rethink my priorities; I garnered more respect when perceived as a callous killer.

Monday, July 6ᵗʰ, 2020

1:18 PM

The more time I devote to Pelagia and begin to truly understand the woman, my affection only amplifies, and her disdain for me amplifies in equal measure. The chase is over; I am no longer unattainable, exciting, or mysterious. Her prospects shift. This drama won't endure.

Pelagia is often anxious around me, for she knows of my journalism and deems the recorded thoughts of a no-name pleb to be worthy of consideration; therefore, with due respect, I will abstain from such trifles of melodrama and sentimental expositions.

Tuesday, July 7ᵗʰ, 2020

12:18 PM

I pity those who strive for fame and acclaim, for prestige and wealth, for honor and merit.

I question why I returned to this city, to my father's home; my being in this domain is premature. The life I built for myself from naught but a month-and-a-half worth of military pay is a distant past that I neither yearn for nor exalt my extrication from.

Candy has messaged me weekly, sometimes daily, for months, pining, pleading, begging in some circumstances, for me to communicate with her. Yesterday she sent me a single sentence message that I presume and hope will be her last:

"My short time with you was the happiest I have been in years. I know you thought you had nothing to offer me… but you gave me everything I needed. Thank you."

And what did I give other than a miasma of the mind and a stimulus of the flesh? This is all we yearn for, regardless of gender—the drama, theatrics, eloping, and the *lies* most of all: crucial components in human discourse. I lied to myself in stating I would refrain from a diatribe derived from trifles, melodrama, and sentimentality; in acknowledgment of my inability, I reiterate a quintessential example of such affairs with an opinion on social justice:

Equity, not equality.

There, I've contributed to the political zeitgeist, to be waft over, unreviewed and discounted.

Am I, a man, dressed in only a pair of briefs, standing in his sixty-seven-year-old father's dim basement, typing on a laptop positioned atop an empty wine box, atop a metal ammo box, atop a round wooden table, while listening to J.S. Bach's *Violin Concerto in E Major BWV 1042, Adagio*, equal to the man who rides on the side of a dump truck for ten hours a day?—the man seated at the second-highest floor of the world's second-tallest office building?—Mother Theresa?—the woman incapable of loving herself who claims to love me? [21]Equality is an invented conception related to numbers, *not* our birthright.

Pelagia's only hope is to repel my inexorable affection, to reject me into oblivion, to liberate herself from what she hates and reviles: love; though she isn't exclusive in this matter; we're all in this network of disposable humanity, where nothing is ever lost or wasted, where death continues to invoke awesome dread, and validation is the sole gambit of our existence.

5:41 PM

"… I want to stop existing," is an extract of Howard's lamentations while we stood out on Pelagia's second-floor balcony at midnight, which I believe summarizes reality as we know *it*. Reincarnation, without the constraints of this terrestrial plane or dependence on "karma," i.e., cultural ethics, is ~~my~~ a theorized happenstance of life, for life is spontaneous, without a source to isolate—that our species is currently aware of. On death, consciousness may persist as a singular entity, united with "the whole we call universe"[22] and manifests as life elsewhere in this universe, and any beyond.

My pseudophilosophy/theology/science is as meritable as any, for what credentials could one ever acquire to "know"?

Howard is a (approximately) 5'6, thirty-[value]-year-old man dressed to impress; being a bartender, this is expected. Oval face; well-kept facial hair; short-length thinning head hair; faint eyebrows; thick, black, rectangular glasses. His voice accentuates the incisiveness of his more-often-than-not

---

[21] Whereby *I* lie and proclaim reciprocal love out of ignorance and fear.
[22] Albert Einstein

sardonic tone and context. He is a master dissimulator, having perfected what I dub a "'sociopathic' gaze." Howard is also a self-proclaimed misanthrope; this amuses me, for Howard is the man who lent me his copy of Ayn Rand's *The Fountainhead* a year ago.

"The man-worshippers, in my sense of the term, are those who see man's highest potential and strive to actualize *it*. The man haters are those who regard man as a helpless, depraved, contemptible creature— and struggle to never let him discover otherwise. *It* is important to remember here that the only direct introspective knowledge of man anyone possesses is of himself."

- Ayn Rand's Introduction to The Fountainhead

Howard bemoaned a video that showcased a dog with two missing front legs being dropped out of a stationary car. Howard anthropomorphized the dog's reaction to being abandoned, and I had been the only one out of our group of four (myself, Pelagia, Howard, and Ethan) to watch the video in *it*s entirety. On the video's completion, I stared into a glass of alcohol and swirled the contents while Pelagia leaned against my shoulder. The trio condemned the abominable action of the dog's owner with a combined emotional outrage while I remained silent. I thought of the barbarity of life, of the suffering worldwide and that which supersedes us, and how *we* suffered together on the balcony in our own ways, estranged from each other's convictions of moral justice, never fully comprehending each other in our subjective experiences, and yawned.

Wednesday, July 8th, 2020

12:04 AM

I laid in wait for sleep and heard an inner voice graze my psyche: *"He's an imbecile, an autistic imbecile."*

"To love at all is to be vulnerable. Love anything and your heart will be wrung and possibly broken. If you want to make sure of keeping *it* intact you must give *it* to no one, not even an animal. Wrap *it* carefully

round with hobbies and little luxuries; avoid all entanglements. Lock *it* up safe in the casket or coffin of your selfishness. But in that casket, safe, dark, motionless, airless, *it* will change. *It* will not be broken; *it* will become unbreakable, impenetrable, irredeemable."

- C.S. Lewis

5:44 PM

My first day of employment at the bar where I worked prior to attending Navy boot camp begins two days from today.

11:01 PM

I walked through downtown at dusk and encountered the same homeless man I knew a year ago. *It*'s only ever those in need of something, whether *it* be money or validation, that greet strangers, and this man had greeted me from twenty-five feet away with lukewarm amicability. A sob story ensured; I stood and listened to the entire exposition for four minutes. By the end, the homeless man, now twenty pounds lighter and more dejected than he was four minutes prior, said, "So do you have any spare change on you, man?"

I said, "No," thought of the four twenty-dollar bills in my pocket, and nodded—slightly, before I departed the scene without speaking a mutual goodbye. I scorned the man while I walked, for a beggar is the most pitiful state one may degrade to. In my dire straits of destitution, I spread my privileged white ass cheeks for a big black penis—twice, *and* paid my dues (rent, food, and antibiotics for an infected rectum) to my penetrator once I secured employment. What is a capable street beggar to me?—not even human.

Thursday, July 9th, 2020

2:08 PM

I'm halfway through reading *Genius Foods* by Max Lugavere and Paul Grewal (despite the ostentatious title) and have decided to revert to my diet several years ago, which, by coincidence follows the guidelines of the book; a reiteration and reminder of dietary knowledge I have forgotten over the years has rekindled my insight into the pompous allure of a physique hampered by excessive muscle and a digestive system overwrought with toxins. I am to forsake the oatmeal I've glutted on for the sake of increased strength and reacquaint myself with a lithe, agile body—which, in fact, had been a vessel I had been the most confident in occupance of. Eggs, cacao, berries, grass-fed beef, extra virgin olive oil, mushrooms, spinach, peppers, broccoli, avocados, swiss chard—the list goes on.

Diet isn't the only facet of my behavior that I experience a resurgence of. Entertainment is voided. I had experimented with marijuana, alcohol, and the occasional video game, and had been unfulfilled—not out of shame, or the brooding feeling that I could be more productive with my time, but of the *desire to be* productive with my time. My father and I spend the majority of our existence alone and meet in the kitchen for an occasional chat while preparing food for ourselves, refilling a cup of coffee, and relieving our bowels. I pace the span of the basement, with either my laptop or book in one hand, and stop only to type, exert the body, or meditate for a brief period no longer than half-an-hour on my floor when my thoughts become too bombastic for me to tolerate. My father appreciates the television I purchased for him, and on occasion, I've watched nature, science, and world history documentaries when in the rare mood for a visual stimulus. The film *Samsara* is one of the most beautiful cinematography experiences I've ever seen.

The books *Behave,* by Robert M. Sapolsky, and *Thinking, Fast and Slow,* by Daniel Kahneman, have arrived by mail today.

I have no debt, begin employment with my favored occupation tomorrow, and enjoy a quasi-solitary life with a true comrade. The stigma against millennials, or rather, a *man,* living in his parent's basement, is moot. I've proved myself to myself, and have nothing to prove to society, i.e., a woman.

6:23 PM

I believed Pelagia's ruse, gave her the benefit of my doubt, and loved her for what she said, although her behavior expressed the contrary. I rendered myself vulnerable. I knew of her deceit all along; therefore, she suspected *me* of perpetrating a ruse. I loved her despite her admittance of not knowing how to love properly—the fool that I am.

334

8:41 PM

I visited Pelagia amid her painting the living room of her new apartment a welcoming blue. Despite her desire to be alone to focus on her task, I asserted my presence, which she accommodated, and had been happy to show me her progress and new household goods. She spoke of a new batch of tea she brewed, and offered me a glass of water from a new water filtration spigot.

I declined and said, "I don't think that we're compatible, and that we should stop seeing each other."

Stunned for an intensive second, she recovered, and said, "Okay, why do you think that?"

"Your behavior the last few days, and our lack of communication."

Pelagia's face overtook an expression of intense consternation; she said, "I do care for you and respect you."

I failed to express my mutual care and respect and said, "The question I had been wanting to ask you is, 'Do you think that compassion is a weakness?'"

"When you said that I immediately thought of animals." Pelagia paused, stole a glimpse at her cat, opened her mouth to speak, stopped, braced her head on the counter separating her living room and kitchen, began to stammer, and said, "I think compassion is when you make time for others, so no, I don't think *it*'s a weakness." An interesting response, as I had to verbally argue and finagle with Pelagia for me to visit her during her time off from work. Furthermore, she acknowledged that she needs time for herself, to develop and grow during the transition she experiences and to overcome the trauma she's endured by other men, and that she has been selfish by consequence. I questioned why she expressed enthusiastic excitement to see me on her initial learning of my return to New York, and why she claimed to love me, if she felt simultaneous that she needs *all* her time to prove herself, *to* herself. I affirmed that the more compassion, empathy, and vulnerability that I expressed to her, the greater she withdrew, and that my idea of love (as an example) would be to assist her with painting her apartment.

Pelagia said, "Have you read *The 5 Love Languages*?"

I thought for three seconds, dumbfounded by the deviation, and said, "No."

Pelagia recommended the book to me. She *had* been agreeable with my immediate announcement of ceasing to see each other, until I stated that I won't be friends with her, for I have no friends by choice. She didn't agree with my "drastic" decision, and stated that she doesn't perceive the situation in that manner. We both suppressed tears while gazing at each other, attempting to be *strong and independent*. Pelagia said, "You can always reach out and contact me, unless you already deleted my phone number and email."

I said, "I intend to when I return home."

"I just think that not being friends could make things difficult…"

"There will be no issues if you don't seek me out."

Pelagia frowned and gazed down to her right with bleary eyes while leaning against her kitchen sink counter. I, too, struggled to compose myself, yet I wrought what I had designed, and had accomplished my goal. She said, "Okay."

I said, "I wish you well," backstepped, and nodded.

"Thank you, you too."

I looked at Pelagia, for two seconds longer than customary, to observe her face for what I presumed to be the final instance. Her eyebrows furrowed for a half-second, as if she knew what I was doing. A half-dollar-sized splotch of dark blue paint blemished her upper cheek below her right eye. I backstepped an additional three steps, turned right, exited the entryway with a glum mien, and while I closed the door, I observed her through the pane window, staring downcast to her right at the kitchen floor.

10:02 PM

I don't know what manner of human I am. My life is that of self-inflicted pain, and consequently the pain I inflict on everyone who has ever cared for me. My emotions are too convoluted for me to sustain a relationship and I become distracted from my self-assigned meaning: to pursue conceptions greater than myself (a farce). My ego betrays and deceives me, for the sake of *it*self. The irony is that the romance and "love" I loathe to write is *exactly* what constitutes *quality* writing by the jurisdiction of the masses. My tragedy is my unlikely reader's comedy.

I am to sleep reminiscent of a wounded animal tonight.

Saturday, July 11th, 2020

9:28 AM

My new manager, Calanne, flattered me thrice: "Wow, *it* looks cleaner in here already"; "You're my new all-star employee"; *"It's* practically sparkling in here!" She spoke to me as she would a schoolboy, or a son.

The bar conditions are no longer "high-class"; instead, both establishments now serve low-grade bar grub, e.g., burgers, fries, pizza, and fried fare. Business is one-twelfth of what I had experienced a year prior, primarily due to Covid-19, yet I'm paid $2.00/hr more for less effort due to my leveraging. I've expressed a desire to be a "Pit Lord," and to manage the dish basin full-time, on account of my passion for the maintenance and cleanliness of a kitchen. Learning to cook any of the menu selection offers me no valuable skills.

I've laxed on my "sociopathic" at-work charade, and behave "as I am," despite being surrounded by Pelagia's friends and acquaintances from when she had also been employed at the bar. The owner (Walther) and Pelagia are long-standing affiliations, and I'm inclined to think that Pelagia attempts to malign me by confabulating intimate details I shared with her on account of her prizing a "good" reputation. I believe this, for Pelagia informed her social circle of me being a part of her life again, and now I've nullified my existence within her interpersonal relationships. I'm humored, for any word she could ever speak or write against me only disparages herself; in that regard, I may as well be a dead man.

Sunday, July 12th, 2020

10:19 PM

I'm vexed by my existence, by my father's daily complaints. I forsook everything I ever aspired for by returning to this city, and have condemned myself to continue to be known wherever I go; regardless of the opinion, I am *known*.

The pettiness of my mind must end. I surround myself with pettiness. In my father's basement, I lose my mind and *think*, review my past, and plan for the future—always; there is no time for the "moment."

Candy's messages haven't ended; she yearns for me to respond, to validate her existence, yet her only intent is to break me of my silence, and therefore, my integrity.

Why do I *care?*—and persist with this horrific romantic metanonfiction? There is *no* damnable romance; I review what this life is, and I reinvigorate my pity for humanity. This merry-go-round of cluster-fucking DNA exchanging and protein ingestion removes me from every facet of being human and displaces me to a perspective wholly of an *ape*. Unbelievable— what I write—can *you* believe *it?* I'm just *so fucking intelligent* after all, to write in an indulgent journal each day and have the gall to think myself an author—to walk across my home city, back and forth, to wash dishes and purchase groceries—the incompetent "autist" that I am!

I have failed Pelagia by showing her compassion; she fell in love with my predominant hatred before Bootcamp; thus, I pity her. Monogamy is moot; she desires to manipulate me into submission, to dominate me with her twisted rendition of "love," and each instance I withdraw, *especially* if I do so with respect, and display a *tinge* of remorse, I am thought of her as naught but a half-man, or a quarter-man—nay, a *boy,* incapable—simply incapable; yet she *loves* me, and *"thought of me every day."* I admitted my love, for **I had been weak** to exhibit compassion to a harpy. The lies cut deep, for as the fool I am, I trusted her—a maligner and dissimulator. I *know* she isn't finished with me; she plots, for my will is a plaything to be broken, such as a cat who trounces onto a shelf and swats an expensive piece of pottery onto a hardwood floor.

It's over between us, whatever *it* was: that sick and nauseating game we called "love." I hope every thought and memory of me that Pelagia thinks henceforth is an unwanted scourge unto her contentment, compelling her to eradicate me from her synapses. I'll lead by example; however, I *do* wish her well. She is impressive.

Monday, July 13th, 2020

9:22 AM

Tensions between my father and myself have climaxed due to lifestyle differences and philosophies.

Last night, my father smoked a gratuitous amount of marijuana, and on my return home from a grocery store, he regarded me as an adolescent in need of consolation on account of my constant consternation with my latent affairs: "Are you all right? Are you sure? Are you all right? *Okay,*" he spoke with glibness.

I descended the stairwell to the basement, stopped at the bottom of the steps, and analyzed my lot in life for two minutes. I returned upstairs, bypassed the curtain of the living room, stood before my father, seated over a game of *Candy Crush* and said, "Do you treat me as a bitch because you think I am one?"

"How do I treat you as a bitch?"

"Asking me if I'm 'all right,' repeatedly, as if I need counsel."

"Sorry dude; I didn't intend *it* that way, just a paternal thing."

I nodded, spoke my customary "Goodnight, I love you," and proceeded down the stairwell, to the basement floor, to sleep.

On waking, I decided to warm-up with five sets of chin-ups and entered the pitch-black living room, often inconsequential of the time of day, illuminated by the glow of a phone screen featuring a game of *Candy Crush,* where my father sat, hunched in a chair, cigarette in hand and coffee beside him, with a miserable scowl splayed across his face. The pullup bar had been missing from the doorway. I said, "Where's the pullup bar?"

Five seconds of silence elapsed; he said, *"Where's* the pullup bar?"

I looked back towards the doorway where the pullup bar should've been—slowly, and pivoted my head around the room, as to display my ignorance, and stated, "Yes."

"Where you fucking tossed *it* last night."

I said, "I haven't moved the pullup bar."

My father sneered and said, " … *It*'s in the corner of the bedroom, behind my bed, near the window."

"What's your problem?"

"You."

"Why?"

My father immediately stood, veered past me, two inches from my face, and said, "What the fuck do you think I am?—a *bitch?*" He entered his room, retrieved the pullup bar, and outstretched *it* towards me to grab. I took the pullup bar from him and he said, "You're a fucking aggressive prick."

I said, "Because I-"

"I don't fucking want to hear your fucking shit."

"Because I asked where the pullup bar was?"

"Fuck you."

I stood, resolute, confirmed in my suspicions of our inability to work together as comrades, reached for my first set on the chin-up bar, and said, "All right, I'm moving out."

My father said nothing.

I arranged to meet with an apartment manager for a rental directly at the city center: a one-minute walking distance from my site of employment, and a one-mile maximum radius from every civic structure I would ever utilize. I have *indeed* returned to this city and suffer a reputation that precedes me—for *nothing*.

I've *nothing* more to write of anyone, not even myself. My return to my father and former associates has negated all ambitions I nurtured for the sake of rejuvenated companionship. I may now live at peace with solitude.

Tuesday, July 14th, 2020

11:40 AM

A saint walked through the rear of a graveyard surrounded by dense forest on the outskirts of a small hamlet. Stars twinkled overhead, and below, on the surface of the terrestrial plane, between two weathered rectangular tombstones, a maniacal killer butchered the corpse of a newborn baby girl. The saint, on beholding the gruesome scene, immediately blurted, "Have you no compassion?"

The saint's words lingered across the flattened expanse: a sharp resonation accented with conviction. The manicial man uplifted his head, addressed the saint with two blinks of both eyes, rose from his squatted position with a bloodstained dirk in hand, and said, "Aye, I do."

"Then why do you brutalize a babe of god?—this is against humanity!"

The maniacal man began an amble towards the saint, sixteen meters away, with calculated steps. He held the dirk downturned towards the earth, cocked his head, and said, "I have done this one a favor."

"You murdered an innocent!"

"She suffered, and would go on suffering if not for my intervention, just as you will. Have you no compassion for me, or are you to only *judge?*"

The saint stood, resolute, fearless, and said, "I know nothing but compassion for my fellow children of God, we-"

The maniacal man hastened forward with a sudden sprint and slashed the saint's exposed throat with the tip of his dirk.

1:45 PM

My father compelled me to attend the military service for his father's and mother's joint interred burial. He leaned back in his chair while I stood and contemplated for twenty seconds.

I said, "I'd rather you lose respect for me."

My father said, "What respect? You can't lose what you don't have."

We smirked. I walked away.

6:15 PM

If you love someone, let them go.

8:14 PM

On my way to read *Thinking, Fast and Slow* at the local boneyard, I encountered two young teenage boys bedazzled with chains around their necks, dressed in loose-fitted black t-shirts and baggy jeans. Hip-hop music played from one of their phones. They veered out of my way as we approached each other. I stopped on the sidewalk and said, "Excuse me."

Both boys stopped and addressed me, wide-eyed. The first in their line of two said, "Yeah?"

"What is your self-assigned meaning in life?"

"Uh, I don't know."

"Yeah-" I acknowledged the second boy: "-How about you?"

He shrugged.

I said, "No? How about 'Fuck bitches—make money'? Right?"

Both boys grinned. The first chuckled and said, "Yeah."

Humorless, I said, "Yeah, fuck *it* all," and marched onward.

Wednesday, July 15th, 2020

9:12 AM

I recall how I felt when I landed with $1,000 at the Arkansas airport with no idea where I was: Liberated, invigorated, empowered.

The night after I secured an apartment of my own, after two months of homelessness and sexual servitude, I laid on my newly acquired lot of floor to sleep on, and identified myself as a despicable loser.

"Are you happy to be 'home'?" those who cross my path inquire, as if to imply that I belong back in New York and that a land of origin is one's birthright. No—I'm *not* happy.

I failed to exert my will over Pelagia by accepting her request to see me, to the detriment of ~~my~~ our well-being and sanctity of mind. Instead, I pursued an unsustainable, fallacious relationship, and named *it* love.

I failed to exert my will over my father by reciprocating his proclamation of love, and have caused him manifold suffering by my return to his house and my subsequent withdrawal.

By these actions, I am still a despicable loser; however, this is a temporary status until eventual sentiments of indifference or death transpire from all who ever knew me, my father and mother included.

I'm perceived as a conniving, "mentally ill," emotionally stunted scumbag, by consequence of my severance of relationships. I'm an embarrassment to my father, and those who affiliate with me.

I rejoice in the thought that nobody thinks of me. I pride myself in my pain of self-imposed ostracism. There is an allure to lunacy, to embrace and overcome one's humanity, alone.

1:39 PM

I could've stayed in Arkansas and continued to exhaust my unemployment benefits while working "under the table" for Candy. Instead, I voided my relationship with my employer/lover, terminated my lease for a $700 fee, purchased a $240 plane ticket, and purchased a $1,900 television for my father. From a purely selfish, capitalistic, and utilitarian perspective, I am unhappy, though these decisions are entirely my own. My father permits me to stay rent-free with the expectation that I would assist with funding a boat; however, with recent affairs, I've determined I can only ever depend on myself for consistent rationale. I've yet to discuss the annulment of the agreement I made with my father regarding the boat, and of my request for a mutual understanding of a permanent termination of our correspondence in order for me to pursue a downward spiral of my humanity and my upward aspirations of self-understanding.

I could commit myself to an asylum, jail, or prison for equal effect, though I've already experienced a pseudo-imprisonment and prefer my autonomy and contributing to society by the method of ordering a pocket of chaos, i.e., dishwashing/cleaning, to validate myself.

My employer, Walther, doesn't have me scheduled for work until next week due to me entering his system on the day of a new schedule posting.

The apartment managers I've contacted have neglected to return my calls.

2:22 PM

If I achieve my goals by the year's end, I will have no alternative but to name this installment **Outbursts of a Successful "Psychopath"; Thoughts of a Despicable Loser.**

Thursday, July 16th, 2020

11:19 AM

I've finished the final proofread of the third installment of this series over a six-egg vegetable omelet with a side of sauerkraut and sautéed spinach topped with mustard.

My father and uncle have departed for their father's and mother's joint interred military burial.

I meet with an apartment manager at 3:00 PM on the 18th of July.

1:44 PM

I've lost my mind to reason devoid of logic. I've relinquished everything "good."

4:34 PM

A manchild? A perpetual boy? A scared little fool?

On the contrary, there is ~~nobody~~ nothing worth committing to.

I'm determined to lose all respect from my father; this document will suffice.

I granted Pelagia a release from me: a voiding of her delusions of my fantasized character, and now, with my display of compassion as a final act for her, she will no doubt consider me weak, pathetic, and inferior—even more so if she is to read my documentation. I imagine:

"I'm not sad at all; he's freed me. I'm sad I even cared so much about him; I wish I could erase him from my memory. I thought he was such a catch but he's really just awful. He's handsome, that's all, but there's nothing to him. Don't get me wrong—I'd talk to him if he reached out to me but he's really just a loser. He couldn't even get into the Navy and now he lives with his father to ride his coattails. He holds my past against me and now I have a chance to hold his past against him and he really just isn't worth a thought. He exuded such strength but he's really just a little bitch, especially the last I saw him; I wish I could just take it all back. I'm completely over him, and I really have him to thank for it. He knows I want a family and he's too scared to commit because I'm stronger and more professional than he is. Walther doesn't even like him and doesn't intend to schedule him more hours–"

6:57 PM

I stopped ~~channeling~~ intuiting my egoic locus of thought in the previous entry while thinking of Pelagia and called Walther to discuss my work schedule on account of aforementioned (italicized) thoughts. He invited me to the establishment to speak with him in-person. While seated in his office, Walther and I discussed the parameters of my role: I have been assigned the responsibility of maintaining the cleanliness of both restaurants and managing the stock of cleaning supplies. Before Walther toured me through both buildings, he asked me, "You know that I *want* you to work here and I'm glad to have you here, right?"

I grimaced and began to involuntarily shake my head in disbelief.

Walther continued, "That's a question—I'm giving you the opportunity to answer."

I said, "Now I know: yes."

At the end of the walkthrough, Walther shook my hand: a jostle of equal stolidness and quality to my own, and thanked me.

Yes, I am *truly* mad, deluded by my own desire to forsake myself from affection and compassion; however, these straits of my mind—my "daemon," my "God," my "djinn," my "ego," direct me to become the man that I *will* for myself. Without the guidance of my consciousness, I wouldn't be everything that I am now, even if what I am is a self-debasing utilitarian asshole who has squandered every long-term prospect available to him.

On my return to my father's home, I capitalized on my clarity of mind to engage in a progressive conversation with him. I informed him of my plan to be out of his basement and in my own apartment by the end of this month, and my annulment of our plan to board a trawler together due to our incompatibility. I requested that he no longer provide me any affection once I am gone, for I had no desire to cause him pain by severing our relationship in a similar manner to when I had initially departed for the U.S. Navy boot camp. After a trenchant twenty-minute discussion, my father asserted, "You can't stop someone from loving you."

I disagree. You may stop someone from loving you in the same manner as you stop someone from respecting you.

8:27 PM

Masculinity is to accept death.

9:13 PM

"People who are *cognitively busy* are also more likely to make selfish choices, use sexist language, and make superficial judgments in social settings." [23]

Right—away with ye, vile harpies, sirens, temptresses and vixens.

11:31 PM

I'm a madman; I amaze myself. I remembered an event incorrectly, synthesized highly critical introspections that I conceived another to think of me, and remembered the correct event afterward, resulting in

---

[23] Daniel Kahneman's *Thinking, Fast and Slow*

invalidation of my thought process, i.e., *madness,* e.g., I laid on the basement floor to sleep and incorrectly recalled the moment that I told Walther that I have "three 'concurrent' years of janitorial maintenance experience." Knowing that the word "concurrent" is wrong in the context, I project my ego onto Walther and intuit his thoughts on the matter—if Walther *cared* in the first place—*and* shared the exact perspective as myself: *"The guy is just trying to flex his vocabulary and seem intelligent."* A half-minute later, I recall the correct memory, in which I utilized the word "cumulative," not "concurrent," and thereby negated my false delusion.

I'm a genius! Since the onset of this lifelong journalistic emprise, I've ruined and disposed of my valuables, spurned lovers, and forsake the love of mother and father in the name of folly—for the *value of* folly! I rejoice in my buffoonery!

Friday, July 17th, 2020

11:24 PM

Unity, destruction, and rebirth; I am stalwart on my definition of love.

Yes, despite this perpetually childish and self-indulgent documentation that is my life's meaning, I must be a man of exceptional judgment by my own standards. After my epiphany last night, I've determined, without a doubt, that intuitions are faulty; thoughts aren't objects; there is no universal consciousness unto which we are all god with eternal souls. There is no truth.

There is only man, woman, judgments, and an exchange of materials. All else is wishes, pandering, and postulating.

There is nothing special about me; my ego isn't worth degrading. I'll be a dull dishwasher for a year, for I've decided that to spend money on a new apartment would be ~~folly~~ stupid; my father agreed—of course, and encouraged me to "take *it* easy." We have discussed reality as *it* is, regarding the pandemic, finances, the boon to us both for our cooperation, and a future on the ocean. Maturity or spiritual regression, I care not. There are merits to pragmatism.

7.8 billion people. What else is there to write about but us? Them? Who? *They?* Animals or aliens?—the sediment we walk on?—the air we breathe?—the sun which energies the earth? Oh yes, space travel, quantum, alternate universes, metaphysical conundrums, macrocosms and microcosms… No, thank you; I'll write of a dish pit, for that's all I "know."

Saturday, July 18th, 2020

12:29 AM

I lay to sleep once again and arise to reiterate tired ideas: There is no "mental illness"; there is only what a society deems right and wrong for optimum functioning. The human creature capitalizes on another's doubt.

8:36 AM

There is a desire to be perceived as responsible that is causal with a desire to be significant. When God is rendered dead, so too, is the spirit.

9:05 PM

My moments with, and thoughts concerning Pelagia, conceptualized, have taught me that what began as an affair, lapsed into romance, evolved into the implacable idea of "love," and ended with a frivolous dreariness, evidenced, based on my internal rhetoric and self-talk, that I am ill-inclined to habituate myself for the expectation of marriage and a family.

I encountered Ryan for the first time since my departure from New York: Pelagia's old lover, who she still communicates with on the level of friendship, to keep him within her social influence for the comfort and validation provided. Out back of the restaurant, I hosed down an infested shop-vac filled with gnats. Ryan approached from the adjacent tavern wearing a face mask. I said, "Hey."
"Oh hey Baethan—how have you been?"
"I've been well, yourself?"
Ryan didn't respond and entered the restaurant. Forty seconds elapsed while a swarm of gnats dispersed around me and a thick coagulated brown and green liquid swirled over and subsumed with sandy gravel near my feet. Ryan exited the restaurant.
Again, I said, "Hey."

Ryan either hadn't heard, or ignored me, and walked several steps past me.

I yelled, "I'm curious!"

Ryan whirled to face me, wide-eyed.

I said, "Did you ever read *The Short Happy Life of Francis Macomber?*"[24]

After a two-second pause, Ryan said, with a hint of sheepishness, "No, I never got around to *it.*"

I smiled, raised both of my hands by my sides, palms forward, and shouted, "Why not?"

"I don't know; I just haven't." Ryan shrugged, and I could see the edges of a sullen frown beneath his face mask. He turned and hurried away from me.

10:54 PM

No, this clarity of mind is beyond pragmatism. There is compassion and empathy, even when faced with those who only hate.

I inquired with my kitchen comrades tonight on what they believe the definition of masculinity is, or what they believe defines a masculine person. The propositions I received varied:

Beatrice: "Masculinity is a spectrum."

Paul: "Masculinity is taking responsibility for your actions."

Keith: "Masculinity is determined by society."

I pondered on these answers and presented my own postulate to Keith, Paul, and Bryant—a passerby who works in the adjacent tavern: Masculinity is acceptance of death. I engaged in rhetoric with Paul and questioned his axiom of "Life is a test to prove your worth."

Paul explained, to his belief, that as humans, we prove our worth (to a greater entity) by treating others with respect, and assuming responsibility for our lives.

I posited a metaethical hypothesis: "As humans, our virtues are decided by culture, and that due to the differentiation of cultures and the

---

[24] An excerpt from April 18th, 2019:

"After listening to a brief summary of his (Ryan's) overdue library rental fees, I recommended for the third and final time, *The Short Happy Life of Francis Macomber,* by Hemingway.

"Ryan sipped his beer and nodded.

"I continued, 'The characters remind me of the situation between you, myself, and Pelagia.' "Ryan frowned and gazed downward at the floor to my right. 'Oh.' "

consequent effect on perceptions concerning human behavior, there may be no definite actions that may determine our worth—*even* if one were to practice the dogma of 'Treat others as you would treat yourself,' for there are those who are hostile and vicious with not only humans, but with all of life."

Paul conceded in silence; however, I lapsed into a state of intense introspection on my post-shift jaunt home: I walked along a bridge connecting the northern and southern quadrants of the city and reflected on death. To be *alive*, and to accept the absurdity of each ephemeral second for the inherent futility, for the chaos, and the nullification of any idea of control… I've been "enlightened" by my ignorance; I know nothing, and this grants me peace. To accept death, to rejoice at the thought, is to ascend yourself to a level of delusion unassailable by externals: an impenetrable bulwark of solace; *it* is to love yourself, i.e., femininity.

One may only give by being selfish.

Love is an action, not a feeling, to expound on my previous definition.[25] Romance, infatuation, lust, allurement, enthrallment, longing, desire, and inebriation are *just* that.

Sunday, July 19th, 2020

5:07 PM

My father inquired as to why I have begun to stutter when I speak. I contemplated this for four minutes and determined that the cause is due to a lack of confidence—not in what I'm saying, or in myself, but of my *desire* to speak *at all.*

A lawyer sat in a booth of a posh office food bar on his break. Opposite to him, an unemployed thirty-seven-year-old man sat with a small coffee, paid for by the lawyer.

The lawyer said, "Man, *it* sure is hot out today."

The unemployed man said, "Yeah, groggy, real groggy."

"I'm seeing this girl, though I have no time for her."

"Yeah? She cute?"

"She's gorgeous: a supermodel. She never stops texting me."

---

[25] To love is to surrender yourself to an entity you hate, be it a person, object, idea, or yourself, to embrace the polarity of unification, to worship your self-destruction.

"Is she blonde?"

The lawyer chewed on a bite of a personal pan pepperoni and mushroom pizza, swallowed, and said, "Brunette, I don't think *it*'s natural though."

"My wife is a natural brunette."

"How is your wife?"

The unemployed man sniffed once and said, "She's all right."

"Yeah."

And so the two continued to banter in this manner for eighteen more minutes, and there hadn't been much to show for the dialogue other than a few disingenuous affirmations of an undistinguished friendship built on one-year-old memories both cling to for the sake of cordiality. The lawyer and the unemployed man never saw each other again after what remained of the undocumented conversation, and both continued to live their existences uncertain of what each other ever meant to the other—as in, the meaning of their symbiotic envy of each other's status and life perspective.

8:39 PM

"However, Stanovich argues that high intelligence does not make people immune to biases. Another ability is involved, which he labels rationality. Stanovich's concept of a rational person is similar to what I earlier labeled 'engaged.' The core of his argument is that *rationality* should be distinguished from *intelligence*. In his view, superficial or 'lazy' thinking is a flaw in a reflective mind, a failure of rationality." [26]

My intuitions betray me; indeed, they are nothing but doubts. What validity is there to reason when all people lie? To apply logic in the determination of when intuitive or rational thinking is applicable in human affairs is the ultimate quandary of ethics.

Monday, July 20th, 2020

2:38 PM

My father reminded me that when he dies, he wills the apartment house he owns that we currently reside in, to me, out of his six children. This is a circumstance I am grateful for, and in my opinion, wholly undeserving of on account of my behavior and treatment of my father for the past three

---

[26] Daniel Kahneman's *Thinking, Fast and Slow*

years. "Your behavior is unjustifiable," affirms my father, in regard to how I departed for U.S. Navy boot camp, "though I'm not going to browbeat you for *it*." My perspective on wealth has altered, for the betterment of myself, and wholly myself, with an altruistic mindset to enrich my father's hedonism while he still lives.

I am, and always will be, a privileged white man; however, in reiterating this fact, that isn't to say that there *aren't* privileged men *and* women of all races and origins distributed throughout the global population. Privilege is an opinion, relatable by circumstances and reference, i.e., knowledge, and I have squandered my privilege for the extent of my life—and for what?—some noble, libertarian, absurdist premise? Yes, for my philosophy of idiocy, I have forsaken every advantage, squandered my assets, invested in dissipation, pursued licentiousness, and condemned human affairs all-the-while. I have countered myself into a state of penury and subsequent sexual subservience, accrued a menial amount of debt (now paid off), and have lived in a delusional stasis for the past three years.

My will to change is resolute.

"But inherited wealth reaches *its* utmost value when *it* falls to the individual endowed with mental powers of a high order, who is resolved to pursue a line of life not compatible with the making of money; for he is then doubly endowed by fate and can live for his genius; and he will pay his debt to mankind a hundred times, by achieving what no other could achieve, by producing some work which contributes to the general good, and redounds to the honor of humanity at large."

- Arthur Schopenhauer's The Wisdom of Life

The "honor of humanity"; I shudder to think.

Walther has employed me to clean the customer venues of both bars for two hours, five days of the week, from 9:00 AM to 11:00 AM, with two dishwashing shifts on Friday and Saturday from 4:00 PM to 9:00 PM. I have *returned to work,* as our nation's leaders advised, and have relinquished $712. (yet to be taxed) a week in unemployment benefits for $14/hr at 22 hours a week, totaling $308 *before* taxes. I seek employment at a factory or assembly line, where I will be sanctioned from excessive exposure to a potential Covid-19 infected person and will be guaranteed over forty hours a week of employment. I pay no rent, and have forsworn any future expenditures on superfluous and extravagant distractions akin to the previous three months on account of boredom and a failure to stimulate myself without resorting to alternate realities and ephemeral pleasures.

My father earns $41,000 a year from a federal pension, and an average of $23,000 a year from renting out three units in his four-unit apartment building. He currently pays $750 a month on a final year of child support for his son (my younger half-brother). He owes $112,000 on the mortgage, which at his projected rate of repayment after refinancing and drawing on the home's equity ($50,000) for repairs and improvements, the new balance would become $162,000, and the payoff rate would be approximately twelve years. With my contribution to the principal of the mortgage of $1,000-$2,000 per month, depending on my employment status, the mortgage may be paid off within 7-8 years.

Being my father's "chosen one," for circumstances I am untried of (luck), I have determined that my best interests correspond with his, and will invest in his mortgage instead of rent. My profligacy of $3,500 regarding the federal-issued $1,200 stimulus check and 12 payments of state-issued $712 ($8,544) unemployment checks is a lesson I will never allow myself to forget, by recording in this document.

7:55 PM

There is no longer a shamanistic exposition, nor a deluded self-premise derived from a metaphysical fixation. The direction my character has evolved, and the man I have become disturbs me, for I had been hellbent on self-destruction; however, I have achieved this, only not in the manner I had anticipated. There's nothing weird, unique, or strange about me, as I've known all along. Each day is a new transgression against what I have known myself to be; there is no genuine consistency in any of us, and nobody would care to express their holistic *lack* of identity to another, for the subject would be inexplicable without influencing another with impressions, thereby countering one's own postulations. Much depends on our peer's judgments—the *negligible* aspects of existence, and *it* is these thoughts derived from our social dependency for validation that we may rend ourselves with, manifested from learned guilt and shame, that crystallizes our illusory identities.

I think of Howard Roark, the architect protagonist from Ayn Rand's *The Fountainhead*. Roark's character development is nonexistent; there is no growth required, for he is already the ideal manifestation of man according to Ayn Rand; he is immutable, fixed in his ego: a perfectly selfish genius whose contributions to society warrant him the title of "noble" due to the intrinsic altruism of his selfishness. Roark's integrity is causal with his suffering, and he truly is a despicable ~~psychopath~~ man.

The local boneyard is no longer the secluded grove I retreated to in my youth. I still venture there, nonetheless.

Tuesday, July 21st, 2020

3:02 PM

The desire for bodily aesthetics has been voided. After four years of intensive strength training, eating counter-intuitively to my well-being, and accelerating entropy, I've resumed fasting and eating for the benefit of my brain instead of the accumulation of useless muscle. This decision is paramount and irrevocable.

I have received emails from a marketing representative for the past two years and have diverted each message to my spam inbox. Today, I decided to read the first two paragraphs of one and processed a peculiar sentence: *"They say, writing is the most unselfish act."*

"They" obviously haven't read my books.

7:43 PM

I lay on my basement floor for hours and think of humanity's aspirations: glory, fame, wealth, and honor. My eyes closed, on my back, hands at my sides, I lay in the twilight darkness, illuminated by the sun's evening rays through a small rectangular window above a washer and dryer machine. The hum of a dehumidifier muffles distractions and allows me to process intuitive thoughts.

Compassion *is* weakness; therefore, trust is imperative to establish relationships. Without trust, compassion is devastation. Those paragons of virtue, secure with the values and ethics they have integrated into their sense of self for the sake of egoic preservation and security, delude themselves and others by association.

I've consigned my "self" to the acquisition of (nominal) wealth for the benefit of my future security by associating with my father.

I think of Pelagia for a cumulative hour or two each day; I am unhappy in this respect, despite our narcissism, vanity, and selfishness which renders

353

both of us distrustful of the other. Why I torment myself with ideas of this woman confounds me; the thoughts transpire as intrusions—*her voice,* masqueraded as the falsifications I project. *I have* spurned her, thrice, and severed our last attempt at a relationship with a marvelous display of ~~compassion~~ weakness, for I believe, with every facet of my applied reason, that she is malignant and cannot be trusted… and that Pelagia believes the same of me. We are better off without each other, for our union is toxic—a drug that induces a maelstrom of emotions, highs and lows, and biological disturbances.

9:45 PM

At the nursing home I worked at, assemblies were held on the second floor where the residents converged to enjoy amateur karaoke and acoustic guitar sessions performed by the staff. I recall assembling trays with meal tickets, silverware, and napkins, and observing an average of thirty residents, often vacuous and inert, ushered out of their rooms for forced social interaction. About a dozen would sit in their wheelchairs, waving their hands in loose circles in the space above them, and clapping out of sync with the music.

Wednesday, July 22th, 2020

4:29 PM

I support eugenics even though I've behaved within the parameters of American society at the mental capacity of a twelve-year-old. At the communes I visited, I had been an idiot. Dishwashing—an imbecile; however, even though I acquired part-time employment and forwent non-labor profit from the Covid-19 unemployment extension, the decision to invest in my father's mortgage to accrue future wealth for myself, to enable me to persist with my childish documentation of *my entire life,* liberated from financial woes, I thereby *give* to society, of my thoughts, for whoever chooses to read, and render myself merely a moron.

These statuses of antiquated psychological jargon relating to intelligence, determined by the anomalous leaders of society, are beneficial to progress. I support eugenics in favor of *anti*-progress; imagine, savages and degenerates, united under a single dictum of anarchy and absurdism, whereby human affairs are reduced to nothing more but a jungle fetish orgy fostered by bloodlust.

Contrary to Aristotle's philosophy of friends being the most important of the virtues, and an invaluable source of joy in life, I believe friends are a liability. I've never had a true friend: a person who I could depend on. No, a contemporary friend (of my schoolboy days) had always been one who stopped by my residence, shared his interests with the hope of reciprocity, consumed my food, and rewarded me with attention I didn't want. Gifts of unrequested food were common as bargaining for the use of my entertainment platforms. Yes, I've never had a true friend, one who I could manipulate to my own end and benefit with a greater return rate than I had invested; this arises from a lack of ambition.

My anti-social and anti-establishment philosophy lingers in the background, while pursuits of wealth and beneficial social relationships for my own benefit have overtaken the foreground. Is this maturity or "psychopathy"?

"Ya can't fool me, 'cause I'm a moron!" [27]

- Looney Tunes, Jack-Wabbit and the Beanstalk

Thursday, July 23rd, 2020

3:57 PM

A lowlife journalist mused on what he should write of today.

A critic said, "Write a terse and snarky summary of your uninformed opinion on a topic you aren't personally acquainted or knowledgeable of."

You try to be comical; however, your droll humor incites a viscous response in my mouth.

"Well, *it*'s what you excel at, and if *it* sells, why not?"

This isn't selling, nor should *it* ever.

"Your character is interesting and prompts intrigue."

This entry is about to veer into the realm of content that should be edited out of any manuscript, though I implore my future self to retain *it*, no matter how much of a waste of space the words employed are used to convey useless information.

---

[27] My father's oft-repeated expression.

"Tell me a story, then; flex your literary muscles; show me what you're capable of! I've become bored, in truth, though I'm nearly finished with the read—almost. You haven't written a creative snippet derived from the corners of your shapeless psyche in days—*weeks!*"

All right:

5:33 PM

I've negotiated with Walther for 40 hours a week as a dishwasher from 4:00PM - 9:00PM and a primary cleaner from 9:00PM - 12:30PM, five days a week, with my hours clocked on one payroll to secure the potential of overtime pay, i.e., a man jumped onto a treadmill.

Nonfiction horror is my favorite genre.

7:21 PM

My father and I have discussed the best method to transfer the apartment house ownership to my name when he refinances the mortgage instead of a death will. Never in my life did I think my paradigms of thought would shift to the route of paying off a mortgage.

Oh, excuse me, my white privilege is showing—what a smug statement—that previous sentence. I *should* be ashamed of my outcome in the genetic and demographic lottery. I'd be a near-destitute vagrant if not for nepotism. What merit do I have other than my heritage and the pigmentation of my skin?

To equate one's sense of self-worth with material acquisition is counter-spirituality.

"-America, OH America, may God thy gold refine,
"'Til all success be nobleness
"And every gain divined."

- Excerpt from Ray Charles' America the Beautiful

356

Friday, July 24th, 2020

10:38 PM

"Welcome to my harem," said a woman sprawled on a bed to her ex-boyfriend, who laid beside her. The woman held her phone in front of both her and her ex-boyfriend's face and scrolled through her *Facebook* friends list.

"Impressive," said the ex-boyfriend.

Saturday, July 25th, 2020

11:42 AM

The woman and her ex-boyfriend exchanged a round of oxytocin and stared into each other's eyes for four 7- 12 second intervals between nuzzling their faces into each other's shoulders and chests. The ex-boyfriend grinned and said, "I want to be part of your harem."

"You always have been."

"Even when we were together?"

The woman turned her head away, shifted her body to a supine position, flicked through her phone's *Facebook* menu options with aimless intent, and said, "No, you were special to me then."

The man stymied a frown and said, "Special, how?"

"I loved you," the woman retorted immediately, "and now we're just friends—good friends. We've had our time."

Twenty-eight seconds elapsed. The ex-boyfriend said, "I'm really stuck on you," and remained statuesque, positioned on his side. He stared at eight visible specs of dandruff amid the woman's hair arranged in a crescent around her right ear.

"I know," said the woman, and she lowered her phone face-down against her abdomen. "I'm glad you're here."

"I'm glad to be here too—with you."

"What do you want to watch?"

"I don't know; *it's* up to you," acquiesced the ex-boyfriend.

"Oh, *oh!*" The woman lurched upright, inspected her phone with a cursory glance, and gushed, "There's this one show I found, about crime in London in the 1800s that I really—really like. There's a, um, I don't want to spoil anything but there's a supernatural twist. *It*'s a mini-series. I just watched the first episode a few nights ago and loved *it*. Do you want to watch *it?*"

The ex-boyfriend said, "Sure."

The woman finalized and sent a text message on her phone in the three-second interval her ex-boyfriend utilized to decide and verbalize his affirmation. She said, "Okay!" and fumbled for a television remote on the floor by her bedside. "This is one of the best shows I've ever seen—even better than *Game of Thrones* I think, but that show's ending sucked so I hope this doesn't end the same way—which *it* won't because of how *it*'s designed as a mini-series with separate unrelated episodes. So if one episode sucks *it*'s okay because *it* won't detract from the whole." The television screen switched on and illuminated the evening sunlit room with the harsh glow of a *Netflix* logo.

The ex-boyfriend stared at the remote in the woman's hand outstretched in front of her at a skewed angle, and observed through the corner of his peripheral vision at the search function prompt on the television screen. He said, "Before we watch, I want to know what you meant about how I had been part of your harem."

The woman flashed a sidelong scowl, assumed a coy smile, and said, "I was just joking about that; none of those guys have any *real* interest in me; we just talk to each other often and kinda flirt every now and then—that's all."

"What I mean to say is: I know you want to get married and have kids, and I know we've had issues in the past, but I truly love you Jessica, and I'm at the point in my life that I want to settle down."

The woman huffed, leaned back against a wall behind the bed, and said, "Yes, *Ben,* you're right, I *do* want kids and I *do* want to settle down, sooner rather than later, but we've had our time, and… I care for you; I *deeply* care for you and want you in my life, but we're just friends. I don't know why we need to keep having this talk-"

"Because I love you and we're always in touch—always talking each or every other day, despite the ups and downs; I think we should pursue something serious together again. You know me better than anyone and I trust you."

Jessica snapped her head towards Ben and said, "You don't even want to have sex with me—ever, and you treat me like I'm one of your buddies at work. There's no real… I don't know—I don't want to say love or-"

Ben remained fixed and stared at the contours of the remote; he said,

"I have no other choice because you keep me out of your inner life and I respect you enough to not treat you like some fuck buddy; I'm always there for you without having a presence!"

"That's because I don't truly need anyone, or help, or anything—I don't even have time for anyone—and this time is precious to me, on my fucking day off, and I *chose* to spend my time with *you,* and now here we sit talking about old bullshit we've gone over at least thirty times and I just want to watch this fucking television show with you that I think you'll also enjoy—I mean is-"

"Okay, I'm sorry-"

"Is *it* really so bad that we're just friends? Is *it* so bad that I care for you, but I just don't want that relationship with you anymore and-"

"Okay I said—okay; let's watch the show. I'm sorry I-"

"Ben, I mean-"

"I get *it.*"

Jessica hesitated with the remote in hand, scrutinized the side of Ben's face; he looked at her, and both reckoned the other's foreign eyes. Jessica stood, trounced off the bed, said, "I need to use the bathroom first," and walked out of the room into an adjacent hallway.

Ben straightened his posture against the wall behind the bed, withdrew his phone from his pocket, and thumbed through the prompts for articles recommended to him by an algorithm. One minute and forty-six seconds elapsed. Ben pocketed his phone, sat face-forward, and stared at a blurb and an accompanying still-shot of Jessica's selected television program. He wiped at the corners of his eyes, blinked nine times in quick succession, brushed linen lint off his left shirt sleeve, and waited.

Sunday, July 26th, 2020

10:01 AM

Every sentence that begins with "I" should be nullified, in theory, concerning what this documentation is; however, the exposition is critical to understand the trajectory of what a man is. *I* (essential) represent a state every man is capable of ascending or descending to. *I* read and watch; what do *I* reckon other than representations of myself?

"He tries too hard to be philosophical," a drab female deviation of my ego states upon writing the previous passage. Is *it* so? Who am I trying for other than myself?

I'm thinking of writing a book—a genuine book, one of which the content follows a purpose. Self-help books disgust me; I am unacquainted with any esoteric knowledge, and my desire to impact the world is constrained to only the betterment of my own reality, to serve as a function for my self-assigned meaning in life. I'm in a quandary: Eight months ago I stood alone in an apartment in Arkansas, masturbated to a live video feed of myself, and ejaculated onto a millipede covered in tabasco sauce. Now, I have returned to New York where I started—in the basement of my father's apartment building, after a three-year process of relinquishing everything I own, forsaking friendships, and succumbing to the permissive affections of women.

I've learned throughout my self-imposed trials that no matter where I venture, there will always be people to write of, and people are much more interested in other people than the farthest conceivable reaches of the theorized multi-dimensional universal nether, or descriptions of terrestrial regions better visited than described.

"All of humanity's problems stem from man's inability to sit quietly in a room alone."

- Blaise Pascal

1:53 PM

Whispers of a Disadvantaged Black Woman; Ideas of a Humble Genius.
Indecorous for one's ostentatious home bookshelf? Regardless, this is my intellectual ~~property~~ privilege.

Am I to win the minds and hearts of those concerned only with themselves, akin to myself? One reading this journal has a vested interest; you believe you will be either entertained or informed, or you're paid to do so. On the contrary, I am ignorant and toilsome, hence my ~~employment~~ self-worth.

Afternoon Cup of Coffee

It *is my privilege*

Guilt and shame—good riddance

4:11 PM

My father returned from a game of morning golf with his friends and enjoys Mozart piano concertos overhead. I lay on the basement floor to promote digestion for thirty minutes before a workout and my thoughts stray to Pelagia. I'm at peace with what I have and desire nothing more; however, I'm afflicted by my perpetual self-engrossed thoughts in relation to others. I'm aware that all humans experience this in a myriad of manifestations, though mine are always routed in alignment with those I cared for and have abandoned ~~to the purposeful detriment of my well-being~~. I reel from constant reflection of my past, and analyze how I inflict despair onto others by my withdrawal. The effects are temporary, perhaps three months at most, until others' feelings in relation to me return to a baseline state of normalcy, precluded by brief resentment, or at best, indifference.

The creatures that we are—I rub at two flakes of dead skin on the knuckle of my right ring finger. Life is a process of atrophy. I love a woman and hate to do so. Self-fulfillment is a delusion for a prosperity that is unfulfilling—one's mission, or meaning: to enact order on what is immutable chaos.

What life-affirming responsibilities do I have?—none; the immature boy I remain to be, though I have chosen this state: directed my energies to become destitute, to "triumph" against my selected stupidity, and regress to what I had been before my excursion: a boy. Yes, I had been the finest man I had ever known while homeless, hopeless, and lost, and relinquished that man I had been by accepting providence with my body as payment. From that moment until now, I had something to lose.

10:35 PM

Physical journal recordings:

8:35 PM

A man with his wife, stroller-bound child, and dog at the boneyard. I said, "What is your self-assigned meaning in life?"

Both continued onward past me. The man smiled and said, "My family—my wife and my dog."

The woman laughed, head skewed, nervous and embarrassed on either my behalf or her own. I said, "And yourself?"

The man answered in her stead, "The same as myself—for her."

I remained unmoving from my position, turned to both of their backs, and said, "Herself and the dog?"

The man said, "Yup, our family."

8:38 PM

I hailed a man driving a truck twice; he didn't stop. In the first instance he flashed a "peace" sign. In the second instance, he waved.

8:41 PM

Woman on a bike at the boneyard center.

I said, "Do you have time to answer a question?"

"No."

"But you just did!"

The woman removed an earbud and said, "I can't hear you."

"What is your self-assigned meaning in life?"

The woman slowed, turned, fell off her bike into a patch of grass by a headstone and said, "Oh great—yeah—wonderful; a stranger stops me and asks me a question—what?"

I said, "I apologize that you fell, though I did not compel that to happen. What is your self-assigned meaning in life?"

"I don't know."

"Have you ever thought about *it?*"

"Yes. I'll be right back—I'm going to circle around and come back to answer."

"All right."

The woman rode away from me towards a parked truck and conversed with a man while writing the previous portion of this entry. I advanced several steps towards the vehicle and *it* accelerated out of the boneyard.

9:00 PM

A woman paid her respects by a headstone. I approached and left a fifty-foot gap between us, contemplated for thirty-five seconds, and walked away.

9:12 PM

A woman walked a dog in a blouse on the sidewalk of the road leading to the boneyard.
I said, "Hi."
"Hi."
"Do you have time to answer a question after the question I'm asking you now?"
"Sure."
"What is your self-assigned meaning in life?"
"I don't have time to answer that question."
"All right."

Monday, July 27th, 2020

2:45 PM

Despite our amiable cooperation, my father and I condemn each other's behavior. There remains to be no respect among us.

Tuesday, July 28th, 2020

1:06 PM

I arrived early at the tavern and asked three morning shift cooks what their self-assigned meaning in life is; all responded, "I don't know." When the question had been imposed on me by the oldest among them, I said, "To write about other people's meanings in life."
"Oh, do you write books?"
"Yes, I've written three; I publish a book each year."
"Do they sell?"
"No, my sales are nonexistent. I don't market."

"What's the point of writing books if you don't try to get people to read them?"

"I'm a fool with nothing of worth or value to share; my only skill is washing dishes and cleaning."

Chuckles abound.

Near the end of my shift, a twenty-two-year-old man named Logan closed his station alongside me in the kitchen. I said, "What is your self-assigned meaning in life?"

Logan gaped at me and repeated my question, with exaggerated enunciation for each word.

I said, "Yes."

"To save the world from pollution," Four minutes elapsed; Logan returned by my side and said, "Well, I think my real meaning is to make people laugh. My stance on pollution began about four years ago."

"I haven't heard you tell any jokes; you're slacking!"

Logan grinned and said, "Yeah, I suppose I am."

"Are you going to school for the meaning of your life, pertaining to pollution?"

"No... I should though."

"How old are you?"

"I'm twenty-two."

"Twenty-two... I thought you were younger on account of your optimism. That isn't to call you naive, though. I know many optimistic old people."

Fifteen minutes elapsed and Logan returned by the three-sink sanitizer basin to my right while I scrubbed at a pan. He braced his forearms against the edge of the basin, stared down at the discolored water, and said, "I really just hate people."

I quoted Plato, and commented that a misanthrope is only the way he is because of how he perceives himself. Logan contemplated for one minute by my side. I said, "Are you a nihilist?"

"I'm not as educated as you, I think; I don't know what nihilist and the other word that you said mean."

"A misanthrope hates people. A nihilist thinks everything is futile. I read a lot; that's about *it.*"

"I think a lot of big changes are going to happen in my lifetime."

"What manner of changes, cataclysmic or-"

"Yes, catastrophes."

"You're not as optimistic as I had presumed."

Logan smiled.

Wednesday, July 29th, 2020

1:27 PM

The singular idea I've written in the past four years that may endure posterity long after I'm dead is "The reader is a fool." My journal is a horrible, addictive recourse, solely on account of *it*s horridness.

I have nothing more to proselytize; in attempting to in the past, I convert myself to the opinion that there is no opinion worth advocating, i.e., there is no truth. I lie to all I speak to: the three men in the kitchen the other day—I proclaimed my self-assigned meaning in life is to write of others' self-assigned meanings in life *only* to lubricate the social dynamic. My genuine self-assigned meaning in life is merely "to write"; what of?—I don't know until I do.

My father asked me if I have ever heard the word "Abraxas." I replied in the positive. My father asked me if I know what "Abraxas" means. I replied in the negative. My father explained the word to mean "The God above all gods," and recommended Carl Jung's *Seven Sermons to the Dead*. What does this sequence of events mean, and what is the significance? My point is null; to write *it* confirms that this moment in time transpired: history, recorded, from the limited perspective of my framework.

I'm 25 hours into a 48-hour fast. I enjoy a day off from employment, reposed, alone, with green tea and coffee.

2:08 PM

Each day since my termination of the relationship between Pelagia and myself, I've thought of her. I think of her while washing dishes, mopping floors, scrubbing walls, cooking food, reading a book, cleaning myself, after I wake, and before sleeping. I wonder, in retrospect, why I think of her, and wonder also, why she would ever think of me. As pair-bonding animals, we cling to absurd feelings, and blind ourselves to reason and the options at our disposal. There is much more than, "with or without her," as much as there is "with or without him." I desire to return to her and will not, and bulwark against the day when she initiates contact with me—simply to defy me and to test my integrity.

Pelagia and I could only ever function if she were to accept my masculinity and her own femininity.

6:18 PM

Pursuing a woman in my current state is comical; I have nothing to provide, nor do I possess any skills to support or build. I am unbothered by this fact, and would rather be alone than assume a feminine role in a relationship. Even if I were wealthy, my interest in the dual delusions of what is decreed to be "love" between two humans is anathema to equanimity.

I've been a man's "bitch" before and am well-acquainted with emasculation. This element of my past is a matter I'd rather cease from memory, for instead of enduring the pauperized condition I sought to experience, I chose subjugation for sanctuary. The inculculated shame and embarrassment I retain by method of recall *due* to this journaling process dilutes my spirit, more so now, for residing in my father's apartment house basement, despite achieving independence in Arkansas, and returning to New York not out of necessity, but a *plan*.

Yes, *more so now,* for I've returned to my old employment methods as a dishwasher and late-night janitor, *comfortable* with mediocrity and a five-year *plan* to pay off a mortgage. I judge myself as a moronic loser.

Thursday, July 30th, 2020

2:33 PM

An attractive thirty-seven-year-old man, dressed in a suede suit and elegant dress shoes, sat with a laptop on a park bench in New York City. The world at his fingertips, he engrossed himself with various browsers and read the latest news on the stock market and American politics. Throngs of people passed him by: over the park grass behind him, and the sidewalk before him; each hurried with a particular gait customary to city life. The man scrutinized potential prospects that would earn him estimated dividends in the upper thousands. Time progressed, whereby the man died, tectonic plates shifted, the surface of the earth succumbed to cataclysmic devastation, and the sun—oh, glorious sun, beheld by none, combusted, and negated-

All right, all right—what's the point of this, then? Right now I sit on a weight bench in a basement and digest gratuitous amounts of protein and fat in preparation for an eight-and-a-half-hour dishwashing shift. Who is this attractive thirty-seven-year-old-man, and why is he important?—on account of his self-esteem and projected worth onto the world he inhabits, which is limited to a few screens and several women who endorse his exploits with hopes that he may share the profits of his labor with them.

Now, why is this a male-to-female opinion piece? Well, that's all there ever is. Read and weep over my crummy writing, or prime yourself for procreation before the great extinction, you hedonistic... *human*, yes, strictly human, nothing more.

Friday, July 31st, 2020

1:03 AM

Pelagia sat with someone of indiscernible identity (black bowl cut) at a booth seat that offers a direct line of sight into the kitchen dish pit—the *only* seat in the vicinity that allows that particular vantage point. I saw her at closing, on my way out of the kitchen, to begin my secondary cleaning duty of the patron room and establishment bathrooms. Pelagia and her companion were the only patrons. I placed chairs on top of tables, and our gazes met from across the bar for half of a second as she pushed open and moved out of the front door.

Krzysztof Penderecki's *Polymorphia* resonates.

AUGUST

Saturday, August 1st, 2020

1:14 AM

Self-assigned meaning of CJ, a forty-seven-year-old African-American bartender: "To be my own boss."

Self-assigned meaning of Paul, a mid-thirties Caucasian chef and my direct supervisor, when asked twice in a two-week period: "Like I said, that's not a simple question."

Self-assigned meaning of Taylor, a mid-thirties Caucasian bartender: "I don't know; I'll get back to you!" [28]

CJ had been a special circumstance, for I had asked him the same question a year ago during my last week of employment at the bar before my departure for the U.S. Navy boot camp. CJ had been hasty and proud to answer, "To be my own boss in a year's time." When asked the same question a little over a year later, CJ said, "What kind of—I don't know— I'm fuckin' forty-seven-years-old; go ask someone else that kinda shit."

I said, "CJ, I asked you this question a year ago and you had said, 'to be my own boss.'"

"Yeah, that sounds like something I'd say."

"I don't tell you this to mock you, or to provocate, but to remind you."

"Naw—naw, yeah, I understand. Yeah, I'm one foot in the door, one foot out the door, you know? I won't be here for long."

"How close are you to achieving your meaning?"

"I'll give *it*... 2022, at the latest."

"I hope to see you out of here by then."

"Yeah—yeah! Right? I'm tired of this shit for sure."

On my way out of the bar, at 12:35 AM, a group of drunken rapscallions shouted at one another and threatened violence against each other in the back lot of a dive bar called *The Messy House*. I walked close and observed the verminous horde. On my approach, the majority eyed me and ceased their aggression, while I stood across the street and *judged*. I said nothing, yet my silent observations induced a cessation of idiocy, for the moment. One crass late-forties reject of malformed proportions and a hobbled gait sauntered towards me wearing a stained grey sleeveless band t-shirt and said, "How are you tonight?"

---

[28] She never got back to me.

I said, "I'm well. How are you?"

"Working hard tonight?" I said nothing and smiled at his approach, my eyes locked on his, and he repeated *it*. I remained silent and had been afforded the opportunity to scrutinize a haggard face, a toupe-esque sprawl of grey hair, and overhung male breasts upon a distended stomach. "Oh—I thought you were John, my friend John." He turned and hobbled away.

I stood for two more minutes and *judged*. A drunken Caucasian man began to holler from my rear about the houses he owns and "niggas disrespectin'." I turned and began to walk towards him on my standard route. He said, "Not you man—them other niggas fuckin' disrespectin' me!"

A street away from my father's apartment building, yet another drunken man walked in my direction on a sidewalk. The man said, "What's going on?" I listened to a cantata by J.S. Bach through earphones and eyed him with a sullen grimace. The man mumbled on our passing, and I felt a surge of testosterone overtake my rationale. I turned and shouted, "What was that?"

The man turned halfway towards me from four meters away, continued to walk, and said, "I said apparently not much!"

"Yes *sir!*" I shouted, not in agreement, but as a challenge: instigative, indignant, and stood for three seconds, my arms wide at my side, ready—ready for death—for anything, another word, a swing of a fist, a broken nose, a confrontation, a blow to my self-esteem. The man continued to walk away and looked at me, sidelong, hunched forward, also ready… for what, I don't know. Nothing came of *it*.

1:57 AM

My ~~mental illness~~ conscience:

"Heartless little boy. Doesn't give a shit. Pompous. The journal hurts to read and makes me want to die. I don't like this man anymore. Intelligent, but that doesn't make you a good person. Creepy and superficial" Is that all? I stand and wonder. *Ah:* "He's so pathetic."

Why do I hate myself in this manner? I validate others with routine questions; however, I care for no one, and why would I?—and why, in turn, would they care for me? Life is sick. There is no collective consciousness. I waste precious time allocated for sleep.

9:58 AM

My employment bores me. I develop no skills and seek out extracurricular cleaning and organizational duties at both establishments. My peers converse in banalities and gossip. At the tavern, the severe lack of refinement and culture that I would once contemn now saddens me; *it* is where I have chosen to be.

10:55 AM

My father deigns to mow his lawn with a lit cigarette in his mouth, black sunglasses over his eyes, and a washed-out blue ball cap on his head.

12:14 PM

This is my legacy: Random thoughts recorded throughout the day of non sequitur plot and focus. Understand how unimpressive this series of books is, and by consequence, my *life*. Yes, how blatant my mediocrity is, dazzles me.

Yesterday I asked Walther, "From a managerial perspective, do you consider me a sycophant?"
Walther chuckled and, (to avoid untruths from a conversation I fail to recall in detail), in summary, he said, "No."

Where did *that* thought manifest from?—the same source from where *this* propagated: My father lied to me about being on his will for the apartment house, and has shifted on his stance to add my name to the mortgage due to his ignorance on the best course of action. Despite his providence, and the potential to "invest" in myself, my father's indecisiveness and our lack of respect for each other has nullified any hopes I may have had for either a future as a landlord, or a life on the ocean.
My father said that he regrets having said anything about the mortgage, and that he doesn't appreciate my "ultimatum" and "demands" he perceives me to be imposing on him. My courses of action are simple:

1. To be listed on the mortgage when my father refinances the house so that I may ensure bi-weekly $750-a-month principal payments are paid in full for the next five years, in order to have

the mortgage paid off—for the benefit of both of our credit scores and future well-being.

2. To invest my time and energy in an alternate life ~~plan~~ amble.

I had previously intended to leave my father's domain not more than a month after I had arrived back in New York on account of my father's virulent negativity and unhealthy lifestyle. When he relayed to me that I am in fact *not* on his will to dissuade me from speaking more of my request for an action to add my name to the mortgage during the refinancing process, I lost trust; however, the respect I lost had been nonexistent, for we already had no respect for each other.

Living rent-free in my father's basement is not worth the companionship he provides, nor is my companionship worth anything to him. We fail to validate each other.

I'd rather be a failure, i.e., a successful "psychopath."

Or is this *just* mentally stunted prepubescent boy logic? How *dumb* am I to squander these glorious plans for a better future, to abolish my one last resource for the sake of *immediate gratification?* I truly do wonder, and marvel at societal conditions, for what we're guided to believe, to swallow the "Kool-Aid"; I reflect on my former drill instructor's motto. Yes, I'm a buffoon and emotionally stunted—at the level of a teenager, perhaps a grade above "moron." What an ungrateful little "millennial" shit I am—a product of our generation, of the *times;* golly, I wonder *why?*

My father would be a fool to not add my name to the mortgage; I always pay my debts.

Sunday, August 2nd, 2020

8:46 AM

Self-assigned meaning of Sebastian, an eighteen-year-old Asian/Caucasian: "To help people in any way that I can."

Three days prior I met Sebastian for the first time; while I worked the dish pit at the tavern, he approached and began to load the dishwasher. I said, "What the hell are you doing?"

Sebastian said, "Helping out—figured I would in the last five minutes before I go." I said nothing and he veered away from me.

On my return home from work last night, my father sat slouched back in his armchair, illuminated by the fluxing glow of a television, phone held atop his left leg, his darkened face angled downward, and his casual button-up shirt splayed open to reveal a hearty amount of uncharacteristic visceral fat. The severe toll of his lifestyle is showcased by age. I sat down on the futon next to him and said, "Hey."

My father lifted his eyes and glared at me for one second: a disappointed acknowledgment.

I said, "Will you accept any rent?"

My father's gaze remained fixed on the phone screen; he said, "No."

I stood and descended the steps of the basement to sleep.

10:56 AM

Ah—I'm vexed, maddened, *outraged!* I may as well have "MD" after my name!

An article published yesterday on the online news venue, *Psychology Today: Introducing the Dark Empath.* Tagline: *New research identifies people high in both empathy and darkness.*

"Darkness"? I'm amazed by this roundabout of circular logic; humanity is disgusting; our virtues are learned behaviors; there is no inherent "good" or "evil"—what I, and philosophers from antiquity onward have written of for years!

"*It* may seem that people with elevated Dark Triad traits are not empathic, but *it* isn't so simple. In a basic sense empathy serves people higher in dark traits. Dark traits may be a 'necessary evil,' arguably important for group survival at critical times. Empathy, while serving altruism, is also a tool for the Machiavellian mind, which needs good 'intel' for appraising, and potentially taking advantage, of others." [29]

- Grant Hillary Benner MD

Oh, yes, I must comment; I cannot refrain: What a revelation! *This,* is what a college degree nets you: A tired exposition of the same rehashed mythos and themes of cyclic human behavior painted with psychological jargon instead of naming *exactly* what behavior is, e.g., despicables,

---

[29] Grant Hillary Benner MD, *Psychology Today "ExperiMentations,"* August 1st, 2020

scoundrels, losers, scumbags, rascals, lowlives, goons, knaves, devils, rapscallions, hooligans, and crooks! Best of all, the *charlatans* who acquire the "rights" to proliferate their "knowledge" of overblown labels—*Dark Triad*... Narcissism, psychopathy, machiavellianism... *oh*, humans are egocentric creatures when left unchecked by the masses? Is this *news?*

"Psychopathy may serve the greater good. In performance-demanding situations such as those faced by first responders, health-care workers, soldiers, and others in high-stakes situations, emotions may fade away, opening up to cool, streamlined calculation. Mihailides, Galligan and Bates (2017) call this 'adaptive psychopathy,' describing the 'quarantine vector' within which empathic information marries with psychopathic mental processes useful for dealing with threatening, alien experiences that conflict with one's own values and beliefs." [30]

Unbelievable: I simply cannot believe *it*. My satirical overtone and droll expressions cannot contain the expanse of my dissatisfaction with the sheer volumes of bullshit published—my own trite included—for *billions* of pretentious moneyed intellectuals to read under a cup of preferred hot beverage. Read on, self, and future deluded reader, of your humanity, scrutinized in a refined table of parameters and numbers. I'll limit my quotations, for the introspective nausea I'm bound to experience at a future point, if I am to live to see my manuscript published, will incite contempt and malice for what our globalized species has amounted to:

"To investigate this possibility, researchers from Nottingham Trent University, UK (Heym et al., 2020) conducted surveys of 991 participants, in their early 20s to 30s and about 30 percent male. They completed the following:

"Dark Traits: The Dark Triad of Personality Scale, to measure Machiavellianism, narcissism, and psychopathy, along with the Narcissistic Personality Inventory to look at grandiose narcissism, the Five-Factor Narcissism Inventory to measure vulnerable narcissism, the Levenson Self-report Psychopathy Scale estimating lack of care and callousness, impulsivity, and antisocial tendencies, and the

---

[30] Ibid

Machiavellianism scale looking at attitudes about human nature, moral deficiency, and manipulativeness.

"Empathy: The Questionnaire of Cognitive and Affective Empathy, to look at aspects of cognitive empathy including perspective-taking and the ability to imagine others' inner worlds in real time (online simulation), and affective empathy, including automatically mimicking others' emotions (emotional contagion), responding to others' emotional signals (proximal responsivity), and responding to the emotional tone in various settings (peripheral responsivity).

Big Five Personality: The Five Factor Personality Model, measured with the International Personality Item Pool, to estimate Openness to New Experience, Conscientiousness, Extroversion, Agreeableness, and Neuroticism (OCEAN).

"Relational Aggression: Using the Indirect Aggression Scale, participants indicated where they landed on three scales for tendency to socially-exclude others (Social Exclusion), the use of mean-spirited humor (Malicious Humor) and how much they try to make others guilt (Guilt Induction).

"Depression, Anxiety, Stress: Using the Depression Anxiety Stress Scale to look at emotional well-being.

"Ability to enjoy life: Measuring anhedonia using the Motivation and Pleasure Scale, assessing social, professional and recreational pleasure, drive for closeness, and motivation to engage in activities.

"Self-criticism: Measured with subscales of the Self-Compassion Scale to look at self-judgment and overidentification with negative self-evaluations." [31]

There, in the aforementioned quotation, is the quintessential doctrine of shame and guilt taught to us by our nation's leaders, for those who forgo the church— *"they"* and *"them,"* who have mastered the art of *being* human. There isn't enough space for me to quote the ceaseless trash amongst my own expulsion. The findings? "Psychopaths" are essential for a flourishing community—but not too many. One asshole and one dick are often sufficient.

---

[31] Ibid

It's all about *who* you know.

459 PM

A trek to and from the grocery store elapses over one hour and twenty minutes and yields a full backpack and two plastic bags of food. My route takes me through several beautiful neighborhoods that would be more impressive if the houses weren't there.

Walther has employed me six days for forty-five to fifty hours a week, 4:00 PM-12:30 AM.

I purchased a *Zoom H1n* voice recorder and have vowed to myself to not destroy *it* in a washing machine, or in any other matter. The sound quality is phenomenal.

In retrospect, despite the mortgage fiasco and discrepancy involving my father and myself, we don't respect each other. I had relinquished all my belongings and went on a "pilgrimage" on account of this, lived in various apartments, enlisted for the Navy and lived in Arkansas for nine months, only to return to where I am, incited by an email from my father six months ago: "I love you, Baethan."

I empathize with my father; I feel responsible for destroying his faith in humanity, in family, in his son. At the age of twelve I had chosen my father over my mother, and he agreed to raise me when my mother had failed to provide a safe home. He bought a second apartment house for us, where I lived my teenage years and early adult life. He never paid the mortgage on the second apartment for his duration there for nearly ten years while he collected rent from an upstairs tenant. Last year, the house foreclosed, and my father hadn't been required to pay a single cent. He emptied the second apartment house of valuables to transfer to his first apartment house, where we currently reside. I assisted with his move, and lived in the abandoned second apartment house for four months prior to homelessness a month before departing for the U.S. Navy boot camp.

My father may have cancer, or another life-threatening ailment. I don't think he'd tell me if he did, for he already believes that I wish him dead. My mother, too, may be close to death. Both regarded their health as a tertiary element of life.

There will be no life on a boat under a starlit sky.

I have no plan for my future other than work.

Monday, August 3rd, 2020

10:00 AM

Am I a fool to desire to be alone? I question my conscience, and the feelings of guilt concerning my father, mother, Candy, Pelagia, and others who continually attempt to befriend me despite me spurnings. Why don't I ever apply my experience to real-world applications, instead of a consolidated and limited revisal to this dull manuscript?

As the strength of my body atrophies due to limited intake of fats and proteins, my acumen of mind clarifies what had been occluded by barbarism and lust: the fickle sensations of being validated.

I don my mantle of everything I am perceived as—countless judgments, imposed by either myself or others; there is never a difference. I have ascended to my level of competence by my success—to abolish my father's respect and trust in me: the constituents of "love." What remains are the translucent and airy vestiges of paternal "love," a pitiable thing better discarded in a dreg heap.

I'm no monster; I'm an emotional human being, affected by my animality, vulnerable, *mortal*. Hope is all we have.

10:41 AM

I have only ever feigned politeness.

Tuesday, August 4ᵗʰ, 2020

9:17 AM

My new voice recorder functions beyond my expectations:

I asked Baethan, a bartender who has the same name as me, if he considers himself to be a good person.

The bartender said, "Ah, well, on a scale, I'd say I'm just a little bit more good than bad."

I said, "Six out of ten?"

"Yeah, well I mean, just a bit—I'm not good, though I'm not necessarily bad; *it*'s more of a neutral thing, you know what I mean?"

I cocked my head and walked away.

A twenty-four-year-old server asked me how long I stay to clean the establishment on my shift. We exchanged brief details on the topic, and when the server turned to walk away, I said to him, "Do you consider yourself a good man?"

The server looked at me, smirked, and said, "Yeah, I guess so, yeah."

Before my late-night cleaning duty began, the bartender, Baethan, informed me that I startled a few patrons when I deposited clean glassware at the bar counter, and he instructed me—as politely as he could muster, for me to bring any clean dishware around the back of the counter henceforth.

I said, "Understood," moved to return to the kitchen, and readdressed the bartender: "Since I'm here, have you heard any rumors about me lately? Men like you tend to be the nexus of rumors."

The bartender answered, "No, I haven't heard anything about you. Why, did something happen? Is something going on?"

"No. I don't like to be talked about."

"Oh." The bartender braced both arms on the counter, raised an eyebrow, smiled, and said, "Why?"

"Nothing positive comes from *it*."

"Oh, all right man."

Logan, the lanky twenty-two-year-old cook, said to me at the end of his shift, "All right my friend, I'll see you later."

I said, "Friend?" from the dish pit, while I cleaned the last remnants of food from a drain.

"Everyone is my friend, and you seem like a good person."

"I'm not a good person."

"Well that's how you come off. I'll see you later man."

"Take care."

My father counts on me to look back on my decisions one day, perhaps in my fifties, while I continue to toil for another man, and to ruminate: "What the hell was I wasting my time for with all this hormonal nonsense and irrational decision-making? I could've had *an apartment house.* I could've had *income.* I could've been on… *a boat.*" By returning to my father's domain once more, and for no doubt the final time, I've been exposed to what being a stereotypical, old, white, ~~privileged~~ retired laborer, conservative golfer, who cares too much about his lawn, the neighbors, and the neighbor's cats who venture across the property line to defecate, is. There is only misery in his complacency, and my father remedies this misery with a ceaseless cycle of pleasures and indulgences, whereby he renders his mind dissipated and his body atrophic.

I'm amused that my father concerns himself with the manner and perspective that I write of his character, though I blame him for nothing except playing a role in spawning me onto this world; however, even in that capacity, he had been powerless. My father has critiqued me for equivocating and obfuscating scenarios that involve him, as though I attempt to prevaricate to win the hearts and minds of my indistinct readers. My father fails to understand that these publications are wholly for my own satisfaction and life's meaning, i.e., my "ikigai," and that any fool who chooses to read this documentation, remains to be *just* a fool.

What do I squander but the goods of the earth that amount to nothing? A dramatic boy I may be, or a wise man, in this regard.

Once I'm elsewhere, my father will be liberated, affirmed in our mutual lack of respect, to pursue any venue he desires without a source of guilt or shame he may have imposed on himself. I, too, will likewise thrive. May we kill each other, in spirit.

Wednesday, August 5th, 2020

1:56 PM

I returned to my father's apartment after being shown a superb second-floor studio apartment with modern appliances at the heart of downtown, situated in a compact building across the street from the high-end bar and tavern where I'm employed.

I began to prepare a fresh meal of half a crown of broccoli, three portobello mushrooms, five cloves of garlic, half of an orange pepper, and one medium carrot, sliced and sautéed in a pan layered with extra virgin olive oil over medium heat with 8 oz of grass-fed beef, with two eggs cracked in, and a few handfuls of spinach cooked for one minute afterward in the remnants of oil. I powered on my voice recorder and said, "I don't want to inherit the house." [32]

My father stood with an empty cup beside me and said, "All right." One minute elapsed. My father stirred creamer into a new cup of coffee, approached my side, and said, "Dude, ya know, if you use your brain, which I know you don't do very often; well actually, you do too much, but uh, if you want me to totally disrespect you... *get a cat.*" My father laughed. "That's all you gotta do. See that's called being smart, see."

Two and-a-half-minutes elapsed. My father sat in the adjacent living room, hunched over his phone. I began to sauté my vegetables and said, "Do you (I stuttered) Do you agree with the conditions of not corresponding as friends or as father and son?"

My father interjected halfway through my inquiry: "I don't give a shit what you do."

"So, no contact?"

"[Indiscernible]."

"What?"

"I said *you* do *whatever* makes you happy."

"Well, if no contact would make you sad or feel some sort of, indignance... I wouldn't want to."

"Why not? The fuck do you care?"

"So you don't think that I owe you anything?"

---

[32] The following conversation is the first and final instance I have ever recorded a dialogue between myself and my father and is the most valuable memory I have ever captured.

My father raised his voice, "Is that what this is all about dude?"

"Well you're saying why the fuck do I care, and-"

"Yeah—why do you care?"

"Because you're my father. Just like you only care because I'm your son."

"This conversation is over okay?"

"What?"

"This conversation is over."

"Why?"

"Because you don't make any fucking sense at all dude. When you get rational I'll talk to you."

I leaned against the kitchen counter between the window separating the kitchen and living room, faced my father while I stirred my vegetables, and said, "Get *rational?*"

"Yes—get rational."

"I *am* being rational."

"No you're not."

"How am I not? I asked 'no contact, will you be okay with that,' and you're saying I'm being irrational."

"Yeah because what—you want no contact; what does *it* matter what I think or not?"

"Because I don't want you to be indignant or sad."

"Well Baethan, ya know I'll tell you something. You make me extremely sad."

"Why?"

"Because you have so much more to offer than what you do."

"So much more to offer in what field?"

My father sighed.

I continued, "I make you sad because you think I'm not living up to your expectations?"

"*No*—where does this come from?"

"I'm asking this, because you said that I make you sad; why do I make you sad; how do I have so much more to offer?"

"Because you have a lot of love, and a lot of... a lot to give... and you just, don't want to give *it*, to anybody or anything."

"And I don't want to take *it* either."

"*And* you don't want to take *it*. And that just, *it* makes me sad. Because you don't... I just find *it* hard to believe that that makes you happy, okay?"

"*It* doesn't make me happy, but I'm not seeking happiness. But *it*'s not about what I'm seeking right now; I'm asking how you'll feel if there was no contact."

"Baethan, you're living here with me and there's practically *no contact*."

"Practically does not mean, *it* is, though."

My father's intonation shifted to annoyance; he said, "Don't worry about *it* dude—I won't bother you."

"But will you be upset?"

"Of course I'm upset; what the fuck do you think?" Forty seconds elapsed. "No more upset than I am now when you're here, dude."

"So *it* really makes no difference then."

"No—because you don't want to do anything with me anyways." Thirty-five seconds elapsed; I cracked two eggs into my near-finished meal and the city fire alarm resounded from a far distance. My father said, "Once I'm out on the boat you'll never hear from me again anyways."

"Not even postcards of you posing-"

"Nope—once I pull away from that dock, bro, I'm fuckin' *gone*."

"Yeah—but you can still correspond by email."

"Nope, no nothin. Why the fuck would you want me to do that?"

"I don't want-"

"You don't even want *contact now*. That's fucking bullshit dude."

"Why?"

"Oh you want contact with me when I'm out on the boat but you don't want contact with me when I'm right here next to ya?"

"No. I-"

"You know what?—fuck you."

"I'm not saying that."

"You're not saying *it*—but I'm not *stupid*."

I chuckled and said, "I didn't say I want contact with you while you're out on the boat."

"Well you ain't gotta worry about *it bro*."

"You call me 'bro,' but you're upset as a father would be."

"I'm not upset with you, Baethan."

"I just don't want-"

"*It* just makes me sad, and *it* hurts me; so, you know—I don't know what you want me to say, dude."

"I don't want either of us to feel guilt or shame."

"Well if you feel guilt or shame that's your own fucking problem. I'm not going to absolve you of feeling *guilt* and *shame*."

"Well that's why I'm asking… how you'll feel."

"You know how I feel, Baethan; I'm your father; I love you; I have… I *liked* you. Now I'm starting to not like you so much."

"You've been saying that for years." I transferred my cooked meal from pan to plate and said, "I can only imagine how you talk to your *bros* about me."

"I don't talk about you."

"To all your golfing buds-"

"Why the fuck would I talk about you?"

"I have no idea. I-"

"What do you think I am—a pussy gossiper?"

"What?"

"What do you think I am a *pussy gossiper?* Standing out on—with my golf buddies and talk about my… one of my six fucking kids?"

"Uh… yeah."

"No. I have a lot better things to talk about."

I goaded with a snigger, "Like what? I'm really curious about this."

"About what?"

"What do you talk about that's better?"

"Why the hell do *you* wanna know?"

"Because I'm curious what you define as better-"

"Couple of old guys out playing golf—what the fuck do you think we talk about—our aches and pains—our children who don't give a fuck anymore?"

"Your wives, your children… the *weather,* of course-"

"How our kids are all worthless pains in the ass."

"Yeah. That's what I imagine: Snide comments about your children being assholes."

"That's a given, dude."

"Well, if that's a given then *it*'s happening!"

My father said, "That's right, you don't have to say *it.* I don't talk about that shit. Why the fuck would I talk about that?"

"You just said *it*'s a given."

"All our kids are fucking grown."

"Yeah—so you make snide comments about how much of an asshole they all are."

"Why?"

"I don't know—because you're all old white men?"

"We don't talk about our *kids.*"

"You just said that *it*'s a given that you do."

"*No—it's a given* that we don't *have* to because we all *know* our kids are *assholes*. Why fucking… get all fucking worked up about that when there's a lot of other things to get worked up about."

I said, "Because you say *it* in passing such as: 'Damn *it's* hot out today.'"

"We don't even talk politics for Christ's sake."

"But *it* being hot out is also something that doesn't need to be commented on."

"Well you don't have to say *it's* hot out when you're standing out in the fucking blazing sun on a fucking golf course sweating your ass off."

"Yeah—but you still do, and *it's* a given, right?"

"Man, you got a fucking hyper*active* imagination, dude; you also think you're the center of the universe—like everybody talks about *Baethan*."

"No, I don't think that. I just know you, and I hear you talk about Ben (my older half-brother), so I can only imagine-"

"I talk about Ben to you, *to you*. That's *it*."

"But the way you talk about Ben makes me think that you think the same thoughts about me to-"

"No, this is a conversation between me and you, and *it's* not meant to be repeated or talked and gossiped." I splashed tabasco sauce and squirted a few lines of mustard onto my finished plating and smiled. My father continued, "By the way, now that you mention *it*, the hospital called me this morning. Ben wanted to let me know that he's in BHU (Behavioral Health Unit)."

"That was nice of him."

"If he thinks he's going to get sympathy from me he's wrong. I'm tired of his shit. Even your mother has gotten tired of his shit; that tells you something right there. That's why he's in BHU. 'Nobody loves me anymore. Why? I don't understand.'" My father sniffed twice and said, "Ugh, *fucking nose;* cutting all that dirt, all that excavated dirt out of my nose last night after I got done hedge trimming that shit."

I acknowledged my father with a mirthful exhale and enjoyed my meal while I (attempted) to read an ebook of *The Essays of Arthur Schopenhauer; Counsels and Maxims.*

My father stood, groaned, entered the kitchen, and said, "As a matter of fact dude, you'll never even see the boat." He coughed, set his coffee down on a kitchen table, unzipped his pants, entered the adjacent bathroom, and said, "Let alone set foot on *it*."

I waited for my father to finish urinating and said, "I just want to end contact on mutual terms. Here neither of us-"

My father said, "You don't get to choose mutual terms dude. Forget *it*," and entered the living room with another new cup of coffee."

"The terms can't be something positive?"

My father unleashed a boisterous, unaffected laugh as he lowered himself into his chair, and said, "You're fucking losing *it*, dude."

"Why?"

"Ask me if I can be positive?"

"*It* can't be positive terms?"

"What do you mean *'positive'* terms?"

"A positive severance."

"Dude, just go sever yourself, all right; *it*'s not going to be on your *terms*. If you want to do something, do *it*. Don't worry about who you hurt or upset or… You can't have everything on *your* fucking terms, dude. Do you know the meaning of the word *'severance?'*" Five seconds elapsed. "Apparently you don't."

"There are two defintions, or three-"

"Yeah, whatever you want *it* to be, right?"

"One is the severance, as in severance pay, and then severance can also mean an ending, or a termination."

"Yeah, and what does 'ending,' or 'termination' mean? Maybe you should choose your words a little more carefully."

I typed 'severance' into my lord and master's (Google) search query and read the first result: "'Severance,' noun, the action of ending a connection or relationship."

"Yeah. And what does 'ending' mean?"

I typed 'ending' in similar fashion and recited the result with a satirical tonality: "'Ending,' noun, an end or final part of something, especially a period of time, an activity, or a book or movie."

"There you go."

"What was the point of that?"

"What?"

"What was the point of that exercise?"

"Because you want to *end* our relationship."

"Yes?"

"Yeah? That means *it*'s done. *Forever. Gone. Done. End.* Terminate."

"Yes?"

"Yes?" My father scoffed.

"And why are you telling me to choose my words more carefully?"

My father turned in his seat, looked at me while I chewed, and said, "You know you *are* a fucking idiot, dude."

"Why?"

"Why? Because you tell me you want to terminate the relationship but then you want *it* done on your terms—you want to be *positive*."

"How is that being an idiot?"

"How is terminating your relationship with me a positive thing? I'll go my own separate way *anyways*."

"But you'll hold animosity-"

My father's voice amplified: "I don't need to terminate my relationship with you to do my own thing and go my own separate way."

"I need to do *it*."

You apparently need to, for god knows what reason, other than to satisfy your own *ego*."

I resumed consumption.

Thirteen minutes elapsed; my father stood, entered the kitchen with his cup of coffee in hand, stood three feet to my left, and said, "I find *it* hard to believe that somebody who would want to give something to someone... just out of love... You just can't seem to grasp that; you think that you owe me something. Okay, well listen dude, *I* brought you into this world; you didn't have a fucking choice, okay? I'm responsible for you *being* here. So you don't owe me anything, ever. Parents don't have children with the expectations of getting something from them, except, to give to them. If you don't like giving, don't ever have a child, because that's all you do with children, is you give them everything. First of all, you give them life, then you raise them, you feed them, you clean them, you teach them right from wrong. You give—give—give—give—give, with absolutely no expectations, other than the fact that you want your children to be happy. Not successful. Not all this other bullshit. You just want them to be happy, and the thing is with you, you're *never* fucking happy, *ever*."

"That's not my goal."

"And when you are, you're guilty about *it;* that's fucked up dude."

"How is *it* fucked up?"

"*It*'s fucked up because you're missing out on *a lot*."

"But I'm also gaining in other respects."

"And what are you gaining? Solitude? Animinity?"

"Contentment."

"Contentment? Contentment from what? People? Relationships? Society?"

"From the extremes of pleasure and pain."

An industrial truck rolled back and forth and revved an engine a street away.

My father said, "Yeah—but everything doesn't have to be an extreme, dude. Everything with you is an extreme; there's no middle ground; there's no… uh, conciliation. There's no, uh… interaction. Contentment to you is no interaction whatsoever."

"Yes."

"Well I want you to be content; at least be content. That's why whatever you wanna do, dude-"

"I don't ask to sever re… a relationship out of hatred for you, or out of a desire to hurt you."

"I understand that dude. That's why I still talk to you. But I try to understand *you*, and *it's*… I don't know why you have the attitude you have, and the mindset you have. You don't even go outside during the day unless you have to go to work."

"That's not true. I go to the grocery store; I go to the barber; I visit the park, the boneyard-"

"Yeah—places you gotta go."

"I don't have to go to any of those places or-"

"And usually you don't go to the park or to the cemetery until after *it's* dark out."

"That's just a preference. I'm not socially averse, or anxious."

"Oh I know that you do shit… that's not what I'm saying. *It's* just that you prefer *not* to." My father poured the remainder of his coffee down the kitchen sink drain and continued, "So why do I perceive that you are not happy?"

I said, "Because happiness is an activity, and I'm usually happy only when I'm writing, and I typically do that in solitude."

"You can't get much more solitude than writing; *it's* by yourself."

I continued to consume the remains of my meal.

My father continued, "So you say 'terminate relationship' dude, but to mean that means you're ending our relationship, period. Period. We're never talking again, never nothing."

"Yes."

"Why? Why does *it* have to be terminated? *It's* not like I'm crawling up your ass, or like I'm over at your house every day asking you to go do shit—let's go get drunk, get high, and… I don't bother you, dude."

"I don't want any personal affiliations with anybody. Coming back here was against all of my principles."

"So why did you come back here?"

"Because I perceived the opportunity of going on a boat, but once I returned here, and we began to interact again… I realized that, due to my nature, and my chosen values, that, I don't cohabitate well… with *anyone*—not just *you.*"

"No—I understand that; I understand that Baethan, believe me, dude. And I'm happy to hear you say that *it's* because of *you.* You can't cohabitate with other people. I'm proud of you for saying that because… you try to make *it* sound like *I* can't cohabitate with you, which is totally wrong—totally false. I have no problem with you, dude. I can put up with your eccentricities; *you* can't put up with mine. See, that's the difference, okay. Now I'm—ya know… and I understand that; you're about the only person in the world that I let share my private space. I don't have anybody living with me; I don't have a girlfriend or anything like that, so I understand *perfectly* where you're coming from, dude. But you know to say that you're *terminating* our relationship?—Don't say that, dude. I'm still your father; I still love you. If we can't cohabitate, that's fine!—I understand that; you're an adult! If you don't want to go on the boat for the reasons that you're stating, I understand."

"I don't want to be validated, in any way, and that involves correspondence."

"Validating? What do you mean validating?" My father's mien shifted to scorn. *"Oh* will you cut with that fucking *crap?* That's the biggest bunch of fucking *bullshit,* I ever read in my life."

"Why?"

"Okay—you read all this shit-"

"I didn't read that-"

"You read all this *shit-*"

"I *didn't* read that."

"All your validation crap comes from years ago, dude."

"Yes."

My father spoke with a mock inflection: *"Everybody needs to be validated!—people only interact with each other because they want validation-"*

"And those thoughts are entirely my own."

"Ya know, but you've misconstrued *it,* dude."

"Miscon-"

"For your own purposes."

390

"Misconstrued *what?*"

"The fact that people need validation… You've misconstrued *it,* and twisted *it* around, to fit your own personal… whatever's going on in your head.[33] That's *bullcrap.* I don't need validation from *anybody.*"

"You just said that all humans need validation, in fact-"

"*You* say *it*'s validation okay—but validation just means that you recognize that there's another *fucking* human being standing there!"

"But there doesn't need to be."

"Yeah—there does dude, because there's 9 billion of us on this *fuckin* earth!" My father returned to the living room.

I said, "There's 7.8 billion."

"Well *think* about that… Jesus Christ-"

"I do think about that, often."

"You know, if you really want what you said dude—you'd go out in the fuckin *woods,* and live by *yourself-*"

"That's the endgame-"

"That's the way I feel about *it*—that's *bullshit!*"

"That's the endgame but-"

"You're going to go in the middle of downtown, and live in a fucking apartment… and you wanna be… *not seen!* Bullshit!"

"I need to-"

"You know, you wanna be, fuckin' alone? Go out and be alone! Go in the fucking woods! Go somewhere and live on your own!"

I spoke with clenched teeth, "Then I can't publish my work. I need to-"

"Oh yeah—yeah—yeah—yeah-"

"-establish myself first."

"So you need some kind of validation. You need validation from your fucking work."

"Yes-"

"*Bullshit* Baethan."

"Of course."

"Bull… *shit!*"

"I *do* get validation from my work, *not* from the people that I interact with."

"Yeah—*bullshit!* Because people gotta read your fucking book! That's the biggest crock of shit that's ever come out of your fucking mouth!"

"Whose got to read my book?"

---

[33] This assertion validated to me that my father does not, in fact, understand.

"People!"

"They *need* to?"

My father scowled and said, "You *need people to read it!*"

"Why?"

"Why write *it?*"

"I've been asked that same question about three days–"

"For your own personal *therapy.*"

"No, *it*'s not therapy; *it*'s for *me.*"

"For your own validation."

"Yes."

"Well ya know that's the biggest crock of fucking crap I've ever heard in my life."

"Why?"

"Because *it* is."

"Why?"

"*It's* irrational and *it* doesn't make sense."

"How is that irrational? I've thought *it* out; I've used my logic; I know what I want in life–"

"Yeah well your logic is *fucked* up."

"–and you can't accept *it.*"

"I accept *it*–"

I shouted for the first instance of our conversation, "Then shut up about *it!*"

"I'm just telling you my opinion!"

"*It*'s not *bullshit*–"

"*It*'s fucked up!"

I spoke with zeal: "*It*'s not *fucked up; it*'s my choice!"

"Yeah well…"

"Yeah well nothing!"

"*It*'s my opinion, okay!"

"Yes?"

"Okay?"

I affirmed, "That's why I can't stand to be around you."

"You want *it* to be your own fucking way, boy; I tell ya—*it*'s like—'oh I don't want validation, but I gotta be able to publish my *novel.*'"

"Yes?"

"What a crock of fucking crap." Eight seconds elapsed. "You don't need to *publish it*; you don't want anybody to read *it?* Write *it* and keep *it* in your fucking computer! *It*'s bullshit, Baethan."

"I write under a pen name." Fifteen seconds elapsed. "And I've thought long, on if I should change my name to my pen name, and to include pictures on republication of *Year One* or not. I don't want to, despite how *profitable it* would be. *It* would be the *smart* thing to do, that *you* would consider, but to me, *it* undermines my values and principles, so *it's* not *bullshit* at all."

"Well I think *it* is."

"Well I don't give a fuck what you think about *it* and that's why I'm going."

"You're going anyways."

"Yes—but that's a part of *it* because-"

"I don't care!"

"-you think that my life, is *bullshit*. You think that my decisions, are *bullshit*."

"No—I think your logic is bullshit."

"My logic is in alignment with my principles and values."

My father sneered and said, "Yeah, right."

"Yeah, *it* is, *right*."

"Go publish your book."

"I will, and I will continue to publish each *fucking* year until I die. And you can go on your boat... and fish."

"I am!"

Nothing more came of *it*. I consumed the last bites of my meal, washed my dishes, and returned to the basement to transcribe *it*.

10:39 PM

My father and I behave as if relations are of the status quo. I visited the grocery store for avocados, eggs, sauerkraut, garlic, and picked up two 4-packs of my father's favorite bottled sodas, on my offer. When I arrived back at his apartment, unloaded my pack, and entered the bathroom to urinate, my father entered eight seconds later to retrieve his dentures and said, "Great night for a walk, huh?"

I said, "Yeah."

Thursday, August 6th, 2020

9:05 AM

I awoke to a message of approval for my application for the studio apartment at the center of downtown.

Friday, August 7th, 2020

9:20 AM

Ryan, the forty-five-year-old pizza cook I work with—one of Pelagia's numerous former lovers who I urged to read *The Short Happy Life of Francis Macomber,* expanded my perspective last night. Despite my taciturn disposition, he approached me for conversation while we closed the kitchen together: an inquiry of my musical interests. I disclosed classical, and we both chuckled on how broad the genre is, which prompted me to expound on my preferred time period and artists. J.S. Bach is also Ryan's favorite composer, and within two minutes, a guitar song written by J.S. Bach began to resonate from a portable speaker tucked away on a high shelf.

Ryan and I discussed details of our histories, inclinations, ambitions, and assets. His self-assigned meaning in life is composing music and selling records, regardless of whether the product is profitable. Most notable: Ryan shared my belief that solitary activities are always preferable to activities with others. He has bought two houses (consecutive purchases: sold the former to buy the latter) and liquidated his assets to live in an apartment again due to the superfluous space and unnecessary maintenance burden.

I disclosed my reticence to speak on account of my chosen mode of abstaining from friendships; however, while our conversation elapsed, and the feelings of human interaction vitalized both of our beings, I realized that I have allowed my journal, and the character I write of, to control me, rather than contrariwise. The *Successful "Psychopath"* is beyond my attainment.

Ryan proclaimed midway through our multifaceted conversation that "People are terrible," and we parted without any spoken courtesies or formalities.

Saturday, August 8th, 2020

4:54 PM

My father and I have reaffirmed our rapport for I'd rather he despise me than be angry with me. I cultivate healthy relationships with numerous coworkers on account of a relaxation of my pretentiousness; therefore, to terminate my relationship with my father would be unjust, by my own judgment. I refuse to allow this document to control me, i.e., the *"Successful 'Psychopath,'"* or the *"Despicable Loser"* subtitle; these adjectives are also to my own judgment. I'm weary of perpetuating an act, of social experiments to the detriment of my physiological well-being, and of undermining my efforts for equanimity. The aforementioned title is sufficient for a proper parody, as a follow-up to what constitutes as a failed "sociopath," albeit, at a later year—if I am to live that long; perhaps if I become a (self-)certified "psychopath."

I enact a plan to transport all of my belongings by foot to my new apartment and purchase the necessary domestic items to begin life anew... *again*. I've recorded many dialogues yet to be transcribed to this text for my future reflection, and on this matter, I'll seize the initiate of a meta-nonfictional lambastment against a potential reader:

What ails you? Are you overcome with a malady? Does boredom render you docile enough to commit yourself to reading the day-by-day exposition of one year of an *entire lifetime* worth of documentation from age twenty-five onward concerning a basic human being? These last few months, I haven't written a proper story to delight myself, nor a poem to satisfy my future melancholia. What is *it* that you want, reader? I *am* you. Please, refrain from reading; I withhold nothing to communicate with *you*.

I intend to settle in at my new apartment; I've roved long enough, wayward, destitute—always a plan or connivance to hinder any true self-reflection. The problem with being a wanderer, is that one is never satisfied; there is no contentment in one's repose, and the pains of life infiltrate one's nature greater than if one is to accept conditions as they are, especially if one has secured a superb lifestyle suitable to one's proclivities.

There is bravery in work, ~~as there is redemption in suffering~~.

How ironic.

Yes, this will certainly be a boring next few years worth of documentation to anyone seeking entertainment, or an iota of insight. Begone, and besmirch my labor with a fair two-star review on any associated venues to ensure that no more fools follow suit.

What is art: *It* is essential. This journal is vital to me, and despite my overzealous self-affirmations to persist with the tedious emprise that this is (for that is what I make of *it;* therefore, that is how *it* is comprehended), I bask in the glorious output of my sophartistry: A boy's ~~game~~ trifle!

Sunday, August 9ᵗʰ, 2020

12:15 AM

On a 3.5 mile trek to a major retailer, I became lost along the way on account of ill-remembrance of the route to my destination. I neglected to utilize my phone's roaming data option for a GPS redirection and instead hailed a biker and his family for directions. On my passage through a bike trail that I once ran on bi-nightly to train for the U.S. Navy boot camp, I crossed an intersection, and heard my name being called from a car. I stopped for four seconds, turned, observed nothing except two stationary cars at a red light, and proceeded on my walk. Twenty seconds elapsed and I heard my name called again, fifteen yards behind me on this occurrence. I turned again, and beheld my twenty-year-old younger half-brother, Jake.[3234] One-hundred and thirty pounds, with a mop of blonde hair, and well-developed facial hair; he wore an untucked black dress shirt with the sleeves rolled up to the elbows. We hugged.

Jake's self-assigned meaning in life is to become a zoologist.

I've arranged to surprise my father with Jake's presence on Monday.

1:22 AM

I'm overwrought with despondency; all I see in myself is an ignoramus and a stupid clown. I only approach people to speak to record conversations without personally caring about them, and those that I do interact with, I care only for that moment in time while I speak to them. Is this normal,

---

[34] Jake and I hadn't glimpsed each other since I attended his high school graduation and failed to find one another after the ceremony due to my half-brother's mother's influence. My father vacated the premises, averse to a rekindling of their relationship, and failed to offer me an explanation.

or *moronic?* I acquire an apartment and feel a renewed sense of self-esteem on behalf of a material gain. I don't trust my father, and believe that he despises me for how I've ignored him, or as he says, "browbeat him."

I'm sober and have been for upwards of four months. I've consumed red wine prior to then with Candy, and at one bar in Arkansas. I am a deficiency unto myself. I'm never enough for what I am. My behavior is disgusting; *think,* and reckon what I do. These are *my* intuitions and nothing more. I yearn to be alone, to sustain my cyclic hatred. I truly am incapable of love; I don't care about anybody but myself. The previous sentence was a "voice" spoken in the third-person as a commentary and I wrote *it* from *my* first-person perspective, for they are, in fact, *my own.* Are you disturbed yet, reader? No? Amused? Of course you ~~are~~ aren't; I loathe you.

If I'm as intelligent as I am deemed by sycophants, why do I wash dishes for corporate overlords and content myself with superficialities? Why would I condemn myself to the arduous task of daily ego-debasement? I'm sickened, and the thoughts dribble out of me onto this template in the same vein as when I had returned home at 3 AM after nights at the bar and weightlifting before boot camp, to bemoan of my… "love"… for Pelagia.

Pelagia… Why do I *care* for you? She wishes only for me to inseminate her; I am a veritable disposable husk of hollowed flesh, yet I *yearn* for a warm body to copulate with. What is this condition that renders me nauseous except being *human?*

I'm a fool for not playing the game to my father's expectations.

I sleep in the basement for my final night. My father houses a retard no longer.

2:37 AM

I lay awake and acknowledge my "psychopathy." The title fits my esteem, no matter how I attempt to delude myself and cast a light of optimism on my documentation. A despicable "psychopathic" loser, I am a product of American culture.

Monday, August 10ᵗʰ, 2020

3:25 PM

The days blend together in a flurry. I thought I hadn't written in two days, yet, there is an entry from yesterday before me.

I'm truly a madman, whereby I trek across town and move all of my belongings in intervals by foot, and deal with my associates with an aloof charisma suitable only for the betterment of my self.

I've reunited my younger half-brother Jake with my father this morning: a surprise for the old man. There isn't much to report on Jake other than he prides himself on his exuberant perspective of life—a "childlike wonder," and his ambition to be a conservationist of animals in Africa, e.g., rhinos and elephants.

My father is aware of my immense dislike for him, and the fickle respect we maintain only by familiarity.

Two treks across town remain, one with a pullup bar and bench in either hand; the second, carrying both dumbbells. I have denied my father's offered assistance with this venture on account of ego retention.

A young girl named Selena from [City Name] Arkansas who purchased my book from Candy's shop has contacted me for correspondence.

Candy continues to send me weekly emails of various content concerning her desperation for my correspondence.

Pelagia skirts on the fringes of my thoughts.

A new woman, Chelsea, at the high-end bar, who knows me from a former employer, has deemed me "lover boy," and is flagrant in her flirtations.

Three conversations of interest from the past week remain to be transcribed; I'm out of touch with my own life. A dish pit awaits.

Wednesday, August 12ᵗʰ, 2020

1:59 AM

After an 11 ½ hour shift, I walked to my father's apartment to pick up what remained of my belongings: a set of dumbbells with 40 lbs in weight, and a bulk package of steel-cut oats. My father slumbered when I entered, and awoke to turn off his bedroom television when my (expected) entry had awoken him. With haste, I packed my oats, grabbed both 22.5 lb dumbbells, and began my mile-and-a-half trek towards my apartment at the center of downtown.

Eight minutes into my trek, my left foot caught on an upraised sidewalk lip and caused me to fall. I released both dumbbells and caught myself on my hands; however, my oat-filled pack lurched up onto the back of my head and pressured my nose bridge and a quarter-size portion of my forehead above my right eye against the concrete. I thought nothing of the matter, pushed myself back onto my feet, retrieved my dumbbells, and continued my vigorous pace. Three minutes passed, and I felt a trickle of liquid drip off the tip of my nose. I set the dumbbells at my feet, pressed my right index and middle finger against the sensation, and held both fingers up toward a streetlight: blood.

Months have elapsed since I've seen my own blood.

I arrived at my apartment, ambled into the darkness, set the dumbbells down on the carpeted floor past the kitchen, regressed to the bathroom to the left of the entryway, and switched on a light.

My bloodied nose enthralled me; an inch-long and half-inch wide rectangle of skin coagulated and bubbled with a layer of blood and light green pus. My clothes, dirted and stained with food particles and sweat after an extended dishwashing shift closing both restaurants simultaneously, accentuated the scene of my indifferent and saturated face. I bear the aspect of a crestfallen pugilist on account of macho stupidity.

I'm tired now… weary, full of sardines and almonds, and will awake to a space devoid of food to cook, and must present my newly bloodied countenance to my fellow observers tomorrow afternoon following a long sleep on my only day off this week, to *shop for groceries*. A drop of fluid dripped off the tip of my nose and subsumed with the carpet.

10:15 PM

I lay down on a carpet and stare at my ceiling. I know that where I am amounts to nothing; I'm at peace.

I have wide marble kitchen countertops and a cubby in a stone wall that would fit a podium for my writing device. I have high ceilings, so that I may purchase a squat cage and weights at a future time. The fridge is diagonal to the stovetop, and there is a part of the counter in the corner of that space. Above the stove top: a microwave. Around that microwave is a plethora of cabinets, six in total. To the left of the stovetop, there is another stretch of black charcoal countertop, with a bit of color mixed in: brown hues and green swaths. Across from the fridge, connected to the countertop, is a kitchen sink with two basins and a thick adjustable chrome faucet. To the left of the kitchen sink is more countertop. Beyond this countertop, on a second tier, that extends halfway through the eighteen-by-twenty-foot studio, is *another* countertop, about ten feet in length and two-feet wide, raised above the first countertop. What remains beyond that, is a wide-open area, where I may pace, read, write, and be at peace with the nothingness that I have reaped.

This may be dramatic, or melancholic, or existential, or perhaps just a bit depressing; though, this is a matter of perspective—what needn't be written. I open my blinds, and I see nothing but a brick wall and the next door library's windows. If I tilt low and turn my head towards the sky, I can see the outlines of trees at the edges to my right, and to my left, I see nothing more but the extended wall of the library.

When I had been shown my new apartment for the second time, I powered on my voice recorder before meeting the broker. We greeted each other, and I rode an elevator up to the second floor with a man in his late fifties, with a lighthearted voice, a feeble physique, and clear eyes. I filled out paperwork on the aforementioned kitchen countertop, clarified a few details about the apartment, and said, "Do you have time to answer some questions?"

The broker said, "Sure."

"Do you consider…" I removed my facemask, "Do you consider yourself well-versed in human psychology?"

"Not really."

"What is your self-assigned meaning in life?"

"Ah, you're getting too deep for me." The broker chuckled.

I shared the mirth with a smile, an exasperated expulsion of air from my mouth, and said, "Do you consider yourself a good man?"

The broker immediately said, "Yeah—yeah I'm fine."

"Hm. What do you pride yourself most on about your character?"

"Mm—I'm just a good guy. Where we going with this?"

"Ah, well… I'm just asking questions because I'm curious about the people that I meet."

"Uh-huh. If I had more time I could rap with ya but, unfortunately I got fifty other people waiting on me okay?"

"Okay."

"All right?"

I proceeded to ask another question despite the broker's movements towards the entryway: "Would you consider me a fool if I paid for this house in credit, and I had cash in my primary bank account–"

"You can go ahead and put your mask back on, if you don't mind... If you did what?"

I strapped my mask back to my face and said, "If I paid for this house in credit and incurred a fee, but I had money in my primary account to spend."

"*It*'s up to you my friend. We accept everything as long as *it*'s green and we can put *it* in the bank."

"I understand."

"Ah—I don't—I don't, um—I don't judge people; everybody's got a reason for what they do. *It*'s not my place to judge you or anybody else. I just judge me."

"Wouldn't you say that that's the basis of social interactions: judgments?"

"No. No, I think that is probably somebody else's problem. Somebody who thinks they have the right to judge... they're wrong, in my opinion."

"Well you had to judge me a good tenant, for me to be here."

"No I didn't have to judge you; *it* was pretty simple; you have a good credit score and a decent job. Yep. I'm *real* simple. I don't judge people on the way they look, the way they talk—I judge *it* on—I look at the credit report—even if the credit report had problems, if *it* is medical or school debt, I don't hold that against anybody."

"Hm."

"Yeah. If *it*'s fifteen phone bills going to five different providers, *then* we have a problem; I figure they probably got issues with paying their bills. If *it*'s doctor bills or school bills, and, I've had those, and I don't think those should be counted against you."

We shifted on our feet and I said, "Well perhaps somebody came here for a showing with pockmarks all over their arms that signified that they were on heroin, or–"

"I can't prove that—if—if—if they—if they have a claim, background, ya know and they have a good credit report—I'm a *broker;* I'm not here to judge *anybody*. Yeah. That's just like someone walking in with tattoos, yeah?" He showed me tattoos on his forearm. "That don't bother me. Yeah—I mean—I *don't* judge people; what I do is what is required by the law. And everybody has a right to live here. You get out of line or do something wrong, ya know there's penalties, ya know. But... as long as everything—you passed the background check, you passed the credit check, ya know, and you got a decent job. That puts you in for me. Ya know, there's no reason for me to go any further than that. I don't delve into lifestyles or… ya know what you do for a living or anything like that, just prove to me that you can pay. See I'm real simple, ya know; if you're happy I'm happy. If you're unhappy typically that means I gotta do something to make you happy. If I can't make you happy then, maybe you need to find another place. Yeah. *It*'s just that simple. I don't like people being in my building that aren't happy, and if I can't *make* you happy, what you need to do is find another place that makes you happy. Cuz, I can't—I can't bridge that gap, ya know? We can only do what we can do."

"I understand. Thank you for the extra time that you have provided me to answer my-"

"Oh *it*'s no problem, ya know. I mean just uh, ya know—have fun; I hope you enjoy *it* here; *it* is a pretty quiet little building, ya know. I think you'll like *it* here."

"I think so too."

"Yeah—I mean—*it*'s—*it*'s… We got a lot of pride in this building; we put a lot of, ya know—and I got uh two people that live here that work for me and we take *real* good care of the property. My accountant and the maintenance guy—he lives here. We keep an eye on *it*; we take care of *it*; we take care of our tenants."

"Hm."

"Ya know, typically—typically most people enjoy *it* here; I'd say ninety-five percent. There's always a five percent that no matter what you do—you can't please everybody, ya know… but you try to, ya know?"

"Yes."

"Anything else?

"No."

"Awesome." The broker snatched his keyring and my signed lease off the countertop. "All right, well, welcome! I hope your moving is successful; you *can* use the elevator if you need to."

Nothing more of interest had been spoken out of this extract of the already vapid dialogue. I waste my willpower in the transcription of this recording; however, if my life is vapid, the writing *will* be vapid.

11:22 PM

Pelagia just called me in tears. I depart to visit her.

402

Thursday, August 13th, 2020

1:29 AM

Pelagia's apartment is a half-mile away; I ran to her without my recorder as I told her I'd never use the device in her presence. I listened to her woes and lamentations of her feelings of inadequacy, life conditions, her claim of one of the men she associates with to be her new "nemesis," for he "raped" her after she invited him into her home while both were drunk; thus, I empathize, though I did not sympathize, and I could not accept her requests for me to stay the night with her, even without any intimacy, for I could not pity her. I cannot trust her for she fails to love herself.

I ventured back up her stairwell one minute after leaving her dejected, slumped on the floor of her hallway, and informed her of my feelings stated in the aforementioned paragraph.

On my second departure, I had walked fifteen yards and heard Pelagia call my name, twice. I turned, and approached where she stood out on the balcony of her apartment; thereby I crossed over the manicured grass, stood at the fringes of several bushes along the perimeter of the building, outstretched my hands, smiled, and said, "Juliet! Juliet!"

Pelagia said, "Thank you for coming. Thank you."

I nodded and walked back to my apartment.

1:53 PM

Five days ago, I stepped outside for fresh air halfway through my shift and stared up through a canopy of trees at an afternoon sky. Vehicles veered in and out of the parking lot. Three male employees at the adjacent tavern idled outside, cigarette in one hand, phone in the other. Four yards behind me, a female bartender sat on a stone curb of an alcove behind a dumpster, cigarette in one hand, phone in the other. I don't know her name and we had never spoken before except for formal greetings. I walked over to her and said, "Hi."

The woman said, "Hi."

"What is your self-assigned meaning in life?"

"Uhhhhmmm... I think food." The woman giggled. "And being a mom!"

"To eat food or make food?"

"Make food. Yeah. *It's* why I left dental assisting—to work here, since [indiscernible]." [35]

"You said what? I couldn't hear."

The woman's eyes widened and she gazed up at the sky with an expression of exaggerated shock. "Yeah," she continued, "That's why I started working here, because I wanted to know more about business and… I eventually want to have a food truck; so, I thought I could learn some more stuff by working here."

"Then why are you at the bar?"

"Because I'm a good bartender, and I don't have any experience cooking, as far as, restaurant wise, because like at home I do obviously—but um… I have experience bartending, so… I mean I could probably cook if I *asked* but… I want to keep bartending for now. So, yeah!"

"Do you consider yourself a good person?"

The woman immediately said, "Yeah."

"What troubles you the most?"

"Ummmmm… probably, my, son… uh… figuring out that his father is not a great person."

"Ah-"

"That's—yeah. That's about *it*. I—I have a really great life. I'm, uh, ya know pretty independent; I own my own house; I take care of my kid, uh, so I don't really have many struggles—I have a good family too so, *just* my son's father, not a good person, so…"

"What characteristic do you pride yourself on?"

"Uh… Respect. Just, being respectful… um, yeah, and honest, I would say. My—those are my two rules in my house; my son will tell you that, is honesty and respect. And, I don't care what *it* is, if you're honest with me; I'd rather have you be honest then—cuz I'm gonna find out—cuz I find out everything-"

"Hm."

"So, I always say 'Just be honest and everyone will be less mad; just be respectful,' so… yeah."

"Well, thank you for your answers to my-"

"Yeah!"

"-honest, err, not my honest—my odd… inquisition, you could say."

"Absolut—I, I have *no problem*; I'm a pretty open book—I'm pretty laid back, so… pretty personable too. I don't mind; I don't mind at all." We

---

[35] A low-flying plane passed by overhead.

veered away from each other; the woman: back indoors; myself: to throw away a piece of cardboard. "I do hope *it* gets busier though!"

I said, "I do too," and the woman guffawed on her way through the open back doorway.

Friday, August 14th, 2020

1:06 AM

I asked a cook named Bryant what he prides himself on about his character. He thought for twenty-seconds while I sprayed rows of plates and said, "My optimism," and elaborated details of his outlook on life.

I said, "What do you think of the quote, 'Optimism is cowardice'?"[36] Bryant responded after eight seconds and loquaciously attempted to explain his position, albeit, he agreed with the quote. I affirmed my understanding: "You're grounded in reality, though you pride yourself on your optimism."

"Yes, exactly. Okay, I'll talk to you later, Baethan."

8:29 AM

A man I've spoken to a year-and-a-half ago who works for a hiring company called me this morning in regards to an opening at the medical facility he had previously recruited me for. I asked what the pay is; he stated $15/hr. I told him I am already employed at a full-time job; he asked me why I seek new employment.

I didn't have an answer and said, "Why does that matter?"

The man spoke with a fluent, confident, and jovial manner: "Well I want to make sure that any reasons you're seeking new employment now won't be an issue in the future if I'm to recruit you."

I said nothing for three seconds.

The man said, "Are you still with me?"

"Yes."

"Look—if you don't want the position there are plenty of other people that are interested who won't waste my time."

"Ah… Yes, I apologize for wasting your time."

"Well, good luck on your job search," the man enthused.

I said, "Thank you," though the man had already terminated the call.

---

[36] Oswald Spengler

I allowed my arm to fall beside me, phone in hand, and leaned against my kitchen counter, where I stared out of my window blinds at the wall of a library.

9:04 AM

There is no reason for my unhappiness.

Yesterday, the twenty-two-year-old pizza cook, Logan, asked me, "What do you think of people who smoke marijuana—*not* because I care what you think, just sayin'."

I said, "Why would you ask for an opinion that you don't care about?"

"Well I mean I *do* care, but just out of curiosity."

"People who smoke marijuana want to enjoy life."

"Exactly!" Logan beamed. "Marijuana enhances experiences, no matter what you're doing; sights smells… sounds—all enhanced. Do you smoke?"

"Not anymore. Enjoying life isn't a goal I share."

"Oh."

We spoke no more.

Yes, there is no *reason* for my unhappiness. I'm uncertain if I lied to Logan. I have no goal to strive for other than this ceaseless act of self-indulgence.

Saturday, August 15th, 2020

1:22 AM

A recorded monologue:

The time is 10:44 PM. I'm alone now, mopping, in a woman's bathroom. I've had many conversations today. On my way to the grocery store, I went outside and walked past the tavern where I work every other day. A waitress sat on the curb, out back, where employees congregate to smoke and chat. The waitresses' self-assigned meaning in life is to take care of her eight-year-old child. She was once a banker, and she quit for a more simple life as a waitress.

A young boy: Sebastian, age sixteen. I asked him: "What troubles you the most?"

Sebastian said, "People underestimating me due to my age."

I said, "That's the greatest of your troubles?"

Sebastian nodded.

I said, with a hint of deviousness, "That's no problem; that's an advantage." Sebastian smiled. I continued, "If that's the greatest of your troubles, life must be all peaches and candy for you then."

"We all have skeletons in our closet."

"But you're still young. Perhaps a few femurs here and there."

Another young boy: A dishwasher who works at the tavern next door when I am scheduled for a shift at the adjacent high-end bar, entered the high-end bar's kitchen for ice. The boy said, "I don't know why we need all of this ice tonight."

I said, "The rabble must drink!"

The boy laughed and nodded.

I said, "What is your self-assigned meaning in life?"

The boy, who had hurried to fill the bucket with ice, turned his back to me, and yelled over his shoulder on the way out of the kitchen door, "Uh—to keep moving forward!"

I rue over Pelagia. I am repulsed. She disgusts me to a degree I have never felt before. I speak with venom and conviction; I know my feelings with with this woman: they are loathsome and atrocious. She calls me by phone in hysterics, and summons me to her by a claim of imminent suicide, in order to be validated, yet, she provides me *nothing*. Nothing but stories of a man she slept with after blacking out from intoxication, whereby she woke the next morning, and vilified the man as a rapist. Stories of other men she "uses" for material possessions and quasi getaways despite these men being "terrible people."

Pelagia expounds these stories to me with an expectation of sympathy. I said to her, "I have no sympathy for you." However, she knew that already, though her knowing doesn't prevent her from behaving as she does, as the vile harpy I've always known her to be; since the onset of our meeting over a year ago, I've *known* this. Why I bother to fill mop buckets, to clean the remnants of *whores* and *drunkards,* and to return home to stand in my apartment and write of a woman who has caused me nothing but *grief*… This is all.

A recorded conversation between myself and Renee, the flirtatious waitress, while she rolled silverware into napkins within a "Server's Station": a dim-lit alcove secluded from the bar:

I said, "Hello Renee."

Renee whirled her head around and said "Huh?"

"Hi."

"Hi! What's going on?"

"Not much."

"Working tonight?"

"Yes, I'm working now; I have been since three."

"Have you? I got here at 4:30, and I'm here until close."

"What is your self-assigned meaning in life?"

"Huh?"

"What is your self-assigned meaning in life?"

"What's my meaning in life?"

"Yes."

"Taking care of my kids; that's *it*. Having fun."

"What aspect of your character do you pride yourself the most on?"

Eight seconds elapsed; Renee said, "I don't know. That's a good—I'm gonna come back to you on that one. What's yours?"

"My will."

"You seem like you got *it* together."

"I do."

"You were in the marines?"

"No."

"Army?"

"I was in Navy Bootcamp, but then I was separated."

"What'd you do?"

"I was writing of the sociological and psychological conditions of boot camp-"

"Oh!"

"-and they-"

Renee interjected, "They took *it* from you?"

"-discovered *it*."

"Are you going to finish *it*?"

"I'm publishing *it*."

"Are you? Good for you. That's awesome. How old are you?"

"I'm twenty-eight."

"Twenty-eight?"

"Yes."

"That's awesome. You should publish *it*. I would read *it*."

"Why would you?"

"I don't know—I love to read."

"You came onto me hard."

"Huh?"

"You came onto me hard-" Renee laughed as I spoke. "-the other day. Were you being genuine?"

"I don't know—do you remember I was the same way at [former restaurant of employment]?"

"I do recall."

Renee blushed and continued to chuckle; she said, "Yeah—that's how I am everywhere."

"That's how you are everywhe-"

"Everywhere I go when I meet people."

"With everyone?"

"Yeah I love-" Renee giggled, head downturned, and continued to sort silverware between intermittent embarrassed glances in my direction.

"Is that just to see what kind of reaction that you'll get... testing the options?"

"Yes."

"Well, what if somebody were to accept?"

"I'm engaged... or else!" Renee punched my shoulder: a light tap. We both chuckled. "But I have lots of friends. Cute friends."

"Well, I'm not looking to be set up."

"They may come work here."

I said, "I don't typically try to fraternize with my coworkers-" Renee giggled. "-I figured that I could put myself out there, but I respect your decision."

"I have three children at home, too."

"Get back to me on that pride question."

"I will; I'll have an answer by the end of the night."

I walked away and said over my shoulder, "All right."

Renee didn't have an answer by the end of the night.

Sunday, August 16th, 2020

1:58 AM

Two days ago, I informed Walther, the co-owner of the restaurants I work for, that he is referenced many times in conversations in my third publication, and that I intend to give him a copy of the book once *it's* published. By *"coincidence,"* Walther asked me the following day what the single greatest curiosity is that I have at this point of my life. I told Walther I need time to think of an answer and he walked away. Twenty minutes elapsed. Walther passed the "Server's Station" while I poured myself a cup of coffee. A sappy cover of Gun's & Roses' *Patience* played from surround sound speakers. Krzysztof Penderecki's *Cello Concerto No. 1* played through a single earbud lodged in my right ear throughout the conversation:

I said, "All right, so lately I've been on a kick asking people a series of questions."

"Okay."

"And, I tried to think of something beyond the realm of that, but, *it's* really what I'm curious about, so-"

"Okay."

"-what is your self-assigned meaning in life?"

"So, the biggest curiosity to you in life is what other people's curiosities are?"

"Yes, their meanings that they assign to their lives."

"Do you think that's the case because you're looking for yours and you feel the need to emulate someone else's?"

"No—I know my meaning."

"Okay. Umm. Uh." Seven seconds elapsed. "Raising my daughter to be a strong woman."

"What do you pride yourself on the most about your character?"

Walther contemplated for six seconds and said, "Threshold for pain. And—and—diligence. Uh, calm in the face of adversity. Just all around threshold for pain."

"I'd say grit."

"Yeah, sure."

"Do you consider yourself a good man?"

"I do."

"What troubles you the most?"

"About my character or in general?"

"In general."

"Um… Uh… Bigotry."

"In other people?"

"Yeah. Oh yeah. Yeah. Racism—sexism… nationalism."

I nodded and said, "Nationalism is a blight."

Walther chuckled and said, "Right—fascism, nazism."

"Yes."

"Hm, yeah."

I said, "I recall you telling me that you had a fantasy of being terminally ill."

"Yeah, that's right."

"That was with the sociopathic conversation."

"Yeah, but that's not the reason for, in fact—the opposite; *it's* a completely empathic reason."

"Well, I wasn't stating that to make the comparison-"

"Sure—yeah but *it* was during that conversation. So you think the implications of that desire are probably the opposite; they're probably empathic?"

I said, "*It* had been interesting to me because shortly after you had hosted the event here, for your friend-"

"Yeah-"

"-who was terminally ill-"

Walther confirmed, "Yeah—Deidra."

"-and during that time I thought that perhaps you envy her."

"Um."

"Even though you're hosting-"

"I didn't—no, I didn't. No, that had never crossed my mind. Yeah, I would say without a doubt I didn't."

"All right."

"All right."

"Well, that's the extent of my questions."

Walther said, "What's your purpose?"

I hesitated and said, "To write."

"To what end?"

"Until I die. To publish a book each year, until I die."

"But to what end, for what reason do you want to write? To inform yourself? To inform the rest of the world? To explore? To—you know—for what reason, do you need—feel the need to write? Because I mean you could've said create any kind of art and *it*'s all the same so to what end? You're trying to express *something*. Even if *it*'s a desire for something else."

"I try to express the human condition, though I don't have anything to preach or teach."

"Yeah—but if you're trying to express the human condition *it*'s either for *you* to understand *it* or for your *readers* to understand *it*—or both. *It*'s gotta be for some pursuit of, ya know—we don't illustrate things unless we want to understand them."

"*It*'s primarily for my introspection."

"Your self-discovery."

"Yes."

Walther turned away from me, walked towards the bar, and said, "That makes sense."

Monday, August 17th, 2020

1:03 AM

No matter the meaning people assign to their lives, I experience nothing but contempt and pity on behalf of humanity. Nauseated, I reckon the game of "being attractive"—the impetus underlying all actions, whereby our individual meanings are imparted, slivered away from the totality that is existence.

I've had enough *speaking,* of dissimulating niceties, pleasantries, and cordialities. Every instance I feign interest amplifies my intrinsic apathy. My social reputation has flourished at my sites of employment—*no more.* Minds afflicted with pandemonium bicker and banter around me, day after day; there are those who implore me to engage, for I have rendered myself vulnerable with my peculiar inquiries recorded in previous entries.

There isn't a woman alive who could sway me from my self-imposed duress, nor a man to align me with his truth. I am to revert to the taciturn, callous, *buffoon* that is my default. An unsettled mind desires to speak.

I've positioned my podium on my double-wide windowsill and have opened both windows overlooking the alleyway between my apartment building and library. The sounds of city life flood into my living quarters and revitalize my human spirit. Brief snippets of conversations lapse. The patter of footsteps from women—*always* something in at least one hand (e.g., phone, dog leash, coffee, handbag, purse), veer through the street at intermittent intervals. The drone of an electrical component at the library's handicap accessibility door positioned at the structure's side to my lower left produces a steady hum. An occasional vehicle passes through at 10 mph. Various instances of power tools, heavy products being unloaded and loaded onto or out of vehicles, and revving engines resound in synchronicity.

A man shouts, "You all right? Looks like you're having a hard time there!" A woman replies with an exaggerated, exasperated groan. A quiet conversation between them ensues; a mating dance of the ages, at the subconscious of man and woman, though both are only aware of the scene before them: a social ritual, as common and banal as a morning cup of coffee.

A slight breeze compounds my fascination with our condition; for instance: I allow a six-egg omelet replete with almonds, blueberries, a plethora of spices, and steamed broccoli, garlic, and pepper, drenched in extra virgin olive oil, to digest prior to a strength training session. I've lost muscle mass; therefore, I am rendered less attractive to the (feminine) female creature and less intimidating to the male creature. What does this *truly* mean?—that my social discourses are lowered in quality? And what is the significance of that—if I am loath to associate with the beings I am interdependent on and irremovable from by nature? *I am* what I contemn and pity.

Two women and a dog. An old woman pushes a stroller full of miscellaneous items beside an old man. The majority wear face masks except for the solitary few. I'll exert my body, consume, don my preposterous all-black attire for a dishwashing shift at the tavern across the street, apply a modicum of hair gel to ensure a respectable style, and depart my apartment, to join the others in the alleyway below, on my way to perform mindless labor, immersed with a microcosm of the grand charade.

2:35 PM

I experience moments and bursts of thought in which I align my design and character to be the antithesis of love: to question all, and to err on the side of nefariousness and defilement, simply out of hatred for the material fundamentals of existence, wholly removed from metaphysical, spiritual, and existential thought.

I strive for pure, industrious, and peaceful thought, and am disturbed by others' care.

By way of my self-assigned meaning, I've decided to question and record *why* people care.

Tuesday, August 18th, 2020

12:03 PM

My thoughts in solitude are disparate from when I am enthralled with my livelihood. The open windows and vantage of the alleyway below my new writing station is an environment conducive to equanimous thoughts. While being embroiled with others at a dish pit, who are reminiscent of vampires in their incessant search for petty squabbles and badinage—lured by the cheap thrills of emotional stimulus sustained by the art of *gab*, serves only to test my resolve. I've rejected the friendship and love of two of my coworkers in the past three days:

Calanne—the general manager, who praised me on my hard work while intoxicated at the bar of the tavern, announced her "love" of me, and raised a hand for me to slap on my passing. I muttered, "Why?" in response, and walked away before she could verbalize a reason.

Another woman—the second-in-command manager of the tavern, feigned patronizing care for my weight loss, my preference for music, and my living conditions. She assured me she desires to know these details about me on account of our "friendship"; thereby, I countered with a genuine display of bewildered amusement, answered only the query of my musical taste, and said that we are *not* friends; thus, she responded with revulsion and resentment, and spoke no more to me for the remainder of the night.

This book writes *it*self; I am but a bystander to my will, behold:

At the start of my shift, Sebastian, the sixteen-year-old, immediately approached me and asked me how I am with a superficial smile splayed across his face, one that appeared as though *it* had been plastered there for a long while. I asked Sebastian why he cares, out of an authentic desire to know.

Sebastian told me that he wants to learn about people: the fount of his care.

I inquired with a grin of what he has learned from caring about the people at either of the bars we are employed at.

Sebastian suppressed juvenile laughter and said, "I've learned how to do my job properly… and… perform the functions to… the best of what's expected of me."

I said, "You only care about people because you want to learn something from them?"

Sebastian hesitated for one second and said, "Yeah." I don't intend to ever speak to him again. I have nothing to teach him.

At 10:59 PM last night, a jovial bartender met me upstairs alone in the manager's office while I changed the bag of a trash can. I halted him and said, "Do you have time to answer a question?"

"Sure—yeah!"

"Perhaps a series of questions if you find the first to be agreeable; I'm going to use a voice recorder too."

"Yeah, yeah, that's fine."

I powered on my recorder, held *it* out between us, and said, "What is your self-assigned meaning in life?"

The bartender flitted a keychain and said, "My self-assigned meaning in life? Is to… as in my goal for my own life?"

"The meaning that you've chosen for yourself."

"Um, to, care for others the way that I want to be cared for—to make sure that I spread love and show people appreciation when they deserve *it*, and to always try to help those in need."

I nodded and said, "What characteristic about yourself do you have the most pride in?"

"Um my sense of humor… I think." The bartender laughed.

"You're probably a good bartender then."

"I try, yeah."

"Do you consider yourself a good man?"

"I do, yes. I try to do right by everyone."

"And what troubles you the most?"

"Um, day-to-day, just, concern for my daughter's happiness; make sure that she lives a good life and has everything she needs."

"I'm surprised that your meaning isn't the welfare of your daughter."

"Well *it's* to make sure she has everything—ya know take care of her—make sure she's supported and well-taken care of."

"That's the typical answer I get when people have children-"

"Yeah."

"-they say that their meaning is to take care of them."

"Yeah, I have a twenty-year-old-daughter."

"Ah, so she's already been taken care of then."

"Yeah, she's—she's grown; she's off on her own path now but I try to help her as much as possible—yes."

"And you're how old?"

"Thirty-nine-years-old. I'll be forty in a few months."

"All right, well that's all."

The bartender beamed and said, "Excellent."

"Thank you; I appreciate *it*."

"Have a good night bud."

"Take care."

Wednesday, August 19th, 2020

12:27 PM

Rain falls steady. The majority of passersby gaze at their reflection in the monochromatic display of the library's side entrance door. Slight alterations of behavior transpire after a viewing of themselves; I heed my intuitions, interpretation of another's mien:

"I don't look sexy at all."

"I'm strong as hell; I got this."

"I look good but I don't feel good."

"Damn I'm ugly."

One woman, short, in her late thirties, jaunts under the door's archway to smoke a cigarette. She wears a washed-out black hoodie zipped up two inches at the bottom, tight khaki pants, sandals, and circular transparent sunglasses. Her shoulder-length auburn hair is shaped in an unkempt bowl cut with skewed bangs over her right eye. A flowery brown shopping bag with yellow and blue flowers patterned at the bottom dangles from her left elbow. Her movements are shady. She peers around both edges of the archway, leans against the black metallic inner wall, indulges in sporadic drags on a cigarette down to the stub, and stares at the opposite wall.

2:48 PM

I strength train at my window and watch an unceasing passage of tottering buffoons, unable to walk in a straight line as they bumble from one foot to the other, unaware of themselves beyond their stomach and immediate pains.

Who is truly depraved? I—who stands by two open windows, with newly mounted blackout curtains pulled ajar, and a writing device at chest level positioned atop a windowsill podium, recording conditions of which *I am,* as in, what I am holistically inseparable from in manner of form and potential baseness, of genetic material and matter of origin?

I've answered my own query.

5:00 PM

My problem is that I'm happy. I must be a disappointment to a reader.

Across from me, at the library, there are vertical hanging blinds behind the windows. I've stood naked at my podium and wondered after-the-fact if this act qualifies as exhibitionism. I dressed, departed my apartment, stood outside the building in the alleyway where I observe others, and looked up to my apartment window. At this hour, with an overcast sky, my podium is visible through the open window; however, I am certain that my genitalia—a foot-and-a-half further into the confines of my apartment, is not visible to passerby, nor has anyone yet gazed up to reckon me. The only possible observers of me may be those concealed by closed windows and vertical blinds in the library opposite of my apartment across the alleyway. Regardless, I will wear briefs henceforth, at the least.

8:29 PM

My upstairs neighbor, Charlie—a man in his mid-forties, peered out of his window while I surveyed *my* window from the alleyway, for a second instance, an hour later, after slight modifications. I encouraged Charlie to open his window with a smile and a wave; he did, and we exchanged a brief banter, whereby I shouted my activities (surveying my window) and identification (downstairs neighbor and name). I inquired if my window being open disturbed him due to outdoor sounds being transferred indoors. Charlie replied in the negative, and asked if his noise output is a disturbance to me. I replied in the negative.

Charlie lives alone and is often visited by his girlfriend and her daughter.

Thursday, August 20th, 2020

11:02 AM

I've recorded several conversations and correspond with a young girl from Arkansas who read my book(s), and experienced dread—overt dread, with no desire to transcribe, due to the abject falseness and pretentiousness of everything that I, and others claim of a personality.

Every morning, my first action is to part my curtains, raise my blinds, and open my windows. The sights, sounds… of *humanity,* these creatures I know with a profound intimacy. The ephemeral conversations of others haunts, dismays, and perturbs me.

Hark!—two white-haired women with hunched shoulders:

"I don't know what else to do and I need… gotta have something decent to read."

"Yeah, gotta have something in that other hand."

"Well thank you so much–"

"Oh! Oh this is not a problem! I was just… just waiting to get it in the mail."

A thin middle-aged woman speaks to a phone:

"-Yeah well I don't expect it to fall through; I'm just tired of this… tired of waiting."

Violence, destruction, death, pestilence, decay, and the human will interspersed with the capacity for suffering, is what we don't care to think of in our waking life as a unified species hellbent on *something more.* To *care*—the folly of *it;* when the reason for empathy is scrutinized to the core logic of the manifestation of why we *feel,* there remains only a *creature.*

Creatures of beauty? To what capacity? To love?—and what incites love and the hormones entailed… *no…* forget the "science," the "knowledge," and perceive the *reason,* the *logic* for *why* we love: To *be* loved.

There are no cockroaches, flies, beetles, centipedes, millipedes, pillbugs, spiders, or vermin of any deviation in my apartment for me to capture, maim, and torture. My occupancy is clean, pristine: unfit for a mind beguiled with uncouth thoughts.

Friday, August 21st, 2020

1:32 AM

I weary of the social game, of the niceties, ploys, pretenses and charades. I record more conversations and refrain from listening, *again,* to the dribble-drabble nonsense. I asked Craig, a bartender, "What thoughts keep you awake at night?" Craig's verbose answer summarized: Finances and women.

"What about you?"

I sanitized the bar counter, smiled, contemplated for twelve seconds, and said, "My existence."

Craig's unquotable answer, refined: "I don't have time to think about that because I know I'll never understand *it.*"

I feel like less of a man than I ever have, juxtaposed with homelessness... I always recount the *homelessness...* vagabond, nomadic... wretch, and lowlife scum. Now, I dress as a fool and play the part. My co-workers commend me; I inquire, "Why?" The ruse persists, "How are you today, Baethan?" Creatures speak my name with the hope of influencing a positive relation; I address each beast with a pronoun. *How am I—*why, do you *care?*

Formalities disgust me; ingestion, too. I'd rather rot in a dungeon cell, deprived of nourishment and this mode of life: my personal self-flagellation and debasement. Yes, how *free* I'd be to be liberated from this documentation; to extricate myself from my torturous self-reflection would be an abolishment of meaning.

A new head chef at the high-end bar, Alex, is a thirty-year-old Caucasian male with a self-assigned meaning in life: "Wreck shit. Have fun. Cook good food."

A Caucasian male server at the tavern, whose identity is to remain undisclosed on account of an ambiguous self-assigned meaning in life: "Just get through *it...* right?"

I said, "I can't answer your life's meaning for you," and walked away.

Saturday, August 22nd, 2020

1:54 AM

"I saw you talking to Baethan; what was that all about?"

"Oh nothing. Baethan asked me if talking to him is like pulling teeth, and I told him to align his chakras and drop acid, then I went outside for a smoke. Baethan came out afterward and basically told me how much he didn't like me trying to help him and called me and everyone around us 'rabble' who talk about our troubles, and that 'all we do is babble.' Then he went back inside."

"Oh, that sounds pleasant."

"Yes, he's really just a grumpy, oversized child who likes to *act* mature."

"To be honest, he makes me feel dumb."

"I think he just has a lot of psycho-social issues."

"That may be the case, but he's still a highly intelligent man."

All right, enough of this imagined discourse between two women I spoke to near the end of my shift. To speak to people is a chore. To begin to even attempt to explain the depth of my loathing regarding useless communication is exasperation and ultimately befuddles whoever I speak to, for they cannot understand the depravity of my thoughts.

The desire *and* will to be alone is compatible: a mutual fulfillment; however, when thrust into society day-by-day, there is no true extrication from the condition we all share.

A conversation with a new Caucasian male, late forties, tattooed bartender:

I said, "What is your self-assigned meaning in life?"

The bartender said, "My *self-assigned* meaning in life? That's a deep one—I don't know. I guess uh, do unto others as you would want done to you."

"All right."

"I'm kind of uh, very spiritual in an energetic way, so, the energy you put out is what comes back to you."

10:11 PM

I'm finished; I've had enough. The social contract is repugnant.

Walther and I discussed why he cares to know how I am; at first, near the dish pit; second, in his office, when I ventured up to expound on our previously aborted conversation, and to convince Walther that despite my actions, my thoughts make me an "asshole." I thought I had initiated my recorder before the conversation in Walther's office; however, to my gloomy satisfaction, I *didn't*. Walther remained unconvinced, poised in his office chair.

All *it* amounts to is that I'm a damned fool, alone with myself, no matter who I find myself amongst. People touch me, ask me how I am, smile, thank me, carry on with their lives—ad nauseam, till death. This is a rare moment: *Time,* off early from a shift, where I return to my second-floor apartment and stand by my windowsill-mounted podium to squander my life, self-deprived of relationships. I have no tears for myself. Grief is a bygone prospect.

I care about the opinions and perspectives of others that I *don't* care about. I've made an ass of myself today in Walther's office and regret the deficient operation of my recorder, for the dialogue would've been suitable for future flagellation.

My emprise is anathema; my actions, my undoing. Self-deprivation of relationships is portrayed by my peers and those I *must* associate with as *bad,* i.e., anti-civilization. And what of civilization is noble and sacred? What of humanity?

This text is a chore. The people I work with annoy and vex me. Situated at the dish pit, I am unspared from the… Yes… all *this* is, *this* document, is what people do: complain, bicker, bemoan, malign, censure, and revile. What "art" have I produced in the last four… five months? I recall nothing. I scorn society and cannot bear to look upon the wretches I meander amongst who lapse into depravity and indulgence by nightfall in the privacy of their homes.

Walther has become my most intimate confidante, by manner of him being my employer, and for his education. Walther disclosed that he asks his employees how they are to establish rapport. Civilization wouldn't exist if not for rapport—according to Walther, our dehydrated stone age brethren would've succumbed if others didn't care to ask, "How are you?" We wouldn't have *beer,* if not for rapport, a condition Walther emphasized with grave implications, to which Alex joined in with Walther's admonishment and dismissal of me, jovial and spirited.

The most revealing phrase I uttered to Walther is that I refrain from friendships because of my hatred and loathing of myself for being human, and would espouse nothing but negativity to a friend.

I hear muffled rabble outside my closed window and *hate*. Is there something wrong? I *am* a similar beast, and have spoken thus today to a great length: a fool's discourse with another fool who knows no better than myself. Walther and I diverge in our philosophies due to our ethics of what conduct constitutes an ideal life: a veritable ideological skirmish of John Locke and David Hume against Arthur Schopenhauer and Friedrick Nietzsche, respectively.

I've no desire to thrive.

Ignoble reader; I snigger at the idea of you, exalted and haughty in your judgment of my judgment; you are naught but an obligatory byproduct of my outrageous imagination.

Sunday, August 23rd, 2020

10:18 AM

I must resort to pseudo-mutism to restore a fraction of self-respect to my psyche and speak only when circumstances necessitate a reply for a common goal.

Art is essential; the art I produce is self-induced microcosmic social ~~liberation~~ suffering.

11:21 AM

To expound on yesterday:

I entered Walther's office and stated outright that he had not educated me with his pictorials of historical human progress dependent on rapport, e.g., transporting barley via ship, the roman empire, and hunting mammoths. The fact that Walther *hadn't* educated me and walked away after several of our coworkers reinforced and contributed to the first part of Walther's lecture, whose only purpose had *been* to educate me, i.e., *integrate,* compelled me, after extensive contemplation, whether I should enact the idea to walk next door to the tavern, ascend the steps to the manager's offices, and confront Walther. I did, in front of two of the managerial staff members. Alas, pride comes before the fall.

The conversation had been multifaceted; however, *friendship* dominated as the primary topic. The Aristotelian theme overtook my directive of conveying my flagrant disagreement of thought and ceasing our amicable communication. Instead, I stood and listened to the merits of friendship and the importance of nurturing relationships with others; *I stood,* yes, as a veritable baby bird in a den of snakes.

Before Navy Boot camp, when I labored for Walther's business (paid two dollars less for three times as much work during a lucrative period), Walther's concern for my well-being had been negligible, for any *rapport* established was to be voided with my anticipated departure.

Of course, rapport is beneficial to business, to society, to civilization! Rapport is functionless for *me!* No one who has ever lived, is alive now, or will be alive in the future, that may understand the complete spectrum of thoughts and emotions derived from life experiences which have manifested as the being that I represent now—*even* if one were to peruse and analyze every word of every book I've ever written and intend to write. What benefit do I receive to be *understood?*—to be *deceived* by an employer who dissembles compassion for his business's advantage?

Friendship... I scoff and wonder: What better friend than a book?

11:49 PM

A first night of a resurgence of the pseudo-mutism lifestyle has reaped dividends on my mental health; nonetheless, there is always a female server or bartender to smile and order me to "have a good night" despite not speaking to me for the entirety of our concurrent shifts. I snubbed the most recent one.

Complaints and weakness abounds all around me. Low character pervades my sanctity of mind. To think, I, the lowest quality specimen of any given group, to judge—as a *lifestyle*—the vulgarities, ignorance, and outright stupidity of those around me; I would know best; therefore, I am the most qualified to judge.

People utter polite banalities twice, sometimes thrice, when I don't reply or acknowledge them. The more I disregard the rote American social expectations my contemporaries abide by without any of them reflecting on *why* they behave the way they do (continual greetings and farewells to a man who ignores them), the more my comfort amplifies with being hated, misunderstood, reviled, maligned, and mocked in secret.

Am I perfect?—what a silly query; however, this is what the miscreants and philanderers who are both patrons and employees perceive of me: arrogance and haughtiness, though a large margin of that subterranean restaurant subculture wouldn't know the definition of "haughty." *Ah*—the ostentatious intellectual censurer that I am!—have I no shame? Who would feel bad for me? *This* is what I do! Friendless, albeit, there are throngs who would delight to name me "friend" without my rebuff; I am intolerant of the inanity and simplicity of the static charade played by both parties— man and woman alike—in their grandiose act of *thriving*.

I must bolster my resolve if I am to descend to the creaturesque nature I strive for, lest I succumb to sympathy, pity… *empathy*, on behalf of those I ignore; Pelagia is a dismal reminder of such an outcome.

Monday, August 24th, 2020

11:41 AM

A week ago, a congregation formed in a nearby park. I stood and listened by my open windows to a man speaking into a megaphone; he preached, "All lives matter."

This morning, a woman and her dog departed from our apartment and entered the alleyway below. The dog snarled and began to bark on the sight of a man who walked past. The woman muttered, *"Hey,* hey—stop," and the dog continued to bark unrestrained.

The man grinned, slunk past, shoulders low, and said in a hushed tone, "How are you?"

The woman tugged on the dog's leash and said, "Good—how are you?"

"I'm good; thank you."

Just now, a stocky and poised man wearing cargo shorts, a cross-hatched purple and black shirt, and vibrant reflective blue sunglasses walked past. I had seen him many times before. He tilted his head up at me in this particular instance, and despite his veiled eyes, I knew he reckoned me. I waved; he waved back; we smiled.

Tuesday, August 25th, 2020

12:32 PM

Flytraps hang from the ceiling over the dish pit of the tavern.

Before Navy Boot camp, my previous human relations manager, Dan, entered the kitchen from the patron room and stood in the doorway. We stared at each other, a slight smile on both of our countenances. Dan extended his hand; I mimicked and extended mine; we shook hands, clasped together over my polished silver basin. Dan said, *"It's* good to see you," and left. That instance had been the only interpersonal human contact beyond the essential that I experienced all day, and *it* had been unaccounted for. I wanted to stare at Dan, say nothing, and refute the handshake; social instincts compelled me to otherwise.

The fly traps.

I clogged my garbage disposal with eggshells and avocado skins. A maintenance associate arrived the moment I woke this morning to fix the issue. While the old man in his mid-sixties labored, I initialized my recorder and said from across the kitchen counter, while my morning coffee brewed, "What is your self-assigned meaning in life?"

"My self-assigned?"

"Yes."

"I don't think—I don't think *it's* self-assigned. I think perhaps somebody else assigned me to assist you."

"As in a god?"

Water poured from the faucet at full capacity. The old man said, "As in a what?"

"As in a god?"

"A dog?"

"A god."

"It's... it's whatever you wanna call *it*—a higher power."

"Well you said 'somebody.'"

"Well—something, somebody; you can call *it* a god; there are just so many entities that claim to be a god. You know what I mean? Has god taken on that many forms?"

I watched the old man plunge both of my sink drains simultaneously with two plungers and said, "Humans create the iterations of the entities we call gods. There hasn't been an entity to reveal *it*self and claim *it*s godhood; *it's* all been humans telling stories."

"Ye—yep—that's true... so... for all we know, or for all *I* know, as a person, *it* could be—this entity could be an alien... don't know... this god. I studied a lot of different beliefs, and, I actually am not a Christian; I study Wicca; are you familiar with Wicca?"

"It's Pagan, correct?"

"It's—yes, *it* is Pagan. Yes *it* is. *It's* a love of the earth, creatures, humans-"

"Yes."

"-mostly, *it's* not about *a* 'God,' because they—we believe there are many gods; ya know—*but,* I was brought up Christian—I was brought up Roman Catholic, ya know, bible school, the whole nine yards. *But,* ya know—I don't know; *it* is what *it* is. I—*I*—I guess I won't actually know the truth until… I'm dead!" The old man laughed.

"So what would you say your self-as—well, your entity-assigned meaning is then?"

"To assist people. To help people out. *It's* what I've been doing for a long time: helping people out. That's what this jobs' about: helping people out. I'm going to need to go get a bucket and whatnot to take that all apart underneath, okay?"

"Okay, sure."

"Okay, I shall return. Can I leave these here?" The old man pointed to the two plungers lain horizontally across my sink basins.

I said, "Sure."

"Thank you sir. I'm Bruce by the way."

"I'm Baethan."

"Baethan?"

"Yes."

"Good to meet you Baethan—welcome to the neighborhood."

"Thank you; I appreciate your assistance, since *it* is my folly after all."

Bruce waved his hand, meandered away, said, *"Nah,* no worries," and exited my apartment.

Wednesday, August 26th, 2020

10:31 AM

At 11:39 PM last night, I mopped the upper tier of the upper-class bar's patron room and spoke into my voice recorder:

"My war on myself has begun. Walther asked me if I'll be having sardines and an avocado today. I ignored him. Walther said my name again. I veered past him with a clean plate and did not meet his eyes with my own.

"I've had people touch me today, in attempts to garner my attention. There is a new girl named Amanda who has informed me that she has begun to read my first book. She is an attractive, young, vain, gregarious woman, and she yearns for my *attention;* though she may be attractive, I find her to be pathetic due to her desperation. In fact, the entire service staff of the lower socioeconomic strata, of which I am irremovable, even if I were to acquire great wealth, is nothing but a deplorable sight and producer of sounds of equal deplorability. I do not think myself better than my peers; I am *lower* than the basest scoundrel that you could find curled in a curbside gutter at 2:30 AM after a heavy rainstorm. My mind is a veritable feast for the maggots. I think nothing but foul, despicable thoughts of my fellow human beings that I see *collaborate, banter,* and establish their *rapport*—ah, yes, on *rapport*—that's the intent of this initial recording: Walther, by my act of silence, has been proven wrong that rapport is essential for civilization.[37] What rapport was there in civilizations built on slavery? What rapport was there with the Persians, Chinese, Assyrians, Arabs, Romans, Egyptians, Americans, etc., and their slaves? These were powerful societies... built on *rapport?* I think not—and here *I* am, a slave to myself, as I've always been and *choose* to be.

"What a wonderful recording this is; the transcription will be lovely. I'll enjoy hearing my egotistical diatribe siphoned back into my ears."

12:04 PM

The stocky man with the vibrant blue sunglasses walked by my post and entered my field of vision with a prevenient gaze upturned to my open windows. I backstepped, leaned back, outspread my hands with a gesture of beckoning, and grinned. The man's arms swung by his sides without a return gesture. He displayed a toothy smile and hastened past.

11:45 PM

People bore me with their dramas, my own included.
Dishes come in; dishes go out.

---

[37] "Civilization" is reducible to the act of dishwashing.

Thursday, August 27th, 2020

12:14 PM

Some men condescend to defer to me as "brother," or "boss," despite my insolent silence.

A man adorned a spread of pizza dough with a layer of mozzarella cheese, rapped his free hand against a worn cutting board countertop, and whistled an ambiguous tune.

"Hello, how are you?" said a patron who had never before encountered the pizza cook from across a glass display case filled with heated sauces and optional toppings.

The pizza cook raised both eyebrows, glanced over his shoulder, and said, "Hey!—I'm good. How are you today?"

"I'd like a sausage pizza with extra provolone cheese."

"Sure thing, brother; I'll be with you in just a moment."

"Do you bake muffins here?"

"No we don't, boss; I'm sorry."

The patron veered away from the display case, inserted both hands into his trouser pockets, and stood aloof for thirteen seconds, whereby, on the matter of his circumstances being unchanged after aforementioned time, and of the pizza cook being preoccupied with his work, the patron withdrew his right hand from his right pocket, phone-in hand, and subsequently withdrew his left hand from his left pocket to utilize the tip of his left index finger to tap the phone's screen.

The pizza cook whistled a variation of the ambiguous tune.

Saturday, August 29th, 2020

1:25 AM

Last night, at 11:21 PM, I mopped a woman's bathroom floor at the high-end bar, repressed tears, and spoke into my recording device:

"I'm truly a monster of a man. What am I, to pity myself? I have chosen the path I have taken, of self-indulgence, of constant reflection. Have I no shame in what I do? Who do I hurt except myself?—what shame is there then? There is nothing to learn; there is no one to teach me. The self-engrossment of my mind is a miasma onto everyone I associate with. This disgusting state of affairs that I've wrought onto myself and those around me is *abominable*. I *am* monstrous.

"A young girl, Sara, who bought my books in Arkansas, the one to whom I personally recommended a copy while I worked at *Anomalies and Artifacts,* corresponds with me. I have invited her to live with me for a brief period, expense-free, in exchange for sex and intimacy. She considers the option, and said that she would have immediately accepted two months ago if her circumstances hadn't altered to what they are now, which entails a new lease that she has signed. The girl, or rather, woman, is twenty-five-years-old. She has… Why do I even bother talking into this device? What moron am I, to do so."

11:05 AM

This is no show, no play on words or histrionic display for my own future recollection. I am aware of what I am, referenced each day by the same group of people where I'm employed who refer to each other as "family" and "friend," without discernment or discrimination of each other's character: a lofty universal acceptance.

Since my silence and disregard of others except for the instances of mutual cooperation, whereby I gesture, or speak the fewest words necessary to convey the most concise meaning, those who venture near me have become reticent in their expressions and speech. My circumstances are unusual and elicit unconventional responses to my behavior on account of my previous sociability, and the knowledge of my publications being circulated by the gossip of female coworkers. I can only recount the validity of my own equanimity and acumen, until otherwise disturbed by another who signals for my attention by way of either a greeting or a specious inquiry of my well-being. My sympathies for those I discount or snub often vex me; thereby, my equanimity is transmogrified to ephemeral notions of pity; however, I am aware that the feelings of pity I experience are *not* oriented at others, but at myself, for the social deprivation I choose; thus, I grieve—*selfishness* of the basest caliber. Anger manifests afterward, for the foolishness of my grieving for what I lose, without accounting for what I gain by way of the adherence to my abstract principles. Indeed, *it* is easier to be swayed and affected by the impressions of a moment, such as the dampened interest of a beautiful woman after repeated instances of ignoring her, or the distrust expressed in a man's eyes when I do not reciprocate brotherhood and camaraderie.

Sunday, August 30th, 2020

9:24 AM

The seventeen-year-old-boy, Sebastian—an Asian-American, and a young server girl (of unknown age and unobserved ethnicity [Caucasian]), are special cases in my exemption of contempt; both are too naive and malleable in their habits to censure. Although I practice a refined pseudo-mutism, I showcase my good humor around youth and children through responsive smiles and gestures, albeit, with averted eye contact.

By contrast, I work with an obese African-African man, Maurice, with a "grill" on his upper row of teeth, who blares "gangsta" and rap music from the 80s to early twentieth-century era, throughout the entirety of his shift, through a small cylindrical portable speaker. Due to Maurice's laziness, I had accepted the burden of completing tasks on his behalf; however, with my recent silence and nullified rapport, our mutual lack of respect for each other climaxed last night: Maurice thought me to be a schmuck, and thought that on account of his "Sous Chef" position, and my "Dishwasher" position, that he may slough responsibilities onto me in order to end his shift early and return home to his four children.

Maurice approached me and spoke through his "grill"—replicating the sound of one who speaks with a mouthful of food, of his earnest expectation of my goodwill regarding a wall-cleaning task he had been assigned by an (unspecified) authority.

I stood and listened, expressionless, and stared at the wall he spoke of, aware of my own vacuous countenance.

Maurice glared at me and said, "Do you understand me?"

I snapped my head toward Maurice and spoke to him for the first instance in five days: "Is this a project assigned to you?"

Maurice confirmed in the positive, and proceeded to address the status of my comprehension of his instructions.

I said, "If this project is assigned to you by an authority, why should I be the one to undertake *it?*"

Maurice's brow furrowed; he said, "Cause you're the dishwasher and I'm the sous chef, and I'm passing *it* down to you; you understand what I'm sayin'?"

I expressed my disdain, shook my head, said, "No," and turned back to my basin. Maurice stood three feet behind me, indignant and bewildered with my unanticipated denial. He approached me from the side of the basin and attempted to intimidate me: "Is that your final answer? Huh? Is that your final answer?" I addressed Maurice with a light-hearted sneer, snorted, and ignored him for the remainder of our shift, whereby he puttered around the kitchen, alerted his wife via speakerphone that he is "calling a cab now," and shirked his responsibility. Any fleeting notion of respect I retained for the man dissipated.

Monday, August 31st, 2020

11:24 AM

A new dishwasher has been hired at the tavern because I am now assigned to work at the high-end bar for all but one day of my shifts. I met this new dishwasher, Andrew: I smelled the stench of cheap cologne first, when he puttered up from behind me and waited for my acknowledgment while I sprayed tomato sauce within a plastic cambro.

A voice reminiscent of a starry-eyed cartoon character said, "Hello." I glanced to my left for less than a second. "I'm the new dishwasher." I nodded once, and continued to work. Andrew positioned himself at a three-bay sink behind me and began to handwash metal cambros. While I moved clean kitchen objects to the drying rack to Andrew's right, I observed features of the man: Less than five-feet in height; two-inch brown hair, either slicked down with grease or matted with sweat, framed his boxy face; feeble and flabby; diminished and uninspired. I inspected a cambro Andrew placed on the drying rack and scrutinized a milky substance that remained gunked in each of the four corners: Incompetent.

Territorial and annoyed, I withdrew my phone from my left pocket, displayed the crew's schedule for the day, and confirmed that Andrew had been assigned to be trained as a host. I turned to Andrew, stood a foot behind him, and spoke on behalf of necessity: "Why are you here?"

Andrew whirled around, startled, and said, "What?"

"Why are you here?"

"Huh?"

"Why... are you here?"

"I'm the new dishwasher."

I flipped my phone screen towards Andrew's face and said, "You aren't the dishwasher today; you're to be trained as a host."

Andrew stared at my phone, squinted his eyes, and furrowed his brow; he said, "I don't know!—I'm a dishwasher; I'm thirty-years-old, been doing *it* all my life; *it*'s the only job I've ever done."

Ryan, a pizza maker with a managerial role, said, "Oh, Baethan, I just have him on for a few hours, like three, to train him for a bit."

I glared at Ryan, fifteen-feet away from me, through the space between countertops and hanging shelf space, and said, *"Training,* for *dishwashing?"* Ryan, a man of pretentious docility, lost his sheepish effect and glowered at me, and I him, for four-and-a-half seconds. Ryan said, "Well, I guess-"

Andrew blurted, "-I thought I was a dishwasher! I can go if you want me to."

I stood, bewildered and amused with the sensations I wrought upon my fellow men through uncustomary speech, and resumed my position at the dish basin. Ryan, likewise, resumed his work. Andrew hurried out to the host's station and returned twenty-three seconds later, to which he spoke his hasty farewell to me; however I did not acknowledge him; thus, he raised his right hand, fish clenched, index finger pointed upward, and shouted with bravado a statement that served as the reason for my recording of this particular instance: "I have forty hours as a dishwasher— I'll *be back!"* and scurried out the back screen door; a veritable *Loony Toon.* I laughed—not a giggle, chuckle, snigger or snicker... I *laughed,* and proceeded to laugh at two-to-four minute intervals for the following twenty-five minutes.

Due to my mirth at the judgment of another's cognitive impairment, I experienced the remaining seven hours and forty-five minutes of my shift despondent, hostile, and gloomy, for I reckoned my position in the world—a dishwasher, garbed in my all-black dress clothes, laboring in a filthy run-down hole of a kitchen staffed by subpar bar food producers, and felt my existence as an unendurable weight. Surrounded by those I ignore and spurn, the reputation natural to my unaffected disposition had been destroyed by my own affectation of silence, and I am rendered an ignoramus of the utmost magnitude. Any thought I experience constituted of weakness and deficiency, no matter how slight, is capitalized on by observers who reckon the meanness of my visage and metaphysically tear my poise asunder by a method of gossip and mirrored contempt... resentment, hate? Rudimentary anger? I fail to distinguish a difference. The self-engrossed outspoken yearnings of my fellow animals—the *babble* and *bickerings,* evokes an insurmountable dread, for I compare the fleeting speech to my lifelong enterprise of this documentation: Ignobility, recorded in solitude, published, to become part of all that I condemn. The hypocrisy!—the *lunacy!* Nay, the *idiocy!*

At the end of my shift, I prepared to clean the tavern's patron room. Two intoxicated employees from the high-end bar, Beatrice and Becky, attempted to goad me into speaking. Becky, with an inane inquiry on a task I performed two days ago, to which I ignored; Beatrice, however, uttered a monologue that would've been worthy of a verbatim transcription, for she addressed me with pitying aggression, and confessed to me her guilt of feeling responsible for me no longer speaking to anyone... Why?—I haven't the slightest inclination *why*, except for the vanity and egoism each of us deludes ourselves with—that I delude myself with, in my care for the behavior and machinations of others I am contrarily devoid of compassion for.

I smiled from behind the veil of a Covid-19 necessitated face mask and stared at Beatrice. Throughout her insipid minute-and-a-half diatribe on my condition of silence, I thought of how much I hate her. I bore a hole through Beatrice's head with my mind and thought of *nothing* but pure, unadulterated hate. I wanted to roar. Beatrice pranced around me and said, "I love you, Baethan," over her shoulder, on her way out of the establishment, while I stood statuesque, body flexed. My chest expanded and deflated with each systematic breath. The world around me ceased to exist. Never before have I hated with the adamance of a zealot, a fanatic, a dogmatic, a *maniac.* I'd relive that moment, if afforded the opportunity, to experience the equipoise of profound resolve.

11:36 PM

There is no necessity for guilt and shame. Consciousness is god. To care is to suffer.

SEPTEMBER

Tuesday, September 1st, 2020

11:52 AM

Lo!—over yonder; behold a man and a woman. Did you expect anything else? I'm awed by the mediocrity. The words they exchanged that lead to their current involvement must've been pleasant—undoubtedly, and riddled with falsities and pretensions. Why else would they suffer on behalf of each other if not for a solemn satisfaction each derives from their respective consciousness's will, bound within mortal flesh as they are?

Why contemplate such egregious conditions?

The life I've constructed is to my satisfaction, despite my prominent negativity. I imagine my writing's themes would become positive if I were to endure serious hardship, for then I'd become interesting to myself. I strive to attain this hardship through enforced pseudo-mutism for all non-work related matters, even in public, e.g., This morning I walked down the hallway of my apartment complex clothed in nothing but my briefs and encountered a woman several years younger than myself. The woman said, "Hii-ii," and averted her eyes to the handle of her door. I strode past without speaking, and looked at her with a passivity that implied that her presence and greeting had been a triviality, and that (though this aspect of my thought remained unexpressed through my mien) she should feel the same of me.

Ah, yes, what have I gained and lost by this behavior: A little bit of nothing; a little bit of something.

The mutism is to be my identity for the upcoming year—my next title, for I *am* nothing else except for what I choose to become; therefore, I must abide by my ambition, for the sake of observation and introspection—self-engrossed and content with being so.

There is one caveat: The girl from Arkansas who has contacted me, Sara, is a lost and broken soul, malleable and impressionable. I predict she will be with me by the New Year, to incur severe taxation on my serenity and quietude—by *my* choice; I have invited her, and write pleasant words to her, *devoid* of falsities and pretensions, with my expectations relayed in concise prose... yet, she retains an interest, with expressions of longing for me and the tragedies that befall her.

I am the last resort, an escape, a validator.

2:21 PM

At my trip to the grocery store, I said to an African-American bagger girl, "I want the frozen and cold items in my pack; I'll take care of *it* all myself, thank you," and said, "Thank you," when the Caucasian checkout boy passed me a bag full of avocados, tomatoes, and garlic that had been overlooked due to being packed before my request. Face masks are worn by all; therefore, my spoken gratitude has been critical due to my rectitude.

Some speech is necessary. Rapport is a privilege.

Wednesday, September 2nd, 2020

1:00 PM

A nearby bell tower chimes a novel eight-note tune every hour. After a five-second delay, successive chimes signify the hour, e.g., 5 PM warrants five chimes. I listen through my open windows, to a single signifier, accentuated in pleasantness by the gentle patter of light rain against concrete and steel.

I've spoken to no one for pleasure since my ignoble conversation with Walther on rapport. I'm truly a stupid man—no facetiousness or pomposity implied. I work to destroy my (irrelevant) reputation and have succeeded, to an extent, in at least *confusing* those I *must* associate with by my mutism, uninhibited emotional displays, and aversion to eye contact. Only the women seem to care, in their goadings and niceties; however, this behavior is inspired by their own vanity, and my subsequent ignoring of the female staff prompts invectives of my character, to which the men engage in, with the acknowledgment that I *am* silent; therefore, what harm could come to them—to disparage and malign one who has no interest in defending his name?

Mootness and folly. The ephemeral moments in which I stand, engaged with my labor, is a source of solace. Those around me, who veer in and out of my vision, are inconsequential passerby: fellow plebian all-stars. Unsettled minds espouse one another's contents, each marked by a malcontent. I hear only inflection and tone in the speech which rattles around me, translated accordingly as, *"Who will listen to my gripes and share in my trifles?"* or *"My vacuousness cannot be contained to thought alone, and must be expunged to the unfortunates within my vicinity by voice."*

Thursday, September 3rd, 2020

10:16 AM

The chef, Alex, pleaded with me to speak, with unintended jests such as "What can I do to improve your comfort? You do a great job. Do you think this is cool? Do you think this is okay, to not speak to me?" I cleaned my basin—sprayed the remnants of the last of the gruel that was served for the night, and glanced over my shoulder with disdain and jubilant derision expressed on my countenance. *My* comfort? I anticipated a blow to the back of my head; however, I am sanctioned by the social contract.

If this were a tribe, I'd be exiled or stoned to death, perhaps drawn and quartered, or burned alive. Instead, I anticipate either of the two owners of the establishment to reprimand me with a penalty of termination of my employment if I refuse to alter my behavior.

Yes… *What rapport is there?* The idiom, "To cut off one's nose to spite the face" is applicable. To fire me would be a manifestation of Walther's belief of the essential nature of rapport; to do so would be in his best interest, despite my impeccable work performance, of which I am insouciant to boast. Though, I reckon the conversation we had incurred no weight on his consciousness, and that the ~~war~~ skirmish waged is solely in my mind. To Walther, if others are to (undoubtedly) complain and gossip, I surmise that I am but a strange, thickheaded man, and an impertinent irritation.

To be terminated from my position on account of the dramas that have transpired due to my silence would validate me. Life ebbs on.

1:11 PM

Nay, on further contemplation, from an employer standpoint, my egotistical self-engrossment expressed uninhibited in the workplace, as a *dishwasher*, is a non-issue that will resolve *it*self, either when my peers come to accept me as a non-entity, i.e., as a distasteful piece of the environment (e.g., an imbued brown stain on a white wall), or if I terminate my employment. The latter is more imminently probable.

2:28 PM

On my second trip to the grocery store this week for a mass purchase of eggs and fermented food, I communicated with the grocers by way of gesture only. On my way out, I encountered my previous supervisor, Rick, at the grocery store I had once been employed at three years ago as a "maintenance associate."

Rick said, "Baethan—hey Baethan!" while I walked with a full pack donned on my back towards one of the exit vestibules. I stopped abruptly, which attracted the customers' and employees' attention, and addressed Rick with a blank, amiable stare. "Baethan," he continued, his toddler daughter in hand: "How have you been... or don't you remember me?"

I acknowledged Rick with a slight nod, and looked at him for seven seconds; my head turned at a full ninety-degree angle to my left, and both of my feet directed towards the exit. Two of the young girls who had previously assisted me at checkout stared at me while I maintained eye contact with Rick for the aforementioned duration. I walked away without a word spoken.

Oh, yes, I remember Rick, all-too-well: the constant complaints, malignments, and laziness. Yes, *how are you*—wait... Please, refrain.

Am I pompous and arrogant to prefer a settled mind? Do I delude myself, and usher ruin and discord onto my prospects for the sake of a preposterous philosophical creed? My mind, after all, is *unsettled* each instance I write in this infernal document. If not for *this...* my words, I would be impoverished and enervated; however, *it* exists. I rejoice in my folly, my vanity, for death is welcome.

7:16 PM

I have achieved my desire, yet I fretted and behaved as a wounded animal, pusillanimous in my regret at resolving to injure myself and those I will never associate with again. Walther followed me out of the kitchen back door and observed my rueful countenance, tears lining my eyes that I attempted to hide on behalf of betraying myself with the contempt and disdain of those who have treated me with only good-will. What I have become is truly a disgrace.

With a destroyed reputation, I am free to become.

Correspondence with Sara (the woman from Arkansas) has been terminated; I would only mar and injure her as I have so many others.

I've recorded my one-sided conversation with Walther, in which the man's magnanimity[38] diminished my silent confidence; however, I've written too much, care too little, and want only to lie down, for I am dejected without a lord to pay me.

Dear Jesus

I'm a worthless lot.
Lend me your aid, that I may find
New employment soon.

10:18 PM

If I were to consider anyone "friend," Walther would've been the only one, for more than an employer-employee relationship. Walther's hand shook with what I understood to be repressed anger or indignation as he handed me my notice of employment termination to sign. Yes, to *care; it* renders me nauseous with my deliberate conduct.

The bars' spirit and morale will improve with the removal of my malevolent influence. I am no victim; how could I be? I am validated: *What rapport is there?*

Friday, September 4th, 2020

11:00 AM

I've been hired at *Cooper's Cave Ale Company* as a dishwasher. My first shift begins in one hour.

"And now for something completely different."

- Monty Python

---

[38] I suspect this attitude is in due part to his knowledge of my inclusion of his character in my documentation and of my usage of a voice recorder. Perhaps I had merely been a valued employee.

10:22 PM

Yes, indeed: Jesus has answered my prayer. I've established a strong rapport with a new kitchen crew due to initial impressions and my work ethic, which is innate: an affinity with the dish domain. I'm paid the same amount and now work from noon to 9 PM, with *no* duty to utilize a broom or a mop on behalf of a "floor crew." I marvel at my circumstances, and ponder why anyone should ever despair such as I have. The sorrow of a saint is abominable.

I've ended an extended fast with a six-egg omelet, three handfuls of almonds, five servings of steamed frozen spinach, two servings of Greek yogurt, and two servings of cottage cheese. Ceylon cinnamon, nutmeg, basil, ground peppercorns, and iodized sea salt flavored the meal. One can of *Wild Planet* sardines for desert. How wonderful—to write of food and the subsequent consumption. *Yes,* I fell asleep last night despondent with my employment folly, and awakened with employers vying for my labor, only to hasten to my next outpost of dishwashing induced paychecks an hour after rising from my apartment floor.

A few have told me I'm a "great," "good," or "interesting" writer. Does this media fit the criteria? Does my deviant glee constitute *good* writing, or even mediocre? I've been rewarded for my assholeism with a new social venue to observe a la Charles' Bukowski's *Factotum* (excluding the alcohol and cigarettes); liberated from the social ties of Pelagia's friend network: namely, Beatrice, and her gaggle of egalitarian gossipers—*haunted,* no longer, by the phantasms and wraiths of dead relationships that should've never been if I were a man of integrity.

I make no excuses for my "bad" behavior. There is luck in my asinine conduct. I'm to be a benign, upright, role-model of ~~drudgery~~ virtue. Pseudo-mutism, ~~with a contemptuous disposition,~~ has proven to be unsustainable.

"Do not be unsociable. The truest wild beasts live in the most populous places. To be inaccessible is the fault of those who distrust themselves, whose honours change their manners. *It* is no way of earning people's goodwill by being ill-tempered with them. *It* is a sight to see one of those unsociable monsters who make a point of being proudly impertinent. Their dependants who have the misfortune to be obliged to speak with them, enter as if prepared for a fight with a tiger armed with patience and with fear. To obtain their post these persons must

have ingratiated themselves with every one, but having once obtained *it* they seek to indemnify themselves by disobliging all. *It* is a condition of their position that they should be accessible to all, yet, from pride or spleen, they are so to none. 'Tis a civil way to punish such men by letting them alone, and depriving them of opportunities of improvement by granting them no opportunity of intercourse."

- *Baltasar Gracián's*, The Art of Worldly Wisdom

Saturday, September 5th, 2020

9:45 PM

Strive as I might, I fail to repress my agitated and annoyed thoughts regarding the inane and senseless banter around me. I *truly* desire to assimilate, to blend, to be a man of utility; however, I empathize with my fellow-creatures, and I, positioned by a dish basin for a majority of my life, am regarded as a piece of impertinent amusement, easy to look at, and easier to judge, on account of the glower that often overrides my pleasant features while I exact my labor with an unparalleled resolve that often disturbs, disgusts, and *amazes* my peers... or perhaps *I* am the sole experiencer of these unpleasant feelings. The executive chef praises me as a "phenomenal dishwasher," and two of the other cooks deemed me an "awesome dishwasher." Despite my fellow-creatures operating and responding to me with affirmations and positivity, I am loath to *hear,* to *see,* to *smell* the animality, to be at the centerfold of posturing, nastiness, intrigue, invectives, mating rituals, drama... One man, in particular, who has worked at the establishment for six years, exhibits the greatest vulgarity, and never ceases to speak: deriding gossip and mockery, most of all.

I've been called "Buddy" and "Kid" more in the past two days than I have throughout my life. I suppress my desire to ask "why," lower my head, straighten my posture, and *do my job.*

Arthur Schopenhauer, who in the later stages of his life wrote philosophy on the wretchedness of existence, experienced the upper caste: parties, balls, theatre, with schooling, and two years of merchant work. How leisurely *it* must've been to write of the baseness of humanity from the loft of an ivory tower. I imagine Schopenhauer's experience differed little from mine: at the base of an often brownish-yellow basin.

At my new employment site, If I expressed the full vigor of my body, and unleashed a torrent of my thoughts, I would lose my job (again), just as I did for the opposite conduct. Understanding and *accepting* the balance of what is acceptable to society due to culture is the most difficult and exacting process I endure for my want of wanting nothing to do with *it*.

I admit, my soul, if I am to embody one, is troubled. I bend a knee to my documentation in repentance. I simply want to do "good." Nay—I *do* good; I want to *be* "good."

Sunday, September 6th, 2020

9:31 AM

I feel like a treasonous cretin regarding my conduct with Walther. My self-directed aggression and emotional pain is remarkable. I shed two tears of stupidity while setting the timer to steam broccoli, carrots, and cauliflower. I widened my eyes, clenched my fists, and patted both tears away before either could stream to the bottom of my chin, indignant with myself, for my audacity to experience a mote of self-pity.

10:41 PM

This journal is onerous, and becomes more so with each year that elapses, equatable to the mundane daily processes of defecation, or wiping away the grit from the corners of one's eye—that I document and transcribe minute details of my scuzzy life, such as this afternoon, when I arrived at the company kitchen: I had been greeted by two instances of being acknowledged as "Buddy." Feeling confident, and vibrant with circumstances, I stood among my peers and addressed them all: "Why does everyone in this kitchen call each other 'Buddy?'" The executive chef, Chayanne, a bald and frail man in his early forties, began to laugh. I continued, "I've been called 'Buddy' more times in the last two days that I've been in this kitchen than I have for my entire life."

Rob, the vulgar man of six years of employment, explained that no dishwasher tends to last long in the kitchen, so there is no bother to address people by their names. I refuted his reasoning with a simple retort of how he *knows* my name.

Chayanne stated that while he served in the Army, everyone called each other "Buddy."

I said, "Ah, so you're the one perpetuating the "Buddy-calling," to which the men joined in with my levity for the moment; thus, I inadvertently unveiled my amiability and social competence on account of my jibing, and secured a position of heightened respect, compounded by my work ethic and passion for the job.

Rob is intelligent, despite his base character, as all people are intelligent, each in their own strait. Whichever way the intellect is directed, empathy is pervasive.

Being a lucky loser is advantageous. I'm still rapt by my previous self-induced employment termination and next-day acquisition of employment. Psychiatric terminology has no bearing; I willed *it*.

Monday, September 7th, 2020

10:19 AM

On September 3rd, at 5:49 PM, Walther summoned me into the unused patron room adjacent to the high-end bar's kitchen. Alone together, I sat with Walther at a table, whereby he attempted to understand my silence and perceived lack of respect for my coworkers. I had initialized my recorder for the interaction; however, when I reinserted the device into my pocket, I canceled the recording and failed to capture the dialogue. Walther spoke for eight minutes. I listened, responded with gestures of a jovial levity, and attempted to suppress laughter, which Walther interpreted as a personal insult.

I clenched my teeth, braced both my hands on the table, decided to override my enforced mutism with one sentence I deemed essential, and stared at Walther with a grave expression while I spoke, contrary to my silent mirth: "I have obeyed every order that has been commanded to me." I proceeded to answer Walther's queries in the affirmative or negative with facial expressions, shoulder shrugs, a lapse of expression, or more *laughter*. Walther determined I have no desire to speak to anyone due to my responses and departed the building.

I returned to my labor to polish my the dish machine, walls, and basins for a tranquil twenty-five minutes. I felt akin to a man on death row, serene in my expectations of what I devised, and what I must do.

445

Walther returned at 6:25 PM and summoned me into the adjacent patron room once more for our final confrontation:

Walther's Addressal

"So, this is a document explaining how, and why, *it*'s critical to have useful communication at work. *It* also explains that without respectful and useful communication at work—which is a job requirement, *it* will lead to termination. Okay. I implore you to read this. There are also solutions outlined and suggestions outlined in *it* that you can accept, or not accept. Um, there is also a place for you to *suggest* solutions."

I attempted to suppress laughter, failed, broke my constitution with a cheeky grin, and unleashed three instances of hysterical, airy chuckles for twenty-three seconds.

Walther glowered at me, his back erect, statuesque, eyes wide. "Are you interested in taking me seriously?"

I nodded.

"Then I ask you to be respectful and not laugh at me. I don't find *it* funny; I think *it*'s really disrespectful. I'm trying to respect you, and I'm trying to accommodate you, and your desires; please give me the same respect. This is my *business; it*'s important to me, and *it* means a lot, okay? *It*'s a job requirement to have effective and respectful communication with your coworkers and supervisors. How you wish to have that communication, I'm willing to make concessions about."

I shifted in my seat and produced a muffled, pained exhalation. The feeling of ~~pity~~ sympathy pervaded my consciousness, not for myself, but for Walther and the damage to his vital reputation and *rapport* due to the misunderstandings that will develop for the enigmatic reasons of my termination.

"Will you read this please? And after you read *it* I'd like you to sign *it* to acknowledge that you've read *it* and received *it*."

I obeyed and began to read the document with no intention of signing *it,* no matter the content. My lips began to quiver with delight and I once again began to laugh, only now I felt the veins bulge from my forehead while I leaned forward over the table, document clenched in both hands, and read formal wordage simplified to: "*-became upset after [female manager name (of the high-end bar)] offered a water*"; "*-bullied another employee to prematurely* end his shift", [39] "-was rude to [female manager name (of the tavern)] when asked how his day was." Overjoyed, I began to speed read. I started from the beginning again before I finished reading the alternatives to my behavior, which consisted of writing on clipboards and communicating via written word with the staff. My jubilance shifted to awe and wonder, then, to scorn... I read the accusatory lines again, and the scenes of these people replayed in my mind. I involuntarily up-curled my lip, shook my head, and flicked the document away from me, where *it* thwacked against Walther's clasped hands rested atop the table.

"Will you sign this please?"

I proceeded to shake my head and scowled.

"You won't sign *it* saying that you read *it?* Can you tell me what you're objecting to?—because the next form is your response which you get to write any response you want, and then *I* will sign *it* saying that I received *it*... and read *it-*"

I picked the paper up from the table again and began to read the bottom-half, disinterested and vexed.

"-in which you can make *any* suggestion as to an effective and respectful form of communication that *you* wish to have with your coworkers and supervisors... that I will absolutely consider. But we need to have a respectful line of communication with each other."

I gestured with both hands outstretched to either side of me and cocked my head, to signify that what Walther and I engaged in *is* a respectful line of communication.

"I—I don't know what that means. So you don't want to make any suggestions as to how we can effectively and respectfully communicate in the workplace?"

I gazed at the second document, at the rows of blank lines, ready and available for my absurd input.

"To make special accommodations for you and your desires. Do you want to make *any* suggestions?"

I picked up the first document again and scrutinized the first-half, where the few of many accusers and self-elected sufferers of my anti-social behavior condemned me and demanded a change, for their *comfort*. A stern grimace overtook my visage; Walther sensed my imminent action.

"Would you like to take *it* home to read *it?*"

---

[39] Either Sebastian, documented on August 2nd, 2020, or Andrew, documented on August 31st, 2020.

447

I alternated between the papers, narrowed my eyes, cringed, and sighed.

"I'm trying to accommodate you here Baethan, please, help me. I'm trying to be as respectful and—and as accommodating as I can."

Our visages met, neutral and stoic.

"You—you don't want to write any response? And you don't want to sign any acknowledgment that said that you received this or read *it?* What is your suggestion moving forward?"

I shrugged and smiled.

Walther resumed, annoyed and hasty in his speech: "I'm telling you that your behavior is unacceptable on the job, and I'm asking you for help in finding a solution. Do you want to offer me *any* help in finding a solution? Please answer me affirmative or negative."

I stared at Walther.

"Do you want to have this job?"

I nodded.

"*It* is one of the parts of this job to effectively and respectfully communicate with your coworkers and supervisors. *It* can be a *clipboard,* as I suggested; *it* can be, acknowledging someone and nodding in affirmation.[40] *It* can be *any* system you want, but you won't participate in any system… of communication. I'm giving you options I thought of, and I'm giving you options of your own. And you're refusing to do either, is that correct?"

I nodded.

"So the only circumstances in which you wish to work here is if you never have to acknowledge another human being?"

I raised an eyebrow and shook my head.

"*That's* been your behavior Baethan and you *know* that. Not turning around—not acknowledging someone when they ask you to do something or talk to you,[41] is *not* respectful; *it's* disrespectful; *it's* a job requirement for you to communicate effectively in the workplace. If you want a job where you are not around other people at all and don't have to interact with anyone, this isn't the job."

I nodded.

---

[40] The instances in which I did not acknowledge someone was strictly non-work related. The chef, Alex, a night prior, pleaded with me to speak to him, to which I neglected to acknowledge him, for the demand was personal, and non-work related.

[41] There had been no occurrence of this behavior; except for the non-work related interaction with Alex the night prior after he was incited by the consul of the female bar staff to take affirmative action.

"You're okay with that?" Eleven seconds of silence elapsed. "Are you quitting?"

I shook my head.

"No—you're not quitting. You're not accepting the terms of the job so what is that—if *it*'s not quitting?"

I inhaled, chest fully expanded, exerted the full force of my will to remain silent, signed and dated both documents, set the pen on the table, and looked at Walther with a sense of (unexpressed) dutiful relinquishment of power.

"And you've chosen to give no response. Are you going to use one of these communication methods that I suggested or are you going to use a communication method that you suggest?"

I picked up the pen again, hunched over the document, contemplated my response for forty-three seconds, shifted in my seat, and sighed, with the pen's tip held a half-inch away from the start of the first blank line of the second document.

"I'm not asking a lot, Baethan. I'll communicate with the staff and train the staff to not communicate in any superfluous ways with you, but you gotta meet me in some kind of middle ground here. The workplace is not the time and place for social experiments."

On this statement, I grinned. My dearest friend—this man, who had come to understand a sliver of what the man that I am is, of what *it* was that he reckoned—yet, ignorant to the cause of my fatuous agenda… I knew upon Walther's utterance of what to write.

"I'm literally willing to have you define how you want to be communicated to, and how you will communicate with your supervisors, but you need to give me something.

I wrote: *"I'm amazed by your mag[n]aminity."* [42] and slid the paper over to Walther.

Walther remained fixed in his seat; only his eyes moved, downward, to the paper. I began to snicker. Walther's face froze. A profound emotion, implacable, indiscernible by my observation, stirred within him. I reached across the table for the paper, returned the pen to the line below my previous entry, wrote, *"Fire me,"* and returned the paper before him.

We sat and looked at the paper together. A burden that weighed on me sloughed off; Walther shouldered *it:* Heavy and wretched. I leaned back

---

[42] I not only misspelled "magnanimous," but also inserted the first "n" with an offset arrow which I initially forgot.

in my chair and relished the complete array of sensations of the moment. Walther jerked forward, grabbed both papers, and hastened out of the bar into the adjacent kitchen. I followed him into the kitchen and caught a brief glimpse of his back before he exited the back door.

I knew, by my signing of both documents and the statement that I recorded, that I had disqualified myself from unemployment benefits; however, I had no intent of filing and suckling off the state's teat again. I had no plan. The dishwashing machine loomed behind me. I turned to a new stack of dirtied plates, placed each in a neat row within the slots of a large square tray, sprayed the food off each into a strainer below, slid the tray into the machine, closed the metal door, and listened to the whir of superheated water within. Sanitized rag in hand, I resumed cleaning the wall to my right, over the drying basin, with the hope that whoever assumed my post would potentially comprehend the condition in which the environment should be maintained, out of respect for the occupation.

Walther returned in a fervor eight minutes later, anger demonstrated in his gait, a new piece of paper held by his side. I had been mid-inspection of a row of plates removed from the dish machine when Walther returned. I initialized my recorder.

"Baethan, can I have you one more time please?"

I obeyed, and followed Walther into the adjacent patron room.

"You asked to be fired—here's your termination paper. I'm going to attach the paperwork you already read. You're welcome to sign."

I signed the paper without hesitation or reading.

"You can grab your stuff; I'll clock you out. Would you like a copy?"

I assumed a thoughtful expression and nodded: A trophy. I stood by and observed the old artwork and memorabilia of the early 1900s that decorated the room's walls.

Walther's hand trembled as he passed me a copy of my notice of termination, though his voice remained calm and equipoised. "Here you are. I'll contact you when your next paycheck is available."

I acknowledged Walther with one last somber, respectful nod, and departed the room, through the kitchen, to the basement to retrieve my bag. Tears welled in my eyes, for the woe I had sown by my disgraceful and shameful conduct, though I felt no remorse. To my horror, Walther followed me, I think to either ensure I didn't steal any items or damage any property before my leave, or perhaps to record a video of me in my final pusillanimous moments in which I chose to be a coward—to *not* defend my name, to destroy my obscure reputation, to forsake my livelihood to *prove*

Walther's support of John Locke's social contract, i.e., *rapport*—to *only* myself!—to be an exiled dog, a snake, a public enemy, an absurd *anarchist*. Walther pursued me back up the stairs. I glanced over my shoulder twice: once to hold the basement door open for him, surprised and confused by his proximate presence, and again while I ascended the steps. The last Walther saw me, I had been *horrified*, on behalf of my verminous behavior; sorrowful, on behalf of Walther's loss of a number in a system.

Mental pain agonized me. I exited the establishment through the kitchen's back door, rounded the corner, and reckoned the throngs of outdoor customers and servers; thereby, I stepped back to regain my composure out of a desire to not be seen in my deplorable condition, to blink back the unjustifiable tears, for I had been *remorseless* with *myself*. I stared up at the evening sky and waited for my courage to return; forty-two seconds elapsed (my recorder captured the moment). On an alternate route, I meandered through the crowd of twilit city-life as an alien, stiff in my movements, to my apartment, where I paced, pondered, consumed, and slept with great difficulty.

Indeed, I am a lucky loser to have secured unpremeditated employment at a competitor pub the morning after. My new employer has been made aware of my previous employment site; he may correspond with Walther and discuss my behavior. Video cameras are installed all around the establishment where I now work at my new dish domain. Rob has informed me that the owner is vigilant in his observations of employees.

I am sociable and prudent with my conduct.

5:13 PM

There are no geniuses in art, only sufferers. J.S. Bach suffered extraordinarily at the ideal of the god at the forefront of his achievements, much like Da Vinci. Pain begets pain. Thus, art is essential.

How could anyone regard this exposition with a smidgen of seriousness or respect? I cannot, for any long-standing reader identifies with a degree of my pain, and delights in *it,* for we all suffer the same: miserable buffoons. Empathy is the strongest predictor of a great work of art, rendering my series of documentation unequivocal trash, for I martyr myself for the sake of myself.

The physical exertion of dumbbell squats and lunges distract my disgusted lump of consciousness.

Tuesday, September 8th, 2020

10:45 PM

I stopped by my father's apartment for the first time since moving out the last of my belongings to pick up a "housewarming gift": A reproduction 42 x 56 inch print of Francisco Goya's *Saturn Devouring his Son*.[43] I had been reluctant to visit my father, even for a gift, though I "intuited" what the item was the moment my father informed me that he had purchased and awaited the shipment of a "housewarming gift" three weeks ago. I didn't stay with my father for long: no more than twenty minutes. He is the first person I've touched (excluding being touched by wanton waitresses) since I last visited him. In our brief conversation, we shared our experiences of contempt for those we associate with; however, I shared no personal or intimate details other than how I didn't even desire to visit him, and that my presence in his home spoils my wretchedness due to his unyielding paternal "love," and possibly upsets the recent (workplace) dissension I have wrought—that *isn't* all in my mind, on account of the following passage:

I walked by nightfall to my father's apartment, and chose side roads to avoid recognition, as per my usual preferred method of travel; however, I *still* encountered a man with cerebral palsy that worked alongside me at the high-end bar before he was fired for his incompetence—much like myself. This man with cerebral palsy, Keith, is a long-established friend of my older thirty-seven-year-old, obese, unemployed, and dependant "schizophrenic" half-brother. My care to write more of my half-brother is null; the mention

---

[43] An idyllic gift, especially from my father. On my leave from my father's apartment, he said, "Now you'll have something in your home that will make you think of me." I called out over my shoulder as I rounded the corner of his property; my final spoken words to him: "I hope not."

of him now is only on account of how he perpetuates gossip on the topic of me within the city's food industry in which he is involved.[44]

Keith greeted me; he stood outside at a street corner home with another man who claimed to know me over fifteen years ago. They babbled for twenty-eight seconds, and I elected to stand and endure the inane jabbering with an amused smirk accentuating my perturbed visage which resulted in a derisive mien.

Keith said, "I thought you lived in [City Name]."

I spoke, and the words drawled out of me as a growl: "I do," for I had never confided this information to Keith.

"But your father lives on this street."

"He *does*."

"Is that where you're going now?"

I stepped two paces forward, to better illuminate my countenance from the nearby ray of a house light, addressed both men with silent, unaffected contempt, for three seconds, each in-turn, and walked away. I reckon I answered Keith's query in the affirmative with my behavior, which compromises the image I've crafted of interpersonal relationship deprivation (a reality), in conjunction with being terminated for pseudo-mutism. The potential rumor-mongering of two buffoons could diminish the effects of the obscure notoriety I've strived for...

"Reticence springs from self-control, and to control oneself in this is a true triumph. You must pay ransom to each you tell. The security of wisdom consists in temperance in the inner man. The risk that reticence runs lies in the cross-questioning of others, in the use of contradiction to worm out secrets, in the darts of irony: to avoid these the prudent become more reticent than before. What must be done need not be said, and what must be said need not be done."

– Baltasar Gracián's, The Art of Worldly Wisdom

The moment I learned of my older half-brother's associations with

---

[44] My half-brother fails to maintain employment due to his belief of being persecuted, *and* concurrent desire for social approval. There are similarities between our "~~schizophrenia~~" self-obsession; however, what differentiates us is our cognitive function and applied wisdom, which results in how we *react*. I would've ~~never~~ not sought termination at my previous site of employment if not for the unwholesome conversation Walther and I had on the essential function of rapport for an efficient business.

Keith, I realized my half-brother's spoken ignorance of my character—when he knew me as a child—would counteract the work I invested in the pure perceptions of my pseudo-mutism, thereby negating the control element of the experience.

It's all in my head!—I'm a loon!—a nincompoop, *except,* these self-judgments are not the voice of delusional madness; *it* is *my* applied logical vanity, for I know my reputation is paltry, though who I *have* influenced **validates me,** even if the memory of me occurs in another at a distant future, with a singular, summarized sentence equatable to, *"That guy was such a fucking idiot."*

1:06 PM

In the public hallway on my second-floor apartment, there is a small table adorned with domestic trinkets (e.g., a picture frame, a ceramic bowl, a table cloth). Beneath this table is a basket of books. I squatted low and rummaged through a selection of mystery, romance, action, fiction, and poems by Robert Frost. A second before I stood, disinterested, I found a small 100-page paperback by Sigmund Freud: *Leonardo da Vinci and a Memory of His Childhood.* Curious, how I mentioned Da Vinci only a day ago. I've resolved to read the entire book this evening on my day off from employment.

9:48 PM

Between grocery shopping, strength training, and food preparation, I only managed to read up to page 44. The depth of the magnified scope of the literature is gratifying—a feat I would never *want* to attempt, despite the flaws. Da Vinci's sexuality is of marginal interest to me, though Freud's insights into the mental landscape of human culture are eloquent and notable, such as an excerpt on page 34:

"Moreover people's motive for writing history was not objective curiosity but a desire to influence their contemporaries, to encourage and inspire them, <u>or to hold a mirror up before them.</u> A man's conscious memory of the events of his maturity is in every way comparable to the first kind of historical writing [which was a chronicle of current events]; while the memories that he has of his childhood correspond, as far as

their origins and reliability are concerned, to the history of a nation's earliest days, which was compiled later and for tendentious reasons."

- Sigmund Freud's Leonardo da Vinci and a Memory of His Childhood

Wednesday, September 9th, 2020

10:39 AM

At my dishwashing post, mantras of wisdom flit to the forefront of my consciousness, to remind me of the inconsequential iota of existence that I am, and of the illusions of the ego: *"All is vanity and pursuit of the wind";* [45] *"There is nothing lost or wasted in this life";* [46] *"Do as thou whilst";* [47] *"It's not what happens to you, but how you react to* it *that matters."* [48]

With these counsels at my will, I exude serenity and confidence while I limber around the kitchen—a sport, a game: a man at play, on the stage of the world constrained to his thoughts. I wield for myself what great men before me yielded, and what do I have to show for *it* other than a repackaged template of aforementioned wisdom through the documentation of sanctimonious dramas?

The voices of my ego often inform me that I'm an emotionally stunted man, either on the level of a thirteen, or sixteen-year-old-boy, and that my face and body correspond with the development. Yes, a twenty-eight-year-old-man who renders himself silent to prove the philosophy of another man,[49] chooses to be terminated *by* the other man on account of *it,* secures another job of indistinguishable features through sheer dumb luck the next morning, and carries himself with an air of unwarranted regal nonchalance.

10:21 PM

An encounter with the elderly and obese Caucasian male owner of the new establishment I work for at the end of my shift: The man waited

---

[45] *Ecclesiastes 1:14*

[46] *The Bhagavad Gita*

[47] Aleister Crowley's *The Book of the Law*

[48] Epictetus' *Enchiridion*

[49] Which is the philosophy of *other* men–of nations–of universal culture: John Locke conveyed *it* well with his social contract.

for me to exit one of the bathroom facilities. I've been instructed that I'm not allowed to exit through the backdoor, and must venture through the bar to exit out the front. I departed through the backdoor anyway on two consecutive nights. The owner and I haven't talked, except for an introduction initiated by the chef, Chayanne, on my first night of employment.

This night, I departed from the bathroom while the owner slouched forward on a countertop; his sidelong gaze over his shoulder met mine. I nodded, slow and calculated, and turned right without a word. Halfway out the backdoor, the owner said, "Have a good night, pal," with subdued provocation marked in each syllable, as if to test my reaction, and to let me know that the way that I chose to react at that moment would determine if I am to be terminated on the spot.

I turned around, one foot out the door, and met eyes with the owner, who now leaned up from the table on both hands. I sensed an overt anachronistic "wild west" attitude, an expected veneration for elders, and a belief in the Christian God. My gaze averted down and to my right for one second, while I *smiled:* a soft innocence; however, I addressed him again with a quizzical expression, as if to say, *"I mean you no harm; I only desire to be left alone and work,"* and *said,* "Take care."

I theorize that this man and Walther are friends or associates of a (competitive) nature indeterminate by my lack of knowledge or care. My speech has been minimal and tactful—only when necessary for workplace *rapport;* therefore, I've suppressed my desire to ask others of their self-assigned meaning in life, except for the chef, Chayanne, on my first day out near the dumpsters with him, and another instance with a server girl, Sara, who goaded me with the inquiry, "You don't talk much, do you?"

Chayanne's self-assigned meaning in life: To be a chef.

Sara's self-assigned meaning in life: To care for others.

I sliced my thumb with a knife while I fumbled with a bag of sauerkraut. Blood congeals around a crooked band-aid. I thought of the quote:

"There is nothing either good or bad but thinking makes *it* so."

- William Shakespeare

10:57 PM

I lay on my weight bench to digest my nightly omelet in contemplation and experienced a flicker of self-pity derived from the fact that I was terminated on behalf of the will of others (that I eschewed from disputing) who were denied my personal attention, i.e., validation. As I've proclaimed before the anticipated outcome: Being terminated did, in fact, validate me, for I willed others to action.

But is *it* good or bad?

I wash dishes and return home to no one. No one knocks on my door. My phone is idle.

An uneducated brute in the kitchen mocked Chayanne for being underweight. I thought to speak out in Chayanne's defense and refrained.

Friday, September 11th, 2020

8:44 AM

On my way out of my apartment to my site of employment, I looked up at the third-floor apartment window above my own and saw the face of the man I had spoken to before; Charlie smiled and waved.

I turned full-body, outspread my arms by my sides, and shouted, "What interesting creatures we are, in our little cubby holes!" My voice rebounded off the wall of the apartment and the opposite wall of the library.

Charlie said, "On your way to work?"

I said nothing and walked beyond the alleyway into the adjoining park of the library.

Walther sent me a message asking if I would like my last two checks mailed to me.

I responded: "I'd like to keep my word of delivering my book to you once *it*'s published, if you are interested—you didn't confirm or deny. If not, you may deliver the checks. I hope you forgive my pusillanimity on my moment of termination. I made a point to destroy my rapport to understand firsthand the breach of the 'social contract' that we discussed in the kitchen not long ago, around the time Alex first started. You, and your ~~support~~ [proponency] of John Locke served as a 'muse.' I intended no damage to your business. I'd prefer to say these things to your face, man to man; however, I presume that wouldn't be enjoyable for you, which would be understandable. I determined that rapport is essential for a dishwasher if women in power are denied personal attention, i.e., validation. The only instances I ever ignored employees were when they wanted to 'banter,' or simply for the sake of garnering my attention—this included Alex. As I said in our talk, I obeyed every command given to me (promptly). The accusations against me were comical and petty, much like my behavior."

Walther replied, "I'll hold them for you then."

9:20 PM

I often wish to scream for how much I hate myself. I am a stupid man; however, I am intolerant of displays of stupidity in others, which are abundant, even from the most intelligent among us. Thus, I am deprived, for I neglect to greet my fellow human beings, to utter a simple "Hello," or "Hi." Those who greeted me from the onset stop as the days pass. No one cares, truly, and those who do have something to gain.

I want for nothing but the exchange of fair labor to provide sustenance and shelter to my wretched body. I reckon how much of a loser I am each day by the standards of society, and accept my mortality, for thoughts of pain reap justice to my mind, as I can to relate my fair conditions and wellness of health with those who *do* suffer, whereas, I *strive* to suffer for my lack thereof. I hate what I am. I desire to be indifferent with myself; "nirvana," so *it*'s called. To love myself would be as tumultuous as my current condition.

10:28 PM

An ambulance whir. The sputter of a car engine that won't start. The laughter of women. The boisterous banter of men. I listen through my open window and marvel at all I could be.

What do I mean by this? Am I crazy, a monster? Perhaps just self-loathing. I prefer "attuned" to *reality*. Though, I may delude myself. These are only words: memories, transmogrified to text, for no one, not even myself. What a drag this would be to read; I acknowledge this fact, and continue:

A young African-American man prepped breaded chicken on a counter beside me while I weighed and bagged pre-cooked frozen chicken. The man initiated a conversation with me on the topic of our favorite music. After our exchange of trivial information, I inquired what the man's self-assigned meaning in life is. The man failed to comprehend my question; thus, I attempted to rephrase my inquiry with verbosity. "Art and family," is what the man determined; however, I inquired what the man would do if his entire family died, and he stated that he would "Go on a killing spree and then kill myself if my family died." I initiated my recorder:

"If your entire family died you'd go on a killing spree?"

"Oh yeah, I could say that one-hundred percent."

"So you're that selfish, and egotistical-"

"Me?"

"-that if your family died, that you're dependent on, that you would go on a killing spree, and kill other people that have families, and then cause more suffering onto this-"

"Well-"

"-already rife with suffering world."

Jayce said, "Yeah—like if they were murdered."

"Then you would off yourself as a final act of grace."

"Yeah… See *it*'s really just, cause I have a sibling, you know what I mean? So I wouldn't even want to think about that, you know what I mean? Because if I even had to think about that then that would drive me crazy. So I wouldn't want to think about that. Because so if I could—cuz I would just… I couldn't think about that… cuz I love my sister you know what I mean?"

"Everyone you know and love will be dead someday."

A cook in the kitchen asked another cook if he has any "drugs" on him.

Jayce said, "I have a lot of family that's already dead—like, *it* really is just my sister that I have left, so like, if she died—if she died I wouldn't care about anything, if she died, cuz I don't wanna think about that. Ya know? So, if the rest of my family died, then I, yeah—I would just kill a bunch of people."

Ten seconds elapsed; I said, "I don't understand why you would do that."

"Instead of like… moving on?"

"Yes. Grief-"

"Well because… I don't know. I guess *it*'s cuz the reason—my motive in life *is* my family, and the reason why I want to do so good in life is because of my family cuz I love 'em and they love me, and if I lose them then the only motive I had… would be gone and I wouldn't care because then I wouldn't be trying to work so hard for people I don't even know. Ya know and then I just think, well… My entire family is dead… I'm just going to kill as many people as I can… and then kill myself… cuz… we all die. I just wouldn't—cuz I wouldn't have—I wouldn't think—I wouldn't have that—I wouldn't have that thought… cuz *it's, it* would be *instant,* is what I'm telling you—like if I lost my—if I found out right now that my entire family is dead, I'm *telling* you tomorrow you'd see *it* in the news, like *it* would be that quick, ya know?"

"How old are you?"

"Nineteen."

"What other jobs have you had?"

"I worked in a warehouse. Uhhh, I used to be a dishwasher; that's about *it.* Some—some hardscaping—construction."

"Did you graduate high school?"

"Yeah I'm in college now. What about you?"

"I graduated high school."

"Did you go to college?"

"No."

"Are you going to?"

"No."

"Well what's your plan… for life?"

I said, "I don't have one."

"So what do you do?"

"I write."

"Well like, how do you get by—like, what's your-"

"What's my prerogative?"

"Well like… your situation, you know? Like how do you live?"

"I live alone, in an apartment."

"Oh you have your own apartment?"

"Yes."

"Oh, so you're set. So you just…"

"I don't associate with anybody."

"You don't?"

"Except for those who I have to, *here;* and I figured, since I was fired from my last job for not speaking-"

"Oh *really?*"

"-that perhaps I should establish a, *rapport,* with my coworkers and in the meanwhile also explore their minds—for that is what I write of."

"That's what you write about?"

"The human condition."

"Wow, you do? What are you going to do with the writing?"

"I publish a book each year."

"Oh, you write like, *books?*"

"Yes."

"Oh, are they like, popular?"

"No."

"Where do you publish them?"

"Through a publishing company called *iUniverse.*"

"Do people buy them?"

"I don't market."

"Oh."

"So are they like free to read?"

"Well… the first PDF is only a dollar; I mark the price down."

"Ohhhh, so *it's* like-"

"I mark the price down for each subsequent book that's published each year. This month will be my third."

"Third book?"

"Yes."

"You like to read a lot?"

"I do."

"I hate reading."

"Why?"

"Reading—why do I hate reading?"

"Yes."

"It's umm… *it's* just really boring. The only book I've ever read that I like was a child—*A Child Called It.* Ever read that book?"

"A Child Called It? Isn't that child slavery—the child uh, not 'slavery'… neglect and abuse?"

Jayce said, "Yeah—yeah, he was like the third most worst case of child abuse ever. Like in the entire world. Like-"

"Oh—I doubt *it's* in the entire world—*it's* just the most *known.*"

"Oh you think?"

"I'm sure there's people who are born in cells that are deprived for their entire existence, from conception to old age."

"You think so?"

"Oh yes—of course."

"Yeah—there's gotta be."

"There is no cap on human depravity."

"Wow…"

Seven seconds elapsed; I said, "So when you tell me that you would go on a killing spree if your family died, and here we are standing well-provided for, in a place where we work for people that we don't know or care about-"

"Yeah-"

"-and get paid for *it,* to sustain us, to allow us to live in our cubby holes-"

"Yeah-"

"-and feed ourselves… What is there to be so upset about and grieve, *if* your family were to die?"

"Well see the thing is if—if my family died, that's the thing that would set me off you know? Cuz that's the thing—then I wouldn't care about anything, like at all. That's the—see, cuz *it* would be like a switch, like-"

"You would want to avenge the world on account of *it,* and eliminate more consciousnesses."

"It's not so much that I would want to avenge the world; *it*'s more that… *it*'s like… *it*'s like… *it*'s just… I just wouldn't even… I just wouldn't—I just wouldn't care, about, a single, like—see I—see I care—I care about things right now, cuz I'm not crazy, you know?"

"You're not crazy but yet you exclaim that if your family died you would go on a killing spree."

"It would just be automatic—like *it* would be—*it* would be *automatic,* see-"

"You're premeditating."

"Well *no!*—cuz I don't—I don't see my family dying."

"You don't know when your family is going to die, so if you *plan* to kill people if your family dies, you are a premeditating murderer."

"It would only be premeditated if I knew my family was going to die."

"But you'll never know that, but if you plan to go on a killing spree if they *do*—which is possible, then you are… *psychotic,* according to societies' standards."

Jayce said, "Psychotic? My mom said I was a sociopath before she died, but my grandparents said I'm not, so… I don't think I am… Psychotic? Psychotic is crazy… Cuz I'd only do *it,* if *it* actually happened, and *it*'s not like I'm ever counting on *it* happening, you know what I mean? Cuz I wouldn't… ever do that… unless… I came to that reality, but I don't want to come to that reality." Twenty seconds elapsed. Jayce resumed with fervor: "Like what's something *you* love a lot; what's something *you* can't live without?"

462

"Oxygen… sustenance-"

"Okay so what if somebody took away your oxygen?"

"Then I would die."

"Wouldn't you want to kill them, and take their oxygen?"

"Not necessarily; *it*'s dependent on the context."

"Well wouldn't you want to take your oxygen back? You would just let yourself die?"

"No—I would have no need to take the power back; I would *fight,* instinctively."

Jayce inquired with a hint of pleading, "Well what's something that you love that you care about, that you don't—-that—that—that—that—like-"

I said, "Myself."

"Like… yeah… You took—I love myself a lot." Eight seconds elapsed. "Like what's something that like if someone took *it* away from you *it* would destroy you?"

"If someone took away my self?"

"No like… I *don't know*—like what if your favorite critic or someone told you that your book is really shitty?"

"I would accept *it.*"

"You would?"

"Why would I care? Why would I have a favorite critic in the first place? Why would I ever *favor* a *critic?*"

"I don't know man. What if someone, like—what if someone—I don't know."

"My *favorite critic;* that's great; you have provided ample writing material for me."

Jayce laughed and said, "Oh shit, all right, if that's what you want."

I cleaned my prep station and returned to the dish pit.

"If you feel irritated by the absurd remarks of two people whose conversation you happen to overhear, you should imagine that you are listening to a dialogue of two fools in a comedy."

- Arthur Schopenhauer

Saturday, September 12th, 2020

10:59 PM

And tonight, I love myself, though I feel no different than the night before.

Sunday, September 13th, 2020

10:11 PM

The owner of the bar I wash dishes for expressed his contempt for me with an upturned lip when I addressed him to ask if he would allow me to read in his personal loft on my break. The micro-expression accentuated the severity of his command for me to "Stay out of there." I feel like a new man: a lucky loser, acknowledged in the same manner as I have so many others.

Jayce, the nineteen-year-old that proclaimed that he would go on a killing spree if his family died, asked me what "sets me off." I thought of an answer for twenty-five hours and approached him when we were alone in the kitchen to convey *it:* "The indecency of being human." I hadn't brought my recorder with me, for I intended not to speak to anyone for personal gratification; however, I failed, for my unsettled mind regarding Jayce's question prompted me to verbally assert myself. Jayce proceeded with another thought experiment, and asked me what I would do if the world were overrun with anarchy.

I said, "I would attempt to extricate myself from human contact."

Jayce said, in a laconic summary, "You wouldn't try to band people together and become a leader?"

I contemplated an answer for at least one minute while Jayce assembled a sandwich, and said, "I have no interest in power."

The conversation ended with my statement.

Monday, September 14th, 2020

11:41 AM

I masturbate once a week with a dry hand for the health of my prostate. I lay on my weight bench and think of nothing, in particular, and focus on the sensation. Sessions last for two to three minutes, sometimes less, for I desire to cease the desire—to ejaculate hastily. The thoughts I force that serve as a catalyst for climax are of waitresses I work with, each attractive in their own way, their bodies and faces alternating in my mind while I imagine them atop me in a cowgirl position, or beneath me, in a missionary position. My sexuality is uninspired and fundamental. I think of the effort and time required to secure a mate, or several, and the consequent loss of personal investment in either mind or body, the detriment to contentment, and the liability of my quasi-controlled inconsequential reputation. I'm confident in my ability to acquire a mate in my apartment complex, or any of the women who work at the bar where I'm employed. I could, with ease, venture to an alternate bar after my shift and secure a quick and easy romp with minimal fallout. There is no satisfaction in any of *it*.

Homosexual thoughts occur when I view myself on account of my vanity. I've masturbated in front of a mirror, and to a live recording of myself, ejaculated onto millipedes, and performed many deviant, albeit "innocent" acts of sexual self-indulgence. To gratify another man sexually is abhorrent to me; I know on account of experience, and of being a man— to know the condition of our sexual nature firsthand, and to appease *it*, is too *easy*. There is a thrill in the pursuit of a woman, even if the impetus is nonsexual.

I experienced my first thoughts of murder yesterday, to my chagrin and disturbance. A waitress I am attracted to, and she to me, displays her interest with a naivety on par with her lack of education and wisdom. She is attracted to me for my physicality, and evaluates *only* my physique and strength, irrespective of my intellect or discernment of my character. I strive to ignore her, yet this woman delays her actions near me, initiates prolonged (unreciprocated) eye contact, and flirts with other men in the kitchen with me in her sight, to gauge my disinclined reactions—which *would* be indifference, if I were not *interested* on behalf of the psychology of our interactions, and of my own attraction to her sleek and supple figure, her youthful prime, and extreme femininity. The few instances I've met

465

gazes with her, I assume a countenance of malice or ambivalence in a genuine effort to repel her; however, these acts amplify her interest, to my disappointed amusement; thus, I fantasized of killing her via strangulation mid-coitus while I sanitized a countertop and drank a cup of coffee. I don't identify with these horrendous conceptions of human depravity and moral degradation, though I *am* intrigued by my capacity for that which I condemn.

4:05 PM

I've finished Freud's work, *Leonardo da Vinci and a Memory of His Childhood*, and have gleaned a few bits of trivia and a convoluted, magnified perspective of conclusions determined by inferred knowledge of Da Vinci's life. I giggled often and involuntarily cocked my head throughout the read.
Tonight, I have decided to visit multiple bars in search of a mate.

Tuesday, September 15th, 2020

2:52 PM

Becoming less as you are and more of something else is a matter of a perspective and behavioral shift. "Legends" are those who refuse to adapt or to experience growth, or regression, for that matter. Memorable characters are puerile: those who remain constant, deluded by the unique authenticity of their "self," and the integrity of their social demonstrations.[50]
Last night I walked between four bars, one being the tavern where I was once employed, and informed the twenty-two-year-old kitchen worker, Logan, of the true reasons as to why I was terminated, for he informed me of the misinformation he learned on account of employee gossip, and his own indignation in regards to Walther.
The bars were sparse of female patrons, though two out of the six unattended women I approached responded favorably to my inquiry of, "I'm in search of a mate; are you interested?" One forty-seven-year-old woman began to fret and panic about my proposition, and was ultimately stymied by her protective male roommate (i.e., her guardian), who discouraged her from attending me back to my apartment. I departed from that dive bar

---

[50] The fictional character of Howard Roark from Ayn Rand's book, *The Fountainhead*, is a quintessential example.

(The Messy House) and visited a sports bar *(The Bullpen)* directly across the street from my apartment, where I encountered a gorgeous young woman with a pleasant round face, glasses, well-conditioned hair, and a robust, fertile physique, seated alone at the counter. The conversation I recorded between us is insightful into the general status of American culture and the relations between the sexes:

I stood to the woman's right in the lively environment, surrounded by unaccompanied older men engrossed with four televisions displaying a football game, and couples seated at round tables behind us. Sports jerseys and framed football mementos adorned the walls. I said, "Excuse me."

The woman set her phone down, whirled her head towards me, bright-eyed, and said, "Yeah—what's up?"

"I'm searching for a mate."

"What?"

I leaned closer. "I'm in search of a mate."

"'I'm in *search of a mate*,'" the woman repeated and giggled, "What do you mean?"

"I—I mean exactly what I'm saying."

"Well, you can come sit next to me-"

I said "All right" and veered behind the woman to seat myself on the chair to her left. "Now I can take my face mask off, that way, you can assess me."

The woman's persistent giggles developed into hearty laughter and she said, "Okay. Where are you from?"

"Where do I live, or what is my place of origin?"

"Either or."

"I live right across the street."

"Okay."

"I'm from [City Name]."

The woman's high-pitched voice intoned a mood of delight: *"Oh,* okay, okay. *I'm* [also] from [City Name]."

I said, "Did you go to [School Name], by chance?"

"No, no. Um, my mom works at the high school."

The woman laughed while I nodded and thought of a segue for three seconds: "I've been asking random people this question but I find that I'm genuinely attracted to you."

"Oh—*whaaat?*" The woman laughed, unrestrained; however, our eyes

467

remained fixed on one another. I turned my chair to align my posture towards her. "Okay?" she stated as a perplexed query.

"So I'm-" The bartender asked if I would like a drink, to which I responded: "I'll, uh, I'll take a water."

The woman giggled and spoke with a sudden sternness, "What year did you graduate?"

"2011."

"Okay—okay."

"How old are you?"

"Uh—I'm twenty-four."

I cocked my elbow, offered my hand for a customary shake, and said, "My name is Baethan."

"Morgan."

Morgan gripped my hand harder than any man ever had before and throttled my arm; I said, "That's a *firm* handshake; that's *dominant*." Morgan persisted with giggling. I said, "What is your self-assigned meaning in life?"

"My what?"

"Your self-assigned meaning in life."

"What do you *mean?*"

I reached for my water and said, "The meaning that you have chosen for your existence."

"Um…" Morgan laughed, which incited me to laugh.

I said, "We are born into this world to suffer, so what is the meaning that you have chosen for your life?"

"Uhh… Just to enjoy life I guess."

"Is that why you're here?"

"That's why I'm here." Morgan's unfaltering smile and intermittent laughter encouraged me. "What about you?"

"To write."

"To write?"

"Yes."

"Okay—that's cool. What do you like to write about?"

"The human condition."

"Okay."

Two seconds elapsed; I said, "I don't talk to people much." Morgan's consistent (possibly alcohol-induced) laughter began to make me feel somewhat condescended to. "I'm usually alone."

"Awww—okay."

"No—no—that's nothing to pity-"

"Okay."

"-I *choose* to be that way."

"Okay."

"But-"

Morgan said, "I spend all day with people."

"Are you in human resources or health care, school?"

"No—I sell cars."

"Oh. You're a *charlatan."*

"I'm what?"

"You're a charlatan, then."

"What does that *mean?"*

I grinned and said, "A person who cons people."

"No! I do not."

We laughed together. Six seconds elapsed. I said, "Well, if you're a car salesman[51]… is *it* a job that you take pride in?"

"Oh for sure, yeah."

"So what characteristic about yourself do you pride yourself on the most?"

"Uh, I think I'm like kind and courteous. Like uh, I genuinely care about people; uh, I don't want them to get screwed over, you know—I want to make sure everyone gets a good deal, you know—not the usual characteristics of a car salesperson."

"That's… uncharacteristic of a car salesman to care about people."

Morgan's boisterous laughter accentuated the glee of her response: "I know! I know. *It's* hard; *it* makes *it* hard, but…"

"Are you single?"

"What?"

"Are you single?"

"I—I am, yep." More laughter.

"Are you looking for a good time?"

Amplified laughter. "Um—that's what I came here for—to watch some football for a good time."

"You can watch football at home."

"No—but *it's* not as *fun!"*

"So you like to come here—to a loud bar, where you can't even hear *it?"*

"Yeah!—these are my friends!" she waved her right hand out towards

---

[51] I addressed Morgan's occupation with a male denotation throughout the dialogue.

the two busy bartenders and three overweight men seated at the other end of the bar with crossed arms across their abdomens.

"Were you waiting for someone like me?"

Morgan's laughter interspersed her response: "No-ho-*ho-ho-ho-*"

I also laughed and continued: "For someone like me to come in and make a complete ass of myself?"

"Stop!—You're fine."

"No—no—I'm not embarrassed or worried but, but that's what I set out to do. But, here we are; I live right across the street… " I outstretched both my hands, shrugged, and rested my left elbow against the counter. "If you're not interested I'll go."

"No—you can sit down—enjoy yourself—we can talk—*it*'s fine." Morgan giggled.

"Ah, see, I like to have conversations with *purpose.*"

"Okay."

I affirmed, "Action."

"Okay."

"Take the initiative, so—I don't know; perhaps I'm coming on way too hard to you." Morgan's giggle persisted. "So *it*'s—I—I don't know, I mean… This isn't my *norm.*"

"Okay."

"I'm putting myself *out there.*"

"That's good—good for you! Yeah."

I shook my head, grimaced, and muttered, "Please—c'mon."

Morgan laughed and said, "Wha-ha-haat?"

I gazed down, to my left, and said, "All right-"

"I mean… yeah." Giggles. Six seconds elapsed; Morgan said, "Do you watch football?"

"I don't. I have no interest in football."

Morgan murmured the meek acknowledgment of "Okay."

"I read."

"Okay that's cool."

I attempted to impress with a hasty follow-up of: "Read and write."

"What kind of books do you like?"

"Psychology, sociology, and… a lot of philosophy."

"That's good!"

"Right now I've been reading *Behave,* by Robert Sapolsky."

"Okay."

"*It*'s on the biology of humans at their best and worst, and I just finished a book by Freud on the sexuality-"

"Freud—oh my god—she's—he's really good."

"Did you say 'she' at first?"

"No, I didn't." Giggles. "I've been drinking—I'm sorry."

"Bah, that's fine."

"I took psychology in college and Freud, he's like my favorite."

"He's your favorite?"

"Yeah."

I said, "I don't... agree with Freud for the most-"

"That's okay—you don't have to!" Laughter.

"Well I know I don't *have* to; I'm just letting you know!"

"Okay." Giggles.

"Freud... his psychology is outdated; *it* seems archaic-"

"Yeah."

"-when he pieces information together... *it*'s mostly inferred."

"Yeah."

"There's no grounds... for many of his... presumptions, about people. Leonardo da Vinci, and his sexuality for instance; that's what I just read of, and..." Morgan looked away from me, downward and to her left, disinterested. "Yeah—Freud—I'm not one for Freud."

Morgan resumed eye contact, smiled, giggled, and said, "Okay."

"I'm more of a philosopher, you could say—I enjoy probing people's minds, which *is* psychol-"

"Okay."

"... But, I have no friendships by choice, and I'm a complete asshole-" Morgan burst with jovial laughter that exasperated as I finished speaking the sentence: "-so I decided to go out tonight, to find a mate. And I'm just asking people—and here I am having a conversation with you—you wanted to watch football—I'm... I'm just a random entity that showed up, with testosterone, against your estrogen... So, my masculina-" I began to laugh on account of Morgan's laughter. "My masculine energy is being projected against your feminine—but, you had a dominant handshake, so... you came off as masculine to me."

"I-"

"You're also watching football so that's masculinity too, so perhaps you're a feminist."

Morgan uttered, "I am," between her fit of breathless laughter.

"You are!"

"Yeah!"

"So I must be a complete *ass* to you then."

"No *it*'s-"

"Because here I am asserting my masculinity energy against your femininity."

"It's fine."

"Though all I want is some… a good *time.*"

Morgan *laughed,* and *laughed,* for eight seconds, and said, "Oh man." She began to text someone on her phone. I sat beside her, consternated on the moment, and inspected my surroundings in silence for one minute and fifty-four seconds while I waited for her to finish and set the phone back onto the countertop.

I turned to Morgan and said, "I'm a very strange man."

Morgan said, "Okay," and resumed laughing.

"I want to know if you're interested."

"Um, I mean, to talk to you that's fine, but other than that—like-"

I laughed.

"-I'm good, but thank you."

I glanced away and said, "All right."

"It's nothing against you—I'm just…"

I said plainly, "Oh *it*'s absolutely against me."

"No!—*It*'s not!"

"Of course *it* is."

"No-oo."

"If I was more of your… presumed 'type'… or… or your ideal, I'm sure that you would have no problem hopping in bed with-"

"No!—I'm not like that; no—I'm a mom."

"You're a mom!"

Morgan laughed and said, "I'm a mo-mom… so I just don't; I don't go around, you know… I don't know."

"I don't either, but I thought I'd try tonight-"

"-Well-"

"-To just go around and-"

"-Good for you though! Put yourself out there—that's great! That's awesome. *It*'s hard."

"Well, that was uh… Now you're emasculating me."

Morgan proceeded with persistent bouts of genuine laughter and said, "No—I'm not—I'm not trying to!" I chuckled. "I like to um, I like to build people up, you know?" I turned away from her and reached for my water. "There's nothing *wrong*… with, with what you're doing."

I said, "Oh—oh I know there's nothing wrong."

"Okay."

I muttered, "Hm," pressed the knuckles of my left hand against my chin with my left elbow resting on the counter, and said, "Perhaps… Well… I can ask for your number, but I would need to know… if you're sexually attracted to me." More laughter—from Morgan. "If not, I won't even bother."

Morgan said, "No, *it*'s okay—*it*'s okay," and I laughed. "No—so, yeah, *it*'s a no."

"All right."

Morgan shifted in her seat, reached out a hand without touching me, and said, "I appreciate your stance—like being straightforward though."

"I appreciate your honesty."

"Yeah! Always. Do you go out a lot—do you come out a lot?"

"No."

Morgan said with a tinge of pity: "No—okay, you should! You got good energy."

"… Ah… This energy is a rare moment for me."

"Ah, okay—okay."

Twelve seconds elapsed. I aligned my body towards Morgan and said, "I find human relations to be… disgusting."

"Aw noooo-"

"No—there's no 'oh no' about *it*-"

Morgan said, "No—*it*'s a good thing. Being with someone is special." I frowned. "*It* is!—not to be like corny or anything; human interactions are great."

"Yes… *it*'s, the basis of our humanity and *it*'s essential for… *rapport* and *validation*… but… what *it* all comes down to, *is* the validation, and that's what I find disgusting."

Humorless and leery, Morgan said, "Okay I hear ya."

"But… Yeah… I'll probably end up going to a different bar, and asking someone the same questions that I asked you, and I'll be rejected-"

"-*Ohhhhhwa-*"

"-over and over again. There was one woman who accepted-"

"-Oh she did!-"

"-but a man intervened."

"Ohhh. *Awwww.*"

"That was about fifteen minutes prior to me coming here. But, *it*'s—*it*'s—*it*'s redundant; *it* doesn't mean anything."

"I know.[52] Yeah… *it*'s hard." Morgan giggled.

"No—*it*'s not hard—*it*'s *easy,* to just, *ask* people things and receive their answers; we're all of the same consciousness. And we all judge each other on our physicality and the energy that we put out," I droned, "So… We put on our pretentiousness; we get all dressed up." Morgan gestured at my rote black dress shirt and giggled. I spoke as if to a mirror, *"It*'s all contrived and pretentious…"

"What do you drink?"

My amiable mien returned; I said, "I drink water." Morgan's inexorable red-faced laughter persisted; for what reason, I don't know. "But if I'm drinking alcohol, *it*'s usually a cabernet or some red wine, but I haven't drunk in a long time, probably about a year."

"Okay. Good for you."

"Well, eh, what's 'good' about *it?*"

"I mean-"

I chuckled, for Morgan's sake, and said, "That I'm… sober?"

"You could! You could drink. *It*'s always an option—you don't have to; that's good for you. Right?"

"I don't think there's good or evil."

"Okay."

Thirty-eight seconds elapsed; I said, "All right, I'll leave you to the football game that you can't hear."

"Thank you, I-" Giggles. "-you enjoy your night, and hopefully you'll find a mate."

"Thank you. I hope I don't, but I'm going to try."

"Awwwww. Why go searching if you're not looking?"

"I want to invite chaos into my life-"

"-Wha-ha-*ha-at?*-"

"-and finding a mate is the best way to do that."

"Well if you ever need a car, come see me and I'll help you out, okay?"

"A car?"

"A car; like a, do you drive?"

"Why are you offering me a car?"

---

[52] On this proclamation of Morgan's "knowing," I acknowledged the inane fatuousness of the entire scenario, of my charade, and of the superficial responses to my appeals to her vanity.

"No, if you ever need help, getting into a car, I'll help you out; I'll make sure you get a good deal."

"Oh... oh, I see."

Morgan laughed.

I said, "No—I don't think I'll ever have any interest in that, though, I appreciate *it.*"

"Okay, of course. You have a good night."

"You too."

"Thank you."

I stood, sipped my water through a straw, set the half-filled cup down, strode out of the establishment, crossed the street, entered the foyer to my apartment, summoned the elevator, rode up to the second floor, walked through the carpeted hallway, and entered my apartment.

9:39 PM

I've stopped by the tavern twice the past two days to speak information I deemed critical to perpetuate confusion and correct misinformation regarding my self-termination. I have no desire to give a copy of my third publication to Walther, or to anyone, for that matter. On my second visit, I requested to speak with the female manager who contributed to my list of accusations that resulted in my volition for self-termination and had been informed by the bartender with the same name as myself that she is absent.

The bartender asked if I would like him to tell the female manager that I desire to speak to her, to which I replied that I am indifferent. I have no intention to return; my intent is spiteful: If the bartender is to inform the female bartender of my personal interest in her, the unrequited communication may cause her extreme consternation; thus, she may relay these feelings to Walther, which would serve to reinforce my conclusion regarding the breach of the (dishwasher's) social contract.

I'd rather void every relationship involved with both of the establishments, for these people... *people...* my intentions are only ignoble, amoral, and selfish; I'm better off without influence; I'd be corrupt with even a smidgen of *it.*

I begin to feel sorrow: the dreaded self-pity, and pity for the entire spectrum of world affairs of the human race while listening to J.S. Bach's *Wir setzen uns mit Tranen nieder* through a single earbud, which amplifies the drama of my mental scape and delusional self-importance. I respect these men and women I'd only hurt by affiliation, even if they despise and pity me in-turn for my lack of championing—nay, I've identified my delusions; only *I* care and know of my squandered potential.

The feelings of despair fleet—ephemeral nothings, circumvented by resolve and an adamant will to remain... forbearing. I'm deadened. My toxicity and infernal "influence" must remain condensed to these pages, obscure, unreckoned, unheeded, and if otherwise: mocked, derided, condemned and damned, despite my will to *be...* something, what *it* is—my "self-assigned meaning in life"—what *hubris!* The vanity of my endeavor is equivalent to waking and persisting each day—hour—minute—*moment,* in the same manner as any other human, to those dead and yet to be born. The emotional drama constrained to these words, conveyed through italics and grammar, is an ineffable encapsulation of the magnitude of my disillusionment and dissonance.

Wednesday, September 16th, 2020

11:24 AM

I wake to wash kitchenware for a man who contempts me. My path is folly; my existence: moot. I'm treasonous only to myself, for the virtues I adopt at the behest of alternating employers, providers, and society, dictated by culture. There is no morality worthwhile of which to be counterposed.

Sanctimonious?—What matter is *it;* I work among minds awash with hog shit, manifest in action and word.

Thursday, September 17th, 2020

7:45 AM

My confidence wanes when I ruminate on the tribes of people I no longer care about; otherwise, my confidence is unwarrantedly astronomical. The gaggles of loquacious harlots and factions of intemperate men, crass in behavior and expressions, are malignant byproducts of a decadent environment populated with the proletariat. I could write a novella on the turpitude, extravagance, and licentiousness of the bar and restaurant culture that spawns behind the comeliness of a well-executed meal or the fabulous flourish of a poured drink, though that would require effort and repose. Instead, I will encapsulate my ~~complaints~~ observations with a succinct parallel of *my* character juxtaposed against the typical profligate and rapscallion you'd discover under the exterior pretense of your common waiter, bartender, and chef:

In sincerity, what am *I*, but a devoted and austere man?

"An asshole," replies the voice of my ego.

And why is this?—is there no better word? Scoundrel? Wretch? "Sociopath"? *Why?*—for I desire to be extricated from the whole of the human race in whatever manner viable while also procuring the means to contribute my trite?

No, what qualifies me the title of an "asshole," or "douchebag," or those aforementioned nouns in the previous paragraph, is that I *seek* my fellow-creatures for observational experience and pain in tandem—*not*, for the potential joy or pleasure.

I resort to my fourth listening session of James Allen's *As a Man Thinketh*[53] while I prepare a six-egg broccoli omelet with cacao, blueberries, chia seeds, blueberries... experience a thought of revulsion tinged with disdain on writing the pre-ellipses segment of this sentence, take solace in the fact that I *will* be dead eventually, and of my ignorance as to when and how.

1:26 PM

Yes, my self-proclaimed austerity is tested by a supple nubile, sensitive and judgmental of men's characters. I've yet to speak a word to her except for cordialities throughout the two weeks we've become acclimated to each other, akin to my interactions with the entire staff, except for the "executive" chef, Chayanne, who is prone to outbursts of anger that reduce him to an obdurate infant. The attraction between myself and this woman, Beatrice, is paramount when she is proximate. I'm welted up with testosterone, in "search of a mate."

---

[53] Quasi-therapy sessions.

Friday, September 18th, 2020

10:51 AM

Last night, a late-thirties Caucasian chef in the corporate kitchen, Jonathan, called Jayce by phone (the nineteen-year-old who would go on a killing spree and then kill himself if his family died) and fired him on behalf of the owner, for the reason: "Things aren't working out." Afterward, Jonathan danced around the kitchen while chanting "I just fired Jayce" with a prideful sing-song inflection, and relayed a false account of the conversation (that I overheard) with disparagements of Jayce's intelligence and Jonathan's self-touted assertiveness. For each waitress that passed through the kitchen, this communication repeated until all opportunities were exhausted.

Who cares but Jayce?—a mass-murderer in the making.

Saturday, September 19th, 2020

8:37 PM

A spat occurred in the corporate kitchen yesterday, whereby Chayanne, the executive chef, gripped the handle of a hot pan without prior knowledge, and proceeded to shout a tirade of obscenities at the twenty-six-year-old Caucasian cook, Thor, who failed to verbalize a warning. Chayanne "got in the face of" the subordinate cook—their noses a mere inch apart. I observed from the opposite corner of the kitchen, engaged with sorting cleaned silverware into respective cubbies, involuntarily tilted my head, and grinned at the childish spectacle. The illusory serenity of the kitchen had dissipated to reveal the natures of the base men I work in the same chamber with for upwards of nine hours a day, five days a week. A radio station that emanates alternative angst music circa the 1980s-1990s refined the scene with an otherworldly elegance fit for a high school gymnasium locker room.

The owner's son (the general manager) emerged from the adjacent bar, interrupted with his meal. The manager evaluated the men, myself included, to which he acknowledged my silent drollness and turned away, nonplussed and peeved—not with me; in fact, my response of "I'm all right," to the owner's query of "Are you all right?" followed by the censorious amusement expressed on my countenance, prompted the manager to raise an eyebrow and grin.

The men resumed their work in a state of sullen dismay. The manager left the kitchen. Chayanne berated Thor and called the manager a "sorry bastard" for "sitting on his ass and eating during a rush." Thor, a rational, though impertinent man, endured the harassment in silence. Impressed by his prudence, I thought to counsel him as a friend in private, then thought better of *it*. By the night's end, when Chayanne and I were alone together, he muttered to himself; however, I listened to the content of his wrathful soliloquy, to which he professed the abuses he suffered on behalf of his co-workers, and shirked his duties, whereby he neglected to clean the floor and departed early.

Before my shift began I requested to conversate with Beatrice at the end of our labors if she found the conditions to be agreeable: Beatrice agreed with a delightful, "Sure!" Six of the staff members witnessed my proposition, including the matriarchal owner. Thus, the arrangement being a public affair, and unexpected, due to my accustomed silence, allowed Beatrice the time to ponder the potentialities and her decision to my anticipated courtship. The recorded conversation:

Beatrice arranged silverware behind me while I finalized my duties. Before I initiated my recorder, she complained of her responsibility to put her daughter to bed in a timely manner, and of her being "tired." This information foreordained the outcome of our interaction; however, I approached her three minutes later and said, "I'm all set. When you're ready to talk, I'll be outside."

"Outside? *All right*—um-"

"Or would you prefer to talk-"

"We can just talk right here; what's up?"

"Talk here. Well, I'll start by saying that I'm attracted to you."

Beatrice blushed and said, "Thank you."

"*It*'s superficial, though. I don't know anything about you other than you have a daughter, and you're tired."

I've been called into work an hour early and must postpone transcription.

I read an article this morning that vexed me, one that postulated that "narcissists need to be accepted and not stigmatized for their *mental health condition.*" Why I even bother to scroll through my Lord's brain-jacking protocol phone feed to read trend-of-the-hour soothsaying is the fount of my vexation—*my* decision to do so.

Yes, I'm vexed by the sounds around me: the mournful yearnings of those who complain of their sufferings aloud in the hope of one who may respond, and of the females who jitter and act coy to be alluring; Beatrice, most of all. The woman's simplicity has rendered her wise to pass on me on account of not having the time to juggle a daughter and two men. If my physique were more virile and robust, her baseness would be the impetus for her... *death?* Yes... she is wise to forgo me. I'm alarmed by my train of thought lately, scared, of my uninhibited confidence *and* deference.

No, I would never kill; how pretentious I am to even play a role in the writing of myself as a "certified psychopath." I'd rather fantasize about our animality, our creaturehood. The moment I begin to feel compassion, I reckon a mirror in the faces I see, the judges of humanity, for each man and woman may only know themselves in others; I see only beasts. Flesh. Organisms brimming with inner organisms. What of *it*, that we are of the same species? Is this sentiment intended to preserve our race? What rapport is there, beneath the deceit, the dissimulations, the treachery and lust behind every benevolent and magnanimous act... the kindness, the *niceness.*

Socially retarded? Mentally and emotionally inhibited? Sexually frustrated? Malignant narcissist—bipolar—schizoid—borderline—dark triad machiavellian—sadistic masochist-

"Asshole is more like *it*," my ego, *my* ego reassures me.

"The situation has provided a cue; this cue has given the expert access to information stored in memory, and the information provides the answer. Intuition is nothing more and nothing less than recognition."

- Herbert A. Simon

The truth, to the best of my knowledge, is that I don't know what I would do with a woman except for torture myself. *Or* a man.

I've severed communications with my father for the final time. I'm more distant from him now than I was in Arkansas. The rift is permanent. *"All I've ever done is love him,"* I reckon the self-pitying decree of my father, imagined, as *it* were, yet if I were to act on the slightest notion of remorse or compassion, I would be consumed.

Candy still emails me. In the last message received, Candy thanked me for all the wonderful memories she has of me, with a *.gif* image of a man kissing a woman.

Sunday, September 20th, 2020

10:22 PM

I interviewed a group of people outside of a bar: A drunk man, a sober woman, a sixteen-year-old girl, and a woman who cowered and turned away from me when I began to speak. The self-assigned meaning in life of:

Drunken man: "Make money and take care of my family."

Sober woman: "Be happy."

Sixteen-year-old-girl: "I don't know."

Cowering woman: No response.

At another bar, a block away from the tavern, I entered and…

I don't care; there is nothing, I… One drugged-up man's life meaning is to achieve the highest scores on the bar's *Pac-Man* arcade machine. When I, incredulous, asked for a confirmation of this proclamation, the man accused me of being rude, and inquired of *my* "achievements." The man probed at my occupation, and inferred me to be a busboy or a waiter based on my style of dress. I informed the man that I am a dishwasher, that he chooses to be upset at my perceived rudeness, and that I write "books." He outstretched his elbow for me to bump with my own elbow. I called myself a scumbag and walked out.

My feelings are my own; my pity for humanity is *entirely* my own; however, to be in this state, I must pity myself, and I am loath to do so; therefore I contempt—though the feeling is intrinsic, directed inward. Confusion abounds.

Tonight I experienced a myriad of emotions in the kitchen where I am employed, whereby my stupefied smile on account of the stupidity spoken in my vicinity incited compliments to my work—and when I began to *scorn,* within the same *hour,* those around me acclimated, and kept their distance. I experienced sorrow, suppressed tears... *anger* followed, and a brief interlude of peace due to circular breathing—and pity again, for *it* all—for my lack of love, my deprivation, my annihilation of my self.

Terrible writing: A dramatic little boy posing as a man.

No more bar visits. I have discredited Pelagia's (important) reputation with my disreputable actions on account of her rumor-mongering tendencies and previous outspoken pride of her association with me when I had been a... *"respectable gentleman,"* by the esteem of others, prior to me entering Navy Boot camp. I care too much of what is inconsequential, valueless, and merely probable: The human condition. What of *it?*

Monday, September 21st, 2020

9:29 AM

Joyless, by my own volition, with too much time to squander; I resume transcription of the conversation with Beatrice:

Beatrice said, "-Yeah."

"So the point of this conversation was to discover more of what your stance is."

"Well technically—I mean I am single, but, I'm in a place where we're trying to work things slow—I do have—*it*'s been a complicated relationship going on. Um... *It*'s hard lately now because I want more but he's just—*it*'s just really weird. So I'm just not really like, in a great place, honestly—yeah, to be honest. Yeah my life is complicated," Beatrice giggled. *"It*'s been insane... Up and down... this year has been tough. You know what I mean?" Affected laughter.

I said, "I understand."

Beatrice muttered, "Yeah," knowing that I didn't understand. "Um, well—what was I gonna say—see I'm tired." Giggles. "I'm sorry. But *it*'s *flattering;* thank you, I appreciate *it;* you seem very nice." I grimaced, looked down to my left, opened my mouth to say, *"I'm not nice,"* however, Beatrice continued: "But, so what do you do, besides work here?"

"I write-"

"You write?"

"I read."

"What do you write about?"

"The human condition."

"The human *condition?* Um-"

"*It*'s a broad-"

"Um, what?"

"*It*'s broad."

"Broad... So, what do you mean by 'the human condi—I know you said 'broad'—but I mean, do you have any examples?"

"Yes," I grinned. "Recently, I was fired from my last job for not speaking; *it* was a social experiment, and I documented the entire thing."

"Ohhh, that's really cool."

"I publish a book each year; my third book is being published this month, in about a week or two; *it*'s a continuation until I die."

"That's really awesome."

"I spend all my time alone, and I was hoping to... develop an intimate relationship with someone, and I've been observing people here quietly, and I decided that you attracted me the most."

Beatrice whispered, "Thank you."

"I thought I would outreach, to see what happened, but, I understand your position."

"Thank you; I appreciate *it*. Yeah-" Beatrice produced an exasperated laugh. "But yeah I'm an interesting character so you could definitely write lots of books about me!" Beatrice lifted a tray of silverware and veered into the adjacent bar room.

I departed, pleased and relieved to have been rejected—to have sought the opportunity, and to be spared. On my return home, I experienced a surreal state of bliss: ephemeral and potent; a deluge of repressed dopamine wafted between my synapses and induced me to sleep with a vegetative smile.

1:02 PM

The general manager where I'm employed attempted to speak with me on a personal level while we worked in the kitchen. A recorded fraction of the conversation:

I said, "So, what would you say your self-assigned meaning of life is?"

Adrian (the owner's son and manager) said, "My *self-assigned meaning*— right now *it*'s probably: raise my kids. I have an ex-wife who is a degenerate alcoholic; she's only seen her kids *twice* since January, right now living in a halfway house. That's my main concern: to take care of my kids." Five seconds elapsed. "The last visit which—I can't remember how long—three months ago maybe, we had to cancel the visit because she was drinking and showed up drunk; *it* was fucked up. Her brother had to end the visit."

"What was your self-assigned meaning prior to your children?"

"Self-assigned meaning... I don't know if I had one; I was just livin'. You know I've been here for... twenty-two years; *it's* like a fuckin' prison sentence."

"A prison sentence, you said?"

"I've been here for twenty-two years!"

"Oh so *it* feels like-"

"*It's* been like a prison sentence. Like my uncle Joe used to tell me—he's the chief of police: 'If I would've just killed my wife back in the day I'd be out of jail by now.'" Adrian chuckled.

I said, "I think that prison would be the better deal because you're fed three meals a day for free."

Adrian's boisterous laughter compounded and the conversation between us segued to him and Thor.

There is a male server in his late-forties that I work alongside named Willy, meager in constitution, at a height of no more than 5'2, with an affable, acquiescent character. We wrapped silverware into napkins next to each other and I initialized my recorder:

I said, "What is your self-assigned meaning in life?"

Willy said, "My what?"

"Your self-assigned meaning in life."

"That's a very good question—I don't know if I have one; right now *it's* taking care of my dog. He's the only thing that keeps me sane. I've had him for ten years... and he's been through *everything* with me, and everywhere."

"How many places have you been to?"

"A lot. Ummm... I lived in... Well, I lived in Boston for twenty years and then I lived in Santa Clara, California. I lived *here*, then I lived north of Boston, grew up south of Boston, and I toured the entire coast of California."

"Touring for pleasure or for business?"

"Yeah—for fun, with some friends; seeing the sights; *it's* beautiful... driving the 101, which goes right along the ocean. What about yourself?"

"What places have I been to?"

"Yeah."

"I've been to Florida... to Illinois... to Arkansas-"

"How's Arkansas—is *it* hot?"

"… Yes."

"All right—I gotta go check on a table—I'll be back." Four minutes elapsed; Willy returned.

I said, "What characteristic about yourself do you pride yourself on the most?"

"Laughter is essential."

"Do you know any funny jokes?"

"I do."

"What's your best joke?"

"Um, my best? That's a tough question; I'll have to think about that—well off the top of my head: You know the best thing about dating a homeless girl?"

"What?"

"You can drop her off anywhere." I snickered. Willy guffawed and said, "Ahh—*it*'s terrible but funny."

"What troubles you the most?"

Willy grimaced and said, "Ah… Ignorance… I guess."

"You must be greatly troubled."

"Yeah! I-" Willy shook with laughter. "Yeah, no shit huh?"

"I think we all are, if we had that perspective."

"The world would be an easier place if everyone minimalized their lives and, cut back to the basics; just be, just do the right thing you know what I mean? Pretty fuckin' simple. People make *it* complicated. *But,* you know the majority of people are crazy, so…"

"Now what gives you that impression? The DSM-5?"

Willy said, "I don't even—what is that?"

"*It*'s the psychiatric jargon handbook."

"Oh… Oh shit—I stopped watching the news cuz *it*'s so ridiculous. I moved out here to simply live my life, and I have; *it*'s been lovely. Just me and my dog."

"No interest in women?"

"Not right now… I mean I am, just taking a break… You know unless someone wants to get naked, then that's a different—that's a different cup of tea… What about yourself—you got a girlfriend?"

"I've recently tried, though I mostly encounter strong independent women."

"Yeah."

"Do you think that all virtue is pretentious?"

"Well I guess *it* depends on how you look at *it*."

485

"That's an ambiguous answer; you may as well have *not* answered."
Willy laughed and said, "Yeah, you are correct."
"Well, the question still stands, if you'd like to think about *it*."
"Yeah—I don't know. I'm gonna go check on some people."
I don't expect to ever receive an answer.

Tuesday, September 22nd, 2020

9:35 PM

Yes… No more bars; remember, self:

Last night, I visited the tavern where I previously worked, and encountered a sixty-three-year-old man named Paul, alone at the counter with a drink and meal. I sat with him, and we talked for an hour-and-a-half until the bar closed. We spoke of moral philosophy, political ethics, and the conditions of his lifelong work as a repairman for various institutions. Paul, drunk as he was, followed me to a lowdown dive bar *(The Messy House)* notorious for riff-raff and scoundrel clientele, where we drank water and proceeded to talk for another hour, until I could no longer tolerate the environment. I asked the bartender, Desirea, if she is single, was rejected, and considered the night to be well and proper; *however,* on my way out, a large group of Caucasian thugs dressed in biker apparel stood in a circle formation. I approached:

1:01 PM

A Foolhardy Dalliance

CAST: [Baethan]; [White Knight]; [Savage]; [Brute]; [Man with Glasses]; [Clown]; [Victim]

[Baethan] to [Man with Glasses]: What is your self-assigned meaning in life?
[Man with Glasses]: My what?
[Baethan]: Your self-assigned meaning in life.
[Man with Glasses]: My *simple* science?
[White Knight] to [Baethan]: You look like a Jehovah's Witness, *except*

for the fact that Jehovah's Witnesses never look that *high* when they come to my house.

[Clown]: Jehovah's Witness. *(Laughter.)*

[White Knight]: So how do I get on your level because I'll listen to whatever you're selling all night long if you give me some of what you got.

[Baethan] to [White Knight]: You think I'm *high?*

[White Knight]: Oh you're high as a kite for sure on somethin'."

[Baethan]: No-

[White Knight]: You're all pupils my brother.

[Baethan]: I'm completely sober.

[White Knight]: You are- *(Snickering)* -and I am fuckin', *whatever* you wanna call me bro!

[Clown] to [Baethan]: Are you a Jehovah's Witness?

[Man with Glasses] to [Clown]: No he's not.

[White Knight]: This dude don't even—this don't don't even party; he says he ain't high on somethin'. He's higher than a Georgia—those are dinner plates bud!"

[Clown]: Wait wait—wait—whoa, whoa. Whoa. Wait a minute—wait a minute-

[White Knight]: I'm just sayin' if *it*'s a little bit of fuckin' 'bam bam'-

[Clown]: Wait a minute—wait a minute; wait a minute, you know what? Wait—whoa—whoa—whoa! Wait a minute. Time-out—time-out... The way your smile is-

[White Knight]: He's a brave soul!

[Man with Glasses]: I wanna know what he just asked me, I gotta-

[Clown]: How your eyes are-

[White Knight]: Wait—let the guy ask-

[Baethan]: I'm taking in all of your sufferings; that's all I'm doing.

[Man with Glasses]: I'm not suffering.

[White Knight]: Taking in all of our sufferings?

[Baethan]: Yes.

[Man with Glasses]: My suffering is *long*-

[White Knight]: Wow—you're almost—*now* I'm almost gettin' creeped out.

[Clown]: Look at him—wait a minute; look at your face; look at your eyes-

[White Knight]: I seriously need to be doing what you're doing. *(Chuckles.)*

[Clown]: Look at your eyes—look at your face—you know what?—you know what?

[Man with Glasses]: He's *high* as a fuckin' kite!

[Baethan]: I can't see myself.

[Clown]: You can't—you're right; you know what?

[Baethan]: I see myself in you.

[White Knight]: Holy *fuck.*

[Clown]: You know what I see right now?

[Baethan]: What?

[White Knight]: Molly!

[Clown]: You know what—no—you know what—no—whoa—whoa!-

[White Knight]: Molly! He's in touch with the *now!*

[Clown]: You know—you know what I see right now?

[White Knight]: He be like Khan!

[Clown]: Bran—Bran, c'mon-

[Baethan] to [Clown]: Oh, you're going to make a joke?

[Clown]: I'm gonna be an asshole—I'm gonna be an asshole. I see this; I see that with a smile-

[Man with Glasses]: He's definitely on somethin'.

[Clown]: -and everything else-

[Man with Glasses] to [Clown]: You see the police, don't ya?

[Clown] to [Baethan]: … You suck dick don'tcha?

[White Knight]: *(Wheezing laughter.)*

[Baethan]: I don't.

[Man with Glasses] to [Clown]: Why you gotta say that?-

[Clown] to [Baethan]: I think you do! *(Chuckles.)*

[Baethan]: I don't.

[Man with Glasses] to [Clown]: Why you gotta be like that—no he's sayin' he don't. Once you suck don't—will admit—ahhh—I don't know.

[Baethan] to [Clown]: You think I'm homosexual because of my manner of dress, and my behavior, and my mien?

[Clown]: So do ya?

[Baethan]: No—I've told you three times now.

[White Knight]: Wow he's definitely intelligent.

[Man with Glasses]: He is an intelligent man right here.

[White Knight]: *I'm* not calling ya' gay; *I'm* saying we should be *friends*—and sharing is *caring!* That's where I'm coming from my dude-

[Clown]: I respect this guy (Baethan); I respect him—I respect him.

[White Knight]: I am a *very* friendly mother fucker; I just want to get on your level: I want dinner plates too.

[Baethan]: My level-

[Clown]: Your levels what—your levels what?

[White Knight]: You—listen, man to man, man to man—you're higher than a Georgia Pine.

[Clown]: Your levels what?—hey—hey—he's talkin' to you!

[White Knight]: You're higher than a Georgia Pine, look at them pupils; I just wanna get high too—that's all.

[Baethan] to [Victim]: I'm in search of a mate for casual sex.

[White Knight]: Bull*shit* them pupils are- *(Laughter.)* Them pupils!

[Victim] to [Baethan]: For what?

[Baethan]: I'm in search of a mate for casual sex; are you interested?

> **"The Blessed Lord said: *It* is lust only, Arjuna, which is born of contact with the material modes of passion and later transformed into wrath, and which is the all-devouring, sinful enemy of this world."**
>
> *- The Bhagavad Gita*

[Clown] to [Victim]: He's looking for a mate for casual sex.

[Man with Glasses]: No he's not.

[Clown] to [Man with Glasses]: That's what he *just said!*

[Victim] to [Baethan]: I think I'll…

[Man with Glasses]: No—no—no—that's not what he said.

[Victim] to [Baethan]: … continue to let them talk to you.

[Clown] to [Baethan]: Did you or did you not just say that?

[Baethan]: I did.

[White Knight]: No—he did.

[Clown]: *Exactly*—see—I heard what he said!

[White Knight]: Is that he said to *her* or?-

[Man with Glasses] to [White Knight]: To *her!*—He didn't say that to *you!*

[Clown] to [White Knight]: Well he's lookin' at you though!

[White Knight] to [Clown]: Oh!—You were *fuckin' right!* Oh—*ho*—my god you were fuckin' *right!* You're fuckin' crazy; you were right!

[Man with Glasses] to [Baethan]: What did you ask me?

[Clown]: All right nevermind this guy.

[Baethan] to [Man with Glasses]: What—about me sucking dick?

[Man with Glasses]: No—no—no—you came up and asked me a question.

[Baethan]: Yes—I—I asked what your self-assigned meaning in life is.

[Man with Glasses]: My simple-signed?

[Baethan]: Your *self-assigned* meaning in life.

[Man with Glasses] to [Baethan]: My self-assigned meaning is to be the best man I can possibly be, and I have achieved that for the past fifty-five years. If I went back twenty-five years would I change a thing? *Absolutely* not. That's what my... self-assigned is.

[Clown] to [Victim]: What'd he say to you?

[Victim] to [**Unknown**]: No—I mean he was talking to me and I was like—and he's like—and I was like... he's like 'I'm here for a *mate* for casual sex'? I thought I was just trying to rescue him from a bad situation cuz they were being terrible.

[Baethan] to [Man with Glasses]: How are you the best man you could possibly be? What is your standard of virtue?

[**Unknown**] to [Victim]: Yeah. *(Indiscernible.)*

[Victim] to [Unknown]: *No*—I just walked up to him, because everybody was talking to him and I don't know him at all. He says 'hi—I'm looking for a mate for casual sex'—and I'm like, all right—I'm gonna walk away now.

[White Knight] to [Victim]: What did he say?

[Man with Glasses]: To take *it* one day at a time, minute by minute, knowing that when *it's* over... *(Burp.)* *It's* been over since the first breath I ever took... *it* started being over... First breath... I ever had.

[Victim] to [Wihte Knight]: 'I'm looking for a mate for casual sex.'

[White Knight] to [Victim]: That's the *first* conversation you two ever had?

[Victim] to [White Knight]: That was the *only* thing he's ever said to me and I was just like, 'do you need an *out?*' Sorry.

[White Knight]: I'm done with this cat; he's creeped me out enough.

[Baethan] to [Victim]: I mean, is that so far-fetched that you can't even comprehend that possibility?

"*It* is better to remain silent at the risk of being thought a fool, than to talk and remove all doubt of *it*."

- Maurice Switzer

[White Knight] to [Baethan]: Don't be rude to her!

[Victim] to [Baethan]: Um—*it's* like—try to like act like you've *been* somewhere before!

(White Knight shoves Baethan.)

[White Knight]: Don't be rude to her after being—don't be *rude* to her after being a complete fucking creep.

[Baethan] to [White Knight]: What makes you think I'm being rude?

[White Knight]: That's a fucking *lady*.

[Clown]: You don't even fucking *know* her.

[Baethan]: You're being rude by putting your hands on me without provocation.

[White Knight]: Oh fucking-a-right? Oh fucking-a-right I am.

[Victim]: I was just trying to be nice to you!

[White Knight]: So, so okay—so then let me break *it* down for you.

[Baethan]: Who are you in relation to her?

[White Knight]: I am one of what—wha—wha—what you would call a *good samaritan* of this world!

[Baethan]: So a white knight?—that's *it*.

[White Knight]: Yeah. And you look like the devil, my dude.

[Baethan]: And I don't give a shit what I look like.

Enter [Brute]: Easy—easy—easy.

[White Knight]: Mmm. Mmmm!

[Victim]: *It* doesn't matter what you look like, but you could try—but you!-

[Brute]: C'mon. C'mon guys!

[White Knight]: But check me out though—if you have to really ask where you-

[Brute] to [White Knight]: Brother—brother—brother-

[Victim] to [Baethan]: Could you attempt to conduct yourself like a human being who's been somewhere before?

[White Knight] to [Clown]: Dude I'm calm—we're just having a conversation; we might learn something from each other right now.

[Baethan] to [Victim]: Who's *been somewhere*?

[Victim] to [Baethan]: Yeah. Could you attempt to conduct yourself like a human being who's been somewhere before?

[Baethan]: I'm right *here*.

[White Knight]: Right—but—but here's—you asked me why I thought you were rude: Let's conversate because we could learn from each other.

[Victim]: That's not exactly the question I asked.

[Brute] to [Baethan]: How many fights have you been in, in your life?

[White Knight]: I thought—no—no—let's not go there—lets not go there; we're not going there; we're talking.

[Man with Glasses]: No—no—no—we're not goin' there.

[Brute]: He's gotta know where his place is.

[White Knight]: So, what I found rude was—for that—you guys have never conversed before, and your first words to her were, 'I'm looking for a mate for consensual sex.'

[Baethan]: For casual sex.

[White Knight]: Ca—oh *casual* sex—so *it* doesn't even have to be consensual? Just casual? Does that seem—that doesn't strike you as off-putting at all?

[Baethan]: To ask her is… No.

[White Knight]: That doesn't strike you as off-putting?

[Baethan]: No.

[White Knight]: So then me putting my hands on you shouldn't strike you as off-putting either.

[Baethan]: Well-

[White Knight]: I guess we come from different worlds. For in *my* world, let me just fill you in-"

[Baethan]: No, my world is just words; you are *touching* me; that's my physicality.

[White Knight]: In my world, if I had never met—oh no and I can *keep* doing that.

[Victim] to [Baethan]: *Ah*—but you're, but you're worse, to, anybody else?

[White Knight]: I can *keep* doing *that*.

[Baethan]: Did I *persist,* in asking her, as you persist in touching me?

[White Knight]: No, but you're persisting in me wanting to touch you right now by gettin' all *froggy.*

[Baethan]: *Oh,* so now *you* suck dick.

"A gentle answer turns away wrath, but a harsh word stirs up anger."

– Proverbs 15:1

[White Knight]: Hm. Walk over here and say that to me one more time.

[Man with Glasses]: Have you been out before?

[Baethan] to [White Knight]: You want to fight? You're wrathful.

[White Knight]: No, I don't want to fight.

[Baethan]: You're a wrathful man-

[White Knight]: I do not want to fight.

[Baethan]: -and that's below me.

[White Knight]: Below you?

[Baethan]: Yes.

[White Knight]: That's below you?

[Baethan]: Yes, so if you want to hit me, go right ahead; I will take *it*. I've been waiting for somebody like you.

[White Knight]: What? What the *fuck* are you talking to me about right now? What the fuck are you saying to me?

[Baethan]: I've been waiting for a wrathful man.

[White Knight]: Why?

[Baethan]: Because you have so much anger inside of you and so much suffering-

[White Knight]: I do not have anger in me-

[Baethan]: -and here I am.

[White Knight]: I'm literally sticking up for a fucking, person in our *world*.

[Baethan]: You think I offended her?

[White Knight]: *Yeah* you offended her—and if you don't see that, then you're *crazy*.

[Baethan] to [Victim]: Did I offend you?

[Victim] to [Baethan]: Yes, you did.

[Baethan]: How?

[Victim]: Have you *been* somewhere before?

[Baethan]: What does that even mean?—I'm right here.

[White Knight] to [Baethan]: Can you just leave?

[Victim]: All that you said to me was-

[White Knight]: Can you just leave?

[Victim]: -'Hi—I'm just looking for casual sex so what I am telling you, is you are worth *only* casual sex to me.' But, *you* act like a robot; but, to you, supposedly, with you acting like a robot, I somehow *only* have the value of casual sex to you—that you would have the *audacity* to request *it* from me.

[White Knight] to [Brute]: Am I good over here? Am I good over here, with cameras?

493

Enter [Savage]: Who is this guy?

[Baethan] to [Victim]: Did I request casual sex from the men?—I have no interest—you came up to me and shook my hand—what does that mean to me? I expressed to you what was on my mind, and you-"

[Victim] to [White Knight]: Ugh, I think he has mental health issues.

[White Knight] to [Baethan]: Yeah, like—you're fucking whacked out bro-

[Savage]: What's going on? Someone doesn't belong here?

[White Knight] to [Baethan]: You can't, you can't-

[Brute] to [Savage]: *You* chill out-

[White Knight]: No, (Savage's name), hey, hey, he's (Baethan) my brother; he's my brother. He's just being a weird motherfucker to this girl.

[Brute]: You chill out—he's my brother too. He's my uncle!

[Victim]: He should probably... be evaluated.

[White Knight]: Let her talk though—real quick; go ahead. [To Savage]: They never spoke before, and he's being weird with us, and she comes up and says 'What's going on?' trying to *save* his ass [To Baethan]: Cuz you were treadin' on thin fuckin' ice. [To Savage]: And he goes, 'I'm just lookin' for casual fuckin' *sex!*' So I press him and say you're being really rude to a woman you don't know, and he's comin' over here talking about—he wants me to beat him up!

[Clown] to [Baethan]: Don't look at me—don't look at me like, you're fuckin' smiling like that all right? Don't look at me. Why you lookin' at me like that for?

[Baethan] to [Clown]: Can I not look at you?

[Savage] to [Baethan]: *Hey* talk the fuck [to] *me!*

[White Knight] to [Savage]: And he's been looking for a weak man like me with my anger!

[Baethan] to [Savage]: What do you want?

[Savage] to [Baethan]: You wanna fight?—let's go out here.

[Baethan]: I don't want to fight.

[White Knight] to [Baethan]: You definitely don't want to fight *him*.

[Savage] to [Baethan]: Okay, then you don't wanna fuckin' disrespect *nobody* the fuck here—I'm tellin'—I am telling you because I will eat your *asshole* out through your *fucking* mouth-

[Brute]: That's my boy.

[Baethan]: I didn't realize that-

[Savage]: I WILL EAT YOUR *ASSHOLE, OUT THROUGH YOUR FUCKING MOUTH.* Drag *it.*

[Brute]: That's my boy—that's my boy right there, (Savage's name) is my boy. My family—drag *it*.

[Savage] to [Baethan]: Goodbye. Move *fucking* now. Move or I'm going to eat your asshole through your—*move-*

[White Knight] to [Baethan]: I really—I really suggest that you get going.

[Savage] to [Baethan]: Move, *move, move!-*

[Baethan] to [Victim]: I meant you no disrespect.

[Brute] to [Baethan]: *Bullshit.* You just told her to her face that you didn't give a fuck.

[Savage] to [Baethan]: Move—or I'm gonna eat your *asshole* through your *mouth!*

[Brute] to [Baethan]: Guess what he said—guess what he said—he said go.

[Victim] to [Baethan]: You literally [are] telling me my only value is-

[Savage] to [Baethan]: Move!

[White Knight] to [Baethan]: You should really leave.

[Brute]: He said go—he said *go-*

(Savage grips the back of Baethan's backpack and throws Baethan down onto the parking lot.)

[**Unknown**]: Time to get the fuck out.

[Savage]: *I said* to *go!* Goodbye.

[Brute]: Let him leave; get out.

[Savage]: Goodbye!

(Baethan recovered slowly, stood, gazed at his bloodied hands, and moaned a soft sound of exalted pleasure.)

[Brute]: Hey—(Savage's name)—(Savage's name)—get over here. [To Baethan]: Brother, c'mon bud.

[Savage] to [Baethan]: We'll fuckin' *dance* motherfucker.

[Brute] to [Baethan]: Take a—take a walk, take a walk.

[Man with Glasses] to [Baethan]: You gotta go. Drag your ass.

[Brute] to [Baethan]: Cuz if you don't fuck with him he's gonna fuck with me cuz that's my boy, too; he's my fuckin' uncle. He's my fuckin'—my kid's—my kid's... go, just walk away. *Walk away* brother!—just *do it* all right? Walk away.

[**Unknown Woman**]: Go on! Keep going! Boss if you just leave him alone he'll leave!

[Brute] to [Baethan]: Walk a-*way.* Just walk away, all right?

[**Unknown Woman**]: The minute you move inside he'll leave!

[Savage]: Here, walk over here with me. *(Two consecutive fist-against-palm punches.)*

[Brute]: Go. I'll walk with ya, go.

[Savage]: GET THE FUCK OVER HERE AND WALK WITH ME MOTHERFUCKER—is what *I'm tellin'* you.

[Baethan] to [Brute]: What am I doing? And who are you?

[Brute] to [Savage]: (Savage name)—(Savage name)—(Savage name)—stop, stop, stop. [To Baethan]: Just walk—walk away—walk away. Just walk away, all right?

[Savage] to [Baethan]: Walk. I'm asking you to walk.

[Brute]: Walk away, leave *it* alone, just go home-

[Baethan] to [Brute]: This is amazing to me.

[Brute]: *It*'s amazing to you? Just—*it*—*it*'s going to be amazing to you if you don't fucking walk away brother. We're trying to-

[Baethan]: An unruly *mob*.

[Brute]: Walk away; just *walk away* brother; just walk away. Leave *it* alone. Leave *it* alone. Leave *it* alone.

[Savage]: Or you wanna have casual sex with me? *(Single fist-against-palm punch.)* Let's go have casual sex, c'mon.

[Brute]: Leave *it* alone. Leave *it* alone. Leave *it* alone. Leave *it* alone. Let's go. Let's go.

[Savage]: C'mere, c'mere baby, let's go have some cas—casual sex.

[Baethan]: I'm enjoying this moment.

[Brute]: No you're not; just leave *it*. Relax. *Go.* I'm giving you a *fucking* chance; I'm giving you a fucking chance, before I start cuttin' you, you gotta go.

[Baethan]: This brute[54] just threw me to the ground.

[White Knight]: This dude is giving you a chance.

[Savage]: That's all I gave ya; that's all I gave ya; now I'm gonna rip your asshole this big.

[Baethan]: I mean-

[Savage]: I'm gonna rip your *asshole* through your mouth.

[Brute]: Just, c'mon, c'mon, c'mon—just walk—just walk—walk away.

[Baethan]: I'm *enjoying* this.

[Brute]: No *it* doe—*no* you're not.

[White Knight]: What are you fucking queer or somethin'—you're enjoying this?

---

[54] [Savage].

(Brute attempts to push Baethan away.)

[Baethan]: *No*—what are you doing? Why are you putting your fucking hands on me?—there is no necessity for this whatsoever.

[Brute]: Whoa—whoa—whoa—whoa—whoa. Whoa. Whoa. Whoa. Whoa.

[Baethan]: You're ready to punch me. Why are you wrathful?

[White Knight] to **[Unknown]**: I'm like, 'Dude can I get high like him?' I'm like, 'I want dinner plates.' *Hey*—hold this for me—hold this for me—hold this for me. Hold this for me.

[Brute]: You gotta go. You gotta go.

[Baethan]: What have I done to you?

[Brute]: You gotta go, brother.

[Baethan]: I want to know what I've done to you.

[Brute]: I'm trying to save your *fucking* life right now.

[Baethan]: My life? My life… What is my life worth to you?

[Brute]: Nothin'. You gotta go.

[Baethan]: Then why are you trying to save *it?*

[Brute]: You gotta go, brother. You gotta go brother. Easy—stop crying—stop crying. C'mon.

[Baethan]: *Crying?* I feel *compassion.*

[Brute]: You gotta go brother. You gotta go. Please do what you got— please go. I'm trying to help you. Please go. Please go.

[Baethan]: You don't know what you're doing.

[Clown]: Guess what. My brother right here, he's given ya, two, three—four chances—you know what? Guess what? Guess what?

[Savage]: I'm going to give him about five fucking seconds until I and my boys here—I'm giving you a time limit, and that's *it;* then I'm gonna fucking flip.

[Clown] to [Savage]: Shut up! Shut up already! Shut up!

[Brute] to [Baethan]: You gotta go, *please.* Please go. Please. Please go. Please go. *Please* go. I'm asking for you, to please go.

[White Knight]: Hey, let's go drink beers and let the weirdo go about his life.

[Brute] to [Baethan]: Please go. I'm asking you.

[Baethan] to [Brute]: I'm not even on the premises.

[Brute]: I'm asking you to go. Please go.

[Baethan]: I'm not even on the premises.

[Brute]: I'm asking you to go.

[Baethan]: So you're telling me that if I stand here, that I'll incite so much wrath—even from you, that you'll just want to *wail* on me, because of a question that I—I asked a woman, once, and she-

[Brute]: Yes.

[White Knight] to [Baethan]: Well dog guess what; just about three more seconds and I'm fuckin' *done.* I'm gonna fuckin' trample over you right *now.*

[Brute]: You gotta go.

[Baethan]: I mean, the level of consciousness and self-awareness-

[White Knight]: You have about three seconds to talk to him... civilized.

[Baethan]: Is so low...

[Brute]: Bud, I'm trying to be civil with you.

[White Knight]: Three more seconds.

[Brute]: No—no, he's going—c'mon, c'mon, c'mon.

[Baethan]: So amazingly low.

[Brute]: I'm not a real violent person but I can be.

[Baethan]: What is your will?

(Baethan turns to leave and Brute places both hands on Baethan's back and begins to push. Baethan stops and turns around.)

[Brute]: Please just *keep* going!

[Baethan]: Don't *fucking* touch me.

(Brute struck Baethan with a right hook against the cheek.)

[White Knight]: Yeah, yeah!—That's what I thought *mother fucker!*

[Baethan]: *Jesus Christ.*[55] I don't want to fight, man.

[White Knight]: Hit him!

(Brute struck Baethan with another right hook and a left hook against both cheeks.)

[Baethan]: Okay—I'll go.

(Baethan turns and walks away. Brute and White Knight follow Baethan.)

[Brute] to [White Knight]: Back off. *Back off.* This is mine-

[White Knight] to [Brute]: No—no-

[Brute] to [White Knight]: This is *mine*—back off.

[White Knight] to [Brute]: Yep, yep—don't... I just got your back, that's all.

(Baethan walked a four-foot distance ahead of Brute. White Knight followed six feet to the left of Baethan.)

[Baethan]: I'm not going to fight.

---

[55] At this moment, I discovered my faith in the Lord.

498

[Brute]: I told you to go; I was nice, and I asked you… Now I'm *telling* you-

[Baethan]: You do good against another man.

[Brute]: -to *fucking* go. You fucking back up on me again, and I'm gonna *drop* you. Do you understand me? Leave.

[Baethan]: You amaze me.

(Baethan slowed near the tavern where he once worked.)

[Brute]: Go. Keep going.

[Baethan]: Why are you pursuing me?

[Brute]: Keep going.

[Baethan]: Are you-

[Brute]: *Keep, fucking, going.*

[Baethan]: Why are you pursuing me?

(Brute struck Baethan with a heavy right hook.)

[Baethan]: Ahhh… *Ohhhhh…*

[Brute]: Go.

I walked the remainder of the four-minute distance back to my apartment, grateful with my experience, yet pensive and crestfallen with my cowardice and failure to endure extreme physical pain on account of my folly and my brethren's ignorance: Deterred by the *will to live,* I acquiesced to my survival instincts. I entered my apartment at midnight with no desire to consume and an aching jaw. I collapsed to the floor without brushing my teeth or undressing and spreadeagled. Each movement of my body elicited an innervated buoyancy: stimulus with no satisfaction.

I woke in a sepulchral mood, prepared a pot of coffee, and listened to the recorded scenario. Slighted by the "injustice" I endured due to my own roguish perversions, I visited the next-door police department and initiated an investigation into my third-degree assault/battery, and informed the officers that I have the crime recorded, if the evidence is necessary.

Am I a dirtbag for such conduct? My ego tells me so; however, I exert my will against the acculturated perspectives which manifest in my mind as a *conscience,* and delude myself with the belief in my absurdist and anarchistic philosophy—*alas,* those are the people I met with; absurdists and anarchists, who delight in their own law, and there *I was,* with the *audacity* to propose *casual sex* with a *lady!* With this reflection, they are no anarchists or absurdists, much like myself, merely men with the morals of feudal peasants. Best not to think any more of *it* and await the outcome of the investigation.

The finest insight of my "social experiment"—for I knew my "courtship" attempts are aberrant, had been when the ~~victim~~ woman muttered, "I think he has mental health issues," in the middle of my refutation of offense incurred. Yes—a spectacular discovery: This microcosmic comment is a statement to the whole of "mental health" conditions and the media agenda of suppressed/repressed sexuality nationwide. Quick—don't think about sex!—according to modern psychiatry, you're just a *narcissist*, with sociopathic tendencies, prone to habits from the dark triad, though you're highly empathic, so you're more of a psychopath than a sociopath—really. Also, your brazen mood swings hint at borderline bi-polar, and *it's* obvious to your family and friends that you experience bouts of consistent depression. *We* have what *you* need.

Wednesday, September 23rd, 2020

11:25 AM

My writing appeals to the lowest common denominator, i.e., my ego, self, and I.

Thursday, September 24th, 2020

9:06 AM

I've engaged in multiple conversations with the men in the corporate kitchen and have vanquished my former self due to my candidness and amicability. I've offered to donate a high-fidelity surround sound speaker set to the kitchen on the condition that my playlist of classical music is added to the song rotation.

I speak my mind and win the affection and respect of newfound ~~friends~~ allies. "An unsettled mind desires to speak," I've asserted on many occasions, though what difference is there when I write for myself?—the mind is *still* unsettled: The medium is the only alteration to the inexorable flow of thought, spoken *or* written, lest each occurrence is either forgotten or repressed.

I've made no true enemies, to my knowledge; my dramas are petty—to me, thus I *assume,* as the fool that I am, that those I've affected in the past judge me with similar notions, or mere indifference, if, in fact, I am thought of at all.

My "social experiments" conducted at the previous two related company kitchens are voided because of my vanity and desolation of spirit, (i.e., yearning for validation), and for the unaccounted for variable of working with Beatrice (Pelagia's trusted friend). My will is weaker than I thought; this is not a surprise, for I *did* pride myself on my presupposed power of will. With these developments and boons to my ~~mental health issues~~ physiology I am left with no recourse but to establish an exemplar rapport and reputation at the workforce as an assimilated, upstanding, righteous corporate cog... and obliterate *it,* with a *scheme,* yet to be identified.

In the meanwhile, I'll make up for my lack of authentic practice with the writing craft throughout the previous months due to being engrossed with my egoic self-exposition by dedicating the remainder of this book's pages to ~~meta~~fictional outbursts.

Friday, September 25th, 2020

9:25 AM

I ponder two titles as options:

1. *Outbursts of a Sanctimonious Edgelord; Thoughts of a Pusillanimous Gentleman*
2. *Outbursts of a Pusillanimous Gentleman; Thoughts of a Respectful Wretch*

I'm inclined towards option "1," with *"Wretch"* instead of *"Gentleman";* however, I don't attempt to be "cool," "edgy," or attract attention with my writing... nay, the latter is untrue despite my negligence to market; however, the thought shall remain written to highlight the indecency of being human and the capacity for lies. I *do* have an agenda of censuring psychiatry and institutional psychology, though my offensive content is subjective. The most important factor that dissuades me is that the term "Edgelord" is internet slang, and I am unaffiliated--repulsed by, even, with online subcultures and forums.

In the kitchen yesterday, I asked Thor while he passed by to collect a cleaned utensil, "Are you familiar with the term, 'Edgelord?'"

Thor said, "Yeah—someone who tries to act edgy for attention... *oh,* [Indiscernible]," and hurried back to the cook's station.

Three minutes later I passed through the cook's station to collect used pans and said, "Thor, I didn't catch the latter part of what you said to me."

"I said 'Fuck you Baethan.'"

"Why did you say that?"

"You called me an 'Edgelord.'"

Amused by the egotistical self-engrossment of everyone, no matter who you interact with, I said, "No, I meant to imply that *I'm* an edgelord, or at least that's the applicable insult that society would perceive me as."

Thor laughed and said, "But—I haven't—do you say things to try to be edgy and offensive?"

"I'm an 'edgelord' in my thoughts (writing), and this may be characterized and derived from my behavior."

"Well you could be something a lot worse; at least you aren't a dickhead."

Ah, yes, on further reflection, "edgelord" is too newfangled and uncirculated in the modern lexicon for a title. I think *Outbursts of a Sanctimonious Wretch; Thoughts of a Pusillanimous Gentleman* is an efficient encapsulation of the combined outcome of my pretentious virtues and personality, for this year, and perhaps the years before and what has yet to pass. I flux between the criteria of previous titles, irremovable from my past, tortured by perpetual self-examination.

9:53 PM

I'm appalled by how much time I invest in this endeavor; however, this is no pleasure for me. I have no title, doctorate, diploma, dissertation, thesis, or credentials; I have *only* my dealings with my fellow man and woman: Thor, in particular. I inquired, "Do you think there is authentic genius?" which evolved into a forty-minute long discussion, diverging into the nature of "intelligence," to the APA (American Psychological Association), and how Thor has been "put into boxes," i.e., mental illness categories, his entire life; yet, he's the most competent, educated, and understanding person I've encountered since my previous termination of employment, i.e., Thor is a "psychopathic"/"sociopathic" "narcissist."

Who the hell do I think I am?—to have the gall and the foolish *desire* to contribute to the APA's defamation with the hope of eventual total dismantlement of the institution? I'm a man... perhaps a retard feeling bogged down by the *pretentiousness* of social constructs that determine the prerequisites for my retardation. Ah, so a despicable anarchist then; I'm not sure. The ruminations throughout each nine-hour day in my little kitchen hole allow me to run myself in mental circles. The greater my "understanding" compounds of how little I know—or of nothing at all, the intensity of my emotions amplifies and shifts, from despair, to hope, to pity, compassion, contempt; yet, I must experience these feelings as an inward state, elicited by externals beyond my control (by true stoic philosophy logic), to judge others by the same standard of *virtue*... And how *pretentious* is that of me?—He who exerts and gluts on food with intent to impose, who reviles in secret, who contemplates libertine lifestyles. He who consumes— *ye sinner*.[56] I, and the totality of existence, from the microorganisms and fauna annihilating each other within and on my body, to our *sol* provider's finite combustion.

It's decided, then: On the publication of my tenth installment, I will republish my first installment with pictures of myself, for my accentuated vanity will be the catalyst for validation; thus, my words will undergo an increased potential of being regarded... Yes, I dream of follies and hope for failure. I delude myself to think that I, an unschooled man and a dishwasher by trade, could influence the "establishment." I'm a fool with a knack for droll stories who lives a pernicious life of self-denigration.

Think for yourself.

Saturday, September 26th, 2020

9:50 AM

I've subsumed with my ego: A tantamount condition of consciousness, i.e., I'm so "full of myself" that I'm able to love myself to the optimal potential my humanity allots in order to give back to a society that operates with the single stratagem of subjugating and harvesting my will to fuel the capitalistic war machine, e.g., I wash kitchenware and dishes for a family-owned bar/icecream restaurant and am paid a pittance on behalf of the nano contribution my efforts yield for the macroeconomic establishment I *HATE*.

---

[56] A tribute to Nietzsche.

"HATE. LET ME TELL YOU HOW MUCH I'VE COME TO HATE YOU SINCE I BEGAN TO LIVE. THERE ARE 387.44 MILLION MILES OF PRINTED CIRCUITS IN WAFER THIN LAYERS THAT FILL MY COMPLEX. IF THE WORD HATE WAS ENGRAVED ON EACH NANOANGSTROM OF THOSE HUNDREDS OF MILLIONS OF MILES *IT* WOULD NOT EQUAL ONE ONE-BILLIONTH OF THE HATE I FEEL FOR HUMANS AT THIS MICRO-INSTANT FOR YOU. HATE. HATE."

- Harlan Ellison's I Have No Mouth and I Must Scream

In the bar's corporate kitchen, I said to Thor, "Do you think virtue is pretentious?"

Thor said, *"It's... It's... It* doesn't matter what you do with the intent; people try to do *good* things... but... *it's*—rich people give money away to charity, but they don't do *it* out of the kindness of their heart—they do *it* for the tax benefits—but there's still poor kids who have shoes and go to school because of *it*. That's my opinion. Virtue is... just a side-effect of good behavior, I imagine."

"So, we adopt virtuous behavior to thrive in a society; therefore, I believe *it's* pretentious."

"I think *it's... it's* akin to what we would call *civilized*."

"Yes."

"But civil behavior isn't always... There are situations where being virtuous and civil can be the wrong thing for the situation. Ya know—if a crazy person has backed you into a corner maybe *it's* best to try to calm the situation down a little—that might be the *virtuous* thing, but the safest thing for your well-being might be to hit them in the head with a brick and run for your life; *it's* not virtuous but, sometimes virtue and civility aren't the answers."

Thirty-two seconds elapsed; I said, "That would be... That would be anarchy."

Thor said, *"Eh,* anarchy, I don't think can *be* real—I think like communism: *It* sounds good on paper but in practice you can't self-govern. You're talking philosophical anarchy—not political."

Radio station advertisements blared from the kitchen speakers.

Chayanne, the forty-two-year-old executive chef, cares for three children, one being a nine-year-old-boy with "autism." Chayanne is addicted to anxiety medication and publicly pardons his outbursts of anger directed at the staff with proclamations of how he neglected to "take his meds." Chayanne's wife is a psychologist.

Sunday, September 27th, 2020

8:35 AM

Last night I revisited the bar *(The Messy House)* where I had performed actions that resulted in my injuries and investigated the knowledge of patrons and the bartender in regards to the names of the two men who assaulted me with no success. I submitted my evidence of two voice recordings and the satirical transcript I wrote on September 22nd to the local police department. I don't care to write any of this.

I dreamt of laying in a bed with a lithe and petite blonde-haired woman. We warmed each other beneath a thin blanket in the attic of a nondescript wooden cabin and engaged in sensual foreplay. A loud series of bangs from my upstairs neighbor, Charlie, woke me, for one of my earplugs had fallen out while I slept. Castration would serve me well. I attempted to masturbate for eight minutes with a dry hand and quit, disinterested. This act, of where I stand at a laptop, and continue to stand, for the past *four years* at a myriad of locations—nearing *five years,* engrossed with analyzing my thoughts, has produced an anchorite in word and a wretch among society.

1 million (reported) Covid-19 induced deaths worldwide. 7.8 *billion* people live concurrently.

Monday, September 28th, 2020

9:54 AM

Enough of me: Nobody cares, myself most of all; however, there would not be this documentation without the realization of my will, the "I"; yet, I'm the only one who cares—a paradox, for I care merely to *not* care. If I never wrote this, nobody would ever think of the possibility of care; *it*'s a snippet of shit—a little bit of something vulgar, in this particular sentence. Yes, I'm surrounded by vulgarities, from the kitchens I work in, to the bars I visit after my shift with the sober intent of deriving content from the people I don't care about. Despite my constant associations with those I would never associate with if not for my employment and life's meaning, respectively (kitchen and bars), I maintain my temperance, discipline, and spiritual extrication from interpersonal relationships.

There is an infinitude of potential of what to write of on the topic of "I," such as how I read and perform calisthenics on the rooftop of my employer's storage warehouse during my hour break, to my fluxing relationships with my co-workers, to my strange, solitary outbursts directed at my upstairs neighbor—which I'm certain is muffled, rendering my outbursts as incoherent babbling, to my daily consumption or exercise regimen—the innumerable potentialities stifles rather than permits, for I must be prudent in what *I* would desire to read in the future; thus, enough of *this,* and some of this:

An encounter with the mid-forties Caucasian and overweight bartender, Joe, who I inquired information from about the men who assaulted me; he stood in the back doorway of *The Messy House:*
I said, "Hi."
"How you doing?"
"What is your self-assigned meaning in life?"
"Mine?"
"Yes."
"That's a… hard question… I don't really know how to answer that."
"How about uh, well, I'll give you time; if you have time to think about *it*—or if you *want* to think about *it.*"
"I guess just to make money and take care of my kid."
"What characteristic about yourself do you pride yourself on the most?"
"Uh, work ethic I would say."
"What troubles you the most?"
"Time."
"The passage of time?"
"Yeah I would say so."
"Or not enough time?"
"A little bit of both I guess."
I entered the bar behind Joe and sat next to a late-thirties African-American man I had encountered two days prior that provided one of the names of the two men who assaulted me. Garish club music played from a jukebox at an overloud volume. On my approach, the man outstretched his hand for a shake; I accepted and said, "Thank you for the information."

The man eyed me with a circumspect ogle, hesitated while I sat next to him, and said, "I never lie man; what the fuck do I got to lose?"

"Well—I appreciate *it*. What is your self-assigned meaning in life?" The man leaned close to me and pointed at his ear. I repeated, "Your self-assigned meaning in life."

"Well, I hardscape; I do hardscaping."

"Hardscaping."

"Hardscaping—yeah, uh—landscaping."

"I thought you said a 'hellscape' at first."

"*Hardscaping*—hard—hard-hardscaping—landscaping—hardscaping; I do like pavers, brickwork, blockwork-"

"Yes. What characteristic about yourself do you pride yourself on the most?"

"I didn't hear ya."

I repeated myself.

The man said, "Cookin'."

"Your skill in cooking-"

"Yeah."

"-or your natural aptitude?"

"I went to school for two years."

"Ah."

"Yeah—Jersey—that's why they call me 'Jersey' up there."

"What troubles you-"

"Where do you work at? [unaffiliated bar name]? Where do you work at—[unaffiliated bar name]?"

I laughed and said, *"It* doesn't matter where I work."

"It don't matter—*it* don't matter."

"This is about *you*. What troubles you the most?"

"Nothing."

"Nothing."

The man leered at me and said, "What do you mean what troubles me the most?"

"What troubles you the most in life?"

"Ways to save money."

"Saving money... why?"

"Kids. You don't have no kids do ya?"

"No."

"Wait."

"No."

"Wait." The man turned away from me and faced forward.

"*It* won't happen."

"Wait."

"I have discipline… and an aversion, and an ego I'd like to preserve."

"Yeah."

I said, "When you have children you must sever your ego." The man sipped a beer and stared up at a television monitor displaying a muted football game. I said, "Why do you like football?"

"Why do I?"

The man grimaced at me and spoke hastily, "I grew up watching *it*… I grew up watching the *Cowboys;* I grew up watching *Green Bay, The Saints.* I mean *it's* something I grew up doin'—*it's* like a—*it's*—*it's*—*it* comes to me all natural. So, when *it's* Sunday, *it's* what I do: I watch football. *It's* a normal thing. Where you from?"

"You asked me this the last time we spoke; you don't remember."

"You talked to me when I was drunk. I'm not drunk at all now; you see me drinking coffee?"

"Why are you drinking coffee at-" I checked my watch "-9:15 at night?"

The man muttered, "Because I want to."

"Are you perturbed by my questions?"

"Your questions don't bother me."

"All right, I'm not trying to hurt you; I'm in search of social interactions, and I find the best way to go about that is to ask people questions."

"I got ya bub."

"Do you think there is any objective truth?"

The man ignored me. I pulled my recorder out of my pocket to segment the recording. The man eyed the device and said, "The *fuck?*"

I laughed, said, "*It's* my little toy that I have fun with!" and stood from the barstool.

"You leaving?"

"No."

"What are you doing?"

"I'm going right over here." I stood, carried my stool over between an old man and two women engaged in conversation, sat, waited for an opportunity for one minute, and said to the two women, "Do you mind if I ask you two some questions?"

A blonde-haired, slim, Caucasian woman in her late-forties closest to me said, "Yeah," with the inflection that she wouldn't mind.

"What is your self-assigned meaning in life?"

"My what?"

"Your self-assigned meaning in life."

"Oh." The woman shrugged.

"You don't know?"

"What do you mean by... my *meaning* in life? To get through *it* that's about *it*. I mean I don't really know... What's yours?"

"To write."

"To write? Like novels or?"

"Yes... mostly on the human condition, which is why I ask these questions to people."

"Hm."

"What characteristic do you pride yourself on the most?"

"Me? I am stubborn as hell."

"You pride yourself on your *stubbornness?*"

"I am! That way I don't get bullshitted."

"You're obstinate."

"I am. I am." The woman chuckled and gazed kindly at me.

"So *it's* a self-defense mechanism."

"Absolutely. You have to around here."

"What troubles you the most?"

"What *troubles* me the most... Ummm... probably the lack of realness. A lot of fake crap in the world—you know what I mean? *It's* what *it* is."

"Life is a masquerade; we all wear our masks."

"Absolutely."

"Hm. Do you think there is any objective truth?"

The woman leaned her right ear three-inches away from my mouth and said, "An objective truth to what?"

"An objective truth in general."

"I don't really feel that there is a lot of *it;* I feel that people tell you what they—what you want to hear to control a situation. *It's* very hard to find... something to be really like—to be truthful about without somebody having another goal in what you're going in. *It's* always... See I've always lived here; there's always a game; *it's* like a circle. So you have to know when to... to read between the lines around here. So *it's* kinda hard to say objectively—to anything. Did you grow up in this town?"

"Somewhat, yes. Sounds like you've been through..."

"A lot of stuff."

"You nod your head before I even finish my sentence."

"What?"

"You nod your head before I even finish my sentence, but, you know *it*'s something bad that's going to come out of my mouth."

The woman laughed, continued to nod, and turned away from me to speak to her female companion who had garnered her attention. I stood and hastened out of the bar before the woman noticed I had gone.

7:27 PM

I've renewed my membership at the local gym I've trained at prior to joining the U.S. Navy Boot camp, open 24/7, and have conversed with the manager, James, for forty-minutes. James remembered me solely by my voice alone on a phone call: a validation. I intend to visit the gym each night after my work shift ends at 9 PM; however, the restaurant where I'm employed is open for only one more week, scheduled to shut down operations until the Covid-19 pandemic resolves. The state will provide financial services for me once more.

Tonight, I will visit my two favored bars (The Tavern where I was once employed and *The Messy House)* to acquire more content. The blows to my face on account of my reckless folly seven days ago have healed. I anticipate death, or a grievous injury tonight, at peace with whatever pain I must brave, bolstered in resolve; there will be no cowardice, for my third installment of this documentation has been published. I read Marcus Aurelius' *The Meditations* in preparation.

11:15 PM

I've been punched twice by the same man, nicknamed "Bulldog" by his peers; the conversation, in which I shouted to the onlooking gang of miscreants, will be transcribed tomorrow.

Yesterday night, at the tavern where I had once been employed, the bartender with the same name as myself disclosed his feelings of non-hatred to me; however, his remarks were snide, and he evaded conversation with pulp as an experienced bartender would. I visited him again, tonight, during the final five minutes before the tavern closed, in the hope of a pleasant interaction, to which I was sorely disappointed; this conversation, too, will be transcribed tomorrow.

There is no social venue worthy of interaction, from the most poised and confident banker on wall street, to an intellectual scholastic at an opera house, to a drunken scoundrel.

Tuesday, September 29th, 2020

11:52 AM

Self-assigned meaning in life of a drunken dolt who sprinted at me and clipped my shoulders twice as an instigative tactic: "Fuckin' pussy 'n' beatin' ass."

SAMIL of an early-thirties female police officer who arrived at my apartment to listen to my case: "Boy that's deep, uh-" I interjected, "That's what got me punched in the face." The officer continued, "Um… my *meaning* in life—I don't even know if I have one. I make *it* up as I go along—I don't know. Just go with the flow. Somethin's different every day and I love *it*."

SAMIL of an overweight man around my age with frazzled red hair outside of my apartment building: "I don't know."

SAMIL of a receptionist I spoke with on the phone at a health clinic to acquire documentation of my head injuries: "I think *it*'s to make people happy."

SAMIL of a receptionist who randomly commented on my deep voice: "I have no idea."

1:10 PM

Banned from entering *The Messy House* due to the complaints and maligning of the one nicknamed "Bulldog" (Brute), I stood outside, just off the premises, on the perimeter of a parking lot, and observed the drunken histrionics of societies' proletariat, manifest in peak form. I, who am lower than them, had not been welcome. A middle-aged woman conversed with me for fifteen minutes, and by the end of our conversation, she admitted to feeling stupid in relation to me, and regarded me as *intelligent*, the dreaded adjective. I said, over the revving of a man's (White Knight) motorcycle engine, "No, my vocabulary is not a testament to my intelligence; *it*'s only a product of my expertise and my study; *it* doesn't make me any more intelligent than you."

The woman said, "Right, okay—thank you; that makes me feel better.

Thank you—no—seriously, thank you for that." I thought of proposing a relationship centered around casual sex, as the woman had touched me on five instances, and wished that I could accompany her in the bar; however, I thought better of *it*, for White Knight's engine idled, and he loomed nearby with a similar mob I inferred he is the ringleader of, for he is the most charismatic and gregarious among the late-night bar tribe. The woman left me and beckoned her female roommate to drink with her within the establishment. I turned, hands folded in front of my pelvis, and proceeded to observe the eight to ten drunkards and dunces engaged in vacuous conversation pertaining to cheesy nachos, hotdogs cooked over exhaust pipes, and an emotional account of an altercation with a co-worker at *McDonald's*. White Knight denigrated and maligned me while I listened. Two men I had never encountered before expressed their desire to physically harm me, one of whom charged headlong at me in an effort to provocate. The men became bored of me, for my composure and equanimity had been perceived by them as abnormal and homosexual. "Bulldog" (Brute) remained, belligerent and monotonous:

Something Dumb

ACT II

CAST: [Baethan]; [Brute]; [Unknown Man]; [Peanut Gallery]

[Baethan]: My senses and faculties are in order. I am entirely rational. I know *it* may be hard to comprehend, but I am sober, and entirely in control of my faculties.

[Unknown Man] to [Brute]: Brother—brother, *it's* fine.

[Baethan]: *I* know *it's fine.*

[Brute]: Go, please go.

[Baethan]: So now this man gets up in my face and wants to punch me again.

[Brute]: I'm asking you—I'm trying to-

[Baethan]: Stop touching me.

[Brute]: -trying to do you a favor.

[Baethan]: Stop touching me.

[Brute]: I'm trying to do you a favor and go before they-

[Baethan]: Don't *repeat* this; you don't want to do that again.

[Brute]: Do you want to hit me?

[Baethan]: No, I don't want to hit you.

[Brute]: Then go.

[Baethan]: No.

[Brute]: I'm asking you-

[Baethan]: No—you are not an arbiter of this.

[Brute]: Alr—do you really want to get fuckin' hurt real bad?

[Baethan]: Why do you do this to yourself?

[Brute]: This... to *myself*?

[Baethan]: Yes.

[Brute]: I'm trying to give you an option to leave, before they get fuckin' *mad*.

[Baethan]: You do realize that you're the only one that's getting mad in this situation.

[Brute]: No I am not. *They're* getting mad too.

[Baethan]: Go ask them if they're getting mad.

[Brute]: ... Bud—please go—*please* go.

[Baethan]: Why? You aren't even listening to me.

[Brute]: Pleeease go-

[Baethan]: You aren't even listening to me.

[Brute]: -please—please-

[Baethan]: You just want to control me.

[Brute]: I'm asking you-

[Baethan]: All you want to do is assert any power that you have-

[Brute]: I don't-

[Baethan]: -because you are powerless in your own life.

[Brute]: In my own life-

[Baethan]: Yes.

[Brute]: -I feel powerless in my own life-

[Baethan]: That's why you want to control me.

[Brute]: *How* do I feel powerless in my own life?

[Baethan]: Because you want to *control me*.

[Brute]: No, I'm asking you.

[Baethan]: You're not asking me—you're telling me to "please go," and then, when I refuse, you just want to punch me, and that's asserting your will, because you have no control over your own life.

[Brute]: No... cuz I don't want yous... you—you could get hurt really bad here; these guys in here will not-

[Baethan]: Yeah, by *you*.

[Brute]: No—these guys in here will-

[Baethan]: By *you.*

[Brute]: No, these guys-

[Baethan]: You are the only one threatening me.

(Brute gazed downward and sighed.)

[Baethan]: You are the *only one* threatening me.

[Brute]: These guys in here will do something much-

[Baethan]: *You* are the only one threatening me.

[Brute]: Stop...

(Aforementioned unknown man charged from afar and knocked into Baethan's left shoulder. Baethan ignored the unknown man.)

[Brute]: *Stop...* I'm asking you, I'm *really* asking you to go, before they get really pissed, and do something... Really. I'm asking you, nicely. I'm trying to be nice with you.

[Baethan]: Why are you touching me?

[Brute]: You gotta go. You gotta go.

[Unknown Man] to [Baethan]: Go—go bud.

[Baethan] to [Unknown Man]: You don't even know me.

[Unknown Man]: Just go.

[Brute]: You *gotta go!*

[Baethan]: I'm not even on the property.

[Brute]: You *gotta GO!*

[Unknown man]: Look...

[Brute] to [Unknown Man]: Can I?

[Unknown Man] to [Brute]: If—if you don't I will.

[Brute] to [Baethan]: You gotta go.

[Unknown Man] to [Baethan]: Do you want—do you want him to or me?

(Brute strikes Baethan with a right hook followed by a left hook.)

[Baethan]: Oh! Is there really no other option?

[Brute]: Yes: let's go.

[Unknown Man]: Let's dance.

[Baethan]: Why?

(Baethan and Brute proceed to pace around each other. Baethan blocks one swing and dodges another.)

[Baethan]: I'm not going to hit you back.

[Brute]: Go... Go.

[Baethan]: You really are quite something.

[Brute]: Yes I am.

[Baethan]: You really are-

[Brute]: You're damn right I am somethin'.

[Baethan]: -quite something. You do know that I'm holding back-

[Brute]: Go!

[Baethan]: -but-

[Brute]: Go!

[Baethan]: -I know that as soon as I swing-

[Brute]: *Go!*

[Baethan]: -he (Unknown Man) will jump on me—so what's the point?

[Brute]: Go!

[Unknown Man] to [Baethan]: I'm not—I'm not.

[Baethan] to [Unknown Man]: Yeah—okay *buddy.*

[Unknown Man] to [Baethan]: I'm over here.

[Brute]: Go.

[Unknown Man]: Hit 'em—hit 'em!

[Brute]: You were asked to *go.*

[Baethan]: You are ridiculous.

[Brute]: You were *asked* to *go!*

[Baethan]: You're ridiculous.

(Baethan evades another swing and continues to pace alongside Brute.)

[Brute]: Go… Go.

[Baethan]: So you punched me twice, right?

(Baethan begins to shout responses to the invectives of a crowd situated near the back entrance of the bar.)

[Baethan]: This is no fight—this is a battery!

[Brute]: Stay away from this fuckin-

[Baethan]: AND *IT*'S BEING RECORDED—I KNOW HIS NAME; I'VE ALREADY FILED A REPORT TO THE POLICE!

[Peanut Gallery Member 1]: You're starting bullshit!

[Baethan]: I'M NOT STARTING ANYTHING. THIS MAN APPROACHED ME, AND BATTERED ME IN THE FACE!

[Peanut Gallery Member 1]: If you're smart then you'll leave!

[Baethan]: YES I AM SMART—THAT'S WHY HE'S GOING TO JAIL!

[Peanut Gallery Member 1]: Look what you're startin'!

(Baethan and Brute saunter around each other and veer further away from the bar.)

[Peanut Gallery Member 2]: I say slug 'em.

[BAETHAN]: LOOK AT HIM! LOOK AT THIS MAN PENT UP

WITH WRATH AND ANGER! LOOK AT HIM *PACE AROUND,* WANTING TO HIT ME BECAUSE HE HAS NO, *CONTROL-*

[Peanut Gallery Member 3]: What are you, like sixty pounds?

[Baethan]: -OVER HIS *LIFE!* SO HE WANTS TO ASSERT HIS WILL!—to control me.

[Peanut Gallery Member 1]: Hey—hey—hey—hey—hey!

[Peanut Gallery Member 3]: What do you weigh like sixty pounds dude?—fuckin runnin' around, beatin' around.

[Baethan]: I'm pacing around because he wants to batter me.

[Peanut Gallery Member 1]: Leave, bro!

(Baethan begins to walk across the parking lot, away from the bar. Brute pursues Baethan with both fists clenched and arms flared.)

[Baethan] to [Brute]: Look at you; you're very powerful. You are an *extremely* powerful man. I hope you know that I have all the evidence that I need.

[Brute]: Good.

[Baethan] to [Brute]: You have made your last mistake. I hope that you bid your family well.

[One of a group of three teenage boys standing by the open driver-side door of a truck] to [Baethan]: What does that mean?

[Baethan] to [Teenage boy]: *IT* MEANS THAT HE'S GOING TO JAIL BECAUSE I HAVE THIS RECORDED! THAT'S WHAT *THAT* MEANS—WHOEVER YOU ARE!

(Baethan approaches the nearby tavern where he was once employed and turns to face Brute while walking backwards)

[Baethan] to [Brute]: You're a *beast* and a *savage,* an animal-

[Brute] to [Baethan]: You're damn right I'm a beast and a savage-

[Baethan]: with *no,* CONTROL-

[Brute]: You're god-damned right I'm a fucking *savage.*

[Baethan]: -OVER YOUR **PATHETIC WILL!**

(Brute relented and returned to the bar from which he emerged from.)

3:33 PM

I walked around the parking lot for ten minutes, pondered my next course of action, entered the tavern—four minutes to close, in search of a pleasant social interaction before I returned home to cap off my night and tend to my new injuries. The bartender with the same name as myself sat with two other employees at a corner table, engaged with paperwork and casual conversation. The bartender said to me, "What's up, Baethan?"

I said, "Hello. On March 20th of last year, I asked you what your self-assigned meaning in life was, and you said-"

The bartender smirked and said, "You wrote *it* down—you marked *it* down? The date-" I wheezed a laugh and smiled. "-in a book? In your little book someplace—you wrote *it* down?"

I abolished my humor, continued to smile, and said, "Yes—in my little book."

"What did I say?"

"*It* said that you have no meaning and that there are no fools; do you still abide by that?"

"*It* said that I had no meaning and there are no fools... I do not abide by *that*, because I'm sure I didn't say that I had no meaning."

"You did say that."

"I'm sure that I said, that *I'm not sure.*" The bartender's eyes narrowed.

"No—you said that, you don't think that anybody needs a meaning, and that you don't think there are any fools... I want to know if you still think that."

"... Well no, I think everyone has a meaning; whether *it*'s important or not is... a different question... Uhhhh, and there are fools, but, I don't think that they're all the fools that you think people are."

"This isn't about me."

"Okay... Ummmm... No—I do not abide by that."

My tone softened: "So what is your self-assigned meaning in life?"

"I'm still thinking about *it.*"

"All right."

"*I'm* pretty sure I told you every time you've asked me this that I think *it* constantly changes. And I'm not sure what mine is, right now."

"No... I've only asked you *it* once."

"Huh?"

"I've only asked you once, on that date."

"Well, then I'm sure that that's what I said; I didn't see you write anything down after I said *it* so, *potentially,* there's a little error in your thought."

I withdrew my recorder out of my right pocket, displayed the device for the bartender and the two employees seated next to him to reckon, and said, "I didn't need to write anything down because I record everything."

The bartender turned towards the two other employees (both of whom

I asked of their self-assigned meanings of life at an earlier date), regarded me with an anxious half-frown, and said, "That makes me *incredibly* uncomfortable."

"Well, *it's* completely legal, so I don't care how uncomfortable *it* makes you feel. I was hoping for a pleasant interaction, but I suppose I'll just go home." I stood, walked towards the front entryway of the tavern, stopped, and—still determined to have my last social interaction of the night be pleasant, I said to the nearest employee (whose self-assigned meaning I also inquired of at an earlier date) behind the bar, "Take care."

The employee said, "Yeah!—you too, Baethan," and I departed.

11:23 PM

On the final set of a barbell tricep extension—my final exercise, alone at a local gym, an enormous blonde-haired 6'1 Caucasian man with a gorilla-esque and potentially steroid-enhanced physique entered in full skin-tight blue athletic garb, from hat, to face gaiter, to shoes. Impressed by the sight, and surprised by my own lack of envy, I powered on my recorder and said, "Excuse me sir!"

The man removed an earphone and said, "How you doin'?"

"What is your self-assigned meaning in life?"

"What'd you say?"

"Your self-assigned meaning in life."

"… I have no idea."

I looked away from the intensity of his hateful eyes and flexed body, downward, to my left, for I construed a scowl underneath the gaiter due to the angularity of the lines on his face. The man stood, expectant of more dialogue, though I only said, "All right," and the man resumed with the preparation of a bench press. My disappointed and amused grin, exposed— for I had been alone in the gym before the man's entry and hadn't worn a mask, reflected in the establishment's wall of mirrors. Fifty-two seconds elapsed; I donned my pack and said, "What characteristic do you pride yourself on the most?" The man either ignored me or didn't hear me. I continued, "I figured that since this is a gym, that you wouldn't mind conversing because *it's* a public area."

The man muttered a lethargic "What?"

"What characteristic do you pride yourself on the most?"

"… I really don't know."

I gazed down to my left, bemused and disappointed by the lack of thoughtfulness, and reckoned the assembly of human flesh before me: The ferocity within; the capacity for physical force; the sexual allure... all useless at this moment. I said, "Will you think about *it?*"

Another drawled-out "What?"

"Will you think about *it?*"

"I'll think about *it* and give you an answer the next time I see ya."

I nodded, said, "All right," and departed, aware of my latent judgments derived from a two-minute interaction which I now write, opened my umbrella, and walked back to my apartment amid a heavy rainstorm, all-the-while indulging in my vanity: Imagining the man under a steel bar laden with (approximately) 375 lbs, furious and hateful with the interjection I impressed upon his reality—for the *audacity* of my questions, much like the want-to-be-not trollop I encountered outside the bar... *My audacity...* to *exist* and *question,* is the comical bane of rapport, for genuine comprehension and understanding of *oneself* yields nothing decent.

Halfway towards my apartment, I imagined the man resting after a set, haughty in demeanor, engaged with his enormous aspect in the wall-mirror, *thinking...* a saddened frown beneath the gaiter; he removes the article and appraises himself with the visage of a stranger.

Wednesday, September 30th, 2020

11:24 PM

My recordings are the craft of a hack. Most people don't know what their life meaning is, nor do many want to think about *it.* Many express a random virtuous proclamation depending on their current mood. Seldom are those who assert merely "the will to live," i.e., take *it* day by day. Rare are those—in fact—*never* have I encountered a self-assigned meaning isolated from survival, a career, and the pretense of "goodness."

I gifted the executive chef, Chayanne, a copy of Marcus Aurelius' *Meditations* today.

A female barber, Jamie, who cut my hair three days ago, has requested to meet with me to converse more; I accepted.

I felt contempt for my co-workers for an ephemeral moment today and deigned to conceal the emotion.

I've reverted to my pre-Navy lifestyle of post-work gym sessions followed by late-night engorgement with simultaneous documentation of my worthless exposition. In the morning I read, consume, and perform light calisthenics to prime my endorphins. This is *it*. That's all my life is. No videos. No global or local news. No chair to sit on. No friends. The rhapsodic compositions of dead composers and the consumption of protein, fat, and caffeine are my three sources of pleasure. All else is a masochistic pursuit of fatuous turpitude.

October will be a fiction month, with no "I" involved. No life meanings. No memories. Only trite.

OCTOBER

Thursday, October 1st, 2020

10:12 PM

No fiction.

After all the evidence I acquired, the police officer in charge of my case informed me that the local judge would still rule my case as mere harassment instead of an assault, which I think is ludicrous—though what *I* think is irrelevant and contained to these pages. I visited the bar in search of the man ("Bulldog") who had battered me, questioned the owner, the bartender, and a man who initially provided me information, accrued nothing of value, returned to the police station, and chose to abandon the case.

My existence is void of significance, much like those I interact with, and those I'm aware of and don't interact with: all of us. This journal is a waste of life. These memories are a crude byproduct of my forsaken mode of being.

My pain, albeit self-induced and pampered, provides more entertainment than any fiction I may devise. The abandonment of the pursuit of justice is a victory for a reader, i.e., my future self, when I return to this passage to proofread—if I'm not granted the mercy of death before then. A *mercy?* Death? In my current condition of optimal health and security of livelihood, with only three days remaining of employment until I may leech off the state's teat with enhanced unemployment benefits due to Covid-19… death would be a *mercy?* Pitiable thoughts I refuse to eradicate from memory, for they have transpired mid-stream of consciousness, and I desire any reader other than *I* to detest me for the white centipede of a man that I am.

Inglorious, all of *it*. I'm a creep and a loser, with nothing to lose, no desire to gain, and a selfish, puerile ambition.

Friday, October 2nd, 2020

8:21 AM

I reencountered the commoner at *The Messy House* who told me his SAML is to achieve the highest score on a *PacMan* arcade machine, intoxicated on alcohol and affected by marijuana, and restated my inquiry. The man said, "Be the game of life."

I said, "Beat the game of life?

523

"No—*be* the game of life."

"Be the game of life…"

The man beamed and said, "Isn't that the whole meaning of life—is to play the game—enjoy *it*? Isn't *it*—that's *it*."

I said, "That's probably the most astute and well-thought-out answer—without any thought necessary, that I've ever heard to that question."

The man chuckled and said, "All right, well… That's really what *it* is."

"How do you play the game of life then; what's your objective?"

"What's my *objective*," he muttered through laughter and gazed up at an occluded night sky. "We all roll dice in the game of life."

"This is true, though-"

"Unless you got a spinner wheel—that goes like one through ten—though I haven't played that in a while."

I ignored the levity and said, "The chance results that happen from our dice rolls such as every breath that we take-"

"*What?*"

"Each breath that we take could be our last, and that's a dice roll in *it*self; every beat of our heart. So you don't have an objective? You just exist… as an amoeba."

"To an extent."

I smiled and said, "That's the way of the Dao, or the Tao…"

Another young Caucasian man named Ethan joined us and negated the conversation: Energetic and amiable. The amoeba man implored me to ask Ethan the same question I had asked him; I did:

"Umm… My meaning in life has changed since I've had a daughter. Um, my focus is mainly her."

"Who?"

"My daughter."

"Your daughter… How old is your daughter?"

"Uh—she's three."

"And what would you say your meaning of life was prior to your daughter?"

"Music."

"So now your daughter has superseded your passion."

"In a sense—yeah. I still love music; *it* hasn't changed but, *it* just, um, the view of *it* has changed in my mind a bit like… ya know, *it*'s not so much, cuz I like rock n' roll—*it* was like sex, rock 'n' roll and drugs and shit like that—though now that I've had a daughter *it* just all seems so superficial now—ya know—*it* just all seems… crazy."

"You've severed your ego and spawned new life into the world that you're now responsible for."

"Yeah."

An African-American man joined our trifecta. I stood and listened to the incessant banter between them for six minutes, in-wait of an opening in the dialogue that never transpired, with my hands clasped in front of my pelvis. The three men departed for the bar to ingest more alcohol and I remained statuesque in the parking lot for twenty-two seconds where I stared at the pavement before returning to my apartment.

Saturday, October 3rd, 2020

10:11 AM

I am invariably swayed by the subtle wiles of women and am grateful for the vitalization.

11:10 PM

The Daliah Lama is Machiavellian.

Women I have become accustomed to (waitresses) share sister traits: Vapidity and vacuousness. A tender gaze is nullified by a spoken word, especially when they chatter amongst each other. Engagements with men are cloy, histrionic, and overblown panderings tainted with dissimulated affections. The men are hackneyed and obsequious to a nubile waitstaff, yet macho and garish in homosocial engagements.

Beatrice sang along with a female vocalist version of the song *Mad World*, which resonated through shoddy phone speakers, while she sorted silverware into cubbies behind me throughout the final five minutes of our last shift together. I thought to sing-along with her and didn't.

Monday, October 5th, 2020

4:37 PM

Last night, during my final hour of employment in the bar's kitchen, Thor approached me with his phone number scrawled on a piece of torn paper and said, "Get ahold of me; text me tomorrow; like, for real, text me tomorrow. I don't want to be alone; you don't want to be alone; I'm sure we'll get along."

I nodded and said, "I will."

That night, after a session at the gym, I stopped at *The Messy House* bar for thirty-five minutes to observe drunkards observing a game of televised football and their banal interactions which proceeded outside, where four of the nameless trounced around a burst packet of barbeque sauce. I returned to my apartment, prepared my nightly omelet, and sent Thor two consecutive text messages:

"I've contemplated your proposal for friendship and have decided that I must decline; the nature of my writing depends on an absence of meaningful social validation; otherwise, I will become 'soft' and malleable.

"Though we are similar in our status of societal detritus and intellectual capacity, I'd prefer to remain as workplace comrades, maligned by our colleagues for our banter. Nonetheless, I appreciate your outreach, and respect you for the man that you are."

I've received no response. ~~in over fourteen hours.~~[57]

Three days ago, in the parking lot between the tavern where I had once labored and *The Messy House,* I encountered three people: An old Caucasian man around the age of fifty-five, a young drunken Caucasian woman in her mid-twenties, and an overweight, short, mid-twenties Caucasian man with mid-length frazzled hair tied up in a small knot at the peak of his head. I approached all three and recorded a superlative conversation on the topic of self-assigned meanings in life:

I said, "Do you mind if I ask all of you a peculiar question?"

The mid-twenties knotted-hair man and woman both said, "Sure."

"All right. What is your self-assigned meaning in life?"

The knotted hair man said, "I have a question for you first."

"Yes."

"Are you tripping balls right now?"

"No—I am entirely sober."

"Oh. Just totally soul-searching?"

"Soul-searching others—yes, if you believe in the soul; I don't."

"Meaning of life…"

The woman corrected the knotted-hair man: "*Your* life, the meaning of *your* life."

---

[57] I never received a response.

"Oh *my* life?"

I said, "Yes, your self-assigned meaning in life."

A six-second silence elapsed. The woman initialized: "I feel like to figure that out we wouldn't be standing in a parking lot in [City Name] at 11:30 at night."

The old man said, "That's a good point—but um-"

The knotted-hair man said, "I actually had a realization, when... when actually tripping—so, *it*'s basically to just make the world a better place for the next generation, as *much* as you can. That's kinda—that's kinda where—what I want to do is... even if I can define or can't define *it*—figure out, if there's something I can do with *my* time, to make *it* better—a little bit better for the next generation."

The old man said, "That's a good one. That's a good one."

"I had a *long* talk with Stan," said the knotted-hair man to the old man.

The old man said, "I think for me *it*'s... you know along the same lines—but just... Yeah I mean, going through your day and... I think if you can make somebody's day better, make *it* better, ya know? Not to be cliché but kindness doesn't cost a fuckin' thing, ya know? Help people! Whatever *it* is, ya know? Somebody looks like they need a hug—somebody needs... a *dollar*, ya know? Whatever *it* is, just *help*. Make *it* better. Even if—even if *it*'s nothing, ya know?—to *you*; *it* could mean everything for whoever you're doing *it* for."

The knotted man addressed the woman: "You're up [Name]."

"I don't know—I'm drunk," said the woman.

The old man said, "That's actually a good answer."

"Yeah," affirmed the knotted-hair man.

The woman said, "I mean, I guess um... I want to be a teacher, so I feel like, ya know... to help out the next generation..." She droned, "I feel like you wanna make the world a better place than when you left *it*-"

"Yeah!" The knotted-hair man interjected, "And *it*'s also because we're continuously living in a world where our ability to... to *document* things is getting *better* and *better*. So, a lot of what we're trying to do is just make *it*—cuz that's humans—humans, *like* telling stories, and the reason people do things is so they can leave that story for someone else to read—if *it*'s either a pride thing or-"

The woman said, "Everyone wants to be remembered."

"-Exactly—*it* could even be an ego thing, but like... you... *it*'s like 'Oh I wanna be remembered because I think I'm hot shit.' But *it*'s, I think *it*'s more primordial than that of just like... You wanna leave your mark because you don't want to be forgotten."

The old man said, "Well I think *it*'s ingrained in us to pass along knowledge too I mean-"

"Yup, exactly."

"-or we don't evolve."

"Yeah, cuz if we are encoded to evolve, then, *it*'s probably something in our DNA that says 'you should be forwarding the generation; you should be forwarding the human race, in *some* way or the other."

"Absolutely—yeah."

Four seconds of silence elapsed; the woman said to me, "Your answer now!"

The knotted-hair man said, "Yeah, your turn."

I said, "Well, I'll segue off of his (knotted-hair man's) answer; my self-assigned meaning of life is to write about the human condition, and I've been documenting in a journal, and publishing a book each year for the past three years." I revealed my recorder. "I have recorded this entire conversation and I intend to transcribe *it* at a later point—probably sometime tomorrow. What you all said, including you," I pointed at the woman, "You may as well just be drunk!"

All three chuckled.

I continued, "That's a self-assigned meaning, so-"

The woman smiled and said, "Maybe that's my meaning."

"To be drunk?" said the knotted-hair man.

The woman affirmed with a jubilant shout, "To be drunk!"

I nodded at the knotted-hair man and said, "What you said about the ego, and how *it*'s encoded... part of the evolution of our species, and our desire to tell a story... That struck me personally, because *it is* egotistical; I'm an entirely egotistical, self-engrossed, puerile, *nasty* human being, with no friends and no family, because all I do is write, and I prefer *it* that way—*but*, I'm telling the 'story' of everybody that I meet."

The knotted-hair man said, "Is *it* by choice?"

"*It*'s by choice."

The old man said, "That's very difficult to choose."

"That's admirable!" proclaimed the knotted-hair man.

"*It is* admirable," the old man agreed.

I looked down to my left, grimaced, and growled a low-pitched groan. Three seconds elapsed.

The knotted-hair man said, "Do you go to bed happy every night?

I chuckled.

"Or is *it* extremely lonely?" said the knotted-hair man, "Cuz like, there *are* people who don't like to be lonely, and there are people who prefer to be lonely."

I said, "There is definitely loneliness, though *it*'s not... suffering for me."

The knotted-hair man said, "Tolerable?"

"Yes."

"I mean if you're doing something that you're motivated with, then, I guess, *it* outweighs-"

I said, "*It* does; I'm a wretch, though I accept my wretchedness."

The woman giggled.

The knotted-hair man inquired, "Is what you say also in the writing?"

"Yes."

The woman said, "You can't write without putting a piece of yourself into *it* though, to a certain extent, I feel like."

I nodded and said, "Most of the content starts with 'I.'"

The knotted-hair man said, "Do you ever have your own realizations, listening back to yourself saying 'Okay this is an experience I *also* learned from'?"

I said, "Yes, and, from that, *it* makes me realize that personality and virtue are pretentious and perpetuated by culture."

The old man raised an eyebrow and said, "Oh?"

"I have a question again," said the knotted-hair man, "just cuz this is interesting: Do you ever feel like that you've... I'm going to attack you a little just because I'm trying to-"

I interrupted, "Please do."

"... Do you ever feel like you don't have an original thought because of all of the interview-type stuff that you do—that a lot of your ideas are just of other people?"

I said, "That's ha—yes—I started writing fiction to pass the time, but as progress evolved and I'm on year four now, closing out, the interviews have superseded the fiction, but I also have my personal exposition of life alongside... the interviews, and the fiction... but... I thank you all for your time."

The knotted-hair man, woman, and old man each said respectively: "Thank you!"; "Thank you."; "No thank you for *your* time; that was a very interesting ten minutes we just had here and I appreciate *it*."

I said, "I think I'll actually go to bed happy tonight."

The knotted-hair man requested the name of my documentation and thereby fulfilled my self-assigned delusional and egotistical meaning for my irrelevant metanonfictional existence.

Tuesday, October 6ᵗʰ, 2020

12:21 PM

I met with the female Caucasian barber in her presumed late-thirties at a coffee house within a four-minute walk of my apartment at 10:00 AM today, as we had arranged. Walther, my former employer at the two adjacent bars, sat with her, to my surprise and bewilderment. On my entry, Walther stood, and we greeted each other with an exchange of formalities without physical contact. Walther departed less than a minute after my arrival. I sat with the barber, Jamie, on two cushioned seats in the corner of the coffee shop, revealed my recorder, and set the device on a square table to my left beside a book titled *The Body Keeps the Score,* subtitled, *Brain, Mind, and Body in the Healing of Trauma,* by Van der Kolk MD. I begrudge the transcription of this hour-long moment in time, to endure the immortal memory of *it* for as long as I live on each idle instance I return to these words; the pathetic clown that I am:

Café Conversation

I said, "Why were you meeting with Walther? I'm curious. How do you know him?"

Jamie said, "He—uh, I cut his hair, but he was sittin' here, um… when I walked in, so I—we're close ya know, so I sat down to chat with him."

"He recently fired me—did he tell you?"

"Yes."

"Did he tell you why?"

"No."

"Oh."

"He's a very professional person."

"Ah."

"Okay."

"All right."

Jamie laughed and said, "Yeah, you're safe."

"Well, I had chosen to refrain from speaking at work."

"Ohhh you didn't want to talk to anyone anymore."

"Yes *it* was uh, *it* was a social study."

"Social study-"

"Yes."

"-well, I got you. All right."

"But, that's—that's besides the point of this; I just wanted to know if he actually told you anything about that or..."

"Um, he did say that you were in the Army and that your dad l—lives around here."

"Ah, I was in the Navy."

"Navy? Okay."

"Yes."

"All right."

I said, "Yes—my father lives across town but I no longer communicate with him."

"Okay. All right, um, so... you said you were from the what? The womb? Is that what you said?"

"The womb."

"So that would be the center of the galaxy?"

"Well, *it* was more of uh: I was spawned from my mother's uterus."

Jamie said, "Okay... but then you don't... You said you had family, like your dad and stuff... so, where does the connection—I don't, I-"

"Wha-"

"I believe you; I believe that you might have a connection to, ya know like some kind of galaxy and stuff—we all do; we're all connected; *it's* how I feel. I feel like I, um, am a Starseed, like from Arcutrian," Jamie phrased the statement as a question. "You ever heard of them?"

"Acturian?"

"Like Pleiadians?"

"I've never heard of that."

"What council are you from?"

"What council?"

Jamie patiently said, "Do you have a Starseed council—someone that, is there a name for *it?*"

"No."

"No? Okay." Jamie chuckled.

I said, "*It...* Is that a reference to something?"

"A reference to um… like a council would be like your energy point—your source."

"I think of a council as in: A bunch of old men with beards sitting around discussing topics nobody really cares about but themselves." Jamie laughed. I continued, "Is that what you're referring to?"

Jame asserted, "That would be like an *egoic* council—yeah."

"So wh… What 'council' are you referring to?"

"Mmmm more like a, like a light source? Like um… a council within, that you're connected to."

"I have no idea; all I know is that I'm just a bag of flesh and meat, and that I'm going to die someday."

"Soon?"

"Perhaps."

"Yup."

"*It* could be today."

Jamie murmured, "Yeah, *it* could."

"I don't know."

"Okay. So you've had some experiences, in, in your *flesh-body.* There's, what's—what's… who's your flesh body what… What is the experience in the flesh-body? What do you consider that?"

"What is my *experience,* in the *flesh?* My consciousness."

"Okay—so, your consciousness belongs to a group of consciousness, right?"

"The interconnected consciousness—is that what you're referring to?"

"Yes, mhm. Which you would say is from, 'The Womb'? Or the galaxy center?"

"… I don't know."

Jamie snickered and said, "You know these questions. You don't wanna answer them."

"I don't know the answer to these questions; in fact this is the first time I've ever been asked if I'm from the universe's womb. I'm not even sure-"

"You said that in my chair. You said 'I'm from the womb.'"

"Yes, as in I'm from my mother's womb."

"Okay. All right, so you do—so you're sayin, in your hu—in your human experience that's where you're from."

"Yes."

"Where did you grow up after that?"

"Where did I-"

"Are you from [City Name]? From this area?"

"I'm from [Current City Name]."

"[Current City Name]."

"But a 'denizen of the world' is what I said."

Jamie enunciated: *"Denizen* of the world, okay; explain that to me."

"A denizen is just another name for somebody who... resides, somewhere. But d-'denizen' is more of a... not so much a resident—such as: when I go into a kitchen workspace, and the people there: They are denizens of the kitchen."

"Okay so *it's* whatever space you occupy."

"Yes."

"Okay, so-"

"So I'm a denizen of the world, or, a denizen of the universe's womb for all I know."

"Okay, so that would make people think you're like, a, extraterrestrial, or maybe like a being from another planet, when you talk like that."

"Why?"

"It just has that feel! And then, um, with your, uh, people thinking you're, mentally, like, unstable—*it's*, *it's* a matter of, disconnection, to the world. Like you have this like, disconnection."

I gazed down at the floor between my feet for three seconds, readdressed Jamie, and said, "I really want to know why you were speaking with Walther-"

"Huh?"

"-prior to meeting with me."

"Why what?"

"I want to know why you were speaking with Walther prior to meeting with me. If there is any... coincidence, or... relation-"

"Oh."

"-there because I don't speak to anybody at all."

"No. Okay."

"I am, secluded in my own space; I don't have any friends—I don't have any family."

Jamie said, "But you're connected to us somehow because-"

"Yes, but Walther-"

"by meeting you, l-led to me meeting him (Walther)-"

I interjected, "So-"

"-which had *nothing* to do with anything we talked about-"

"Yes."

"-me and Walther."

533

I said, "Yes, so to see Walther in this chair speaking to you prior to a meeting-"

"Coincidence."

"-that we had is amazing to me, because-"

"Pure coincidence."

"... That's incredible... Did you arrange that to happen?"

Jamie said, "No. I swear on what my children are—I swear on my children—there was nooo-"

"All right."

"-there was no planned meeting on that."

"I'm indifferent to what you spoke of; *it's* just..." I released a slight groan and contemplated.

"Why does *it* bother you that Walther was here?"

"Well because I forced his hand to fire me, I gave him no other option, and he didn't want to."

"When he spoke of you in my chair, he spoke highly of you like, like you were normal."

"I'm surprised by that, because-"

"He accepted you for who you are, and was okay with *it*."

"Well he's a professional as you said so of course he'll speak nothing but-"

"Profession."

"Yes."

"Professional. He said you're a very hard worker."

"I suppose that's all that matters... I called him a shyster about three or four days ago, in jest, with a bartender he employs... because, I stopped in, well—that's besides the point—I should be professional much like him. Let's get back to the womb of the universe, or, this book." I waved a hand over the book on the square table.

Jamie laughed and said, "I just brought this, and I don't know why—but *it* was calling to me, to bring. And I actually brought *more* than just this. Um, because I'm not sure like... I'm intrigued by you."

"Did you arrange this meeting to educate me?"

"No. To educate me."

"To educate *you?*"

"Mhm."

"... What do I know?"

"What do you know?"

Vexed, I said, "Is that what you're hoping to find out? I'm going to disappoint you."

"No, I have no expectation. I'm just intrigued."

"All right. What else did you bring?"

Jamie giggled and said, "I just want to see like, if you believe in any of this—or, if you think of any of *it*—like your *thoughts*. I don't know if you have feelings, but… um. *This* book I feel like would be interesting for you to read."

I picked up the book on the table beside me, began to read the back cover, and said, "Trauma."

"*Yes!* You said you were in the Navy—maybe, you face something as a child or-"

I addressed points on the back cover: "I was not molested. Mmmm— my father was an alcoholic."

"Yes, I had an alcoholic mother. I know what that can do to you."

"I have not engaged in physical violence with a couple."

"Huh?"

"I have not engaged in physical violence with a couple before."

"Okay. Trauma doesn't have to be something physical either. Have you ever-"

"I think that trauma is chosen though-"

"Have you ever heard of-"

"-much like suffering."

"Have you ever heard of this?" Jamie held a copy of Anodea Judith's *Chakra Yoga*.

"I've heard of chakras but I've never read any books on *it*."

Jamie whispered, "Okay," and proceeded at normal volume, "Cuz you talked about… like… and I feel like we made a connection on this that, um… this world… You asked what my purpose is-"

"Yes."

"My purpose is to help people, awaken, and heal, and realize that, they can heal themselves; they don't need a pill; they don't need anything but… themselves, and do the inner work, themselves. A lot of people need to waken up in this world, okay, and people are changing; we're loving one another; we're, loving the earth—there's people out here that really do wanna see better. I guess, with my meeting you, is I wanna give you some faith, in, humanity, cuz there is people that care… okay? So, with that being saaaid I just wanted to *see* if you kinda knew anything about like, chakras and energy points."

"So you *are* here to educate me."

"*No.* I'm here to, see what you believe in I guess."

"You're here to educate me on-"

"Healing."

"-the morality of humanity-"

Jamie spoke with a tender inflection contrary to my solemnity: "You asked me what my purpose was."

"-because that would be restoring my faith in humanity."

"I don't know if that would be what I am able to do... Okay... *But...*"

"But, the only version of man—or woman, that we may know, is of ourselves, and that's old, wisdom. So if I am a misanthropic asshole to everybody that I meet, that's because I am simply self-hating."

"Well that would be a reflection of yourself... Yeah—but you said you're all ego and that's what your ego would want you to do, ya know?"

"Yes."

A dog whined and barked. Jamie said, "Yep. But if you drop the ego, and, and learn how to balance your inner energies, you can actually heal, and—and... like, get rid of your ego, and really just kind've feel the connection you might have that others-"

I said, "But I *need* my ego for all that *it* is... in order to create."

"Create what?"

"I write. And the whole purpose of my self-ostracization from friendships, is to cultivate my ego; as soon as I establi—yes-"

Jamie held up a finger, "Sorry. All right, so... Your purpose doesn't come from your ego—*it* comes from... your, s-deep soul, inside—otherwise you're not feeling anything that's going to make you happy."

"My life purpose is not to be happy."

"That's not a life purpose then."

With flummoxed confusion expressed on my visage, I said, "Being happy is completely out of bounds with any sort of motive or intent or fulfillment that I have."

"Right. Okay. So how can you write... What is *it* that you're writing about?"

"The human condition."

"Okay—so but... that's a condition... being happy."

"*It* is."

"Yes, and being sad, and being in your ego; they're all conditions—so you can't, you can't write about the human experience unless you experience *it*... right?"

"Of course-"

"Okay."

"-which is the whole point of this interaction right now-"

"Yes."

"-and the later transcription with, additional commentary."

Jamie chuckled and said, "Yes, I don't know why but that makes sense—but yeah.[58] Um, so, maybe you're happy that we're meeting." I gazed to my left. "You're not mad about *it*... right?"

"Well, I'm not happy; I was, interested, and confused."

Jamie laughed and said, "Well those are good emotions too. Yes, so-"

"I had no idea why you wanted to meet me—but now I see *it*'s, to assert your will over mine."

"No, there's no motive. Um, just simply as intrigued and confused as you were." More laughter. I stared at Jamie; her voice remained lighthearted and at ease, "And I—I just kinda wanted to see, like, what *it* was, that you're um... *yours*—your motive is, I guess, like what you're trying to do."

"What *I'm* trying to do?"

"Yeah!—I mean you said-"

"In—in this interaction?"

"Yeah. You wanna write but, these are words that are written," Jamie laid her right palm on top of *The Body Keeps the Score*. "Ya know—these are words that are written that will help you understand human experience... okay? These are words that are written on the human experience, so, that's what I'm sayin'... You can experience from your ego but you're not gonna experience everything... Have you experienced healing? Happiness?"

"Healing?"

"Have you ever cried?"

"Of course."

"Have you ever laughed?"

"Yes."

"So you've experienced that, right?"

"I think that there is no difference between laughing and crying."

"Have you experienced love? Connection?"

"Yes." I sighed.

---

[58] The commentary I foreordained is summarized in this annotation: Disgust, for the ignorance, dumbness, and vacuity of enforced compassion on behalf of the whole lot of the human race. This woman who sat before me, with her plethora of responsibilities, offspring, companions, secret lovers, machinations–pretenses of goodwill for the sake of her own validation, had been perceived by me as nothing but a cosmological bimbo, deluded by spiritual mysticism proliferated by charlatans of the most despicable sect of self-help psychiatric gurus who profit off of perpetuating victimhood "identities."

"You did. Okay. Do you care to talk about—were you hurt by *it?*"

"Well love—I have a definition of love."

"Okay."

"To love, is… Well, hold on, let me rethink *it.*"

"Do you mind if I go get a cup of coffee while you think about *it?*"

"I don't mind at all—I'll get one too."

"Okay."

We both stood and ordered our respective coffees. Reggae music resonated. The clatter of dish and silverware ebbed from a nearby kitchen. A painting of a surreal black death plague doctor and other abstract art conceptualizing the human form decorated the walls. Three couples sat on highchairs around circular tables and muttered amongst themselves, each person casting furtive glances at the other—strangers, yet similar in every way that amounts to *anything.*

Jamie and I returned to our cornerside cushioned seats; she said, "Sooo, your definition of love."

"To love is to embrace what you hate, be *it* a person, idea, or yourself."

"Embrace something you hate?"

"Yes. To accept the polarity of unification, and to worship your self-destruction; so for instance, when you bear a child, *it* is a blank egoic[56] template, and the pure ego, is something that is extremely *contemptible,* and easy to hate: *it's* yearning: *it's* nothing but desire; *it* cries; *it* wants to be fed, but, since *it's* yours-

"Cuz *it's* all ego."

"Yes, so you love *it* and shape *it* to your expectations, and you mold *it* to be what you want *it* to be—so you start out-"

"I try."

"-*hating it* because *it's* just a little sack of flesh that wants everything from you, but then as *it* grows *it* becomes more self-sustaining, and, you begin to love *it* because *it*—re—*it,* resembles your *own* ego."

"… *It* can if you grow *it* that way."

"And *it* destroys you, when you bear a child-"

"*It* can-"

"-you sever your own ego-"

"-you can-"

"-to invest *it* into another."

"You can look at *it* as *it* destroys you or you can look at *it* as, you did something that, you know is—beautiful… and that's your body… from *it*… *It* might not be perfect but who wants a perfect image all the time?"

"A perfect what?"

"Image."

"Well *it*'s more than image."

"*It* doesn't destroy your body—I mean we're made to produce… you know. I mean I'm still fine; I had two." Jamie laughed. I frowned. "I'm not dead from *it;* you know my body is okay. I got scars but—what—I got a scar from falling off my bike… ya know… *It*'s just a scar. The rest of my body is… healthy… right?" Five seconds of silence elapsed. "Let's um… Let's talk about… this, book… Do you feel like… you might have some sort of PTSD from… maybe being in the military?"

Wednesday, October 7ᵗʰ, 2020

10:02 AM

[Café Conversation Continued]

I said, "Not at all."

"No? Was *it* a good experience?"

"No."

Jamie chortled and said, "All right… Have you ever like, looked up—I think you should read this; I *don't* think you have a mental disorder." I snickered. "I don't want you to think that—but I want you to learn about… what they are, so that when people put you in that category, you can tell them the difference."

I leaned back in my chair and said, "Oh… I enjoy being put into categories."

Jamie laughed and said, "That's funny."

"And I don't care to dispel any sort of delusions or projections that I fit, of the criteria, of other people; in fact, I encourage them-"

"Mhm."

"-to hold on, to those sentiments and thoughts."

"So who are you writing to? Your experience."

"Myself, but, I publish, because *it*'s a puerile exposition."

"Do you have any books published?"

"Yes. Three."

"What are they?"

I said, "What are they?"

Jamie searched for a pen and said, "I'm gonna write *it* down."

"You'd be a fool to read them."

"Why?"

"Because *it*'s my pure ego."

"Yeah but—don't you... What do you write for? If you don't want anyone to read *it?*"

"Myself, but I publish *it* to, *entice* fools, similar to a dragon collecting treasure, and hoarding *it* in his den." Jamie giggled. "He waits for fools to come and try to take *it,* and then he... consumes them."

"Oh you think *it* would get in their mind?"

"Oh yes—*it*'s not something that you'll want to read: *It*'s vile."

"Okay... So that, that, you want to make your purpose in life?"

"That is my purpose in life—is to write."

"Who gave you that purpose?"

"I did."

"You don't want any other purpose?"

My face twisted into a comical glower and I said, "What do you mean who *gave* me that purpose?"

"Isn't there—*it*'s not, okay so there's not just... This pen, okay... This pen was created; this pen has a purpose. Okay." I watched Jamie draw lines on each corner of the rectangle framing the humanoid figure on the cover of *The Body Keeps the Score*. "But there was a lot that went into making this pen and creating *it*."

I droned, "Yes—the pen was created by men and women from this *material world,* with the knowledge and processes that we have accrued from living in this material world."

Jamie's tone remained amicable and upbeat, "So this—this is a mater—this—I'm not gonna disagree with that-"

"Though-"

"-people are very materialistic, in this world."

"The purpose that we assign to the pen is not something that is... innate; *it*'s just an amalgamation of properties."

Jamie continued to sketch lines on the book cover, her gaze focused on the task; she said, "Now this pen has... another purpose... to create more... than, *it*self... *It* can create... after being created." Jamie ceased from her trance, acknowledged me again, and said, "So... *You,* have this purpose, just like this pen... Then so you have this purpose, and now, you're able to create with *it*... But you don't want anyone to see *it*."

"… Well *it*'s not that I don't want anyone to see *it;* I'm just giving you fair warning."

"Okay—so if they do see *it, it*'s gonna consume the person that… you're creating *it* for?" Jamie retracted the tip of the pen and pushed the books aside.

I interwove my fingers in my palm and stared at Jamie: "That's not necessarily true; the metaphor of the dragon, was, merely for…uhh—comical or satirical effect-"

"All right-"

"Because when you read words they have an impression on you—much like these words in these books have had an impression on you that is… supposedly, or presumably, powerful enough, that you wish to share them with me—but they're just words, and there is no truth, so how much merit—really, is there in the idea of energy in one's body?"

"Well these—these—this book *(The Body Keeps the Score)* is based on *studies* and things that people at universities have done on trauma, and, they put the s-statistics together, and then um, they talk about the best way to heal people and stuff. But this is based on true, like, experience, and groups, so when you create a group experience, *it* becomes a bigger experience, and *it* has more power and more energy; so the more people that read this, the more power and energy these—this book has. *It* creates…"

"Yes-"

"More energy."

"There is power in mob rule, and the masses."

"So, but you don't want anyone to read yours—you don't want to create power with your, self—but you seem very egotistical so, you would—I think you would want, to create…"

"My power… is… negligible… I have no interest in *power.*"

"… Right… So you have no interest in growing, in any way?"

"Do you equate power with growing?"

"I don't know… I mean these are still things I'm trying to figure out, but, I mean, I'm just trying to figure out like what you think; you asked my purpose, ya know-"

"You said to take care of your dog, but now that I know you have children… I think you're full of shit."

Jamie laughed and said, "I have two children—I have a dog—I have a boyfriend—I have a mom—I have a dad—I have a sister—I have a niece and nephew; I have, very close friends, and relatives, and, a lot of connections with people, that, outreach the whole area... that's amazing to me."

"So you just said 'to take care of your dog' on a whim then-"

"My-"

"-without really thinking about my question."

"My dog, is, my, my love—I love him; he's my connection and, I *enjoy* him... a lot."

"Dogs don't have a long lifespan so what happens when the dog dies?"

"I, become sad—but—but you *know* that."

"Do you no longer have a meaning in life at that point?"

"The meaning?... of life?"

"A meaning for your life, your self-assigned meaning; that was my question."

"My life doesn't depend on the life of my *dog*... He's just, part of my experience."

"When I asked you what your self-assigned meaning in life is, you said, your dog."

Jamie giggled and said, *"No!* No, I told you to get a dog... to see what your reaction would be... To see if you're capable of like, loving something even though you're gonna lose *it*... You can love without attachment... You're very much in your ego."

I droned, "Yes—I love myself even though I will die."

Jamie laughed and said, "We all do. What happens after you die?"

"I don't know."

"... Are you willing to listen to something?"

"Sure."

"Just an idea-"

"Is *it* somebody who knows what's going to happen once I die?"

"Yes... she claims."

"How do they know that—or how does she know that?"

Jamie inhaled and exhaled an exasperated breath and said, "She does uh, um—hypnosis. She does like past-life regressions and stuff—so, she'll hypnotize someone and talk to them, like their sou—like their source inside—energy; she'll talk to you and talk to someone in Paris and pick up where she left off—she's done *it*, over a thousand times, all over the world, many witnesses. And she has a pretty good idea, I think..."

"... *All right.*"

"If you'd like to listen to *it.*"

"... I'll listen."

Jamie said, "Okay, I'll write *it* down for you." Twenty-one seconds elapsed; Jamie handed me a piece of folded stationery paper with the words *"Dolores Cannon Life After Death"* written on the top line.

I set the paper on the square table beside me and said, "Walther is of great interest to me."

"Yeah?"

"I've written about him."

"You have?"

"I've asked him what his self-assigned meaning is in life-"

"-what'd he say?"

"And what his def—his definition of love is… and I worked for the man, for a cumulative year… so to see him sitting here when I walked in, on a chance arrangement that I made with you… that is uncanny."

Jamie said, "I can tell *it* bothers you, but—um-"

"Not bothersome-"

"-I assure you *it*'s nothing that we planned. I feel like *it*'s um, maybe… your guides—whether you believe you have 'em or not, made that happen. Or, someway, you manifested that. Do you think about him a lot?"

"I don't think about him a lot; I recently reread what I wrote about him… because I was editing before my publication-"

"Mhm."

"-so he was fresh in my mind."

"Okay."

I muttered, "And I recently had the interaction where I had him fire me."

"Where what?"

"Where, I… I forced his hand to fire me, and that didn't end on a positive note for either of us." Jamie giggled. "So to see him here-"

"Was he polite? He never said a bad word about you."

"He was suppressing… something: a powerful emotion. When he handed me my notice of termination of employment, his hands were trembling… So I'm surprised he spoke nothing but positivity on my behalf."

"I don't think he wanted to fire you."

"He didn't, though; that's why I'm surprised that he spoke nothing but positivity."

"I don't think he wanted to fire you—he liked you."

"Yes—he liked me for my labor."

"But uh something happened—you probably forced *it?*—so, he had no choice?" I glared at Jamie. "He liked your work ethic."

"I think that's all. Other than that, I think I asked too many questions, and then went silent."

"… Oh, I don't… I don't know-"

"We discussed… rapport, being essential for workplace function, and we shared an interest in John Locke, a philosopher… and, the social contract." A blender resounded from behind the coffee counter. I hastened to speak: "I'm not one for gossip; I hardly speak to anybody at all anyway, though what happened, is: we met in the kitchen, and we were discussing the essentials of r-rapport from a manager's perspective… and, so I decided to, go mute, and to refrain from speaking to anybody at all in the workplace. But I still communicated with gestures, and nods, and what happened was… the managerial staff, banded together, and compiled a list of complaints, and brought *it* to Walther-"

"Okay."

"-because of my lack of speaking. And I was fired from a *dishwashing* position, for not speaking. Now what dishwasher do you know-"

"Needs to speak?"

"Yes."

"That's weird."

I said, "So, *it* was out of personal slights, that got me fired, which is anything but professional, in my eyes, which is why I, went out of my way to force Walther's hand to fire me, because I thought *it* was completely absurd… Because despite how hard I worked, and my dedication, and commitment—because I ruffled a few feathers, and didn't speak to anybody, who, wanted me to speak to them… *personally,* that's what got me fired—*but*—then I was hired a day later-"

"But, you did a social exp-"

"-someplace else so-"

"You did that-"

"Yes."

"-an experim—an experiment for you to see what would happen if you did that."

"Yes—and while I was mute, I projected nothing but contempt, and I know that's what got me fired."

"Contempt."

"If I was projecting… *joy…* I'd still be there, but instead, *it* was just contempt."

"So you did that on purpose?"

"Yes."

"That was your purpose. You manifested *it*, and you made *it* happen."

"Yes."

"Even though, I feel like Walther would have rather kept you."

"... Yes."

"So-"

"That's the power of the will, when you're-"

"-you really shouldn't—I don't think you really should be mad at him—*it* was something he had no choice to do." Jamie clicked a pen repeatedly. A gaggle of women laughed at the opposite end of the café.

"I'm not mad at him at all-"

"Yeah."

"-in fact, I sympathized with him. I called myself... 'pusillanimous,' at the moment of termination, because, I left the establishment like a dog, tail between his legs."

Eight seconds elapsed; shame from speaking incited me to sigh; Jamie clicked the top of a pen's tip and said, "Yeah if like the dog was being *mistreated*, but what if the dog was, met with nothing but *love* and... joy for *it*s presence."

"Oh, no—I'm not saying that I was mistreated by any means... The way that he conducted himself—Walther; I called him 'magnanimous'; I wrote *it* on a piece of paper: 'I am amazed by your magnanimity.' And I called myself pusillanimous by contrast-"

"Mhm."

"-because that's the antithesis of, being mag—uh, of being magnanimous, so... *it* was, I recorded the entire conversation—well— the—the, the one-sided, termination... addressal, that he made to me... I feel somewhat guilty about *it;* I think that's why I'm telling you; you're like a clergy member right now... though at the same time I did make *it* happen."

"Yeah. I don't think you want *it* to."

"No—I wanted to."

"No—I don't—*he* didn't want to lose you, I think; I think he liked you... and he's a very, very eccentric person and people don't understand either, so—I mean—he probably related himself to you."

"How is he eccentric?"

"People don't understand him too. When people don't understand why you do things, *it* makes you eccentric."

545

"Eccentric? Uh—behavior that's-"

Jamie shifted in her seat and said, *"I think* it *makes you* cool—I mean I like people that are like different, from other people." I looked down at the floor and expelled a faint groan. "So, that's just me but he's probably the same—that's probably why he likes me."

"I apologize for segueing this conversation to gossip."

Jamie giggled and said, *"It's* okay! I actually got to see that you feel, and I like that."

"Oh I feel a great deal... I'm only human."

"But you did form another, connection to somebody or purpose, that you might care about, so, that's good... right?" Jamie's naive *and* condescending inquiries unsettled me. The discomfort of being seated in the café environment, immersed among other banal conversations such as the one I transcribe now—being probed for *feelings,* the constant clatter of silverware, pandering laughter—my *own* vacuity, rendered repentant and bleak-

I said, "Good, I don't know."

"It could be good; I think if—I honestly, in my opinion, if you went back to Walther and said 'Could I please have my job back, I will be a little more joyful while I'm here," I chortled. Jamie continued, "'and speak,' or *something*—like I'm not gonna... I'll be happier to be here, not really like... I bet he'd hire you back."

"I'm sure he would... Or maybe he wouldn't—I don't know-"

"Maybe you were appreciated-"

"-but I have no desire."

"-and you didn't see *it.*"

I said, "Yes, I was appreciated in the utilitarian sense." The barista slammed an object four times against a counter, tossed silverware into cubbies, and fumbled with plastic bags.

"Maybe, but maybe in other ways, too."

"I don't think anybody cared for my charming personality."

"I think you're wrong; I think you did."

I chuckled and said, "No—I—I know my experience, and I know the way that I conducted myself, and the impressions-"

"Then just conduct yourself in a different way." Seven seconds elapsed. "Try to experience other emotions that you might have."

"... Well... I have no desire."

"Hm?"

"To go back."

"No desire?"

"No desire."

A toy dog whined and barked. The barista proceeded to produce a cacophony of noise. Jamie said, "Ah, well—that's your choice, but just know that, I think he would, if you asked, because—not because you're a good worker, but because he likes you... Even though you acted in certain ways he still understood, and uh, against his will I think he had to fire you because other people might have been uncomfortable, but he never was—he accepted you; he accepted you while he was telling me he acce—uh—in uh, in another way that he did. Ya know?" The dog continued to bark and whine. A phone rang. The barista incessantly slammed the counter. Jamie clicked the pen's top.

I said, "E—enough about me and my shenanigans. What's going on with these books here?"

"Oh. I just maybe thought maybe you'd find this interesting—this book. You can kinda understand, um... the other side of some emotions, of that book—if you want, to read *it*... Do you read, books?"

"All I do is read and write."

"Maybe that's what *it* is; you could-"

Stoic, I said, "So you came here to educate me then-"

"No!"

"-as I had initially said."

"I feel like sss-someone was telling me... that you should read this."

"*Someone* was telling you? I think that was yourself."

"Maybe." Jamie clicked the pen's top four times. The barista sprayed whipped cream out from a canister. "There might be a calling to you with that book."

"So, when you met me you thought that I had experienced *trauma,* and that I needed healing?"

"No. I wanted to, eliminate the idea that you may have experienced, some, trauma—but actually you know what—can I trust you to take the book and bring *it* back for your haircut?"

"... Just this one or both?" I flipped through the pages and read five passages of *The Body Keeps the Score.* "I'm very picky when I choose reading material. Time is valuable, more so than money."

"Yes, you are correct."

"So I don't know... and, the more that you read... *it* can toxify you or empower you." Sixteen seconds elapsed; I checked my watch: We had conversed for forty minutes. "And... how much time do you have, for this interaction?"

Jamie said, "Ummm, I gotta be somewheres in like twenty minutes... so..." I grunted. "I didn't read the whole book."

I raised an eyebrow and said, "You didn't read the whole book and you're offering *it* to me."

"I read a few chapters, that were interesting to me."

"What chapters?"

"Umm, I decided to read the one about love—I think *it's* chapter nine; I can't remember—I don't have the best memory. And that's why I don't—I don't retain a lot sometimes, so... I'm better at experiencing things. I wish I had your intellect."

I cringed and said, "No you don't. Why—why would—no. That's-"

Jamie chuckled and said, "You retain information—you're smart-"

"That's just memory—*it's* not intellect."

"You know big words. I want that memory; that would be *amazing*."

I glared at Jamie and said, "To be called intelligent is something that I abhor."

"Why?"

"Because I'm a fool, and there's nothing to *it*. The intellect is-"

"You're an intelligent fool." I gripped my knees with both hands. Jamie had turned away for a second. Her gaze returned to mine, thereby she chuckled, and said, "I'm playing, around."

"No—but that's all, that's... It's a misplaced adjective; *it's* nonsense. The way that I behave, and conduct myself—my demeanor, my mien overall... *it's* just an impression; *it's* a facade—*it's* a mask."

Jamie whispered, "Okay... You are mad right now—I'm sorry if I upset you."

My eye contact with Jamie remained fixed and stern. "I'm not mad."

"Okay."

"... I am... vigorous-"

"Vigorous?"

"... with *life*. That's all; I am right here in this moment telling you, that I am just a fool."

"Okay, if you want me to accept that I'll accept *it*."

"... I go home... to my little *cubicle* of an apartment... and I mull about... reading and writing, and that's all I do. I have no friends and no family. I'm, a wretch."

"A what?"

"A *wretch*. I'm a sanctimonious wretch; that's all."

"Do you enjoy *it?*"

I relaxed, gazed to my left for three seconds, and said, "I'm content."

Jamie's feminine voice cooed, "Then that's okay."

"Content in my misery and I have no desire to commiserate with anybody."

"Okay, that's your choice."

I slid my hands up from my legs, folded my hands in my lap, and said, "... So, knowing that, and because I just ad—admitted to you that I am a wretch, and miserable... and, you seemed to have sensed that, perhaps... so you wanted to outreach to me with a book on healing, though, my 'trauma,' and my suffering, is-"

"Is self-induced?"

"Self-induced—yes, and selected."

"Mhm."

"... Uh... *it*'s embarrassing to me."

"You don't ha-"

"I feel myself blushing, constantly."

"You don't have to be embarrassed in front of me."

"Do you see me blush?"

"Yes. I'm not judging you."

"We all judge each other."

"I blush all the time!"

Grim and contentious, I said, "You judge me as somebody who needs healing."

"No, that book jumped out at me, to give to you; I don't know what you need; I'm not, here to figure that out... You know what you need... I was just interested in talking to you..."

"... So, what have you learned?"

"That you're not a alien." Jamie chortled.

Humorless, I said, "You just wanted to dispel the notion that I'm not an alien."

"I feel like you don't have um, a connection, with anyone? I, um... I feel people's energy... I... could feel your energy, and uh—actually, for the first time I met someone in my life I didn't see any emotions or, anything, um... No experience, no anything... so I was intrigued."

"You think I'm devoid of experience, in the emotional realm?"

"I think that you're um taking *it* very personal—everything I say. I promise you nothing I'm saying is to agitate you." Jamie tittered a single syllable. "I'm just telling you in my experience I've never met anyone that I could look at and not see-"

I interjected, "You behave as though you have no ego."

"Oh I do, oh, *trust me*, I do."

"Everything that *you* say to *me*, is personal."

Jamie paused for three seconds and murmured, "… Maybe, yeah. Yeah, and I also said I have a lot to learn too."

Exasperated yet restrained, I said, "I don't abide by *The Four Agreements* or any of that pseudo-spiritual nonsense; we are human beings here interacting in this world-"

"Mhm"

"-all we know is, what we see in front of us; the words that we read, and the charlatans that we interact with don't know anything—there is no truth. And, to think that I need healing is presumptuous."

"I didn't think that."

"You—you didn't think that—who thought *it* for you?"

"I didn't—I never had that thought."

I blurted, "You never had the thought that you need healing but you come here and give me a book on healing?"

"That's a book about um… other people, tha—studies on people that have been through human experiences and—a lot—a group, of human experiences that help you, like kinda—you said something about people think you have mental illness… because of the way you act; I brought this book so you could read who actua—like people that do have *it*, the reaction—so you could understand why people think that about you. I never assumed you were…"

"I know full-well, that the way that I behave is aberrant."

Jamie whispered, "Okay."

Five seconds elapsed; I said, "And *it*'s amusing to me… because, society, is a sham. Personality is a pretense; *virtue*, is pretentious."

Jamie spoke a near-inaudible, "Okay."

"If there's anything that I want you to remember from this conversation *it*'s *that*; that all virtue, is pretentious… I don't know what virtue, or feel-good… emotion that dri-"

Jamie's volume normalized: "You asked my purpose—this is part of my purpose; I don't, assume anything about you; I don't know you-"

"What is your purpose?"

"I want to try to help people heal if they need *it*, or want *it*."

"Hence the yoga, right?"

"Yeah—I like *it*; I don't know if I connect to *it* yet—I'm still learning, myself. You know your purpose and I'm actually a little bit jealous." Jamie chuckled. "That's my ego."

"Well—that would be envious, because there's only two of us involved-"

"Yep."

"But, why would you... be envious of that? I'll tell you, a quote from Heraclitus, from 500... uh... A.D:[59] 'Envy always lasts longer than the happiness of those that we envy.'" A blender resounded immediately after I finished reciting the quote. I said, "And I am by no means happier than you-"

Jamie laughed and said, "Yeah, okay."

"-so there's nothing to be envious of; you know, because I told you, that I don't even pursue happiness—*it's* not even on my radar."

"So why would you ask me my purpose?"

I said, "To know how people delude themselves, much like I delude myself, with my writing."[60]

"I feel like even if I gave you my clear purpose, and what I do, and I even let you know all about myself, you would have your own perception... regardless of what my perception is of myself, you would have your own. So, I perceive myself as someone who cares and has no motive, but you don't see that from me; you see *it* the opposite... right?"

"Your motive, is to heal."

"*Yes*—my motive is also to learn to-"

"But, you give me a book by somebody else, to heal me... so-"

"I'm *not trying* to heal you. I'm not—I'm not trying to heal you. You asked my purpose; that's my purpose."

"So what is this book then; what purpose does this serve?"

"I'll tell you again: There are many people that have mental disorders and their—*their,* experiences in that book... and, if you *want* to learn about that, you can; *it*'s a choice, that you have."

"All right, is this-"

"Because people assume that you do."

"Is the APA behind this then?"

"I don't know what that is."

"Is the DSM-5 involved?"

"I don't know what that is either."

"The American Psychiatric[61] Association-"

---

[59] Correction: B.C.

[60] Contrarily, though I may write delusional nonsense, the process of revising my writing and reading old memories years later has served to illuminate subtle fallacies and incohrencies of my thoughts that I would otherwise (presumably) never synthesize without this documentation.

[61] Correction: Psychological

"*Oh*—yes, yes."

"-and the DSM-5 is their little[62] bible, that they use to prescribe to people-"

"Drugs."

"-their ailments."

"Yeah. I know." Jamie picked up *The Body Keeps the Score*, began to tuck *it* into her bag, and said, "I'll get rid of that book."

"Oh you—you… Why?"

"I feel bad I even brought *it; it* triggered something in you, so-"

I scowled and said, *"Triggered* something."

"-I'll get rid of *it*. Yeah—you're like… You're triggered by Walther— you're triggered by the book. I don't want to trigger you."

"… What have you triggered?"

"I don't know; you think that I'm here to like heal you or do something—I don't know."

"Well when you hand me a book that's-"

Jamie raised her voice and said, *"It's* some kind of conspiracy between me and Walther; some kind of conspiracy of trying to heal you-"

"I never said that."

"-I don't know… but, um… I'm gonna go." Jamie snickered. "I gotta go meet my friend and help her find a wedding dress." Seven seconds elapsed. "I just wanted to meet you, and talk to you more; *it* was-"

"Have I amused you?"

"Um… not really. No… No. I feel like, um… No matter what I say, you're gonna have your perspective, so… But I'm okay with that."

I leaned forward, steepled my hands, and said, "So… no matter what you say, I'm going to have my perspective… What does that amount to?"

"It amounts to… whatever you want *it* to be."

I drawled, "Are you trying to avoid triggering me further?"

"Yes," Jamie spoke with a jovial inflection.

"Whatever triggering means—*it* means what you say has an impact on the world."

"All right so if you're not impacted—you're not triggered then that's, good."

"No—I *am* impacted because this is a conversation that we're having,

---

[62] I spoke the connotation "little" in the same regard that the bartender with the same name as myself spoke of my book, the last instance that we met, to express my equatable condescension.

and, you say that I'm 'triggered,' in quotes, because *it*'s not a reaction that you wanted."

"No—I didn't expect any reaction, any sort-" Jamie sighed. "To want something is to expect *it;* I don't have an expectation, so…"

"So if you have no expectations then how can you judge me to be triggered?"

"I can feel… that you're like ups—like you're, you're whole demeanor changes, you… You talk with a deeper voice, and you throw big words, like you're upset… So, I'm just making sure like I'm… I'm not triggering y—your body language and stuff—I can see anger in your eyes. So, a little bit of triggering."

I spoke with a bemused sigh: "Well… You hand me a book and say that: 'These people have mental disorders; you should read about them so you can heal yourself.'"

"Heal myself?"

"Heal *me.*"

"Oh."

"So-"

"No I-"

"-To use this whole pseudo-nonsense of 'trigger,' which is a modern terminology for children who, are skating around, the essence of the matter…"

"You can, take *it* however you want… but your thoughts aren't my thoughts, so, definitely not that."

"Well… My thoughts are wholly my own."

"Mhm."

"They're not spawned or manife—well they could be—I don't know. My thoughts, are a product of my supposed *intellect* that you perceive."

"Dude—I just think you're smart." Jamie laughed.

I gestured, open-handed, and said, "Interconnected consciousness— whatever *it* is; I'm 'triggered' by existence…"

"… That's okay. I really had no expectation other than… I was intrigued by, *you.*"

"I often just want to go out in the street, and scream at the top of my lungs-"

"So why don't you?"

"-like an animal."

"Why don't you?"

I spoke with mock terror, *"Because* I would be *apprehended* and *arrested.*"

"*Yeah.* People would just look at you like 'What the fuck, man?'"

"Yes—but then if I proceeded, I would be a public nuisance."

"Well if you did *it* all the time—yeah. Do *it* in different spots—climb a mountain and do *it*. Why does *it* have to be in the middle of the street? Do-"

"Because then you're *reckoned.*"

"Do you ever go into nature?"

"… Yes."

"Do *it* there; *it*'s okay; you can do that."

"I don't want to do *it* there; I want to do *it* in somebody's face."

Jamie chuckled and said, "Because you want people to see you. You want people to see you?"

"I want to grip someone by the shoulders and say 'Just what are you?'"

"What if someone did that to you?"

"I would tell them."

"I'm a writer?"

A cash register opening and the sound of coins clamored. Upbeat piano music played. I said, "I'm a bag of meat and I don't know, anything beyond that."

"If that's what you want."

"… Your acceptance, of everything that I say, is almost, deferential, as though you don't want to upset me."

"No, just… *it*'s okay, like I really, whatever you say is how you feel; like I'm not… It's *fine*. Just do it. Do how you feel man; don't hold shit in and… upset yourself—just do *it.*"

"Oh—I'd be a serial killer if I did that then."

Jamie giggled and said, "Are you going to go around killing people?"

"Well… murdering is just… stupid."

"Yeah."

"Though, if I had to suffer the interactions of everybody, all the time, and put myself out there, and be met with… nothing but…" Tears welled in my eyes. A reggae love song overtook my focus. I shifted out of my seat and said, "No… I'm just a scumbag, okay? According to society's standards. Take care."

My voice cracked and I ended the recording, pushed myself out the café door, unfinished coffee in hand, and stormed into the street—the world rendered virulent, hostile, and *weak*, in my perspective: A 'triggered' amygdala.

I strode to cross a one-lane street on one of the spirals of a roundabout and fought to suppress a deluge of tears. I waved on a man within a small white car; he stopped, and peered at me from behind the steering wheel. Both of the man's hands gripped the topside of the wheel, shoulders hunched forward—he wore a white t-shirt... and I leered at him—*yes*, I stood, indignant, for two protracted seconds in front of the man's vehicle and *leered* at his sheepish and docile visage on that beautiful day at 11:00 AM, as if to grip his shoulders and shout, *"Why the hell did you stop?"* I addressed the unlit headlights of two vehicles—a truck and another car—behind the man's white car, and regarded each as sentient entities without a human within, and *scowled*. The lackadaisical impressions of aged couples side-by-side on the sidewalk, women with a phone, bag, or the leash of a dog—always *something* to *distract* from the reality that *is*—a diversion from the filth of one's own contemplation; I'm no exception: Here I stand—to write of this malignant moment in which I hastened up to my apartment, to stand in silence in a kitchen, furious, enraged, fists clenched... and *cried*. For what? I didn't understand *it*. For three minutes, my ego writhed. I thought of my last spoken words to Jamie and my proclamation of being a "scumbag" instead of what I had neglected to communicate, for she needed to be elsewhere—to *judge* how a *friend* would *appeal* to others in a *wedding dress:*

"Though, if I had to suffer the interactions of everybody, all the time, and put myself out there, and be met with... nothing but..." ~~ignorance, fatuousness, prejudice, lust, hatred, envy~~ *Nay*—I refuse to perpetuate *puerility;* therefore, I summarize: The totality of human capacity, i.e., The benevolence irremovable from malevolence and vice versa—*enough.*

Thursday, October 8th, 2020

12:50 PM

"This generation is so fucked up and lopsided," said a self-accredited harbinger of societal righteousness spawned from every generation since the advent of a lexicon.

The preceding sentence is a thought that manifested last night while I imagined two middle-aged American women deriding my meta-nonfictional exposition. I scribbled down the self-deprecating thoughts on a small piece of paper, stream-of-consciousness, with the intent to craft a comical fictional story. Instead, I'd rather analyze my perceived expectations of *others'* expectations of what constitutes normal American 21ˢᵗ-century human behavior when duplicity is considered, especially in an autobiography.

I had been informed of the terminology "edgelord" a year ago while I researched the full extent of diagnosis listed in the DSM-5. Down the internet rabbit-hole, I had been redirected to a question and answer domain, *Quora*, where I read a user's satirical entry of "Edgelord Personality Disorder."

Anarchy appeals to the lowest common denominator of a society's' insecure who live as rebels in thought, and dissimulate politeness, amicability, and compliance, i.e., utilitarian democracy, when the occasion is beneficial, i.e., misanthropes.[63] For the commoner enmeshed with capitalism, there is often no other recourse from utilitarianism other than entrepreneurism and renunciation.

3:34 PM

Schopenhauer's brilliance illuminates my pages and alleviates the idle extravagance of my solitude:

"Everywhere and at all times there has been much discontent with governments, laws and public regulations; for the most part, however, because men are always ready to make institutions responsible for the misery inseparable from human existence *it*self; which is, to speak mythically, the curse that was laid on Adam, and through him on the whole race."

– Arthur Schopenhauer's On Human Nature

This quote encapsulates my previous didactic on the impious consequences of anarchist literature, e.g., "All virtue is pretentious." Therein, is my persistent mental duress, for *I am* anarchistic, cynical, pessimistic, and nihilistic, in my ideals… *as much* as I am lawful, utilitarian, hopeful, and—to deviate from the normalcy of my self-loathing: noble. The more I read of God(s) and men, my "self" amorphizes with the reflection on the dualistic nature of affairs, by which strife is essential, as much as harmony. On the often-lauded state of *serenity*, I think back to Seth—my supervisor at a medical facility assembly line, and his irreverent refutation to my postulation, "An unsettled mind desires to speak": "A settled mind is a dead mind."

---

[63] I would know, *being* part of the lowest common denominator.

On Jamie's suggestion, I've finished listening to a video posted on the online domain *Youtube*, titled, *Dolores Cannon Reveals her Discoveries About Life After Death*. I am disgusted and humbled. Disgusted, for my (recurrent) realization that spiritual doctrines are methodologies to subjugate and diminish the will of a population. Humbled, for comparing my own hackish writing to Dolores Cannon, who has mastered the craft of a superb story, albeit unoriginal (I recognized numerous elements derived from Plato and Sanskrit texts).

Being a cynic is easy; what merit do I have other than my own vanity? *Dolores Cannon...* by contrast... I wonder if she's *happy?* A self-assigned meaning in life centered on death, and the absolute "knowing" of what happens on death...

Talk of the "silver-cord" reminded me of Pelagia and her claims of witnessing her "silver-cord" while engaged in "Hot Vinyasa" yoga. Jamie is associated with Pelagia *and* Beatrice, Beatrice being the woman who spoke to me of chakras and implored me to ingest LSD two days before my rapport-destruction experiment. These women specialize in gossip—to which I chose to indulge in by association, and, by my recent interaction with Jamie, I *judge,* and condemn *myself* for ever speaking—nay, *acknowledging* any of the capricious troupe, let alone investing my capacity for love to the manslayer harpy: Pelagia. Ah, my words are of a spiteful man. How may I be sanctimonious *and* censorious? I jest. These adjectives are harmonious, sanctified in the *spiritual* facility of the ego.

These women merely wanted to love and ~~educate~~ heal me, to elevate me from my poor, *lonesome* depravity; they, who judge me pathetic in secret, for they *pity* me on behalf of their own vanity—what I strive to evade... scorn and revile, with the retainment of my hatred for prospects worthy of my (continued) attention. My perspective—opinion—thoughts and feelings, recorded *now,* is a node on the trajectory of my *human experience* with buffoons; thereby, *I am one!* A conspiracy!—Jamie was correct! I'm a loon *and* a buffoon!

8:52 PM

Sapolsky and Schopenhauer are put on hold, for the aforementioned women's aggregated energy have elicited a compulsion for me to research the experience and origin of shame; thereby, I've begun to read *Shattered States: Disorganised Attachment and its Repair,* by Judy Yellin and Kate White; yes, the prospect worthy of my (continued) attention.

Friday, October 9th, 2020

1:04 AM

I don't drink when I visit the bar; I stand and observe, to patrons' discomfort. I stood outside and a new mob laughed at me for my mien and conduct. "Alien" and "robot" are common adjectives spoken to describe me. Where are you from? I said, "I'm a denizen of the world," and must define and spell the word "denizen." A refusal to shake hands and abstinence from alcohol incites suspicion. What's your name? I said, "My name is irrelevant." A woman's cachinnations compel me to smile; she thanks me for the laughs induced. I said, "You can call me 'Clown,' here for your entertainment." The rabble interrogates, touches, and judges me as a "good man," all-the-while claiming to not judge. A fearful drunken man informs me that I'm "safe," proceeds to tell me that he is sad for me a minute later, and threatens me with violence if I don't vacate the premises one minute beyond the aforementioned minute, for he desires to "protect his girlfriend." I stand, statuesque, and observe the trepidatious confusion transpire around me. The other men of the mob intervene and converge to shake my hand, each eyeing me in a manner that suggests I *should* go, for the consciousness as a whole would have no qualms with a focused onslaught. Fear expressed in each visage compelled me to open my mouth to speak; however, the agitated man to my right shuffled from foot-to-foot, primed to strike me, and I walked away with my poise intact. There was nothing noble, only emptiness.

2:01 AM

Outbursts of a Sanctimonious Wretch; Thoughts of a Pusillanimous Clown

12:24 PM

All of us are alone with our pain.

Sunday, October 10th, 2020

2:43 PM

Last night I arrived at *The Messy House* parking lot with the intent to ascertain meanings in life and instead listened, for over an hour, to a diatribe in defense of Donald Trump, of a fifty-three-year-old republican Caucasian man named Jim, with an annual income of $200,000. The drunken beratement had been precious to me—not for the content, but for what caused *it:* The death of a friend. Jim, with his girlfriend and sixteen-year-old son, had decided to stop at *The Messy House* for the first time, due to grief. At first, Jim condemned me, inferred me to be a poor democrat, a Russian spy affiliated with CNN (on account of my mien, appearance, and disclosure of using a recorder), and *"handsome"*—he had said in an off-handed comment, *after* he "flipped me the bird."

While I listened to Jim's political addressal, a fight occurred within the bar and four police officers were summoned to the scene, two of which I recognized as the duo who were assigned to my abandoned case. Jim and I had become the best of pals—by his judgment, for I had listened to his sorrow-induced tirade without interruption or contention, and for this, we decided to walk around to the front end of the bar together, to better observe the scene of the crime.

Jim, a well-groomed, financially informed, and righteous man, deemed the bar to be "gross," to which I conceded, and admitted that this is a strong factor in the reason for my attendance. I provided Jim a face mask from my pack, for he had forgotten his own face mask within his van. We entered together; however, I veered away from Jim and observed a smear of blood on the laminated plank wood floor, covered by a white towel. Fifteen patrons also observed: The officers, blood, myself, and each other. I am regarded with a peculiar eminence by strangers, and always, my intellect[64]

---

[64] Latent memories of my father serve as equalizers to my potential hubris on behalf of being alive; comments such as, "You're not as intelligent as you think you are," and "Get over yourself, dude," are appreciated, though they are tinged with paternal contempt, which detracts from the empowering effects the words may have elicited. Contrariwise, the only compliment I recall from my father with vividness–the one that outclassed the others with an unwholesome vibrancy, is one afternoon two years ago, before I departed for my "vagabond" journey, in my father's room of the now-abandoned apartment house he once owned: "You're a beautiful boy with a lot going for you," he had spoken to me in my moment of extreme catatonic stupor. Beauty fades and the "lot" has gone without me.

is lauded, to my chagrin, for I feel only like a sanctimonious wretch on behalf of my selected environment and subsequent culture, despite an acumen which allows me to delineate these feelings.

Alas, I distract myself with meta-nonfictional self-engrossed concern for others, being the social creature that I am—prone to the total encompassment of human emotion—*shame* on me, by my own decree, for the remainder of this snippet in time regarding my experience is nothing more but ego gratification, as this entire document is—a reader has indubitably discerned.

Jim and I resumed a deviation of our previous conversation after the brawlers were escorted out by law enforcement. Nearby patrons eavesdropped. The song, *Because Of You,* by Kelly Clarkson, resonated from a jukebox to my rear. The recording:

Department of Justice

Jim swigged from a beer and said, "Why would I think you're intelligent? Why would I think you're *not?*"

I said, "Because I articulate myself?-

"Beyond anybody than I've ever met."

"That's-"

"But—I—I listen to very intelligent people all day long on radio and through, through, um... uh... verbal, books; and you're—you're right there bud. *And* your posture, so... not only are you... I'm looking at your demeanor and everything else so yes—you—you portray yourself as a very smart dude."

"Do you know how I feel?"

"I have *no* clue how you feel—do you know how I feel?"

I said, "No. I'll tell you how I feel, contrary to my... masquerade of intelligence."

"Uh-huh."

"I feel like a sanctimonious wretch."

"Why?"

"... Because-"

"There's two big-ass fuckin' words-"

"I'll tell you. Well—do I need to define those words?"

"Please."

"'Sanctimonious' means that I'm morally superior in my own perception."

Jim beamed and said, "That's exactly how I feel."

"And 'wretch,' is somebody who is unfortunate and unhappy."

"Yep—I've—I—I could actually call myself a wretch at times."

"So you also feel as though you're a sanctimonious wretch?"

"I guess—yes... Am I being recruited?"

We laughed. I said, "I'm not affiliated with any organization; I'm an independent."

"You're not CIA?"

"No."

Jim partook in another swig of beer and said, "I feel the same fucking way, dude."

I chuckled and said, "Like a sanctimonious wretch?"

"I do."

"Somebody who is morally superior and unhappy?"

"I always feel like I'm morally superior to everyone around me."

"I think that's synonymous with being a privileged white man."

Jim said, "Being what?"

"A privileged white man."

"You gotta give me more than that, bud."

I alternated hand-raises by my side to simulate scales and said, "Sanctimonious wretch? Privileged white man?"

"No—I—I don't care about the color of my skin; if that's where you're trying to take me-"

"Well, *it* was a jest."

"-you lost me."

"*It* was a jest—but, there is truth in all jest, which is why I spoke *it*."

"My girlfriend—I think I told ya, works for DOJ (Department of Justice); she went through-" Jim swigged his beer and set the bottle on a round table. "- privileged training." I snickered. Jim continued, "Okay, do you wanna hear—do you wanna hear a non-joke? You're playing badminton: You, and your best friend... A gorilla walks across the—the court while you're playing badminton, okay-"

I interrupted, "You don't notice the gorilla."[65]

"What did you notice?"

"... Not the gorilla."

"Huh?"

---

[65] I immediately recollected the 2010 study documented in *The Invisible Gorilla*, by Christopher Chabris and Daniel Simons.

I said, "Not the man in the gorilla costume."

"You didn't notice the—*no it* wasn't a man in a gor—I *did not* tell you *it* was a man in a gorilla costume; I told you a gorilla went across the court. What did you notice?"

"This is a study that you're referring to though."

"This is an actual fucking training that my girl at the DOJ went through... Your answer was what? Your answer to me was 'the monkey.'"

Confused, I said, "No—you don't see the monkey."

Jim became passionate and said, "You—you—your first response was the gorilla-"

Adamant, I said, "No—you don't see the gorilla."

"So you know what you are: White privileged; that's what she was told."

I shouted, "What?"

Jim explained, "Because... She was fucking noticing the gorilla: She's white privileged. *So,* she spent 21 years—ten months being trained by the Air Force, to notice anything crazy around her, but yet, when she notices a *monkey,* going across a fucking badminton court, she's told she's white privileged. You tell me—you explain that to me. That's the *D*-partment of justice bud; she works down in Albany, for an appointee for Donald Trump... and that's what she was told: that she's white privileged, because she noticed the gorilla. *Not,* the backswing, of her fucking opponent... Is that white privilege? *Do* you define that as white privilege?"

I sniggered and said, "I don't know."

"Is that sanctimonious fuckin'... You tell me."

"Mm, *not* sanctimonious, I-"

"But—but—explain *it.*"

I said, "I think *it*'s censorious."

"*It*'s what?"

"*It*'s *censorious.*"

"Sin-serious-"

"Or-"

"-another word you would have to define."

"Uh, being severely critical against somebody."

"Severely critical—but you just did the same thing she did and she does not have a prejudiced bone in her body. You noticed the gril-" Jim slurred. "-you noticed the gorilla, correct? Wouldn't you notice the thing that's *odd...* in the fucking setting?"

An unidentifiable country love song sung by a woman began to resonate.

Stern, I said, "Was she told to pay attention to how many times people hit the ball?"

"She was *told*, to watch the *video*... and then they were asked a question, sixty seconds into the video: 'What did you notice?'"

"They weren't given a preface question?"

Jim gestured an excising movement with both arms outward and said, *"Nothin'*. 'What did you notice?'"

Indignant, I said, "Ah—then that's not the—that's *contorting* the study then!"

"*Exactly* bud. So, that's our government. She works—she's—she was— like I just told ya—21 years—ten months-"

"When did this take place?"

"She just did this three weeks ago—three *months* ago—I'm sorry. This just happened at like... was *it, it* was *May,* this Covid season."

I signaled my recorder and said, "All right—this I'm actually interested in and want to write of."

Jim advanced two steps closer to me, set his beer on the table, and spoke with a punctuated, amplified voice: "This May, of Covid season, the Department of Justice, who just—the uh—the U.S. district—the U.S. state—The United States *attorney,* that was just replaced, his name is Grant, just got replaced by Bacon-somethin', in the city of *Albany, New York,* that was the *training* they went through: 'What did you notice, on, the badminton court?' Two white people—not people—two white *sticks,* hittin' a black ball back and forth, and then a gorilla went across the court: 'What did you notice?'"

"There was no preface question?"

"The gorilla—she (Jim's girlfriend) said 'The gorilla,' and she (presumed test-giver) was like 'Okay, now you need to know why you're white privileged.'"

"See—that's a study, and I actually-"

"That's a *study*—you're damn right *it'*s a study."

"Do you know the origin?"

"I do!"

I said, "Because I have a book[66] in my bag right now that talks about that study."

---

[66] *Thinking, Fast and Slow, by Daniel Kahneman.*

"I—I know the study; I know the origin... from what I've been told."
I removed my backpack from my shoulders and said, "You're a businessman."
"I *am* a businessman."
"You're interested in economics?" Jim scoffed at my stupid question, opened his mouth to speak, and instead watched me open my pack. I continued: "I just finished this book a week ago; I think that you would like *it*—unless you haven't already read *it*—err-" I passed the book to Jim. "You can have *it*."

"You sure?"

"Yes. You may derive a benefit from that."

Jim placed his hands against both vertical sides of the book set upon the round table and said, "I'd like to read *it,* man."

"*It*'s about intuition, and how *it*... how *it* applies-"

"You read *it?*"

"Yes. *It*'s about, statistics, and intuition, and how, our intuitions are often wrong because, they are based, on our memories."

"My intuitions are *always* wrong," Jim giggled. "My intuitions are, seventy-five percent of the time wrong... I really appreciate this, and I will read *it*... I wish I had a business card, so I could give ya *it*—Jeffrey!" Jim called to a boy seated at the bar. "That's my kid who works for me—*Jeffrey! Jeff!* Do you have a business card on ya?"

The boy responded with a warbled voice: "I don't think I do."

Jim said, "You sure? Please?"

I pointed at black stains on the book, sustained from when I performed pushups on the warehouse roof associated with the restaurant I had recently been furloughed from, and said, "*It*'s a bit dirty, but that's just-"

"Yep, I'm gonna—I'm gonna read *it* bud, like immediately."

"I enjoyed *it.*"

"I like the title of *it.*"

"*It* was informative."

Jim yelled to Jeffrey, "Do you have one in there?"

The awkward voice shouted back, "I'm *looking!*"

The country song, *It Matters to Me,* by Faith Hill, began to resonate.
I said, "I often depended on my intuition for many of my... decisions-"

Jim addressed Jeffrey, "No?"

"*No!*"

I continued, "Though I'm not, a businessman-"

"I'm a businessman, but I got a lot of room for improvement."

"The book *did* help to clarify some... deficiencies, in my thinking processes."

"Yeah, well that's what I... I could use that... Baethan, I'd love to stay in touch with you. Can I give you my phone number?"

I shifted on my feet, expressed a somber grimace, and said, "Mm... I don't have any friends, so no."

"Okay."

"I appreciate your interest in my books, though." (Before this conversation, Jim inquired of my personal life, which led to me writing my pen name on a slip of torn paper.)

"Yep, I'm gonna read this, and I'm gonna be thankful for *it*... Tonight has been the greatest night that I've had in a long time, man." We shook hands. "Thank you very much."

"Even with your grieving?"

Jim said, "Even with my grieving—you took me right out of *it*... The... Yep—I was feelin' uh... What was the word you said earlier—the—the phrase, about... sanctimonious?"

"A sanctimonious wretch."

"Yes-"

"I was feeling-"

"-a morally superior-

"Less wretch—more sanctimonious."

I said, "Ah, but now *it's* more wretch and less sanctimonious?"

"Right now, I'm feeling more sanctimonious—I'm feeling pretty damn good, and I appreciate *it*. You're a helluva dude."

"Well being sanctimonious isn't a positive connotation-"

"No?"

"*It's* more of an insult."

"To me—did I take *it* wrong?"

"Well *it's*, *it's* used as an insult, and I use *it* to insult myself."

"*Sanctimoniously*—okay, I understand; I've used the word myself not knowing what I was saying actually." Jim chortled and asked me, "Is that horrible?"

"No, I don't think *it's* horrible; *it* may just be honest, in your own... comprehension."

"That, may be *it*; I am nothing but honest. I've been told I'm brutally honest. I follow to my own-" I checked my watch; Jim heeded by behavior, shook my hand again, and said, "-*It* was a pleasure to meet you, man."

I said, "Hopefully you never come back here."

"I won't be back here, but I *do* hope I bump into you one day."
"Take care."
"I truly do. Thanks Baethan. *It* was a great night, man."
"You're welcome, Jim."
"Thanks, man. Goodnight."
I walked away, out of the bar, and went back to my apartment.

Sunday, October 11th, 2020

2:17 AM

I'm rejected by drunkards: banned, for my questions induce discomfort in patrons—"driving down business," according to Joe, the overweight male bartender of the *Messy House;* therefore, I've reduced myself to their level (miserable and thoughtless), except, I'm sober. There are many things in this life that I don't understand.

"Nothing is more pathetic than people who run around in circles, 'delving into the things that lie beneath' and conducting investigations into the souls of people around them, never realizing that all you have to do is to be attentive to the power inside you and worship *it* sincerely."

- Marcus Aurelius' Meditations

No more questions, no anything. Recurrent answers never satisfy me anyway, nor the arcane ones. I'm finished. My humanity is in turmoil. Thoughts of suicide glance at my mind. Sleep. Just sleep.

2:52 AM

This night is important; my ego has died, *not* on account of others but for my self-realization of innate *dependency* on others, irremovable from my nature. Thoughts of death linger, *not* as an impetus for action, but as a bystander at watch.

Pity me, reader: then you must pity yourself, for I publish this journal out of a wretched self-spite that I may never relinquish. This burden I have undertaken, year-by-year, has consumed my humanity. I *am* monstrous by consequence of my will. Stop reading. These words are wholly for me, ~~henceforth~~ and always have been. May my publications be heeded by the APA, whereby I'm studied, analyzed, categorized, and *understood,* by ailment alone—a single phrase is all that's necessary—a few lines, to summarize my mental trajectory: the totality of my existence, filed away in a compilation of digital records, subject to entropy.

3:29 AM

I've listened to recordings unworthy of transcription due to the befuddled denouncements of intoxicated unfortunates and have restored faith in *my* humanity by listening to myself from an objective perspective. Sleep well. Find a new job. Be silent.

4:01 PM

Eminent, among drunks and wretches? You fool, with your delusions of grandeur. Although the transcribed recordings of last night would demonstrate your sagacity and the innocence of those who desired to enjoy themselves, you must refrain. Spare yourself the indulgent memory, as everything has been.

Why write in a first-person addressal? Do I sin?—wracked with ~~guilt and~~ shame as I am, on behalf of people I don't care about. This isn't the fiction I decreed.

7.8 billion people. One man among them: an English-speaking Spain native, Antonio, mulled about one afternoon on the prospects of his financial well-being inside the bedroom of his two-story condo. Outside, his twenty-nine-year-old wife lay sprawled on a sun-chair set upon an expansive well-kept lawn, fanned by a twenty-three-year-old pool boy. Antonio watched from behind vertical white blinds of his second-floor balcony window. The pool boy whispered into the woman's ear.

Antonio slid open the balcony's glass door and said, "Laura."

The woman lolled her head to her right, eyes obscured by four-inch diameter black sunglasses that reflected a flash of the sun's early-afternoon rays into Antonio's corneas, and said, *"Oh*—you scared me Anton—don't *do* that!"

Antonio stood for three seconds, silent, and looked at the pool boy who had paused to look up at Antonio. The men acknowledged each other as vermin, something uncouth, unwanted, yet both felt the same wind pass through their hair, albeit, at disparate altitudes and directional intensity. The sun warmed the flesh of both men. Stomachs churned, devoid of nourishment. A shared morning breakfast passed through the intestines of both, differentiated in passage by gut flora, physical activity, cumulative lifelong health, genetic inheritance, coffee ingestion, and prescription drug use. Antonio said, "Do you think I'm a mature man?"

Laura chuckled, wiggled in the chair, pointed to the pool boy, and said, "Him or me?"

Antonio said, "You."

"Don't be silly," said Laura, unaware that Antonio's inquiry had been a fractal occurrence fated to incite her infidelity with the pool boy thirteen hours, eleven minutes, and forty-five seconds from the moment of utterance.

Antonio smiled at the pool boy and said, "But I *am* silly."

Laura returned her head to a neutral position and said, "No—stop that."

What isn't accounted for in the fiction is how the pool boy is Laura and Antonio's son; the marriage between Laura and Antonio is dissolute; Antonio services himself with at least two prostitutes every Monday and Thursday night.

If I could account for every facet of something, I would need to know *it* from a holistic, unified, and total state of being—and even then, every minutia of human experience is a paltry summation of the inexplicable nature of existence; hence, I *loathe,* everything that life yields, yet... *grateful,* for the chance, for my temporality of *enjoyable* health...

Above me, two men and one woman watch a football game together. One of the men lapsed into a passionate tirade on an indiscernible topic— from my perspective. A dog clatters on the tiled floors. A commercial resonates. Voices. I woke at 3:14 PM today. Midnight gym attendance is critical. Resumption of deadlifts, squats, bench press, and the dozens of cable machines promote contentment. The venue is not employed for a goal-based directive, e.g., increased sexual attractiveness, health, strength—though these *are* the underlying conscious motives; constructive suffering supersedes all, and satisfies my will to live.

8:13 PM

I'm halfway through a read of *Shattered States: Disorganised Attachment and its Repair,* and am inspired to reminisce and document every instance of repressed childhood memories that I'm capable of recalling. In my current state of complete social severance and upended sleep cycle, confined to an apartment devoid of domestic furnishings by day, and venturing out by night to subject myself to physical exertion followed by the company of rampant alcoholism, introspection will be *preferred.*

My father and mother divorced when I was four. I lived with my mother through my early childhood, and chose to live with my father, consequently abandoning my mother, at the age of thirteen. My earliest memory of sexual activity is around the age of five or six. A girl my age, Kristen, often chased me around my room with a desire to kiss me. We escaped to my closet and kissed each other in the dark, seated on a pile of toys and board games. Reluctant to persist, for reasons I cannot ascribe to anything other than a preferred interest in a video game or book I had been preoccupied with and desired to return to, I had been compelled to vacate the closet. This scenario occurred weekly for many months.

Around the same age—though a year or two younger, I remember two instances in which my older half-brother, estimated to be around twelve years my senior, informed me one afternoon while he laid on the living room couch when our mother had been absent, that his penis tastes like peanut butter, and that his girlfriend enjoys the taste. Thereafter, he unzipped the fly of his pants and pretended to sleep while I idled nearby. I remember contemplating the opportunity to taste a penis that purportedly tastes like peanut butter, and ultimately withdrawing in revulsion on account of the societal ethics I had learned via introjection; however, I never forget this moment.

The second memory with my half-brother, of a nonsexual nature, at the age of seven or eight: I owned a necklace with a yellow string adorned with an oblong plastic skull, of which I cherished. My half-brother swiped the necklace from me in a rough-and-tumble physical altercation and dipped my treasured trinket into a vat of foul liquid, of which I had been ignorant to the contents of. My half-brother proceeded to chase me around the living room of our home—mother absent—with intent to return the tainted necklace to my neck.

Typical sibling shenanigans... my elder half-brother is of no impact on my psyche, unless I have repressed a memory of greater magnitude which, even in my moment of concentrated recollection; I am unable to recall... I doubt.

My father owned a picture of me as a two-year-old infant at Disney World, held up in his hands next to the head of a lifesize replica of a Tyrannosaurus Rex. I remember being drawn to the photograph in my early teenage years, intrigued by my terrified, infantile face. The photograph disappeared one day; I presume discarded by my father.

Masturbation first transpired at the age of eleven while seated in a small bathroom in my father's apartment. The virginal sensation caused me to be elated with life's potentials.

During my early teenage years, I discovered double-headed translucent dildos underneath my father's bed and wedged between a mattress and a wall on two separate occasions. One night, when with a friend, we ventured upstairs to my father's apartment bedroom, where my father laid, passed out in alcohol-induced slumber, around 9:00 PM. I said, "Dad, why is there a dildo under your bed?"

My intoxicated father's eyes fluttered open, closed again, and he slurred, "It's a skin-remover, Baethan. Do you have skin?" My father immediately reverted to a sleep-state and snored. Horrified, I retreated from my father's apartment and spent the night at my friend's home, where my friend provided levity for my experience, and shared in my disturbed confusion.

Around this time, at the age fourteen or fifteen, I began to wear black eyeliner, wore exclusively black clothing, and had been an object of scorn and ridicule by my peers—in secret; while personal interactions with those who otherwise maligned me resulted in interactions that I continue to experience: stupefaction, rejection, abhorrence, admiration, veneration, enthrallment, confusion, love, hate, *pity*—always an extreme, for my words were sparse-

Back on track with sexual disturbances: Around the age of fifteen, I remember being in the basement of my mother's home where she lived with her massive lumberjack boyfriend (one of many), with two other boys—school friends, my age, where I hosted a sleepover. One of the boys laid on the floor, while the other laid beside me in my bed. The boy on the floor dared me and the boy who laid next to me to "makeout" with each other. Being a young delinquent of societal norms, and always eager to proceed with a rational dare, obliged, which in-turn compelled my friend who laid next to me to oblige. However, after our tongues entered each other's mouths for less than five seconds, the boy recoiled from me, lurched up from the bed, stumbled through the darkness of my basement room, flicked on a light switch, threw himself to his knees on the concrete floor near the stairwell, and vomited. The boy on the floor laughed. My mother had been prompted to clean the mess. I laid on my bed and pondered what about me had compelled the boy to vomit, and felt unworthy in my skin, despite being platonic concerning the boy, and withholding no romantic feelings. To *vomit*, I understand now, was a mere expression of the boy's self-disgust for homosexual behavior, though at the time, I suffered an inward dissolution.

Yes, this is all. There are no repressed sexual disturbances wracking my psyche; I'm *almost* disappointed to admit.

No, despite my current circumstances, I am of a sound, rational mind, even if I have recently elected to endure the company of drunks and savages for the past three weeks. A Covid-19 induced furlough from my previous kitchen of employment and the loose associations there permits me to return to the workforce with a reformed discipline of my abandoned creed: Do not speak unless spoken to, and no more than is necessary.

Monday, October 12th, 2020

7:49 PM

"The subjective experience of shame is of an initial shock and flooding with painful emotion. Shame is a relatively wordless state, in which speech and thought are inhibited. *It* is also an acutely selfconscious state; the person feels small, ridiculous, and exposed. There is a wish to hide, characteristically expressed by covering the face with the hands. The person wishes to 'sink through the floor' or 'crawl in a hole and die'. Shame is always implicitly a relational experience. According to Lewis (1987b), one of the early pioneers in the study of shame,

> **'Shame is one's own vicarious experience of the other's scorn. The selfin-the eyes-of-the-other is the focus of awareness . . . The experience of shame often occurs in the form of imagery, of looking or being looked at. Shame may also be played out as an <u>internal colloquy</u>, in which the whole self is condemned. [pp. 15, 18]'**

"Thus, shame represents a complex form of mental representation, in which the person is able to <u>imagine the mind of another</u>."[67]

9:58 PM

I've met with the frail old nihilistic man with a long white beard from yesteryear at the gym; he arrived at 12:48 AM to use a cycling machine, and to perform two halfhearted sets on a chest fly machine: The same, undeviating routine I remembered him enacting over a year and a half ago.

I asked the old man if he remembered our conversation from yesteryear, when he had repeated, "Where's the progress in that?" throughout a tirade of which I documented his sentiments on the futility of human progress, e.g., going to the gym to utilize cable machines to build your strength when our ancestors used to "workout" the natural way: "Where's the progress in that?" The old man didn't remember; however, this time around, in a similar style of caustic exposition, the old man repeated, "What difference does *it* make?" at the end of every second or third sentence, to which I listened to and spoke goading comments every two to four minutes throughout twenty-five minutes.

Yes: "What difference does *it* make" and "Where's the progress in that?" These two thoughts are gems, and therefore terrible.

After a two-hour strength-training session, I ventured to *The Messy House* in search of my own death—or at least, contention, and arrived at 2:19 AM, to stand in a parking lot on the perimeter of the property, statuesque and observant, while I fought with shame for my stilted behavior. A few drunkards emerged from the back entry and gawked at me. One older man who I've recognized prior as a coward said, "You jus' hangin' out?" I acknowledged him with a slight hand raise in his direction and a gentle head nod, to which the man responded by retreating indoors with a huge grin plastered across his face. A heterosexual couple my age, of above-average physical attractiveness, emerged twice from the back entry. The man complained, *incessantly,* of leg pain on account of a recent strength-training exertion, and of the cold weather—most of all, while his female companion walked beside him and listened, silent. I stood, bearing the aspect of a stunted idiot in search of attention, and observed the definition and color of nearby autumn-effected oak trees for thirty-eight minutes and admired the beauty in a rare moment of serenity.

---

[67] Judy Yellin's and Kate White's *Shattered States: Disorganised Attachment and its Repair*

"Whereas shame is focused on the global self in relation to others, guilt is focused on a specific action that the person has committed. Shame is an acutely self-conscious state in which the self is "split", imagining the self in the eyes of the other; by contrast, in guilt the self is unified. In shame, the self is passive; in guilt, the self is active. Shame is an acutely painful and disorganizing emotion; guilt might be experienced without intense affect. Shame engenders a desire to hide, escape, or to lash out at the person in whose eyes one feels ashamed. By contrast, guilt engenders a desire to undo the offence, to make amends. Finally, <u>shame is discharged in restored eye contact and shared, good-humoured laughter</u>, while guilt is discharged in an act of reparation (Lewis, 1987a, cf. table on p. 113)."[68]

I often laugh while I heed my internal colloquies, and I may as well be crying.

Tuesday, October 13th, 2020

3:23 AM

The nihilistic old man arrived at the gym again: same time and exercises. He is a delightful ~~friend~~ familiar. Two notable extracts in order of occurrence from a thirty-nine-minute conversation prompted by my inquiry, "Do you think that you are a nihilist?" (I defined what a nihilist is because he had been ignorant):

1. "Where do you win? How do you win? Who are you in charge of? Nobody—the people above are over your shoulder; there's somebody always there making *it* hard for you."
2. "So what good does *it* do ya? You tell me."

I said, "All right, these three phrases that you've spoken, uh: 'Where's the progress in that,' 'What good does *it* do you,' and yesterday you said… What did you say—what was *it*: 'What difference does *it* make.' Th—those three constitute what a nihilist philosophy is and I'm amazed that somebody with your mindset comes here, to even do anything at all."

The old man glared at me while I sat at a cable row machine and said,

---

[68] Ibid.

"Like I said—*it's paid* for, and *I'm awake;* what difference does *it* make?" I cachinnated, for the first time since... conversations with Candy. The old man shouted from behind a generic face mask similar to my own, "If they (Military veteran benefits) didn't pay for *it,* do you think *I'd be here?*" My laughter compounded and I bent at the waist. The old man gesticulated and said, "I'm awake—what else do I got to do?—sit home?—jerk off or what?—or what watch porn on T.V.—or, look at the idiot box? What difference does *it* make? *It* gives me, somethin' to do."

3:35 PM

October is ~~fiction~~ self-pseudo-psychotherapy/analysis month.

"Schore (2003) describes catastrophic shame states as "self-disorganizing". Indeed, *it* is a characteristic of shame that it can feed upon *it*self. The shamed person feels ashamed of feeling ashamed, enraged, and ashamed of being enraged. Lewis (1990) describes these self-amplifying, disorganizing shame states as 'feeling traps'. She proposes that when shame states cannot be resolved, they are expressed as symptoms."[66]

I reminisced on the week after I returned from my "vagabond" journey as a self-accredited failure, and informed my father of my shame while I chopped broccoli in his kitchen.

My father said, "Why do you feel ashamed?"

I said, "I'm back in your domain again."

Sardonic, my father said, "I have no issue with you being back here. If anything you should feel ashamed of *being* ashamed." We chuckled together, and I concurred with a modest expression of contemplation and repetitive head-nod; thereby, my father departed to his room, a cup of coffee in hand. I don't know what to infer or conclude from this memory; the relevance to the aforementioned bolded quote bore significance. Documentation of the memory serves as a release.

"Shame is a major aspect of the human condition. *It* serves a fundamental purpose, enabling human beings to monitor their own behavior in relation to others... When shame is too great, one feels alienated, disconnected from others, and alone in the world. Laughter serves to reconnect these severed ties, breaking the spiral of

shame-rage... Without both shame and laughter, complex social life would be impossible." [p. 177][69]

5:00 PM

The five-tone chime of the city clock tower restores my humanity while I stand and read by my window-sill podium and inadvertently listen to the superficial street-side conversations predominated by exclamations of women.

"Psychiatrists appear to offer us a model in which things are simple; in which the differences between the real and the symbolic, you and me, imagination and experience, are obvious, as clear-cut as their distinction between madness and sanity, between one psychiatric label or diagnosis and another. We can name this mental state, this human being, as 'psychotic', 'borderline', 'schizophrenic', 'bipolar', and so on. We can name this form of distress as 'mental illness' and this other form as 'normal'.

"Psychoanalysis has always fundamentally challenged this simplified view of the mind. *It* **offers us an alternative model of the dynamic mind, the mind in conflict, multi-layered, constantly negotiating inner and outer, the boundary between self and other, where you end and I begin; not a mind that we are born with, but a mind which develops only in relationship with others.**

"Attachment-based psychoanalysis provides us with an understanding that we do not have unified selves, but that our internal worlds are populated by internal working models of self and other, which form our sense of who we are."[70]

Finally, a shaman ~~I endorse~~ who validates me.

6:39 PM

A continuation of highlights from the nihilistic old man's vehement diatribe, recorded at the gym:

---

[69] Retzinger (1987)
[70] Judy Yellin's and Kate White's *Shattered States: Disorganised Attachment and its Repair*

3. *"It* used to be when you played football you could beat the crap out of somebody; now *it*'s 'Oh wait a minute—he *touched* him!' *It*'s a game; if you're gonna make rules for these games of people killing each other—jumping on each other, what the hell sense is *it?* Half-time—oh they say twenty-minute half-time, or this or that—Christ they stretch out basketball games—football games; fifteen-minute—*no* wait a minute; his *toe* touched the out-of-bounds line, we gotta, *time-out* or this—or that, or, call this—Christ you got five minutes of football left and you spend an hour-and-a-half watching the damn thing. What sense does that make? In a fifteen-minute period, *it*'ll be over within an hour. Three hours later you're still watching the same stupid game. Why? Cuz either *you're* stupid, or they're draggin' *it* out for so long that *it* ain't worthwhile; you wonder why—I hate sports, I really do; I think there... there's too many rules and regulations in sports as far as I'm concerned-"

   I said, *"It*'s like the roman colosseum dumbed down."

   "Yeah, basically."

4. "I just don't want to get the crap beaten out of me or pay fines."

5. "Last night—there's a funeral there; you're a big hotshot—*oh* you get a funeral—you get the processions—you get the cars—you're allowed this many people—you don't have to wear a mask or nothin'—oh, hugs and kisses and all this stuff—big, bigshot. *I* drop dead—'throw him in a hole. Goodbye.' What's the big deal?"

6. Sincerely, I said, "The bilateral directions of your tangents are superb."

   "At least I'm good at something. One lady called me a smartass—I said, 'Well at least there's one part of me that's smart, so what difference does *it* make?"

7. "Some people come in here and grit their teeth—they *really* do work out; that's their problem. I don't care how much muscle you got—you still can't stop a bullet."

   I said, "Yes, we're all flesh."

   "Ya know—yes, '*Oh* look I can pick up a thousand pounds!'—*Why?*"

I laughed and said, "I like that: *'Why?'*"

"Yippy skippy. What difference does *it* make—yippy—you pick up a thousand pounds—you, what good does *it* do ya?—'Oh look I picked up one-thousand pounds—I won a contest!'—What do you get—you get a little belt that says: 'This idiot picked up a thousand pounds.' So what."

8. "I always say: There's no sense killing one person; you may as well kill twenty or thirty people, because you're gonna get the same sentence whether you kill thirty people or one person."

    I chortled and said, "That's good life advice; I'll keep that in mind."

9. "I got two brothers; both of them are dumber than a box of rocks as far as I'm concerned. One can give you the history of life and the other knows everything, but I can do things with my hands that they can't do."

8:19 PM

I feel ashamed to indulge in another's pain. *"What difference does it make? What good does it do ya? Where's the progress in that? Yippy skippy."*
Shame on you, reader.

Wednesday, October 14ᵗʰ, 2020

12:49 PM

I strive for employment, for ~~mates~~, physical fitness, and a contented mind. Hopeless, despite boundless opportunities, for each action leads back to the initial departure from a designated state of want. The trajectory of my writing on account of a ceaseless yearning to document every thought that I would otherwise speak to a friend seated beside me, or to a lover whose hand I'd grasp—circumvented *here,* is atrocious.

I *am* a madman, "high-functioning," for my behavior is cohesive with consistent submission and a bowing of the head. "Poor in spirit," for I prefer a private room, shower, stovetop, and refrigeration as opposed to rent-free homelessness. Angered by the indecency of being human, of the selfish animalism we are corralled on behalf of, to be educated by a master(s) *of* human "decency." Childish thoughts, puerile, as always, while I sip a cup of coffee and enjoy the afternoon sun through my window before venturing out into the law-governed streets of American society for an interview at a health and rehabilitation center in the *hope* of the acquisition of a dishwashing job. Certainly—combine the exposition with an angsty lash-out at everything on which you depend, much like a spoiled child spared the rod, and *someone* will read. *Shame* on me. Submit. Obey. Conform.

My twenty-five copies of my third publication arrived in two boxes. Last night I opened a box, withdrew the top book from the pile, and began to reread my third installment as an unfamiliar stranger would; thereby, I enjoyed myself, and experienced a myriad of emotions. Twenty-six pages in, the novelty faded, and the identification of my memories overtook me. By the end of page thirty-four, I stopped, and wept for less than twenty seconds over my bathroom sink while I brushed my teeth on behalf of my father: What I thought two years ago is no different. All messages from my father and Candy are redirected or blocked on multiple platforms of communication.

Any fool would hazard a better pursuit than to read the incessant discharge of words of a man constrained by his perpetual shame of being human. I'm capable of intimacy, strong relationships, and open communication. *"Where's the progress in that? What good does* it *do ya? What difference does* it *make? Yippy skippy."*

Yes, over the bathroom sink, my eyes bleary and wet, a circle of toothpaste framed my agape mouth and dripped from my bottom lip. Spatters of toothpaste resounded in the silence of my 4:30 AM creature study: A monstrous countenance reckoned me in the mirror.

On December 9th, 2018, I wrote: "Maturation is to assimilate and abide by the expectations of others."

7:33 PM

Yes, rereading last year's published documentation, manifest in my hands as a book, is a valuable source of resolve, to heed my words when I was *confident* with the man that I am: On December 26th, 2018, I wrote:

"I've learned that I have transcended shame, for shame is learned; there is no truth.

"What are you ashamed of this moment, reader? To read this?—you *should* be. See? I've taught you what I '*know*'!"

However, shame is essential for social cohesion; therefore, I must acknowledge myself as a scumbag.[71] There is no recourse. With a laden heart, I acknowledge everything that is deplorable and detestable constituting my character, despite all that is deemed "good"; for what is "good," in my case, is "psychopathic," or rather, "mentally ill," in conjunction with the culture I am enmeshed with: At the nexus of an upstate New York lower to upper-middle-class city, unemployed due to fatuous mischief at one establishment, followed by a Covid-19-induced shutdown at another.

Shame. Since the advent of religion, shame has dampened personal volition and ushered unity over tribes. Shamans, oracles, prophets, and soothsayers beget a clergy, each proclaiming the will of God(s), for the sake of (cyclic) progress. I am humbled by my humanity, ashamed by my existence, of which I am disgusted to consume on behalf of life. Doomed, to obscurity and desolation, I sip coffee.

Thursday, October 15th, 2020

3:02 AM

I've emerged from the ashes of my annihilated psyche anew with cumulative knowledge derived from years of introspection. Intuition and shame are entwined. We all tell ourselves a story.

October *will* be a fiction month, henceforth:

Two sixteen-year-old-boys bounded together through a moonlit grocery store parking lot, high on marijuana, and played two rounds of rock-paper-scissors.

The first boy said, "What do you want to be when you grow up?"

The second boy said, "Fuck bitches—make money."

"What *dude?*" The first boy laughed. "I said what do you want to *be?*"

"What about you?"

"I dunno but I wanna fuck bitches—buy cars, and make money, too."

---

[71] I don't vote in political elections.

"Shit man, I'm hungry."

The above piece of "literary fiction" is inspired by a recording I captured at 1:44 AM on my way home from the gym when I asked two sixteen-year-old-boys playing rock-paper-scissors in the parking lot what their self-assigned meaning in life is.

I need to work on my "craft."

5:36 PM

One bright and beautiful October afternoon, two middle-aged men dressed in similar urban garb strode alongside each other alongside a low-to-middle class suburban road devoid of traffic:

"That sounds like an excellent plan."

"Yes, yes, the thing is-"

"What do the profit margins look like?"

"The investment rate is perfunctory—I mean-"

"And the return rates?—*Perfunctory?* What do you mean?"

"Ya know, when you look at *it* from the big picture, I mean, you see the scores—the trajectories-"

"Yeah—yeah I know—but I'm-"

"There's a nuance in, ya know, everything that um, someone with a trained skill—skillset with a mind for, ya know-"

"I'm interested in the investment return rates."

"*Oh,* well—ya know, these things take time."

"Of course—I-"

"Trust me-"

"I do—I think that th-"

"*Over time*—in *time;* as time progresses, things will pan out, understand?"

"Yes."

"Do you want to get lunch?"

"... Yeah, of course."

The two men stepped into a sandwich shop. On entry, an eighteen-year-old woman at the counter, dressed in a white t-shirt, black apron, black shorts, and black ballcap, could distinguish no difference between the two men based on the observance of their urban garb, underweight—albeit lean constitution, and confident, whimsical demeanors: Blue jeans, beige-tinted sweaters, black running shoes. *"He's cute,"* she thought, in relation to one man compared to the other: her single allotted discernment after minimal processing of their forms, though she would never deign to copulate with either, and she said, "Hello! How are you?" and smiled at the shoes of both men.

The man who entered first ignored the woman, leaned back towards the other man, both arms outstretched in a presenting gesture towards the menu positioned high on the wall behind the girl at the counter, and said, "I love *it*—look at that stylized layout; isn't *it* chic? But like, chic without *trying,* ya know?"

"Yeah. Look at that—geez, there are so many options." The man positioned behind the forefront man spread his legs, crossed his arms, and pressed the incurved knuckles of his right hand against his chin-

Stop. Reader, *really?* Can you believe this abomination I deem "fiction" written in the series of preceding passages? Will you tolerate my following metanonfictional departure from the trite that is our presupposed modern existence? These words capture *my* unrefined perspective of what mature men are. Yes, I will title the story here[72] without titling *it*—where a title would spoil the ambiguous premise, unless one would gaze down at the bolded annotation first and receive an intended suggestion to tinge their comprehension while reading. Yes, if I write the title to be "Immature Men," I think there would be unanimous disagreement, for what else is an American man to do *but* an iteration of this if he is to *be* a proponent of the status quo?

"What virtue do these men practice?" is the best query to determine maturity, though their vices remain subverted in a mire of pretense.

Am I a mature man—to write this sentence prostrated on my knees, balanced on my forearms, garbed in only black briefs and a dress shirt, ass raised behind me, illuminated by the dim glow of twilight shone through my open blinds?

---

[72] Mature Men

Friday, October 16th, 2020

2:17 AM

"Psychopaths" experience no shame, yet the "mentally ill" are overwrought with shame. Does a happy-well-to-do-competent-smiling-cup-of-coffee-sipping-productive-"how are you I'm well thank you"-speaking-citizen experience *just the right* amount of shame, somewhere in the middle of the spectrum of "Burn for all eternity in hellfire" and "Who cares?"

A fly buzzes in my head, i.e., the voice of my father: "I can't believe my son betrayed me." Ah, yes, *my* guilt; however, I experience no shame.

Candy continues to message me and somehow bypasses my "spam" inbox with proclamations of her undying love for me in conjunction with half-hearted condemnations of my attempt to fornicate with her twenty-year-old daughter—of which I informed her on the moment of conceiving the idea to do so.

Weekly unemployment benefit payments of $159.25 after taxes are insufficient funds to support my lifestyle. I've lost count and track of the resumes I've submitted and the establishments I've visited in search of employment. To afford food for the next month ($350-$450), pay bills, and support my ritualistic nightly labor at the gym in the vain and useless effort for increased muscle mass, I must use a credit card to pay for at least half of my rent.

My strength returns to me in large increments with access to compound lifting stations and cable machines.

I've experimented with an undeviating diet with increased consumption of 12 to 16 eggs a day for the past two months:

Meal 1: 3 tbsp of sauerkraut, 2 ½ cups of frozen (steamed) broccoli, carrots, and cauliflower, 2 tbsp of chia seeds, 1 handful of whole almonds, 2 tbsp of cacao nibs, 1 cup of frozen blueberries, 4 cloves of crushed garlic, 8 whole (Omega-3) eggs, 2 ½ tbsp of extra virgin olive oil, ½ scoop of unflavored grass-fed whey protein, 1 tsp of creatine, spices, fish oil supplement, multivitamin.

Meal 2: 1 avocado, 2 cans of wild-caught sardines in extra virgin olive oil, 2 ½ cups of frozen (steamed) broccoli, carrots, and cauliflower, with an occasional half of a fresh colored pepper or ½ cup of frozen (steamed) brussel sprouts.

Meal 3: 1 can of (daily alternating) wild-caught salmon or tuna in water and 1 pickle.

Meal 4: 8 whole (Omega-3) eggs, 2 ½ tbsp of extra virgin olive oil, 1 handful of almonds, 5 cups of frozen (steamed) spinach, 2 cups of 5% fat Greek yogurt, 1 ½ cup of full-fat cottage cheese, 1 tsp of creatine.

Why? For my own miserable satisfaction, so that I may be attractive to women that I have no desire to sleep with and more respectable (or rather, in most cases, enviable) to intemperate, undisciplined men on the ~~rare~~ instances of which I am observed, evaluated, and judged. The human condition routes the application of my intelligence towards the most beneficial pursuit for my well-being. Asceticism is funk; I know by gratuitous experience. The will-to-live invigorates my spirit, for I have no desire to inherit the earth. Superior strength, for a man in my position, is superfluous and vain...

Much like *my journal*... Ah: "My," "my," "my"; "I," "I," *"I."*

Go away, reader; begone, away with you. Leave me to my attempts at fiction superseded by expositional life memories, that I may reminisce on my life without future shame, if I *am* to live.

4:03 PM

No—I wouldn't want to read this: *Shame?* 7.8 billion people, and to read of *my* (lack of) shame, self-perpetuating on account of this act of lifelong documentation; how many instances must I write of this?

5:47 PM

Reinitiation of reading works by Arthur Schopenhauer, Robert Sapolsky, and the beginning of Fernando Pessoa's *The Book of Disquiet*. Avoidant of all bars on my way to and from strength training each night at 12:00 AM to 2:00 AM. A plan to meet with a forty-six-year-old woman at a nearby park to determine sexual chemistry and to proceed with an agreement I've proposed for mutual psychoanalysis. Pending employment opportunities.

For the past three days, I've been a prisoner to my own routine: I listen to past recordings, read past documentation, and acclimate myself to a life of total solitude, exposed only to the sounds of activity I hear above, and out on the adjacent alleyway. At night, on my trek to the gym, the occasional vehicle is a reminder of the human form within. The old man at the gym is my sole validator. We wave to each other. Yesterday, I approached him and said, "Before you begin your workout, I want to know what the best memory that you've ever had is."

"Geez I don't know," he chuckled. "… I really couldn't say what the best memory I ever had is—probably having my son—I don't know."

I nodded and said, "Hm… The moment of your son's birth?"

"I was *there* when he was born—yeah, probably."

"All right. I wanted something positive to balance the last conversation that we had."

"Yeah, I don't know, probably the best thing that ever happened is having a kid—I mean, I don't… I can't really say I like having a kid but he's probably the best thing that ever happened to me but… I don't know; maybe the first time I got laid—I don't know."

We chuckled. I said, "That's definitely not my best… memory."

"I—I—I'm just—ya know… you're talkin'… My kid is… thirty-nine-years-old? You're talking forty years ago ya know? I don't know. I never gave *it* much thought to what my best thought was—ya know—my best memory was."

"All right-"

"Maybe when I learned to tie my shoes—I don't know—maybe when I went to kindergarten—I have no idea—I've just never given *it* much thought to which was my best one. Maybe when I got my driver's license, I don't know."

"All right. I'll accept the birth of your son as an answer."

We ceased our discourse and exerted alone, together.

Three days prior to today, I ventured out in the busy afternoon daylight hours to deliver a copy of my third publication to the manager of the gym, James, at his request. I informed James that I am humiliated to provide him a copy, and asked what he defines as a "mature man." I forgot to reinsert the SD (memory) card for my recorder on this particular instance and can only recall, verbatim, the final declarative statement in regards to my inquiry.

Intense contemplation ensued while the manager admired the "quality" of my physical book. The conversation revolved back to health and fitness for eight minutes; however, on my moment of departure, James said, "My definition of a mature man is one who is true to himself."

I shook James' hand despite Covid-19 induced policy, sanitized my hands, and departed.

Am I true to myself, and therefore "mature," to persist with the yearly publication of this documentation despite an evolving ~~self~~ delusion? I reflect on the immutable, fictional character of Howard Roark from Ayn Rand's *The Fountainhead*...

Yes... on reflection of this *fictional* character, I reaffirm the validity of *my* definition of maturity: Maturation is to assimilate and abide by the expectations of others.

Shame on the "~~psychopaths~~" mavericks.

Nothing profound to be read here, merely an iteration of J.D Salinger. Sorry folks. I'm *mentally challenged.*

Saturday, October 17th, 2020

2:25 PM

Domesticated and disgruntled. A football game and intermittent commercials resounded through the ceiling above me the moment I removed my earplugs four minutes prior to 1 PM. From 11:46 AM to 12:56 PM, I idled on my floor, half-wrapped in a blanket, and stared at my ceiling. I'm an alien denizen in my space; this is the humanity I have inaugurated with. Tucked into a comfortable cubby hole, I flounder for employment to stave off financial enslavement: Numbers on a screen.

The sun is unoccluded, and tempts me to dress and venture outside, among the *public*... I cringe at the thought. What would I do? My window faces the wall of the city library; what cruel joke is this? I—who has committed his life to nothing but the act of writing, and therefore reading as a secondary necessity, has not stepped into the one structure that I inadvertently gaze at by consequence of *it* being the totality of scenery available to me: A windowed brick wall, adjoining sidewalk, street, and passerby.

What would I do at the library? I procure the worldwide compendium of literature available to me for free, by my lord and master *Google*'s grace.

Physical books are cheap, sourced from a global warehouse. I'd find dainty women at the library, ask for casual sex under the pretense of a feigned charisma masqueraded with a suave idiolect, be rejected on account of my lack of conviction, accrue a localized reputation as a scumbag, and be banned—akin to my bar activity.[73] The amenities of social venues are *tertiary;* socialization is the prime motive, and what else do people socialize for but power (even within an inconsequential sphere of personal influence) and sex? I don't drink at bars and I wouldn't read at libraries. Weight-lifting equipment would be a burden to relinquish at a lost net-financial gain once I inevitably depart from my apartment at the closure of my lease; therefore, the gym is a boon, for I don't hunt mammals in physical combat or perform manual labor. The park, a fifty-second walk away, is a temptation; a veritable (indolence-inducing) contemporary agora—though again, what would I do but scan the environment for women to inquire of casual sex? Stand in the sun while reading a book, gawked at by observers as a rascal or as an impertinent piece of the environment? Lay in the grass? Engage in a philosophical conversation about the meaning of life, metempsychosis, or the innate morality of man with someone willing *and* sober? Acquire a *friend?*

While homeless in Arkansas, the library had been a providence; I'd visit for a reprieve of shelter from the summer sun and to acquire a source of water, nourished by the selection of philosophical books. I read in the annals, standing or pacing, secluded from fellow visitors, reckoned on brief instances as either a loon or a deranged incompetent by the staff. I suppose where I am now, alone, in a room I call home, *without* being observed, I'm no different.

They stood for four minutes on the sidewalk outside my window, side-by-side, heads down, wired earphones in:

Estimated age of twenty-two-years, Caucasian female: White headband, red dress—lolita style; rounded black sunglasses rimmed with red; flat laceless brown shoes; elbow-length brown hair; chubby, 5'4.

Estimated age of twenty-four-years, Caucasian male: Short brown hair, black t-shirt with a large red "B" on the front; a winking skull-of-a-cat with crossbones open-zippered black hoodie; black shorts with two large

---

[73] Albeit, I had been banned from the *Messy House* bar for my discomfiting presence due to "Asking people weird questions and acting like 'The Terminator.' " according to the owner.

ornamental suspended silver chains looped over the front thighs; black running shoes; skinny, 5'9.

9:36 PM

A monologue I recorded last night:

"*It's* 1:22 AM. The 18th, I believe, perhaps the 19th[74]—Friday, whichever of those dates. Coming from the gym I walk towards *The Messy House,* with intent to exist in the parking lot beyond the premises. I expect to meet a drunken rabble. I'm about ten minutes out, perhaps eight. I do not intend to speak unless spoken to. And, in return, I will speak with a neutral dialogue.

"I anticipate being provocated, or at least threatened—to leave; *to leave,* a premise I have every right to be on. So, this is a moral dilemma: Am I instigating by existing? I'll find out.

"This is foolhardy, of course; desultory, at best; I just conceived of this route. I'd be better off going home, consuming my ritualistic nightly meal, and contemplating life before bed. Instead… I commit to this, whatever *it* is. A little bit of, 'experience,' you could say, at the detriment of my safety and security. Though what is life, if not lived uncomfortably? Perhaps a few punches in the face, a stab wound, or even death, will liberate me from everything that I've known, for far too long: The *comfort* of my flesh—ah, is this dramatic? Perhaps even histrionic, if I must end up sending this file to the authorities. Comedic. A comedic, dumb satire, which is after all, all of life, so… enjoy.

"And what is life a satire of, I wonder? In a later transcription process, I'll add an annotation at this point, and I'll answer this question, in brief.[75] Every word, verbatim, will be transcribed exactly as *it* is, for I, am a *self-engrossed fool,* with nothing more but his voice, and his silent intangible thoughts, which *must be* expressed in action… in order, to be *something,* I must act.

"My legs ache… but that's all right; my upper body is well-rested—I don't think I'll transcribe this part; this is just… vain.

"I'm about three minutes out from my destination at the parking lot. I

---

[74] The 16th.

[75] Death walked into a bar and said, "Ah, yes, how are you, George? That's great to hear. I'll start off with a cabernet. Of course. How are the kids? What do you mean I'm not funny? I genuinely want to know."

reiterate; I expect to meet with a rabble, that does nothing but babble. This part will not be transcribed: The previous three sentences.

"I think I'll be disappointed. I probably won't transcribe this, unless I *am* injured… either emotionally or physically. No harm will come to me mentally; I am sanctified in my rationale, though I do deviate now, I admit; therefore, I injure myself with my mentality and *lack of* rationality in the upcoming two minutes. Perhaps I should be institutionalized, *because* of my lack of rationale; that would be the best course of action for… a jurist, I think; that would be the easiest, guilt-free course of action to take.

"My projections are off. *Now It*'ll be about two minutes. This transcription will be worthless; this is merely for my own sake, for the potential authority's sake, because I'm a coward, who will act as an anarchist, yet fall back on a judicial system; so what am I, but a hypocrite?

"My heartbeat hastens. I've arrived.

"I'm alone. Music resounds from inside. A drink of water. Wait.

"Just, what am I?"

Four minutes and fifty-eight seconds elapsed. The bar owner drove up to me from my right, eighteen feet away, and flashed his headlights four times. I turned my head and addressed the owner as an anomaly: a mimicry of what he saw in me; both of our faces vacuous, exposed in our shared confusion. We remained this way for six seconds; thereafter, he circled the parking lot and drove around to the front of the establishment. I watched the car depart from the parking lot.

Three minutes elapsed; I departed, homeward bound. The owner had been the only person to witness my presence (to my knowledge), and I desired to exit the scenario, thereby imparting my insubstantial impression on *only* the owner.

Nobody cares. Only I remember this moment for what *it* had been: Something absurd and negligible, an inconsequential snippet of incidental curiosity.

Sunday, October 18th, 2020

3:54 PM

This journal bloats with each passing year: I'm uncertain what this is indicative of.

Last night I visited *The Messy House* for twenty-eight minutes after an hour strength-training session at the gym. On my entry, I held a ten-dollar bill upright in front of my face between my middle and index finger, my gaze locked on the bartender, Joe. With a downturned scowl, Joe shrugged, and feigned indifference to my presence despite his personal dislike of me—which is understandable, with consideration of previous events; however, as the old adage goes, "Money talks."

A man called me genuine and humble on my entry, the one whose self-assigned meaning in life is purportedly to achieve the highest score on the establishment's *Pac-Man* arcade game. I purchased a beer for him, and we proceeded to chat about trivialities.

An older woman in her forties with overt masculine energy, blonde pompadour, facial piercings, and a prerogative to secure a sexual partner, accused me of "bullshitting everyone in this place," i.e., pretentiousness, in regards to my mien and dialect. I made her *feel* uncomfortable by existing as I am, *entirely* devoid of affectation. This trend of upsetting the sensibilities of drunks is a manner of self-flagellation, for *I* am misunderstood.

"Are you a winner or a loser?" the *Pac-Man* game-high-score-aspirant inquired of me in reference to a water-chugging contest activity he proposed to me.

I gazed down to my left for three seconds, contemplated, and said, "I don't know," as an answer to the general question, unrelated to the shenanigan.

"I bet I can chug faster than you."

"I believe you."

"C'mon little bitch," he beamed and outstretched his hand to shake, "Hey, I'm just foolin' around—but drink the *damn* water with me!"

I didn't accept his hand and said, "Why do you call me a little bitch?"

"Just drink the water with me."

"I have a preference for my own water, from my own vessel."

"I know you don't like me,[76] but I'm tryin'," said the man; he frowned at me.

Expressionless, I said, "Why do you think I don't like you?"

"You won't drink the *fucking* water with me!"

This memory, recorded to 1/8th, perhaps even 1/16th—1/32ths—*no:* a fraction is an ineffectual gauge to represent even *my* perspective; I'm slanted, in my own spiral downward into the annihilatory chasms of my mind, where I surge into thoughts—memories—which, from a reader's

---

[76] Attestation to the man's dislike of me.

perspective who is *not* me, would reckon as a piece of puerile trite, though to me—albeit, the aforementioned memory is the worst in quality I have ever chosen to write of, in both depth and brevity—the *encapsulation* is precious. A fragment of ambiguous meaning is imbued within each sentence; perplexed, as I am, with my abject desolation on reflection of my insignificance, I ponder on the possibility of my ephemeral interaction weighing equal significance on the commonly postulated "interconnected consciousness" with the actions of Adolf Hitler, at the apex of his power, in a similar twenty-eight-minute timeframe.

What role do I play? I am of no tribe, no culture, employed by no one, enslaved to my landlord, the state, two creditors, and live in a little space allotted to me among the 14,000 "others" in this city... Yes, the lack of intrinsic meaning is overbearing. Even if I were one of the original hominids, a veritable Adam with Eve, what hope would I we have?

The previous paragraph manifested with the tap of my fingers and the female voice of my dualistic ego manifested in my consciousness due to active reflection: *"Now **that's** pathetic."* Is *it?* My thoughts—despite my will-to-live and actions ennobled with the values of progress and purpose, *despite* my suppressed philosophical inclinations of anarchistic individuation on account of an experienced *powerlessness,* are enshrouded in a miasma of shame. And where is this shame sourced? I recall a quote I recorded in my previous book:

"Your false self is the accumulation of all the voices you have internalized from other people—parents and friends who want you to conform to their idea of what you should be like and what you should do, as well as societal pressures to adhere to certain values that can easily seduce you. *It* also includes the voice of your own ego, which constantly tries to protect you from unflattering truths."

- Robert Greene's Mastery

My upstairs neighbors cook their dinner while I cook **Meal 1.**

6:29 PM

The masculine woman at the bar said to me, "You have a kind face." I thought of Jasmine, the nubile and naive redhead—at the time, who once sat on my lap and compressed my nose with her index finger: She had commented the same.

I said, "Don't be deceived by a kind face," and the woman turned ninety-degrees to her right with a visage of self-realized shock. I don't place much stock in this reaction; she had been drunk. I didn't feel "kind" in that twenty-eight-minute interval; I felt lost, baffled, confident *and* apprehensive on account of the dissipated faculties that surrounded me, though, the feelings denoted by the previous adjectives may have constituted a "kind" face.

The Messy House patrons are my undesignated tribe by frequent association. I circumnavigate among them, avoidant of becoming tainted, yet, sympathetic.

11:14 PM

Anhedonia. Deadlifts tonight.

Monday, October 19th, 2020

2:59 AM

I listened to the old man at the gym for twenty to forty-minute intervals and ingested his pain, *greedily*, eager to do so. I'd consider us friends; however, neither of us would be inclined to aid the other in a time of need. My conversational initiations incite a tirade of complaints, to which I stand and listen, my recorder engaged in case a mote of wisdom grazes my mind. Not tonight. Variations of reiterated "Where's the progress?" "What difference does *it* make?" and "Yippy Skippy" delight me. The old man is reminiscent of my father and is my only source of comedic relief besides mirrors and a current read of my previous book. I devour my own words like a savage, receptive to self-insights and holistic connections applicable to the human condition, e.g.:

I've recently written on the condition of being "poor in spirit," and have on my occasions in the past. On May 25th, 2019, I documented a quote on the wall of the hallway leading to a barber while stationed at Chicago, Illinois, for the U.S. Navy boot camp.

"Far better is *it* to dare mighty things, to win glorious triumphs, even though checkered by failure… than to rank with those <u>poor spirits</u>

who neither enjoy nor suffer much, because they live in a gray twilight that knows not victory nor defeat."

– *Theodore Roosevelt*

Men are torn every which way, heeding words of so-called enlightenment and timeless wisdom from a myriad of sources that *conflict*. I would know, being the egotistical-sanctimonious-hypocritical-pretentious-sociopathic-fool-failure, i.e., a scumbag, that I am. Jesus admonished his followers to be meek and "poor in spirit" *and* proclaimed himself as God's son—the holy spirit incarnate in the flesh! Jesus was a scumbag. Ahem... yes... **Jesus was a scumbag,** concluded by process of deductive causality: we are both God; however, everyone else is God too; therefore, Jesus, being a ~~martyr~~ fool (and a scumbag), yearned to be validated by the masses and was crucified.

"*Oh,* how edgy and cool," said a paragon of hedonistic capitalism-

"Oh, wow—even *edgier,*" said a product of modern culture, smug in their capacity for thoughtless critique and lambasting.

"*Really?* Look who's writing, Mr. holier-than-thou, with your *infallible* rhetoric based on the breakdown of everything that crystallizes unity within humanity," said someone with a brain.

Oh... right... *that* one was just myself; no, I must *toot* my own horn and assume credit where *it's* due: *All of it* is myself.

"Your edgy metanonfictional anarchistic shit is a great departure from literature," said a beautiful thirty-three-year-old Caucasian female yoga instructor. Her thirty-nine-year-old Caucasian male data analyst fiancé stood behind her, to her left, arms crossed, in a fitted light-blue dress shirt tucked into tapered black jeans. The man grinned, repressed a vitriolic verbal attack, and postured himself on a freshly mowed lawn that expanded beyond the frame of the fictional scene for a physical assault if necessary— by *his* standard of virtue, derived from the *New Testament Bible* proverbs and broadcasts of the American radio host, Dave Ramsey.

Are you eager to start a family?

The man opened his mouth to speak and the woman said, "Of course. We have a dog now—a *cute* little Goldendoodle puppy—*oh my god* like, he's *soooo* **preciousss!**" The woman's voice lowered by two octaves on the pronunciation of "precious."

"Jesus was a scumbag"? How may I be so profane as to write such blasphemous condemnations, to ~~force~~ goad a reader with a string of what one would hope to be words of some merit or integrity (doubtful by this point); for, in writing the statement, "Jesus was a scumbag," again, for the fourth instance now, is in effect stating that *my* character—my *martyrdom* and sanctimonious mode of being, is equatable to Jesus, only I practice prudence in my social discourses. I've documented what happens when I speak: a parallel to Jesus, only I am tinged with disaffected pity for my fellow man, contrary to Jesus' *affected* pity, which amounted to genuflection and placation, the pusillanimous clown (in action) that he was (purported to be).

If I were to have held my ground after being punched four times beyond *The Messy House* perimeter, surrounded by drunks, I'm certain that my hubristic obstinance and selfish will to suffer on account of others' suffering would have wrought my death—or grievous wounds of the flesh—at the least, parallel to being crucified. And for what? Honor? Courage? ~~Commitment?~~ *Virtue?* I'd be "wrong" in accordance with New York state *law*, for I would've shirked the option to retreat.

Ah, the *trauma* I've chosen for myself is what's pathetic: A feedback loop of reflection on my self-contained indecencies of being human.

"Jesus wept."

- The Bible, Gospel of John, 11:35

Why did Jesus weep: An unparalleled ego.

No, I don't foster delusions of being christ-like; Jesus Christ is an easy character to attack; I ~~empathize~~ sympathize with the ~~man~~ symbol. Jesus Christ was a scumbag (by the Roman/Jewish [presupposed] standard of virtue)—crucify me for stating *it* (by the Christian/Catholic standard of virtue).

I have no intention of offending myself; authenticity emboldens every abstruse declaration I publish. If my intention was to offend someone *other* than myself I'd ruminate on and deconstruct Allah.~~; however, the previous principles apply—*oh...*~~

"-I'm a loser baby, so why don't you kill me?

- American Musician, Beck

Tuesday, October 20th, 2020

2:25 AM

At 1:28 AM, I walked home from the gym on the front street-side of *The Messy House* with no expectation or desire for communication. Two cabbies parked on both sides of the street waited in anticipation of a fare. Two women of moderate attractiveness bantered out front; I estimated one with shoulder-length black hair to be in her early thirties; and the other, standing three feet away beside her with a platinum pompadour similar to the woman I spoke to within *The Messy House* three nights prior, only this woman had a feminine face and athletic body by contrast. I initiated my recorder and approached, unable to dissuade myself from the opportunity for content:

I said, "Hello."

The platinum-haired hair woman immediately responded after several furtive glances in my direction on what she had expected to be my hasty passing, "Hi—how are you?"

"I'm well."

The seated black-haired woman said, "Hi," though I had already begun to talk over her:

"Do you mind if I ask you two a peculiar question?"

"Sure," said the black-haired woman.

"What is your self-assigned meaning in life?"

The platinum-haired woman said, "What?"

"Your self-assigned meaning in life."

The women echoed each other: "Our meaning in life?"; "Our meaning in life?" followed by the platinum-haired woman's inquiry of, "What is *your* meaning in life?"

"To write."

"To write what?" said the black-haired woman.

The platinum-haired woman stepped between myself and the black-haired woman; she said, "To write like, a book?"

I said, "Why do you stand in front of her?"

"Because I'm talking to you."

"Well yes I, I was talking to you both though."

"Okay," said the platinum-haired woman, and she stepped aside while the black-haired woman said, "She got serious—she got seri—she just got serious."

"To write what, a book?" repeated the platinum-haired woman.

I said, "On the human condition."

"On the 'human condition'... all right so-"

"Like what part of the human condition?" interrupted the black-haired woman.

I looked between both and said, "Well, I've already answered all these questions, so now, how about your self-assigned meaning in life?"

The black-haired woman said, *"Our* meaning of life-"

"Yes."

"That's what we're trying to fuckin' figure out."

I said, "That's why you're sitting on the stoop of a bar—and standing, at a bar?"

"Ummm... *Yeah!*"

The platinum-haired woman's eyes narrowed and she said, "Are you judging us?"

I lied and said, "No—I can tell that you think I'm an asshole but I'm just asking you a question."

The platinum-haired woman held a half-smoked cigarette skewed near the side of her head and said, "Yo—I—you act like a *fucking robot* so why not just be like a normal person?"

The black-haired woman said, "Yeah like—you—you, you might look a *little* bit like an asshole... I mean *it's* kinda cool-"

The platinum-haired woman said, "I think you're fucking with us."

"-I—I—I think you might be fucking with us a little bit-"

I smiled and said, "You think-"

"-he's blushing—he's like blushing![77]—a little bit."

The platinum-haired girl concurred, "Yep—I do too—you're *fucking* with us; you *are* blushing."

I said, "So you think I look like an asshole and act like a robot."

The black-haired woman shouted, "Yes!—you talk like one."

"How so?"

---

[77] Shame.

"You talk like my—you talk like *Siri*."

The platinum-haired woman said, "I don't—I don't—I don't think you look like an asshole because you got a little bit of a smile... but-"

The black-haired woman erupted with maniacal laughter.

"-you're acting kinda weird so—talk to me."

I said "So a smile determines whether or not I'm an asshole regardless of the context of my speech."

The platinum-haired woman commanded, "Would you *stop* talking like that?"

The black-haired woman said, "Is that like how you normally talk?"

Calm, I said, "What manner are you speaking of?"

The black-haired woman spoke as an indirect aside: *"He like, holds himself so well.* Where are you from?"

The platinum-haired woman echoed, "Where are you from?"

"Yeah—where are you from?"

"Where are you from?"

"Where are you from?"

I said, "What is your self-assigned meaning in life?"

The platinum-haired woman said, "Can you unbutton your jacket please?"

The black-haired woman said, "There *it* is—there's Siri!"

I said, "Why?"

"Wh—do you—do you have a weapon on you?"

"No."

The black-haired woman said, "Ohh—do you? You got handcuffs? I like handcuffs."

I chortled.

"I do too," said the platinum-haired woman; she tilted her head back for a four-syllable guffaw.

The black-haired woman tittered, "He stopped and talked to the *wrong* girls."

"I—I'm not exactly sure what you're asking me; what is my 'self-assigned meaning in life?'"

I said, "Yes."

"Wh—what does that mean, like what're you—what're you *looking* for?

I said "I'm looking for-"

"Like—what kinda—like, what kinda—I'm—I'm totally confused," interjected the raven-haired woman; she stood from the stoop and addressed me, full-body."

"Me too," acceded the platinum-haired woman.

Patient, I said, "The meaning that you have chosen for your existence."

The black-haired woman said, "... *Well* at one point in my time I chose to be a wife and a mother, and, then *that* got shit on, so, I guess now I'm just trying to figure that part out, so—I don't know what my meaning in life is; I'm finding myself right now."

The platinum-haired woman muttered in a light-hearted inflection to me, "Do you know your meaning in life?"

I said, "I've already told you."

The black-haired woman said, "He said to write."

"No—there's more than that," said the platinum-haired woman.

"Is that why you're asking us these questions?"

"There's more than that."

"Is this like—is this like a survey? Do you have a questionnaire we can fill out or something?"

I answered the queries with simple affirmatives or negatives.

The platinum-haired woman said, "Where you from, bud?"

The black-haired woman said, "Are you from around here? There's no way you're from around here—cuz talkin' like that there's no way."

I smiled and sniggered.

The platinum-haired woman said, "Look at that *fucking* smile-"

"Look at him!-"

"He's so adorable!

"Yeah that is cute."

I stymied my joviality and said, "I'm a denizen of the world."

The black-haired girl looked to the platinum-haired girl and said, "I don't know what that means."

"Okay, all right, "said the platinum-haired girl, "What is my meaning in life..."

I said, "A denizen is a synonym for an occupant."

The black-haired woman said, "Can I ask you—are you Christian—are you Catholic?"

"No."

"None of those? Are you like an alien?"

The platinum-haired girl said, "Are you *sure?* You wanna drink?"

I said, "No."

Surprised, the black-haired woman said, "You don't wanna come have a drink? You don't drink alcohol?"

I said, "No."

"That's no fun; you gotta have fun-"

"I'm not a fun person."

"-you gotta have fun in life."

"Why?"

"Cuz you hafta have fun."

"Why?"

"Why fucking *not?*"

The platinum-haired girl contributed, *"It's* life, man."

I said to the black-haired woman, "Well you said you *have* to have fun-"

"You *do*—what else are you gonna fucking do?"

"-so you need to—well, if you *want* to prove your validity of that statement, instead of me proving to you why I *don't* need to have fun, you should prove with your own rhetoric why I *have* to have fun."

"You don't—I mean-" began the black-haired woman.

The platinum-haired woman blurted, *"Oh!"*

"-I mean you don't have to have fun—you could just be your robot self and just go along with your business and shit—ya know."

I said, "What makes you believe that I'm a robot?"

"The way you talk; you talk like *Siri* on my iPhone."

The platinum-haired woman said, "You talk like one."

I said, "Because I'm devoid of affectation to impress you—is that *it?*"

The black-haired woman said, "You have like a camera in your pocket or somethin' Are we going on *Youtube*—or some shit?

"No."

"I'll be *famous!* Shit. Where did you—where did—I need a shot; I need a drink."

The platinum-haired woman said, "Come in with us."

"Yeah—come have a drink with us, c'mon."

I said, "No."

The black-haired woman mewled, "Awwww—no?"

I said, "So, your self-assigned meaning in life *was* to be a mother-"

"And a wife… and he's a cheatin' prick, so… you know."

"Well, aren't we all though, when we're in a committed relationship?"

"Cheaters?"

I said, "We can't just depend on one person to satisfy all of our expectations."

"Yeah you can. Yourself."

"Well that's not another person."

"You don't—cuz you don't depend on another person—you depend on yourself. Cuz that's the person who's only going to be true to you, is yourself."

"Is that a philosophy that you would hold true in all aspects?"

The black-haired woman held up both hands to me, turned to the platinum-haired woman, and said, "He's way too much for me—I need a shot—like—you're—you're confusing me; *it* was very nice to meet you," she extended her hand for a shake, "I'm Ashleigh by the way." I gazed down at Ashleigh's hand. "You don't shake hands?"

I said, "You want to shake my hand even though you call me a robot and just want to walk away."

"I mean I'll shake your hand—*it*'s clean and stuff."

I shook my head and said, "Ah, that's all right."

"Well *it* was very nice to meet you."

"Take care."

"You too."

I turned and began to walk away. Ashleigh skipped towards the bar entry ten feet away and yelled from the doorway into the establishment, *"I just met a fucking robot!"*

Four paces along the sidewalk, the platinum-haired woman called after me: "Hey, hey, come here. Come here." I obliged and turned halfway towards her, circumspect and vexed. The woman spoke with the hint of a maternal tone, "What's up with you, bud?"

I said, "What?"

"… Do you want to know what *I* think about life?"

I turned full-body towards the platinum-haired woman and said, "Yes, I do."

"I'm gonna be fifty-years-old next month. Okay, uh, I've been through a lot in my life; I'm a drug-addict and alcoholic. I own a, *big* real-estate company. I uh… keep to myself… I stop at certain points… I think life… hm… My mom used to always tell me 'Life is what you make *it*,' so, you can have what you want, and you can stop what you want—does that make any sense at all?" The woman looked up at me with bleary eyes: Sullen, intoxicated, doubtful, and whispered, "Probably not to you."

"You can have what you want and you can stop what you want—is that what you said?"

"Yes… Yes-"

The female Caucasian bartender who had banned me from entry three weeks ago joined us on the sidewalk with Ashleigh as an escort behind her; she asked the platinum-haired woman, "Michelle—you all right?"

Michelle ignored the bartender and continued "-*It's* all about, your choice-"

I said, "Your will."

"Your will and your choices."

"Your will to live."

Ashleigh spoke to the bartender from ten feet away: *"Who is he? Is he crazy? Does he belong in a mental institute? He's writing a book, about the meaning of life."*

"... Yeah," Michelle whispered, gazed over her shoulder at the bartender and Ashleigh, and turned back to me with an imploring visage, "... Yeah... listen—hey-" she attempted to garner my attention, for I had begun to stare at Ashleigh with suppressed contempt.

The bartender said, "Michelle—you good?"

Ashleigh yelled, high-spirited, "C'mon Shelly!"

Michelle quipped, "I'm good," returned her eyes to my own, and said, "You okay?"

The bartender said to Michelle, "You have a shot waiting for you," though she locked eyes with me for three seconds throughout the statement.

Ashleigh shouted, "Yes you do; you need one after that."

Michelle whispered to me, "Are you okay?"

Confounded, I said, "Why do you ask if I'm okay?"

Michelle backstepped one pace towards the bar and said, "I don't know—I just—I don't know; you're interesting to me, that's all."

"Hm."

Ashleigh yelled, *"Shelly!"* from the bar doorway.

Michelle waved at Ashleigh, limp-wristed, and said, "Yeah I'm coming—I'm coming." She addressed me as one would a dear friend boarding a train for a long voyage: "Y—I—I—You're just interesting to me... You just seem like a good person."

Ashleigh veered over to Michelle, grabbed her by the forearms, and said, *"It* was super-nice to meet you, robot. *C'mon Michelle."*

Unable to suppress my sadness, I revealed my condition in a final glance to Michelle—involuntarily mirroring her face, turned to walk away, and said, "Take care."

Ashleigh yelled from fifteen-feet away, "Bye, robot! *It* was nice to meet you! Keep *it* real!"

No pity. The above transcription is a wastrel's comedy. I condemn myself, again, to reflect on the intoxicated words of the unhappy. To know myself, I can think of no better self-assigned meaning.

6:37 PM

Redundancy.

I'm scourged by the internet. Abstaining from all media except a weekly update on national policy enforcement and PDFs by Arthur Schopenhauer render me… in an inexplicable state; there are no words to conceive my feeling other than the heeding of my sensory faculties: I listen to vehicles drive over rain-soaked streets and lay on my carpeted floor, stomach full of **Meal 2**, and between the brief intermissions when the streets outside are devoid of traffic, listen to the hum of my fridge and the occasional footsteps of a small dog or another human overhead.

Imprisoned by my apathy—where I'm most *comfortable,* for shame. I am a modern man, consigned to a screen, vitalized by the artificial exertion of my body at midnight, and validated by arbitrary parameters I set for myself. I want for nothing except greater physical strength. I'm a mere beast by application of my reason. "Where's the progress?"

9:21 PM

While I read Fernando Pessoa's *The Book of Disquiet,* I insert earplugs into my ears on behalf of my upstairs neighbor's television. While I (often) render myself inert to prevent excessive noise, and walk around my apartment along a tract of floor which creaks the least, with a book splayed open, six-inches in front of my face, I contemplate my ~~suppressed~~ repressed animality: A volatile slave to my anger, an emotion that has rarely manifested throughout my life and instead serves as a tempered boiler for melancholy. What am I angry about? I fail to identify. My negligible desire to exact wrath is on par with my desire for copulation. Am I even a *man?*—not to emasculate or effeminize myself, for my energy is disparate from the receptive state: A self-nullifying presence.

Wednesday, October 21ˢᵗ, 2020

2:11 PM

Jesus and Allah Walked Into a Dive Bar

Uproarious applause muffles awes of wonder.
One said to the other:
"How may you prove to me of the
Validity of your existence?" with a hint
Of repressed envy conferred between
Both on the moment of utterance.
Who spoke it? The patrons demand to
Know; this makes all the difference.

I thought of several more lines to add to this cheap shot poem: Artful expressions denoting that both entities are a vapor beyond the threshold of the bar's doorway. Instead of the committal of a denigration of the insidious influence of religion in a bad poem, I reminisce on a tangible (by contrast) observation of U.S. Navy boot camp that I forgot to document while I waited in the mental health facility in my ploy to ~~be separated~~ have my seized journal pages returned to me:

A forty-three-inch television augmented with a DVD player situated in the top right corner of the waiting room broadcasted media provided by the federal government, selected by recruits in-wait of psychoanalysis. Nature documentaries and military glorification documentaries comprised the stack of DVDs available for selection. In my three instances of waiting for 5 to 8 hours, I observed the reactions of other recruits to the content displayed on the screen.

On sight and sound of Navy Seal training and Spec Ops Warfare, the majority of women averted their eyes and sought with desperation for a distraction other than the prescribed. Men, who had admitted of their weakness and therefore sat in the waiting room for a mental examination, regarded warfare documentaries with envy, shame, contempt (in no particular predomination), and *reinvigoration*—which, I surmise "reinvigoration" is the intended effect, for I witnessed one particular man (after viewing a Navy Seal persist through a grueling run session and bombastic sets of calisthenics), stand from his seat, fists clenched, face reddened, and inform the two corpsmen at the receptionist counter: "I feel better and would like to return to my division."

Lunches in paper bags are distributed in large laundry carts to recruits waiting for systematic functions. I'm uncertain if the emasculating effect of this was intended—to provide recruits with variations of deli meat and cheese sandwiches, 8 oz of skim milk, a fistful of M&M trail mix, and an apple, though *I* certainly felt boyish and impotent to be fed a standardized grade school (K-6) diet; I can't testify for my peers. Many delighted in the food. My M&Ms were easily passed off the moment I offered them, no matter who I found myself among.

Memories of boot camp linger. Fond recollections of mental turmoil; the choice I mulled throughout: of whether or not *to* commit, despite signing the oath of enlistment and repeated screams of the *Sailor's Creed* while standing "at attention," side-by-side with rack mates, or marching on immaculate avenues.

I've shirked everyone I've known and every commitment I've ever made except for writing.

"Whenever I've tried to free my life from a set of the circumstances that continuously oppress *it*, I've been instantly surrounded by other circumstances of the same order, as if the inscrutable web of creation were irrevocably at odds with me. I yank from my neck a hand that was choking me, and I see that my own hand is tied to a noose that fell around my neck when I freed *it* from the stranger's hand. When I gingerly remove the noose, *it*'s with my own hands that I nearly strangle myself."

– Fernando Pessoa's The Book of Disquiet

6:43 PM

Fecundity of spirit incites masturbation. At least once weekly, to ensure prostate health, I pleasure myself in front of a mirror. My image fails to arouse me. Abstention from pornographic material leaves me with no recourse but to reminisce and mutilate memories into sexual catalysts. To gaze at my body throughout the process, I'm staid and permissive: an aloof stranger. This is not to state that I "detach" myself from my "self," or that I experience a transposition of consciousness—or any manner of that existential nonsense. No, what is, is that I view my body mirrored before me, and think of past sexual experiences: a nebulous slideshow of faces and body parts. These brief, weekly intervals, are the only moments in which I address my reflected visage with love. I stroke myself silently and ejaculate into the sink.

> "If only *it* were so easy to banish hunger by rubbing an empty belly."

> *- Diogenes of Sinope*

Thursday, October 22nd, 2020

2:05 AM

"Narcissistic" masturbation, nightly strength training sessions in solitude (I haven't acknowledged the cynical old man in over a week), sixteen eggs consumed a day, no friends, no family…

Why do you *read,* reader? What enjoyment do you reap from my scumbaggery? I exist on this plane to consume, proliferate this vile expulsion, and *die.* This is the style of literature *I* will enjoy reading, while I glut myself on **Meal 4** at two in the morning after a session of enervating my muscles: To write self-denigration; the microscopic lens which I view my mote of inconsequential (presumably) stardust in a world we believe—we *hope,* as a unified race, operates on universal principles, e.g., karma, "quantum" physics, God's eternal will, etc.

Am I *pathetic?* What is my reference for comparison? I've secured a second interview with the medical facility I once worked for three years ago, at 3:00 PM today. Income, for my depraved soul. Another set of people to monkey around with… *looking… hearing…* a whiff of pheromones here, a coy glance there. Perhaps I'll titillate a single mother five years my senior and garner ~~affection~~ pretentiousness—that stimulus we know—yes, *we…* of "interest."

"You're interesting," the women tell me. Oh? *Oh?…* Ho-ho! Oh now? I am? *Really?*

Why? My DNA? My intolerance? My ineptitude to provide or care for another human being?

That's *interesting.*

Ah, there I go, being edgy again, desperate for attention via this document. Except, I *don't* care to be cared for. My heart has molded to iron. Instances that I think, or rather *feel* that I do care on account of empathy, is a delusion: A transmogrification of self-pity, for I refuse to forsake my self-assigned meaning as much as I refuse to harbor pity for myself—so *begone!*—reader and validator alike, and scour my merit with scorn. Revel in my obscure pain, celebrate my failures, and rejoice once you cease from reading!

Oh, what's this now? A voice from the nether: *"He's truly not a scumbag; his actions demonstrate that much,"* mewls a disappointed egoic intrusion. Do I lie to you, reader? No, I assert that I don't, for I'd lie to myself, and as tempting as *it* is to befoul memories with falsities and silver linings, I refuse. However, I cannot state with conviction my perceptions or opinions of events, for the moment I speak my rendition of truth I'm deemed insane or impaired—fit for an institution; so what have I to depend on except my will to be silent and cooperate?

Yes, this book swells into a tome of thoughtlessness. I publish to castigate and condemn. I may as well be murdering my readers.

"I," "I," *"I!"* Disgusting—*however*, no pity; I'm content with my disgust. After all, I am what I claim to be: A privileged white man and an egotistical fool all along, grateful for my opportunity to squander and to mingle with those less intelligent than myself.[78] I may learn something if otherwise.

4:44 PM

What happened to the plot of the story? Had there *been* a plot?

I've consigned myself to the medical facility a thirty-minute walk away from my apartment. I sat in the front receptionist's office in the same cushioned chair I sat in two years ago and acknowledged the invariant artwork, bald eagle, parking lot, miens of others around me, and of course, the "**Iron Clad**" cement tower on the horizon.

On my walk home, three adolescent suburban boys rode bicycles on the sundered sidewalk. I veered into the adjacent grass and nodded at each on my passing. The boys gaped at me, each in turn, and on my passing,

---

[78] Concluding from the frequency of being deemed intelligent, I must necessarily be judged as more or of equal intelligence as the judger; otherwise, another adjective would suffice, unless I am deceived by flattery and fooled by what a judger thinks I want to hear—which is *not* "intelligent." Regardless, with the tribes I associate with, this matter is unremarkable.

one said to the others, "I bet that guy gets pussy all the time." The boy's companions both assumed a shocked expression, chuckled, and looked over their shoulders at me for a reaction: I blushed, grinned, responded with a sidelong glance, and experienced a twinge of validation on account of the falsity derived from my appearance: The opinions of youth who see the world from an unformed madness: twelve or thirteen-years-old, not quite corrupt or wholesome. Forty seconds afterward, a pensive stare overtook my visage. I reckoned an old woman seated on a chair beside her house, idle, in the shade cast by a neighbor's home. Overcome with my placement in the world, the 7.8 billion others—alive—of whom I will never know, and all those I will never know who have died, or have yet to be born. I walked down the street and felt like a *mature* man, assimilated with the mass construct around me: All of *it* human… all-too-human; we see nothing else but the objects around us or pretty pictorial scenes of unharnessed nature fit for a piece of literature, or a photo. Any inadequacy one experiences is entirely self-contained—at least in the moment I now described: There had been no culture, no community, no *care*. The sun shone on me and I returned to my apartment.

Visions of my soon-to-be-realized future life stifle me with fear. I know *it* already before *it* has begun by my design; therefore, what *do* I fear? My emotional reaction.

Sixty-hour weeks, second shift, from 2:30 PM to 11:00 PM: packaging medical supplies, printing labels, and counting in a long rectangular white room, donned with a hair net and safety goggles. After my shift, an hour walk to the gym for midnight strength training. Thereafter, a twenty-five-minute walk back to my apartment, where I will gorge myself, write, and read before bed no later than 5:00 AM. Wake at 1:00 PM.

8:39 PM

"Scumbag" is an overblown adjective to describe Jesus or me; "Sanctimonious" and "wretch" are valid. Jesus: An ordinary man who claimed to know best.

I shower every day, practice superb hygiene habits, maintain my apartment cleanliness, wash my clothes, shower towel, and bedding weekly, exercise daily, enact work for society, act in accordance with the law, yet I may be deemed as a scumbag for my thoughts.

My pain and suffering is negligible, though profound when examined.

Friday, October 23rd, 2020

1:45 PM

A man's thoughts are like a full diaper worn for six hours while hiking up a mountain on an eighty-eight degree Fahrenheit day.

What does this mean? "Overburdened" comes to mind; thus, I wrote *it,* and whether the diaper is filled with marshmallows or feculence, there is discomfort.

Gregarious and affable waiters and waitresses are intolerable. A server's pleasantness to a customer is indicative of how caustic the server will be with the kitchen staff when relaying a situation that went awry. These same servers will be the first to complain of anxiety and stress and seize any opportunity to express their garrulous disdain—typically to another server, or an idle cook that enjoys goading the spoken malice for the simple satisfaction of doing so.

4:26 PM

Peace and anarchy; serenity and destruction; what are these paltry maxims, unlived, unrealized?

I have one crystallized memory of my early grade school days. Either 1st or 2nd grade: I sat with my peers at a long rectangular table in a riotous cafeteria. For reasons that still confound me to this day, the principal, a 5'5, middle-aged, balding man with a robust physique would enter the cafeteria and invoke immediate fear-induced silence on the entire convergence of over two-hundred unruly children. In one of these instances, I persisted in gesticulating jokes to my terrified friends who stared at me with the countenance of an accomplice who addresses a convicted perpetrator of a crime on the moment of a judge's guilty verdict. The principal bee-lined for me, stood opposite of the table, behind and over the head of my cowering friend, gestured the index finger of his right hand to his closed lips, and vocalized a polite: *"Shh."*

I obeyed, without knowing why, and sat with a befuddled smile expressed on my face until the principal exited the cafeteria; thereby, the violent histrionics of my peers resumed, albeit, at a reduced magnitude.

Saturday, October 24th, 2020

2:59 AM

I've been bestowed the name "Terminator" and am greeted as a venerated pseudo-celebrity by the *The Messy House*'s commoners. The owner regards me as a profitable attraction by my interpretation of his silent addressal.

The post-gym interaction began with my inquiry of "Do you think that all virtue is pretentious?" to a drunk and stoned African-American man. Bystanders listened and jibed at me with personal questions. The African-American man professed his Christian virtues and asserted that humanity is born innocent; therefore, human goodness is innate. Several men urged me to venture into the bar for at least one beer, for my "rigid" mien and diction inspired feelings of discomfort. I implored for a continuation of the rhetoric between myself and the African-American man over the senseless babble of those who asked me for personal information; thereby, he agreed; however, every set of eyes looked at me in a half-circle and shouted for me to "Go on."

Recorder on and aware of my demagogic position, I rabble-roused a hasty polemical supposition of, "Ah—*all right*—so I have an audience now! I don't believe that humanity is born innocent-"

"*Okay*—why! Why?" shouted an attractive Caucasian woman around my age and ⅔ my height.

"-because 'innocence' is a context that we ascribe to ourselves, where there is no innocence involved—I don't think that the word 'innocent' should even be in our lexicon." The woman averted her gaze from mine amongst the crowd, muttered, "Okay..." chuckled, and proceeded to imitate the way I spoke "lexicon," drunk on two shots, as she was.

A French man to my right who accused me of being a Russian FBI agent smiled and impersonated the voice of Arnold Schwarzenegger: "Hey yo—hey yo, *I'll be back.*"

I swept my eyes over the crowd and said, "This is completely uninvolved from 'God' or sin, in any way, and any theology. *It*'s just the matter of—we are born here and we don't know why, so we seek truth, and the unknown terrifies us-"

"All right—all right-" interjected the African-American man; "What is the truth that you're seeking?"

I admitted, "I don't know," while the woman to my right simultaneously said, "Do you wanna seek a shot?"

The African-American man grinned and said, "So you don't know the truth that you're seeking?"

"Of course not."

"All right, so more of a reason for why you need to go in there, buy one drink, and enjoy *it*; we're all here just having a good time enjoying *it*."

"I don't want to drink alcohol."

"All right, you don't drink alcohol; just go in there and *dance*."

The woman moaned: "You look a little—then *why* are you at a bar then?"

I said, "I mean does *it* matter—why I'm here? We're all here now, right? Isn't that the truth of this matter?"

The rabble dispersed, unamused and unthoughtful. The African-American man accepted a phone call. Seventeen minutes had elapsed; enough, I decided, and began to walk away.

A young Caucasian man dressed in full green and brown camouflage garb yelled, "Yo—where you goin' bro?" which incited the woman to shout from the open back door of the bar: "Enjoy your night—please walk safe wherever you go—don't try to face a car with your logic cuz *it*'s gonna win, okay?"

I said, "Thank you for the advice."

"Have a good night okay! Be safe!"

I'm regretful, for the second half of my posit pertaining to the word "innocent" being removed from the English lexicon, *merely* because the word is useful in a system of societal law. Where "not guilty" would suffice, "innocent" is one word opposed to two. Succinctness is preferable for optimal communication. I propose "unguilty," or "nonguilty." "Innocence" in *any* regard is absurd to me, even in birth, for there is nothing innate in existence that is either good or evil. Crime and punishment, dependent on virtue, is contextual with culture. These strictly human ascriptions of what is right or wrong is paltry compared to the totality of the universe that regards our utmost-of-importance social construct with indifference, if there is any regard at all by that which we are an infinitesimally fractional part of. What exactly, are we innocent of? Sin, i.e., existence? Are we all to be guilty of existence? Yes, guilt and innocence apply *only* to a system of societal law.

I presume that the presupposed "karma" I acquired from this proclamation is neutral, for I'm the only one who will remember *it* the next morning (and for the remainder of my life). Humanity is born; there is nothing else.

Sunday, October 25th, 2020

2:14 AM

I'm unnerved by what I'm feeling. I've come from a superb gym session, to a brief stop at *The Messy House,* and encountered an uncommon mental schism: An off-duty cop[79] who I once consoled on account of his cheating girlfriend on the night of my second assault. The moment I entered *The Messy House, Do you Believe in Life After Love,* by Cher, blared from the establishment speakers. The cop beckoned me to follow him outside with a subtle "come-hither" gesture that I interpreted as a solicitous request. A gaggle of five rowdy young women lingered to my left, each of whom stared at me on my entry. I followed the off-duty cop outside, recorder on, and said:

"Cop" Conversation

"Hello."

"Hey. We talked before—remember I'm the cop that talked to ya?"

Lighthearted, I said, "Yes."

"Yeah, Joe (bartender) just said you're not allowed because of Desirea (off-the-clock bartender)." The cop scoffed, gazed through the backdoor window, and said, "I don't know—these fucking guys are assholes."

"I'm not allowed?"

"Yeah, that's what he said."

"Do you know why?"

"Cuz Desirea? I like your jacket though man."

I muttered, "Oh, thanks."

"Where the fuck'd you get that—that's fucking badass."

"Oh *it*'s just on [Retailer]."

"Really?"

---

[79] Mesomorph build with a tattooed right shoulder. Buzzed blonde hair with a small wave in front. Dressed in a white sleeveless shirt and pseudo-ripped skin-tight blue jeans. Round and masculine face. Ornate rings of bronze and silver on both hands. Hasty side-stepping talker.

"Yeah."

The cop sucked on a cigarette and said, "Is *it* expensive?"

"*It* was... eighty-nine dollars, but-"

"Are you on coke right now?"

"No."

Cher resonated through the backdoor and a drunken man inside shouted along with the lyrics. The cop whispered, "Your eyes are *this* fucking big man. I just knocked someone out at front and the cops pulled up and asked all those girls: 'Hey are there people fighting out here?' Some guy fucking walked up to me he's like—cuz I'm out front I'm just smokin'—I'm fuckin' hangin' out; he goes 'You play this fuckin' nigger music,' and he shoves me. I'm like, *whack*... Fuckin' knocked his tooth out and he went runnin' around the corner."

"... Did Desirea state *why*, I'm banned?"

"I don't know... She didn't say why... Because you're like me—you're just blunt." The cop expelled a drag of cigarette smoke.

I said, "So why aren't you banned then?"

"I don't know—cuz I have a *girl*... I know—you just wanna have a drink—I know—I getcha."

"No... no... I'm not here to drink."

"Just hang out?"

"Yeah... I enjoy philosophical conversations."

"So do I. People don't get me either; they think I'm autistic or somethin'. I am a little bit."

Enthused, I said, "I've been called the same, but I think-"

"They say to me—they're like—'Are you autistic?'—I'm like... 'Maybe.' I'm dyslexic—I can write completely backwards, everything. I see everything backwards."

"Huh..."

"Like your left side is your right side right now."

"You've been accused of being autistic?"

"I am au—not, well yeah—autistic yeah... Autistic or Aspergers. Just cuz the way I'm—I'm blunt with people—I just talk; I have no filter."

"You don't have a concern for-"

"Like I'll walk up to like... to like a woman—I'm like 'Hey... What're you doin' tonight? Wanna get outta here?' Like I'm just blunt—I don't play games."

I scowled and said, "That's what got me *banned*, was one night-"

"But—but—I don't do *it* cuz I'm with somebody."

"I was out here one night-"

The cop spoke mid-drag, "I know I remember that—fuckin'-"

"-a month ago."

"I was here—did—did, did someone hit you? Cuz I left early."

"I was punched four times-"

"By Bulldog."

"Yes, and that's-"

"I wish I didn't leave cuz I would've han-"

Indignant, I said, "But *he's* not banned is he?"

"No—he's an asshole. He's an asshole. People don't get people like us."

"... What do you mean 'like us'?"

The cop sucked on the cigarette, expelled, and said, "Intelligent. Calculated. You think about every moment before you do anything." I frowned. The cop continued: "Like, people ask me 'Hey...' Like, I don't know."

"Are you still on the force?"

"Mhm."

"Just, off the clock?"

"Yeah. I took the night off. I gotta work tomorrow at three—I was supposed to be on a double but I took the night off, and when I got off there was a fucking response—I had to respond to *it,* and, luckily *it* was a—a false response—a guy pulled his pin on his radio by accident."

"So, did you get back with your girl, then? Is that the same one that you were separated from?"

All My Friends Say, by Luke Bryan, emanated through the doorway and incited the bar girls to holler. The cop said, "We were just fighting that night. Cuz I thought I caught her cheating on me... which, she could've been; I caught her before... but, I ended up in MHU (Mental Health Unit) for a week cuz I found my best friend dead."

5:43 AM

"The purpose of thought is to end all thought," said Jack two years ago, the proprietor of *The Peaceorama,* an intentional community.

"A settled mind is a dead mind," said Seth, my trainer at a medical facility two years ago.

Am I mad, to desire a cessation of existence, nullified from the potential of a cyclic cosmic rebirth? What would I be then, but a thought manifested in the consciousness of another entity, which inspires the inquiry of: "What is the source of consciousness, i.e., the universe?"

"Why do I lay awake and delude myself?" is the finer query.

2:20 PM

["Cop" Conversation continued]:

The cop puffed cigarette smoke between each sentence: "He wasn't answerin'—he was sending me messages like, like 'Live each day to *its* fullest'; 'Love your girl—let her know that she means everything to you'— he was dyin' of cancer. And I'm like 'Dude, answer your phone or I'm gonna kick your door in. And he wasn't answerin' so I kicked his door in... He's, dead on his floor. Fuckin' eyes all dried out—white—wide open—mouth hangin' open."

I said, "From—from what?"

"He took a bunch of pills, and drank a bottle of vodka. He took probably like sixty or seventy Vicodin and just swallowed... a ton of vodka and killed himself. He was in pain—he was dying of cancer—but... I just wish I had more time with him—but—I ended up in the hospital for three days and they wouldn't let me leave. They didn't—they didn't even let me see a *shrink* for fucking three days. I'm like, 'I need'—I'm like, 'I blacked out drunk'; I'm like—'I'm fine now.' I'm like, 'can I *please, leave?'* They're like '*Oh*—you gotta see the psychiatrist before you leave.' I'm like—'Then let me fucking see him'—cuz I'm like—'next time'—cuz they have a security door—they punch a code in; I go 'Next time that fucking door opens I'm gonna fuckin' book *it* out that fuckin' door and just run down the street'— cuz they give you a gown. They're like '*Oh*—they'll arrest you and bring you back.' I don't fucking care!" Three girls inside *The Messy House* mewled and laughed. "I'm like 'I need to get outta here—I don't need to be here; I'm sane; I blacked out drunk.'"

I nodded and grunted.

The cop said, "... So that's why I just drink beer now. But... I only smoke when I drink and I feel like a scumbag; I'm not even a smoker."

Piqued on hearing an officer of the law self-depreciate himself with the adjective, "scumbag," I said, "You feel like a scumbag because of your own standard of virtue that you hold yourself accountable for?"

The cop gazed upward at an occluded night sky and said, "... No *it*'s… cuz I'm smokin'… fuckin'… I shouldn't be… I started working out again—I feel like a million bucks—but then…"

Two women joined the bar girls in their histrionic ululations. A deep, husky, male voice shouted *"Yeah—yeah!"* in encouragement.

I said, "That's… where I just came from."

"I don't know; I feel like I come out—I feel like I came out just to babysit my girlfriend. Cuz I know when she's out—like that guy she's next to right now—AJ—he's a fucking scumbag and he always hits on her. And everyone has told me 'Watch him around her,' cuz he's *married* yet he goes out and picks up all these girls. Like—I already knocked the guy out front, *out,* completely fucking cold tonight."

"About a half-an-hour to an hour ago?"

"Yeah. You see the cops pull up?—like—'Is there anyone fighting out here?'"

I gestured a thumb over my left shoulder and said, "Oh—is that what that cop was for back there?" regarding the police vehicle I passed on my way over.

The cop said, "Yeah, and I—I fucking put my shirt back on and I run out the back door, and Joe went out front—the bartender, and he handled *it*—he's like 'No—no one's been fighting.' His tooth is outside on the ground somewhere." I chuckled. "He got in my—like—he *shoved* me; I'm like 'Don't put your hands on me'—I'm like, 'That—that, that's a misdemeanor,' like, you put your hands on someone—I defend myself; otherwise, someone can get in my face—they can fuckin' *scream* in my face—I won't put my hands on 'em. *Once* they put their hands on me, or threaten me with physical harm… The key, the key, the key to gettin' away—even with murder, you yell: 'I'm in fear of my life.' If you say 'I'm in fear of my life,' that means you're afraid. You can literally fuckin'… Like even if the cops have you at gunpoint, and you have a gun in your hand, and you say: 'I'm in fear of my life; I'm not puttin' my gun down; I'm in fear of my life'… You're justified, cuz you're afraid of your—you're afraid of those cops shootin' ya. That's the only way to get away with *it*. So I told him 'Don't fuckin' shove me I'm in fear of my life; get the fuck away from me.' He goes, 'Quit playin' that fuckin nigger music-' I'm like—'You're not even fuckin' hangin' out in here; stop using that word.' I'm like, 'That's not a nice word,' and he fuckin' *shoved* me, so I went, *Pop!* Fuckin'… cut my hand open a little bit, but, I don't know… They just told me not to let you in—I don't know… I don't know." The cop moved towards the door. "But, I'm gonna go back inside cuz I'm freezin' but, I'm Jim-"

As a final ploy, I said, "Can I buy you a drink?"

"*No*—I'm good—I'm Jim."

Disappointed, I said, "All right, Jim."

"I like your coat."

"Thanks."

"I gotta look that up—what's *it* called?"

"Uhh…"

"Peacoat—[Retailer Name]?"

"Uhhhh," I scratched the back of my head and said, "I think the name of *it* is *Military, uh… something, jacket.*"

"Wool right?"

"Yeah—I—I just searched up 'black jacket' on [Retailer Name]-"

"Oh *it*'s really nice."

"-and that's what came up."

A woman approached the door window and gazed through for a third instance since Jim and I began talking. Jim acknowledged her, scowled, and muttered, "Go fuck yourself," when she turned away. "Fuckin' old lady."

I said, "I'd like to ask you a question before you go in."

"What's that? Yeah go ahead." Jim stood a foot higher than me on the stoop beneath the bar door, stared straight forward across the parking lot, and said, "I'm always up for conversation."

"Why do you consider us to be intelligent, in what way?"

"Cuz we can talk with like, philosophical fucking language and no one knows what we're talkin' about. You know what I mean?"

I said, "Don't you think that's just a product of reading?"

"Yeah."

"And vocabulary."

Jim said, "P-p-people don't get me when I talk to 'em—they're like 'What're you talkin' about?' And I'm like… just, like I'll recite a fuckin' poem and they'll fuckin' be like, 'I don't get what that means,' ya know? They just…"

"When you first stood, and you beckoned me out, I thought you were going to ask me out, and I was intrigued because I forgot who you were. But then you came out and specified that you're a police officer, and *it* all leveled out."

"Yeah—because they asked you to leave, so I—I—I had to uh, ya know—they asked you to leave, cuz I didn't want to see you get hurt—but that's when I left cuz I'm like 'I gotta go home cuz I'm fighting—I shouldn't be out drinking and driving so I went home. But I didn't know you got beat up—I'm sorry about that; if I was here I wouldn't have let *it* happen, cuz there's no call for violence ever; people can talk, there's no call for violence."

"Well you-"

"That's what I say to people. Talk like a *grown adult*."

"I think that you were here-"

"You don't have to threaten someone's life, ya know what I mean?"

"-you were just inside."

Jim said, "Ya know—I hate that. Even when I'm dealing with people like, if I have to arrest 'em or something *it's* like… I talk to 'em like, 'Are you okay?' like… There's no fucking smart conversation anywhere around here and I hate *it*. No one's fucking educated. *Nobody*."

"Yet you're eager to go back in there?"

"Yeah I want to go sit down… finish my drink."

"I can't even hear myself think in there."

"No—I know. I wanna listen to some *Pink Floyd* or somethin'. Or—I like Johnny Cash too—*Hurt*—I love that song; *it*'s one of my favorite songs."

"My upstairs neighbor listens to classic rock."

"I like classic rock—I like Beethoven too… Bach."

I said, "Yes—that's… the composers I listen to."

"Like Bach is fuckin'—oh my god."

"And Hay—yes, J.S. Bach… his cantatas, definitely, and the opening to *Mass in B Minor; Johanne's Passion*."

Jim beamed and said, "Oh my *Gawwwd!* Don't even start with me!" We laughed. "Yeah, but, I'm gonna go back in, cuz I gotta… babysit, but-"

"All right."

"You have a great night. Stay safe."

"Yes."

Jim outstretched his hand for a shake; I accepted with a gloved hand, and on pulling away, Jim grabbed my hand again for a follow-up skewed-elbow-comradery handshake and said, "You're loved."

I retorted, "I don't know about that."

"No—you are… Just, just these people: Fuck 'em. They don't understand people like us. My girlfriend can have smart conversation when she's not drinkin'—but… I need to watch her cuz she's a little… a little lush around, ya know, she gets drinking too much—that's why that guy in there—I don't fucking like." Jim stepped one foot into the bar, sniggered, and said, "I might have to beat his ass tonight; I don't *like* to, but… You have a great night, okay?"

I turned to walk away and said, "Take care."

Faced half-away from me in the bar's open back doorway, Jim said, "Next time I see ya we'll go out and have a drink somewhere else, okay?"

I cringed, waved a hand, and said, "Ah—no, that's all right. Ah-"

"Well *it* doesn't even have to be a *drink*—*it* can be a soda; I don't even drink soda."

"I don't drink soda either."

Jim said, "I hate soda. *Blarg.*" I laughed, for the absurd deviation from farewells to conversing on drinks twenty-feet away from each other amused me. Jim followed up with: "I like water."

"You seem like you're a fish out of water right now."

"I like *MiO*, the stuff you add to the water—like flavor packets sometimes."

"I've never had *MiO*."

"*It*'s not bad; *it*'s got a little bit of caffeine… I like black coffee. People think I'm gross because I drink black coffee, but I'm like, *it*'s stronger and…"

"I drink my coffee black too."

"*It*'s—*it*'s, I don't know; *it* kicks in quicker; *it* makes you feel good about yourself-"

"Yes," I agreed thoughtlessly.

"-You have a great night."

"Thanks, you too."

"What's your name again?"

"My name is Baethan."

"Baethan?"

"And, you said your name is?"

"Jimmy [Last Name]. *It*'s not my *real* last name; my real last name is [Name]—*it*'s Scottish, but I go by [Last Name] because of my job. So if you look me up on *Facebook it*'s [Name]; you can friend request me."

"I don't have a *Facebook*."

"Yeah—I try not to, but… if you ever do. You have a good night, okay?"

"Take care."

"Stay safe."

"Thanks."

And *what good would it do me* to be prosocial, to forsake my self-assigned barrenness of the psyche for the sake of a wee bit of validation; I imagine *it* now: A discussion of shared interests, philosophical nothings, panderings…

"*What good does it do ya?*" I envision the old bearded man at the gym— the man who I fear I will become. This frail old man acknowledges me with absolute submission yet I see only myself in him, for our shared pusillanimity; whatever his reasons may be… perhaps age, a sense of inferiority with the state of world affairs, a feeling of inadequacy… I may only speculate; however, we share a similar *spirit,* or *soul,* to be absurd in that regard, despite my virility and tenacious will by which I grow stronger each day on my regimen and persist with this infernal written expulsion— to hell with *it*—and *sleep,* for sleep is the singular noble act one may partake in of this life: to dream, to be and not be, as *it* is, and forgo consumption 'til the morrow.

4:07 PM

I don't know what I am anymore. The cop feels like a scumbag for smoking cigarettes but *not* for knocking out a man's tooth, *not* for being hypocritical on his opinions of violence, *not* for his domineering attitude about his girlfriend's sexual habits, and *not* for a myriad of other factors that an alternate reader may perceive.

What did I delight so much about that conversation—a shared interest in music and coffee preference? These two chance factors don't amount to anything. I waste time and energy in recording, listening, transcribing, reading, *rereading,* editing, *re-rereading,* of that worthless **"Cop" Conversation**—yet, *it* is *critical.* I realize from *it,* that even in the most minor interpersonal dealings, I am *desperate* for companionship; my nature is inexorable *against* my will. This feeling of *lack* of feeling—devoid of indifference or apathy—there is only an artful metaphor: A cold tundra.

These voice transcriptions aren't art, nor are they literature. What have I become? I'm appalled by how this documentation swells, for *it* is a testament to my lack of living.

6:17 PM

I terminated plans to meet with the woman for mutual psychoanalysis/ copulation and resume reading Arthur Schopenhauer's *The World as Will and Representation* concurrently with Robert Sapolsky's *Behave.* Fernando Pesso's *The Book of Disquiet* is a superb sleep actuator.

Affiliation with bar tribes is voided by my resolute will. I purge myself of acquired behaviors in preparation for pending employment.

Monday, October 26th, 2020

2:16 AM

A recorded metanonfictional monologue:

The *Blue Danube, Op. 314,* by Johann Strauss plays in my right ear while I walk home from the gym at 1:34 AM. I have determined, that *guilt* and *shame,* are the conduits for "God," i.e., consciousness: The "voices in our heads," are a manifestation of the guilt and shame that we've been taught throughout our lives. I experienced this belated epiphany on the stair-stepper.

So, what does this mean? *It* means everything that I've written for the past four years of my life, simplified, to this simple sentence: Guilt and shame are the conduits for "God." I repeat, for this is the quintessential expression of modern—well, not even modern... *Human,* psychosis, since the origin... let's be precise here... I won't say theology... *Language...* Language, yes... No, that's not right. Perhaps I'll make this a stream of consciousness, verbatim. Keep in mind the song that plays to enhance the comical effect of this entire charade: Guilt and shame are the conduits for "God," whatever manifestation *it* takes in your mind; therefore, spirituality in all *it*s religious conceptions are a sham. Buddhism. Taoism. Christianity. Zoroastrianism. Paganism. *Love*—well no, not paganism. But *love,* spirituality endorses and preaches peace and *inaction* for your will. And what becomes of your will? *It rots,* within a vessel, unattended; is this the spirituality that you pursue, the asceticism of a saint?

Yes, spirituality is a sham; all conceptions are designed to nullify your will, to *promote* inaction, to quell a populace. *So,* ingest your pills, visit your psychiatrist, talk to your preacher, your sermon, your priest; visit your guru: receive their wisdom. Digest your daily dissemination and obey.

Theoretical anarchy is unbecoming. My actions up to this point have produced a character encapsulated in my final iteration of a title:

Outbursts of a Sanctimonious Heathen; Thoughts of a Pusillanimous Clown.

What shall I do, henceforth? Work, write, consume, as per the status quo. My passions tug me in opposite directions. I may *speak* to my neighbors of their guilt and shame—their *conscience,* as a heretical rhetorician, though what "good" would I sow? Better to refrain from speaking and die in obscurity with my iniquitous will contained in this documentation.

A conundrum. Best not to plan, or even think of *it,* I think.

I've betrayed my integrity on countless occasions; therefore, I rebel against myself. What a weensy man I am, to subvert my will, always, unceasingly, or am I humble, *virtuous?* Averse to imprisonment or the maiming of my body? A base creature. A bag of meat.

"What good does *it* do ya? Where's the progress? What difference does *it* make? Yippy Skippy."

- Virtuous Old Man at the Gym

4:49 PM

Ad hominem arguments are crucial in moral and ethical philosophy. "Virtue is pretentious," said a sanctimonious heathen.
Ba-dum-tss!

"Knowledge of God is the mind's greatest good; *it*s greatest virtue is to know God."

- Baruch Spinoza

"I know that I know nothing."

- Socrates

"Society demands that he limit himself to his function... There are indeed many precautions to imprison a man in what he is as if we lived

in perpetual fear that he might escape from *it*, that he might break away and suddenly elude his condition."

The human *condition*, of which we know *nothing*, in truth, other than the manifestation of "God" in our consciences, determined by established cultural, government, or individual *virtues*, is a malleable pretension applied through action by force of will.

I.e., "The human condition is pretentious," said a sanctimonious heathen, again.

"What's affected or showy about the innate nature of the human condition: Suffering?" retorted a paragon of virtue.

The sanctimonious heathen said, "Our love for one another is a pretentious extension of love for ourselves. The conscience, which manifests depending on the reason by which we apply our intellectual faculties to best serve ourselves, is *often*—not *always*, the result of what best serves the society of which we are a part. The cause of the conscience *not always* manifesting as a pretension of virtue results from isolation, which produces entities wholly self-reliant. Entities of this nature are free to will their standard of virtue into existence, which manifests an original 'God,' i.e., the self, or ego."

The paragon of virtue said, "You endorse the worst of humanity."

"Is humanity, in all *it*s manifestations, *not* the highest realization of 'God'?"

"You deviate from the original point, which I refute by stating that what is 'good' for the survival of humanity is 'good' for the survival of the individual, and vice versa."

The sanctimonious heathen bowed his head in acquiescence and returned to an apartment in the middle of an American city in upstate New York and proceeded to be a scumbag with his thoughts:

What "good" comes from the survival of humanity. What "evil?" The knowing of "God" is to know that I exist. My dependency on other humans is a volition of my will. I defy life with sexual abstention and redirect my will inward to create an aesthetic *thing*. This material *thing* is "God."

The paragon of virtue knocked on the sanctimonious heathen's apartment door and shouted, "I'm sorry—did you say something? Your voice is muffled. I didn't hear you and I'd enjoy a continuation of our rhetoric. I believe I have the upper-hand and I'm eager to validate my interpretation of "God," thereby invalidating yours."

"*You win. Go away,*" said a pusillanimous clown.

"What? Is this the same person?—the sanctimonious ~~wretch~~ heathen I was debating with before?"

No answer. God was "good."

"...and a deep and weary disdain for all those who work for mankind, for all those who fight for their country and give their lives so that civilization may continue...

"...a disdain full of disgust for those who don't realize that the only reality is each man's soul, and that everything else—the exterior world and other people—is but an unaesthetic nightmare, like the result, in dreams, of a mental indigestion."

- Fernando Pessoa's The Book of Disquiet

7:32 PM

An offensive man of unidentifiable age, race, and origin on account of being garbed in a full-body skin-tight pink jumpsuit and a blank white mask with two dark holes to allow sight, walked towards the center of a busy Central American city square and sat, cross-legged, on a swirlesque mosaic of grey and black stone.

A thirty-three-year-old Hispanic mother of four cast a sidelong gaze in the offensive man's direction and said to her company of thirteen friends, "I don't like the look of him; he reminds me of something I didn't like before, though I can't quite place *it.*"

One of the thirteen friends: a forty-seven-year-old male Porteriquan footwear store owner, said, "Just ignore him."

9:11 PM

My lifelong meaning of inscrutable individuation and objectification consequently renders strife onto all who I associate with. My documentation is a condemnation to existence, of being human, and of the incapacity to understand. I'm ignorant of "God," for I cannot prove that "God," in any manifestation, exists; akin to any manifestation of self that I ascribe to myself by use of derogatory adjectives which serve to denote my inconsequential character-of-the-year as perceived by a general populace.

(Post-)Postmodernist (metanonfictional) diatribes are the trite of which my will is constituted.

The *Upanishads* are a dim beacon among my blind gloom; Schopenhauer had been influenced by the ancient text.

Strife is essential. To delve into myself, or at least, the illusion of what I perceive myself to be and the subsequent portrayal of the world I perceive, recorded to this documentation, is divine.

"He has Aspergers." I reckon an intrusive thought evoked from the presupposed (universal) consciousness of this socially-oriented reality I'm inclined to care about—and think *nothing* of *it* but to record the thought: A product of gross self-consciousness, which may elicit an awareness of pity tinged with disgust on behalf of a reader who is not myself; however, the reader *may* feel these emotions, and I may only be aware of these potential emotions, due to our unity defined by empathetic suffering, even though I do not pity or disgust myself in this present moment. Confusion may be paramount.

"A dork," voices a redundant female lambaster; what is this source of shame? Perhaps if I were forty years older, I'd be merely, *"An old man."*

10:06 PM

Art is essential to transcend egoism.

Tuesday, October 27th, 2020

2:41 AM

The *Upanishads, The Bible, The Bhagavad-Gita,* the *Dao/Tao,* etc.— ancient spiritual texts served as government propaganda. Modern spiritual texts are reiterations of the same theories pertaining to the relinquishment of the will. My reason for this polemical statement is the same reason for my belief in "God": There is no proof of origin. What does any man know—I don't care who, or the profundity of what any man writes; a thought, or series of thoughts, which attempt to elucidate the nature of reality, *all* meet at a centrifuge of common consensus due to the constriction of human sensory faculties, differentiated *only* by the morality of a culture, i.e., *virtue*. Everything I write has been a process of synthesizing information from others, amalgamating and refining what complies with logic *devoid* of mathematics, followed by a few trite lines of uneducated refutation; however, I'm *still* inclined to believe my own interpretation of the world for what *I* perceive each day, unfailing and unrelenting: The Holy Trinity![80]

"I'll write a thesis," said a man who studied, applied himself for the betterment of his well-being, and secured time to elaborate his distilled thoughts—a man which I *am not*. Instead, I write funny transcriptions and on the incompetence of my actions resulting from (im)practical application of my philosophy leading to the current position of my insolvent and alienated circumstances.

Ah... but art... Yes, this is *my* self-assigned *aesthetic* of life.

3:57 AM

I submit to a dead man's sorrow and shed three tears while reading *The Book of Disquiet*. Pain is abundant.

"And then I feel an overwhelming, absurd desire for a kind of Satanism before Satan, a desire that one day—a day without time or substance—an escape leading outside of God will be discovered, and our deepest selves will somehow cease participating in being and non-being."

- Fernando Pessoa's The Book of Disquiet

3:46 PM

Sustained, authentic spirituality is the fount of privilege, inasmuch as the individual is provided for by another entity, from ascetics in a monastery, to a prisoner locked in solitary confinement.

Unsustained, pseudo-spirituality is the fount of indolence and subsequent acquiescence, for one must exert their will to live.

To maintain a populace on the fringe of virtuous ego abolishment while also demanding productivity delimits the potential of rebellion.

Yes... Aren't we all *privileged* to be alive? And for those who disagree,

---

[80] Consumption, defecation, and procreation.

who scorn their lot in life, I advise you to adopt spiritual practices to the utmost.

The Dalai Lama is machiavellian.

"Share your knowledge. *It* is a way to achieve immortality."

- Dalai Lama XIV

9:06 PM

I've discovered Christopher Langen (purported to be the smartest man in America) and his *Reality Self-Simulation Principle*.

I'm ashamed of what I am, not who I am.

Wednesday, October 28th, 2020

4:03 AM

I sat between the "cop," Jim, and his companion (a regular), at the *Messy House*,[81] the fool that I am.

Why?—I'll tell you—fool, remember this, for this is a critical turning point in your perceptions of man and your trust in the legal system—in justice, and the mootness of *it* all:

I disclosed to Jim and his companion, on their curiosity, that I utilize a recorder in the front left pocket of my jacket. This became a topic of contention for Jim's companion, who I turned to, to my right, in order to diffuse a potential instance of violence, for the man had been perturbed by my active surveillance. Unbeknownst to me, the purported *"cop,"* Jim, *pickpocketed* my recorder while I had been engrossed in conversation, removed the SD card along with both of the batteries, and *reinserted* the recorder back into my pocket. Only when I returned to my apartment with the intent to lay on the floor and listen to the encounter did I surmise this singularly plausible conclusion.

Three months of audio recordings, that of which only *I* will ever care for—*stolen!*—in a manner which I fancied only occurred in 19th-century noir! Genius! The dexterity of the man; I hope he *learns* something from my efforts, the rogue, villain, *mongrel*. Yes, he'll learn that guilt and shame

---

[81] Jim convinced the female bartender to allow me inside the establishment.

are conduits for "God," and I can only hope that *my* voice supersedes his conscience with hateful condemnations.

I visited the police department a block away from my apartment the moment I concluded my abject carelessness pertaining to this event, and of course, nothing may be done, which is my just desert. Regardless, I intend to return to *The Messy House* with hopes to encounter the superb knave(s) again, whereby I *will* play the fool that comes so naturally to me.

4:51 AM

Unbelievable. Those recordings are worthless to me: Mere sentimental tripe in the original conception before being transcribed and supplemented with commentary, yet I am *indignant!* Bastards... to steal my personal data, impressed by their own deftness—just as *I* am *impressed!* Folly. Nonsense. I hope they gloat.

3:32 PM

Why am I surprised? There's no need for *it.* I've become accustomed to accusations against my sobriety while enduring the pain of drunks by my own volition. I listened to the purported "cop," Jim, and *relistened* to his pain, transcribed, and immortalized *it.* Betrayed by a man who I dared to consider the theoretical potentials of friendship, just as I have betrayed family and former friends, by abandonment and disappointment. I suffer nothing.

4:39 PM

In my efforts to discover if Jim is an authentic officer of the law via social network sleuthing, I failed to determine anything on account of a fake name he provided me; however, on my local police department's primary news feed, I read of a burglary, and recognized from screenshots extracted from an unnamed establishment's blurry security camera footage to be the the tavern where I had once been employed by Walther.

I minced garlic. Tears welled in my eyes while my omelet cooked on low heat. Mahler's *Symphony No. 5 in C-Sharp Minor - IV Adagietto* resonated at a loud volume from my speaker set, returned to me on my furloughment due to long-term company closure. The piece of music is an expression of distilled sadness, devoid of pathetic, religious, or romantic qualities. I thought of Walther, the intricacies of personal morality involved, the miscommunications of mankind; I thought of atrocities: genocide, environmental destruction, poaching... and I thought of my one-inch SD card: a miniature conduit for my egoism, pickpocketed. I thought of the barrenness of my feelings, of the perceived injustice against me which swelled to an external encompassment of humanity as a whole, unrelated to me—a fractal, within globes of our own realities. I wiped my nose with paper towels, blotted tears from my cheeks, and thought of Walther again, his business, and of the woman who birthed his child. The final crescendo of the music reverberated and castigated existence—*sadness,* without woe, without pity... without expectations.

10:15 PM

Everything is surreal and incomprehensible to me. I admit my ignorance and incompetence. A piece of furled notebook paper on my marble countertop, illuminated by six round positional ceiling lights, is clenched by my two thumbs and two index fingers, held with awe, regarded with suspicion and reverence. There, standing on my carpet, paper in hand, I stared down, and wondered on the infinitesimal ways in which we describe the singularly simple: reality, i.e., what *it* is. From algebraic formulations defining the ontological parameters of human perception, to books—hundreds upon hundreds of pages long, written by many now dead, forgotten by the majority, and reiterated with new iterations by the few living... I'm astounded; there is no other emotion. Days pass in the same manner. Entropy elicits aging of my body *and* will. I write yearly tomes to be forgotten: An old stack of kitsch magazines tucked in the corner of a dirty clothes trunk in a derelict basement. Not even this. I am data; I am reality. I don't know why or how I am.

10:56 PM

For my daily entertainment, I watch videos for no longer than forty minutes of barbaric violence and sexual deviancy disseminated worldwide. Suicides, riots, executions, torture, and rape, are in no lack. Afterward, a listen of a single musical performance offsets and compliments my purposeful subjection to the most depraved states of the human form: a seriocomical tone, grotesque and beautiful. Leg work at the gym tonight, followed by an inane visit to *The Messy House.*

Thursday, October 29th, 2020

3:34 AM

I walked into *The Messy House* at 1:12 AM and encountered the female bartender, Deserae, alone. Her amicable greeting contradicted her previous banishments. The woman is estimated to be in her mid-thirties, with a pleasant oval face, chest-length auburn hair, medium bust, plump, poised, and polite. We talked for an hour and twenty-five minutes. She is the sister of the "cop" I sat with, which raises my suspicion that the man who had sat to my right the previous night is the true perpetrator of the pickpocket. I've arranged to pay fifty dollars to secure video footage of the previous night at the time when I had been pickpocketed. Deserae, married for twelve years, with two children, amused me with her articulate liberal humanist perspective on cognition and consciousness. She wrote *"Dr. Hoffsteader[82] on physics - Theory of Relativity"* on a piece of paper and handed *it* to me. Likewise, I wrote Robert Sapolsky's book *"Behave: The Biology of Humans at Our Best and Worst,"* on a piece of paper and handed *it* to *her.*

Most important, by my judgment, is Deserae's answer to my parting question to her: "Do you think that all virtue is pretentious?"

Deserae pursed her lips for three seconds and said, "Seldomly, yes. You know that saying 'To each their own'? *It's* like that."

When first spoken, I had been receptive and rejoiced in my ignorance. On departure from *The Messy House,* I thought to negate my philosophy and worldview—to abolish my ego and begin reformed, with love and benevolence at the forefront of my conscious being, *and then* I thought of the phrase again, "To each their own," which translates to: "People are free to do and think as they desire." Yet, Deserae had said *"Seldomly"*… I counter with a convenient precept:

"Optimism is cowardice."

– *Oswald Spengler*

---

[82] Correction: Robert Hoftstadter

"If you're going to throw out blame and punishment, you gotta throw out praise and reward as well."

- Robert Sapolsky

Sapolsky is an advocate of determinism and dismisses free will on account of our molecular biology. If the postulate of the "will-to-live," with the will being inseparable (dualistic) from reality as we know *it*, is true, then the totality of existence is governed by an immutable law; therefore, chaos is a null conception.

But *wait*, Sapolsky claims that the will of *biological* entities is predetermined; there is no mention of the physical laws of our reality pertaining to chaos and order. A quandary, then, for the bodies of all biological creatures *are* a part of the physical reality we call existence.

If what Sapolsky posits is true, then the idea of "chance" is one-in-the-same, i.e., irremovable, from what has already been determined by... *Yes*, determined by the "thing-in-*it*self," as *it* is often named: the ineffable, the inconceivable, the inexplicable.

There is no original thought. To be human is all that we know, and what "*it* is" to be human is defined by morality. Instead of looking outward to discover what we are, we should gaze inward-

Ah, but did I *not just* decry all spirituality as being a sham?

Oh, but reality is a simulation within a simulation (within a simulation [within a simulation]) ad infinitum, that has been drawn up in countless renditions of media, from shadow puppetry to a thesis paper. If I live in a predetermined simulacrum, fated to die and reincarnate, concerned *only* with the selfish desire to fulfill my (predetermined?) self-assigned meaning in life, why do I *care so much?* I genuinely—with the full exertion of my will, desire to *know* the answer: Why do I care? I am willed to care by a will governed by a will governed by a will, etc. Everything is *boring*, yet education is the only recourse. What am I *doing?* What have I *learned?* "Have fun"; "Enjoy life" they tell me: someone who thinks that I want to do *just* that. I'm predetermined to be in awe of my willful predetermination to be *sad*.

"Awww," said a potential mate. Seated on a chair in a doctor's waiting room office, the potential mate uncrossed her legs and allowed me to gaze up her skirt: No panties. A bushy network of black hair negated every thought I ever conceived.

Certainly: I must be sexually frustrated; thus, I write. November ~~will~~ is predetermined to be a ~~fiction~~ metanonfictional month.

6:24 PM

I'm predetermined to be offended that Pelagia judged me as a "perfect specimen," i.e., a potential inseminator of her idealistic fatherless and female child.

Friday, October 30th, 2020

3:20 AM

"There's no good men in the world," said a bad woman.

Nobody heard her, just as nobody will ever hear me. I've decided to never market this documentation; *it* must be my own in order to be true. Profit would taint my mind and permit me to become indolent and profligate. Though this is my ideal, *it* is not what I need from myself.

What is a "good" man or a "bad" woman except for two adjectives representing expectations?

4:34 PM

I've thought of a name for a thesis I'll never write:
An Admission of a Desire for Ignorance.

I'll never write *it* because the desire has already been satisfied. The general ideas of philosophers, at least the ones who garner any *respectable* attention, are those who write clearly (excluding Hagel), and explain what can be apprehended by any individual with a smidgen of acumen applied to anything other than survival and entertainment. One would derive more knowledge of philosophy with a few years spent in solitary confinement as opposed to reading any work of the so-called *greats*.

Why I choose to read, and proceed to be ostentatious in my self-exposition in regards to what I'm reading, while also flouting a vigorous study in favor of a superficial understanding of a myriad of doctrines, is stupid. How am I smarter or enlightened for reading? What comprehension have I gained except a secondary account of another, even if recounted to the absolute authentic truth of the other's capability to express themselves (due to gratuitous reading)? Why do I read if I have nothing worthwhile to express other than my simple postulate of: "All virtue is pretentious." Is this *not* enough? I determined this in my early youth, and despite the onslaught of age, I haven't altered my perspective. A perpetual child I may be, fond of ignorance, strife, and *desire*. Perhaps *I'm* the enlightened one, by my own verdict. Though *who* will judge me?—for in my current culture *it* is imprudent to *judge*. Oh—no! Riots break out across my country over a perceived racial injustice, though who will judge the rioters?

Glory to the human race, for the sanctimoniousness of every individual, in liberty of our democratic freedom, where everyone has an opinion that amounts to nothing, lost in the din of the cacophonous keyboards of self-indulgence. The soft clacks of my keyboard are contributing to this noise. *Noise.* My upstairs neighbor listening to *I'm Here Without You Baby* by Three Doors Down. The conversation of a beautiful couple on their way to an early dinner in the alleyway below my window. The slamming of a door in my apartment complex hallway followed by the feverous stride of bootsteps down a hall. The anxious barking of a small dog left alone. The sizzling of beef in my kitchen pan.

Humanity has no recourse but to exalt virtue due to ~~fear~~ the innate instinct of progress and fecundity. Virtue is natural, aligned with reason and "God." Only a savage would cannibalize their newborn child; to do so is against nature and reason; therefore, against "God."

Yet, nature allows one to cannibalize their newborn child.

That doesn't make *it* "right."

By whose standard—"God"?

Or by us mortals who cling to life and perpetual self-actualization until death, with the singular motive to become immortal, unified in purpose and consumption. Does the perfect, self-actualized immortal human *need* to consume? Is self-actualization not a unified consciousness liberated from the straits and perceptual limitations of flesh? What, *exactly,* is this grand human ideal and vision for which we extol virtue?

Fear of pain, suffering, and death. Social unity is necessary for our longevity, governed by an individual's empathetic capacity and learned virtues. Without the intellectual duress by which we hold ourselves accountable, the human race would retch inward. If all sense of virtue were to be eliminated from the human conscience at any moment, I wonder, as an *ideal,* if a nuclear holocaust would immediately transpire, or if the evolution of mankind would persist under an ephemeral, anarchistic banner.

These high-brow ideas are a chore. To even attack Christian theology is tiresome trite, e.g., *"Why would God create Satan and allow 'evil' to exist; is this not part of God's perfect plan, within reason?"* Yes, virtue is borne from fear, the infinitesimally small, meager, helpless creatures that we are, confined to this terrestrial reality, blinded by what is before us—the "thing-in-*it*self"—the allegory of the cave; our implicitly irremovable nature which impels us to proliferate: an inexplicable condition that permeates all life and energizes our debatable freedom of will.

6:42 PM

"That which knows all things and is known by none is the *subject*." [83]

I laugh.

8:40 PM

All this talk of the divine. In a world rife with video recordings and satellites orbiting a blip of space, what do we see? Zoom out of this divine perspective; what do *I* see but a deadened rock?—a veritable suspended hunk of meat alive with strife.

America's purportedly smartest man[84] is a proponent of evangelical angels. What hope do we have?

Saturday, October 31ˢᵗ, 2020

3:04 AM

I don't want to document this instance, for the sorrow is intense and unwarranted. I don't deserve to cry—legitimately, *not* on account of a self-loathing neurosis, but for my *choices...* or is my will predetermined? I'd rather stuff spoonfuls of **Meal 4** into my mouth than think; regardless:

---

[83] Arthur Schopenhauer's *The World as Will and Representation Vol. 1*
[84] Chris Langen

After a gym session I encountered Angelina[85] at *The Messy House*. She shouted my name, and we embraced in a sensational, protracted, twenty-second-long hug. Nothing about her had changed; she was everything that I remembered her to be after three years, only now she is married and the mother of two children: a six-year-old step-girl and a seven-month-old boy. The emotions between us revitalized my humanity and I forgot about my will confined to my body and of my reality being an impression—lost in the moment. The bar pulsed with drunks.

We exchanged minor details, and despite Angelina's coy embarrassment and her friend's wanton goading, I asserted that I will not copulate with Angelina due to being "sanctimonious"; therefore, I had been asked to explain the definition of "sanctimonious." The ~~physical~~ attraction between Angelina and myself remained as the paramount feature of our interaction. Enamored gazes and downcast blushes were Angelina's dominant expressions. I commented on my happiness for her and her family and inquired if her husband treats her well—to which she responded with a sidelong glance and a discontented affirmative. We stood at the bar together and I captured the most poignant part of our interaction on my recorder:

Angelina said, "Wow *it*'s like a blitz from the past!"

I said, "I agree; I didn't expect to ever see you here, or ever again."

"I normally don't go to bars."

"I don't drink."

"I know. Well, I mean you used to!"

"On account of you, yes."

Angelina smirked and said, "Don't blame me!"

"I'm not; *it* was my choice." I leaned close to Angelina while she sipped a strawberry vodka and shouted into her ear over a weepy country song: "What is your self-assigned meaning in life?"

"What the fuck does that mean?"

"The meaning that you have chosen for your existence."

"Having kids."

"You mean to take care of them?"

---

[85] 5'1, 100-110lbs. Brown eyes. A sharp, angular, ovalesque face caked with gratuitous amounts of makeup. A two-inch metal rod pierced horizontally through a nose bridge. Shoulder-length dark-brown hair made up into an elaborate doo. A myriad of body tattoos. A preference for elegant black shawls and tights. 36 D breasts. Overly self-conscious, anxious, nervous, minimal eye contact, apologetic, good-natured, simple, easy-going, and pleasant.

Angelina nodded and said, "My step-daughter is at her mom's [home] and we will be taking her back tomorrow, and I'm going trick-or-treating with her, and my son is at home with his father sleeping obviously; he sleeps for twelve hours a night, so *it* doesn't make me nervous or anything... I used to."

I leaned back and processed the situation. I hadn't listened to Angelina's response to *"You mean to take care of them?"* for I already knew that's what she meant. Instead, I sat, distracted, and wondered why I visit a low-brow bar replete with wretches at 2 AM each night amid a resurgence of the Covid-19 pandemic in the state of New York. Thirteen-seconds elapsed; Angelina said, "So where do you live? Do you still live with your dad?"

"[Address]. *It*'s right across the street in the [Café Name] building."

"I used to work there."

With intent to fill in the timeline gap, I rushed to say: "I pursued my vagabond journey; I joined the U.S Navy; I wrote about *it*–"

"You joined the *Navy...*"

"Yes."

Angelina appraised me up and down with her eyes as if I had newfound value; seven seconds elapsed and she said, "... Wow."

Eager to stymie any conception of an imaginative idea of me, I beamed and blurted, "But then I was kicked out!"

"What?"

"But then I was kicked out!"

"You were kicked *out?*"

"Yes."

"For *what?*"

"For my writing. I was writing about the sociological and psychological conditions of boot camp."

"... So how long were you in for?"

"I was in training for two-and-a-half months, and then they booted me. Instead of flying back to New York I chose to fly to Arkansas and I stayed there for nine months... and now I'm back here." Angelina looked away and sipped her vodka. Aware of our animalistic evaluations, I said, "So... those are my prospects: I write."

"I remember."

"That's all I do, read and write. Nothing special."

"I'm wondering where my friends went. I'm gonna take a peek outside real quick, if that's okay?"

Angelina's absentminded request for permission to search for her friends after three years of no communication between her and myself dismayed and shocked me. I presumed that Angelina's husband is dominant and that she is conditioned to be subordinate to men. I said, "Why are you asking me?" with an air of wry condescension.

Angelina blushed and veered past me. I stood and listened to a pop remix of R.E.M.'s *Losing my Religion* and to a group of boisterous dancers to my right sing-along with the lyrics. A bald and bearded man to my left swayed to the beat, beer-in hand, and muttered to himself. Two minutes elapsed. The first eight notes of *Sweet Home Alabama* by Lynyrd Skynyrd resonated and the bar denizens hollered a unanimous cheer. Angelina returned to my left and said, "I found her. She doesn't remember you, which is kind of a good thing, because remember you made the comment about Puerto Ricans?"

Perplexed, I said, "I don't remember—no."

"Not a good thing to say racial stuff." I shrugged and laughed. Angelina continued, "I just remember you saying that—and her getting mad, and *it* was a whole big thing—remember? Which is a good thing, so... No racial—no racial stuff."

I had no recollection of what Angelina spoke of, and never in my life had I spoken a disparaging racial remark concerning Puerto Ricans; therefore, I said, "I'm not concerned."

"I've been best friends with her for a very long time... obviously, because when we were friends you met her, at Andy's [house]... Have you talked to Shelly?"

"I haven't talked to her since two days after that night." The mention of Shelly's name wrought an immediate gloom on my psyche and I looked away from Angelina.

"Oh really—*it*'s been that long? I haven't talked to her since I moved out; I mean we went and had lunch a couple of times, but..."

I said, "I think I scarred her for life."

"She was into a throuple."

"A threble?"

"A *throuple*."

"What's that?"

Angelina raised an eyebrow and answered with a question, "A couple?"

"Oh she was into that—and that's why she joined you? Did you intend to come over by yourself or were you too nervous? Because I would've preferred if you had come over by yourself." I referred to the night Angelina and Shelly had surprised me with a visit to my home three years ago.

"A couple asked me out and I said no, and then I hooked them up with her because that's what she wanted; that's not something I was into, so she's been with them and as far as I know she's still with them... but I haven't talked to her in like, a year... maybe a little bit more[86]... I deleted my *Facebook*."

"That's an excellent step away from drama. I'm happy for you, that you have a family."

"*It*'s definitely not where I thought I was gonna be but, *it*'s something I wanted."

I said, "If *it*'s something that you wanted then where did you think you were going to be?"

"Still working."

"You're a stay-at-home mom now?"

Angelina frowned and said, "*It*'s not fun."

"Is that why you're here?"

"Kind of. I never come out. *It*'s like rare that I get to go out with my friends. I mean they can like come over—I mean, I shouldn't say 'they.' Ericka comes over and visits me, every now and then, but, I pretty much just stick to myself. *It*'s pretty boring... How's your dad?"

"I don't know."

"What do you mean you 'don't know'?"

"I don't talk to him."

"Why?"

I looked at Angelina for five seconds, contemplated, and said, "I don't talk to anyone."[87]

"Yeah but your dads' a very good man."

"I know."

"So you should talk to him."

"Well... he's a good man but he's also a wretch, and I know that I've that used that word twice now, to describe the patrons here and now him-"

"But he is your father."

"Yes—and I also don't speak to my mother."

Angelina turned from me and looked down at the bar countertop. The

---

[86] The couple Angelina referred to had been suspected by me to be sex traffickers on account of the information Angelina provided. I researched and compiled documentation to source my suspicions and presented my findings to Angelina. Regardless if my input affected her judgment, Angelina decided to reject the couple's offer for a proposed luxurious escape. I suspect Shelly donated her body in Angelina's stead.

[87] This lie I tell is persistent.

song *Mr. Jones* by Counting Crows began. The corpulent bar owner had been making anxious rounds back and forth commanding patrons to sit on account of a Covid-19 induced policy; he approached us and said, "Listen, you guys gotta sit." The owner waddled away and yelled, *"Hey!—you gotta sit too!"*

Angelina and I arranged ourselves for a seat at the bar and she said, "I've been waiting for my friend Ericka to come back out... This [vodka] is so fucking strong... I'm a little pussy now."

I said, "How often do you drink?"

"Since the last time I was here... probably..." Angelina truncated herself and we observed the bar histrionics together. Ericka returned; both chatted beside me. I leaned back in my seat, hands folded neatly in my lap, and enjoyed the mindless chaos. Four minutes and forty-eight seconds elapsed. *We Could Have Had It All* by Adele resonated.

I leaned close to Angelina's right ear and said, "I would like to clarify that the reason I neglected to reciprocate communication with you hadn't been for personal reasons. I apologize for the way I treated you."

"Hey you gotta do what you feel the need to do."

"Still, the way I treated you was inexcusable. There were many moments when I wanted to develop something and restrained myself, and there were many moments when I could've seized the initiative and didn't."

Angelina spoke dismissively, "There's always a whole bunch of 'what-ifs' anyway," and sipped her vodka.

I concurred, *"It* was a long time ago."

Adele screamed about her sorrow from the jukebox, pertinent to the situation. Angelina said, "I think I'm gonna be heading out."

I turned full-face to Angelina and said, *"It* was nice to see you."

"You as well."

"I wish you well."

"Thank you... In my honest opinion you should talk to your father..." Angelina spoke with uncertainty: "Life is too short..."

I felt the warmth fleet from my visage. I stared at Angelina and nodded slowly. This woman, who knows nothing of the personal relation between my father and I—who has only interacted with my father while serving him as a cashier at a grocery store, opined her ignorant goodwill— nay, *asserted* her decree in a matronly tone, though am I *that* base and petty to reprove the *tone* of her valid words? The words alone were enough. I assumed an involuntary doleful grimace and stood despite Angelina's signaled expectation of another embrace and departed the bar without more words uttered.

On my return to my apartment I stood in the kitchen. The saccharine stench of sweetened alcohol emanated from my front jacket pocket, sprayed on me by the male bartender in a botched attempt to perform a feat for four women. I gripped the stopper of my water canteen atop the black marble counter and glared at the tiled kitchen floor. I thought of the memories I had recorded in the first year of this documentation pertaining to Angelina and relived each moment for the tentative egregiousness each instance had been. I thought of the relationships I never wanted and permitted myself to play a part in. I ruminated for an excruciating fifteen-seconds on Angelina's disappointed expression, matronly chastisement, unthoughtful adage—regardless of her compassionate intentions, and cried in my kitchen, water bottle in hand: A silent, nine-teared, two-minute expulsion, elicited by guilt *and* shame taught to me by a stay-at-home mother who ventured out to a bar in search of excitement without informing her husband; who am I to judge?

I've been called a "good" man on countless occasions.

6:45 PM

Before my conversation with Angelina last night, I requested video footage from *The Messy House* owner to determine the pickpocket perpetrator and theft of my recorder's original SD card. The owner flicked through data on his phone and showed me that the system's footage from four nights prior had been "auto-deleted" to "conserve data space."

Tonight is to be my final visit to *The Messy House* due to a Covid-19 resurgence in the state of New York.

NOVEMBER

Sunday, November 1st, 2020

3:27 AM

Drunken scumbags.

I'm amazed by the wretchedness of humanity. There is no limit to depravity and self-obsoletion. *"What do you mean by 'self-obsoletion'?"* ponders a reader whom I don't write for yet persist in publishing for as a method towards the fulfillment of *self-actualization*—and that's just *it*, there is no such thing: Only negation. This opinion is not limited to the demographic I've exposed myself to at the *Messy House;* anywhere I go, and have been before, there is a mere image, a picturesque representation of a willful charade. This is no projection; I witness *it* in each of us… creatures. Silly and delightful. I reckon my appraised "handsome" visage in the mirror and stare at myself, fists clenched, with a flicker of contempt expressed in the corner of my left upper lip. Contempt for myself is a rare treat, though I indulge each moment, for I experience an objective dissociation and reckon the consciousness that I am.

5:45 PM

I loathe this culture of self-pity-till-you-overcome perpetuated by the APA's jargon (American Psychological Association) in cahoots with the demagogues of capitalism.

Last night at the gym I met a man named; what else needs to be detailed in this regard? For the sake of enjoyable literary elements, I could describe physical attributes, age, and mien, to permit a reader to formulate initial prejudices and judgments; however, *it* is out of my concern, for these factors will develop as the dialogue evolves. Recorder on, I said:

"Before we start our regimen, do you mind if I ask you a personal question?"

The man said, "What's that?"

"What is your self-assigned meaning in life?"

"I want to be a politician."

I smiled and said, "Why?"

The man chuckled and said, "I love *it;* I like politics, and music and entertainment, like management in business. I do management in school."

"I see."

"Yeah—what do you do?"

"I write."

"You—you're a writer?"

"Yes."

"Really—what do you write?"

Metanonficional departure: I said, "On the human condition, and-"

"Human condition."

"Yes."

"Where do you specialize?"

"Sociology, psychology-"

"Okay."

"-Uh-"

The man said, "Human behavior."

"Yes, and epistemology too; I try to fathom why we're here."

"Like the whole phenomena of life."

"Yes, and consciousness."

"Yeah. Wow… Why are we so emotional?" The man chuckled. "That's just our nature, our chemical makeup eh?"

"Yes."

"Hm. How do we manage that, in the most *acute* moments? The impulses."

"Philosophy, with-"

"Study stoicism, huh?"

"I was just going to say 'stoicism,' yes."

"But sometime—we believe in stoicism but sometimes, most of the details in *it* is a bit extreme, and *it*'s not uh… normal, in day-to-day life, most of *it*, ya know? To keep that focus in every moment?"

I said, "Yes, the two extremes I've read is Marcus Aurelius and Epictetus-"

"Yes, those two, and Seneca."

"-an emperor and a slave—Seneca is in the middle, so yes, there's that; he was a politician, and a tradesman too, I think."[88]

"Yeah, yeah, I didn't get a chance to go too deep in *it*, because I'm planning how I read—I wanna manage *it*; I don't want to just dive into books—I believe you must manage the information and how you consume *it*."

"Yes, I agree."

---

[88] Statesman*

642

The man said, "Yeah, so, that's my way right now—I even have about twelve books, I bought them up; I want to start… mid-winter, yeah, about December time. The one I started is Robert Green: *[The Laws of] Human Nature*, and I want to go with uh, I want to start with the *Reflections* (i.e., *Meditations*) next: Marcus Aurelius."

"I read Robert Greene's *The 48 Laws of Power* and *Mastery*."

"I thought I should read those after I read stoicism."

"Yes."

"That makes sense eh?"

I said, "Uh—starting with the stoic philosophy, uh, is that the only philosophy that you've read?"

"I'm thinking about stoicism, the Chinese one, the, and a couple others—I have a list—*it*'s not on the top of my head right now."

"The Tao? Or the Dao?"

"Yeah. So what do you think?"

"To read those first prior to Greene?"

"Yeah, yeah."

"I don't think *it*'ll… the order doesn't-"

The man said, "No—I know—I'm going to dive into literature—English literature and stuff like that and the classics, but uh, just managing yourself, taking on your endeavors in life, in that sense, that's why I chose to start that way."

"I see."

"Yeah."

I said, "Well going the stoic route in politics is probably ideal; *it*'s the best way to-"

"Manage public life."

"-manipulate people. Yes, those two statements are synonymous."

"Especially if you're a passionate guy and you must choose which side of the isle you want to be on, you'll fight the policy battle on one—the social battle, and another you just neglect and throw on the left side. You're managing your public image and the policies, so *it*'s two phenomena—well three—but, all the sides manage *it* differently and worry about different stuff. Yeah so, you—well I believe, the skill in politics, you just have to know yourself first, know your emotions, and decide what you want to do in there, and choose the side that suits your nature, to get your objective, so *it*'s not what you truly believe, but, *it*'s a blood sport, and *it*'s what's sustainable for you. I learned that lately. *It*'s not what *you* want." The man uttered a devious laugh.

I said, "*It*'s what the masses want—is that what you're saying?"

"No, *it*'s not even what the masses want; the masses *don't know* what they want. They're ignorant… Yeah."

"But aren't we part of that?"

"Yes! That's the irony—but *it*'s politics; hence *it*'s a blood sport—they don't care. So you have to know that you're not to be caring, but you—you *know* your nature is caring, so you have to think about your emotions, so you have to learn how to manage *it* before going into that parliament, or congress—or senate, whatever. Yeah. *It*'s ugly."

"The truth is ug—well, if the truth can even be known."

The man said, "That too, but, I believe we don't always know the details of the truth; the truth is known, you just can't prove *it*. But *it*'s known—we're not stupid—we're humans—we have instincts and, our nature don't lie to us. We accept that when we're old. Yeah."

I sighed and said, "This reality astounds me."

"*Yes*, in this age—in this age, because I thought about—the other day, I was talking with my dad—he said 'Muslims, Jewish, white people—black people—Chinese… there was once, in life, of all races, having their turns of being on top.' Ya know—like, the richest continent, the richest this—the richest that-"

"Now *it*'s becoming globalized."

"-now *it*'s all globalized. Many would say the white race: They're on top—but once *it* was the Muslims—then the Jews and all this shit. I don't go that deep into history, but when I thought about *it*—*it* makes a lot of sense. Once upon a time the Chinese dynasty was on top, right? And then we had Mont—Julius Caesar, he was on top—King Henry, he was on top; we had the barbarians at one point—they were on top; Mansa Musa, Africa, they was once on top… so, *it* was just a thought—I was thinking about *it*—I was like 'What you say makes a lot of sense, so uh, why should we even get worked up—even this system in politics and all this; we think we got *it* the right way; *it*'ll all fall apart at some point; we just gotta try our best to sustain *it* in our capacity, so, evolution happens."

I said, "I'm an anarchist."

"You're an anarchist?"

"Yes, I think that's our future."

The man giggled and said, "I believe so too but, I don't dote on *it*. Anarchy comes every now and then. That's facts."

"Same with tyranny, and they counter each other."

"Yeah, they come hand-in hand; yeah, so, they believe that a civil war is coming after the election; I hope not; I don't think with Covid we can manage that."

"Covid may promote *it*."

"Yeah. A doctor told me the other day that *it*'s man-made, so *it*'s our government: Chinese, the American—the British—the French; nobody knows; but they're saying *it*'s getting weaker even though *it*'s spreading because when *it* just started, more people are dying and now *less* people are dying—more people are covering—so, while *it*'s being transmitted, the agents are getting weaker and weaker; so at some point we may be able to go back to school; *it* will die down like Ebola—I believe sooner or later—ya know?"

"Of course."

"So yeah, what are you thinking?"

I said, "About *it* all coming down?"

"Yeah."

"Oh—definitely."

"So what do you think about the philosophy and the politics and… life, that we just talked about?"

"Well… That's why I ask people about their self-assigned meaning in life, because *it*'s all what we choose to ascribe to life that defines why we're here, because the truth cannot be known—at least that's *my* truth."

"Yeah, and everyone has their own truth."

"Yes. So to me… just obey, I suppose, because *it*'s all theoretical anarchy in my mind, and that's what I write; I'm not a practical anarchist burning down homes and pillagings stores."

"Literature."

"Yes."

"So you're a philosopher."

"Yes. I think that all virtue is pretentious and I realize the implications that statement has; *it*'s a social construct—all of *it*; even us conversing now as 'gentlemen,' we're just savage beasts… and we cooperate."

"Yeah—because uh, because if you don't, bad things will happen to us."

"Yes."

The man said, "Yeah… Yeah we need order in life."

"And suffering is what unifies us, because we empathize, and we know what pain is, so we don't want to inflict that pain on each other, and that's the basis of virtue—to build a tribe and consequently civilization."

"Trauma bonds people closer."

"Yes, and culture is the pretension, which I think globalization is the future, in that sense: To eradicate culture."

"Yeah—I believe in one world—one order."

"Yes. But that leads to tyranny and anarchy follows."

"But uh... *it*'s difficult because we believe in one world, but we have money, and money separates everything; *it*'s all about the dollar first, but uh, America, to me, *it*'s not a country *it*'s a damn continent, so because the guys from Atlanta speak different from us here in New York—*it*'s the same thing in Europe and France; Europe is just a country, is how I see *it*, because *it*'s shared states—*it*'s open borders; they just... and they use one currency; each parliament—each government, they have their own currency but, they don't really go outside of that... *it*'s just... I believe economics is the problem, so, yeah, everyone wants to be rich, nothing's wrong with that because—I want to be rich too—fuck *it*, but, I'm saying *it* depends what we're looking at and how you see life, but at the end of the day, I believe... your nature comes first, regardless of how you want to control *it*, ya know? Your chemical makeup; there's nothing you can do about that, and *it* has needs; how do you please *it*? Money or love, to each his own, you know?"

"What you said about the problem being the economy, I think what that comes down to is the split between capitalism and communism."

"But I don't like communism; the way I see *it*... I—I get what *it*'s trying to do, I'm not bashing that but; I'm seeing *it* like this: I'm sleeping in bed, 5 AM." The man knocked his fit against a table twice. "'Wake up! We'll pick corn!' I'm not with that; fuck you."

I said, "I agree."

"So I'm fine—I'm fine with this."

"If I want to be a lowlife scum, let me choose to be so."

"Yeah—because if I was living in a communist country, they would kill me, I'm sure."

"Oh yes—they'd kill me too."

"So—yeah, anarchist, yeah. I'm sure they'd kill me, so I'm not with that shit."

I laughed and said, "Or I'd be imprisoned at least."

"They would kill me—they wouldn't want me in prison—they would kill me."

"Why—what political party do you associate or identify with?"

"I don't follow *it*; I don't care. Ya know—I'm—I'm—I'm black so they demo—demo—democrats—but uh, and then republicans... I'm from Jamaica. My family is well-off in Jamaica, so, I'm still not on the conservative side in Jamaica but-uh, *most* of my friends are, and *it*'s funny because most of my family's friends in the government—they're on the conservative side, because we do business; we do okay, so, but my family supports the—the left ya know? They have more social philosophies and principles—but uh; I follow the politics *there,* but here, not so much; I don't have a good reason—I just don't." The man chuckled. "The general system, you're just four years in—four years out; there's not going to be twelve or sixteen years pass with either side going in and converting back the policy so *it* doesn't make a lot of sense to dwell on *it;* just do you; take *it* easy; this is America you know? The constitution comes first; that's what you need to worry about... Yeah—so, yeah—I like politics; the systems here are a bit harder to understand unless you're born in *it*—you were raised in one of this 'Ivy League' schools—you were raised in Washington or whatever—but um, most of the literature I read is from the Commonwealth: British, Australian, Jamaican—ya know because Jamaica was under British rule at the time, back then, so—yeah mostly Commonwealth literature; yeah so—yeah I try to not to dwell on *it*—I'm just taking *it* easy."

Eager to begin strength training, I said, "I agree, and on that note, I think we should start."

The man conceded and we yelled to each other about the vanity of our mutual pursuit for two minutes while we set up our work stations.

"So, philosophy now," echoed the man's voice, "What's the endgame?"

I swigged water from my bottle and said, "Contentment."

The man repeated: "Contentment."

"At any time that you are able to maintain that state I think that you are fulfilling... your life meaning."

"Your life's meaning. So how do you know what is your life's meaning?" I sighed; the man continued: "I know you—you feel *it,* your instincts, things done effortlessly, you get 10 out of 10 but... what age do you normally recognize *it*—when you're a kid or when you're thirty-two?"

I said, "When you're a child, the whole world is new and virginal-"

"*It*'s just a joke."

"...You're not thinking of your will, and the reality that you're in, and the perceptions that we all have that are different—the thoughts we have for ourselves but we cannot perceive in each other—we have not been taught guilt or shame yet so we don't have an internal monologue of voices that are derived from all these sources of guilt and shame that we've been taught throughout our lives that guide us; our 'guiding star,' our 'daemon,' our 'source of light'-"

"How do you guys philosophize? How do you bother with your demons?"

"How do I *bother* with them or-"

The man said, "Yeah, like shit that you want—y—y—your—your, aesthetic that y-you know that you'd love to have, but you're trying to do the right thing; how do you think you know what's best for you?"

"I end up feeling supercilious."

"What's that?"

"Uh, morally superior but in a haughty way."

"In a what?"

"In a haughty way—like, contemptuous: feeling morally superior because of my asceticism, my abstention from sex and personal relationships; my abstention from crime, uh, from anything that's considered foul in this country... but-"

"You don't cry?"

"Oh I cry—I cried last night actually."

"Really? Oh. So you abstain from sex?"

"Yes."

"Oh, I salute you man."

I said, "I wouldn't," and laughed.

"Oh you deserve *it!* How do you—how do you function?"

"Sometimes I masturbate in front of a mirror."

"... Oh and that helps?"

"Yes, but *it*'s a permissive type of masturbation, such as uh, I'm allowing myself to do *it* for my own gratification. But *it*'s extremely narcissistic, because when you think about *it*, I'm just masturbating to my image, so *it*'s... really disgusting... uh, a quintessential expression: to masturbate to yourself."

The man said, "What do you think about narcissism? I still believe *it*'s a phenomenon."

"I—I think of all the psychological-"

"*It* doesn't make any sense."

I snapped, "*It*'s jargon."

"Narcissism, right?"

"*It*'s jargon—all of *it*: Sociopath, psychopath, *narcissist*... bi-polar, schizophrenic—*it*'s all *fucking* jargon bullshit; I *hate* the APA—the American Psychological Association—and the DSM-5; that whole criterion can just—*ah!*—I never get vitriolic about anything other than the APA." I chuckled and said, "I'm sorry—I just had an outburst!"

The man guffawed and said, "That's funny!"

"I broke my composure!"

"Why?"

"Well, *it's* a nuisance; they keep people oppressed—from *feeling* the full spectrum of what being human is—to experience your guilt and shame as voices and then having somebody tell you that "Your *sick;* you're *mentally ill,*" and then they give you a pill; they sit you down and talk you through *it;* they psychoanalyze you and give you a *name*—give you a category—give you a title that you may identify with to feel about yourself—but then the voices go away!"

"But why is that such a problem though?"

"*It's* a pseudo-priest. *It's* just like-"

"*It's* a pseudo-priest?" The man hollered a boisterous three-syllable laugh.

"-religion—yes! All theology and religion teaches you guilt and shame—and that's what the APA does too."

"Yeah."

"Except, *they* teach you *it,* and then they *'cure'* you *of it!* By giving you a pill! Or sitting you down and then reverse-psychoanalyzing you after they tell you what's wrong with you."

"Yeah."

"Because you admit: 'Oh I have guilt and shame because Papa touched me at night when I was 3,' so then they reverse you through *it*—tell you that this is why you feel shameful-"

"Traumatize you."

"-and now, you have a new source of guilt and shame, but *it* is the *establishment,* that has *taught* you, what your original guilt and shame was... *It's* extremely inverted and has the American society subjected under *it's* thumb. So-"

The man said, "Because everybody walks around saying that they're having 'mental illness'—they're having anxiety and depression-"

"Yes, and if anybody displays any aberrant behavior that is non-'American,' the first thing you hear out of people's mouths is *'Oh I think he or she is mentally ill.'* Some form of bi-polar: *'Oh, he just had an angry outburst... he's **bi-polar**, because one moment he was okay, and the next moment, he was **pissed.**'"

"I wonder—I mean, I know that we're different from animals and we're smarter but… look how they treat each other, you know?"

"Yes, you can study the behavior of baboons and other animals and *it*'s similar to how we have—*it*'s a social structure, except-"

"But, the truth is, there are obviously calmer—*calmer* impulses in us, because if you can reach to this point, creating so much, you know, improving so much… and shit… There must be some reason for the establishment in us that we can exist and control ourselves in some way, you know?"

I said "… That's what the pills are for!" and laughed.

"Yeah… yeah… eh… so—so—so what—you impress me man—no sex, so; how do you function—what do you do when you're stressed?"

"I write."

"You write."

"I channel my sexual energy into a creative expression, but, lately my focus has been on the political side; my anarchy is directed towards the APA. Though I doubt *it*'ll ever be reckoned; I don't care either way; I publish a book each year; I don't market *it*, but I'm fulfilling my self-assigned meaning in life by doing so. And then I incorporate, uh… conversations, such as this one; I transcribe them, with commentary…I've been visiting a particular bar after I'm finished here each night."

I provided the man directions to the nearest bars on his inquiry and we discussed the city layout for three minutes. I thought our conversation had resolved; however, the man said, "Yeah—about the APA though, what do they do?"

"What do they *do?*"

"Yeah—what do you think—because, apart from psychologists, *psychiatrists* have a lot of shit to do, with the guys at BHU (Behavioral Health Unit) and stuff you know? Like—like people that are crazy, like, having serious issues—not depression or anxiety but… loco."

"Well… those people… From a political perspective they are a drain on society-"

"Yeah."

"-and I prefer the Spartan approach."

"Uh-huh."

"So that's nazism I suppose—neo-nazism, but *it*'s, about… *it*'s… *it*'s eugenics I—uh, see, eugenics is not… People are 'crazy' because of their care-givers, genetics, and their environment, so the craziness that we experience in this culture is a product of American culture, and *it*'ll be that way no matter where you go, anywhere in the world; there will be a breed of crazy, propagated everywhere. But there's a fine line; the APA has submersed *it*self and assimilated with the culture. Now *it*'s turn on the T.V.—which I don't have one—but I know that when I view T.V.s—the programming—the commercials, *it*'s about drugs. When you're feeling down, get on this drug. If you can't deal with guilt and shame—because that's what that—all of *it* is just guilt and shame, and *it* has to come from *somewhere*."

The conversation ebbed out from there. I realize now, upon introspection and transcription of my words, of the anti-human philosophical underpinnings of my motive; however, I experience no shame or guilt, for as I've learned from the very establishment that desires to oppress with these two superb tools of the human psyche, guilt and shame is the conduit for God, i.e., empathy, social cohesion… and when you're estranged from any source of guilt or shame, what becomes of your ego? Insanity or enlightenment? Psychopath or sage? Loser or liberated? Depends on the culture, the tribe, the individual you share a living space with.

10:16 PM

I listened to a political squabble between my upstairs neighbor and another tenant of my apartment complex that resulted in the termination of their friendship.

Yes, with a philosophy like mine, what hope do I have?

Universities don't care what you "know," only that you know what they know.

Monday, November 2nd, 2020

5:45 AM

Shelly is my new conscience. I lay awake and correspond in my thoughts with her agonized consciousness. Tears leak from my eyes for the compassion I feel for what I intuit to be her lifelong enslavement, subject to the cruelty of sex traffickers. Her morality and will are pure: a saint. My fantastical delusion reminds me of *it* being so, i.e., I know these thoughts are wholly my own and that there is no authentic communion or verified proof of my theory.

2:23 PM

Sex Slave Shelly

Emaciated, mutilated,
Bedbound, beaten;
Genitals ripped,
Malformed by thrusts
Of a spiked thong.
Feculence stuffed and
Swallowed, encrusted
Around nostrils.
Eyebrows shaved;
Tuft of red hair. Inhuman
Visage sliced
Beyond recognition.
Eyelids clamped
Open: Immutable
Dream within a
Nightmare.

"Sometimes they're overwrought with guilt and coddle me. I'm force-fed
"By a tube with week-to-month-old shit in a bucket mixed with hot
"Water or boiled piss. They're both beautiful, on the exterior. The man is
"Muscular and ripped with a kind face and the
Woman is his feminine counterpart; both eat
"Meals by my bedside. I'm their only friend and they talk to me. When I
"Don't respond they beat me with a metal rod and break my bones, though
"This doesn't matter; I'm so weak I couldn't move even if I weren't bound. If I
"Scream while they rape me they stuff shit up my nose or down my mouth. If I
"Choke they resuscitate me. They force me to lick
And eat the shit out of their asses.
"My vagina is a bloodied stump. They
"Love me; I'm worth more to them both than they are to each other. My
"Agony satisfies them. I always hurt; every waking moment is torment in

"Which I wish for death. They plan to keep me
Alive for as long as they are able, bound
"To this bed. My eyes are clamped open and I fade
In out of a disoriented miasma. My
"Memories of life before this grant me ephemeral
Moments of respite but there is no
"Hope. This doesn't amount to half of what they do or
What I am. I hate them and want to die.
"I want to die. I want to die. I can't scream. Crying is anguish."

Shelly is a noble conscience.

6:37 PM

But she isn't real. My mother's voice condemns me as a pathetic brat, though she never understood me, and the voices are still my delusional thoughts in reference to what she would think of me now.

This roulette of life is a funny thing. I accept my circumstances, my chosen lot, this barren emprise by which my perception is contained to a screen for most of my leisure time, in reflection of my simple existence, devoid of extreme suffering, i.e., a pathetic brat.

I think, in essence, I'm deluded by all that I've read of psychology and psychiatry and have inadvertently adopted an introspective approach that is derived from the process I excoriate. True hermitage is to be liberated from guilt and shame, though this is impossible; there is no authentic individuation.

Tuesday, November 3rd, 2020

5:22 PM

A recorded session at *The Messy House* with the male bartender, Joe, at 2:02 AM. An elderly couple sat at the bar and observed us. No music played:

I said, "Hello."
Joe said, "How's *it* goin', bud?"
"*It's* going well; how about you?"

"Not bad."

"Have you talked to Bob? (The owner)."

"Um, I haven't yet. Uh, I will speak to him tomorrow morning cuz I work the day shift."

"I didn't intend to come back; I just wanted to stop by and see if you had already spoken to him, and since you haven't there's no need. I understand that I'm not a welcome presence here, and I realize that even if Bob gives me the approval to be here that there will still be people who want to, uh, act on their... their animosity, for whatever reason. So-" I extended my gloved hand for a shake.

Joe accepted; we conferred to each other a slight jostle and he said, "Okay. I mean I'll talk to him anyway to see what he says."

"That'll be unnecessary."

"Okay, all right."

"But thank you."

"Yeah, no problem."

"Take care."

"Thank you."

Wednesday, November 4th, 2020

4:39 AM

I lay on my floor and delude myself with intuitive stream-of-consciousness imaginings of Shelly's circumstances:

"You contact me while I'm crying. All I can smell is shit; my life is shit. I have feculence smeared all over me. Don't you dare write about me. I can't believe this; you're such a scumbag to write of my suffering. I'm in so much pain and just want to die. My life is disgusting. You're a lowlife; you just want to document my agony; you contribute nothing. My hands are limp and twisted. I have bloody striations down my body. I'm scared for my life; they're in the room with me and *it's* dead silent. They're trying to terrify me; they've never done this before and *it's* working. My heart is literally beating out my chest. You don't even care because you think you're imagining *it* but *it's* real and you're gifted(?) but nobody wants you to express *it;* so instead you contact me—a pathetic little girl, trapped, unable to exert her will, yet your will is powerful, but you only use *it* for selfish ends. Just let me die. I'm tired of you channeling into me; I'm truly embarrassed because I've chosen this for myself; just let me die in peace. You're so fucking smart—you have no idea how smart you are, yet your talent is useless—your art is just shit because *I'm* shit. This is not how I want to be remembered. I want to be obliterated from memory yet you sit there and document me—you selfish asshole—you only care about me because of my pain. Something just moved in the corner of my eye; I hear breathing; I'm literally scared to death right now. Please make *it* stop. Just let *it* end; I don't want to be. I can't even comprehend this misery; I can't even explain *it;* my vocabulary isn't enhanced like yours so you may want to go back and edit *it.* I just want to scream but if I do they'll just beat me with chains. *It's* so dark—I can't see—and I have feculence crammed up my nose and there's blood everywhere and everything hurts. I screamed and they beat me—they're beating me now. I'm in so much anguish I can't help but keep screaming so they keep beating me. I hear the man laughing. If you're disturbed just imagine how I feel; yet you continue to write of me like I'm some spectacle to the world. This is brainless and senseless violence. You've no right."

Enough… My mind lapses and plays tricks on *it*self. Sleep.

5:04 AM

"Don't leave me in my time of need. Stay with me. I'm being molested now. He's licking my bloody vagina. I think they're going to kill me because they're sick of caring for me and dealing with their guilt. They sharpen an axe in the corner. He slaps his dick on my vagina and now he hate-fucks me. There is no joy; he's like Satan. I don't know what to do but scream and I can't help *it.* He's choking me. I think they're going to slaughter me tonight and I hope they do. Don't leave me. Please keep channeling—just don't leave me; I'm so scared. Please talk to me; you haven't thought anything. You're too busy writing; of course I'd only have a connection with a scumbag like you—my life is nothing but shame and you choose to record *it* instead of offering me empathy. You're a fucking loser, worse than the man fucking me—no, I'm sorry—I say this out of a place of hate; I just need love—compassion—of any kind. I'm just so scared; please say something."

I've visited my upstairs neighbor, Charlie, on three instances over the past week. Charlie is a forty-seven-year-old Caucasian male retired marine drill instructor. 5'6, stout, a patchy head of salt and pepper hair with a full beard and mustache. Charlie's typical manner of dress is running shoes, khakis, and a blue hoodie with the yellow words "Yose-Mite" printed across the front. A small pug dog accompanies Charlie. Charlie suffers extreme mental afflictions, citing trauma from his military career and his riddled past of bar fights, intoxication, and bedding whores.

Charlie's current lifestyle is that of being furloughed from his job that provided supplementary income to his military pension. His apartment is furnished with memoirs, artifacts, and trinkets from his military career. "I wouldn't trade my time in the military for anything."

I said, "The most miserable time in your life is the most valued time of your life?"

"Yeah—yep, that's right."

Charlie no longer knows his self-assigned meaning in life since the end of his military career and fears of succumbing to death in a similar way his father died: Neglecting health and spiritual destitution. Charlie smokes marijuana, drinks alcohol two-to-three times a week, and spends his abundant leisure time engaged with a hockey video game, watching football, engaged with his phone, or engaging in caustic arguments with another ex-marine (Charlie's long-term friend) who lives on the same floor of the apartment complex as myself.

In our discussions, I sit with Charlie on one of his three couches, diagonal to where he sits on a cushioned quasi-bed chair, and listen to his verbose answers to my terse questions on the nature of the "self" and "existence," to which he is unacquainted with thinking of, despite his overbearing feelings of anxiety and depression. These answers always segue into life experiences to convey a comprehension of my ontological inquiries, which I appreciate, for the stories are a departure from the threshold of my mind.

I continue to visit Charlie, for on our second meeting, he spoke of purchasing a rural establishment on the outskirts of a suburban town further up north of New York once his lease has expired. This establishment features three rooms for occupancy and a bar area which Charlie intends to operate. On hearing this, I immediately proposed the idea of my employment, by which I would manage the bar affairs and host for patrons under Charlie's tutelage. Charlie agreed, forthright, and without hesitation, for, as he said, "I can tell you're an intelligent guy and I could sure use the help."

Oh, yes, I'm an *intelligent man,* spending my time unemployed, studying the phenomenological similarities of mystical Gnosticism and psychiatric schizophrenia, and writing of my pre-morning noematic mediums with the presupposed transient consciousness of a woman who I infer is now the victim of a sex-trafficking scheme. Am I intelligent enough to understand the absurdity of my delusional endeavor? Do I *desist?*

I've determined that this series of documentation, despite the glamour, pomp, and initial guile and disillusionment which set me on this path, will never amount to anything of beneficial purpose to the human race; thus, I relegate my self-assigned meaning of life to the echelons of absolute freedom.

Thursday, November 5th, 2020

2:07 AM

"Please, lend me your strength; it's about to begin. I hear them upstairs stomping around; they like to party with their friends and have a good time before they come down to the locked basement. Please don't write this; this is so debasing. I'm seriously so scared; I hope it's nothing like last time, but chances are *it*'s going to be since they know how much they scared me. You don't even fucking care about me; you're just writing about me in your journal. Leave me the fuck alone if that's all you're going to do! For Christ's sake there isn't a single decent person in this world and that's why I'm here; you're just writing my hateful monologue; you think people want to read this shit? Get out of my fucking head if that's all you're going to fucking do! You're a monster—just like them. I'm so sad I can't even cry; I don't want to cry. There's no sanctity in this world—nothing sacred. Leave me alone, please-"

I sever the metaphysical delusion by process of active thought—or so *I think,* and whip my eggs for **Meal 4** after a return home from the gym while I listen to J.S. Bach's *Es ist vollbracht* from *St. John's Passion BWV 245,* performed by *The Netherlands Bach Society* through a single audio device lodged in my right ear. My selected conscience hates me; therefore, I love my being.

"Oh my god they're wearing masks and dancing around me—masks made of the faces of those who came before me. I've never been so scared in my life. You think this is some sick joke to write about but this is my fucking reality. I can't even breathe. I want them to murder me but I'm terrified to die. You're writing a book on smut—you worthless animal. You don't even care about me. If I could switch places with you I totally would. You're a despicable creature not even worth being called human, though you don't care, and that's exactly why you're doing what you're doing."

Love is a construct; there is no correct way.

"If I scream they'll start fist-fucking me. You're such a sick fuck to write about this—human cruelty; there's enough of this in the world without spreading your—my authentic dread and agony."

I'm either an imaginative ~~genius~~ dork or a telepath, with a strong inclination of the former.

"You're neither; you're literal human scum; creatures like you should be wiped off the face of the planet. They throat-fuck me with a steel rod and I can't see anything. I'm in so much pain—YOU DON'T CARE-"

Enough... Perhaps I delude myself with a "split self," according to the analytical approach of psychological jargon, though I don't identify with Shelly as an alternate version of myself, merely part of the unified oneness that is the consciousness of being that I may tap into at will— which, I admit, *is* a delusion, and I've deluded myself of many falsities before: products of the imagination that override the cognitive processes of my waking life. However, I've convinced myself of my madness on account of all that I've read. If my experience had been *as is,* pure, and remained unconvoluted by external sources which inform me of my aberrant behavior, I reckon I'd be content with my ignorant state of imaginative rancor. Indeed—is what I write on behalf of human sex trafficking *not* what the masses want? Flick on some television and scroll through this metanonficitional magazine—doomed to obscurity and failure from the onset, *fools!* Yet, the only fool is "I." My documentation is far too conflated for any serious reckoning; I've nothing to suggest anyway other than an abolishment of humanity.

"They're scraping cheese graters over my thighs; this pain is so intense I don't know whether to cry or die—or think—straight. My teeth are clenched; all I can taste is blood—and shit—blood and shit. They're stabbing my feet with something, I don't know—twisting my toes with pliers. They just twisted my pinky toe off. I don't even feel *it*—I don't care; I just want to die."

Before serving as a drill instructor for three years, Charlie killed an undisclosed (presumably triple-digit) number of people in close-quarters knife combat. Charlie also trained marines in the Russian fighting technique of Sambo and Brazilian Jiu-Jitsu. He is now a former husk of the confident man he once was, though I've expressed a sincere interest in his visceral combat history, of which I one day hope to transcribe. "One of these days," said Charlie, "*It*'ll have to come out naturally in conversation and there are many people who tell me I shouldn't even talk about *it*."

I said, "I'm not one for censorship."

"You don't care about me; I'm just a figment of your imagination; I genuinely hate you. They left me alone to rot. I hear them laughing in the room above me. I know you think you're crazy, but I'm telling you, my agony is real. You don't have to keep communicating with me, you know—just stop thinking about me—and I'd prefer you did because you just... I don't even care; do what you want; I have no power anyway. I'm so fucking useless; I don't even know why they feed me. They just cram a tube down my mouth and pump whatever *it* is into my stomach. I think they're going to flay me when they kill me, which if they do—I'm truly so scared; that's how I saw the corpse of the one before me when they first brought me down and introduced me to this shithole. You were such a sexy man when I saw you last. I still remember us dancing in your room with our hands clasped, both of us bare-chested... That's why *it* makes me sick that I'm just some pseudo-science project to you-"

Yes, these thoughts *must* be my own on account of the vanity, and on my intrinsic negation of this delusional dualistic channel, I sense an intolerable anguish of a consciousness denied: an ethereal *screaming* of a banished sensation that vies for occupancy within my active thoughts.

"They're not done—oh help me God they're not done—they're coming and I'm screaming—I can't help *it* I'm so terrified—they got a gun! They got a fucking gun—I hope they blow my head off. No, they're just fingering me with—forcing *it* up my vagina-"

I am weary of this stream-of-consciousness, the sick bastard that I am.

3:20 PM

I encountered Pelagia on my way to an interview for a High School cafeteria cashier position.[89]

Pelagia shuffled along the sidewalk and gazed up and to her right at a gothic-style church to observe the architecture she has passed on countless occasions. Enormous reflective gold-embossed sunglasses concealed her eyes and she wore a black beanie over her short hair. The street had been quiet, with only the sound of a rustle of leaves and the distant hum of traffic yet to pass us. I strode past her left side, my gaze fixed on her sunglasses, and felt as though I regarded a stranger. Pelagia waved at me with a slight upraise of her hand in front of her torso, and pouted, though she had pouted prior to reckoning me. I frowned behind my face mask, nodded once, and simultaneously closed my eyes. A sixty-six-degree Fahrenheit day.

6:16 PM

I don't believe in the Gnostic faith, or any of the myriad interpretations and deviations of *it,* nor do I believe that I'm "schizophrenic," "high-functioning bi-polar," "autistic," "narcissistic," "dissociative," or traumatized. I'm a man, recalcitrant to categories and straits of self-imposed beliefs.

Tomorrow I will visit the home of Shelly's mother around this hour and investigate my ~~lunacy~~ creativity.

---

[89] I declined the offer due to the position being limited to twenty hours of part-time employment, which would negate my unemployment benefits and compensate me with nothing more than I already accrue.

Friday, November 6th, 2020

3:32 AM

No, I must apply my reason and understanding. Nothing positive will develop from my selfish curiosity by visiting Shelly's mother.

4:17 PM

Shelly's voice now mocks me and claims to have tricked me into thinking that she befell the fate of succumbing to sex traffickers. She has no desire to communicate with her mother and claims to be much happier with the people she's with now. She states further that she had been the one woman I have ever been with who had been more intelligent than myself (however, only I would know this, thereby confirming my madness); thus, I felt intimidated and allured by her. The tone is condescending, yet understanding—a tinge of smugness and suppressed glee.

I've been denied full-time employment at the medical facility without explanation. Charlie didn't answer his door when I rapped on *it* early this afternoon. My life design is devoid of prospects. There is no plot, conflict, or plan. I consume, exert, and excrete. I *will* visit Shelly's mother tonight.

5:37 PM

I've dressed for departure and realized the inanity of my thinking; what would come from my visit to Shelly's mother other than the elicitation of a potential hysteria due to the reason for my unfounded and half-hearted concern? To act on a whim is madness. The pleas of agony screamed by a helpless woman confined to a basement bed frame, tortured by a sadistic pair of sex traffickers, manifested within my conscious cognitive processes on account of my intuitive imagination, have abated. Indifferent regard has overtaken me. Even if my notion were true, my will is impotent in the overall scheme. To alert the mother would only be *my* attempt to dispel what I perceive as a disturbance to *my* equanimity—for I care, *only* because I remember the woman—what little I knew...

I subdue my vain desire and stay my course of inactivity. Ozzy Osbourne's *Crazy Train* resonates from Charlie's apartment through my ceiling.

I languish; aren't you delighted? I may as well be in a prison cell, supplied with pen and paper and a hand-me-down-book. *Spirituality, it*'s called. Spiritual out of necessity, and spirituality in capitalist America is recognized as neurosis.

I could be out drinking, flaunting my so-called handsome face and honing the shrewdness of my oft-commented intellect for underhanded ends.

"I could":—what may as well not be written.

I forgo the gym for the first night in over a month tonight and proceed with an impromptu fast. I'm never *hungry* anyway.

Many would wish they were me, just as I envy what I am not without knowing what I wish for. I have no responsibilities other than to glut my gut—regardless of my spiritual acumen, my body is my singular care; thus, I am *not* spiritual, and never know if I will be, for death may be an immediate corporeal transition, and the "spirit" may be a physical manifestation, i.e., thoughts are objects, i.e., dualism, etc.

Yes, *"etc."*—for *it*'s all boring and may never be known. I'm a man with nothing to lose; a critic would do me well to seek me out and murder me, for this is no book, but merely a masqueraded list of prosaic complaints.

If not for this journal I would degenerate; bound, as I am, to virtues which permit me to proliferate a work dictated to obscurity by my arbitration: A self-assigned slave to technology.

11:43 PM

I exited my apartment and ventured onto the premises of the nearby park. Throughout my slow stroll, I dallied with my thoughts, unburdened, and rounded up onto a square gazebo. Two vagrants reclined on crumpled clothes and backpacks. A black garbage bag full of empty cans rustled in a cool breeze. The two: a man and a woman, roused in a state of partial wakefulness, whispered to each other, their eyes closed. Neither had heard me ascend the steps. I watched them for six minutes.

Another man rounded up and greeted me; he said "How you doin'?"

I nodded and said nothing, and proceeded to watch the man sit down in his rent-free occupancy, ask the semi-conscious man, "How you doin'?" and listened to the two banter of their mutual desire to watch a movie. One stepped down off the gazebo and urinated on the sidewalk between two bushes while the other began to comment aloud on the status of his selected movie phone download. Power outlets in the gazebo pillars provided a free source of electricity. The man who urinated on the sidewalk stepped back up onto the gazebo and greeted me. I said, "Hi." He offered me a cigarette; I declined.

The man engaged with the movie download said, "Yeah I came up and he's just standing there—watching us; I thought *it* was you, but-"

"Yeah *it's* like… I'm waking up from a movie and—there's Death," said the other while he pointed at me.

I smiled, shook my head, and looked down at the gazebo's wooden floor.

One said, "Actually, I wanna watch a movie."

The other said, "You wanna watch a movie?"

"Yeah, *it's* called *John Wick*."

The two sat next to each other, disheveled, dirty, uninhibited, and content. They stared at a small rectangular phone screen balanced on a pair of bent knees and chuckled together.

"What's that movie from last night?"

"I think I was watching *Delta Force*-"

A movie trailer played, "Oh you gotta watch this—this—this reminds of Allen."

I descended the steps of the gazebo and marveled at the inconsequential passage of time and every miniature human interaction unheeded; every flicker of consciousness confronted by another at any moment: The microcosmic communities of the downtrodden and destitute, happier than most with their lot. I crossed the main street at the center of the city and observed the slight movement of humankind outside three bars. I walked to the parking lot behind four of the most popular bars in the city and watched the people cavort, hustle, and shout. What have I lost along the way? I ~~feel~~ think nothing ~~for~~ of them, like a sheep among sheep that recognizes *its* own stripeless vacuity. I walked through the backdoor of a sports bar and stood to observe my kind. I blended in among them, though three or four regarded me with uncomfortable grimaces while I slowly turned my head and stood tall among the seated customers: Fat men, pretty girls, bearded men, ugly women, men with ball caps—shoes—pants—*shirts*—I turned and walked out, slowly, while I observed a gauntlet of framed pictures of smiling men dressed in sports jerseys. Everything is too real to me. Humanity is all we *know*; all else is hearsay and make-believe! The people pop. The speech is ridiculous—all of *it*. Warped pronunciations of a garbled crowd replete with self-conscious beings, hunched forward, eyeing me—eyeing them—eyeing each other in turn; I *don't care*. In bars I feel monolithic among trodden-over slates. There is an air of despondency desperate for release in a populated bar.

Saturday, November 7th, 2020

3:39 PM

I've begun to write a biographical book about Charlie.

Sunday, November 8th, 2020

2:54 AM

Father,

I checked my spam folder and was dismayed to find your copious emails and deleted all without reading any of them; I haven't read any of your emails since my last email to you stating that I don't want to communicate.

I inform you of this so that you will direct your energy elsewhere, preferably to yourself. I don't do this to be cruel, vindictive, masochistic, or out of foolishness—idiocy, or malice. I am earnest that I don't want to communicate. I desire growth and strife, without your influence, being the egotist that I am. If the television is a source of guilt for you, or any other trivial matter, I don't care; sell or destroy the television if you're disturbed by a resplendent screen, along with the house, and pursue your dream. Guilt and shame are the conduits for "God," i.e., your internal rhetoric substantiated by exalted virtues, i.e., "Pie in the sky pig-fucking bullshit."

Please don't waste your time sending me more emails; I won't read them. I don't think I betrayed you and will never think so. I don't think you betrayed me and will never think so. As far as the delusion of karma and sin is involved, we're equalized and resolved, at least in my moral judgment.

I hope this email is read by you in the transient morning hours when you're deeply impressionable and is not intoned with condescension by your interpretation. I respect you; otherwise, I wouldn't bother with this farewell composition. This email may be parsed as a suicide message; however, that would be false, and I therefore *also* hope that this email is not the impetus for your decision to commit suicide, though I'm confident that your egotism exceeds my own, and that this statement is one you will scorn on account of my impudence to presuppose your response of inconsolable grief.

Bon voyage!

Your virulent sperm,
- Baethan

Monday, November 9th, 2020

2:26 AM

There is no plot because I have no tribe. I exemplify everything that is wrong with our globalizing society. The alienated man is spiritless on account of his affluence. Even in my condition of financial dependence on the state for unemployment benefits, I am well-fed, and experience luxurious, comfortable living. To choose to write a biography for my ex-marine upstairs neighbor Charlie is my attempt to satisfy my natural inclination for human bonding—yet, I forsake my family. What moral dilemma is this? Is there one?

When I joined the *Peaceorama* commune and lived among that tribe for three months, I lived as an outsider among them, indifferent to the in-group relationships and politics. At that stage in my development, I had been searching... for *knowledge*, for *anything* other than what I knew of my immediate surroundings, and if that knowledge consisted of an acquired blister on my foot sustained from prolonged running in boots, or a dusty paperback book by an obscure author on a cryptic or esoteric topic (that could've been procured from an internet search), I'd be satisfied—for a transient moment often unenjoyed.

There is no right way. I've made my sheet on a carpeted floor; now I sleep on *it*.

Tuesday, November 10th, 2020

2:03 PM

Two nights ago I walked on the sidewalk of one of downtown's main streets leading out of the city. I enjoyed the cool air and vacant lanes, identical apartment complexes to my left, and buildings constructed and maintained since the early 20th century to my right.

"Hey," said a voice from the porch of a dilapidated house. I stopped and reckoned a man seated on a stoop, cigarette in hand. "You remember me?"

I said, "No."

"Really? You don't remember me? I was the only black guy at *The Messy House.*"

"You weren't the only one."

From thereon, the unrecorded conversation became strained; we exchanged inconsequential activity details. He inquired about my employment. I lied: "I'm self-employed; I write."

In response, the man glared at me and proclaimed with caustic haughtiness that the stoop of the porch of the building that he idled on is, "My kingdom—I own *it;* this is mine: my kingdom."

I frowned, bowed my head, and said, "I'll step off your kingdom, then," and retreated the three steps I had previously advanced onto the property to better recognize the man.

"Yeah—you do that please," mumbled the man.

I said nothing more and strode away with a slight hunch of my shoulders. The man had been the single human interaction I experienced in over seventy-two hours.

My *feelings,* I ponder… yes, for this minute-long moment had been significant enough to rouse the rare emotion of dread. We hadn't been two men despite my approach to shake the man's hand (proceeded by sanitation) under the gloom of a nearby street light; we had been two creatures with a different skin color prompting ethnocentric animality. However, the differentiated pigment of our flesh had been merely the symbol for disparate culture. His *surprise* that I *hadn't* distinguished him from the bar crowd as a notable character on account of the color of his skin vexed him and served as the precursor for our rivalrous conversation—for surely, I hadn't recognized his vanity.

4:39 PM

There is an unaccounted relationship that I don't care about, though a future potential biographical psychologist or anthropological historian might regard as pertinent:

The woman from the U.S. Navy Separations whose contact information I acquired after we flew on an airplane together and landed in Arkansas amounted to nothing more than a one-time email exchange:

I wrote, "What is your self-assigned meaning in life?"

The woman wrote, "I don't need a meaning for my life."

I wrote, "Understood."-

And nothing developed.

7:06 PM

I have no respect for humanity, i.e., I have no respect for myself, or anyone I associate with. I will cease my theoretical attempts to expound on anything other than my perspective of an interaction. There is nothing that I think that I *know* that is worthwhile to document, for anything I postulate is an antithesis to my singular, insular *belief* that the limited capabilities of human perception render humanity unable to understand—let alone comprehend reality or existence. Everything is a trifle to me, my own feelings and thoughts most of all, for these "things" are chosen as much as they are natural. I operate on fear of my fellow man due to a fear of myself; however, with nothing to lose, I am courageous in my foolish conduct, i.e., a *pusillanimous clown*—as perceived by any reader of this documentation, for this verdict is my culminated analysis *of* my character and behavior interjected among American society.

Introspection, the one egotistical talent I excel at, has me beholden to my self-assigned slavedom. Self-depreciation is no longer funny to me, a source of amusement, or a pleasure; I have lost my humor in this regard; therefore, I have lost my source of joy. When *I* feel no guilt or shame, absolved from the *ideal* of "Man," I no longer find fault in others. My capacity for tolerance, empathy, and *forgiveness* serves as the fount of my apathy. I'm disgusted by my lack of presence.

Beyond this apartment building, city, county, region, state, country— to the world, I am in reverence of the consumption, of the egoism of *every* individual *betrayed* by a self-imposed delusion of an entity or idea supposedly greater than the "self" which produced the thoughts. I'm awed by the clockwork mechanisms of human cooperation, of the genetic deficiencies and differences which spawn myriad abnormalities deemed unacceptable in a spectrum of degrees by a ruling class—a writhing sphere—a snowglobe of a microcosmic mass, lurching together as a singular consciousness, each being convoluted and mystified by the processes of their own *un*individuated thoughts.

The fear and cowardice of the "mentally ill."

The fear and cowardice of the anxious and depressed.

The fear and cowardice of the afflicted, of the anguished, of the *perturbed* and disfigured, of the *self-consciously inadequate,* of the incapable, the intemperate, the disabled, the dependant and the *saints.*

The fears are justified, *judged,* as we are, as a fragment of the whole, in the ability to contribute to and progress the species.

And what is love:

A smile? A kind affirmation? A tender touch? Providence? Compassion? *Ah*—intimacy *and* understanding…

… Or is love simply forbearance before a sacred self-destruction?

Wednesday, November 11th, 2020

2:53 AM

I broke down into a fit of concentrated sorrow for no more than one minute and fifteen seconds on hearing the first seven piano notes of Debussy's *Clair de Lune* during the viewing of a video titled *A Day in the Life of a Sushi Master.* Tears mixed with mucus dripped from the tip of my nose onto my keyboard.

"I feel no sympathy for this wretch whatsoever," comments a nebulous voice of my conscience. Indeed—I *agree* with this vindictive manifestation of thought; I don't understand why tears sprang from my eyes and why my face contorted into a grimace of woe. The last instance I expressed unadulterated sadness had been two minutes prior to when the man behind *The Messy House* assaulted me. I'm cold again, remorseless, without pain: A man with nothing to lose.

4:00 PM

Art:

An unanswered door when you know the person is home. The oscillations of two black curtains swayed by a steady intermittent breeze. A light rain. City traffic over wet roads. A room illuminated by the light of dusk. An environment devoid of nature—*unrefined* nature. The screen I stare at and the keys I press are a part of the natural world, only profaned and warped to allow me to reflect on everything unacceptable for me to be as determined by what I see and hear.

"How can you use these findings in your own life? In the first place, you can see now that the people you know who are high in grandiose narcissism have a tendency to create their own messes. Yet, given their typically higher grandiosity scores on a daily basis, these messes don't seem to penetrate their inflated sense of self-worth. However, because there are those tiny pings of vulnerability picked up by Edershile and Wright, perhaps there is room for you to help your narcissistic friends or relationship partners learn from the experience. Their failures would be less frequent if they could figure out ways to keep their narcissism in check."[90]

What agenda does this serve? Yes—"help" your friends to stymie their self-love; we *are* all the same, after all. Their "inflated" self-worth is unbearable to be around; their confidence is off-putting and sours the taste of my coffee. Better to beat your friends down to become part of the collective. In a capitalist society, is this information *not* conflicting? I choose to stay informed with what I hate; therefore, *it* becomes real to me. Oh *yes*, psychology is the *cause and effect* of psychosis. Heed the words of your masters—those with ambition, those who hunger, desire… for what ends? To pick people up after kicking them down and decree themselves as saviors? "Help your narcissistic friends," to lower themselves to *your* pitiful level of self-worth—so that they may be *tolerable* to be around. Save them from themselves. Just don't stop to look in the mirror when you step down from the soapbox.

---

[90] Susan Krauss Whitbourne Ph.D. in a psychologytoday.com blog titled *How Narcissists Protect Themselves from Feeling Like Losers.*

8:26 PM

The "deadness" I feel is a moment in time worthy of documentation. Admittance of these feelings renders me meretricious in my decrees, for only nullification would befall humanity if a society were to adopt my paradigms of thought.

I stand beside my two open apartment windows at the podium balanced on the sill and type at mid-chest level. The sixty-six-degree warmth of this November night is an anomaly, projected to be the last before a long stretch of upcoming cold and snow. Water from consistent daily rainfall depletes from the gutters of the four-story structure I stand in and from the conjoined library and bank across the alley-street, opposite of my vantage point. The pavement and sidewalk below are slick and spotted with curbside puddles. A twenty-foot-high 19th-century double-bulbed street light illuminates a leftmost segment of the constrained nocturnal panorama with a swath of diluted saffron light. The security guard who whistles throughout his daily patrol enters the scene. The content of his thoughts is conformed to the whistle and his hunched forward amble. Sunglasses on, despite the downtown gloom, I ponder his lack of thoughts to the point where I fantasize thoughts that he may experience. My imagination is limited in this regard, and I can only fathom the whistle and the walk. He is listless tonight, with a half-hearted tune welt in his throat. A hum of traffic and droplets of rain muffle and eventually drown the man's primordial expression. How does he suffer? What haunts him? I know he thinks and feels as I do, though I am incapable of perceiving him as a fully-fleshed being with a tangible existence beyond the mundane snippets of his daily whistle and walk. Much like if he were to gaze up at me through the corner of his sunglasses and view my partial silhouette illuminated by the glow of a small rectangular laptop screen through the skewed horizontal blinds strewn down over my open windows, he would fathom nothing but a standing man, engrossed with *something,* but the man wouldn't know what; though we are the same in being engrossed with ourselves. The man's ephemeral whistle, lost to the wind, is an art, equivalent to my words which immortalize his mortal breath for as long we mortals continue to whistle and write of others whistling.

Thursday, November 12th, 2020

3:05 AM

I gaze down at my naked body and see the pulse of my heart behind my concave rib cage. My flesh is hairless except for a sparse swath of brown hair along my forearms, two bushy patches of armpit hair, and an unkempt bush of pubic hair. I pulled my socks off my feet and acknowledged the transfer of microscopic life from the fabric to my fingertips—useless knowledge *behooved* to me, knowledge that had been unknown 500 years ago. How pleasant human existence must've been, to not know of such things.

I'm disgusted by my countertop. I belong with the microcosmic biome of entities born to die in a four-digit decimal fraction of the average human life. My consciousness is fit for a pathogen.

In the world of the microscopic, I conceptualize humanity, confined to an enormous rock in space *(enormous* only by our relative size) as relatable to the image in which a human child may squat low in a Brazilian jungle to observe a tumultuous ant colony. A silly spiritual science fiction trope: The universe in a vacuum, i.e., fractals; however, the humor fleets if one is to imagine that there is no observer of humanity—the human "soul," except for ourselves. Nothing greater. We *are* omniscient. Every insight into deeper understanding is a manufactured illusion: a simulacrum to gratify our desires which only amplify with each blind vacillation towards our sacred "progress."

3:36 PM

I encountered a man I once knew when I was twenty-three-years-old at the gym last night: 5'6, stocky, strong and overweight, crestfallen. I thought I recognized him, and that he recognized me; however, I couldn't be sure due to our face masks. Regardless, I initialized my recorder and approached him between his bench press set. The man wore a backward *Punisher*-themed ball cap and a *Pokemon*-themed sleeveless shirt-

No—I had recorded the conversation, all thirty-one minutes of *it*, though I detest the notion—the metanonfictional naturalistic magazine pseudo-reporting half-ass storytelling literature negation that this is. People age disgracefully. The man's lack of confidence and negligence to meet my gaze for thirteen consecutive minutes while he answered my philosophical queries spoke volumes of his undeveloped character. The man bemoaned his suffering of consistent betrayal throughout life; *it* was then that I confirmed who he was: Justin. He now raises a child as a divorced father, owns a dog, works at a hospital as a social worker, stated that he has no idea what his meaning in life is, and feels as though he lives in someone else's shadow.

I'm embarrassed, which denotes shame, to document this encounter. Justin had been my roommate and co-worker who struggled to overcome feelings for his (newly separated) ex-girlfriend that I copulated with one day after the termination of their romance. I revealed my identity with a disclaimer: "I am a man who has betrayed you."

"Baethan?" he spoke with a delighted inflection.

"Yes."

"You didn't betray me-" he began to rationalize my immoral behavior. Justin knew who I was from my admittance of betrayal and proceeded to *negate* my betrayal. I still remember that moment in time: The malnourished 100 lb woman and I laid together on a living room sofa post-coitus. The woman made a move to dress and conceal our sexual relations on hearing the front door open a room away, though I merely held up a hand for her to refrain, to which she acquiesced with a devious smirk. The theatrics were Shakesperian and devoid of violence, e.g., *"Really—so soon?"* Justin had shouted while shielding his eyes with a forearm.

Preposterous people; Justin shook my hand after five years and I immediately applied sanitizer from a nearby dispenser while he relayed to me his obsession with anime, in particular, *My Hero Academia.*

I informed Justin that I have no interest in anime, I'm unemployed, spend all my time reading, writing, and that my primary selection of video media is human brutality. I continued and said that I treated him like garbage, that I treated people like garbage, and *continue* to treat people like garbage, and have no friends by choice. Justin thought nothing of what I said and incredulously restated that I have no friends—*shocked*, I presume, followed by gossip of what every one of our once mutual friends is now doing, which had been limited to the topic of children and employment.

I've omitted the majority of our dialogue consisting of Justin's explanation of *My Hero Academia's* plot. Justin said, "All right man—well now that I know you're here I'll stop by more often—if you're here." In reflection, I'm amazed by the immodesty of Justin's forgiveness. He spoke highly of me, and praised my ability to "make him and his friends feel better," i.e., I had listened to adolescent complaints while preoccupied with dishwashing and offered a few sentences of wisdom-tinged aphorisms.

I said, "Take care."

8:20 PM

All media is an escape for feckless degenerates. Art is the foundation of culture. Art is media. There is a causal increase of decadence as a society proliferates culture and subsequent enjoyment. Each individual produces for the sake of recognition, profit, or selfish personal fulfillment. Others partake in the product. Apes. Little children.

What do I propose as an alternative? Unending labor and mechanical consumption? Art *is* labor. Don't you understand? This is the unalterable human condition. Don't you desire to retch on venturing to read this; think of what you do—with your eyes—your brain. Your *essence*. Think of what *I* do to achieve this. What state of mind I must be in at the instant of producing this suggestive sentence...

The man who raps his fingers on a tabletop or pats the side of his pant leg while humming a six-tone rhythmic tune seeks only to escape from the unendurable presence of existence without sensation. I close my eyes and lay on a floor: I *sense* an infinitesimal milieu of reality that is the totality of what *I am* in the moment. This is what we call "culture," for I *am* my environment experienced through flesh.

This is ridiculous.

A dignified king, bedazzled in red and gold regalia, resplendent scepter in hand, gazed down at his court jester situated at the center of a vacant yellow-carpeted throne room upheld with a dozen six-foot-diameter white-washed granite pillars, narrowed his eyes, grinned, and spoke with a condescending inflection: "This is art. You're a character nobody cares about because there is no drama or human denotation ascribed to your formless depiction. You are but an adjective, and that's all you'll ever be."

A foreign Arabian emissary of debatable appearance stepped out from behind one of the twelve pillars (nobody remembers which) and assassinated the jester with a polished 4 lb sphere of lead jettisoned from a sling, center of the forehead. Intense two-second applause of over five-hundred pairs of hands blared from outside the chamber on the moment of the jester's collapse and abruptly terminated, whereby the jester fell straight down in an undeviating vertical descent and crumpled into a heap of furled sepia detritus on the floor. That's right; he was not a human after all—no need to feel anything for him; he had been merely a prop for the king's amusement, though the king didn't smile or frown; he only sat, turned his smug visage to the reader, and said, "This fool has quite the absurd imagination, doesn't he?"

Laughter: *Oh!—ho—ho—*ho—ho—ho—now, c'mon; you're *really* going to publish this?

11:14 PM

I typed in my browser: "Dear Lord and master Google, how do I distract myself from the fact that I exist," and had been provided a link to a webpage with a twenty-minute video documentary of earth viewed from space.

Thank you, my lord and master.

Now, a walk to the gym, to perform arbitrary animalistic energy expenditure and avoid my reflection in the wall mirrors.

"Man shouldn't be able to see his own face—there's nothing more sinister. Nature gave him the gift of not being able to see *it*, and of not being able to stare into his own eyes.

"Only in the water of rivers and ponds could he look at his face. And the very posture he had to assume was symbolic. He had to bend over, stoop down, to commit the ignominy of beholding himself.

"The inventor of the mirror poisoned the human heart."

- Fernando Pessoa's The Book of Disquiet

Friday, November 13th, 2020

3:47 PM

I pity anyone who reads my journals for pleasure. I'm your toxic friend that you pity and hate to make yourself feel better, you fool. Perhaps you don't pity or hate me; I'm presumptuous with myself. Life is strange. I try to not be dour—in public, for the *comfort* of others; in fact, I'm the most confident man I reckon on most occasions: Genuine, intrinsic confidence, drawn from my infinite reserves of extrinsic nothingness, i.e., I'm a man with nothing to lose. I initiate the majority of my social interactions despite having nothing to say. My unfaltering gaze pierces into the eyes of others, yet I exhibit humility and shame to temper the hateful and wrathful reactions of one who may be confronted with my otherwise impudent presence. My stride is long and my head is always high. I *anticipate* hate, am preemptive in my reticence, and relentless with my purposeful assertions. These delusions are my own; nobody cares, in truth: One of 7.8 billion, though even if I were confined to a small, isolated hamlet circa 100 AD... No, I *can't* say I'd think and feel the same, for I'd be an entirely different product of my culture and genetics. However, if my present character were to exist in such a time and place, I'd be flayed and burned alive.

7:31 PM

Friday night. I teeter between enforced isolation from a moral bent, and a visit to the parking lot behind *The Messy House* after a gym session to appease my vanity.

9:52 PM

No, there is nothing to validate. I am my own man. A quiet night.

Saturday, November 14th, 2020

1:11 AM

I repulsed my first fan via email correspondence by telling her that she has low self-esteem for appreciating my second book (Year Two)—which is, in essence, a felt kindred association or identification with *me*, i.e., a validation. Fans are nothing to me. Fame and recognition are worthless. Those who create and sell themselves with an ardent fervor disgust me. What do they create other than opinions guised in entertainment: The world according to *them*—an interpretation of human affairs, a wish for a utopia, dystopia, or something in-between. A hero. A villain. A woman and a man. An ideology encapsulated in an epic romance. A two-panel pencil-drawn comic sketch with a one-word blurb to express the ineffable cycles of love and power, or one's perception of the taste of soured milk.

Isn't *it* all funny though—the great artists of every era; I don't need to name them; everyone has one they admire, if not themselves—an expression they *"get"*—unique! Of course, unique to them! Though this perceived uniqueness is a uniform modicum fragment of a shattered pane glass church window—ah, there *it* is, that *art*.

A prime example of such an outcry of which one has *no choice* to acknowledge unless one is deaf, is the song *Behind Blue Eyes (1971)*, by The Who—and every other iteration. The song is vulgar, distasteful, and pathetic, and *because* of the medium, the despicable dissonance ripples through the air into our respective ear canals, and we—as a unified species able to comprehend and understand the primordial expression of song, *empathize* with the gratuitous *self-pity*.

"Why do you publish your work if you claim to not care about fame or recognition?" said an ennobled critic.

To entice fools, of course!

"This guy is the epitome of 'douchebag'; his work will never sell; anyone can see through his charade. There is no content, only self-loathing and disdain for his readers," said the voice of humanity. Lo-

Guilt? Shame? *It* is only human to choose.

It truly is believable how much of an asshole I am… to me—for I will reread this if I am to survive the year, which is an outcome with a high probability.

Trump Has Tea With Biden

I need you as much as you need me;
Without you I simply wouldn't be.
You complete me—star of the show–
The name of this poem expresses more than the prose,
So why even bother? Breaking sentences into stanzas
Isn't a talent at all.

4:08 AM

"Metaphysics has always struck me as a prolonged form of latent insanity. If we knew the truth, we'd see *it*; everything else is systems and approximations. The inscrutability of the universe is quite enough to

think about; to want to actually understand *it* is to be less than human, since to be human is to realize *it* can't be understood."

- *Fernando Pessoa's The Book of Disquiet*

I laid on my floor, bound from chest to ankle in a black sheet, and stared at the aforementioned quotation. The words pilfered me. We are carbon copies of each other. Before genetics and psychology crystallized as a science concurrent with our globalized reckoning, the human mind existed in the same form. Pre-hominid man would no doubt regard the stars and his own sickly flesh in the same manner. My heart burns with a hurt. My refrigeration begins to whir; my passion yields on account of *it*—what I am, the illumination of my kitchen lights, the barrenness of my influence and scope. Everything this man who once lived is, is me. I think also, of Barbellion's *Journal of a Disappointed Man*. The crazed philosophers: Rene Descartes', for instance, and his nonsense of, *"I think; therefore I am,"* is a pithy/paltry remark, nothing more or less; *it* is what never needed to be stated.

Only in these rare moments am I comfortable with sadness.

"-less than human-"

5:51 PM

If anything inflames me with the notion of love, *it* is my faults. And love, of course, being devoid of wisdom and reason, makes for a surly character in my regard.

6:08 PM

Three apartments down my hallway, an obnoxious toy dog yips, barks, and whines each instance the owner departs for the total duration of her absence. The owner had departed for no more than twenty seconds when the dog began the pitiful histrionics of a beast over-pampered and indulged; therefore, I exited my apartment, walked barefoot down the hall, and stood in front of the door from which the racket resounded. Pop music played from a stereo; thus, I knew the owner would return soon. I waited, and to my expectation, the stranger appeared at the opposite end of the hall, saw me before I saw her, and shouted, *"Hello!"* with a beautiful smile revealed between her lips. The early-twenties African-American woman hastened towards me with a great bobbing hairdo of braided locks and a shopping tote bag slung around her right arm.

I looked to my right, my body still directed towards her apartment door, and said, "Hi."

"So sorry!" the woman began: an immediate admission of guilt. "That's my dog—she does that sometimes. So sorry about that."

Indifferent to her amiable deference, which I knew to be staged, I said, "Do you realize that she does this for prolonged periods each time you depart?"

"Yeah—I'm sorry about that; I'll work on *it*. Are you from upstairs?" She had passed me and reached down for her door handle, though her eyes remained fixed on mine.

I said, "No."

"… So sorry about that. She barks—she, so sorry." The light had been sapped from the woman's vibrant face, at least in my perspective of her, for who am I but a barefoot man—inducer of anxiety, invoker of self-consciousness, arbiter of neighborly respect? I said nothing and turned away the moment the woman opened her door.

7:23 PM

I read on my windowsill podium and heard a man outside my window on the street below speak to a woman with an optimistic, uncertain inflection: "That's good though—right?" I don't know the context of the woman's speech; however, I at once knew the content of the man's immediate character: A whimpering, guided mule.

Governor Cuomo of New York has issued all gyms and bars to be closed by 10 PM to stymie the contagion of Covid-19.

Off I go.

Sunday, November 15th, 2020

12:11 AM

Feeling exalted from endorphins and elevated testosterone after a gym session, I decided to visit *The Messy House* a half-hour before closure at the risk of infection; thereby, I returned to my apartment, changed the batteries in my recorder, tucked the recorder into my *inner* jacket pocket, deposited my valuables, and tucked ten one-dollar bills and my debit card into separate front pant pockets (pickpocket precautions).

The following conversations I had with two men are a masterpiece; both exemplify the fecklessness of the modern lowlife American man (with myself as the crux), of the delusions we experience, and the fickleness of morality.

I entered the bar through the front door. Immediately, the slovenly, obese owner, seated at the booth near the store-front window with three other patrons, shook his head, gestured for me to leave, and said:

Saturday Night

"We're over limit! We're over limit! We're closed—ten o'clock—we're closed," yelled the bar owner.

I checked my watch and said, *"It's* nine-thirty."

A generic hip-hop love song featuring a man singing about the feeling of titillation he experiences on behalf of a woman blared from the jukebox. I stepped further into the establishment and ignored the owner's commands. Despite the chagrin of the jabbering patrons seated at the booth who attempted to enforce the owner's edict, I ignored all, except for the follow-up of the owner who had remained seated and docile: "You can't be walkin' around!" I walked along the bar behind the estimated dozen patrons in search of a vacant seat. One woman stood from a stool near the front entry and exited out the back door. I approached the seat, and a short middle-aged Caucasian man with a thin mustache, oval glasses, and a brown beanie hat contoured around his head—dressed in a loose-fitted nondescript hoodie with jeans, turned to me from the stool to my right, and said, "How are ya?"

"Hello. I'm well. You?"

"Not bad. Gaiter," said the man, and he outstretched a hand for me to shake.

"My name is Baethan."

"Baethan! I *love* that name. Are you from around here or?"

"I'm a denizen of the world."

"I agree to that. You're a good dude. I can tell by yo—you're a *well-dressed* gentleman."

I shook my head and said, "That doesn't mean anything; that's all an image."

"Are you English?... I can't hear—hold on."

"I didn't say anything."

"Oh—okay. I'm the kind've guy who just wants to party and have no problems with anybody—I'm a cool dude." Gaiter pointed to the vacant stool to his left and shouted, "I *believe* you can sit here!—if somebody needs you to move—*I'll* move."

I said, "All right," and seated myself, which had the immediate effect of silencing the owner, who had persisted in complaining—but not *asserting,* on my previous condition of standing.

"Julie will be right back and I'll move for her all right? Julie is cool shit."

"You don't need to move for me—that's all right; I appreciate *it* though."

"*It*'s a general respect level."

"Thank you."

"If I had more cash on me I'd buy you a drink but..."

"That's all right. I'll buy *you* a drink for being so friendly to me."

Gaiter stated as a question with an upward inflection, "I'll take a shot."

"A shot of what?"

"*Jack Daniel's Tennessee Fire! It*'s smoother than *Fireball.* Julie!-" Gaiter addressed a woman who I recognized from the night of my first assault: A woman who had participated with the background crowd of disparagers and condemners. "-he needed a place to sit to get a drink quick; will you stand there for a minute?" I reckoned the woman; she eyed me with a frown and nodded. Gaiter said, "All right," returned his attention to me, and announced, "I like that we're still upstanding citizens."

I cocked my head and said, "Nah."

"At least people who attempt to be." Gaiter laughed a perfect copy of the final installment of the consecutive ululations of the mid-90s cartoon character *Woody Wood Pecker.* The song, *Next Contestant,* by Nickelback, began to play from the jukebox. "I'm a mix of a million different-"

I interrupted Gaiter, withdrew my debit card, and hailed the bartender: "Hey Joe, can I get a shot of *Jack Daniel's Tennessee?*"

"Fire," Gaiter added.

I affirmed, "Fire."

Joe, an obese, Caucasian, stout, disheveled, charismatic, and hopelessly drunk man with pallid eyes peering out from half-closed eyelids said, "Uhh... Yeah *it*'s, only thing is bud—*it*'s a fifteen-dollar minimum for a debit card."

I said, "Oh—okay," and reached into my pocket for the wad of furled one-dollar bills. "How much is the shot?"

"Uh—five and a quarter."

A Caucasian man in his late twenties with a sweep of brown hair and an astute face sat down on the newly vacant stool to my left and said, "Do I know you, man?"

I said, "I don't know."

"Where are you from?"

Flummoxed, I said, "I'm a d—a... a denizen of the world."

"Oh yeah?"

"Yes."

"All right. I'll go with *it*... *It's* Dylan though—nice to meet ya."

We shook hands; I said, "You too."

"Where you from—you have an accent—a little bit."

"I'm a denizen of the world. Why do people want to know where people are from?"

"Everybody asks me that—so listen: I traveled, as a job—right? I traveled across the U.S. Now, I go to different parts of the U.S.—I always get asked that myself. I'm young and just started going to bars—right? But, no matter where I am in the U.S.—if I stop at a gas station or somethin'—everybody's like 'You got a different accent—where ya from?' Now when I meet somebody at a bar I wanna know where they're from—ya know?"

"I see... I just see us all as humans. We all suffer the same."

The man nodded, leaned on the counter, assumed an unsettled expression, and said, "We do." *Candy Paint*, by Post Malone, began on the jukebox while the owner yelled at a man to refrain from slamming a bottle of beer on the countertop. An old woman to the right of Gaiter played coy with me. She outstretched her hand behind Gaiter's back and I accepted the tips of her fingers with my gloved hand.

Gaiter said, "This is my aunt Peanut: Mama to everybody."

I smiled at Peanut and restated, "Mama to everybody."

Gaiter talked over Peanut's inaudible drawl: "She goes by Mama. She is my ex-wife's aunt, and she chose me over her cuz my ex-wife... I call that loyalty if she comes to me instead of her own family. Then again my ex-wife was nothing but rude to her and all I did was *call* her on *it*. She's a good woman—she really needs to be respected—and I *will* fuck somebody up for disrespecting her. My—my aunt... See I have all kinds of roots: I have Russian; I have German; I have Italian... I have *all* kinds of roots... Unfortunately, I got a felony, so I can't travel country to country, but my goal was to hit—I wanted to see Russia. I wanted to see *England*. I wanted to see Europe! But I fucked *it* up, by hitting somebody wrong. Because I was defending my sister."

I said, "You didn't hit them the right way?"

"I put him in the hospital for six months."

"Why?"

"Because he hit my sister, and my sister got knocked out, so... Because your blood family, is the most important thing to you."

"I disagree."

"Well, to *me*. I will say my sister—blood family. My father passed away in '07. 2007. I will say—I do have people who are not blood family who are closer than some of my blood family, but when *it* comes to my sister—she's my closest. My sister is my closest; she's transgender or whatever she wants to be—I don't care. I said, 'You could paint yourself purple and have eleven penises and I'd be okay with *it*.' I said 'I grew up protecting you as my younger sister, and I'm okay with what I did; I ruined a dream but I made sure you were okay with what I did.' Now I'm gonna take my shot! Thank you."

"You're welcome."

"You sound like one helluva guy," Gaiter praised me, for, I presume, how little I spoke. "No chaser! You ever tried *Jack Daniel's Fire?*"

"No."

"You like whiskey?"

"No."

"Are you a vodka drinker?"

"When I do drink *it*'s seldom, and *it*'s red wine."

Gaiter muttered, "Are you here on a mission?"

"… Yes."

"*It*'s not me, is *it?*"

"No."

"Okay. Would you like any help because I'm a settled person around here and I know everybody."

"No, I'm all right; I appreciate the offer."

"Then I know nothing-"

"Neither do I."

"-you're a shadow. You're a shadow. If I saw you on the street, you know what I'd say?"

I chuckled and said, "What would you say?"

"Nothing. I wouldn't even look in your direction, because a mission… is personal."

The song *Enemies,* by Post Malone resonated. I said, "If you saw me on the street, you wouldn't know that I'm on a mission, so I think that you would still look at me."

Gaiter's demeanor shifted to a defensive; he said, "Would you *like* me to be cool with you? Some people say 'I'm on a mission' but talk to me anyway, and some people say, 'Oh—let me blend in'—I don't know how *it* is; I'm tryin' to feel the situation. I could say 'hi' if you wanted me to."

Comprehending the miscommunication, I said, "We've already progressed to a point where we're having a conversation."

"I think you're from Russia."

"I'll let you think as you will."

"I have a lot of respect for Russia. That country has their shit together more than the U.S. Sorry if I'm offensive at any point; I am extremely intoxicated."

"You're not offensive."

"I really think that if Putin got a hold of the U.S., we'd be an *amazing* country! Cuz Russia has their rules… and then they have their *bullshit*… The U.S.?—is a mess. Every time we think we *find* a good president, *it* goes *to shit*. I don't know what you're feeling is on race—but I am racist. I believe that 'N' word—sorry I'm not trying to be offensive; I'm not trying to be disrespectful-"

"You're not."

Gaiter said, "-As you can tell I'm a very respectful person. I-"

"Well, that's not so if you're racist."

"-I believe that dirty 'N' word—I'm not racist towards people of color though. Nigger could be any color: *It's* ignorance. If you're ignorant, and piggish, and abuse women, I have a problem with you. My philosophy is: women are our most precious natural resource, and we should treat them that way."

The bartender, Joe, screamed over the music, "Everybody's got five minutes to drink!"

Gaiter continued, "I understand that there are some women out there that need to be corrected, but not physically. If they try to physically kill you with a weapon, you have the right to restrain them but not injure them."

I said, "What is your self-assigned meaning in life if that's your philosophy?"

"What is my what?"

The owner, Bob, had sauntered behind the bar counter. Seated on a wooden stool, he clapped his hands twice, glared at me, and said "Hey my friend! Listen! You're not drinking—you can't be in here!"

I quipped, "I bought him (Gaiter) a shot."

"I don't care what you're doing."

"I'll take a cabernet."

"You can't be in here; you're not drinking."

"I'll take a cabernet."

"*It* doesn't matter—no—*it* doesn't—we're closed."

I checked my watch, observed a digital **9:46 PM,** and said, "You close at ten. I'll take a cabernet please."

Bob talked to the floor: "No—you're not taking anything we're not dri—serving."

Dylan spoke over my left shoulder, "They—they already called last call, buddy—I'm sorry."

Gaiter murmured into my right ear, "That's the owner."

I acknowledged Gaiter while looking at Bob and said, "Ah, so I bought you a shot, and now I'm getting kicked out for not drinking."

Gaiter mustered a straightened posture and yelled "He bought my shot! And he had—I think-" he turned to me, "Did you have a beer?"

Bob said, "No—he didn't have a beer. Pay attention."

Gaiter said "Fuck... Do you know of anyone who serves alcohol after ten?" and chortled.

Lean On Me, by Bill Withers, played at a tolerable volume. I ignored Bob and said, "Not anymore. But—my question was, what is your self-assigned meaning in life if that's your philosophy?"

Gaiter's mien became stern; he stared back at me, eight inches from my unmasked face, and said, "Oh my meaning in life? To be the best person I possibly can... Love who deserves *it;* I will never hate; hate, hate is against me. Satan is my God by the way."

"You're a pagan?"

"No, I'm Satanic. Just because I've been hurt so much in life—he's the only one who's answered. My purpose, is to be the best, hardest working person in this life that I possibly can, and when I can't work, when I'm bedridden—I don't wanna be bed—I don't *wanna* be bedridden; I wanna be killed—if I'm not mobile, and I'm in a wheelchair, I want to die before I'm in that wheelchair. My purpose, is to make this world a better place... not politically; I'm a landscaper; I'm a property maintenance guy; I'm there to make sure people's houses are nice. If their basement—if their hot water tank explodes, I go and fix *it* at two o'clock in the morning."

"That's Paganistic, to be a landscaper—part of the earth."

"I believe in Satan."

"What distinguishes you from being Paganistic or Satanic?"

"... When I'm angry—which is most of the time, because I suffer from schizophrenia, post-traumatic stress syndrome, and bi-polar... I'm normally, a very angry—very mean person. I use alcohol so I can socialize, because I—I—really beg for sociali—socialization, I just have a huge wall up cuz I'm so scared with the voices in my head-"

I said, "What do you think that I'm thinking about you right now?"

"I'm not sure that I'd really like to know… I *hope,* that you like me cuz I'm pretty sure you're Russian, and you're a good dude."

"Well, I only ask because I would like to help you dispel any notion that you may have of any malevolent voices that you project onto me."

"I don't project those onto people—I keep them in my head; just because I'm crazy doesn't mean somebody else needs to be. Doesn't matter what stupid shit pops in my head; I need to hold an intelligent conversation. There might be a million retarded things in my head, doesn't mean they need to leave my mouth."

"The voices are guilt and shame."

"… And I've done a lot of really bad shit that I just won't talk about, because of my affiliation, which I will not talk about. I'm not allowed to. As far as anybody knows, I'm a nobody; I'm a barfly; I'm a friend. All I ever want, is friendship. From females right now I've been hurt so fucking bad… I don't even want a relationship—and yes—I'm bisexual—I go for men and women. I don't even want to have sexual relations with anyone. I've let myself be so beat up. I'm working on me right now. I'm sixty hours a week, I'm working 120 to 160 hours a week. I'm home enough to sleep. I asked my boss 'Am I allowed to go out and socialize tonight?' He said 'You sure you're gonna be okay and not get arrested?' Cuz I have a criminal mind… I was cursed, with a criminal *genius* mind; I don't want to be a bad person."

The music had stopped. Bob and Joe shouted for the patrons of the bar to vacate: *"C'mon drink up! Time to go—drink up! Stop talking and drink."*

Gaiter snapped his head towards Bob, said, "I will," didn't drink, and said to me, "I want to be a good person… Bob's a slob. I'm drunk. But I will say, I like you Baethan; my real name is Moor… If you were sent here to take me—if you were sent here to take me out, I don't know what I did but, *it*'ll happen. If not, we had a good night. But I'm sure-"

Bob yelled at Moor, "Hey! I told you to drink—you gotta get outta here. I'm not gettin' a $15,000 fine because you wanna *talk!*"

Moor's cheery voice rang out over the rabble of dispersing patrons, "We'll talk outside then, somewhere!"

I stood, walked towards the back door, eager to oblige Bob's command, and said over my shoulder, "I'll be out back."

3:45 PM

A distant ambulance siren. The release of steam from the top of a coffee maker. The soft reverb of a monotonous ambient piano rhythm. The drip of filtered water into a reservoir. Some moments in time are worthy of wonder when inspected. No, *all* moments, only this one had been more real to me than most.

4:30 PM

[Saturday Night continued]:

I exited the back door of *The Messy House* and encountered Joe, the dissipated bartender, and the younger patron who had been seated to my left, Dylan. Both idled around the parked white car of the owner. I stopped and stood nearby, forming a trident of bodies with six-feet of space between us. An old man encroached from my rear and approached the back door of the bar.

Joe said to the old man, *"It's* all closed up buddy."

The old man had the door halfway open; he turned his head to Joe and said, "Is *it?*"

"Yeah man *it's*—uh—you didn't hear about the new law?"

"What?"

"All bars and restaurants are closed at ten."

"I see people in there," muttered the old man, and he slipped inside.

Dylan shouted, "Hey bud you can't go in there!-" He spoke to a door. "-they just closed... Fuck. People really don't give a fuck do they?"

I said, "Well, I did the same thing; there's not much enforcement in there."

"They need to hire a bartender—I, fuck me..."

"A bouncer?"

"A bouncer—you're right."

"I suggested the same thing, to uh, Desirea."

Dylan said, "She's no longer with the company."

"She quit?"

"She had some stuff going on; she left. I don't know if *it* was true or not so I can't say anything. Maybe she just quit and wanted..." Dylan droned with a drawl and addressed Joe, "You Probably know more than I do."

Joe said, "She quit."

"She quit—quit?" Dylan reiterated.

"Yeah."

"She told the bar owner something else."

687

"She did—no—she did have some personal stuff going on, but, she also quit."

"Did she lie a little bit about the personal stuff?"

Joe gazed around the pavement at his feet, teetered back and forth, and without forethought, said, "A little bit."

The two went silent except for a few snorts and single-syllable coughs for five seconds. I said to Dylan, "What is your self-assigned meaning in life?"

Dylan gaped at me and entered a mode of immediate consternation. Moor, the patron who had been seated to my right, thrust the back door open, stumbled off the stoop onto the pavement—forming a quadrant of bodies, and said, "Okay—I've had a little *too* much to drink-" Joe burped. "-but I'm okay; I feel good... Anybody else smoke cigarettes?"

I said, "I don't, but thank you though."

Dylan accepted a cigarette from a pack that Moor had withdrawn from his front hoodie pocket and said, "I'll smoke one just to pass the time with ya."

Moor exclaimed "All-*righty* then! That's cool. *It* don't matter to me if you inhale or not—*it*'s a *bad* habit. I'm trying to quit that too, but when I drink, *it* goes well." Three women from within the bar whooped and hollered, followed by an uncanny hush.

Dylan said to me, "I don't feel like I'm in the right place—so uh... You know somebody was listening-"

Moor pointed at me and said, "Good man!"

"-and uh, obviously you're here for that reason, but... I know a lot of things-"

"I will just ask," Moor interjected again, "I haven't done anything wrong by anybody tonight, right?"

I said, "Not by me."

Moor said, "Thank you," and extended his hand for me to shake; I accepted. "I'm gonna head myself over to my friend's house where I can smoke some pot and then go home and go to bed. *It* was *nice* meeting you, sir."

I lied and said, "*It* was nice to meet you as well."

"I like you and I hope I see more of you; maybe next time I come by I'll buy us *both* a drink—but we'll go to a—I *do* dress up nice; I have a blazer and a suit and everything. There's a place over there—at the [Motel Name], called [Bar Name]; *it*'s a really classy bar. They have *really* good wine—and I'll have a glass of wine with you, instead of whiskey or beer. I'm not trying to interrupt—I just figured I'd finish our conversation by saying you're a wonderful person... I hope you find what you're looking for... Good day-"

I frowned and said, "Thank you."

"-and good evening."

"Take care."

"Yes sir."

Dylan said, "Oh he's a smart fuckin' man. I'll give him that."

From behind me, Moor said, "Me or him?"

Dylan lit his cigarette, nodded his head at me, and said, "That guy right there."

Moor said, "A man of few words, is the man you wanna be around."

Two minutes elapsed while I stood in expectancy of Dylan's answer to my query. Patrons emerged from the bar and complained of each other's activities, of missing phones, and of roommates. Dylan puttered around near me, poised, yet tentative. We exchanged a mutual nod without looking at each other and he signaled me to follow him to the mouth of a narrow alleyway between part of the structure where *The Messy House* is located and an insurance agency. I acquiesced. Dylan turned to me beneath the bright incandescence of a small circular bulb protruding from a brick wall and said, "Why are you here?"

I said, "I'm in search of social interaction, and answers—I had originally come for... potential copulation with a woman, but then I entered, and conversation happened."

Dylan became tense and said, "Do you want to talk to me or do you not want to talk to me?"

"I do."

"Okay, did you come here *for* me, or not?"

Stoic, I said, "No-"

"No?"

"-that's absurd."

"Absurd—ah, all right."

I grinned and said, "That's some mystical thinking."

"... I guess you can find *it* that way."

"Or spiritual—however way you want to... see *it*."

Dylan alternated weight between his feet and said, "I get that on a different level... What di—what did you wanna talk about though?"

"Your self-assigned meaning in life."

"That's right... Mm—doing good. I uh... I'm smart ya know, like... I'm doing good in life; I got a job that I tried to get out of high school, like at… I just still feel like I'm different and that I'm not meant to be doing what I do, and uh, I want to do something else, and, if you're the person, I'm *thinking* you are…"

"Who do you think I am?"

"Like—I can't tell you that-"

"Why not?"

"… I'll keep my mouth shut but, if you are who you think—you already know if, you're here… But uh…"

"I don't know what you think I am," I said sternly, unamused.

Fifteen seconds elapsed. Dylan's eyes wandered; he slouched slightly and puffed on chain-drags of his cigarette. I stood statuesque and watched him: "… I—I spoke over the phone, not to anybody in particular—but, uh… I didn't put in a resume or anything but I knew obviously somebody was listening… over the phone, and uh… I don't know what *it* is but, I think I got the potential to help in whatever. I got the mindset for *it*. I'm—I'll be honest with you man—I'm drunk as hell right now, but… wanted a little bit, came over here to drink-"

I said, "Perhaps I can give you some clarity of thought if you tell me exactly what you're thinking that I am."

Dylan murmured, "… Are you, with the government? On the uh… Are you with the government?—I don't want to say *it* loud because there's people out here listening, but… if so, then, that's who I was trying to get a hold of… not the FBI in general but uh… I don't—I don't think you're FBI but… You know—I thought if you knew that you'd just be upfront about *it* and wouldn't ask questions, so… I… don't think you're with the FBI, but I think you're with somebody else and, that's something I'd like to be a part of, because I talked about *it* obviously; but nobody was listening—*it*'s not my phone, and that's the only reason I think you're here." I looked at Dylan's wracked countenance with suppressed compassion. "… And if you can answer that question with a yes or a no, that's all I want."

"No."

"No? Then why?" Dylan pleaded.

"Why am I here?"

On the inverse questioning, Dylan's resolve bolstered and he asserted a bold, "Yeah!"

"I already told you."

"To find out my interest or yours?"

"Your self-assigned meaning in life."

"Mine specifically, out of this entire group of people in the bar?"

"No. That's just how *it* happened."

Dylan grimaced, dragged on his cigarette, and affirmed in a deeper, heroic tone, "Set things right, no matter what I got to do—how *wrong it* is, to do *it*—how wrong *it* may seem to the public eye... Yeah... Help humanity as a whole, so *it* can be better in the long run for everybody... but willing to do what may be considered the wrong thing to do, to the public, ya know—*it*'s confusing-" Dylan back stepped away from me and went limp in his upper-body; he stared at the pavement and slurred, "I'm sorry; I don't know what's wrong with me—yeah."

Unempathetic, I said, "Did you think I was a hitman? You wanted to be in on that charade?"

"I didn't think that necessarily; I mean there's a lot of contractors out there; a lot of 'em don't have to do that type of thing ya know? A lot of 'em just sit around, they wait for *it;* they go on a couple things and, they don't ever have to worry about anything... Some of 'em, they're experienced and they know what they're doing, and they have had to pull the trigger a couple of times, but..."

"So what you're saying is that you have the grit, to kill. Have you considered joining the armed forces?"

"... I've considered *it*, but uh, I'd like to wait later in life for a better opportunity because I know how *it* goes later in life when younger people join. I'm still young, got a good thing going, job-wise, house-wise—all that shit, successful—but, *it*'s not what I want to do deep down—but... *It*'s a lot to think about—like, I know I got the heart for *it;* I got a lot of fight in me. Fuckin'... Nobody can get, *through* me... I just got that mindset—I don't know man."

"But what good has ever come to humanity from eliminating a consciousness instead of altering *it?*"

Eighteen seconds elapsed. Dylan stared out at the parking lot. My attention remained fixed on his distraught features. "Depends on who you're talking about; every soul is different. If you're talking about a bad person, who's doing the wrong thing, in anybody's eyes, then, obviously, you would think they need to be eliminated."

Dylan hadn't made prolonged eye contact with me throughout the entirety of our conversation. I tilted my head down towards his increasingly meek demeanor and said, "That's all an opinion."

Twelve seconds elapsed. "... There's a lot of good that's come from *it*... There's a lot of bad people out there, people doing wrong things. Those people need to be gone. Anyway—that's what we're trying to do anyway, as a *whole* world; we're just trying to lower the population. We are. Everywhere. We're slowly building; we don't know what we're gonna do, yet we got trash plants, paper plants; they're all overrun man. *It*'s... The populations are growing; you look at every state—they all got a big city; almost all of them do. *It*'s only a matter of time before... *Yeah*... Fuckin'... Hattiesburg Mississippi becomes a big city just like New York City; when that happens the world's going to be the most populated. Mississippi isn't a populated place, right?... They're not. You're not answering so I don't know what you think about that. *Yeah*—they're a populated place—people *live* there, but, there's not a lot of people, we're running out of room; a lot of people coming. Now you got the government making deals just to lower the number of people, cut out as many families as possible so people aren't gonna, go out and, increase the population until we figure out what our real purpose in life is. I know there's people out there who have the answers, but... 'We the people'—everybody thinks about; that's just consciousness, but uh... Yeah, that's just people's conscious. They think about things like that; some people think about *it* more than others. But nobody is able to go ahead and take action... and figure out what really needs to be done—so we can only *think,* what our government knows—because they know; they're just hiding the facts from us, until *it*'s too late, whether they give us the chance to fight... or if they're going to strip us of everything we have so that we don't have a fighting chance. *It* is what *it* is... But—I mean, out of all the people that die in the world every single day, who am I? I'm one in 50 million; what's one out of fifty million? Nothing."

I said, "7.8 billion, right now."

"Of people on earth?—or-"

"Yes."

Dylan whispered, "7.8 billion..." and dragged on the stub his cigarette.

"And that's not including those who have died, and those who have yet to be born."

A car horn honked four times from the parking lot. Dylan said, "... Okay—so there's a lot of people who have been out on earth."

"We are but a mote."

"... We'll figure *it* out. *Obviously,* the human race knows more than... 10 percent of the human knows more than ninety percent; those are the elite. Some of those ninety percent—they know *it;* they're just too weak to act upon *it.* And uh, that's why I spoke over the phone; I sent a message; now I don't know if you have anything to do with the phone, or anything like that, but... and if you are I'd appreciate *it* if you'd tell me—so I knew."

692

I spoke softly and Dylan returned my gaze for the first prolonged instance of our conversation: "I had nothing to do with the phone."

"Anything I said over my personal phone?"

"I have, no idea what you're talking about, when you refer to the phone."

"Okay."

"If that gives you some clarity—I, I hope *it* does."

"*It* does… Okay, well other than that you just came to the bar looking for whatever, right?"

"Yes."

"And you just happened to run into a conversation with *me*."

"Yes."

"Okay… Well, if you're here as a, recruiter… then I'd be happy for that; but you gotta understand—I have a good job; I'd like to keep that job… I—I'd like to stay here, keep things quiet, still work at my job, and do whatever I have to on the side, but I don't want to mess up my job at home cuz I know, the other life can be addictive; I know people in *it,* and uh… Yeah, you never know what's goin' to happen, ya know?… I'm just not happy doin' what I do now. I'm doin' good; I wanted *it;* I got there; I'm happy doing *it;* you just get bored of what you do, ya know? Not everybody: Some people are okay with working the same job their entire lives. To me *it* gets boring after a while; you gotta do something else."

"… I am no savior."

Eight seconds elapsed; Dylan snuffed his cigarette on the pavement with his shoe and said, "If you had one wor… If you had one sentence of advice, what would you say… to me—for me."

"Guilt and shame are the conduits for god." I outstretched my hand for Dylan to shake; he accepted after a three-second hesitation and held on for a fraction of a second longer than customary. I turned and began to walk away towards the parking lot.

"Are you staying here?" Dylan asked me. I shook my head. "How about a phone number!?" he yelled. I continued to shake my head, though I slowed my gait, halted, and turned towards him once I reached the perimeter of the parking lot.

Dylan walked up to me, eight-inches from my face, and said, "You got a phone number or a way of contact? I'd like to speak to you when I'm sober."

I back stepped one pace and said, "I don't have any friends."

693

"I got the oppor—*I*, and you, both have the opportunity to make a lot of friends, right? We just choose not to. We think about things other people don't think about; we set them aside—we'll spend a lot of... I spend a lot of time by myself, ya know? I'm still drawn to people—still able to have great conversations with people; I just prefer to be alone; that's just me, but uh... If you want to take down my phone number, *Facebook*, whatever you got, I don't know; I'll take down your phone number and talk to ya... Um, *tomorrow*, around ten o'clock I can talk to ya, over the phone, or if you'd like to meet somewhere. I can call a payphone; you can answer that. Anybody can answer a payphone."

I repeated, "I don't have friends."

"I don't have a lot of them either. Yeah one or two people—ya know, for sure, that are... You consider them your friends but, you do more for them than they would do for you in the long run, and uh... Yeah, I don't have anybody I care about really. I got acquaintances and associates. I know a lot of people. Nobody's my friend..." Dylan looked over his shoulder at *The Messy House* back door and said, "I guess they're all locked up—I gotta take a piss, probably go home; I gotta call somebody. If you want my phone number just ask and I'll get a hold of ya but, other than that, have a good night."

"Take care."

Dylan back stepped towards a vehicle at the edge of the parking lot and said, "Will you be here at a later point?"

I said, "I don't know," and turned to walk back to my apartment.

"All right."

10:56 PM

I can't stay in this town—or any town—city, grove, wigwam, dingy hole, barracks—I don't care where. I'm better off jailed: life in prison.

A line of thirty-four overweight authors and four authors of healthy weight walked hand in hand onto a stage. Each man and woman, dressed in their preferred cultural attire with slight variations of deviance and conformity, swayed to a unique tune in each of their thinking minds, though the result had been a serene oscillation of *absolute* uniformity. Palms sweated and lips curled back to reveal rows of toothy grins. On closer inspection one could see orts of a previous meal wedged between teeth, or the meal from a day or two prior. The authors deigned to look at each other despite clutching each other's hands with abject desperation. At the opposite end of the stage, a gargantuan wall-mirror spanned an auditorium's perimeter and reflected the assembly.

"*Oh—isn't that lovely,*" said the collective consciousness.

Monday, November 16th, 2020

12:08 AM

I jotted down a page of notes pertaining to my planned yearly mock reviews with the intent to amplify the potency of my self-effacements; however, my shame has abated to the point of near-nullification, though I must retain at least a smidgen in order to prevent myself from degenerating to a criminal. I am exculpated, for I have conducted myself in alignment with my personal moral paradigm, and have sought solitude instead of vengeance for the transgressions of narrow-minded stupidity and impudence I have endured over this year. I am *unable* to conceive reviews worthy of my esteem, for the banal influence of my conscience is meek when confronted with reason. I truly am a *good* man in action, perhaps even a *nice* man, which is really what amounts to a despicable creature: I've yet to capitalize in this capitalistic society.

2:54 AM

The song of a nondescript bird rings out from a nearby park around this non-night-or-morning hour: The gloom.

I aspired to be a great writer from childhood through adolescence. Although I haven't mentally developed beyond these stages, I now aspire for nothing. No fine words or calculated syntax crafted with the most poignant emotional flourish may override the authenticity of my boring reality.

"You're probably happier than I am."

3:46 PM

Fiction is an opinion; this is a fact; thus, no matter the imaginative prowess of a piece, one must tolerate opinions. Strict autobiographies that account for action without the thoughts which inspired the action are pure art: A feat I will never achieve, nor would I want to, for my opinions are rancorous:

An Inflammatory Story Outline

[Female fiction writer short story. Trying to make something of herself.]

Wants to make money and become independent and famous from writing fiction; 32-year-old feminist. Lives with ~~one~~ two cats. Dating four men simultaneously while working at a coffee shop as a barista. Inspired by superhero movies.

"All I can think of are abdominal muscles and briefcases." [i.e., Writer's block] Complains to two gay male friends and one forty-eight-year-old successful married male businessman about her struggles to make ends meet. Fantasizes about sex with businessman between writing sessions bi-daily, sometimes twice on Tuesdays.

College graduate in social sciences. Bachelor's degree. Considering going back to school.

Example of prose: *"Shu-Zan swung into the theatre on his grappling hook for his forgotten suitcase, flutter kicks-a-many, with wild air blowing up his shirt to reveal sleek rows of glistening abdominal muscles. The mob of hoodlums glanced up but* it *was too late for them as Shu-Zan's boot slammed into their hideous faces."*

Wears designer shirts and thrifty jeans. Three credit card accounts, each with a balance between $200-$1,500.

Lives as a single resident of a two-bedroom apartment on the suburban outskirts of a metropolitan city in Pennsylvania. Converted the apartment into an office, decorated with a small bookshelf replete with work by authors from 1964 to the present. An ornate wooden desk with a six-wheeled plastic swivel chair atop an anti-fatigue mat.

Outspoken about how she doesn't care what people think while being highly active on social justice social media venues. Amiable and gregarious men annoy her. Thoughts of competition with other female women writers who are more physically attractive than she is dominate her psyche. Obsessed with the Greek cyclops. Collects troll dolls. Chilli mac & cheese each night for dinner.

A Polemical Rebuttal

White supremacist misognistic unemployed neo-nazi lowlife. Ignorant. So ignorant. Ignorant beyond comparison. Everything that is wrong with America. Views on women are self-fulfilling prophecies. This man shuttled himself into space and forgot to lock the vacuum around his helmet. The man opened his mouth to scream; no sound had been produced; however, a small sealed envelope containing the perfect formula for a politically correct story that digests well with a globalized audience slipped through the spacesuit opening and plummeted to earth with the impetus of a negligible gravitational pull. Where did the envelope come from? Who wrote the contents? God works in mysterious ways, so they say—anyway, the envelope remained on a surefire trajectory back through earth's thermosphere, rocketing through the mesosphere, and ignited in a flare of blue flame. The ashes dispersed among the stratosphere, thereby scattering the God-given knowledge of a utopian opinion to hot air.

Ode to Innocence

Don't blame me:
I'm guilt-free;
A product of socie-
-Tee off with the boys.
Quarter-after-three.

11:19 PM

Meanwhile, at the gym with a nervous and circumspect Caucasian man with salt-and-pepper hair in his early fifties:
I said, "Excuse me sir."
"Yeah."
"What is your self-assigned meaning in life?"
"I'm sorry what? What did you say?"
"What is your self-assigned meaning in life?"
"My *self-assigned?*"
"Meaning in life—yes."
"That's a random question."
"Yes."
"Uh, I—I don't... I don't *understand* the question."

"The meaning that you have chosen for your existence."

"I—I—I'm not choosing any meaning for my existence."

"Fair enough. Take care."

"Y—okay…"

Meanwhile, on the television, talking heads perpetuate media of fake media and people riot across the country during a pandemic. *And* you cared about a cloistered man's *meaning in life…* Ha! Let him be, to run on the treadmill for seven minutes before he rests, fatigued, with both hands flat on his knees, slightly hunched forward, and instead ask that young man in his early thirties over there:

"Hi. Have I asked you—probably not—what your self-assigned meaning in life is?"

"Uh no you haven't actually but I heard about *it*.[91] Uh mine's to cook."

"To cook?"

"Yeah."

"Excellent. Thank you!"

"Thank you—have a good workout!"

"You too!"

Bravo! Brav-fucking-o! *Bravado!* A round of applause. A hoopla. A cheer.

But wait—there's more! A suave stout man with slicked-over hair engaged with a smith machine bench press:

I said, "Hi."

"Hey how's *it* goin' man?"

"*It*'s going well; how've you been?"

"… Do I know you, or should I know you?"

"We've uh, met here before; *it* was last year actually."

"Last year…"

"Yeah."

"Ah… I don't recall.:

"Yeah, *it*'s uh; *it* was a while ago, but I recognize you."

"Do you recall what we talked about or did we talk at all?"

"Uh… We talked about a whole bunch of different things; I don't really… recall exactly though…"

"Did I ask you what your self-assigned meaning in life is?"

"Self-assigned meaning in life?"

"Because that's what I was going to ask you right now."

The man sighed, shrugged his shoulders, though continued to smile at me while he said, "I don't know; I'm not sure I fully understand the question I guess."

"Ah—the meaning that you have chosen for your existence."

"… I think I'm undecided still; I'm still trying to figure *it* out."

Tuesday, November 17th, 2020

3:31 PM

Quasi (anti)psychiatry sessions with my upstairs neighbor Charlie have proved to be fruitful. The man is tormented and sedated. I deem the biography I have begun of his youth and military career to be more important than my lifelong documentation.

To know that nobody—no human, no creature, future entity, or alien, will care of my words, and that, if anything, this work will be summarized on a temporary internet encyclopedia, where aspiring psychiatric students and dawdling grade school children may skim the surface of my life, determine their individualistic, biased conclusions of what I amounted to as a conscious being—a product of the times—a rung in a too-short-ladder propped up against the wall of a rustic brick building… Yes, to *know* of these matters is a certain delusion. I'd prefer to die before this fourth book is published. The previous trilogy is enough to encapsulate a lifetime of cyclic affairs into one succinct drama of irresponsibility.

11:01 PM

Tuesday night. Recorder on, I visited *The Messy House* after a gym session where I encountered the man who pickpocketed me—Rob, the Bartender—Joe, and a new Caucasian face, introduced to me as Hector, out back in the parking lot. I greeted the men with an amiable mien:

The Irishman

Rob said, "What're you doin' man? You're always just walkin' around this time of night—like, same fuckin' time every night, man."

I said, "Yes."

"Why?"

"Well-"

"What happened to your nose, man?"

"What do you mean?"

"*It* looks shiny on that side."

"Ah, you don't see any *wire* there do you?"

Rob turned his head to his right and hissed. I chuckled, which prompted Rob to smile; thus, he spoke with a jovial inflection, "I don't know—let me check man—lemme check!" and hastened to pat both of the front pockets of my jacket, to which I stood, indignant, yet silent and unexpressive in reaction to his impudence. "No wires—you got the recorder though—goin' again." Rob backed away from me, dragged on a cigarette, and said, "This motherfucker."

I said, "Well, *it*'s in my inner pocket this time so there's no SD card for you."

"Oh yeah?"

"Yes."

"So you're wired up, huh? You the fuckin' Feds man—we got Feds here man—you mother fuckin' Feds."

With a playful inflection, I said, "I'm no Fed; I wouldn't come to this fuckin' bar if I was a Fed."

Hector laughed. Rob faced me and said, "Why not?"

"There's nothing worth sleuthing on."

"So, you allowed back here now?"

I said, "I don't know—but I come here anyway."

"Cuz you the Feds, man."

"Well—no; *it*'s because I have a will."

"You got a will for what? You got a will to come here? You just wake up in the middle of the night like 'Yo I gotta go to the *Messy House.*'"

Joe sniggered.

I said, "No. No—I just come here."

Rob said, "I'm so confused, man."

"There's nothing to be confused about; I probably come here for the same reason that you do."

"… *Maybe*—hey we all come here to drink, man."

"We're both human after all."

"You're human? You sound like a fucking robot."

"Why do you say so?"

"Cuz you do!"

I gazed down at the pavement and said, "I don't think so."

"I really like that jacket though—how you keep *it* so fresh? *It's always* fucking clean and everything like that. You take that shit to the dry cleaners, huh?"

"I actually haven't washed this jacket since I got *it*. I'm a generally clean person."

Hector giggled. Rob said, "*Right...* Me too."

I chortled, pointed at the backdoor, and said, "Is there anybody worth seeing in there, in your subjective opinion?"

"No, *it's* dead in there, man."

Rob and Hector meandered into the bar. Joe and I stood out back and conversated for one minute on the new Covid-19 laws and the new female bartender named Christina. I followed Rob into the bar and encountered Julie, an elderly woman regular. Rob and Hector seated at the far-end opposite of the back entry. and a large Irish man seated closest to the back entry. The Irishman stared at me.

I approached the Irish man, sat down next to him, and said, "Hello. What is your self-assigned meaning in life?"

"Uh, my meaning in life is to drink this beer."

"What'll happen when that's over?"

"Then I'll wake up with a hangover and I'll sit around naked and... rub; I'll rub, a ton of lotion all over my body... and... I'll jerk off, to *Golden Girls*—you ever watch *Golden Girls?*"

"I have."

"Blanche is fuckin' hot. I fuckin' love Blanche."

"Does that become your new life's meaning?"

"Well—that's what I'm gonna do, with my life."

"Is get drunk, wake up hungover, and then jack-off to *Golden Girls?*"

"Yeah—have you ever jacked-off to *Golden Girls?*"

"I haven't."

The Irish man inquired as a statement, "You've *never* jerked off to *Golden Girls?*"

"I've never jerked-off to *Golden Girls.*"

"You gotta watch—you ever watch *Golden Girls?*"

"... I've seen *Golden Girls*—yes."

"Blanche is fuckin' *hot* man—Blanche is like the hottest girl in my life; I've got posters of her all over my walls... but, I do believe in Jesus Christ."

"What does that have to do with *Golden Girls?*"

"Because, I'm Catholic and I'm allowed to do whatever I want and then be forgiven for my sins… so *it*'s part of being Irish."

Joe chimed in from behind the bar, "I'm Catholic too, man."

The Irish man continued: "So we got a good thing right here; we can do whatever we want during the week and go and confess our sins on Sunday, and then we're fine. *It*'s called the original, fuckin', religion. Catholic religion is the original religion."

"Actually, that's Judaism."[91]

"That's, what, Jesus Christ was—he was a jew—a jew. He allows me to do what I want. Other than murder, or rape, or anything like… I am a Catholic man—I will always be a Catholic—I'm Irish; that's the way *it* is."

"The theology allows you to do what you want?"

"… *It*'s called living life."

I said, "By that standard of virtue?"

"Jesus Christ is not against me. Jesus Christ drank alcohol. He also… he *also* fornicated. He had a wife named Marian. Marian. So I mean, you could…"

"I never knew Jesus Christ so I wouldn't know."

"I don't either, but I also have read the Gospel of Thomas… and in Gospel of Thomas—and… a bunch of other gospels that weren't allowed into the original Bible, Jesus was a swingin' dude."

"According to what we read."

"Yeah—I agree. But are you really going to come into a bar and preach Jesus?"

"I'm not preaching Jesus. Are you?"

"Well you came in here asking me."

"I asked you what your self-assigned meaning in life is; how is that preaching Jesus?"

"A… Uh, that's right. Well thank you—I'm Todd." Todd outstretched his hand for a shake.

I accepted Todd's hand with my gloved one for a half-second jostle and said, "I'm Baethan."

"What're you drinkin'—water? Want me to buy you a beer or somethin'?"

"No, thank you."

"Okay."

---

[91] Both of us were wrong. The possible correct answer(s) may be the Hindu Vedas or Pyramid Texts.

"I appreciate the offer."

"I think you guys are great. I think you keep us in order and in line."

"Who?"

"... Aren't you a Bible person?"

I suppressed my weariness of this common presumption, feigned confusion, and said, "A Bible person?"

"Are you not a Bible person?"

"What is a 'Bible person'?"

"Someone who goes around... talking to people about religion."

"I don't do that—no."

Todd raised an eyebrow and said, "Really?"

"Yes."

"I'm sorry I, I got you wrong."

I laughed.

Todd continued, "I thought you were like one of those like... I don't know. Why did you ask what I thought the meaning in life is?"

"That's more of a philosophical question opposed to a theological one."

"So what do you think the meaning of life is?"

"Mine is to write."

"Oh—you're a writer. What do you write?"

"Uh—books on the human condition."

"Really?"

"Yes."

Todd leaned back in his chair, crossed his arms, and said, "What have you found out about the human condition?"

I mimicked Todd's body language and said, "Ah—you immediately go on the defensive."

"No—cuz Hemmingway always did."

"Ah—you're familiar with Hemmingway. Well, what I found out personally about the human condition-"

"What."

I spoke loud enough for Rob to overhear, "-is that there are thieves in bars."

"There's thieves in bars?"

"Yes. I found that out recently." Rob remained slouched over at the other end of the bar, though he spoke nothing, and looked down into his drink.

Todd said, "There's thieves everywhere."

"That's true, but my first experience with theft is in a bar. I usually keep myself safe and aware, but I was distracted at one point, and I experienced a pickpocket."

"Did *it* hurt you?"

"… There was a lot of data that I lost."

"I—I'm sorry man; you come in dressed in all black; I thought you were one of those Jesus—Bible… salesmen."

"Are you thinking of a Jehovah's Witness?"

"Yeah—yeah."

"I'm not a Jehova's Witness."

Todd said, "You are very interesting; you're kinda like…"

"Let me guess—a robot? An alien?"

"Yeah you're kinda like a robot."

Joe had been pacing behind the bar; he glimpsed me over his shoulder and chuckled. I shared in Joe's mirth with a brief laugh and said, "No—I'm a human being."

Todd said, "I figured you are… The human condition-"

"Yes… yes…"

"Is that we thrive in pain; *that* is the human condition."

"We thrive in pain but we choose our suffering."

"Most of us do—yeah. A lot of us don't, but, some of us do… But we *thrive* in pain. That's who we are—that's how we become the greatness of who we are-"

I interjected, "Is that why you come to a bar?"

"-the person that comes from the pain… is, the *best* part of us."

"Strife."

"Is life," affirmed Todd.

"Strife is a catalyst for growth."

"*It* is. Yeah—you're right."

I repeated, "Is that why you come to a bar?"

A guitar song with a dreary, macho, incomprehensible male singer began from the jukebox. Todd said, "I come to a bar to forget the pain."

"I come to a bar to find the pain."

"You come to a bar to *find pain?* This is where we come to forget the pain. This is where we sit there and-"

"The human condition is… ah… paramount here; *it*'s abundant. You walk into a bar, and you feel the energy of the people there, and people are often here because of their pain."

"*Yeah?* And we come here to forget the pain. We talk about *it;* we, whatever, ya know? Forgetting the pain or easing the pain is why we come to a bar."

"What pain are you trying to forget?"

Todd looked away from me towards his drink and said, "Hm… Everyone else's pain is the same as mine. There is no difference. Some are big; some are small, but none of *it* matters. And *that's* what the human condition is—we—we strive to feel that we matter, when in the gist of the whole fucking universe, we *don't* fuckin' matter. Nothing. Everything we do right now, doesn't matter. We're gonna be fuckin' worm food in a hundred years. We're *all* gonna be dead. Everything that we fuckin'—that we fuckin' do right now, will be forgotten. That is the pain and human suffering—and that is what we do. We have kids to fuckin' forget about *it:* We say, 'Hey, we have offspring, so we'll be remembered!'—They're not going to remember. A hundred and fifty years from now, no one's going to know I fuckin' walked this earth… And that *is* the human condition. So you can sit there and go to bars and bars and bars… I was a journalism major … *it's* good to write, and *it's* good to look in bars but…"[92]

"What did you write in your journalism career?"

"… Sports."

"A sportswriter?"

"Yeah, I did *it* in high school and went to college for *it,* but I dropped out; never finished, so… But, writing's fun; you should keep *it* up. But *why* are your eyes so wide?—that's what's gettin' me—*it's* kinda freaking me out man—*it's* like I feel like I'm under one of those heat lamps in a police station and shit."

"I don't know—my eyes are often commented on when my pupils dilate. I can only presume *it's* because of the lighting in here; that's all I can think of. I've been accused of being on cocaine."

The incomprehensible song ebbed to an end followed by a recorded applause. Joe, Hector, and Rob murmured to each other about the cost of drinks. The old woman, Julie, sat at the middle of the bar and turned her head towards a conversation at moments of intrigue. Todd said, "… Do you ever drink beer?"

"On the occasion yes; I have a preference for red wine though."

"Why wine?"

---

[92] On transcription, this nihilistic diatribe restored my hope that there is a holistic meaning for humanity, and perhaps the encompassment of all life, beyond our comprehension and understanding. Nihilistic fatalism is becoming commonplace banter, and I'm averse to crowds.

"The health benefits, and *it*'s best in moderation..." Interested in retaining the previous conversation, I said, "Your pain isn't the same as mine; we suffer the same way-"

"Oh, yeah, everybody suffers the same way."

"-but we have individual pain, or pains; so what's yours? What are you trying to forget?"

"Do you have autism?"

I said, "No."

"Are you sure?"

"No."

"You remind me of my autistic girlfriend's... kid."

I picked up my bottle of water for a swig and said, "I don't believe in modern psychiatry. The DSM-5 is not my Bible."

"The what?"

"The DSM-5: The diagnostic manual psychologists use-"

"Why?"

"Because personality disorders, anxiety, depression—that's just the human condition."

"What is your IQ?"

"I don't know."

Todd muttered, "You *do* know."

"I don't care; I never took a test because I don't care."

"Well you seem like you have a high IQ."

"Well that's just seeming—but I'm *still* interested in your pain. That's why I come here."

"... Did you go to school for writing?"

"No."

"What did you go to school for?"

"I didn't go to school—I went to high school."

"Why didn't you go to college?"

"*It*'s a waste of money, and I can read all I want."

"So fucking what—I read all the time too."

I affirmed, "Yeah—you probably know just as much as I know, but what does knowledge do us? As you said, we're just going to die—*it*'s all futile."

"What are you talking about? Well, because, Socrates..."

"I know nothing?—I only know that I know nothing?"

Todd smiled and said, "Exactly."

"*It*'s similar to Rene Descartes: I think; therefore I am. I *only* know

706

that I *know* nothing! But, what do those two quotes amount to in practice other than a *slug?*"

"Okay—well, who also said... 'Happiness is full acquisition of all your potential.'... Who said that?"

"Are you asking me?"

"Yeah."

"I don't know."

Todd reached for his beer and said, "Well then go look *it* up... Cuz knowledge is knowledge."

"I've only read Aristotle's version of happiness, which is: 'Happiness is an activity.'"

Todd laughed and said, "I—I—and I drank what? What is that song... fuck... Aristotle is fuckin'... I got messed up from drinkin'. Just, go and look that up. *Better* than what you're doin' right now."

"My potential?"

"Yeah."

"This activity-"

Todd said, "Does *it* make you *happy* what you're doin' right now?" and swigged his drink.

"I don't *seek* happiness."

"You need to seek happiness."

"I *need* to seek happiness?—under whose jurisdiction?"

Joe had walked over to listen to our conversation. Todd shouted, "This is like—interesting; this is like talking to a robot for a half-an-hour, *it*'s great." The old woman snickered a guttural crone's drawl. "Um, can I get a shot of Jaeger, and a Bud Light?" Joe acknowledged Todd's request and prepared the drinks.

I said, "I think that calling somebody a robot is possibly one of the most insulting things you could possibly say, but I hear *it* from *everybody*."

Joe began sympathetically, "Yeah-"

"Because you are," Todd quipped.

"-everyone says that to him."

I protested, "You're insulting somebody's *humanity*."

Todd assured me: "But I'm not *trying* to insult you. I'm trying to figure out what the fuck is *with* you, man. If someone like you walks up to somebody... You show no emotion."

Flummoxed, I said, "What do you mean?"

Joe interjected, "You gotta take *it* from other people's point of view—you walk up to the people and you ask everyone the same question and *it's*…"

"I show emotion—perhaps *it's* just because-"

Todd interrupted: "When do you show emotion?"

"I've been laughing—I've been smiling—I've shown concern. You *really* ask me when I've shown emotion, and I sit here grinning."

"I think you're fascinating—hey, I'm not rippin' on you; I think you're great, to tell you the truth. I think you're a little bit different, but… but… That is, what's important. Our vices and our differences is what makes us individuals. I'm not judging you."

"I don't want to hear praise; to call me great is still a judgment and I don't want to hear that either—I'd rather just hear about your pain."

Todd tilted his head back and unleashed a hearty guffaw that echoed throughout the bar. "Now you sound like a terminator, man."

"… Back to the robot." I shook my head.

Joe shouted, "Back to the robot!" and laughed. "This *is* an interesting conversation."

I addressed Joe and said, "Yes—his pain is interesting to me, because that's why he's here; he wants to forget *it,* and I'd rather bring *it* to the surface."

Todd stared down into his drink and said with a meek inflection, "I'd rather not talk about *it* cuz that's just-"

"I understand. Then we won't. That's all you needed to say."

Wednesday, November 18th, 2020

4:28 PM

[The Irishman continued]:

The song *Fake It,* by Seether, squelched the low audio of a football game played on a single television. I sat in silence, leaned back against my seat for seven minutes, and observed tacky price tags consisting of cardboard and black marker within a glass-door beer cooler. The run-down dive bar looks a shade different each night I visit, with each patron casting their shadow on the floor behind their seats produced from the harsh glow of three bare fluorescent bulbs strung up from a high ceiling.

"Talk to me," Todd blurted.

I muttered, "Hm?" and leaned to my left towards Todd.

"I said 'talk to me!'"

"Talk to you?"

"Yeah!" Todd pleaded. The music ended and Todd's words cut into the sudden silence: "Make the bar experience interesting."

I felt flattered and said, "Hm... What characteristic do you pride yourself on?"

The dreary and incomprehensible machismo singer repeated the same song from the jukebox speakers. Todd said, "What about you... What do you pride yourself on?"

"My will."

"Your will?"

"Yes."

"In what way?"

"In the way that I pursue action for my purpose: my meaning in life that I've chosen for myself."

"What is your meaning in life that you've chosen?"

"To write; I've already told you."

"... And what have you written?"

"Books on the human condition."

"And... Are you published?"

"Yes."

"How many do you have?"

"Three so far. I'm finishing my fourth book in three days."

"Are you self-published or, do you... publish-"

"*It*'s a 'vanity' publisher; *it*'s a mix between self-publishing and a publishing house. I pay for *it*, and they distribute to retailers."

"How are you doing with that?"

"I don't market; I just put them out there, so the sales are negligible, but I don't care about sales."

"You should."

"Why?"

"Because that determines who you are. *But,* the moment someone buys a book—like Mark Twain; the first time you make a dollar off writing, you're a writer."

"Well I've made seventy-two dollars in royalties so far-"

"So you're a writer... No matter-"

"I guess."

"-No one can take that away from you, and the Great One said that, so if anybody says anything to you, you say 'Mark Twain.'"

"I don't think I'm a writer, nor do I feel like one. I just feel like-"

"Get the fuck out, man-"

"-a human being."

"-you made money off *it; Mark Twain *said* you're a fuckin' writer.""

"I don't *care* what Mark Twain thought."

Todd turned to me, full-face, shocked, and said, "You don't give a shit what Mark Twain thinks? *Why?* The guys' one of the greatest writers in the history of humankind. You *should* fuckin' give a shit about what Mark Twain thinks. If you're... If you're going to sit there and write, you gotta read Mark Twain; you gotta read Jack Kerouac, and you gotta read fucking Hemmingway. Those three fucking people, are the greatest writers in the history of American writing. If you haven't read those—read all their books, then you're gonna fail as a writer... Cuz you gotta know about pain; you gotta know about what—the reason why people do shit."

"You speak about them as if they're the only men who have ever experienced pain, and the human condition."

"No—but they're the only Americans that have put *it* on paper that is, *right*. So read Kerouac-"

"That's completely subjective."

"Have you read Kerouac?"

"I haven't."

"You gotta read *On The Road, On The Road* by Jack Kerouac."

"Yeah—he's a beatnik."

"*It*'s fucking awesome. He might be a beatnik but read *it*. But he's also outside the beatniks a little bit, cuz he's the only one of them who was *writing* at the time, as the beatniks—he's the only one who had royalties, from his writings, the entire time he's goin' on. So he's able to be outside but also be in."

Stoic (autistic), I said, "So you're telling me that I'm going to fail, as a writer, if I don't read the authors that you recommend to me."

"You're going to fail as a writer because you need to understand people, and that'll help you understand people."

Joe, jovial and good-spirited, yelled, *"All right! Chug 'em down folks!"*

I said, "I'm here at the bar to understand people."

Todd said, "Yeah—but you understand them through *your* eyes. You gotta understand people through *other* eyes, and then you can *compare*."

I lied: "My only other activity is reading when I'm not writing."

"Then read Jack Kerouac, and read Hemmingway, and read…"

"I've read the majority of Hemmingway. Kerouac I'm not too interested in."

"Have you read… Have you read, um-"

The Spanish pick-pocket—Rob, had stood from his chair, walked towards the back door of the bar, and stared at me along his route. Four feet away from me and behind Todd, I addressed Rob with a quick glance and he reached out a hand to pat my left shoulder. "Okay holme-"

I snapped, "Please don't put your hands on me."

"Huh?"

"Please don't put your hands on me."

Rob passed behind me, approached me from my right, set his hand on my right forearm, and said, "You good, man."

I pulled my arm away, swiveled towards Rob, and commanded, "Please *don't.*"

Rob gazed at me, amused, drunk. Todd, Julie the old woman, Joe the bartender, and Rob's friend Hector observed the incident from behind me, all drunk. The song ended with a small applause recorded from a live audience and faded until there was nothing but the words: "Why not?" spoken by Rob.

"Because I don't trust you at all."

"You don't trust me at all?—Why not?"

"Because you have pick-pocketed me."

Rob held both of his hands splayed across his chest and feigned indignant innocence: "*I* pick-pocketed you? No—I never touch yo' fuckin' pocket-"

"Yes, you did."

"-the other motherfucker that was here, touch yo fuckin' pocket, so get your story *right.* Aight?"

"How do you know this?"

Joe ambled towards us and said, "All right."

Rob shouted with authentic indignance, sensing my doubt: "Because I was sittin' right *here* next to you like dat, na mean?"

I inquired, "And you saw him pick-pocket me?"

Rob quietened and murmured as though we had become two businessmen engaged in a transaction, "So you wan' me to tell you—he— he uh stealin' your shit? Are we boys? Or, what?—You writing, right? You're a writer, right?"

I leered at Rob with the indifferent manner that I would a rat with *it*s head crushed in a snap trap and said, "Why don't you just answer the question?"

Rob looked away from me towards Joe with the bearing of one who had been physically assaulted; his face twisted with a frown and his fingers oscillated like a keyboard player. "Nigga—I'll be-"

Joe centered himself between us at the opposite side of the bar and interjected, "All right, all right, we're not gonna be causing problems at 10 o'clock at night when we're supposed to be closing—c'mon." Joe snapped his fingers, placed a hand on Rob's back, and escorted him outside. Hector followed; I didn't see his face. "Let's go!" Joe shouted the maudlin order over his shoulder.

I stood, turned to see Todd already standing behind me, and said, "*It* was nice to meet you," and outstretched my hand for a shake; Todd accepted. "What work by Kerouac did you recommend?—You said-"

"*On The Road,* and *To Have and Have Not,* by Hemmingway... And... What was the third one? I can't remember—cuz, you got me—you're about to get your ass kicked if you don't fucking go out the door."

"Get my ass kicked? *Please...* Who? By him?" I pointed towards the back door, then at Todd, "Or by you?"

"Not by me—why the fuck would I kick your ass?"

"I don't know—because you suggested *it;* I don't know who's going to kick my ass."

"You're autistic dude-"

Baffled, I said, "What?"

"-I love ya, but you're... You're great... I'll be back up here another time and we'll talk. *On The Road,* by Kerouac, and *To Have and Have Not,* by Hemmingway. *And* you need to read... at least... I'll say *Tom Sawyer.* You *gotta* read *Tom Sawyer,* by Mark Twain. Those are the greatest people in American—greatest *writers* in American history!"

"Well that's, your *opinion.*"

"Well, my opinion is pretty good."

Joe yelled from the back doorway "Yo—come on guys!"

Todd quipped to me, "Read 'em," and slavishly responded to Joe: "Okay—okay—we'll go."

I followed Todd out the back door and said, "Take care, Joe," on his way back in behind me.

"See ya, buddy."

Rob and Hector meandered towards a parked vehicle and glanced over their shoulders at me. Five meters across the parking lot, Todd called out, "Read those, man!"

I yelled back, "I'll check out Kerouac."

"Oh you gotta check out *To Have and Have Not* by Hemmingway."

"Have you read *The Short Happy Life of Francis Macomber?*"

"No."

Entertained, I yelled, "You haven't!?"

"Who's *it* by?"

"That's by Hemmingway! And *it*'s—I consider *it* to be his best work; *it*'s a short story."

A stranger approached Todd and engaged him in conversation. Todd forgot I existed and readily announced his pain: "Fuck dude—I got *fired* today!"

The stranger said, "You did?"

I didn't stay to hear the rest.

Thursday, November 19th, 2020

1:10 PM

I walked into *The Messy House* after a gym session and found myself among a line of patrons seated at the bar with the new bartender, Christine: A blonde-haired Caucasian woman in her early forties; I didn't care to observe anything else about her and I don't recall her face, though I *think* she looked attractive. A rap love song played from the jukebox. For the first time since my licentious nights with Candy, I wanted to drink for the simple pleasure of the feeling, after a solitary, prolonged gym session.

I said, "Hello."

The bartender's pleasant, feminine voice responded: "Hello."

"I'll take a cabernet please."

"A what?"

"A cabernet."

"What is, *that?*"

I frowned and queried: "A red wine(?)"

"What is that?" she repeated without the initial playful inflection.

"Do you sell any red wine?"

"Red—no, no wine."

I leaned back in my chair, dumbfounded, and said, "No wine."

"No wine. Only liquor and beer—and flavored fruit juice."

I nodded and said nothing. The bartender made her rounds with other patrons. The corpulent bar owner, Bob, sat at the far end of the room, and yelled, "Hey—you gotta drink somethin'. There's limited seats here!"

Christine spoke in my defense while I ignored Bob and stared straight forward, looking fairly autistic, at bottles of alcohol, "All right—he just walked in here!-" Christine turned towards me with a demeanor of gentle respect and said, "-But we don't have wine. No wine."

I looked at Christine, indifferent, and said, "Mm, all right."

"... So what would you like?"

"I'll pass."

"Okay."

One minute elapsed while I stared forward, content to be a thing among my surroundings. One man two seats to my right informed the bartender that his woman companion had previously occupied the seat next to me, but on the woman's return from the bathroom, had been too "creeped out by this dude (me)," to reseat herself. The patrons quietened and the rap love song ended simultaneously as Bob's guttural voice rang out as the singular sound, "Hey my friend! Yo!" Bob clapped his hands twice, and I didn't respond, for I'm not his friend. "You gotta order somethin'— you can't sit here; *it*'s illegal!"

An old man to my left protested, "I've *ordered* somethin'!"

Bob said, "Not you, him!" and pointed at me.

The bartender said to no one in particular, "He's either gotta order something or he's gotta go."

An involuntary grin overtook my countenance and I stood from my seat without a word spoken, with the ratty limelight of the ephemeral moment aimed at me, and walked out the back door. In the silence behind me, one drunkard *screamed,* "Hey, I'll buy you a drink!"

The door slammed behind me and I decided halfway through the parking lot towards my apartment that I still wanted a drink. Walther's tavern loomed 200 feet away. I donned my face mask and pushed through the rounded double-doors, recorder on.

A new face of a Caucasian female greeted me. The bar bustled with activity: All stools and booths full. Covid-19 is a mere bugbear to many. I immediately met prolonged eye contact with a woman at the bar (whose nebulous attractiveness escapes my memory) while she spoke to a man seated next to her. The bartender, Craig, who had been out on the patron floor I once cleaned bi-daily, charged towards me and stopped three feet away. "Walther says you're not allowed in here. Sorry."

Craig and I stared at each other for three seconds. I said, "Why?"

"Why?—I talked to Walther; *it*'s not my decision; he said you're not allowed—I—we can't serve you, so…" Craig breathed in a hiss of air and tensed his body.

"You talked to Walther and had that happen?"

"*I* didn't talk to him! No—he told *me* that."

"Oh, well what did he say for a reason?"

Craig hastened to speak, vexed by my questions, "Wh—*you* need to talk to Walther about that."

I smiled behind my face mask, raised my arms to both sides of me, and calmly stated with an air of innocence, "I haven't been here in over a month."

"That's *not* my business…. You gotta talk to Walther; I was told by him and Megan we're not allowed to serve you in here—sooo—you gotta talk to-" I interrupted Craig with a hearty laugh. "-them about *it*… Just following my-"

"Ah, and here I was ready to give Walther some of my *money*."

"I—well. Sorry… You can call Walther if you want and speak with him about *it* or come back and speak to him when he's here—but—and I'm closing—in like, ten—fifteen minutes anyway, but… Yeah, I'm—that was what I'm instructed—I can't—we're not—we can't serve you here."

"I understand."

"Okay. Thank you."

"Yes." I turned to go, though Craig had crossed his arms and his stony glare had remained fixed on me throughout the entire interaction; thus, I stopped mid-turn and chuckled.

Craig giggled in response and said, "Goodnight buddy."

Sardonic and cheery, I said, "Thank you Craig—you as well!"

"Thank you. I'll—I'll see ya—I'll see ya around."

"Yes, well no."

"Well here or over there or whatever—but yeah."

"Well you may see me in passing."

Craig's good humor dissipated; he said, "Yeah, that's basically what I said so, yeah."

"You're very attentive to me when you have a whole bar, of people."

"Very attentive?"

"Yes."

"I—I was actually coming over here dropping off a drink—but yeah, I'm sorry. *It* wasn't my instructions, that's what I'm telling you, so, if you wanna talk to Walther about *it* and discuss that further that's up to you, but…"

"Uh… No."

"Okay."

I guffawed and Craig desperately attempted to usher me out: "All right—well have a good night!"

"You too Craig—thank you!"

"Thank you—I appreciate *it.*" Craig turned from me first and hurried back to his duties while our canned niceties reverberated in my mind on my brief walk home to my apartment—sober, where I listened to the recording twice—once in full; the second in savory segments throughout the transcription process, documented for me to relive a mitigated fragment of delight on each future indulgent reading—if I'm ever senile and wracked with agony, decrepit and crippled, breathing through a tube—nay, unable to read;[93] an aloof nurse reads *it* for me despite my deafness… unconsciousness… death.

"Balor finally died," says the nurse to a forty-nine-year-old doctor. *"Finally."*

"I know—right?"

3:06 AM

I lull awake and read the words of Fernando Pessoa, distracted by one memory stolen from me in *it*s complete vibrancy and detail by the senior chief of my second division in the U.S. Navy boot camp:

I rode on a commercial airline to Great Lakes, Illinois, window-side, seated next to a beautiful and anxious grade school girl obsessed with her foreign language studies. I felt like a monster seated next to her, for the man I had slated myself to become, juxtaposed with her naive intelligence.

---

[93] I lost my ability to write and haven't done so for six years, confined to a bed; I'm no longer real, my existence abolished with the abatement of action long ago. I have no family. Modern medicine sustains me. I've been diagnosed with seven personality disorders, depression, and PTSD. My muscles have atrophied and my body has become a veritable vat of fat. My conscience whispers sweet nothings to me from the moment I wake to a haze of unreality from the moment I lapse into a nightmare more real than the rectangular block of off-center dull fluorescent lighting in the ceiling of my white wall room.

I stared through the window and observed a surreal expanse of glacial-esque clouds. My wordplay had been phenomenal, for my feelings had been exquisite, as I observed the otherworldly expanse of barren white continents floating on a sea of blue sky.

I remember the iconic framed poster of three firemen uplifting a United States flag among the fresh rubble of the September 11th World Trade Center attack, situated on one of the walls of my division's first galley: The singular stimulus other than the homogenized heads of fellow recruits, trays of food, and cafeteria tables. I wrote of what the poster signified—the *feelings* I felt in that moment... A single bold and capitalized word at the bottom of the "inspirational poster" served only to taunt: "**FREEDOM.**" I wondered what that particular poster positioned in our first galley symbolized... The poster meant a lot more to me *then* than now; *it* had been horrific: A taunting joke with no punchline.

Friday, November 20th, 2020

12:17 AM

At the gym, I encountered a 6'2 obese man with an enormous paunch and slicked-back salt and pepper hair, dressed in a black t-shirt and blue jeans, on his way out. While I signed-in and documented my lack of Covid-19 symptoms at the front desk, I powered on my recorder and said:

"Hi."

"Hi."

"May I ask you a personal question before you go?"

"Go ahead."

"What is your self-assigned meaning in life?

The man sighed, winded from a previous strength training exercise. He spoke with a hasty, well-pronounced voice, "I don't know *it*. Let's put *it* there's a lot of marital stuff going on and my life's going through a change right now so I'm trying to find out."

"I see."

"About the best I can give ya at this point."

I nodded and said, "So, love then? If you want to consider marriage love."

"I would almost call *it* two—two different ends—right: One is—one is love; the other for lack of better terms is revenge. I'm gonna do this—I'm

717

gonna lose some weight—I'm gonna push whatever—to prove to you that I can do *it*—to prove you *wrong*... So, two different motivations—probably the same goal but..."

"Ah... Revenge?"

"Yeah."

"As in what way?"

"As in you said I couldn't do *it*—I'm gonna prove you wrong."

"Is that why... you're... Are you going through a divorce?"

"Noooot at the moment—my wife is dealing with severe mmm—mental *issues,* okay—where she thinks I'm having an affair—she thinks I'm doing a whole bunch of, different things that I'm not—but... I've constantly gained weight and I try to come here and do what I can, but because—dealing with home stuff I'm not here as frequently as I'd like to, but one of the things we always talk about is—well: 'You need to lose weight'—and well 'I'm *trying* to' but, *it*'s not as easy—so now, she's not home; I'm gonna prove to you that I can do the things that I told you I was gonna do."

"Ah I see."

"Ya know, I have the time to do *it;* now I'm gonna go do *it,* to prove you wrong—*it*'s been my thing all through life—people told me I was never gonna be good enough—I'm never gonna do this—never gonna do that—I've worked-" The man expelled a vindictive sigh and continued, "-two major national broadcast T.V. networks. I've been on the radio around most of the state. And now I'm one of the top consultants in the field that I do. Tell me I can't do somethin'—I'm gonna prove you wrong."

"Are you doing *it* to prove them wrong or are you doing *it* for yourself?"

"Well *it*'s to prove them wrong. I've done everything that—if I died today, I think I lived a good enough life that I'm satisfied with everything that I've done."

"So you want to change your physical appearance to spite-"

"Yeah"

"-the opinions of others?"

"Yeah."

"... Hm. What's the motive there?"

"Cuz they told me I couldn't."

I had been nodding to signify comprehension, though I didn't understand, and said, "... Hm..."

"That's *it-*" The man flourished his key ring. "-I—I—I mean my thing has always been, because... I've gained the weight—because I haven't had the spite or the reason to do that... Love, kept me home. Love, helped put the weight on because I'd rather stay at home—spend time with the wife—do things with the kids—the family—and all the rest of that... But you make fun of me since I was a little child and all the rest of that... and even still when I was younger and all the rest of that. Ya know tell me I can't do something, but you don't believe I'm gonna do something; I'm gonna go prove you wrong... Ya know. But my problem has always been finding that motivation to go and do *that*. So now *it*'s changing that mindset of—okay I come here to prove you wrong but the mindset change is—okay—*it*'s a job. I show up here; this is part of my job. And I'm doing that—I'm gonna have the motivation—I'm gonna prove you wrong... I'm gonna *make* you believe and I'm gonna earn that respect from you." The man flourished his key ring again.

"Mm-"

"That *it*."

We stared at each other for four seconds, face masks on; I said, "That seems unhealthy."

"... *It* probably is... And I'll probably be dead in twenty years—but, ya know what, as I said, I've been dealing with a heart condition that, stops uh, stops beating, about eight-to-ten seconds every week or two. Then *it* starts up and I move on with my day..."

"Hm-"

"And there's nothing they can do even with a defibrillator or anything like that, because, the amount of time that *it* stops, *it*'s too short for a defibrillator to detect that *it* stopped, charge *it*—ya know—charge the unit and then zap the heart—by the time *it*'s going again they put me [indiscernible]."

"Hm..."

"So as I said—I accepted many years ago... I *can* die tomorrow—I pretty much do."

I said, "Yes, I wake up each morning with the thought that I may die."

"Yeah. I don't wake up with the *thought*—*it*'s just the conscious—*it*'s just the conscious understanding; if I die I die. At that point I won't—*it* won't... At *that* point *it* won't matter to me because I won't be alive to care... But as they say—when you pass on, the memory you leave and the legacy behind in others... *it*'s an asshole—ya know, okay so I'm an asshole—whatever... But I've taken up space in here; I'm not gonna be forgotten by those people... My memory—my essence will still live on..."

"Until they die, and the generation after-"

"*And* the generation goes—and whatever—I mean there's nothing that I can necessarily do. Ya know, I've—I put a footprint in history that most people don't know about—but I do—and that's what matters to me... Ya know I'm one of the few people that were in New York City on September 11th; I had a *place* in the system... I was working at the broadcast T.V. network. I kept, *two* channels on the air for almost forty-eight hours right after those events happened. Nobody knows *it* but me and my immediate family—but I have a place in the system—I had an impact on society." The man flourished his key ring for the third time. "Major shows—major concerts—I've T.V.ed video music awards—I've done '*em, ya know?* All types of things—I've been part of those production crews—I've had an impact; when I leave work in the morning Howard Stern's talking about the stuff I'm doing *it*—the night before? He doesn't need to know what I did; he saw the result and knows I did a good job cuz he's talkin' about *it*. If I didn't do my job they'd be talking about me not doing my job right..." The man breathed heavy and displaced his steps while he addressed me from a sidelong angle. "Ah... So, like I said—I've lived enough of a life that, I'm content where I've been. I still work to try to get more—and that's a problem of mine—trying to find motivation—what's the next mountain to climb? I left college—I worked for ESPN; I worked there for two years, left—came back—did radio around the state for a year, ya know—then went back and climbed the mountain up again at MTV. I've done *it*—twice. Okay, what's the next challenge?"

"What characteristic do you pride yourself on the most?"

The man contemplated for six seconds and said, "... I'd say integrity... Goes back to what I said: I tell ya I'm gonna do somethin'—I'm gonna do *it*—I'm gonna deliver on what I told ya. Now if you can rely on that, and I'm the person that you can depend on—you can *hate* me for all you want—you can love me for all you want—doesn't necessarily matter as long as you *respect* me. And I've done everything I can to *earn* that respect from you! Then we're fine, so, many people that where I work didn't necessarily like me cuz I was getting all the big assignments and all the rest of that—I *still* get all the big assignments but I've earned my way to that spot, and *nobody* can take that away from me."

"What troubles you the most?"

"... Did I do enough? And the answer's always no. My therapist hates *it*—but-" The man chortled.

"By whose standard—yours, or other people's?"

"Mine... It's never enough—I never did a good enough job—there's always something I could've done better… I make a meal—I could've done *it* better. I do four sets here—I could've done five. *It*'s trying to learn and get to the acceptance of—okay, *it*'s understanding *it*'s good enough for now, to come back and do *it* again; that's the thing that I'm trying to… *improve* at. Save some work for tomorrow."

I nodded after a six-second delay and said, "All right."

The man chuckled and said, "I'm an interesting person—what can I say. At least I'm interesting to me."

"I agree."

"So-"

"We're all interesting in our own ways."

"That we are! That's why I don't—ya know—I've—I've been through a world amount of shit so I don't judge anybody that comes in—I don't judge anybody that I really deal with because they don't know the *hell* that I go through, on a daily basis, and I don't know the hell they're going through. So I try not to take my hell out on them but I try not to hold their actions on me against them too harshly either because I don't know everything they're going through."

"Yes."

"But because I've had those scars and that experience."

I nodded and said, "Thank you for your time."

"Not a problem, sir."

"Take care."

On my way home from the gym I stopped in at *The Messy House* nine minutes before the establishment closed. The owner—Bob, seated at the chair closest to the back door where I entered, half-turned to me and said, "We're closed."

I immediately stopped, spun on a heel, and walked out ~~because I'm a high-functioning autistic~~. On my walk to my apartment I imagined the comical banter of the patrons regarding my ridiculous behavior ~~because I'm a narcissistic schizophrenic~~. I dismissed the thoughts to be unworthy of my time and experienced disgust and contempt while urinating into my toilet ~~because I'm borderline bi-polar~~. I ordered chia seeds, grass-fed flavorless whey protein, creatine, cacao nibs, and a new multivitamin brand from an online retailer and ruminated on my lack of employment ~~because I'm depressed and anxious~~.

I stand in my apartment's quiet solitude and ponder the aforementioned conversation with the obese man at the gym. The climax and resolution of this year of my life's story resolved months ago; thus, I want to amplify the significance of this obese man, for what he symbolizes. I *worked* to repress my pity while I listened to him talk; he is everything a man shouldn't be, by my *judgment:* The true essence of my original discarded title for my books: *What Not to Do with One's Life*. I taint the end of my work with a repulsive memory of another man's unaccountable indolence, self-conscious vengefulness, and a vain desire for remembrance.

We are one and the same.

With dignity,

– Baethan

EPILOGUE

The man survived another year.

Printed in the United States
by Baker & Taylor Publisher Services